P9-BYG-730

Guffey's Xtra!

Business English, 9e

Congratulations! Your purchase of this new textbook includes complimentary access to the Guffey Xtra! Web Site (**http://guffeyxtra.swlearning.com**). This site offers a robust set of online multimedia learning tools, including:

Speak Right!
Spell Right!
Ms. Grammar
WebCheck Reinforcement Exercises
Bonus Editor's Challenges
PowerPoint® Review

Tear out card missing?

If you did not buy a new textbook, the tear-out portion of this card may be missing or the Access Code on this card may have already been used. Access Codes can be used only once to register for access to Guffey Xtra! and are not transferable. You can choose to either buy a new book or purchase access to the Guffey Xtra! site at **http://academic.cengage.com/support**

xtra!

ACCESS CODE

PPQS82DP329VT4

HOW TO REGISTER YOUR ACCESS CODE

1. Go to http://academic.cengage.com/login
2. Click on "Create My Account", and then "Student".
3. Enter your Access Code and click "Continue".
4. Enter your account information and click "Continue".
5. For the license agreement, select "I Agree" and click "Continue".
6. Click on Xtra! on your "My Dashboard" page.

Note: the duration of your access to the product begins when registration is complete.

For technical support, contact 1-800-423-0563 or visit **http://academic.cengage.com/support**

SOUTH-WESTERN
CENGAGE Learning

Mary Ellen Guffey's
AWARD-WINNING

BUSINESS
ENGLISH

MARY ELLEN GUFFEY

Professor Emerita of Business
Los Angeles Pierce College

·

CAROLYN M. SEEFER

Consulting Editor
Professor of Business
Diablo Valley College

SOUTH-WESTERN
CENGAGE Learning™

Australia · Brazil · Japan · Korea · Mexico · Singapore · Spain · United Kingdom · United States

SOUTH-WESTERN
CENGAGE Learning™

Business English, Ninth Edition
Mary Ellen Guffey

VP/Editorial Director:
Jack W. Calhoun

Publisher:
Neil Marquardt

Acquisitions Editor:
Erin Joyner

Senior Developmental Editor:
Mary Draper

Marketing Communications Manager:
Sarah Greber

Content Project Manager:
Amy Hackett

Manager Editorial Media:
John Barans

Technology Project Manager:
John Rich

Senior Manufacturing Coordinator:
Diane Gibbons

Production House:
GGS Information Services, Inc.

Compositor:
ICC Macmillan Inc.

Printer:
Courier, Inc.
Kendalville, IN

Art Director:
Stacy Jenkins Shirley

Internal Designer:
Ann Small, a small design studio

Cover Designer:
Ann Small, a small design studio

Cover Images:
© Getty Images and © Jupiter Images

Photography Manager:
Don Schlotman

Photo Researcher:
Andrew A. Garrett

Library of Congress Control Number:
2006908274

For more information about our products, contact us at:

Cengage Learning Customer & Sales Support,
1-800-354-9706

South-Western Cengage Learning
5191 Natorp Boulevard
Mason, OH 45040
USA

Dr. Mary Ellen Guffey
South-Western Cengage Learning

G

Dear Students:

If your language skills are rusty and you can't remember all those grammar rules from your earlier education, **Business English** is the book for you! I've written this book to help you brush up your language skills and prepare for employment in a workplace where communication skills are increasingly important.

Business English has helped thousands of students over the years improve their oral and written communication skills. It has been the leading book in the field for over two decades because it works. Its three-level approach makes the entire topic of grammar less intimidating and easier to grasp. The three-level approach provides small blocks of material that proceed from simple to complex, thus helping you understand and remember.

Tried-and-true features in **Business English** ensure that you will improve your grammar, punctuation, and usage skills.

- **Three-level approach** presents grammar guidelines in three levels proceeding from easier, more frequently used concepts to less frequently used concepts.

- **Ample reinforcement exercises** enable you to apply your learning so that you internalize and retain your new skills.

- **Pretests and posttests** keep you informed about your needs and your progress.

- **Self-check exercises** in the textbook give you even more opportunities to try out your skills and improve through practice.

- **Hotline queries** let you see everyday communication questions asked by workers on the job—questions that you might face in your career.

- **Writer's Workshops** offer you guidelines, model documents, and writing tips necessary to develop work-related writing skills.

- **Editor's Challenge** exercises let you hone your skills as you correct language errors in business documents.

- **Guffey Xtra!** helps you nail down those grammar rules with PowerPoint® slides, Ms. Grammar, Spell Right!, Speak Right!, and WebCheck Reinforcement exercises.

Business English reviews the grammar, punctuation, and usage guidelines necessary for you to succeed in your business or professional career. It's not only a friendly teaching and learning tool, but it's also a great reference for you to keep handy on the job.

One student said, "**Business English** is a gift to any student who really wants to learn how to use the English language proficiently."

Cordially,

Mary Ellen Guffey

E-Mail: *meguffey@westwords.com*
Book Web Site: *academic.cengage.com/bcomm/guffey*

Dr. Mary Ellen Guffey
Your Partner in the Classroom
South-Western Cengage Learning

SKILLS THAT WORK – IN THE CLASSROOM OR THE WORKPLACE

In today's workplace, communication is constant and instant. With a computer at every workstation and increasing reliance on e-mail, everyone must be able to write and speak quickly, correctly, and effectively.

Mary Ellen Guffey's **Business English**, **9e**, is the fast track to success in building language skills. With more than thirty years of classroom experience in business communications, Dr. Guffey knows what students need—and in **Business English**, the market-leading grammar and mechanics textbook since its first edition, she delivers the best of tested and proven grammar instruction supported by in-text and online resources that enhance teaching and learning.

TESTED AND TRUSTED LEARNING TECHNIQUES

Three-level Approach

Dr. Guffey's unique approach to grammar starts with a solid foundation of basic information and then goes beyond, one step at a time. You will move sequentially from what you need to know to all there is to know, with reinforcement exercises, study tips, and *Spot the Blooper* challenges on every level.

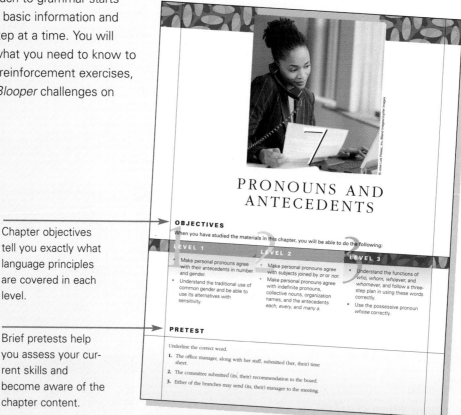

Chapter objectives tell you exactly what language principles are covered in each level.

Brief pretests help you assess your current skills and become aware of the chapter content.

Reinforcement of Skills

Because Dr. Guffey knows that you learn by doing, each chapter of **Business English** includes a wide variety of practice tools, including self-help exercises aligned with the three-level approach.

- **Skill Maximizer** exercises provide more hands-on experience with the most challenging topics.
- **Writing Exercises** apply concepts in composing sentences, while **Writer's Workshops** present a progressive series of composition tips and techniques.
- The new **Editor's Challenge** exercises use realistic business documents that need revision to teach targeted concepts and review previously presented ones.
- Each chapter also begins with a brief pretest that previews concepts and helps you determine what you already know and concludes with a posttest that enables you to evaluate your achievement.

Numerous reinforcement exercises give you many chances to apply your skills.

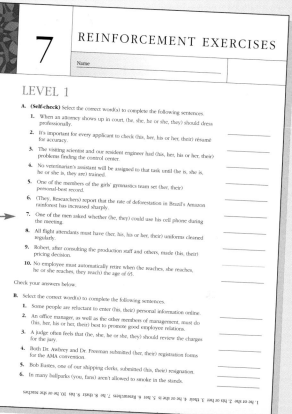

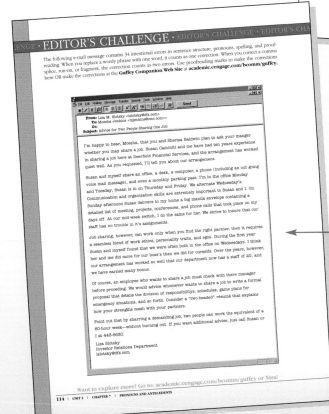

Editor's Challenge exercises ask you to revise realistic business documents to help you learn grammar concepts.

> "I love your book. It is well written with a lot of tools and exercises that will help me with my writing. You make a subject fun that I thought would be boring."
>
> *McKenzie Nichols*
> *Student at Cabrillo College*
> *Aptos, California*

TECHNOLOGY TOOLS AND WEB CONNECTIONS

Business English, *9e*, takes you out of the classroom and into the real world of business with *Learning Web Ways*, end-of-chapter exercises that introduce you to browsers, search engines, online dictionaries, newspapers, encyclopedias, and company Web sites. You will learn to set bookmarks, conduct searches, evaluate Web pages, and navigate the Internet with confidence.

"My students love Learning Web Ways in *Business English*. It's like having an Introduction to Computers class along with the Business Language Skills class!"

Jeanette Walgren
Pikes Peak Community College
Colorado Springs, Colorado

Additional online resources build skills and support the text.

Guffey Xtra!

A robust Web site that serves as an electronic study guide, *Xtra!* is available at no additional cost when you purchase a new book. Xtra! includes Ms. Grammar, Speak Right!, Spell Right!, WebCheck Reinforcement Exercises, and Bonus Editor's Challenge Exercises. If you do not have Xtra!, but would like to use it with your Guffey text, visit http://guffeyxtra.swlearning.com and choose your book. You will be able to order access to Xtra! online.

http://guffeyxtra.swlearning.com

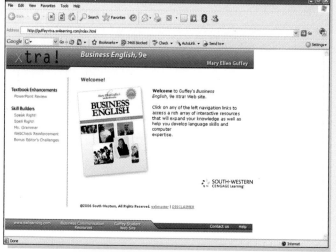

academic.cengage.com/bcomm/guffey

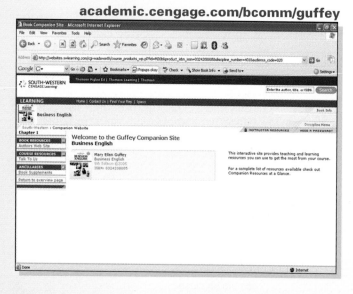

Companion Web Site

In addition to the password-protected Xtra! Web site, Dr. Guffey provides a book companion site, open to everyone. Here you will find chapter review quizzes, Editor's Challenge documents, flashcards of key terms from the textbook, plus links to grammar and writing resources.

"I really like all the extra study tips. The Web site really helped me study for my tests."

Charlene Young
Student at Louisiana Technical College
Natchitoches, Louisiana

WebTutor™ Advantage for Blackboard® or WebCT®

An online extension of the traditional classroom, WebTutor is a content-rich teaching and learning aid that complements textbook chapters with flashcards, quizzes, and additional Web links.
It also provides you and your instructors with a course calendar, chat, e-mail and other rich communication tools. New e-lectures, narrated PowerPoint® presentations of key chapter concepts, are especially helpful for distance-learning classes.

Contents

2   16   28   48

64   82   100   126   144

164 190 206 220

250

268 286 316 334

Dr. Mary Ellen Guffey

Let's face it. Grammar is not a topic that you may find immediately engaging. Yet, **Business English** has been successful in capturing the attention of students and instructors for over two decades. It has helped hundreds of thousands of students improve their language skills and prepare them for successful careers in today's rapidly changing workplace. Today's workers are communicating more than ever before, and sharp grammar skills help them speak and write effectively and confidently.

Although English grammar concepts have undergone few changes, grammar textbooks continue to evolve because students have changed, the work world has changed, and our teaching/learning delivery systems have been improving. **Business English** continues to evolve as it retains its No. 1 position in the market.

TEXTBOOK FEATURES THAT HELP STUDENTS LEARN

Many students realize they must brush up their grammar and language skills before entering the workplace. **Business English, 9e,** with Xtra! Electronic Study Guide provides instructors and students with a structured grammar review aimed especially at students who seek to improve their language skills efficiently and quickly. Many unique features in this textbook ensure success in the classroom.

THREE-LEVEL APPROACH Beginning with Chapter 4, language concepts appear in levels. These levels progress from fundamental, frequently used concepts in Level I to more complex concepts in Level III. Each level has its own trial exercises as well as numerous relevant reinforcement drills. The three-level approach has distinct advantages. First, the overall organization of the complex subject of English is immediately recognizable to students. They feel less intimidated. Second, the three-level approach facilitates comprehension and promotes student confidence by providing small, easily mastered learning segments. Third, this strategy provides blocks of material that can be tailored to fit student goals, institutional goals, and time constraints.

HOTLINE QUERIES One of the most popular features of **Business English** has been its questions and answers patterned on those received at grammar hotline services across the country. These questions—and Dr. Guffey's suggested answers—illustrate everyday communication problems encountered in the work world. In easy-to-read question-and-answer form, she explains important distinctions in English grammar, usage, style, and vocabulary. Updated items related to current events appear in this Ninth Edition.

REINFORCEMENT EXERCISES The most effective way to reinforce and internalize language concepts is by trying out skills in special exercises. Students and instructors using **Business English** have repeatedly told us that its reinforcement exercises are superior both in content and number to those in other books. Every chapter includes abundant exercises for students to practice their language skills. Skill Maximizers provide extra practice with the most challenging topics.

SELF-HELP EXERCISES Special worksheets enable students to check their own learning as they review and internalize chapter concepts. Over 60 pages of self-directed exercises and answers build skills and confidence. Students will find even more reinforcement exercises—with immediate explanations and feedback—in the interactive "Ms. Grammar" software. **Business English** provides the best and most comprehensive reinforcement exercises of any book in the field—another reason for its No. 1 position.

PRETESTS AND POSTTESTS Each chapter includes a brief pretest to preview concepts and to pique interest. Chapters also provide a posttest to enable students to evaluate their achievement.

SELF-CHECK EXERCISES AND UNIT REVIEWS The first student exercise in each level of each chapter is self-checked. Students are able to determine immediately whether they comprehend the concepts just presented. At the end of each unit, a review exercise enables students to check their mastery of unit concepts prior to official testing. Answers to the unit reviews are at the back of the book.

WRITING EXERCISES Each chapter includes a short writing exercise that encourages students to apply chapter concepts in composing sentences. In completing these simple exercises, students move beyond traditional fill-in drills and closer to job-skill requirements.

WRITER'S WORKSHOPS Six workshops feature composition tips and techniques necessary to develop work-related writing skills. These workshops begin with proofreading skills and progress through the writing of sentences, paragraphs, e-mail messages, memos, letters, and short reports.

EDITOR'S CHALLENGE One of the most effective strategies for teaching workplace language skills is providing students with business documents that need revision. In **Business English, 9e,** we provide new Editor's Challenge exercises for every chapter. These documents focus on the content of the target chapter, while cumulatively reviewing previous chapter content. In addition to the new Editor's Challenge exercises, **Business English, 9e,** also gives students additional editing practice with Bonus Editor's Challenge exercises at the **Guffey Xtra!** Web site.

TECHNOLOGY SUPPORT THAT REINFORCES LEARNING

Students require both language and computer skills to succeed in today's information economy and digital workplace. As technology becomes an increasingly important element in the workplace and in the classroom, we are providing even more digital support for a book that is already recognized as the leader in innovative online support. **Business English** offers students the following major digital resources, each one loaded with rich interactive learning tools.

1. **Companion Web Site**
   academic.cengage.com/bcomm/guffey

Open to everyone, the book companion site offers the following:

- **Chapter review quizzes** highlight chapter concepts and give students immediate feedback with explanations for right and wrong responses.

- **Self-check diagnostic grammar test** assesses strengths and weaknesses. New to **Business English, 9e,** this online test is different from those in the textbook and is meant to pique interest. Students receive answers but no explanations.

- **Flash cards** review key terms from each chapter and help students internalize concepts.

- **Editor's Challenge** exercises from the textbook enable students to edit and revise documents online rather than rekeying them.

- **Chapter URLs** list all Web site references and provide replacements if needed.

- **Writing help** in the form of links to OWLs (online writing labs) guides students to the best Internet grammar services where they will find exercises, handouts, and writing advice.

2. **Guffey Xtra! Web Site**
   (http://guffeyxtra.swlearning.com)

Available at no charge to students who purchase new books, this Web site functions as an electronic study guide. Students without new books may purchase access at the **Guffey Xtra!** site. This site offers the following powerful learning tools that are easy to use, stimulating, and cutting-edge.

- **Ms. Grammar** strengthens language skills with chapter synopses and interactive exercises. Students enjoy "Ms. Grammar" because they can learn at their own speed. They also like its colorful, pop-up feedback boxes with snappy, opinionated responses from Ms. Grammar. Reviewing before tests was never easier!

- **PowerPoint** chapter review slides provide a quick review of chapter concepts. Less extensive than the instructor's slides, the student PowerPoint program outlines major points and offers students still another learning medium.

- **Speak Right!** helps students learn to pronounce 50 frequently mispronounced words. Students hear Dr. Guffey pronounce the words correctly and incorrectly so that they can focus on improving their pronunciation. This interactive tool is especially helpful for students learning English as a second language.

- **Spell Right!** provides interactive exercises that review all 400 words in Appendix A of *Business English, 9e.* The entire module is self-checked so that students can learn at their own pace. The module provides separate spelling lists, a midterm exam, and a final exam.

- **WebCheck** reinforcement exercises provide additional reinforcement for all chapter concepts. These exercises develop keyboard and technology skills while reviewing grammar and mechanics. Unlike exercises in the textbook, these online workouts have pop-up answers and feedback for every response. Prompt feedback facilitates comprehension and is an important factor in concept retention.

- **Bonus Editor's Challenge** presents different editing exercises from those in the textbook. Students edit letters, memos, e-mail messages, and reports that focus on chapter concepts but also review previous concepts. This online bonus set of exercises can be used for discussion, homework, or assessment.

ACKNOWLEDGMENTS

I am indebted to many individuals for the continuing success of *Business English.* Instructors across the country have acted as reviewers or have sent me excellent ideas, constructive insights, and supportive comments. I am particularly grateful for the consultation of the following people:

Paige P. Baker,
Trinity Valley Community College

Julie G. Becker,
Three Rivers Community College

Amy Beitel,
Cambria-Rowe Business College

Margaret Britt,
Copiah-Lincoln Community College

Leila Chambers,
Cuesta College

Connie Jo Clark,
Lane Community College

Robin Cook,
Sawyer School

Betty Dooley,
Clark State Community College

Cathy Dropkin,
Eldorado Colleges

Judy Ehresman,
Mercer County Community College

Valerie Evans,
Cuesta College

Diane J. Fisher,
The University of Southern Mississippi

Marye B. Gilford,
St. Philips College

Margaret E. Gorman,
Cayuga Community College

Barbara Goza,
South Florida Community College

Helen Grattan,
Des Moines Area Community College

Ginger Guzman,
J. Sargeant Reynolds Community College

Joy G. Haynes,
Chaffey College

Marilyn Helser,
Lima Technical College

Nancy Henderson,
North Harris College

Janet L. Hough,
Spokane Community College

Marilynne Hudgens,
Southwestern College

Iva A. Upchurch Jeffreys,
Ventura Community College

Edna V. Jellesed,
Lane Community College

Tina Johnson,
Lake Superior College

Evelyn A. Katusak,
Broome Community College

Lydia J. Keuser,
San Jose City College

Marilyn Kilbane,
Cuyahoga Community College

Donna Kimmerling,
Indiana Business College

Ann Marie Klinko,
Northern Virginia Community College

Shelley Konishi,
Kauai Community College

Linell Loncorich,
Hutchinson Technical College

Jane Mangrum,
Miami-Dade Community College

Shirley Mays,
Hinds Community College

Darlene McClure,
College of the Redwoods

Timothy A. Miank,
Lansing Community College

Carol Vermeere Middendorff,
Clackamas Community College

Paul W. Murphey,
Southwest Wisconsin Technical College

Anita Musto,
Utah Valley State College

Jaunett S. Neighbors,
Central Virginia Community College

Mary Nerburn,
Moraine Valley Community College

Jackie Ohlson,
University of Alaska

Mary Quimby,
Southwestern College

Jana Rada,
Western Wisconsin Technical College

Susan Randles,
Vatterott College

Carol Jo Reitz,
Allentown Business School

Judith R. Rice,
Chippewa Valley Technical College

Kathie Richer,
Edmonds Community College

Benelle Robinson,
Ventura Community College

Maria Robinson,
Columbia College

Sally Rollman,
Shoreline Community College

Jan Sales,
Merced College

Marilyn Simonson,
Lakewood Community College

Lynn E. Steffen,
College of Lake County

Letha Strain,
Riverside College

Susan Sutkowski,
Minneapolis Technical College

Evelyn Taylor,
Cincinnati Bible College

Michelle Taylor,
Ogeechee Technical College

Robert Thaden,
Tacoma Community College

Dorothy Thornhill,
Los Angeles Trade Technical College

James A. Trick,
Newport Business Institute

Susan Uchida,
Kauai Community College

June Uharriet,
East Los Angeles Community College

Lois A. Wagner,
Southwest Wisconsin Technical College

Fred Wolven,
Miami-Dade Community College

Special thanks for shaping **Business English** goes to the following instructors who offered valuable insights as current reviewers:

Joan W. Bass,
Clayton State University

Maria S. Damen,
University of Cincinnati/Raymond Walters College

Nancy A. Henderson,
North Harris College

Jared H. Kline,
Southeastern Community College

Ann Marie Klinko,
Northern Virginia Community College

Linda Serra,
Glendale Community College

Mageya R. Sharp,
Cerritos College

Susan Simons,
Edmonds Community College

Many professionals at Cengage Learning companies (including PWS-KENT Publishing Company, Wadsworth Publishing, and South-Western) have helped propel **Business English** to its prominent position in the field. For their support and expertise in producing this Ninth Edition, I sincerely thank Jack Calhoun, Erin Joyner, Neil Marquardt, and especially Mary Draper, my incomparable developmental editor.

Special thanks for shaping **Business English, 9e,** goes to Carolyn M. Seefer, Diablo Valley College, who acted as contributing editor and was instrumental in revising all facets of the book. Her instructional expertise, research prowess, and exciting new material enlivened this edition immeasurably.

Finally, I express my deep gratitude to my husband, Dr. George R. Guffey, emeritus professor of English, University of California, Los Angeles, for supplying exceptional computer expertise, Internet skills, and language knowledge, as well as love, strength, and wisdom.

AUTHOR ACCESSIBILITY

No other business communication or English book on the market offers more instructor support and author interaction than **Business English.** Through teaching seminars, e-mail, author Web sites, personal messages, and online newsletters, I try to stay in touch with those of you in the trenches. My goal is to be an accessible and responsive author who provides relevant, practical, and quality materials for immediate classroom use. As always, I am delighted to have comments about your course and suggestions for improving this book.

Dr. Mary Ellen Guffey
Professor of Business

In the following sentences, faulty grammar, punctuation, capitalization, or number expression may appear. For each sentence, underline any inappropriate form(s). Then write a corrected form in the space provided. Hint: One sentence at each level is correct. In this case, write *C*.

Example: Manufacturers know that the size and design of a product like the iPod <u>is</u> influential in its success.

are _____

LEVEL 1

1. Businesspeople are sending more messages than ever before, that's why communication skills are increasingly important. _____

2. A software workshop scheduled for the fall in Mesa, Arizona will be valuable to some staff members. _____

3. In it's latest online announcement, our Information Technology Department said that even the best-protected data sometimes is lost, erased, or corrupted. _____

4. Jeff and I certainly appreciate your answering the telephone when him and me are away from the office. _____

5. A list with all of our customers' names and addresses were given to the manager and her last week. _____

6. Every field employee, as well as every management and certified employee, is eligible for a company cell phone. _____

7. For you Mr. Johnson, we have a one-year subscription to *The Wall Street Journal*. _____

8. Under the circumstances, we can give you only 90 days time in which to sell the house and its contents. _____

9. We often use WebEx for online teleconferences; but we also recognize the need for face-to-face meetings to exchange ideas. _____

10. In the spring Kathy took courses in history, english, and management. _____

LEVEL 2

11. Please collect all of the graduates names and e-mail addresses so that we can keep them informed of job opportunities. _____

12. Either Jessica or he will be working at the counter on the next two Saturday's. _____

13. Of the sixty-nine e-mail messages she received, Jennifer said that only 9 were legitimate. _____

14. If you expect a three-week vacation, you must speak to the Manager immediately.

15. You should have saw the warehouse before its contents were moved to 39th Street.

16. Chapter 12, which is titled "Controlling Credit Purchases," is one of the best chapters in *Today's Consumer.*

17. Before her trip to the East last summer, my mother bought a Sony Digital Camera.

18. We need only 20 15-cent postage stamps to finish the mailing.

19. Your account is now 90 days overdue, therefore, we are submitting it to an agency for collection.

20. We feel badly about your missing the deadline, but the application has been lying on your desk for 15 days.

LEVEL 3

21. The cost of the coast-to-coast flight should be billed to whomever made the airline reservation.

22. All job applicants must comply to the rules printed in our Handbook for Employees.

23. Los Angeles is larger than any city on the West Coast.

24. The number of checks with insufficient funds are causing the bank to tighten its check-cashing procedures.

25. Our school's alumni are certainly different than its currently enrolled students.

26. Courtney is one of those efficient, competent managers who is able to give sincere praise for work done well.

27. Because she looks like her sister, Kendra is often taken to be her.

28. If I were him, I would call the Cortezes' attorney at once.

29. Three employees will be honored, namely, Lucy Lee, Tony Waters, and Jamie Craig.

30. Surely it was he who put the report on the boss's desk.

LAYING A FOUNDATION

REFERENCE
SKILLS

© Comstock Images/Jupiter Images

PARTS OF
SPEECH

© Jean-Louis Bellurget RF/Pixland/Jupiter Images

SENTENCES:
ELEMENTS,
PATTERNS, TYPES

© JGI/Blend Images/Jupiter Images

© Comstock Images/Jupiter Images

REFERENCE SKILLS

When you have completed the materials in this chapter, you will be able to do the following:

- Understand the content of Business English and its relevance to you and your career.
- Describe several types of dictionaries, including print, electronic, and online.
- Use a dictionary confidently to determine spelling, meaning, pronunciation, syllabication, accent, word usage, and word history.
- Select a dictionary to suit your needs.
- Anticipate what information is included in dictionaries and what information is not.
- Understand the value of reference manuals.

PRETEST

Each chapter begins with a brief pretest. Answer the questions in the pretest to assess your prior knowledge of the chapter content and also to give yourself a preview of what you will learn. Compare your answers with those at the bottom of the page. When you complete the chapter, take the posttest to measure your improvement. Write *T* (true) or *F* (false) after the following statements.

1. Online dictionaries have made printed dictionaries obsolete. _____
2. Dictionary diacritical marks help readers pronounce words correctly. _____

1. F 2. T 3. F 4. T 5. T

2

3. The usage label *colloquial* means that a word is no longer in use. _____

4. Some online dictionaries provide audio pronunciations of words. _____

5. Reference manuals provide information about punctuation and hyphenation. _____

Business English is the study of the language fundamentals needed to communicate effectively in today's workplace. These basics include grammar, usage, punctuation, capitalization, number style, and spelling. Because businesspeople must express their ideas clearly and correctly, such language basics are critical.

WHY STUDY BUSINESS ENGLISH?

What you learn in this class will help you communicate more professionally when you write and when you speak. These skills will definitely help you get the job you want, succeed in the job you have, or prepare for promotion to a better position. Good communication skills can also help you succeed in the classroom and in your personal life, but we will be most concerned with workplace applications.

INCREASING EMPHASIS ON WORKPLACE COMMUNICATION

In today's workplace you can expect to be doing more communicating than ever before. You will be participating in meetings, writing business documents, and using technology such as e-mail and instant messaging to communicate with others. Communication skills are more important than ever before, and the emphasis on writing has increased dramatically. Businesspeople who never expected to be doing much writing on the job find that e-mail and the Internet force everyone to exchange written messages. As a result, businesspeople are increasingly aware of their communication skills. Misspelled words, poor grammar, sloppy punctuation—all of these faults stand out glaringly when printed. Not only are people writing more, but their messages travel farther. Messages are seen by larger audiences than ever before. Because of the growing emphasis on exchanging information, language skills are more and more relevant.

WHAT DOES THIS MEAN FOR YOU?

As a businessperson or professional, you want to feel confident about your writing skills. This textbook and this course can sharpen your skills and greatly increase your confidence in expressing ideas. Improving your language skills is the first step toward success in your education, your career, and your life.

When Jennifer M. enrolled in this course emphasizing language basics, she did not plan to become an expert in the subject. After finishing the course, she didn't think of herself as an expert. When she started to work, however, she discovered that many of her fellow workers considered her an English expert. Most of them had no training in grammar, or they had studied it long ago. Their skills were rusty. Jennifer found that even her boss asked her questions. "Do I need to put a comma here?" "Should this word be capitalized?" Because she was a recent graduate, her coworkers assumed she knew all the answers. Jennifer didn't know all the answers. But she knew where to find them, and this ability made her more valuable in her workplace.

One of the goals of your education is to know where to find answers. You should also know how to interpret the information you find. Experts do not know *all* the answers. Attorneys refer to casebooks. Doctors consult their medical libraries. And you, as a student of the language, must develop skill and confidence in using

CAREER TIP

The lifetime earnings of a person with a college degree are about three times those of a person without a college degree.

SPOT THE BLOOPER

Television producer Kermit Schaefer first defined the word *blooper* to describe mistakes made on television, radio, and film. Throughout this book you will find many written and spoken bloopers. Using the skills you learn in this class, try to identify why these are bloopers.

reference materials. You can become a language expert not only by learning from this textbook but also by learning where to find additional data when you need it.

DICTIONARIES

Using references should become second nature to you. Dictionaries and online resources are invaluable when you must verify word spellings and meanings, punctuation style, and usage. If you have your own personal library of reference materials, you can find information quickly. At a minimum you need a current desk or college dictionary and a good reference manual. Another helpful reference book is a **thesaurus.** This is a collection of **synonyms** (words with similar meanings) and **antonyms** (words with opposite meanings). Many helpful resources are now available digitally, whether online or in a software program such as MS Word.

A **dictionary** is an alphabetical list of words with their definitions. Most dictionaries contain pronunciation guides, parts of speech, word history or **etymology,** labels, and other information, which you'll learn about in this chapter. You can purchase dictionaries in almost every language. Bilingual dictionaries, such as English-Spanish and Italian-French, are increasingly popular in today's global marketplace. In addition, many fields, such as law and medicine, have specialized dictionaries that contain vocabulary specific to that field.

Businesspeople today make use of both print dictionaries and online dictionaries. Even with the availability of online dictionaries, many prefer to have a print dictionary handy to look words up quickly and easily. First, you'll learn about print dictionaries, including how to select one and how to use it. Then, you'll learn about using an electronic dictionary, such as the one that comes with your word processing software. Finally, you'll learn how to use online dictionaries.

SELECTING A PRINT DICTIONARY

Not all print dictionaries are the same, as you will doubtless notice when you shop for one. To make a wise selection, you should know how to distinguish among three kinds of print dictionaries: pocket, desk, and unabridged. You should also know when your dictionary was published (the copyright date), and you should examine its special features.

Pocket Dictionary

As its name suggests, a **pocket dictionary** is small. Generally, it contains no more than 75,000 entries, making it handy to carry to class and efficient to use. However, a pocket dictionary doesn't contain enough entries to be adequate for postsecondary or college reference homework.

Desk or College-Level Dictionary

A **desk** or **college-level dictionary** generally contains over 170,000 entries plus extra features. For college work you should own a current desk or college-level dictionary. The following list shows some of the best-known dictionaries in this category. Notice that the titles of two dictionaries contain the name *Webster.* Because names cannot be copyrighted, any publisher may use the word *Webster* on its dictionary. Definitions and usage in this textbook are based on *Merriam-Webster's Collegiate Dictionary,* Eleventh Edition. Publishers often rely on this dictionary as their standard. Many readers, however, prefer *The American Heritage College Dictionary.* It provides more plural spellings, more usage labels, more readable entries, and more opinions about appropriate usage than most other dictionaries. Any of the following dictionaries is a good choice for postsecondary and college students:

> *The American Heritage College Dictionary*
> *Random House Webster's College Dictionary*

Webster's New World College Dictionary

Oxford American College Dictionary

Merriam-Webster's Collegiate Dictionary, Eleventh Edition (the standard dictionary for definitions and usage in this book)

Unabridged Dictionary

An **unabridged dictionary** is a complete dictionary. Abridged dictionaries, such as pocket and desk dictionaries, are shortened or condensed. Because unabridged dictionaries contain nearly all English words, they are large, heavy volumes. Schools, libraries, newspaper offices, and organizations concerned with editing or publishing use unabridged dictionaries. One of the best-known unabridged dictionaries is *Merriam-Webster's Third New International Dictionary.* It includes over 450,000 entries and claims to be America's largest dictionary. Another famous unabridged dictionary is the *Oxford English Dictionary* (OED). This 20-volume set shows the historical development of all English words; it is often used by professional writers, scholars of the language, and academics. CD-ROM versions are available for easy computer searching.

Copyright Date

If the copyright date of your current dictionary shows that it was published five or more years ago, consider investing in a more recent edition. English is a responsive, dynamic language that admits new words and recognizes changes in meaning, spelling, and usage of familiar words. These changes are reflected in an up-to-date dictionary. For example, the following words were added to the *Oxford English Dictionary* in 2005: *podcast, supersize, gamepad, wiki,* and *offshoring.*

Features

In selecting a dictionary, check the features it offers in addition to vocabulary definitions. Many editions contain biographical and geographical data, abbreviations, standard measurements, signs, symbols, foreign words and phrases, and information about the language. Some also contain CD-ROMs and access to special online features.

USING A PRINT DICTIONARY

Whether you purchased a new one or you are using a family dictionary, take a few moments to become familiar with it so that you can use it wisely.

Introduction

Before using your dictionary, take a look at the instructions located in the pages just before the beginning of the vocabulary entries. Pay particular attention to the order of definitions (senses). Some dictionaries show the most common definitions first. Other dictionaries develop meanings historically; that is, the first known meaning of the word is shown first.

Guide Words

In boldface type at the top of each dictionary page are two words that indicate the first and last entries on the page. When searching for a word, look *only* at these guide words until you locate the desired page. This will save you time.

Syllabication

Most dictionaries show syllable breaks with a centered dot, as you see in Figure 1.1 for the word *signify.* Compound words are sometimes troublesome to dictionary users. If a compound word is shown with a centered dot, it is one word, as in *work•out* (workout). If a compound word is shown with a hyphen, it is hyphenated, as in *old-fashioned.* If two words appear without a centered dot or a hyphen, they

Figure 1.1
Dictionary Entry

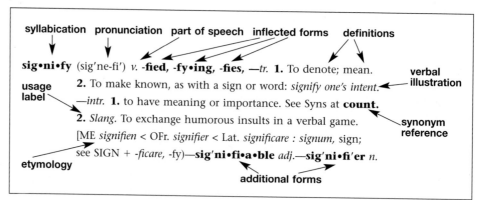

© 2000 by Houghton Mifflin Company. Reproduced by permission from *The American Heritage Dictionary of the English Language, Fourth Edition.*

HOT LINK

To access quickly any of the Hot Links, go to the *Guffey Companion Web Site* at **academic.cengage.com/ bcomm/guffey.** You'll find an updated list of all URLs used in the book.

should be written as two words, as in *work up*. If you find no entry for a word or phrase in a college-level dictionary, you may usually assume that the words are written separately, for example, *ball field*. For newer terms, such as *home page* or *firewall*, you should check an online dictionary.

Pronunciation

Diacritical marks are special symbols that help you pronounce words correctly. A detailed explanation of pronunciation symbols is found in the front pages of a dictionary. A summary of these symbols may appear at the bottom of each set of pages. If two pronunciations are possible, the preferred one is usually shown first.

Accent

Accent refers to the syllable of a word that gets the most emphasis or stress when you pronounce it. Most dictionaries show accents with a raised stress mark immediately following the accented syllable, as shown for the syllable *sig* in our example. Other dictionaries use a raised stress mark immediately *preceding* the accented syllable (*'sig ni'fi*). Secondary stress may be shown in lighter print (as illustrated on the syllable *fi* from our example), or it may be shown with a *lowered* accent mark (*'sig ni,fi*).

Etymology

Etymology shows the history of a word. College-level dictionaries provide a brief word history in square brackets [ ]. For example, the word *signify* has its roots in Middle English, Old French, and Latin. Keys to etymological abbreviations may be found in the introductory notes in your dictionary. Do not confuse the etymological definition shown in brackets with the actual word definitions.

Part of Speech

Following the phonetic pronunciation of an entry word is an italicized or boldfaced label indicating what part of speech the entry word represents. The most common labels are the following:

adj	(adjective)	*prep*	(preposition)
adv	(adverb)	*pron*	(pronoun)
conj	(conjunction)	*v* or *vb*	(verb)
interj	(interjection)	*vt* or *v tr*	(verb transitive)
n	(noun)	*vi* or *v int*	(verb intransitive)

CAREER TIP

Businesspeople are judged by the words they use. Knowing the part of speech for a word helps you use it correctly. For example, if you discover that a word is a verb, you won't try to use it to describe a noun.

Spelling, pronunciation, and meaning may differ for a given word when that word functions as different parts of speech. Therefore, check its grammatical label carefully. If the parts of speech seem foreign to you at this time, do not despair. Chapter 2 and successive chapters will help you learn more about the parts of speech.

Labels

Not all words listed in dictionaries are acceptable in business or professional writing. **Usage labels** warn readers about the use of certain words. In the dictionary entry shown in Figure 1.1, notice that one meaning for the word *signify* is labeled *slang*. The following list defines *slang* and other usage labels:

Label	Example
archaic: words surviving from a previous period	*nigh* (meaning "nearly, almost")
obsolete: no longer in use	*miss* (meaning "a loss")
colloquial or *informal*:* used in casual writing or conversation	*shindig* (meaning "a festive party")
slang: very informal but may be used sparingly for effect	*props* (meaning "respect, recognition")
nonstandard and *substandard:* not conforming to usage among educated speakers	*irregardless*
dialect, *Brit.*, *South*, *Scot*, etc.: used in certain countries or regions	*fixing* (verb used in the South to mean "getting ready to do something")

*Some dictionaries no longer use the labels colloquial *or* informal.

If no usage label appears, a word is considered standard; that is, it is acceptable for all uses. However, it should be noted that many lexicographers have substantially reduced the number of usage labels in current editions. **Lexicographers,** by the way, are those who make dictionaries.

Inflected Forms

When nouns, verbs, adverbs, or adjectives change form grammatically, they are said to be **inflected,** as when *child* becomes *children*. Because of limited space, dictionaries usually show only irregular inflected forms. Thus, nouns with irregular or unusual plurals (*wife, wives*) will be shown. Verbs with irregular tenses or difficult spelling (*bring, brought*) will be shown. Adverbs or adjectives with irregular comparatives or superlatives (*good, better, best*) will also be shown. But regular noun plurals, verb tenses, and comparatives generally will *not* be shown in dictionaries. Succeeding chapters will elucidate regular and irregular parts of speech.

Synonyms and Antonyms

Synonyms, words having similar meanings, are often provided after word definitions. For example, a synonym for *elucidate* is *explain*. Synonyms are helpful as word substitutes. **Antonyms,** words having opposite meanings, appear less frequently in dictionaries; when included, they usually follow synonyms. One antonym for *elucidate* is *confuse*. The best place to find synonyms and antonyms is in a thesaurus.

HOT LINK

How does a word get into the dictionary? Find out by visiting Merriam-Webster's Frequently Asked Questions at http://www.m-w.com/help/faq/words_in.htm.

USING ELECTRONIC DICTIONARY PROGRAMS

Most word processing programs today come with a dictionary/thesaurus feature that helps you locate misspelled words as well as search for synonyms and antonyms. In addition, most e-mail programs now include a spell-check feature that uses an electronic dictionary. You may even be able to program your e-mail program to automatically spell-check your messages when you press the **Send** button.

Locating Misspelled Words

An **electronic dictionary,** also called a **spell checker,** compares your typed words with those in the computer's memory. MS Word uses a wavy red line to underline misspelled words as you type them. If you immediately recognize the error, you can quickly key in the correction. If you see the red wavy line and don't know what's wrong, you can right-click on the word. This pulls up a drop-down menu that generally shows a variety of options to solve your spelling problem. If one of the suggested spellings appears correct, you can click it and the misspelled word is replaced.

Many writers today rely heavily on their spell checkers; in fact, many may rely too much on them. The real problem is that spell checkers won't catch every error. For example, spell checkers can't always distinguish between similar words, such as *too* and *two.* That's why you should proofread every message carefully after running it through your spell checker. In addition, important messages should be printed out for proofreading.

Searching for Synonyms and Antonyms

Electronic dictionary programs often include an online thesaurus showing alternative word choices. Let's say you are writing a report and you find yourself repeating the same word. With MS Word you can highlight the overused word and click *Tools, Language,* and *Thesaurus.* A number of synonyms appear in a dialog box. If none of the suggested words seems right, you can change the search term by using a closely related word from the *Replace with Synonym* column. From the new *Meanings* list, you can also change the word or phrase to help you find the most precise word for your meaning. A good online thesaurus can be a terrific aid to writers who want to use precise language as well as increase their vocabularies.

SPOT THE BLOOPER

A flyer promoting a square dance weekend in Daytona Beach lists the site as the Dessert Inn hotel.

USING ONLINE AND OTHER HIGH-TECH DICTIONARIES

An increasing number of electronic resources are available on the Web, on CD-ROMs, and as handheld devices. The Web provides an amazing amount of information at little or no cost to users. Many excellent online resources, some of which are described in Figure 1.2, are similar to their print counterparts. The big differences, though, are that most of the online versions are free and many also provide audio pronunciations. Some even give you hyperlinked cross-references. Online dictionaries are especially useful because they can be updated immediately when new words or meanings enter the language.

Online sites offer many features. The best-known site is *Merriam-Webster OnLine,* where you not only find authoritative definitions but also can play word games and increase your vocabulary with the *Word of the Day* feature. The site for *OneLook Dictionaries* provides over 975 different dictionaries in various fields. Microsoft's *Encarta World English Dictionary* site is unique in linking to encyclopedia articles to provide in-depth answers to your inquiries.

If you don't want to bother searching the Web to look up a word, you may purchase one of many CD-ROM dictionaries. Installed on your computer, products such as the *Random House Compact Unabridged Dictionary* or the *Oxford English*

Figure 1.2
Notable Online Dictionaries

An amazing number of Web sites offer free dictionaries and usage advice. If any of the URLs for the sites listed here have changed, just put the name into a search tool (**www.google.com**) and you should find it.

- **Merriam-Webster Online (http://www.m-w.com).** Offers audio pronunciations (click on the red speaker icon next to any word to hear its pronunciation), etymologies, and authoritative definitions of a vast number of words. Provides word games and essays on the history of English and the processes involved in the making of dictionaries. The *Word of the Day* feature defines an infrequently used word.

- **OneLook Dictionaries (http://www.onelook.com).** Claims to index more than 7 million words contained in more than 975 dictionaries (at this writing). Accesses computer/Internet, science, medical, technological, business, sports, religion, and general dictionaries.

- **American Heritage Dictionary of the English Language (http://www.bartleby.com/61).** Provides definitions for more than 90,000 entries and audio pronunciations for 70,000. Offers synonym, usage, and word history notes, along with 900 color illustrations.

- **Encarta World English Dictionary (http://dictionary.msn.com).** Not only defines and pronounces words but also links to atlases, maps, and encyclopedia articles from Microsoft's *Encarta.*

- **TheFreeDictionary.com (http://www.thefreedictionary.com).** The dictionary on this comprehensive site is based on *The American Heritage Dictionary of the English Language,* Fourth Edition, with over 250,000 entries. The site also has links to computer, medical, legal, and financial dictionaries. In addition to dictionaries, users will find links to *Wikipedia,* the *Columbia Encyclopedia,* a list of acronyms, and other valuable resources.

- **Dictionary.com (http://dictionary.reference.com/).** Provides links to a variety of references, including English dictionaries, foreign language dictionaries, thesauruses, online translators, and language-related articles. You can also access a word-of-the-day feature and vocabulary games.

Dictionary OED CD-ROM give you access to a large database of words that can be easily searched electronically.

Handheld electronic dictionaries offer another efficient way to check spellings, find meanings, and look up synonyms. Many students and businesspeople find handhelds easy to use. They are especially appealing to people struggling with a different language, such as tourists, interpreters, emigrants, and immigrants. Some are voice-enabled translation devices and even can talk. Two examples are the *Franklin Handheld Dictionary* and the *Merriam-Webster Collegiate Speaking Dictionary.*

REFERENCE MANUALS

In addition to one or more printed dictionaries, every writer should have a good reference manual or handbook readily available.

REFERENCE MANUALS VERSUS DICTIONARIES

A reference manual generally contains helpful information not available in a dictionary. Two popular reference manuals are *How 11: A Handbook for Office*

Professionals and *The Gregg Reference Manual.* Most reference manuals provide information such as the following:

- **Punctuation.** Detailed explanations of punctuation rules are presented logically. A well-written manual will also provide ample illustrations of punctuation usage so that the reader can readily find solutions to punctuation dilemmas.
- **Hyphenation.** Dictionaries provide syllable breaks. Words, however, cannot be divided at all syllable breaks. A reference manual will supply rules for, and examples of, word division. Moreover, a good reference manual will explain when compound adjectives such as *up-to-the-minute* should be hyphenated.
- **Capitalization.** Complete rules with precise examples illustrating capitalization style will be shown.
- **Number style.** Deciding whether to write a number as a figure or as a word can be confusing. A reference manual will provide both instruction and numerous examples illustrating number and word styles.
- **Commonly confused words.** Do you have trouble deciding whether to use *affect* or *effect, its* or *it's, than* or *then,* or *principal* or *principle*? Reference manuals contain complete lists of commonly confused words to help you choose the right one.
- **Abbreviations.** What is the two-letter state abbreviation for Arkansas? Can the abbreviation *a.m.* be written with uppercase letters? Should I add periods to the abbreviation *FBI*? A good reference manual can help answer your questions about using those tricky abbreviations and acronyms.

Other topics covered in reference manuals are contractions, literary and artistic titles, forms of address, letter and report formats, employment application documents, information sources, and file management. In addition, some manuals contain sections devoted to English grammar and office procedures. This textbook is correlated with the widely used *Handbook for Office Professionals* (South-Western Cengage Learning) by Clark and Clark.

REFERENCE MANUALS VERSUS YOUR TEXTBOOK

You may be wondering how a reference manual differs from a business English textbook such as the one you are now reading. Although their content is similar, the primary difference is one of purpose. A textbook is developed *pedagogically*—that is, for teaching—so that the student understands and learns concepts. It includes teaching and learning exercises. A reference manual is organized *functionally*, so that the reader finds accurate information efficiently. A well-written reference manual is complete, coherent, and concise.

Most of the language and style questions that perplex businesspeople and students could be answered quickly by a trained person using a reliable dictionary and a well-written reference manual.

Now complete the reinforcement exercises on the following pages.

Note: At the beginning of every set of reinforcement exercises, a self-check exercise is provided so that you will know immediately whether you understand the concepts presented in the chapter. Do not look at the answers until you have completed the exercise. Then compare your responses with the answers shown at the bottom of the page. If you have more than three incorrect responses, reread the chapter before continuing with the other reinforcement exercises.

A. **(Self-check)** Write *T* (true) or *F* (false) after the following statements.

1. Because all dictionaries contain similar information, it doesn't matter which you purchase or use. _____

2. Students and office workers would find an unabridged dictionary handy to carry with them. _____

3. The label *archaic* means that a word is informal and may be used in casual writing and conversation. _____

4. Knowing which syllable is accented can help you pronounce words correctly. _____

5. Dictionaries usually show noun plurals only if they are irregular. _____

6. Rules for using abbreviations may be found in a reference manual. _____

7. All dictionaries show definitions in historical order. _____

8. Today's spell-check programs can be used to locate all misspelled words in a document. _____

Check your answers at the bottom of the page.

Use a desk, college-level, electronic, or online dictionary to complete the following exercises. The definitions, pronunciations, and usage in this book come from *Merriam-Webster's Collegiate Dictionary*, Eleventh Edition.

B. Select the letter that provides the best definition or synonym for each word shown.

1. pandemic (adj)   a. famous   b. widespread
       c. notorious   d. panoramic   _____

2. entomology (n)   a. study of words   b. study of fossils
       c. study of insects   d. love of outdoors   _____

3. imminent (adj)   a. impending   b. old
       c. famous   d. stubborn   _____

4. integrity (n)   a. value   b. honesty
       c. perseverance   d. loyalty   _____

5. ostentatious (adj)   a. annoying   b. rude
       c. eager   d. showy   _____

6. feasible (adj.)   a. possible   b. unlikely
       c. likeable   d. difficult   _____

1. F 2. F 3. F 4. T 5. T 6. T 7. F 8. F

Want to explore more? Go to: academic.cengage.com/bcomm/guffey or Xtra!

REFERENCE SKILLS | **CHAPTER 1** | **11**

C. Write the correct form of the following words. Use a current dictionary to determine whether they should be written as one or two words or should be hyphenated.

Example: print out (n)   printout _____

1. co worker   _____   4. on line   _____

2. in as much as _____   5. out of date   _____

3. in depth   _____   6. work place   _____

D. For each of the following words, write the syllable that receives the primary accent. Then give a brief definition or synonym of the word.

Word	Syllable	Definition or Synonym
Example: judicious	di	prudent, exhibiting sound judgment
1. comparable	com	_____
2. desert (n)	des	_____
3. desert (v)	sert	_____
4. indefatigable	fat	_____
5. irrevocable	rev	_____
6. posthumous	post	_____

E. If your dictionary shows usage labels for the following words, write them in the spaces provided. If no label appears for a word, which of the following labels would you consider giving it if you were a lexicographer? Put your initials next to the labels you suggest.

Labels: archaic   nonstandard   colloquial or informal   dialect   slang

Example: bloke   dialect (British meaning for "man" or "fellow") _____

1. anyways   _____

2. pushchair   _____

3. eighty-six   _____

4. sheila   _____

5. irregardless _____

6. sawbuck   _____

F. Select the letter that most accurately completes the sentence.

1. The word *chauvinism* derives from Nicholas *Chauvin,* a Frenchman known as a(n)
   a. fanatical bomb thrower   b. extreme misogynist (woman hater)
   c. excessive patriot   d. radical critic of Napoleon

2. If Angelica attends a training session and reports that it was *superficial,* she means that it was
   a. shallow and without substance   b. super helpful
   c. extremely entertaining   d. fun but worthless

Want to explore more? Go to: academic.cengage.com/bcomm/guffey or Xtra!

3. The abbreviation* (actually, an acronym) for the Occupational Safety and Health Administration is
   a. O.S.H.A.
   b. Osha
   c. OSHA
   d. OS&HA
   _____

4. Which of the following is correctly written?
   a. American novel
   b. american novel
   c. American Novel
   d. american Novel
   _____

5. When businesspeople talk about *software,* they are referring to
   a. computer equipment
   b. computer programs
   c. goods that are not durable
   d. uneven profits
   _____

6. If an expression is *redundant,* it is
   a. repetitive
   b. obsolete
   c. clever
   d. awkward
   _____

7. The word *spam,* which now means "unsolicited e-mail," derives from
   a. a slang term for an annoying person
   b. users who hate receiving it
   c. *Monty Python's Flying Circus*
   d. senders who want to remain anonymous
   _____

8. Because Sophia wanted to _____ that all of her friends received her new e-mail address, she sent everyone a special announcement.
   a. assure
   b. insure
   c. ensure
   d. advice
   _____

G. **Writing Exercise.** All employers seek workers with good writing skills. In this book you will find unit workshops devoted to developing your writing skills. In addition, each chapter will include a short writing exercise. Let's say that a friend asks you to explain what a reference manual is and why it might be useful. Write two or three sentences with your explanation.

_____

_____

_____

_____

In two or three complete sentences, tell whether you prefer a print or an online dictionary. Explain why.

_____

_____

_____

_____
*Does your dictionary list abbreviations after the main entries? You'll learn more about acronyms in Chapter 2.

Want to explore more? Go to: academic.cengage.com/bcomm/guffey or Xtra!

REFERENCE SKILLS | CHAPTER 1 | 13

The following e-mail message contains 30 misspelled or misused words, some of which you looked up in earlier exercises. Underline any error and write a correction above OR make the corrections to this exercise at the **Guffey Companion Web Site** at **academic.cengage.com/bcomm/guffey.**

File Edit Mailbox Message Transfer Special Tools Window Help

B *I* U 🔗 ≡ ≡ ≡ A˅ A˄ ⁺≡ ⁺≡ ⁺≡ ⁺≡ 🅰   **Send**

From: Marissa Pelham <mpelham@zyt.net>
To: Heather Martinez <hmartinez@zyt.net>
Cc:
Subject: Thanks for Considering ZyTec Software

Dear Ms. Martinez:

We are happy to learn from your recent massage that Brookline School is considering ZyTec Software Systems as it's source for educational software. Our softwear, which is being used successfully in many area work places and schools, is designed to be especially user friendly.

When we sell a software system to a school, we take great car to insure that we provide suitable training for the school staff. Some companys provide a short training course for there school staff; however, we recognise that most questions arise long after training sessions are completed. Rather then providing the "hit and run" superfitial training that has become common in the industry, weve learned that the best way to train school staff is to provide indepth training for two teachers from each school. After these too teachers work with our training consultant, they are formerly equipped to act as teacher-trainers who can expertly train you teachers and staff.

Unlike trainers who are available for only a few ours, your teacher-trainers would be available to answer questions and concerns when ever they arise. Further more, ZyTec establishes ongoing relationships with teacher-trainers so that your teachers will all ways have the softwear support that they need.

You will soon be recieving a copy of ZyTec's educational softwear training program guide as well as a copy of one of our training cd's. I hope you will find these resource helpful as you consider ZyTec's educational software. In as much as a number of neighbouring schools are using ZyTec software, you might fine it useful to speak with a teacher-trainer from a near by school district. Please call or write to let me know whether such a meeting is feasable.

All the best,

Marissa Pelham
Senior Marketing Manager
ZyTec Software Systems
Phone: (404) 921-1489
E-mail: mpelham@zyt.net

Want to explore more? Go to: academic.cengage.com/bcomm/guffey or Xtra!

14 | **UNIT 1** | **CHAPTER 1** | **REFERENCE SKILLS**

To make sure you enter the work world with good Internet skills, this book provides a short Web exercise in each chapter. If your instructor assigns this exercise, you will need access to a computer with an Internet connection. Additionally, your computer must have a Web browser, such as Microsoft Explorer or Netscape. These programs enable you to see and use Web pages.

All Web pages have addresses called URLs (uniform resource locators). URLs must be typed exactly as they are shown, including periods (.), hyphens (-), underscores (_), slashes (/), tildes (~), and upper- or lowercase letters. URLs are often enclosed in angle brackets < >. You do not need to include the angle brackets when typing a URL.

The following exercise introduces you to an online dictionary. A major advantage of an online dictionary is that it presents the latest information. It also provides pronunciation if your computer has a sound card.

Goal: To gain confidence in using an online dictionary.

1. With your Web browser on the screen, key the following URL in the location box: **http://www.m-w.com.** Press **Enter.**
2. Look over the *Merriam-Webster Online* home page. Move up and down the page by using the scroll bar at the right. Try to ignore the marketing clutter.
3. Scroll to the top and move your cursor to the **Merriam-Webster Online Dictionary** box.
4. Key the word *spam.* Click **Look it up.**
5. Scroll down to see the definition for *spam—noun.*
6. Click the red speaker icon to hear the word pronounced. Then close the box.
7. Print a copy of the definition page by clicking **File** (upper left corner of your browser). Click **Print** and **OK.** Save all printouts to turn in.
8. Click **Back** (upper left corner of browser) to return to the search page.
9. In the **Merriam-Webster Online Dictionary** box, delete the word *spam.* Key the word *firewall* and click **Look it up.** Notice that the dictionary shows that this word is spelled as two words. Read the definition. Print a copy.
10. Click **Back.** Using either the **Dictionary** or **Thesaurus** feature, look up one word from Exercise F. Print the definition or synonym.
11. Click **Word of the Day** (left navigation panel). Read about the word. Print a copy.
12. End your session by clicking the **X** box (upper right corner of browser).
13. As your instructor advises, send an e-mail message summarizing what you learned or turn in all printed copies properly identified.

Write *T* (true) or *F* (false) after the following statements. Compare your answers with those at the bottom of the page.

1. The best dictionary for a college student's assignments is a pocket dictionary. _____

2. When searching for a word in a dictionary, look only at the guide words until you locate the desired page. _____

3. The etymology of a word is usually contained within square brackets. _____

4. The usage label *slang* means that the word may be used in certain regions only. _____

5. A reference manual can help you determine whether to use *capital* or *capitol* in a sentence. _____

1. F 2. T 3. T 4. F 5. T

Want to explore more? Go to: academic.cengage.com/bcomm/guffey or Xtra!

REFERENCE SKILLS │ CHAPTER 1 │ 15

© Jean-Louis Bellurget RF/Pixland/Jupiter Images

PARTS OF SPEECH

When you have completed the materials in this chapter, you will be able to do the following:

- Define the eight parts of speech.
- Recognize how parts of speech function in sentences.
- Compose sentences showing words playing more than one grammatical role.

PRETEST

Study the following sentence and identify selected parts of speech. For each word listed underline the correct part of speech. Compare your answers with those at the bottom of the page.

The **customer and** I **critically evaluated** information **on** the company Web site.

1. customer	a. noun	b. pronoun	c. verb	d. adjective
2. and	a. preposition	b. conjunction	c. adjective	d. adverb
3. critically	a. adjective	b. conjunction	c. preposition	d. adverb
4. evaluated	a. adverb	b. noun	c. verb	d. adverb
5. on	a. preposition	b. conjunction	c. adjective	d. adverb

1. a 2. b 3. d 4. c 5. a

As you learned in Chapter 1, this book focuses on the study of the fundamentals of grammar, current usage, and appropriate business and professional style. Such a study logically begins with the eight parts of speech, the building blocks of our language. This chapter provides a brief overview of the parts of speech. The following chapters will deal with these topics more thoroughly.

CAREER TIP

"Whatever your program in college, be sure to include courses in writing and speaking. Managers must constantly write instructions, reports, memos, letters, and survey conclusions. If this comes hard to you, it will hold you back."
—James A. Newman and Alexander Roy in *Climbing the Corporate Matterhorn*

THE EIGHT PARTS OF SPEECH

Learning the eight parts of speech helps you develop the working vocabulary necessary to discuss and study the language. You especially need to recognize the parts of speech in the context of sentences. That's because many words function in more than one role. Only by analyzing the sentence at hand can you see how a given word functions. It's unlikely that your boss will ask you to identify the parts of speech in a business document. Being able to do so, however, will help you punctuate correctly and choose precise words for clear, powerful writing. In addition, understanding the roles different parts of speech play in written and oral communication will be helpful if you learn another language.

NOUNS

In elementary school you probably learned that a **noun** refers to a person, place, or thing. In addition, nouns name qualities, feelings, concepts, activities, and measures.

Persons:	Stephanie, Dr. Edelstein, teacher, accountant
Places:	Chicago, island, Italy, college
Things:	novel, surfboard, bicycle, horse
Qualities:	patience, honesty, initiative, enthusiasm
Feelings:	happiness, anger, confusion, sadness
Concepts:	knowledge, freedom, friendship, travel
Activities:	snowboarding, dancing, management, eating
Measures:	day, week, inch, kilometer, million

Nouns are important words in our language. Sentences revolve around nouns because these words function both as subjects and as objects of verbs. To determine whether a word is really a noun, try using it with the verb *is* or *are*. Notice that all the nouns listed here would make sense if used in this way: *Stephanie is young, Chicago is in Illinois, horses are beautiful, dancing is fun,* and so on. In Chapter 4 you will learn four classes of nouns and rules for making nouns plural. In Chapter 5 you'll learn how to show that a noun possesses something.

HOT LINK

To help build your vocabulary, check out Merriam-Webster's *Word of the Day* feature at **http://www.m-w.com/ cgi-bin/mwwod.pl.** Each day editors define a new word, use it creatively, and provide fascinating word lore.

SPOT THE BLOOPER

A high school principal quoted in the *San Francisco Chronicle:* "He had some personal issues his mother and him were working on."

PRONOUNS

Pronouns are words used in place of nouns. As noun substitutes, pronouns provide variety and efficiency. Compare these two versions of the same sentence:

Without pronouns:	Scott gave the book to Kelli so that Kelli could use the book to study.
With pronouns:	Scott gave the book to Kelli so that *she* could use *it* to study.

In sentences pronouns may function as subjects of verbs (for example, *I, we, they*) or as objects of verbs (for example, *me, us, them*). They may act as connectors (for example, *that, which, who*), and they may show possession (for example, *mine, ours, hers, theirs*). Only a few examples are given here. More examples, along with functions and classifications of pronouns, will be presented in Chapters 6 and 7.

Please note that words such as *his, my, her,* and *its* are classified as adjectives when they describe nouns (*his car, my desk, its engine*). This concept will be explained more thoroughly in Chapters 6 and 11.

VERBS

Verbs express an action, an occurrence, or a state of being.

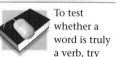
> Jason *built* an excellent Web site. (Action)
>
> It *has* many links. (Occurrence)
>
> He *is* proud of it. (State of being)

Action verbs show the action of a sentence. Some action verbs are *runs, studies, works,* and *fixes.* Verbs that express a state of being generally link to the subject words that describe or rename it. Some linking verbs are *am, is, are, was, were, be, being,* and *been.* Other linking verbs express the senses: *feels, appears, tastes, sounds, seems, looks.*

Verbs will be discussed more fully in Chapters 8 through 10. At this point it is important that you be able to recognize verbs so that you can determine whether sentences are complete. All sentences have at least one verb; many sentences will have more than one verb. Verbs may appear singly or in phrases.

> Stacy *submitted* her application to become a management trainee. (Action verb)
>
> Her résumé *is* just one page long. (Linking verb)
>
> She *has been training* to become a manager. (Verb phrase)
>
> Stacy *feels* bad that she *will be leaving* her current colleagues. (Linking verb and verb phrase)

ADJECTIVES

Words that describe nouns or pronouns are called **adjectives.** They often answer the questions *What kind? How many?* and *Which one?* The adjectives in the following sentences are italicized. Observe that the adjectives all answer questions about the nouns they describe.

> *Small, independent* businesses are becoming *numerous.* (What kinds of businesses?)
>
> We have *six* franchises in *four* states. (How many franchises? How many states?)
>
> *That* chain of health clubs started as a *small* operation. (Which chain? What kind of operation?)
>
> He is *energetic* and *forceful,* while she is *personable* and *deliberate.* (What pronouns do these adjectives describe?)

Adjectives usually precede nouns. They may, however, follow the words they describe, especially when used with linking verbs, as shown in the first and last preceding examples. Here is a brief list of words used as adjectives:

effective	green	sensitive
excellent	intelligent	small
expensive	long	successful

Three words (*a, an,* and *the*) form a special group of adjectives called **articles.** Adjectives will be discussed more thoroughly in Chapter 11.

ADVERBS

Words that modify (describe or limit) verbs, adjectives, or other adverbs are **adverbs.** Adverbs often answer the questions *When? How? Where?* and *To what extent?*

> *Today* we must complete the project. (Must complete the project *when*?)
>
> Mitch approached the intersection *cautiously*. (Approached *how*?)
>
> He seems *especially* competent. (*How* competent?)
>
> Did you see the schedule *there*? (*Where*?)
>
> The prosecutor did not question him *further*. (Questioned him *to what extent*?)

Some of the most commonly used adverbs follow:

carefully	now	really
evenly	only	too
greatly	rather	very

Many, but not all, words ending in *ly* are adverbs. Some exceptions are *friendly, costly,* and *ugly,* all of which are adjectives. Adverbs will be discussed in greater detail in Chapter 11.

PREPOSITIONS

Prepositions join nouns and pronouns to other words in a sentence. As the word itself suggests (*pre* meaning "before"), a preposition is a word in a position *before* its object (a noun or pronoun). Prepositions are used in phrases to show a relationship between the object of the preposition and another word in the sentence. In the following sentence notice how the preposition changes the relation of the object (*Ms. Tokuyama*) to the verb (*talked*):

> Brian often talked *with* Ms. Tokuyama.
>
> Brian often talked *about* Ms. Tokuyama.
>
> Brian often talked *to* Ms. Tokuyama.

Some of the most frequently used prepositions are *at, by, for, from, in, of, to,* and *with.* A more complete list of prepositions can be found in Chapter 12. Learn to recognize objects of prepositions so that you won't confuse them with sentence subjects.

CONJUNCTIONS

Words that connect other words or groups of words are **conjunctions.** The most common conjunctions are *and, but, or,* and *nor.* These are called coordinating conjunctions because they join equal (coordinate) parts of sentences. Other kinds of conjunctions will be presented in Chapter 13. Study the examples of coordinating conjunctions shown here:

> Yukie, Dan, *and* Kristi are all looking for jobs. (Joins equal words.)
>
> You may be interviewed by a human resources officer *or* by a supervising manager. (Joins equal groups of words.)

STUDY TIP

To remember more easily what an *adverb* does, think of its two syllables: *ad* suggests that you will be adding to or amplifying the meaning of a *verb.* Hence, adverbs often modify verbs.

SPOT THE BLOOPER

This headline appeared in a small-town newspaper: "Stolen Painting Found by Tree."

INTERJECTIONS

Words expressing strong feelings are **interjections.** Interjections standing alone are followed by exclamation marks. When woven into a sentence, they are usually followed by commas.

> *Wow!* Did you see what she wrote in her e-mail message?

> *Oops!* I forgot to send the attachment.

SUMMARY

The following sentence illustrates all eight parts of speech.

Well, I certainly will submit a résumé and application letter to them.

You need to know the functions of these eight parts of speech in order to understand the rest of this textbook and profit from your study of language basics. The explanation of the parts of speech has been kept simple so far. This chapter is meant to serve as an introduction to later, more fully developed chapters. At this stage you should not expect to be able to identify the functions of *all* words in *all* sentences.

A word of caution: English is a wonderfully flexible language. As noted earlier, many words in our language serve as more than one part of speech. Notice how flexible the word *mail* is in these sentences:

> Our *mail* is late today. (Noun—serves as subject of sentence)

> This pile of *mail* must be delivered today. (Noun—serves as object of preposition)

> *Mail* the letter today. (Verb—serves as action word in sentence)

> Your voice *mail* box is full. (Adjective—used with *voice* to describe *box*, which is the subject of sentence)

Now complete the reinforcement exercises for this chapter.

Answered by Dr. Guffey

Business and professional people are very concerned about appropriate and professional English usage, grammar, and style. This concern is evident in the number and kinds of questions called and e-mailed to grammar hotline services across the country. Among the users of these services are business supervisors, managers, executives, professionals, secretaries, clerks, administrative assistants, and word processing specialists. Writers, teachers, librarians, students, and other community members also seek answers to language questions.

Selected questions and Dr. Guffey's answers to them will be presented in the following chapters. In this way you, as a student of the language, will understand the kinds of everyday communication problems encountered in business and professional environments.

Representative questions come from grammar hotline services across the country. You can locate lists of grammar hotlines by using the search phrase *grammar hotline* in *Google* (**www.google.com**). Many grammar hotlines have Web sites where you can browse questions and answers. Most grammar hotlines accept questions via both e-mail and phone.

Question

Q: We're having a big argument in our office. What's correct? *E-mail, e-mail, email,* or *Email? On-line* or *online? Website, Web site, web site,* or *website?*

Q: Should I capitalize the word *Internet?* I see it written both ways and am confused.

Q: What is the name of a group of initials that form a word? Is it an abbreviation?

Q: I saw this sentence recently in the newspaper: *At the movie premiere the crowd scanned the arriving limousines for glitterati.* Is *glitterati* a real word?

Answer

A: In the early days of computing, people capitalized *E-mail* and hyphenated *on-line.* With increased use, however, both of these forms have been simplified to *e-mail* and *online.* In regard to *Web site,* I recommend the capitalized two-word form. Capitalizing *Web* is logical since it is a shortened form for World Wide Web. These are also the forms noted by the *Merriam-Webster Collegiate Dictionary,* Eleventh Edition (our standard reference). You might want to check with your company's in-house style manual for its preferred style for all of these words.

A: I recommend writing the word with a capital *I* (*Internet*). However, we are in a time of change with regard to the proper spelling and writing of Web-related words. For example, *Wired News* was the first to spell *Internet, Web,* and *Net* using lowercase letters; others may follow. For now, though, you should continue to capitalize *Internet* and *Web* because that's what many style manuals and dictionaries recommend.

A: A word formed from the initial letters of an expression is called an *acronym* (pronounced ACK-ro-nim). Examples: *scuba* from *self-contained underwater breathing apparatus,* and *PIN* from *personal identification number.* Acronyms are pronounced as single words and are different from abbreviations. Expressions such as *FBI* and *NFL* are abbreviations, not acronyms. Notice that an abbreviation is pronounced letter by letter (*F, B, I*), whereas an acronym is pronounced as a word. An example of an acronym is *OSHA* (pronounced *Oh-shah*), which stands for *Occupational Safety and Health Administration.* Shortened versions of words such as *dept.* and *Ms.* are also considered abbreviations.

A: A fairly recent arrival to our vocabulary, *glitterati* means "celebrities or beautiful people." (The word is actually a blend of the words *glitter* and *literati.*) New words are generally considered legitimate when their use is clear and when they are necessary (that is, when no other word says exactly what they do). If educated individuals begin to use such words, the words then appear in dictionaries, and *glitterati* has made it.

Q: What's the difference between *toward* and *towards?*

A: None. They are interchangeable in use. However, I recommend using the shorter word *toward* because it is more efficient.

Q: Is *every day* one word or two in this case? *We encounter these problems every day.*

A: In your sentence it is two words. When it means "ordinary," it is one word (*she wore everyday clothes*). If you can insert the word *single* between *every* and *day* without altering your meaning, you should be using two words, as in your sentence.

Q: Should an e-mail message begin with a salutation or some kind of greeting?

A: When e-mail messages are sent to company insiders, a salutation may be omitted; however, including a salutation will personalize your message. When e-mail messages travel to outsiders, omitting a salutation seems curt and unfriendly. Because the message is more like a letter, a salutation is appropriate (such as *Dear Courtney*, *Hi Courtney*, *Greetings,* or just *Courtney*). Including a salutation is also a visual cue that identifies the beginning of the message. Some writers prefer to incorporate the name of the recipient in the first sentence (*Thanks, Courtney, for responding so quickly*).

Q: In e-mail messages is it acceptable to use abbreviations such as *IMHO* (*in my humble opinion*), *LOL* (*laughing out loud*), and *TIA* (*thanks in advance*)?

A: Among close friends who understand their meaning, such abbreviations are certainly acceptable. But in business messages, these abbreviations are too casual and too obscure. Many readers would have no idea what they mean. Smileys (or emoticons) such as :-) are also too casual for business messages. Worst of all, abbreviations and emoticons make business messages look immature and unprofessional.

Q: Tell me it's not true! I just heard that the word *d'oh,* which is uttered frequently by the Homer Simpson character, was recently added to the *Oxford English Dictionary.* Surely this is an urban legend.

A: It's true. The word *d'oh* was recently added to the *Oxford English Dictionary*, long considered the foremost authority on the English language. Its editors decided that the word *d'oh* is so universally accepted that it warranted formal recognition. This certainly proves what an effect popular culture has on our language. However, keep in mind that not all words appearing in dictionaries are appropriate for business messages.

A. (Self-check) Complete these statements.

1. Names for persons, places, things, qualities, feelings, concepts, activities, and measures are
   a. verbs   b. adjectives   c. nouns   d. pronouns   _____

2. Words that substitute for nouns are
   a. adverbs   b. adjectives   c. interjections   d. pronouns   _____

3. The part of speech that answers the question *What kind?* and *How many?* is a/an
   a. adverb   b. adjective   c. preposition   d. conjunction   _____

4. Words such as *slowly, very,* and *tomorrow* that answer the questions *How?* and *When?* are
   a. adverbs   b. adjectives   c. nouns   d. conjunctions   _____

5. *I, you, they, hers,* and *he* are examples of
   a. pronouns   b. nouns   c. adverbs   d. adjectives   _____

6. *Wow, well,* and *oops* are examples of
   a. pronouns   b. prepositions   c. interjections   d. adjectives   _____

7. *And, or, nor,* and *but* are
   a. adverbs   b. prepositions   c. interjections   d. conjunctions   _____

8. Words such as *by, in,* and *of* that join noun or pronoun objects to other words in sentences are
   a. adverbs   b. prepositions   c. conjunctions   d. adjectives   _____

Check your answers below.

B. In each of the following groups of sentences, one word is used as an adjective, as a noun, and as a verb. For each sentence indicate the part of speech for the italicized word.

Example: We have little *time* in which to make a decision.   noun _____

   Officials will *time* the runners in the marathon.   verb _____

   Factory workers must punch a *time* clock.   adjective _____

1. He had to *dress* quickly for the awards ceremony.   _____

2. Does your company have a *dress* code?   _____

3. She decided to wear a suit instead of a *dress* to the interview.   _____

4. Doug prefers a casual *work* environment.   _____

5. Susan arrives at *work* early each morning.   _____

6. The entire department *worked* overtime to finish the project.   _____

7. Advertisements promised instruction from a *master* teacher.   _____

8. Few students can *master* Web design in a short course.   _____

9. Warren Buffet is a *master* in the field of investing.   _____

1. c   2. d   3. b   4. a   5. a   6. c   7. d   8. b

Want to explore more? Go to: academic.cengage.com/bcomm/guffey or Xtra!

PARTS OF SPEECH | CHAPTER 2 | 23

Write complete sentences using the word *contract* as a noun, as an adjective, and as a verb.

10. (noun) _____

11. (verb) _____

12. (adjective) _____

C. The italicized words in the following sentences are either prepositions or conjunctions. Write *C* for conjunction or *P* for preposition.

1. Technical skills are important *for* entry-level positions, *but* communication skills are necessary for promotion *into* management.

for _____

but _____

into _____

2. Writing good letters *and* e-mail messages *to* customers creates goodwill *for* business and professional organizations.

and _____

to _____

for _____

D. Read the following sentences and, taking into account the function of each word within each sentence, identify the part of speech of each word shown. Use a dictionary if necessary.

One e-mail message contained a virus, but it was very quickly deleted.

1. One	_____	**7.** but	_____
2. e-mail	_____	**8.** it	_____
3. message	_____	**9.** was	_____
4. contained	_____	**10.** very	_____
5. a	_____	**11.** quickly	_____
6. virus	_____	**12.** deleted	_____

She hurriedly scanned several e-mail messages before the meeting.

1. She	_____	**5.** e-mail	_____
2. hurriedly	_____	**6.** messages	_____
3. scanned	_____	**7.** before	_____
4. several	_____	**8.** meeting	_____

E. Selected verbs in the following sentences have been italicized. Use a check mark to indicate whether these verbs are linking or action.

	LINKING VERB	ACTION VERB
Example: Broadband *is* faster than DSL.	✓	_____
1. An optimist *is* a person who thinks a housefly is looking for a way out.	_____	_____
2. Google Earth *provides* a tool for viewing satellite images.	_____	_____
3. The hotel manager *selected* four trainees from many applicants.	_____	_____

Want to explore more? Go to: academic.cengage.com/bcomm/guffey or Xtra!

4. Her outgoing message *sounds* professional. _____ _____

5. Please *deliver* the computers and printers before April 4. _____ _____

6. The manager and the human resources director *studied* all job
descriptions carefully. _____ _____

7. Words *are* the most powerful drug used by mankind. _____ _____

8. Antonia *felt* bad that too much month was left at the end of her money. _____ _____

F. Hotline Review. In the space provided write the correct answer choice.

1. Those research statistics are available on the _____.
a. internet   b. Internet   c. InterNet   _____

2. Experts suggest that users check their _____ at regular intervals.
a. Email   b. E-mail   c. email   d. e-mail   _____

3. We are considering subscribing to an _____ databank to aid research.
a. on-line   b. online   _____

4. Our _____ has been completely updated.
a. Web site   b. website   c. web site   d. web-site   _____

5. All computer files must be backed up _____ to prevent possible loss.
a. everyday   b. every day   c. every-day   _____

6. Backing up files is an _____ occurrence in most organizations.
a. everyday   b. every day   c. every-day   _____

7. Which of the following is an acronym?
a. U.S.A.   b. IRS   c. PIN   d. RSVP   _____

8. Which of the following is an abbreviation?
a. laser   b. MADD   c. NASDAQ   d. DVD   _____

G. Writing Exercise. In two or three complete sentences, explain why it is important to understand the
parts of speech for this course and later on the job.

_____

_____

_____

In a few sentences, explain the difference between nouns and verbs. Which do you think is more
important to a writer?

_____

_____

_____

_____

Want to explore more? Go to: academic.cengage.com/bcomm/guffey or Xtra!

PARTS OF SPEECH | CHAPTER 2 | **25**

The following memo requires you to supply a single word for each blank. The word you supply should represent the part of speech shown. You may complete the exercise here or at the **Guffey Companion Web Site** at **academic.cengage.com/bcomm/guffey.**

CONSOLIDATED INDUSTRIES
INTEROFFICE MEMO

DATE: January 28, 200x
TO: All Employees
FROM: Brandon James, Manager   *B J*
SUBJECT: Reducing Overnight Delivery Costs

Overnight delivery services are speedy, but [pronoun] _____ are costing us too much [noun] _____. Here at Consolidated, we have seen our use of these services increasingly devour a [adjective] _____ portion of our shipping budget. It seems that anyone who wants to send something to a customer or a vendor automatically [verb] _____ it by FedEx. Although we have corporate rates with FedEx, we are still spending too much on overnight deliveries.

To avoid future restrictions imposed by the CEO, I'm [verb] _____ you to voluntarily reduce your use of these delivery services by 50 percent in the next two months.

Rather than face a ban on all [adjective] _____ services, let's work together to reduce our costs. Here are some suggestions:

1. Ask yourself whether the recipient will [adverb] _____ use the information immediately. If not, [verb] _____ a cheaper method.

2. Send messages [preposition] _____ fax or e-mail. A long-distance fax costs only about 35 cents, [conjunction] _____ local messages cost nothing. E-mail messages are equally inexpensive.

3. Use the FedEx or UPS account number [preposition] _____ the recipient whenever possible.

4. Plan ahead so that [pronoun] _____ can use FedEx or UPS ground service. These ground [noun] _____ take about three to five days.

Some overnight shipments, of course, [verb] _____ critical. However, to retain our budget for those essential shipments, we must [verb] _____ our overall use by one half before April 1. If you can think of [adjective] _____ ways to reduce overnight shipments, please call me at Ext. 213. I appreciate your ideas and your [noun] _____ in solving this problem.

Want to explore more? Go to: academic.cengage.com/bcomm/guffey or Xtra!

26 | UNIT 1 | CHAPTER 2 | PARTS OF SPEECH

Many colleges and universities offer online writing labs (OWLs). These Web sites provide helpful resources for students and businesspeople. You can read online or download handouts that provide help with punctuation, spelling, sentence construction, parts of speech, and writing in the job search.

Goal: To learn to use an online writing lab.

1. With your Web browser on the screen, key the following URL in the location box: **http://owl.english.purdue.edu.** Press **Enter.**
2. Click the **The OWL at Purdue** link.
3. Scroll down to reveal the site's nine areas as listed in the navigation menu to the right. Notice that you can click on each option to reveal a drop-down menu showing the complete contents of each area. Clicking the menu item a second time closes the drop-down menu.
4. Click **The Writing Process.**
5. From the list of handouts, click **Proofreading Your Writing.** The handout will display in the main window.
6. Read the handout.
7. Print a copy. (You can click the **Full Resource for Printing** icon to print any handout.)
8. Select another topic to peruse.
9. End your session by clicking the **X** box in the upper right corner of your browser. Turn in your printout or send an e-mail message to your instructor summarizing what you learned.

Identify the parts of speech in this sentence by underlining the correct choice. Compare your answers with those at the bottom of the page.

Paul **nervously waited** for his turn to interview for the **available position.**

1. nervously	a. adverb	b. pronoun	c. preposition	d. conjunction
2. waited	a. adverb	b. verb	c. preposition	d. conjunction
3. for	a. interjection	b. pronoun	c. preposition	d. conjunction
4. available	a. verb	b. noun	c. adverb	d. adjective
5. position	a. pronoun	b. verb	c. noun	d. adjective

1. a 2. b 3. c 4. d 5. c

Want to explore more? Go to: academic.cengage.com/bcomm/guffey or Xtra!

PARTS OF SPEECH | CHAPTER 2 | 27

© JGI/Blend Images/Jupiter Images

SENTENCES: ELEMENTS, PATTERNS, TYPES

OBJECTIVES

When you have completed the materials in this chapter, you will be able to do the following:

- Recognize basic sentence elements including subjects and predicates.
- Identify four basic sentence patterns.
- Convert fragments into complete sentences.
- Recognize basic sentence faults such as comma splices and run-on sentences.
- Punctuate statements, questions, commands, and exclamations.

PRETEST

Write the correct letter after each of the following numbered groups of words to identify it.

a = correctly punctuated sentence   c = comma splice
b = fragment   d = run-on sentence

1. Jennifer who was recently hired as a management trainee.   _____

2. Guitar Center's stock price increased this year, Jet Blue's decreased.   _____

3. On the ground floor of our building are a café and a bookstore.   _____

1.b 2.c 3.a 4.d 5.b

28

4. Some employers monitor their employees' e-mail others do not want to bother. _____

5. Although many employees start at 6 a.m., which explains the empty parking lot. _____

Sentences are groups of words that express complete thoughts. In this chapter you'll review the basic elements of every sentence. In addition, you'll learn to recognize sentence patterns, types, and faults. This knowledge will be especially helpful in punctuating sentences and avoiding common sentence faults. The Writer's Workshop following this chapter introduces proofreading marks, which are useful in revising messages.

SENTENCE ELEMENTS

To help you better understand the structure of sentences, you'll learn to distinguish between simple and complete subjects and predicates. You'll also learn to recognize and avoid fragments, comma splices, and run-on sentences.

SUBJECTS AND PREDICATES

A **sentence** is a group of words that includes a subject and a predicate and expresses a complete thought. When any one of these elements is missing, readers or listeners are confused. A **simple subject** is a noun or pronoun that tells who or what the sentence is about. A **simple predicate** is a verb or verb phrase that tells or asks what the subject is doing or what is being done to the subject. The **complete subject** of a sentence includes the simple subject and all of its modifiers. The **complete predicate** includes the verb or verb phrase and its modifiers, objects, and complements.

Complete Subject	Complete Predicate
The new *manager* of the office	*received* a warm welcome.
All *employees* in the company	*may choose* from a benefits package.
She and *I*	*will be applying* for jobs after graduation.
The *person* who sent the e-mail	*might have been* a customer.

Notice in the preceding examples that the verbs in the predicate may consist of one word (*received*) or several (*will be applying*). In a **verb phrase** the **principal verb** is the final one (*applying*). The other verbs are **helping** or **auxiliary verbs.** The most frequently used helping verbs are *am, is, are, was, were, been, have, has, had, must, ought, can, might, could, would, should, will, do, does,* and *did.*

LOCATING SUBJECTS

You can locate the subject in a sentence by asking, *Who or what is being discussed?*

Rebecca wanted out of her dead-end job. (Who is being discussed? *Rebecca*)

Positions in many companies are advertised online. (What is being discussed? *Positions*)

Don't be misled by prepositional phrases. Subjects are not found in such phrases.

In many companies *employees* must be promoted from within. (What is being discussed? *Employees.* Ignore the prepositional phrase *in many companies.*)

After January 1 *applicants* for all jobs must submit their résumés by e-mail. (What is being discussed? *Applicants.* Ignore the prepositional phrases *After January 1* and *for all jobs.*)

CAREER TIP

You may be worth an additional $5,000 or more to your employer (and to yourself) if you have writing skills, says one communications expert. Because many companies can no longer afford expensive on-site training, employees with already developed skills are much more valuable to employers.

DID YOU KNOW

The English language has about three times as many words as any other language on earth. English is estimated to include at least 450,000 words. German has about 185,000; Russian, 130,000; and French, 100,000.

STUDY TIP

Many linking verbs also serve as helping verbs. Note that a verb phrase is *linking* only when the final verb is a linking verb, such as in the phrase *might have been.*

Sentences may have multiple subjects joined by the conjunctions *and* or *or*.

> Either the *manager* or his *assistant* will conduct the training. (What two people are being discussed? *Manager* and *assistant*)

> *Artwork, paint,* and *plants* are great ways to bring color into an office. (What subjects are being discussed? *Artwork, paint,* and *plants*)

Although a sentence subject usually appears directly before a verb, in three instances the verb may precede the subject: (1) inverted sentences, (2) sentences beginning with *there* or *here,* and (3) questions.

> First on the program was Jeffrey. (In this inverted sentence the verb *was* precedes the subject *Jeffrey*.)

> There are many jobs listed online. (Ignore *There*, which cannot function as a sentence subject. Read the sentence as follows: *Many jobs are listed online.* Now the subject is obvious because the sentence is in its normal order.)

> Are the best jobs listed online? (To locate the subject, reword this question: *The best jobs are listed online.*)

You'll learn more about locating subjects in Chapter 10.

MAKING SENSE

In addition to a subject and a predicate, a group of words must possess one additional element to qualify as a sentence. The group of words must be complete and make sense. Observe that the first two groups of words that follow express complete thoughts and make sense; the third does not. In the following examples, single underscores indicate subjects; double underscores, verbs.

> Athletic shoe <u>makers</u> <u>convinced</u> us that we need $150 tennis shoes. (Subject plus predicate making sense = sentence.)

> <u>Anthony</u> now <u>owns</u> different sneakers for every sport. (Subject plus predicate making sense = sentence.)

> Although sports shoe <u>manufacturers</u> <u>promote</u> new versions with new features (Subject plus predicate but NOT making sense = no sentence.)

SENTENCE PATTERNS

Four basic patterns express thoughts in English sentences. As a business or professional writer, you'll most often use Patterns 1, 2, and 3 because readers want to know the subject first. For variety and emphasis, however, you can use introductory elements and inverted order in Pattern 4.

PATTERN NO. 1: SUBJECT–VERB

In the most basic sentence pattern, the verb follows its subject. The sentence needs no additional words to make sense and be complete.

Subject	Verb
We	worked.
Everyone	is studying.
She	might have called.
All employees	are being informed.

PATTERN NO. 2: SUBJECT–ACTION VERB–OBJECT

When sentences have an object, the pattern is generally subject, action verb, and direct object. A **direct object** is usually a noun or pronoun that answers the question *What?* or *Whom?*

Subject	Action Verb	Direct Object
Luke	needed	a new car.
He and a friend	questioned	the salesperson.
The sales manager	provided	good answers.

This basic sentence pattern may also employ an **indirect object** that often answers the question *To whom?*

Subject	Action Verb	Indirect Object	Direct Object
This dealership	promises	customers	good prices.
Luke	gave	the manager	a check.
The manager	handed	him	the keys.

PATTERN NO. 3: SUBJECT–LINKING VERB–COMPLEMENT

In the third sentence pattern, the subject precedes a linking verb and its complement. Recall from Chapter 2 that common linking verbs are *am, is, are, was, were, be, being,* and *been.* Other linking verbs express the senses: *feels, appears, tastes, sounds, seems, looks.* A **complement** is a noun, pronoun, or adjective that renames or describes the subject. A complement *completes* the meaning of the subject and always follows the linking verb.

Subject	Linking Verb	Complement	
The instructor	was	Connie Murphy.	(Noun complements)
Our customers	are	friends.	
Your supervisor	is	she.	(Pronoun complements)
The callers	might have been	they.	
My job	is	challenging.	(Adjective complements)
These Web sites	will be	useful.	

PATTERN NO. 4: INVERTED ORDER

In **inverted sentences,** the verb precedes the subject. You might use inverted order for variety or emphasis in your sentences.

Sitting in front is Michele.

Working hardest was the marketing team.

In questions, the verb may precede the subject or may be interrupted by the subject.

What is his e-mail address?

Where should the invoice be sent?

In sentences beginning with *here* or *there*, the normal word order is also inverted.

> Here <u>are</u> the <u>applications</u>.

> There <u>were</u> three <u>steps</u> in the plan.

SENTENCE FAULTS

To be successful in your career, you must be able to write complete sentences that avoid three common faults: fragments, comma splices, and run-ons. You can eliminate these sentence faults by recognizing them and by applying the revision techniques described here.

FRAGMENT

A **sentence fragment** is an incomplete sentence. It may be a phrase or a clause punctuated as if it were a complete sentence. Fragments are often broken off from preceding or succeeding sentences. Avoid fragments by making certain that each sentence contains a subject and a verb and makes sense by itself. You can remedy fragments by (1) joining them to complete sentences or (2) adding appropriate subjects and verbs.

Fragment: *Because cost-cutting saves money.* That's why Wal-Mart works hard at it.

Revision: Because cost-cutting saves money, Wal-Mart works hard at it.
(Join the fragment to the following complete sentence.)

Fragment: We're looking for a potential manager. *An individual who can accept responsibility and supervise other employees.*

Revision: We're looking for a potential manager who can accept responsibility and supervise other employees.
(Join the fragment to the preceding sentence.)

Fragment: My college offers many majors in business administration. *Such as accounting, finance, human resources, and marketing.*

Revision: My college offers many majors in business administration such as accounting, finance, human resources, and marketing.
(Join the fragment to the preceding sentence.)

Fragment: The deadline for the project was moved up three days. *Which means that our team must work overtime.*

Revision: The deadline for the project was moved up three days, which means that our team must work overtime.
(Join the fragment to the preceding sentence.)

Fragment: *Although Ayla will give him some tough competition.* Stephen is confident he'll get the promotion.

Revision: Although Ayla will give him some tough competition, Stephen is confident he'll get the promotion.
(Join the fragment to the following sentence.)

Fragment: *A two-bedroom apartment that was within walking distance of his job.*

Revision: Derek found a two-bedroom apartment that was within walking distance of his job.
(Add a subject and verb.)

COMMA SPLICE

A **comma splice** results when two sentences are incorrectly joined or spliced together with a comma. Remember that commas alone cannot join two sentences. Comma splices can usually be repaired by (1) adding a conjunction, (2) separating into two sentences, or (3) changing the comma to a semicolon.

Comma splice:	Marcos supervises Shipping, Pamela manages the Legal Department.
Revision:	Marcos supervises Shipping, *and* Pamela manages the Legal Department. (Add a conjunction.)
Comma splice:	Let us help you develop your online résumé, visit us at Resume.org.
Revision:	Let us help you develop your online résumé. Visit us at Resume.org. (Separate into two sentences.)
Comma splice:	No stock prices were available today, the market was closed for the holiday.
Revision:	No stock prices were available today; the market was closed for the holiday. (Change the comma to a semicolon.)
Comma splice:	Many applicants responded to our advertisement, however only one had computer training.
Revision:	Many applicants responded to our advertisement; however, only one had computer training. (Semicolons will be discussed in Chapters 13 and 15.)

RUN-ON SENTENCE

A **run-on sentence** joins two complete thoughts without proper punctuation. Run-on sentences can usually be repaired by (1) separating into two sentences, (2) adding a comma and a conjunction, or (3) adding a semicolon.

Run-on:	The work ethic in America is not dead it is deeply ingrained in most people.
Revision:	The work ethic in America is not dead. It is deeply ingrained in most people. (Separate into two sentences.)
Run-on:	Charmayne thought she aced the interview she was wrong.
Revision:	Charmayne thought she aced the interview, but she was wrong. (Add a comma and a conjunction.)
Run-on:	Send an e-mail to all committee members tell them our next meeting will be Friday.
Revision:	Send an e-mail to all committee members; tell them our next meeting will be Friday. (Add a semicolon.)

PUNCTUATING FOUR SENTENCE TYPES

The end punctuation used in a sentence depends on whether it is a statement, question, command, or exclamation.

STATEMENTS

A **statement** makes an assertion and ends with a period.

Laws require truth in advertising.

Manufacturers today must label the contents of packages.

QUESTIONS

A **direct question** uses the exact words of the speaker and requires an answer. It is followed by a question mark.

How many daily e-mail messages <u>do you receive</u>?

What <u>are</u> your peak message <u>hours</u>?

COMMANDS

A **command** gives an order or makes a direct request. Commands end with periods or, occasionally, with exclamation points. Note that the subject in all commands is understood to be *you*. The subject *you* is not normally stated in the command.

<u>Shut</u> the door. ([<u>You</u>] <u>shut</u> the door.)

<u>Insure</u> your home against fire loss. ([<u>You</u>] <u>insure</u> your home . . .)

EXCLAMATIONS

An **exclamation** shows surprise, disbelief, or strong feeling. An exclamation may or may not be expressed as a complete thought. Both subject and predicate may be implied.

Wow! <u>We</u> just <u>had</u> an earthquake!

What a wonderful time <u>we</u> <u>had</u>!

How extraordinary [<u>that</u> <u>is</u>]!

Now complete the reinforcement exercises for this chapter.

HOTLINE QUERIES

Answered by Dr. Guffey

Question

Q: This sentence doesn't sound right to me, but I can't decide how to improve it: *The reason I'm applying is because I enjoy editing.*

Q: My colleague says that this sentence is correct: *Please complete this survey regarding your satisfaction at our dealership, return it in the enclosed addressed envelope.* I think something is wrong, but I'm not sure what.

Answer

A: The problem lies in this construction: *the reason . . . is because . . .* Only nouns or adjectives may act as complements following linking verbs. In your sentence an adverbial clause follows the linking verb and sounds awkward. One way to improve the sentence is to substitute a noun clause beginning with *that: The reason I'm applying is that I enjoy editing.* An even better way to improve the sentence would be to make it a direct statement: *I'm applying because I enjoy editing.*

A: You're right. This sentence has two independent clauses, and the writer attempted to join them with a comma. But this construction produces a comma splice. You can correct the problem by adding *and* between the clauses, starting a new sentence, or using a semicolon between the clauses.

Q: My boss wrote a report with this sentence: *Saleswise, our staff is excellent.* Should I change it?

A: Never change wording without checking with the author. You might point out, however, that the practice of attaching *-wise* to nouns is frowned on by many language experts. Such combinations as *budgetwise*, *taxwise*, and *productionwise* are considered commercial jargon. Suggest this revision: *On the basis of sales, our staff is excellent.*

Q: At the end of a letter I wrote: *Thank you for recommending me to this company.* Should I hyphenate *thank you?*

A: Do not hyphenate *thank you* when using it as a verb (*thank you for recommending*). Do use hyphens when using *thank you* as an adjective (*I sent a thank-you note*) or as a noun (*I sent four thank-yous*). Because *thank you* is used as a verb in your sentence, do not hyphenate it. Notice that *thank you* is never written as a single word.

Q: A fellow worker insists on saying, *I could care less.* It seems to me that it should be *I couldn't care less.* Who is right?

A: You are right. The phrase *I couldn't care less* has been in the language a long time. It means, of course, "I have little concern about the matter." Recently, though, people have begun to use *I could care less* with the same meaning. Most careful listeners realize that the latter phrase says just the opposite of its intent. Although both phrases are clichés, stick with *I couldn't care less* if you want to be clear.

Q: How should I address a person who signed a letter *J. R. Henderson?* I don't know whether the person is a man or a woman, and I don't want to offend anyone.

A: When you can't determine the gender of your reader, include the entire name in the salutation and omit the personal title (*Mr.*, *Ms.*, *Dr.*). In your letter you should use *Dear J. R. Henderson.*

Q: My friend insists that the combination *all right* is shown in her dictionary as one word. I say that it's two words. Who's right?

A: *All right* is the only acceptable spelling. The listing *alright* is shown in many dictionaries to guide readers to the acceptable spelling, *all right*. Do not use *alright*. By the way, some people remember that *all right* is two words by associating it with *all wrong*.

Q: If I have no interest in something, am I *disinterested?*

A: No. If you lack interest, you are *uninterested*. The word *disinterested* means "unbiased" or "impartial" (*the judge was disinterested in the cases before him*).

A. (Self-check) Indicate whether the following statements are true (*T*) or false (*F*).

1. The predicate of a sentence indicates the person or thing being talked about. _____

2. A group of words with a subject and a predicate is automatically a complete sentence. _____

3. The complete subject of a sentence includes a noun or pronoun and all its modifiers. _____

4. Two complete sentences incorrectly joined by a comma create a *comma splice*. _____

5. You can locate the subject in a sentence by asking who or what is being discussed. _____

6. Sentence fragments may be repaired by joining them to complete sentences or by adding appropriate subjects and verbs. _____

7. Sentences that show strong feeling are usually concluded with question marks. _____

8. The verb phrase *might have been* is considered a linking verb. _____

Check your answers below.

B. In each of the following sentences, underline the complete subject once and the complete predicate twice. Circle the simple subject and simple predicate.

Example: The (manager) of our department (will be moving) to the Atlanta office.

1. All _____ in our company _____ instruction and encouragement.

2. Some recent _____ as interns during the summer.

3. Either _____ or _____ will be hired for a permanent position.

4. _____ and _____ to most job applicants.

5. First in line for a parking permit _____ .

In each of the following sentences underline the simple subject once and simple predicate twice.

6. There are more jobs available this year than in previous years.

7. In her presentation Halle used PowerPoint slides to illustrate her ideas.

8. Many job applicants today submit their résumés by e-mail.

9. She and I will be applying for jobs after graduating in May.

10. Are Halle and Sean competing for the same position?

1. F 2. F 3. T 4. T 5. T 6. T 7. F 8. T

Want to explore more? Go to: academic.cengage.com/bcomm/guffey or Xtra!

SENTENCES: ELEMENTS, PATTERNS, TYPES | CHAPTER 3 | **37**

C. Study the following examples. Then fill in the words necessary to complete the four sentence patterns.

Pattern No. 1: Subject–Verb

Example: The boss <u>called</u>.

1. The restaurant _____
2. Our office _____
3. Students _____
4. Health costs _____
5. The committee _____
6. E-mail messages _____

Pattern No. 2: Subject–Action Verb–Object

Example: Administrative assistants use <u>software</u>.

7. Licia answered the _____
8. FedEx delivers _____
9. Salespeople sold _____
10. Congress passes _____
11. Stock pays _____
12. Students threw a _____

Pattern No. 3: Subject–Linking Verb–Complement

Fill in <u>noun or pronoun</u> complements.

Example: The manager is <u>Rachel</u>.

13. The applicant was _____
14. Chandra is the new _____
15. The caller could have been _____
16. The president is _____

Fill in <u>adjective</u> complements.

Example: The salary is <u>reasonable</u>.

17. My investment was _____
18. New York is _____
19. Our new supervisor is _____
20. The report could have been _____

Pattern No. 4: Inverted Order

Revise the following inverted sentences so that the subject comes first. Then underline the simple subject once and the simple predicate twice.

Example: Here are the job applications from four candidates.
The job <u>applications</u> from four candidates <u>are</u> here.

21. There is no Web site listed for that organization.

_____

22. Here is the agenda for the Tuesday board meeting.

_____

23. Where is the meeting agenda?

_____

24. Next door to our office is an Italian restaurant.

_____

25. Who is the leader in online shopping?

_____

Want to explore more? Go to: academic.cengage.com/bcomm/guffey or Xtra!

D. For each of the following groups of words, write the correct letter to indicate whether it represents a fragment, a correctly punctuated sentence, a comma splice, or a run-on sentence.

a. correctly punctuated   c. comma splice
b. fragment   d. run-on sentence

Example: Because the office will be closed on Friday.   b

1. Anyone doing business in another country should learn what kinds of gifts are expected and when to give them.

2. Russian children usually open gifts in private, however, Russian adults usually open gifts in front of their gift givers.

3. In Thailand a knife is not a proper gift it signifies cutting off a relationship.

4. Because one third of all U.S. corporate profits are now generated through international trade.

5. Making eye contact in America is a sign of confidence and sincerity.

6. Although Italians, Middle Easterners, and Latin Americans stand very close to each other when talking.

7. Which means that we'll have to learn how to negotiate when in Chile.

8. Being on time is important in North America in other countries time is less important.

9. Filipinos take pride in their personal appearance, they believe a person's clothing indicates social position.

10. In many countries people do not address each other by given names unless they are family members or old friends.

E. Revise the following sentence fragments.

Example: If I had seen the red light at the intersection. Then I could have stopped in time.

If I had seen the red light at the intersection, I could have stopped in time.

1. Because I am looking for a position in hotel management. That's why I am interested in your job posting.

2. We're seeking a management trainee. Someone who has not only good communication skills but also computer expertise.

3. During job interviews candidates must provide details about their accomplishments. Which is why they should rehearse answers to expected questions.

4. Although an interviewer will typically start with general questions about your background. Be careful to respond with a brief history.

Want to explore more? Go to: academic.cengage.com/bcomm/guffey or Xtra!

SENTENCES: ELEMENTS, PATTERNS, TYPES I **CHAPTER 3** I **39**

5. A candidate who provided a wide range of brief stories about specific accomplishments. That's who was hired.

_____

F. From the following list select the letter that accurately describes each of the following sentences and add appropriate end punctuation.

    a. statement   c. question
    b. command   d. exclamation

Example: Take appropriate steps to prevent hacker attacks.   b _____

1. School and work holidays should always be scheduled on Mondays and Fridays   _____

2. Do employers and workers contribute jointly to the retirement fund   _____

3. How exciting this proposal is   _____

4. Use _Google_ to receive tens of thousands of hits in a nanosecond   _____

5. We wonder whether our new marketing campaign will be successful   _____

6. What a terrific view we have from the observatory on the tenth floor   _____

7. Do you know whether Susan Simons received the purchase order   _____

8. Turn off the power, close the windows, and lock the doors before you leave   _____

G. Hotline Review. In the space provided write the correct answer choice.

1. The reason we are moving is _____ we need more space.
    a. because
    b. that   _____

2. I _____ care less whether Craig becomes manager.
    a. could
    b. couldn't   _____

3. Is it _____ if I leave work early today?
    a. all right
    b. alright   _____

4. It's important to have a(n) _____ judge during a trial.
    a. uninterested
    b. disinterested   _____

5. We would like to _____ for your careful work.
    a. thank-you
    b. thank you
    c. thankyou   _____

6. Which of the following represents better expression?
    a. On the basis of taxes, we are in a good position this year.
    b. Taxwise, we are in a good position this year.   _____

H. Writing Exercise. On a separate sheet write complete sentences illustrating each of the following forms: a statement, a question, a command, an exclamation, a sentence with a pronoun complement, and a sentence in inverted order. Identify each sentence.

Want to explore more? Go to: academic.cengage.com/bcomm/guffey or Xtra!

40 | **UNIT 1** | **CHAPTER 3** | SENTENCES: ELEMENTS, PATTERNS, TYPES

The following e-mail message contains 30 errors in sentence structure, spelling, and proofreading. Proofreading covers errors in spacing, missing letters, extra words, and so forth. When you replace a wordy phrase with one word, it counts as one correction. When you correct a comma splice, run-on, or fragment, the correction counts as two errors. Your instructor may ask you to read about proofreading marks on page 45 and the inside back cover and use those marks in noting your corrections. If you prefer, do your editing at the **Guffey Companion Web Site** at **academic.cengage.com/bcomm/guffey.**

File Edit Mailbox Message Transfer Special Tools Window Help

B *I* U | | | | A˅ A˄ | | | | **Send**

From: Caroline Medcalf, J. Crew <customerservices@jcrew.com>
To: Melinda Jackson <mjackson@yahoo.com>
Cc:
Subject: Our Goof, Your Gain!

Dear J. Crew Web Shoper:

At J. Crew we take pride in ofering fashionable clothes at affordable prices. Recently at our Web site you ordered a sensational zip turtle neck cashmere sweater. Which was offerred at the amazing price of $18.

To ensure accurate pricing, we double-check all copy material before it posted to our Web site. Ocassionally, though, we miss a typo. In the case of this cashmere sweater, that $18 price blew right bye our proof readers. Although this stunning turtle neck should have been list at $218. Because of our error we would like to offer you this sweater for only $118 ($130 for larger sizes. If you check our current Web listings, you will see that this sweater is now correctly offerred at for $218.

The eighteen dollar sweater has been removed from your recentorder, but you may reorder it for $118 (or $130) at this special Web address: www.jcrew.special.html. Only those J. Crew customer affected by the Web price error are being invited to purchase this sweater at this reduced price. Our big goof becomes your big bargin!

You can be sure we'll re-double our proof-reading efforts for all future Web catalog item. Check out the latest must-have cloths for spring that include handsome seersucker, eyelet inspired by an antique lace pattern, and authentic Irish linens. Now is th time to snatch the things you love as the days grow warmer. Thanks for shopping J. Crew. Where you always catch terrific bargins!

Sincerly,

Caroline Medcalf, Manager
Customer Services
J. Crew
CMedcalf@jcrew.com

Want to explore more? Go to: academic.cengage.com/bcomm/guffey or Xtra!

SENTENCES: ELEMENTS, PATTERNS, TYPES | CHAPTER 3 | **41**

A number of search tools—such as *Google* and *Yahoo!*—are available at specialized Web sites devoted to searching. These tools help you find Web pages related to the search term you enter. Anyone using the Web today must develop skill in using a search tool.

Goal: To become familiar with a search tool

1. With your Web browser on the screen, key the following URL: **http://www.google.com.** Press **Enter.**
2. Look over the Google home page. Notice the categories it will search: **Web, Images, Group, News, Froogle, Local,** and **more.** Click each one and study what is available.
3. Click **Web** to return to Web searching.
4. In the search term box, type *"sentence fragments"* as your term. Enclosing an expression in quotation marks ensures that the two words will be searched as a unit. Click **Google Search** or press **Enter.**
5. Google presents a screen showing the first ten hits it has located. Click any of the hits that seem most helpful to someone studying sentence structure. To return to the list, click the **Back** button in the upper left corner of your browser.
6. Select the most helpful site. Print one or more pages (click **File, Print,** and **OK**).
7. End your session by clicking the **X** in the upper right corner of your browser.
8. On the page(s) you printed, explain why this Web page was helpful and why it was better than others you visited. Turn in the page(s) you printed or send an e-mail to your instructor summarizing your response.

Write the correct letter after each of the following numbered items.

a = correctly punctuated sentence　　c = comma splice
b = fragment　　　　　　　　　　　　d = run-on sentence

1. The computer arrived Wednesday the printer is expected shortly. _____
2. On the fifth floor is the Human Resources Department. _____
3. If you agree to serve on the committee. _____
4. On Monday my e-mail box is overflowing, on Friday my box is empty. _____
5. Because Christine, who is one of our best employees, was ill last week. _____

1. d 2. a 3. b 4. c 5. b

Want to explore more? Go to: academic.cengage.com/bcomm/guffey or Xtra!

42 | UNIT 1 | CHAPTER 3 | SENTENCES: ELEMENTS, PATTERNS, TYPES

Begin your review by rereading Chapters 1–3. Then check your comprehension of those chapters by writing *T* (true) or *F* (false) in the following blanks. Compare your responses with the key at the end of the book.

1. Because of advances in technology, you can expect to be doing less communicating than ever before in today's workplace. _____

2. Usage labels such as *obsolete, archaic,* and *informal* warn dictionary users about appropriate usage. _____

3. College-level dictionaries provide in square brackets the brief history or etymology of a word. _____

4. All dictionaries use the same plan for showing the order of definitions. _____

5. Most dictionaries show noun plurals only if the plurals are irregular, such as the word *children.* _____

6. A thesaurus is a collection of words and their definitions. _____

7. Accent marks may appear before or after stressed syllables. _____

8. The usage label *nonstandard* means that a word is no longer in use. _____

9. The terms *desk* and *college-level* refer to the same kind of dictionary. _____

10. An electronic dictionary (also called a *spell checker*) compares typed words with those in the computer memory. _____

Read the following sentence carefully. Identify the parts of speech for the words as they are used in this sentence.

They jumped quickly into the car and looked for the correct address.

11. They	a. noun	b. pronoun	c. adverb	d. adjective	_____
12. jumped	a. conjunction	b. preposition	c. verb	d. adverb	_____
13. quickly	a. conjunction	b. preposition	c. adjective	d. adverb	_____
14. into	a. conjunction	b. preposition	c. adjective	d. adverb	_____
15. car	a. noun	b. pronoun	c. conjuntion	d. adverb	_____
16. and	a. noun	b. pronoun	c. conjunction	d. preposition	_____
17. looked	a. verb	b. adverb	c. conjunction	d. preposition	_____
18. for	a. verb	b. adverb	c. conjunction	d. preposition	_____
19. correct	a. verb	b. adverb	c. adjective	d. preposition	_____
20. address	a. noun	b. pronoun	c. adjective	d. preposition	_____

For each of the following statements, determine the word or phrase that correctly completes that statement and write its letter in the space provided.

21. In the sentence *Excellent communication skills can help you get a job,* the simple subject is (a) communication, (b) skills, (c) you, (d) job.

22. In the sentence *There are your paychecks,* the simple subject is (a) There, (b) are, (c) paychecks, (d) your. _____

23. In the sentence *I feel bad,* the verb *feel* is considered a(n) (a) linking verb, (b) helping verb, (c) subject, (d) action verb. _____

24. The sentence *She sent many e-mail messages* represents what sentence pattern? (a) subject–verb, (b) subject–action verb–object, (c) subject–linking verb–complement, (d) subject–linking verb–object. _____

From the following list select the letter to accurately describe each of the following groups of words.

     a. complete sentence   c. comma splice
     b. fragment   d. run-on

25. Armando hates receiving "spam," he uses filters to avoid unwanted messages. _____

26. Whenever Mr. Jackson calls to confirm the shipping date. _____

27. Turn on your computer when you arrive, and leave it on all day. _____

28. That company's products are excellent its service is slow, however. _____

29. Most of us would rather risk catastrophe than read directions. _____

30. Although he wore sandals, white socks, and a T-shirt with a beer company's logo. _____

31. Complete the form and send it with your check. _____

32. I've never had a bad day, some days are just better than others. _____

33. Your letter arrived today your package should be here next week. _____

34. Many companies feature profit-sharing plans, but some employees are reluctant to participate. _____

35. PepsiCo ran three commercials during the Super Bowl, however, not one was devoted to its core brand. _____

Hotline Review

Write the letter of the word or phrase that correctly completes each statement.

36. We appreciate your work; _____ for completing the report early.
     a. thankyou   b. thank-you   c. thank you _____

37. Is it _____ to leave my computer on overnight?
     a. all right   b. alright _____

38. You may have deliveries _____ if you wish.
     a. everyday   b. every day   c. every-day _____

39. The reason I am late is _____ my car stalled.
     a. because   b. that _____

40. Send me an _____ as soon as you find out.
     a. email   b. E-mail   c. e-mail _____

Name

DEVELOPING PROOFREADING SKILLS

As you complete a set of chapters (a unit), you will find a workshop exercise that introduces various techniques to help you improve your writing skills. This first workshop emphasizes proofreading skills. You will learn about proofreading marks, which are often used by writers to edit printed material. Study the basic symbols shown here. See the inside back cover of your textbook for a more comprehensive list.

≡ Capitalize   ∜ Insert apostrophe   ⊙ Insert period

∾ Delete   ⋏ Insert comma   / Lowercase

∧ Insert   ⊼ Insert hyphen   ⌒ Close up space

Example:

Proofreading marks are used by writers and editors too make corrections and revisions in printed copy they use these Standard Marks for clarity and consistency. If you are revising your own work, Youll probable use these marks only occasional In many jobs today however you will be working in a team environment Where writing tasks are shared. Thats when its important to able to aply these well known marks correctly.

PROOFREADING TIPS

- Use your computer's spell checker. But don't rely on it totally. It can't tell the difference between *it's* and *its* and many other confusing words.

- Look for grammar and punctuation errors. As you complete this book, you'll be more alert to problem areas, such as subject-verb agreement and comma placement.

- Double-check names and numbers. Compare all names and numbers with their sources because inaccuracies are not always visible. Verify the spelling of the names of individuals receiving the message. Most of us dislike when someone misspells our name.

- For long or important documents, always print a copy (preferably double-spaced), set it aside for at least a day, and then proofread when you are fresh.

Writing Application 1.1

After you read and edit the following letter, your instructor may ask you to write a similar introductory personal business letter to her or him. On a separate sheet of paper, explain why you enrolled in this class, evaluate your present communication skills, name your major, describe the career you seek, and briefly tell about your current work (if you are employed) and your favorite activities. Your instructor may ask you to write a first draft quickly, print it, and then use proofreading marks to show corrections. Make a final copy. Double-space the rough draft; single-space the final copy. Turn in both copies. See page 385 of Appendix C for a model personal business letter. The following personal business letter contains intentional errors in typing, spelling, capitalization, and sentence punctuation. Use proofreading marks to edit this letter. You should mark 30 changes.

810 North Miller Road
Marion, IN 46952
September 8, 200x

Professor Margaret M. Sullivan
Department of Busness Administration
Schoolcraft College
Marion, IN 46954

Dear Professor Sulivan:

I enrolled this class to help me improve the way I use language I know that comunication skills are important, and I'm afraid that my pressent skills are below average. They're not good enough for me to get the kind of job I want I also enrolled in this class because its required in my major.

Accounting is my major I chose this majer because I like working with figures. And because I know that many good jobs are available in accounting. Although I thought that accountants worked totaly with figures. My advisor tells me that accountants also need to be able to explain their work to management, to fellow employees, and to clients. My language skills are not terrific, and I want to improve. When I finish my accounting program, Ihope to get a job in the entertainment industry as a Junior Accountant.

I have a parttime job at Pizza Bob's. Where I deliver pizzas to campus dormitories, or to apartments an homes. I like my job because I get to meet people and because it helps me pay for my car and it's insurance.

When I'm not studing or working, I like to surf the internet. My favorite places to visit are World wide web sites devoted to unusual hobbys and businesses. Right now I'm interested in "CyberSlice," a site showing the menus of participating pizzerias in a neighborhood. May be I can get Pizza Bob to participate!

Sincerely,

Mark Watkins

Mark Watkins

KNOWING THE NAMERS

UNIT 1 · **UNIT 2** · UNIT 3 · UNIT 4 · UNIT 5 · UNIT 6

4

NOUNS

© PureStock/Jupiter Images

5

POSSESSIVE
NOUNS

© Rubberball/Jupiter Images

6

PERSONAL
PRONOUNS

© BananaStock/Jupiter Images

7

PRONOUNS AND
ANTECEDENTS

© Jose Luis Pelaez, Inc./Blend Images/Jupiter Images

© PureStock/Jupiter Images

4

NOUNS

OBJECTIVES

When you have completed the materials in this chapter, you will be able to do the following:

LEVEL 1

- Recognize four classes of nouns.
- Make regular and irregular nouns plural.

LEVEL 2

- Spell challenging plural nouns ending in *y, o,* and *f.*
- Form the plurals of proper nouns, surnames, compound nouns, numerals, letters, degrees, and abbreviations.

LEVEL 3

- Recognize and use correctly foreign plural nouns.
- Make special nouns and single-letter abbreviations plural.

PRETEST

Underline any incorrectly spelled noun in the following sentences. Write the correct spelling in the space provided.

1. Several attornies requested tax write-offs for education expenses. _____

2. The two bottom shelfs contain business history books. _____

3. We're considering two logoes for our new business stationery. _____

4. Both of our CPAs asked for leave of absences in June. _____

5. Based on all the criterion, several diagnoses were given. _____

1. attorneys 2. shelves 3. logos 4. leaves of absence 5. criteria or criterions

48

As you will recall from Chapter 2, nouns *name* persons, places, things, qualities, feelings, concepts, activities, and measures. In this chapter you'll learn to distinguish concrete from abstract nouns and common from proper nouns. The principal emphasis, however, will be on forming and spelling plural nouns, an area of confusion for many business writers.

Beginning with this chapter, concepts are presented in levels, progressing from basic, frequently used concepts at Level 1 to more complex and less frequently used concepts at Level 3. This unique separation of concepts has proved very effective in helping students understand, retain, and apply the information taught in this book.

• LEVEL 1 • LEVEL 1 • LEVEL 1 • LEVEL 1 • LEVEL 1 • **LEVEL 1** • LEVEL 1 • 1

CLASSES OF NOUNS

As the "namers" in our language, nouns perform an important function. They often serve as sentence subjects. Although nouns can be grouped into many categories, this chapter focuses on four classes that are important to business writers: concrete, abstract, common, and proper nouns.

CONCRETE AND ABSTRACT NOUNS

Concrete nouns name specific objects that you can actually see, hear, feel, taste, or smell. Abstract nouns name qualities and concepts. Because concrete nouns are precise, they are more forceful in writing and talking than abstract nouns.

Concrete Nouns

bagel	horse	refrigerator
dentist	laptop	software
dictionary	quarterback	stapler

Abstract Nouns

accuracy	happiness	success
ethics	memory	technology
freedom	personality	value

CAREER TIP

Successful job applicants fill their résumés with concrete expressions and quantifiable data rather than abstractions. Instead of *Worked as lab assistant*, try *Assisted over 300 students and 25 faculty members using Word, Excel, and Access in computer lab.*

COMMON AND PROPER NOUNS

Common nouns name *generalized* persons, places, and things. Because they are general, common nouns are not capitalized. **Proper nouns** name *specific* persons, places, and things. They are always capitalized. Rules for capitalization are presented in Chapter 17.

Common Nouns

candy	magazine	professor
company	organization	roller coaster
document	photocopier	television

Proper Nouns

Bill of Rights	Big Dipper	Sony television
Coca-Cola Company	Jan Jardine	United Nations
Forbes magazine	Snickers candy bar	Xerox machine

HOT LINK

What are "count" and "noncount" nouns? Learn more at **http://owl.english. purdue.edu/handouts/ esl/eslcount.html.**

HOT LINK

Remember, at your Guffey Companion Web site you will find an updated list of all URLs used as Hot Links.

BASIC PLURALS

Singular nouns name *one* person, place, or thing. **Plural nouns** name *two* or more. At Level 1 you will learn basic rules for forming plurals. At Level 2 you will learn how to form the plurals of nouns that create spelling problems.

Plural of Regular Nouns

Most regular nouns, including both common and proper nouns, form the plural with the addition of *s*.

advantage, advantages	issue, issues	passenger, passengers
contract, contracts	Juan, Juans	password, passwords
house, houses	Johnson, Johnsons	vendor, vendors

Plural of Nouns Ending in *s, x, z, ch,* or *sh*

Nouns ending in *s, x, z, ch,* or *sh* form the plural with the addition of *es*.

box, boxes	business, businesses	Sanchez, Sanchezes
brush, brushes	dish, dishes	virus, viruses
bunch, bunches	fax, faxes	BUT: quiz, quizzes

Plural of Irregular Nouns

Irregular nouns form the plural by changing the spelling of the word. Dictionaries show the plural forms of irregular nouns, but you should be familiar with the most common irregular noun plurals, such as the following:

child, children	man, men	tooth, teeth
foot, feet	mouse, mice	woman, women

Be careful not to use apostrophes (') to form plural nouns. Reserve the apostrophe to show possession. (Chapter 5 discusses possessive nouns in detail.)

Incorrect:	Many basketball and football star's earn big salary's.
Correct:	Many basketball and football stars earn big salaries.

In using plural words, do not confuse nouns with verbs (*He saves* [verb] *his money in two safes* [noun]). Be especially mindful of the following words:

Nouns	Verbs
belief, beliefs	believe, believes
leaf, leaves (foliage)	leave, leaves (to depart)
loaf, loaves (of bread)	loaf, loafs (to be idle)
proof, proofs	prove, proves

Now complete the reinforcement exercises for Level 1 beginning on page 57.

SPOT THE BLOOPER

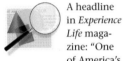

A headline in *Experience Life* magazine: "One of America's most celebrated chef's gives credit where credit is due."

SPOT THE BLOOPER

From the *Democrat and Chronicle* [Rochester, New York]: "Foremans and supervisors will receive training."

SPOT THE BLOOPER

Nabisco introduced a new product as *Teddy Graham Bearwich's*. Not long after, it quietly gave the box a new design and new name, *T. G. Bearwiches*.

SPOT THE BLOOPER

Large awning on Philadelphia restaurant: "Steak's and Hoagie's"

CHALLENGING NOUN PLURALS

Your ability to spell certain challenging nouns can be greatly improved by studying the following rules and examples.

Common Nouns Ending in *y*

Common nouns ending in *y* form the plural in two ways.

a. When the *y* is preceded by a vowel (*a, e, i, o, u*), the plural is formed with the addition of *s* only.

attorney, attorneys	journey, journeys	turkey, turkeys
delay, delays	key, keys	valley, valleys

b. When the *y* is preceded by a consonant (all letters other than vowels), the plural is formed by changing the *y* to *ies*.

city, cities	country, countries	luxury, luxuries
company, companies	currency, currencies	quality, qualities

Nouns Ending in *f* or *fe*

Nouns ending in *f* or *fe* follow no standard rules in the formation of plurals. Study the examples shown here, and use a dictionary when in doubt. When two forms are shown, the preferred appears first.

Add *s*	Change to *ves*	Both Forms Recognized
brief, briefs	half, halves	calves, calfs
belief, beliefs	knife, knives	dwarfs, dwarves
safe, safes	leaf, leaves	scarves, scarfs
staff, staffs	shelf, shelves	wharves, wharfs
sheriff, sheriffs	wife, wives	
Wolf, Wolfs	wolf, wolves	

Nouns Ending in *o*

Nouns ending in *o* may be made plural by adding *s* or *es*.

a. When the *o* is preceded by a vowel, the plural is formed by adding *s* only.

patio, patios	radio, radios	studio, studios
portfolio, portfolios	ratio, ratios	video, videos

b. When the *o* is preceded by a consonant, the plural is formed by adding *s* or *es*. Study the following examples and again use your dictionary whenever in doubt. When two forms are shown, the preferred one appears first.

ADD *s*	ADD *es*	Both Forms Recognized
auto, autos	echo, echoes	cargoes, cargos
logo, logos	embargo, embargoes	commandos, commandoes
memo, memos	hero, heroes	mosquitoes, mosquitos
photo, photos	potato, potatoes	tornadoes, tornados
Soto, Sotos	tomato, tomatoes	volcanos, volcanoes
typo, typos	veto, vetoes	zeros, zeroes

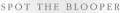

c. Musical terms ending in *o* always form the plural with the addition of *s* only.

alto, altos	cello, cellos	piano, pianos
banjo, banjos	contralto, contraltos	soprano, sopranos

Proper Nouns and Surnames

Most proper nouns form the plural by adding *s* or *es* (*January, Januarys*) depending on the ending of the noun. When making proper nouns and surnames (last names) plural, don't change the original spelling of the word. Simply add *s* or *es* to the end. Note that when the word *the* appears before a surname, the name is always plural (*the Kennedys*).

a. Most proper nouns are made plural by adding *s*.

Awbrey, the Awbreys	Germany, Germanys	Leno, the Lenos
February, Februarys	Holbrook, the Holbrooks	Tiffany, Tiffanys

b. Proper nouns that end in *s, x, z, ch,* or *sh* are made plural by adding *es*.

Bush, the Bushes	Max, Maxes	Sanchez, the Sanchezes
Lynch, the Lynches	Rodriguez, the Rodriguezes	Williams, the Williamses

Compounds

Compound words and phrases are formed by combining words into single expressions. Compounds may be written as single words, may be hyphenated, or may appear as two words.

a. When written as single words, compound nouns form the plural by appropriate changes in the final element.

bookshelf, bookshelves	payroll, payrolls	printout, printouts
footnote, footnotes	photocopy, photocopies	walkway, walkways

b. When written in hyphenated or open form, compounds form the plural by appropriate changes in the principal noun.

account payable, accounts payable	board of directors, boards of directors	mayor-elect, mayors-elect
attorney-at-law, attorneys-at-law	editor in chief, editors in chief	mother-in-law, mothers-in-law
bill of lading, bills of lading	leave of absence, leaves of absence	runner-up, runners-up

c. If the compound has no principal noun, the final element is made plural.

cure-all, cure-alls	no-show, no-shows	start-up, start-ups
go-between, go-betweens	run-in, run-ins	trade-in, trade-ins
know-it-all, know-it-alls	show-off, show-offs	write-up, write-ups

d. Some compound noun plurals have two recognized forms. In the following list, the preferred form is shown first.

attorney general: attorneys general, attorney generals

court-martial: courts-martial, court-martials

cupful: cupfuls, cupsful

notary public: notaries public, notary publics

teaspoonful: teaspoonfuls, teaspoonsful

Numerals, Alphabet Letters, Isolated Words, and Degrees

Numerals, alphabet letters, isolated words, and degrees are made plural by adding *s*, *es*, or *'s*. The trend is to use *'s* only when necessary for clarity.

a. Numerals and uppercase letters (with the exception of *A, I, M,* and *U*) require only *s* in plural formation.

9s and 10s	all Bs and Cs	three Rs
2000s	three Cs of credit	W-2s and 1040s

b. Isolated words used as nouns are made plural with the addition of *s* or *es*, as needed for pronunciation.

ands, ifs, or buts	pros and cons	yeses and noes
ins and outs	whys and wherefores	(*or* yeses and nos)

c. Academic degrees are made plural with the addition of *s*. Notice that degrees are written without periods or spaces. You'll learn more about degrees and other abbreviations in Chapter 16.

AAs	MBAs	PhDs
BSs	MDs	RNs

d. Isolated lowercase letters and the capital letters *A, I, M,* and *U* require *'s* for clarity.

A's	M's	p's and q's

Abbreviations

Abbreviations are usually made plural by adding *s* to the singular form.

bldg., bldgs.	DVD, DVDs	No., Nos.
CPA, CPAs	FAQ, FAQs	wk., wks.
dept., depts.	mgr., mgrs.	yr., yrs.

The singular and plural forms of abbreviations for units of measurement are, however, often identical.

deg. (degree or degrees)	in. (inch or inches)
ft. (foot or feet)	oz. (ounce or ounces)

Some units of measurement have two plural forms.

lb. or lbs.	qt. or qts.	yd. or yds.

Now complete the reinforcement exercises for Level 2.

FOREIGN NOUNS AND SPECIAL PLURALS

Selected nouns borrowed from foreign languages and other special nouns require your attention because their plural forms can be confusing.

Nouns from Foreign Languages

Nouns borrowed from other languages may retain a foreign plural. A few, however, have an Americanized plural form, shown in parentheses in the following list. Check your dictionary for the preferred form.

Singular	Plural
alumna (*feminine*)	alumnae (pronounced a-LUM-nee)
alumnus (*masculine*)	alumni (pronounced a-LUM-ni)
analysis	analyses
bacterium	bacteria
basis	bases
crisis	crises
criterion	criteria (or criterions)
curriculum	curricula (or curriculums)
datum	data*
diagnosis	diagnoses
emphasis	emphases
erratum	errata
formula	formulae (or formulas)
hypothesis	hypotheses
medium	media (or mediums)
memorandum	memoranda (or memorandums)
parenthesis	parentheses
phenomenon	phenomena
stimulus	stimuli
thesis	theses

*See the discussion on page 55.

Special Nouns

Some nouns ending in *s* or *es* may normally be *only* singular or *only* plural in meaning. Other special nouns may be considered *either* singular *or* plural in meaning.

STUDY TIP

Language purists contend that the word *data* can only be plural (*the data are*). However, see the Hotline Queries for another view.

SPOT THE BLOOPER

From *The Journal* [Bath County, Ohio] announcing honors for two female graduates: . . . the award goes "to an alumni who has made a significant contribution or given extraordinary service."

SPOT THE BLOOPER

A headline in the *San Francisco Chronicle*: "Numbers put face on a phenomena."

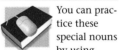

STUDY TIP

You can practice these special nouns by using them with the singular verb *is* or the plural verb *are*. For example, *Genetics is fascinating* (singular); *scissors are useful* (plural).

Usually Singular	Usually Plural	May be Singular or Plural
billiards	clothes	Chinese
dominos	earnings	corps
economics	goods	deer
genetics	pliers	headquarters
kudos	proceeds	politics
mathematics	scissors	series
mumps	thanks	species
news	trousers	statistics

Single-Letter Abbreviations

Selected single-letter abbreviations may be made plural by doubling the letter.

pp. (pages)	See pp. 18–21. (That is, pages 18 through 21)
ff. (and following)	See pp. 18 ff. (That is, page 18 and following pages)

Now complete the reinforcement exercises for Level 3.

HOTLINE QUERIES

Answered by Dr. Guffey

Question

Answer

Q: What is the plural of computer *mouse?*

A: *Mice* refers to both computer devices and rodents. However, some experts prefer *mouse devices*, which is probably less confusing.

Q: What happened to the periods in Ph.D. and M.D.?

A: Over time usage changes. Writers found it simpler and more efficient to write these abbreviations without periods. Who decides when to recognize language changes? Our guide is *The Chicago Manual of Style.* It no longer shows periods in academic degrees (*AA, BA, MBA, MD, PhD,* and so on).

Q: Could you help me spell the plurals of *do* and *don't?*

A: In forming the plurals of isolated words, the trend today is to add *s* and no apostrophe. Thus, we have *dos* and *don'ts.* Formerly, apostrophes were used to make isolated words plural. However, if no confusion results, make plurals by adding *s* only.

Q: One member of our staff consistently corrects our use of the word *data.* He says the word is plural. Is it never singular?

A: The word *data* is plural; the singular form is *datum.* Through frequent usage, however, *data* has recently become a collective noun. Collective nouns may be singular or plural depending on whether they are considered as one unit or as separate units. Therefore, *data* can be considered either singular or plural, depending on how it is used. For example, *These data are much different from those findings.* Or, *This data is conclusive.*

Q: As a sportswriter, I need to know the plural of *hole-in-one.*

A: Make the principal word plural, *holes-in-one.*

Q: In the sentence, *Please read our FAQs,* does the abbreviation need an apostrophe?

A: No. The abbreviation for *Frequently Asked Questions* is *FAQs,* as you wrote it. Avoid using an apostrophe for plural forms.

Q: The company name McDonald's is written with an *'s* at the end. How would I make this proper noun plural?

A: Your best bet is to use the common noun *restaurant* after the proper noun; then make the common noun plural. For example, *We visited several McDonald's restaurants.*

Q: Is there a plural form of *plus and minus?*

A: The plural form is *pluses* (or *plusses*) and *minuses.* For example, *Consider all the pluses and minuses before you make a decision.*

Q: I don't have a dictionary handy. Can you tell me which word I should use in this sentence? *A [stationary/ stationery] wall will be installed.*

A: In your sentence use *stationary,* which means "not moving" or "permanent" (*she exercises on a stationary bicycle*). *Stationery* means "writing paper" (*his stationery has his address printed on it*). You might be able to remember the word *stationery* by associating *envelopes* with the *e* in *stationery.*

REINFORCEMENT EXERCISES

Name _____

LEVEL 1

Note: At the beginning of each level, a self-check exercise is provided so that you may immediately check your understanding of the concepts in this chapter. Do not look at the answers until you have finished the exercise. Then compare your responses with the answers shown at the bottom of the page. If more than three of your answers do not agree with those shown, reread the chapter before continuing with the other reinforcement exercises.

A. (Self-check) Write the plural forms of the singular nouns shown in parentheses.

Example: Several (fax) arrived this morning.   faxes _____

1. Many organizations use software to protect their computers from (virus).   _____
2. The cafeteria uses over a dozen (loaf) of bread every day.   _____
3. Most toy manufacturers employ (child) to test their new products.   _____
4. Wells Fargo has three (branch) in that neighborhood.   _____
5. Tracy made two (batch) of chocolate chip cookies after school.   _____
6. The condition will not change unless Congress passes a law with (tooth) in it.   _____
7. One administrative assistant may serve six (boss).   _____
8. Several (tax) were levied on the new property.   _____

Check your answers below.

B. Correct any errors in the use of plural nouns in the following sentences by underlining the incorrect form and writing the correct form in the space provided. If the sentence is correct as it stands, write *C.*

Example: The advertising agency submitted several <u>sketch</u> of the design.   sketches _____

1. After many delays, the heavy boxs were delivered.   _____
2. Ryan placed all the dishs on the kitchen shelves carefully.   _____
3. News dispatchs from Europe described four new tunnels through the Alps.   _____
4. In the redevelopment zone, several new business's will open this month.   _____
5. We need to hire seven additional waiters and waitress's.   _____
6. Each employee received two free pass's to the exhibit.   _____
7. Mona Jackson purchased two different lens for her new camera.   _____
8. She has three different account with her bank.   _____

1. viruses 2. loaves 3. children 4. branches 5. batches 6. teeth 7. bosses 8. taxes

Want to explore more? Go to: academic.cengage.com/bcomm/guffey or Xtra!

NOUNS | CHAPTER 4 | **57**

C. Write plural forms for the nouns listed.

1. employee _____
2. watch _____
3. witness _____
4. franchise _____
5. quota _____
6. rich _____
7. foot _____
8. glass _____

9. hunch _____
10. goose _____
11. bias _____
12. quiz _____
13. service _____
14. gas _____
15. woman _____
16. committee _____

LEVEL 2

A. (Self-check) Provide the correct plural form of the words shown in parentheses.

1. One of our (attorney) was better prepared than the other.
2. Both (bill of lading) showed excessive shipping charges. _____
3. You'll find the files for our past cases on the upper (shelf). _____
4. Small businesses can afford few administrative (luxury). _____
5. The (Williams) bought a vacation home in Maine. _____
6. Students had to show their (ID) before they were admitted. _____
7. Two (bailiff) are assigned to the courtroom. _____
8. Our organization is prepared to deal in foreign (currency). _____

Check your answers below.

B. Write the correct plural form of the singular expressions shown in parentheses.

1. What percentage of (CEO) are women?
2. The two (company) will merge in February. _____
3. We compared liquidity (ratio) of the two companies. _____
4. President Jared Kline wanted a manager with contemporary (belief). _____
5. The reunification of the two (Germany) occurred in 1990. _____
6. Graduates with (MBA) are earning higher salaries than ever before. _____
7. Do the (Wolf) subscribe to *BusinessWeek?* _____
8. Sales are increasing with all Pacific Rim (country). _____
9. Two of our publications managers were former (editor in chief). _____
10. Congress established the Small Business Administration in the (1950). _____
11. Computer users must distinguish between zeros and (O). _____
12. We will tabulate all (yes and no) before releasing the vote. _____

Want to explore more? Go to: academic.cengage.com/bcomm/guffey or Xtra!

13. The two (board of directors) voted to begin merger negotiations. _____

14. President Lincoln had four (brother-in-law) serving in the Confederate Army. _____

15. At least two employees recently took (leave of absence). _____

C. Write plural forms for the nouns listed. Use a dictionary if you are unsure of the spelling.

1. balance of trade _____   **11.** cure-all _____

2. half _____   **12.** RN _____

3. bill of sale _____   **13.** C _____

4. IPO (initial public offering) _____   **14.** No. _____

5. subsidiary _____   **15.** governor-elect _____

6. TV _____   **16.** if _____

7. Wednesday _____   **17.** avocado _____

8. liability _____   **18.** RSVP _____

9. Sanchez _____   **19.** dept. _____

10. valley _____   **20.** q _____

D. Writing Exercise. Write sentences using the plural form of the nouns shown in parentheses.

1. (Alvarez) _____

_____

2. (standby) _____

_____

3. (do and don't) _____

_____

4. (portfolio) _____

_____

5. (hero) _____

_____

6. (witness) _____

_____

7. (attorney) _____

_____

8. (belief) _____

_____

Want to explore more? Go to: academic.cengage.com/bcomm/guffey or Xtra!

NOUNS | **CHAPTER 4** | **59**

LEVEL 3

A. (Self-check) Select the correct plural form of the words shown in parentheses.

1. Moving lights and other (stimulus, stimuli) affect the human eye. _____

2. Black holes are but one of the (phenomenon, phenomena) of astronomy. _____

3. Numerous (crises, crisis) within education will only be worsened by budget cuts. _____

4. Fund raisers contacted all (alumnus, alumni) of Colorado State University. _____

5. The professor sent four (syllabus, syllabi) to the copy room. _____

6. You will find the index on (p., pp.) 116–120. _____

7. Experts presented conflicting (analysis, analyses) of the problem. _____

8. Economics (is, are) a subject studied by all business majors. _____

Check your answers below.

B. Write the correct plural form of the words shown in parentheses.

1. Researchers collected substantial (datum) to support their hypothesis. _____

2. The girls' school will honor its illustrious (alumna). _____

3. References to video phones may be found on pp. 25 (and following pages). _____

4. Dr. Maria Damen used several (criterion) to judge the success of her experiment. _____

5. Page references are shown in (parenthesis). _____

6. Dr. Lynn Steffen requested information about two related (curriculum). _____

7. Galileo's (hypothesis) about the solar system were rejected by his peers. _____

8. Our catalog shows marketing courses on (p.) 226–231. _____

9. Her disorder has resulted in several different (diagnosis). _____

10. Ratha Ramoo's master's and doctor's (thesis) were both in the library. _____

C. Complete the following sentences, selecting the proper singular or plural verb to agree with the nouns.

1. Genetics (is, are) a dynamic field of study. _____

2. (Is, Are) the proceeds to be donated to charity? _____

3. Mumps (is, are) becoming a critical disease in some states. _____

4. Statistics (has, have) the highest failure rate of all courses offered at our college. _____

5. The proceeds from the Colorado lottery (go, goes) to improving the great outdoors. _____

6. (Was, Were) proper thanks given to you for your efforts? _____

7. Several Chinese (is, are) enrolled in this class. _____

8. Billiards (has, have) become a popular television sport. _____

1. stimuli 2. phenomena 3. crises 4. alumni 5. syllabi 6. pp. 7. analyses 8. is

Want to explore more? Go to: academic.cengage.com/bcomm/guffey or Xtra!

60 | UNIT 2 | CHAPTER 4 | NOUNS

D. Skill Maximizer. To offer extra help in areas that cause hesitation for business and professional writers, we provide Skill Maximizers. In the following sentences underline any noun or noun-verb errors. For each sentence write a corrected form in the space provided. If a sentence is correct, write *C* in the space.

1. The Japanese are renowned for their advances in electronic's and other technologies. _____

2. Many banks have installed multilingual ATMs to serve their customers. _____

3. Her goal is to earn all As this semester. _____

4. The huge number of inquirys resulting from the news announcement overwhelmed their two Web sites. _____

5. Although many stimulus are being studied, scientists have not yet determined an exact cause of the bacterial mysteries. _____

6. Unless the IRS proves that the Kellys owe federal taxs, no penalty can be assessed. _____

7. Both woman asked for leaves of absence during the week of June 7. _____

8. Tomatoes are grown to perfection in the interior vallies. _____

9. Our directory lists RN's and MD's separately. _____

10. Because economics are the primary concern, be sure your proposal outlines a careful budget for the entire project. _____

11. After numerous brushs with the law, Mark became a consultant to a security company. _____

12. The Chavez's named three beneficiaries in their insurance policies. _____

13. Because of many glitches in our software, e-mail messages arrived in irregular batchs. _____

14. Despite the new flexible hours for Mondays through Thursdays, all employees must put in a full workday on Fridays. _____

15. The Martinezes discussed all the in's and out's of the transaction before signing the contract. _____

E. Hotline Review. In the space provided write the correct answer choice.

1. We offer the lowest prices in town for fully functional computer (preferred version)
   a. mouses   b. mouse devices
   c. mice   d. mices _____

2. Despite the manufacturer's list of _____, we managed to blow a fuse.
   a. dos and don'ts   b. do's and don'ts
   c. do'es and don'ts _____

3. Even though he was tired, he maintained a _____ position.
   a. stationery   b. stationary _____

4. Many artists' works are featured on the free e-mail _____ offered with Outlook Express.
   a. stationery   b. stationary _____

5. For a fast answer to common questions about our Web site, please consult our _____.
   a. FAQ's   b. FAQs _____

Want to explore more? Go to: academic.cengage.com/bcomm/guffey or Xtra!

NOUNS | CHAPTER 4 | **61**

The following letter contains 25 intentional errors in spelling, proofreading, noun plurals, and sentence structure. When you replace a wordy phrase with one word, it counts as one correction. When you correct a comma splice, run-on, or fragment, the correction counts as two errors. Use proofreading marks to make the corrections here OR make the corrections at the **Guffey Companion Web Site** at **academic.cengage.com/bcomm/guffey.**

FOREST COMMUNICATION SERVICES
259 Elm Street, Suite 400
Cambridge, MA 02124
(617) 830-2871
conferencing@forest.com

April 12, 200x

Ms. Mary Lou Vasquez
Networking Voices
3540 Freeport Blvd.
Sacramento, CA 95822

Dear Ms. Vazquez:

We apreciate this opportunity to contribute to the magazine article. That you are writing about Web conferencing for *Networking Voices*. My specialty here at Forest Communication is conferening services for North America.

Online meetings are becoming more frequent. And more necessary. Many companys find that such meetings save time and money. Participants can hold live, interactive meetings and share documents and presentations. Without ever leaving their offics or homes. Web and phone conferencing is simply more conveneint then having to attend meeting in person. Nearly all Web conferencing providers offer a common set of user features that increase productivity and collaborative sucess. Let me summarize a few of these features:

- **Participant ID.** This feature displays on your screen the name of all attendees and indicates who are talking over the phone line.

- **PowerPoints/Document Sharring.** Presenters can show Web-based visuals and describe them by talking on the telephone.

- **Polling/Surveys.** A virtual "show of hands" can speed consensus and shorten a meeting. Because these conferencing polls are anonymous, they are less intimidating then those taken in live meetings.

- **Whiteboard.** Just as in physical meetings, a whiteboard is handy for jotting down key points and recording brain storming ideas.

- **Archive.** If requested, all content can be archived so that participants who could not join can catch up as their schedule permit.

Web conferencing eliminates the need for traveling to meetings. Which is especially effective for global teams and large groupes. If you would like a list of do's and don't's for Web conferencing, please call me at (617) 830-8701.

Cordially,

Anderson M. Copley

Anderson M. Copley
Director, Conferencing Services

Want to explore more? Go to: academic.cengage.com/bcomm/guffey or Xtra!

62 | UNIT 2 | CHAPTER 4 | NOUNS

Many Web sites provide summaries of information about well-known companies. Some sites, such as Yahoo Finance, allow you to see a capsule of information at no charge. For more extensive information, you must subscribe. You can find information such as a company's addresses (Web and land), the names of its current officers, its subsidiary locations, its products, and its competition. You can even find out its annual revenue and other financial information. In this short exercise you will search for information about the Coca-Cola Company.

Goal: To learn to search for company data on the Web.

1. With your Web browser on the screen, key the following URL: **http://biz.yahoo.com/i/.** Press **Enter.**
2. Look over the *Yahoo Finance Company Fund and Index* home page. Find the **Search** box.
3. In the **Search** box, key *Coca-Cola.* Click **Search.**
4. Wait for the search results. When the **Search Results** page is fully loaded, scroll down to find the listing for the Coca-Cola Company. Click **Profile** to see a summary of company information.
5. Scroll way down the page to see the Coca-Cola summary. Read about Coca-Cola's main products. What types of products does it sell? In what year was it founded? Where is it headquartered?
6. Print one page from the Business Summary.
7. Click the **Key Statistics** button at the bottom of the description. What is Coca-Cola's most recent gross profit? What is its percent of profit margin?
8. End your session by clicking the **X** in the upper right corner of your browser. Turn in all printed copies or send an e-mail to your instructor summarizing what you learned.

Underline any incorrectly spelled nouns. Write the correct form.

1. The children were warned to be careful of the sharp knifes. _____
2. Three bunches of red tomatos look ripe enough to eat. _____
3. Gray wolves are reported to live in the two vallies. _____
4. In the 2000s many companys will be seeking MBAs. _____
5. After several business crises, we hired two attornies. _____

1. knives 2. tomatoes 3. valleys 4. companies 5. attorneys

Want to explore more? Go to: academic.cengage.com/bcomm/guffey or Xtra!

NOUNS | CHAPTER 4 | 63

© Rubberball/Jupiter Images

POSSESSIVE NOUNS

OBJECTIVES

When you have completed the materials in this chapter, you will be able to do the following:

LEVEL 1

- Distinguish between possessive nouns and noun plurals.
- Follow five steps in using the apostrophe to show ownership.

LEVEL 2

- Distinguish between descriptive nouns and possessive nouns.
- Pluralize compound nouns, combined ownership nouns, organization names, and abbreviations.
- Understand incomplete possessives.
- Avoid awkward possessives.

LEVEL 3

- Determine whether an extra syllable can be pronounced in forming a possessive.
- Make proper nouns possessive.

PRETEST

Underline any incorrect possessive forms. Write correct versions in the spaces provided.

1. Some students loans carried lower interest rates than yours. _____

2. Because of her training, Katherine's salary is greater than Troys. _____

1. students' 2. Troy's 3. weeks' 4. Martz' or Martz's 5. Perrys'

3. Giving two weeks notice is standard when leaving a job. _____

4. Mr. Martz CPA firm will open in June. _____

5. The Perrys stock portfolio contains a variety of holdings. _____

CAREER TIP

"Obstacles are those frightful things you see when you take your eyes off your goal."
—Henry Ford

Thus far you have studied four kinds of nouns (concrete, abstract, common, and proper), and you have learned how to make nouns plural. In this chapter you will learn how to use the apostrophe in making nouns possessive.

· LEVEL 1 · LEVEL 1 · LEVEL 1 · LEVEL 1 · LEVEL 1 · **LEVEL 1** · LEVEL 1 · L

SHOWING POSSESSION WITH APOSTROPHES

Possession occurs when one noun (or pronoun) possesses another. Notice in the following phrases how possessive nouns show ownership, origin, authorship, or measurement:

> Linda Serra's computer (ownership)
>
> Cape Cod's beaches (origin)
>
> Dan Brown's novels (authorship)
>
> three years' time (measurement)

In expressing possession, speakers and writers have a choice. They may show possession with an apostrophe construction, or they may use a prepositional phrase with no apostrophe:

> the computer of Linda Serra
>
> the beaches of Cape Cod
>
> the novels of Dan Brown
>
> the time of three years

The use of a prepositional phrase to show ownership is more formal and tends to emphasize the ownership word. The use of the apostrophe construction to show ownership is more efficient and more natural, especially in conversation. In writing, however, placing the apostrophe can be perplexing. Here are five simple but effective steps that will help you write possessives correctly.

FIVE STEPS IN USING THE APOSTROPHE CORRECTLY

1. Look for possessive construction. Usually two nouns appear together. The first noun shows ownership of (or a special relationship to) the second noun.

> the woman['s] briefcase
>
> the children['s] teacher
>
> a day['s] earnings
>
> both investors['] portfolios
>
> the musicians['] instruments

SPOT THE BLOOPER

From the cover of *Florida Today's TV Week:* "Tune in to see who will win this years [Indianapolis 500] trophy."

SPOT THE BLOOPER

From Lois and Selma DeBakey's collection of bad medical writing: "The receptionist called the patients names." (How does the missing apostrophe alter the meaning?)

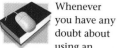
2. Reverse the nouns. Use the second noun to begin a prepositional phrase. The object of the preposition is the ownership word.

> briefcase of the *woman*
>
> teacher of the *children*
>
> earnings of a *day*
>
> portfolios of both *investors*
>
> instruments of the *musicians*

3. Examine the ownership word. To determine the correct placement of the apostrophe, you must know whether the ownership word ends in an *s* sound (such as *s*, *x*, or *z*).

4. If the ownership word <u>does not</u> end in an *s* sound, add an apostrophe and *s*.

> the woman's briefcase
>
> the children's teacher
>
> a day's earnings

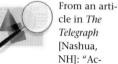
5. If the ownership word <u>does</u> end in an *s* sound, usually add only an apostrophe.

> both investors' portfolios
>
> musicians' instruments

A word of caution: Do *not* use apostrophes for nouns that simply show more than one of something. In the sentence *These companies are opening new branches in the West,* no apostrophes are required. The words *companies* and *branches* are plural; they are not possessive. In addition, be careful to avoid changing the spelling of singular nouns when making them possessive. For example, the *secretary's* desk (meaning one secretary) is *not* spelled *secretaries'.*

Pay particular attention to the following possessive constructions. The explanations and hints in parentheses will help you understand and remember these expressions.

> a day's work (the work of one single day)
>
> three days' pay (the pay of three days)
>
> one year's salary (the salary of one year)
>
> five years' experience (the experience of five years)
>
> a dollar's worth (the worth of one single dollar)
>
> ten dollars' worth (the worth of ten dollars)
>
> your money's worth (the worth of your money)
>
> today's weather (only one today is possible)
>
> tomorrow's work (only one tomorrow is possible)
>
> the stockholders' meeting (we usually assume that a meeting involves more than one person)

The guides for possessive construction presented thus far cover the majority of possessives found in business and professional writing.

Now complete the reinforcement exercises for Level 1.

CHALLENGING POSSESSIVE CONSTRUCTIONS

You can greatly improve your skill in using apostrophes by understanding the following especially challenging possessive constructions.

DESCRIPTIVE VERSUS POSSESSIVE NOUNS

When nouns provide description or identification only, the possessive form is *not* used. Writers have the most problems with descriptive nouns ending in *s*, such as *Human Resources* Department. No apostrophe is needed, just as none is necessary in *Legal* Department.

> Human Resources Department (not *Human Resources' Department*)
>
> the electronics industry (not *electronics' industry*)
>
> Los Angeles Dodgers (not *Los Angeles' Dodgers*)
>
> United States Air Force (not *United States' Air Force*)

COMPOUND NOUNS

Make compound nouns possessive by adding an apostrophe or an *'s* to the final element of the compound.

> mother-in-law's birthday (singular)
>
> editor in chief's office (singular)
>
> sisters-in-law's children (plural)

INCOMPLETE POSSESSIVES

When the second noun in a possessive noun construction is unstated, the first noun is nevertheless treated as a possessive.

> Please pick up your prescription from the doctor's [*office*].
>
> The team members will meet at Patrick's [*home*] after the game.
>
> This year's sales are higher than last year's [*sales*].
>
> Her test scores are higher than other students' [test scores].

SEPARATE OR COMBINED OWNERSHIP

When two nouns express separate ownership, make both nouns possessive. When two nouns express combined ownership, make only the *second* noun possessive.

Separate Ownership	Combined Ownership
landlords' and tenants' rights	the husband and wife's business
Michelle's and Sam's cell phones	Michelle and Sam's apartment

NAMES OF ORGANIZATIONS

Organizations with possessives in their names may or may not use apostrophes. Follow the style used by the individual organization. (Consult the organization's stationery, directory listing, or Web site if you're unsure.)

Organization Name Contains Apostrophe	Organization Name Does Not Contain Apostrophe
McDonald's	Starbucks
Noah's Bagels	Sears
Domino's Pizza	Marshalls
Kinko's	Mrs. Fields
Macy's	Chevys Fresh Mex

ABBREVIATIONS

Make abbreviations possessive by following the five steps in using the apostrophe described in Level 1.

CBS's fall schedule   both CEOs' signatures

NFL's playoff game   Levi Strauss & Co.'s jeans

AWKWARD POSSESSIVES

When the addition of an apostrophe results in an awkward construction, show ownership by using a prepositional phrase.

Awkward:	my sister's attorney's advice
Improved:	advice of my sister's attorney
Awkward:	my company's conference room's equipment
Improved:	the equipment in my company's conference room
Awkward:	my instructor, Valerie Rodgers', office
Improved:	office of my instructor, Valerie Rodgers

Now complete the reinforcement exercises for Level 2.

3 · LEVEL 3 · LEVEL 3 · LEVEL 3 · LEVEL 3 · LEVEL 3 · LEVEL 3 · LEVEL 3 ·

You have learned to follow five steps in identifying possessive constructions and in placing the apostrophe correctly. The guides presented thus far cover most possessive constructions. The possessive form of a few nouns, however, requires a refinement of the final step.

ADDITIONAL GUIDELINE

Let us briefly review the five-step plan for placing the apostrophe in noun possessives. Having done so, we will then add a refinement to the fifth step.

1. Look for possessive construction. (Usually, but not always, two nouns appear together.)

2. Reverse the nouns.

3. Examine the ownership word.

4. If the ownership word does *not* end in an *s* sound, add an apostrophe and *s.*

5. If the ownership word does end in an *s* sound, usually add just an apostrophe. However, if an extra syllable can be easily pronounced in the possessive form, most writers will add an apostrophe and an *s* to singular nouns.

Singular Noun Ending in an *s* Sound; Extra Syllable Can Be Easily Pronounced	Add Apostrophe and *s*
station of the waitress[s]	waitress's station
desk of the boss[s]	boss's desk
den of the fox[s]	the fox's den

MAKING DIFFICULT PROPER NOUNS POSSESSIVE

Of all possessive forms, individuals' names—especially those ending in *s* sounds—are the most puzzling, and understandably so. Even experts don't always agree on the possessive form for singular proper nouns.

Traditionalists, as represented in *The Chicago Manual of Style* and *The Modern Language Association Style Manual,* prefer adding an apostrophe and *s* to troublesome *singular proper* nouns that end in *s* sounds. On the other hand, writers of more popular literature, as represented in *The Associated Press Stylebook and Libel Manual,* prefer the simpler style of adding just an apostrophe to singular proper nouns. You may apply either style, but be consistent. Please note in the following examples that the style choice applies *only* to *singular* names ending in *s* sounds. Plural names are always made possessive with the addition of an apostrophe only. Study the following examples:

STUDY TIP

Remember that the word *the* preceding a name is a clue that the name is being used in a plural sense. For example, *the Rosses* means the entire Ross family.

Singular Name	Singular Possessive— Traditional	Singular Possessive— Popular	Plural Possessive
Ms. Cass	Ms. Cass's	Ms. Cass'	the Casses'
Mr. Morris	Mr. Morris's	Mr. Morris'	the Morrises'
Ms. Sanchez	Ms. Sanchez's	Ms. Sanchez'	the Sanchezes'
Mr. Horowitz	Mr. Horowitz's	Mr. Horowitz'	the Horowitzes'

Here's a summary of the possessive rule that should be easy to remember: If an ownership word does not end in an *s,* add an apostrophe and *s.* If the ownership word does end in an *s,* add just an apostrophe—unless you can easily pronounce an extra syllable. If you can pronounce that extra syllable, add an apostrophe and *s.*

SPOT THE BLOOPER

Printed on a greeting card: "Happy Holidays from the Smith's."

Answered by Dr. Guffey

Question

Q: How do I type the names *Macy*s* and *Wal*Mart*—when the stores actually use stars instead of apostrophes? I don't have a star on my keyboard. And what about *Yahoo!*, which has an exclamation mark at the end? What if a company writes its name in lowercase, such as *eBay*, and that company name comes at the beginning of a sentence?

Q: I recently heard the expression *a stone's throw?* Should *stone* be possessive in this expression?

Q: In preparing an announcement for sales reps, our sales manager wrote about a *two months' training period.* I wanted to make it *a two-month training period.* Who is right?

Q: Where should the apostrophe go in *employee's handbook?*

Q: I'm renewing my license to drive, and it occurred to me that I'm not sure how to write this word correctly. Is it *driver's license, drivers' license,* or *driver license?*

Answer

A: Some companies (and individuals) seek distinction by displaying their names in lowercase or by including atypical symbols. You are under no obligation to reproduce such idiosyncrasies. I agree with outspoken copy editor Bill Walsh, who considers such usage exhibitionism and illiterate. Use only appropriate punctuation. Change the stars to appropriate punctuation (*Macy's, Wal-Mart*). Skip the exclamation mark for Yahoo and capitalize organization names—regardless of the company's preferred style.

A: Some common expressions that refer to distance or geography use the possessive case. Here are a few examples: *at arm's length, for heaven's sake, in today's world,* and *a stone's throw.*

A: Actually, you both are correct! The expression *two months' training period* is possessive (training period of two months). If the expression is *two-month training period,* it is descriptive and no apostrophe is required. Only a slight difference in wording distinguishes a descriptive phrase from a possessive phrase. Sometimes it is hard to tell them apart.

A: This is tricky. If the writer considers the handbook from one employee's point of view, the expression is singular: *employee's handbook.* This is also true of expressions such as *owner's manual.* If the writer is referring to a group, the references are plural: *employees' handbook* (a handbook for all employees), *owners' manuals* (the manuals of all owners). But you should also know that a few organizations prefer to use these terms as adjectives: *owner manual, employee handbook.*

A: That depends on the state in which you live. Some states, such as Kansas, Illinois, and Iowa, use *driver's license.* Most states, including California, New York, and Florida, have dropped the possession altogether, referring to it simply as *driver license.*

Q: I work for the Supreme Court in Arizona, and I have a problem with the following sentence involving the restaurant chain Denny's: *The plaintiff was in fact fired ostensibly for violating Denny's alcoholic beverage service policy.* How do I make possessive a proper name that is already possessive?

A: As you suspected, you can't add another apostrophe. In the interests of clarity, I would consider the name descriptive, thus avoiding an additional *'s*. You would write *Denny's alcoholic beverage service policy*. By the same reasoning, you would not add another apostrophe to anything possessed by *McDonald's*.

Q: Why does *Martha's Vineyard* have an apostrophe whereas *Harpers Ferry* doesn't?

A: The federal government maintains a Board on Geographic Names in the United States. This board has a policy that "geographic names in the U.S. should not show ownership of a feature." British maps, says board secretary Roger Payne, are "littered with apostrophes." To avoid such clutter, the board allows no possessive on any federal maps or documents, unless previously dispensated. Only four geographic names have dispensations: Martha's Vineyard, (Massachusetts), Carlos Elmer's Joshua View (Arizona), Ike's Point (New Jersey), and John E.'s Pond (Rhode Island).

Q: Is there an apostrophe in *Veterans Day*, and if so, where does it go?

A: *Veterans Day* has no apostrophe, but *New Year's Day* does have one. Other holidays that are spelled with an apostrophe are *Valentine's Day*, *St. Patrick's Day*, *Mother's Day*, *Father's Day*, *President's Day*, and *April Fool's Day*.

Q: As the holiday season approaches, I'm wondering whether it's *Season's Greetings* or *Seasons' Greetings*.

A: If you are referring to one season, it's *Season's Greetings*.

LEVEL 1

A. **(Self-check)** Rewrite the following phrases avoiding the use of the apostrophe. Use a prepositional phrase. Does the ownership word end in an *s* sound?

	Revision	End in *s* Sound?
Example: the salesperson's schedule	schedule of the salesperson	No
1. the restaurant's locations	_____	_____
2. a beginner's luck	_____	_____
3. two women's opinions	_____	_____
4. our company's policy	_____	_____
5. your money's worth	_____	_____
6. the children's education	_____	_____
7. three months' time	_____	_____
8. all candidates' speeches	_____	_____
9. this customer's e-mail message	_____	_____
10. her parents' wishes	_____	_____

Check your answers below.

B. Using apostrophes, change the following prepositional phrases into possessive constructions. Ownership words are italicized.

Example: requirements of the *position*	the position's requirements _____
1. qualifications of the *job candidate*	_____
2. interest of ten *months*	_____
3. permit for a *seller*	_____
4. rights of *patients*	_____
5. addresses of *customers*	_____
6. Web site of the *organization*	_____

1. locations of the restaurant, No 2. luck of a beginner, No 3. opinions of two women, No 4. policy of our company, No 5. worth of your money, No 6. education of the children, No 7. time of three months, No 8. speeches of all candidates, Yes 9. e-mail message of this customer, No 10. wishes of her parents, Yes

Want to explore more? Go to: academic.cengage.com/bcomm/guffey or Xtra!

POSSESSIVE NOUNS | CHAPTER 5 | 73

7. prices of *competitors* _____

8. buying power of *Asians* _____

9. delay of a *month* _____

10. meeting of *stockholders* _____

C. In the following sentences, make the word in parentheses possessive.

    1. The (company) annual report is available online. _____

    2. The three (economists) theories created international news. _____

    3. All (customers) personal information is stored on a secure server. _____

    4. An (inventor) patent protects an invention for 17 years. _____

    5. Every (passenger) bags must be X-rayed, and some will be opened. _____

    6. Six (dollars) worth of gas won't take you far. _____

    7. When a bill receives the (governor) signature, it becomes law. _____

D. Underline the errors in possessive construction in the following sentences. Write the correct form in the space provided. If the sentence is correct as it stands, write *C*.

Example: Several <u>students</u> applications were submitted past the deadline.   students' _____

    1. Board members heard all citizens complaints. _____

    2. Passenger's concerns about cell phone use on planes are justified. _____

    3. Some companies are cutting expenses by requiring employees, customers, and vendors to communicate by e-mail. _____

    4. Customers expect a dollars worth of value for a dollar spent. _____

    5. The apartment complex requires a deposit of one months rent. _____

    6. The profits of all companies are being affected by developing technologies and worldwide competition. _____

    7. Many company's sell products and services globally. _____

    8. Nearly all management firms will tailor their services and charges to a clients needs. _____

    9. Success depends on a companies capacity to deliver. _____

    10. Two years worth of effort was put into this project. _____

    11. All depositor's qualify for free online bill paying. _____

    12. Police officers checked all drivers' licenses at two checkpoints. _____

    13. All taxpayers returns are checked by our computer. _____

    14. Many of Disneys animated films are now made in Vancouver, which is North America's second largest film production center. _____

    15. Jared Klines salary is higher than that of other employees because he has greater responsibilities. _____

Want to explore more? Go to: academic.cengage.com/bcomm/guffey or Xtra!

74 | **UNIT 2** | **CHAPTER 5** | **POSSESSIVE NOUNS**

LEVEL 2

A. (Self-check) For each of the following sentences, underline any possessive construction that could be improved. Write an improved form in the space provided. If the sentence is acceptable as it stands, write *C*.

Examples: The uniforms will be stored at <u>Sarahs</u>.   Sarah's _____

1. In our company the Sales' Department made a major announcement.   _____

2. The Dallas' Cowboys signed a top running back.   _____

3. Sue's and Bob's new home is located in South Beach.   _____

4. This company's product line is superior to that companys.   _____

5. The first runner-ups prize of $500 went to Lynn Seaman.   _____

6. The SECs ruling in the securities fraud case is expected today.   _____

7. All teachers contribute to the State Teacher's Retirement System.   _____

8. Her brother's-in-law position was eliminated.   _____

9. Charlies and Toms bikes were stolen from their garage last night.   _____

10. Our Human Resource's Department has several job listings.   _____

Check your answers below.

B. For each of the following sentences, underline any inappropriate possessive construction that could be improved. Write an improved form in the space provided. If the sentence is acceptable as it stands, write *C*.

1. The United States' Marines will recruit on campus tomorrow   _____

2. Web graphics must be designed with the audience's browser's in mind.   _____

3. On the second floor is the chief of staffs office.   _____

4. This year's new home sales are higher than last years.   _____

5. All beneficiaries names must be submitted when we issue policies.   _____

6. The IRSs goal is to simplify the language used on tax forms.   _____

7. Airline deregulation significantly affected the avionics' industry.   _____

8. One of the CEOs children works in the mail room.   _____

9. Numerous employees personnel folders will be reviewed.   _____

10. You can download many new's releases promoting software programs.   _____

11. Lisa's and Greg's daughter is applying to law schools.   _____

12. Most of this companys customers are concentrated nearby.   _____

13. At least a dozen buyers and sellers finances were scrutinized.   _____

14. Some air-freight lines and all bus lines are subject to the ICCs latest regulation.   _____

1. Sales 2. Dallas 3. Sue 4. company's 5. runner-up's 6. SEC's 7. Teachers' 8. brother-in-law's 9. Charlie's, Tom's 10. Resources

Want to explore more? Go to: academic.cengage.com/bcomm/guffey or Xtra!

POSSESSIVE NOUNS | CHAPTER 5 | **75**

15. Your totals for the last three columns are certainly different from Kims. _____

16. Because of the gravity of the offense, the district attorneys staff is investigating. _____

17. Lucasfilm Ltd.s most popular films include *Star Wars* and *Indiana Jones*. _____

18. Microsofts and Netscapes browsers support the latest animation technology. _____

19. They took their complaint to small claim's court. _____

20. Let's plan to meet at Kates before going to the restaurant. _____

C. Rewrite these sentences to remedy awkward or incorrect possessives.

Example: His company's accountant's suggestions are wise.

The suggestions of his company's accountant are wise.
(**Hint:** Start your sentence with the word that is owned.)

1. My sister's lawyer's hourly fee is high.

_____

_____

2. Michael Jordan's father's support was instrumental to the athlete's success.

_____

_____

3. Dan Brown's latest book's success has been overwhelming.

_____

_____

4. The engineer's assistant's computer held all the necessary equations.

_____

_____

5. My supervisor's friend's motor home is always parked in the company lot.

_____

_____

Want to explore more? Go to: academic.cengage.com/bcomm/guffey or Xtra!

76 I UNIT 2 I CHAPTER 5 I POSSESSIVE NOUNS

LEVEL 3

A. **(Self-check)** Select an acceptable possessive form.

1. Bill (a) Gateses', (b) Gates' or Gates's wealth makes him one of America's richest citizens. _____

2. (a) Tesses, (b) Tess' or Tess's e-mail message was forwarded to the entire staff. _____

3. Annie (a) Leibovitz' or Leibovitz's, (b) Leibovitzes' photographs are on display. _____

4. One (a) waitress's, (b) waitresses' service was outstanding. _____

5. Licia Capone took Dr. (a) Fox' or Fox's, (b) Foxes' prescription to a pharmacy. _____

6. All (a) creditor's, (b) creditors' claims will be honored. _____

7. Several of the (a) witnesses', (b) witness's comments were similar. _____

8. Please verify Ms. (a) Lopezes', (b) Lopez's or Lopez' work hours. _____

9. Have you noticed that the (a) Horowitzes, (b) Horowitzes' have a new car? (Tricky!) _____

10. Are you using a computer to schedule your (a) bosses', (b) boss's appointments? (One boss) _____

Check your answers below.

B. Fill in the singular possessive forms for the two styles shown.

	Traditional Style	**Popular Style**
Example: [Mr. Woods] office	Mr. Woods's office	Mr. Woods' office
1. [Barry Bonds] home run	_____	_____
2. [Chris] car	_____	_____
3. [Ms. Harris] desk	_____	_____
4. [Dr. Cortez] office	_____	_____
5. [Mia Metz] son	_____	_____

C. Correct any errors in possessives in the following sentences.

1. Many of Charles Dickens books are considered classics. _____

2. Elvis home, Graceland, is located in Memphis, Tennessee. _____

3. Ms. Lopez paycheck did not reflect the deduction. _____

4. We were all invited to the party at the Thomas. _____

5. Despite a weeks delay, the package finally arrived. _____

6. Chuck Norris films are enjoyed by fans of the martial arts. _____

1. b 2. b 3. a 4. a 5. a 6. b 7. a 8. b 9. a 10. b

Want to explore more? Go to: academic.cengage.com/bcomm/guffey or Xtra!

POSSESSIVE NOUNS │ CHAPTER 5 │ **77**

7. Where can I find the editor in chiefs office? _____

8. After seven years time the property reverts to state ownership. _____

9. I can find other peoples errors but not my own. _____

10. Attorney's salaries have increased significantly over the last decade. _____

D. Skill Maximizer. To offer extra help in areas that cause hesitation for business and professional writers, we provide Skill Maximizers. This exercise reviews all three levels of this chapter, but it emphasizes Levels 1 and 2. Underline all possessive constructions that could be improved. Write an improved form in the space provided. Write *C* if the sentence is correct.

1. We were surprised when Kim married her bosses son. _____

2. The butler stood at the door and called the guests names as they arrived. _____

3. Many artists pictures will be on display at the museum's exhibit. _____

4. To validate the contract, both parties signatures are needed. _____

5. Our mens team placed 12th in the cross-country championship. _____

6. At the CPAs annual conference, we interviewed the graduates of many colleges and universities. _____

7. Does your company routinely monitor employees e-mail messages and Internet use? _____

8. Ryan decided to follow his father-in-law advice in seeking a job using the Internet. _____

9. Barbara always wants to put her two cents worth in. _____

10. Although Jasons car was slightly damaged, Ms. Berkowitz car required major repairs. _____

11. Only one HMOs doctors complained that they were restricted in the amount of time they could spend listening to patients comments. _____

12. If our departments had been aware of each others needs, we could have shared our inventories. _____

13. The discovery of DNAs structure revealed a babys 46 chromosomes arranged in pairs. _____

14. Many employee's are upset about the new policy. _____

15. When jury members heard the eyewitnesses stories, they were stunned. _____

E. Hotline Review. In the space provided write the correct answer choice.

1. Her office is a _____ throw from her home.
   a. stones   b. stone's   c. stones' _____

2. All new service representatives will receive three _____ training.
   a. months   b. month's   c. months' _____

3. On _____ Day we honor those who served our country.
   a. Veterans   b. Veteran's   c. Veterans' _____

4. The office will be closed on _____ Day.
   a. St. Patricks'   b. St. Patrick's   c. St. Patricks _____

5. At all of its restaurants _____ employees are trained to give good service.
   a. Denny's   b. Dennys'   c. Dennys _____

Want to explore more? Go to: academic.cengage.com/bcomm/guffey or Xtra!

F. **Writing Exercise.** Compose original sentences illustrating the possessive forms of the words shown in parentheses. Underline the possessive in each of your sentences.

Example: (two years) You must have two <u>years'</u> experience to apply for the job. _____

1. (Leonard) _____

2. (contractor) _____

3. (Greg and Lisa) _____

4. (Congress) _____

5. (customers) _____

6. (mother-in-law) _____

Want to explore more? Go to: academic.cengage.com/bcomm/guffey or Xtra!

POSSESSIVE NOUNS | CHAPTER 5 | 79

The following letter contains 25 intentional errors in spelling, proofreading, noun plurals, and possessive nouns. When you replace a wordy phrase with one word, it counts as one correction. Use proofreading marks to make the corrections here OR make the corrections at the **Guffey Companion Web Site** at **academic.cengage.com/bcomm/guffey.**

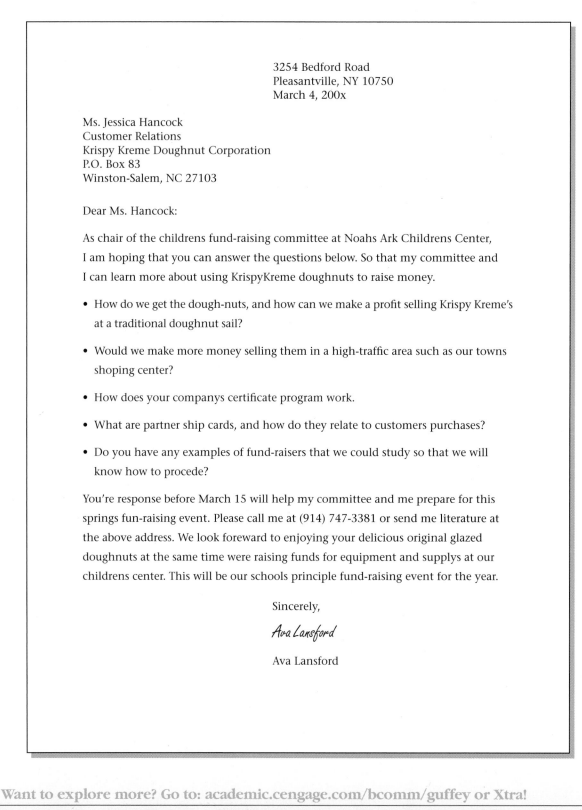

3254 Bedford Road
Pleasantville, NY 10750
March 4, 200x

Ms. Jessica Hancock
Customer Relations
Krispy Kreme Doughnut Corporation
P.O. Box 83
Winston-Salem, NC 27103

Dear Ms. Hancock:

As chair of the childrens fund-raising committee at Noahs Ark Childrens Center, I am hoping that you can answer the questions below. So that my committee and I can learn more about using KrispyKreme doughnuts to raise money.

- How do we get the dough-nuts, and how can we make a profit selling Krispy Kreme's at a traditional doughnut sail?

- Would we make more money selling them in a high-traffic area such as our towns shoping center?

- How does your companys certificate program work.

- What are partner ship cards, and how do they relate to customers purchases?

- Do you have any examples of fund-raisers that we could study so that we will know how to procede?

You're response before March 15 will help my committee and me prepare for this springs fun-raising event. Please call me at (914) 747-3381 or send me literature at the above address. We look foreward to enjoying your delicious original glazed doughnuts at the same time were raising funds for equipment and supplys at our childrens center. This will be our schools principle fund-raising event for the year.

Sincerely,

Ava Lansford

Ava Lansford

Want to explore more? Go to: academic.cengage.com/bcomm/guffey or Xtra!

80 | **UNIT 2** | **CHAPTER 5** | **POSSESSIVE NOUNS**

Your boss is irritated by unwanted e-mail messages, such as "Earn Big Money Working at Home!" She asks you to use the Web to find a way to stop this misuse of her computer. You decide to use a well-known search engine, *Google*.

Goal: To learn to refine search terms.

1. With your Web browser on the screen, key the following URL in the location box: **http://www.google.com** and then press **Enter.**
2. On the *Google* opening page, locate the **Search** box. Key the search term *email* (*Google* seems to prefer this spelling). Press **Google Search** or **Enter.**
3. How many results did *Google* find? Millions? Look over the site titles presented. Do you see any relevant sites?
4. To reduce the number of "hits," you must refine your search term. Scroll back to the top of the screen and locate the **Search** box again. Key a new search term: *unwanted email.*

5. Scroll down to see the number of hits. This refined search term still brings millions of hits.
6. Scroll back to the **Search** box and insert a new search term. Include quotation marks: *"unwanted email."* This time *Google* will find only those sites that include *unwanted e-mail* as a unit.
7. Click one of the pages that looks promising. Find an answer to this question: What can an e-mail user do about unwanted messages (spam)? (If nothing happens on your screen when you click a URL, look at the status line at the bottom of your screen. It tells you whether the site has been contacted. Some sites are slow to respond.)
8. Find and print one or two pages with advice on how to deal with unwanted e-mail.
9. End your session by clicking the **X** in the upper right corner of your browser. Turn in all printed copies or send your instructor an e-mail message summarizing what you learned.

Underline any incorrect possessive forms. Write correct versions.

1. A major vote will take place at the stockholders meeting. _____
2. This month's sales figures were better than last months. _____
3. In just two years time, your profits will likely double. _____
4. Ms. Alvarez secretary located all the accounts receivable. _____
5. One witnesses attire was inappropriate for the courtroom. _____

1. stockholders' 2. last month's 3. years' 4. Alvarez' or Alvarez's 5. witness's

Want to explore more? Go to: academic.cengage.com/bcomm/guffey or Xtra!

POSSESSIVE NOUNS | CHAPTER 5 | **81**

© BananaStock/Jupiter Images

PERSONAL PRONOUNS

OBJECTIVES

When you have completed the materials in this chapter, you will be able to do the following:

LEVEL 1	LEVEL 2	LEVEL 3
• Use personal pronouns correctly as subjects and objects.	• Choose the correct pronoun in compound constructions, comparatives, and appositives.	• Use subjective-case pronouns with subject complements.
• Distinguish between personal possessive pronouns (such as *its*) and contractions (such as *it's*).	• Use reflexive pronouns correctly.	• Select the correct pronouns for use with the infinitive *to be*.

PRETEST

Underline the correct pronouns.

1. Please send the completed form to (I, me, myself) by Friday.

2. (Us, We) employees will vote whether to approve the contract.

3. No one in the office deserved the award more than (her, she).

4. Are you sure it was (she, her) who called me yesterday morning?

5. Reliable managers like you and (he, him) are difficult to retain.

1. me 2. We 3. she 4. she 5. him

As you will remember from Chapter 2, **pronouns** are words that substitute for nouns and other pronouns. They enable us to speak and write without awkward repetition. Grammatically, pronouns may be divided into seven types (personal, relative, interrogative, demonstrative, indefinite, reflexive, and reciprocal). Rather than consider all seven pronoun types, this textbook will be concerned only with those pronouns that cause difficulty in use.

GUIDELINES FOR USING PERSONAL PRONOUNS

Personal pronouns indicate the person speaking, the person spoken to, or the person or object spoken of. Notice in the following table that personal pronouns change their form (or **case**) depending on who is speaking (called the **person**), how many are speaking (the **number**), and the sex (or **gender**) of the speaker. For example, the third person feminine singular objective case is *her*. Most personal pronoun errors by speakers and writers involve faulty usage of case forms. Study this table to avoid errors in personal pronoun use.

	Subjective Case*		Objective Case		Possessive Case	
	Sing.	**Plural**	**Sing.**	**Plural**	**Sing.**	**Plural**
First Person (person speaking)	I	we	me	us	my mine	our ours
Second Person (person spoken to)	you	you	you	you	your yours	your yours
Third Person (person or things spoken of)	he she it	they	him her it	them	his, her hers, its	their theirs

Some authorities prefer the term nominative *case.*

BASIC USE OF THE SUBJECTIVE CASE

Subjective-case pronouns are used primarily as the subjects of verbs. Every verb or verb phrase, regardless of its position in a sentence, has a subject. If that subject is a pronoun, it must be in the subjective case.

I think *she* will be offered the position.

He wonders whether *they* offer wireless access.

BASIC USE OF THE OBJECTIVE CASE

Objective-case pronouns most commonly are used as objects of verbs or objects of prepositions.

Object of a Verb

When pronouns act as direct or indirect objects of verbs, they must be in the objective case.

> Please ask *her* whether she's available to work overtime. (Direct object)
>
> Can you meet *them* at the airport at 10 a.m.? (Direct object)
>
> The attorney sent *them* an important e-mail message. (Indirect object)
>
> The network supervisor issued *her* a new password. (Indirect object)

Object of a Preposition

The objective case is used for pronouns that are objects of prepositions.

> A letter signed by all of *us* was sent to *him.*
>
> Jacques prepared the proposal for *her.*
>
> Just between *you* and *me,* profits are slipping.

When the words *between, but, like,* and *except* are used as prepositions, errors in pronoun case are likely to occur. To avoid such errors, isolate the prepositional phrase, and then use an objective-case pronoun as the object of the preposition (*Every employee [but Weston and her] will work overtime this weekend*).

BASIC USE OF THE POSSESSIVE CASE

Possessive pronouns show ownership. Unlike possessive nouns, possessive pronouns require no apostrophes. Study these five possessive pronouns: *hers, yours, ours, theirs, its.* Notice the absence of apostrophes. Do not confuse possessive pronouns with contractions. **Contractions** are shortened (contracted) forms of subjects and verbs, such as *it's* (for *it is*), *there's* (for *there is*), *they're* (for *they are*), and *you're* (for *you are*). In these examples the apostrophes indicate omitted letters.

Possessive Pronouns	Contractions
Those seats are *theirs.*	*There's* not an empty seat left.
The cat is cleaning *its* fur.	*It's* a household pet.
Your presentation will be fine.	*You're* the next speaker.

As you learned in Chapter 2, words such as *my, our, your, his, her, its,* and *their* function as adjectives when they describe nouns (*my cell phone, our retreat, your address, his car, her condo, its trunk, their vacation*). This concept will be further explained in Chapter 11.

Now complete the reinforcement exercises for Level 1.

CHALLENGES IN USING PERSONAL PRONOUNS

Choosing the correct personal pronouns in compound constructions, comparatives, and appositives requires a good understanding of the following guidelines.

COMPOUND SUBJECTS AND OBJECTS

When a pronoun appears in combination with a noun or another pronoun, special attention must be given to case selection. Use this technique to help you choose the correct pronoun case: Ignore the extra noun or pronoun and its related conjunction, and consider separately the pronoun in question to determine what the case should be.

> ~~Allison and~~ *he* registered for the seminar. (Ignore *Allison and*.) (Compound subject)
>
> ~~You and~~ *I* must write the report. (Ignore *You and*.) (Compound subject)
>
> Tou-Mai asked ~~you and~~ *me* for advice. (Ignore *you and*.) (Compound object)
>
> Would you like ~~Rasheed and~~ *them* to help you? (Ignore *Rasheed and*.) (Compound object)

Notice in the first sentence, for example, that when *Allison and* is removed, the pronoun *he* must be selected because it functions as the object of the verb. In the third sentence when *you and* is removed, the pronoun *me* must be selected because it functions as the object of a verb.

COMPARATIVES

In statements of **comparison,** words are often implied but not actually stated. To determine pronoun case in only partially complete comparative statements introduced by *than* or *as,* always mentally finish the comparative by adding the implied missing words.

> Shelley earns as much as *they*. (Shelley earns as much as *they* [not *them*] earn.)
>
> Nader Sharkes is a better cook than *she*. (. . . better cook than *she* [not *her*] is.)
>
> Tardiness annoys Judy Sunayama-Foster as much as *me*. (. . . as much as it annoys *me* [not *I*].)

APPOSITIVES

Appositives explain or rename previously mentioned nouns or pronouns. A pronoun in apposition takes the same case as that of the noun or pronoun with which it is in apposition. To determine more easily what pronoun case to use for a pronoun in combination with an appositive, temporarily ignore the appositive.

> *We* ~~consumers~~ are protected by laws. (Ignore *consumers*.)
>
> Action must be taken by *us* ~~employees~~. (Ignore *employees*.)

REFLEXIVE PRONOUNS

Reflexive pronouns that end in *-self* or *-selves* emphasize or reflect on their **antecedents** (the nouns or pronouns previously mentioned). Examples of reflexive pronouns include *myself, yourself, himself, herself, itself, ourselves, yourselves,* and *themselves.*

I will take care of this problem *myself.* (Reflects on *I.*)

The president *himself* greeted each winner. (Emphasizes *president.*)

Errors result when reflexive pronouns are used instead of personal pronouns. If no previously mentioned noun or pronoun is stated in the sentence, use a personal pronoun instead of a reflexive pronoun.

Send your request to either James or *me.* (Not *myself*)

Amy Beitel and *I* analyzed the research implications. (Not *myself*)

Please note that *hisself, themself,* and *theirselves* are not acceptable words.
Now complete the reinforcement exercises for Level 2.

3 · LEVEL 3 · LEVEL 3 · LEVEL 3 · LEVEL 3 · LEVEL 3 · LEVEL 3 · LEVEL 3 · LEVEL 3 ·

ADVANCED USES OF SUBJECTIVE-CASE PRONOUNS

Although the following applications appear infrequently, careful speakers and writers try to understand why certain pronouns are used.

SUBJECT COMPLEMENT

As we saw earlier in this chapter, subjective-case pronouns usually function as subjects of verbs. Less frequently, subjective-case pronouns also perform as subject complements. A pronoun that follows a linking verb and renames the subject must be in the subjective case. Be especially alert to the linking verbs *am, is, are, was, were, be, being,* and *been.*

It *was I* who called the meeting. (Not *me*)

I'm sure it *is she* who usually picks up the office mail. (Not *her*)

If you *were I,* what would you do? (Not *me*)

When a verb of several words appears in a phrase, look at the final word of the verb. If it is a linking verb, use a subjective pronoun.

It *might have been they* who left the message. (Not *them*)

The driver *could have been he.* (Not *him*)

If the manager *had been she,* your money would have been refunded. (Not *her*)

In conversation it is common to say, *It is me,* or more likely, *It's me.* Careful speakers and writers, though, normally use subjective-case pronouns after linking verbs. If the resulting constructions sound too "formal," revise your sentences appropriately. For example, instead of *It is I who placed the order,* use *I placed the order.* Remember, when answering the telephone, careful speakers will say, *This is she* or *This is he.*

INFINITIVE *to be* WITHOUT A SUBJECT

Infinitives are the present forms of verbs preceded by *to*—for example, *to sit, to run,* and *to walk.* Subjective pronouns are used following the infinitive *to be* when the infinitive has no subject. In this instance the infinitive joins a complement (not an object) to the subject.

> Mikhail was mistakenly thought to be *I.* (The infinitive *to be* has no subject; *I* is the complement of the subject *Mikhail.*)

> Why would Jennifer want to be *she?* (The infinitive *to be* has no subject; *she* is the complement of the subject *Jennifer.*)

INFINITIVE *to be* WITH A SUBJECT

When the infinitive *to be* has a subject, any pronoun following it will function as an object. Therefore, the pronoun following the infinitive will function as its object and take the objective case.

> The interviewer believed the best candidate to be *her.* (The subject of the infinitive *to be* is *the candidate;* therefore, the pronoun functions as an object. Try it another way: *The interviewer believed her to be the best candidate.* You would not say, *The interviewer believed she to be the best candidate.*)

> Gary expected the caller to be *me.* (The subject of the infinitive *to be* is *caller;* therefore, the pronoun functions as an object.)

> Simon judged the top five performers to be *them.* (The subject of the infinitive *to be* is *performers;* therefore, use the objective-case pronoun *them.*)

Whenever you have selected a pronoun for the infinitive *to be* and you want to test its correctness, try reversing the pronoun and its antecedent. For example, *We thought the winner to be her* (*We thought her* [not *she*] *to be the winner*).

SUMMARY OF PRONOUN CASES

The following table summarizes the uses of subjective- and objective-case pronouns.

Subjective Case	
Subject of the verb	*They* are sky divers.
Subject complement	That is *he.*
Infinitive *to be* without a subject	Josh pretended to be *he.*

Objective Case	
Direct or indirect object of the verb	Give *him* another chance.
Object of a preposition	Send the order to *him.*
Object of an infinitive	Ann hoped to call *us.*
Infinitive *to be* with subject	We thought the guests to be *them.*

Now complete the reinforcement exercises for Level 3.

TYPES OF PRONOUNS

For those of you interested in a total view, here is a summary of the seven types of pronouns, with sentences illustrating each type. This list is presented for your interest alone, not for potential testing.

- **Personal pronouns** replace nouns or other pronouns. Examples:

Subjective Case:	I, we, you, he, she, it, they
Objective Case:	me, us, you, him, her, it, them
Possessive Case:	my, mine, our, ours, your, yours, his, hers, its, their, theirs.

- **Relative pronouns** join subordinate clauses to antecedents. Examples: *who, whose, whom, which, that, whoever, whomever, whichever, whatever.*
- **Interrogative pronouns** replace nouns in a question. Examples: *who, whose, whom, which, what.*
- **Demonstrative pronouns** designate specific persons or things. Examples: *this, these, that, those.*
- **Indefinite pronouns** replace nouns. Examples: *everyone, anyone, someone, each, everybody, anybody, one, none, some, all*, and so on.
- **Reflexive pronouns** emphasize or reflect on antecedents. Examples: *myself, yourself, himself, herself, itself, oneself*, and so on.
- **Reciprocal pronouns** indicate mutual relationship. Examples: *each other, one another.*

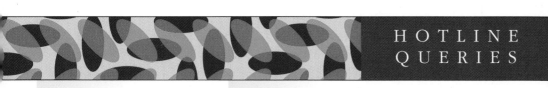

HOTLINE QUERIES

Answered by Dr. Guffey

Question

Q: My colleague insists that the word *his* is an adjective when it is used in an expression such as *his car*. I learned that *his* was a pronoun. What is it?

Q: On the radio I recently heard a talk-show host say, *My producer and myself* . . . A little later that same host said, *Send any inquiries to the station or myself at this address.* This sounded half right and half wrong, but I would have trouble explaining the problem. Can you help?

Answer

A: When words such as *my, our, your, his, her, its*, and *their* function as adjectives, they are classified as adjectives. Although most people consider them pronouns, when these words describe nouns they are actually functioning as adjectives. Your colleague is right.

A: The problem is a common one: use of a reflexive pronoun (*myself*) when it has no preceding noun on which to reflect. Correction: *My producer and I* and *Send inquiries to the station or me.* Reflexive pronouns like *myself* should be used only with obvious antecedents, such as *I, myself, will take the calls.* Individuals in the media often misuse reflexive pronouns, perhaps to avoid sounding egocentric with the overuse of *I* and *me.*

Q: My boss is ready to send out a letter that says, *I respectfully call you and your client's attention to . . .* What's wrong with this?

A: Your boss should have written *I respectfully call your and your client's attention to . . .* However, the best way to handle this awkward wording is to avoid using the possessive form. Instead, use a prepositional phrase (*I respectfully call to the attention of you and your client . . .*).

Q: My supervisor told me that when I answer the telephone, I should say *This is she*. However, this sounds unnatural to me. How can I answer the phone naturally but still sound professional?

A: To sound natural and professional, try saying *This is . . .* followed by your name.

Q: I often catch myself using the response *me too* when I agree or have taken part in the same activity as someone else. For example, my friend will say, *I love that new sushi restaurant*, and I'll respond, *Me too*. Is this a correct use of the pronoun *me?*

A: Although you'll hear this response commonly used, grammatically it's incorrect. When you respond with these words, you're really saying, *Me love that new sushi restaurant too*. However, responding with *I too*, which is grammatically correct, would probably sound too stuffy. If you want to respond correctly but naturally, try saying something like *So do I* or *I do too*.

Q: Is it correct to say *Melissa and myself were chosen . . .?*

A: No. Use the subjective-case pronoun *I* instead of *myself*.

Q: Should a hyphen be used in the word *dissimilar?*

A: No. Prefixes such as *dis*, *pre*, *non*, and *un* do not require hyphens. Even when the final letter of the prefix is repeated in the initial letter of the root word, no hyphens are used: *disspirited, preenroll, nonnutritive*.

Q: I thought I knew the difference between *to* and *too*, but could you provide me with a quick review?

A: *To* may serve as a preposition (*I'm going to the store*), and it may also serve as part of an infinitive construction (*to sign his name*). The adverb *too* may be used to mean "also" (*Andrea will attend too*). In addition, the word *too* may be used to indicate "to an excessive extent" (*the letter is too long*).

Q: Is there some rule about putting periods in organization names that are abbreviated? For example, does *IBM* have periods?

A: When the names of well-known business, educational, governmental, labor, and other organizations or agencies are abbreviated, periods are normally not used to separate the letters. Thus, no periods would appear in IBM, ITT, UCLA, AFL-CIO, YWCA, or AMA. The names of radio and television stations and networks are also written without periods: Station WJR, KNX-FM, PBS, WABC-TV. In addition, geographical abbreviations generally do not require periods: USA, UK, ROC. Finally, the two-letter state abbreviations recommended by the U.S. Postal Service require no periods: NY, OH, CA, MI, NJ, OR, MA, and so on.

6 REINFORCEMENT EXERCISES

LEVEL 1

A. **(Self-check)** Select the correct form.

1. We're waiting to find out whether (she, her) accepts the position.   _____

2. Everyone except (she, her) prefers to use instant messaging for internal communication.   _____

3. Send the contract to (they, them) at their South Dakota address.   _____

4. (They, Them), as well as some other employees, volunteered for the project.   _____

5. We're not surprised that someone like (he, him) was nominated for the award.   _____

6. I'm having lunch today with Nancy Henderson and (she, her).   _____

7. All the purchases made by (I, me) arrived on time.   _____

8. Are you sure (there's, theirs) time to complete the form?   _____

9. Our student business club is having (its, it's) annual banquet in May.   _____

10. Sean is certain that nobody but (he, him) can access these files.   _____

Check your answers below.

B. In the spaces provided, list five personal pronouns that can be used as subjects of verbs and five that can be used as objects of verbs or objects of prepositions.

As subjects: 1. _____   2. _____   3. _____   4. _____   5. _____

As objects: 1. _____   2. _____   3. _____   4. _____   5. _____

C. In this set of sentences, all the omitted pronouns serve as *subjects* of verbs. Write the correct pronoun for each sentence.

1. The manager and (she, her) tested the new Web site.   _____

2. We learned that Betty Dooley and (he, him) will be purchasing the franchise as a joint venture.   _____

3. To prepare for their overseas trip, Emile and (she, her) will take a conversational Italian class.   _____

4. When the product was introduced, other salespeople and (they, them) attended four training sessions.   _____

5. Jean Powers and (I, me) completed our project on time.   _____

1. she 2. her 3. them 4. They 5. him 6. her 7. me 8. there's 9. its 10. him

Want to explore more? Go to: academic.cengage.com/bcomm/guffey or Xtra!

PERSONAL PRONOUNS | **CHAPTER 6** | **91**

In the next set of sentences, all the omitted pronouns serve as *objects* of verbs or prepositions. Selected prepositions have been italicized to help you recognize them. Write the correct pronoun for each sentence.

6. Everyone *but* (we, us) invested in technology stocks.   _____

7. Catherine Bean asked whether the terms of the proposal were satisfactory
   to (they, them).   _____

8. A substantial investment in the McDonald's franchise was made *by* (he, him).   _____

9. Please send Allan Lacayo and (I, me) information about Bluetooth technology.   _____

10. When you update your site, please send the new URL *to* (we, us).   _____

D. In the spaces provided, write the correct letter to indicate how the italicized pronouns function in these
    sentences.

    a = subject of a verb   b = object of a verb   c = object of a preposition

    Example: Please tell *her* that the refund is being processed.   b   _____

1. The office received an announcement that *she* will be the keynote speaker.   _____

2. Professor Amoroso asked *me* for my cell phone number.   _____

3. After Jeff finished his presentation, the supervisor praised *him*.   _____

4. The secret agreement between Shirley Leung and *him* was not revealed.   _____

5. *They* made a good impression on the board of directors.   _____

E. Select the correct pronoun.

1. Everyone except (he, him) took part in the videoconference   _____

2. Please have (he, him) notarize this document.   _____

3. The city is proud of (it's, its) disaster preparedness training program.   _____

4. Nobody but (he, him) has been authorized to use the equipment.   _____

5. Are you sure that this apartment is (there's, theirs, their's)?   _____

6. Tina Wenzel sent the documents to (they, them) for their signatures.   _____

7. (Your, You're) new office is on the third floor.   _____

8. Just between you and (I, me), I think Paul Bernhardt is most qualified.   _____

LEVEL 2

A. **(Self-check)** Select the correct pronoun and write it in the space provided.

1. Her mentor and (she, her) plan to meet weekly.   _____

2. A profit-sharing plan was offered to (we, us) employees in place of
   cost-of-living raises.   _____

3. No one knows technical jargon better than (he, him).   _____

4. Both programmers, Alicia and (she, her), are testing spam-blocking software.   _____

5. (Us, We) delegates stayed at the Westin Hotel during the convention.   _____

6. Ray Goralka and (myself, I, me) were singled out for commendation.   _____

Want to explore more? Go to: academic.cengage.com/bcomm/guffey or Xtra!

7. Proposals submitted by (her and me, she and I) were considered first. _____

8. No one but my friend and (I, me) spoke up during the discussion. _____

9. Separate planes were taken by the business manager and (he, him). _____

10. The announcement surprised Professor Alvarez as much as (she, her). _____

Check your answers below.

B. Select the correct pronoun and write it in the space provided.

1. The presentation on social responsibility inspired him as much as (I, me). _____

2. My colleague and (I, me) plan to take a writing course at night. _____

3. Corey has been with the company six months longer than (I, me). _____

4. The office manager is in charge of (we, us) trainees. _____

5. Our CEO, Laurie Lema, said that no other employees were quite like Steve and (he, him). _____

6. He has no one but (hisself, himself) to blame. _____

7. It's interesting that (us, we) accountants were audited this year. _____

8. Will you and (he, him) have time to meet with the delegate? _____

9. The copilots, Kyle and (he, him), requested permission to land. _____

10. An argument between Nikki and (he, himself, him) caused problems in the office. _____

11. Dr. Douglas Zlock and (I, me, myself) will make the announcement very soon. _____

12. Believe me, no one knows that problem better than (I, me). _____

13. News of the merger pleased President Phyllis Peterson as much as (I, me). _____

14. All employees but Dan Galvin and (I, me) agreed to the economy measures. _____

15. Several of (we, us) candidates plan to visit local colleges. _____

16. Do you think Theresa can complete the work more quickly than (he, him)? _____

17. A proposed annual budget was sent to (we, us) homeowners prior to the vote. _____

18. The signatures on the letter appear to have been written by you and (she, her). _____

19. Contracts were sent to the authors, Pat Tallent and (she, her). _____

20. Everyone except two drivers and (he, him) has checked in with the dispatcher. _____

C. Skill Maximizer. To make sure you have mastered personal pronouns, read the following sentences and underline any faulty pronoun use. Write an improved form(s) in the space provided. Write *C* if the sentence is correct.

1. My supervisor and me compared various wireless packages before making a decision. _____

2. Please send your proposal to Jessica and I by Friday afternoon. _____

3. If neither Matt nor I receive an e-mail confirmation of our itinerary, he and I cannot make the trip. _____

1. she 2. us 3. he 4. she 5. We 6. I 7. her and me 8. me 9. him 10. her

Want to explore more? Go to: academic.cengage.com/bcomm/guffey or Xtra!

PERSONAL PRONOUNS | CHAPTER 6 | 93

4. E-mail messages intended for she and he arrived in the wrong mailboxes. _____

5. Just between you and I, neither Kris nor he met the monthly quota. _____

6. Because of it's success, our organization's diversity program is being expanded. _____

7. Both owners, Mark Messenger and him, agreed to sign the lease agreement by 5 p.m. _____

8. It's surprising that us renters were not consulted about the remodeling. _____

9. Please send you're expense claim to Kim Walsh or me. _____

10. All software technicians except Blanca and she were transferred. _____

11. I think that failing to get to meetings on time is rude, and it angers the boss even more than I. _____

12. To safeguard our passwords, we change our's monthly, but some employees don't change their's at all. _____

13. If a young person repeatedly violates parole, the department pulls he or she back into an institution to try to get the youth under control. _____

14. If you and her are selected, you will both have your expenses paid. _____

15. If the computer continues to give you trouble, check it's wiring. _____

D. Writing Exercise. Provide sentences that use the words shown.

Example: Diana Abernathy and (pronoun)
Diana Abernathy and I agreed to market our invention.

1. My supervisor and (pronoun)

_____

2. The two sales reps, Paul and (pronoun)

_____

3. Just between you and (pronoun)

_____

4. Except for Yumiko and (pronoun)

_____

5. The manager expected Jeff and (pronoun)

_____

6. its

_____

7. ours

_____

Want to explore more? Go to: academic.cengage.com/bcomm/guffey or Xtra!

94 | UNIT 2 | CHAPTER 6 | PERSONAL PRONOUNS

LEVEL 3

A. **(Self-check)** Select the correct pronoun and write it in the space provided.

1. Was it (they, them) who suggested a merger? _____

2. It might have been (she, her) who left the office unlocked. _____

3. If you were (he, him), would you have sent that e-mail message? _____

4. President Barbara Sawyer asked the team and (I, me) to write a proposal. _____

5. If I were (he, him), I would withdraw my endorsement. _____

6. Hyong Than said that it was (he, him) who used the printer last. _____

7. We all assumed the new president would be (she, her). _____

8. The audience didn't discover that Marcelle was (she, her) until the final act. _____

9. They thought Marcelle to be (she, her). _____

10. I'll forward the message to you and (they, them) immediately. _____

Check your answers below.

B. Select the correct pronoun.

1. When Marc answered the telephone, he said, "This is (he, him)." _____

2. If you were (I, me), would you start an internship? _____

3. The committee chair asked Emma and (I, me) to serve on a special task force. _____

4. Most committee members assumed that the chairperson would be (her, she). _____

5. Do you think it was (they, them) who arrived late for the meeting? _____

6. An attempt was made to reach (he and she, him and her) in Paris. _____

7. Voter polls indicate that the new supervisor will be (he, him). _____

8. I'm sure that it was (she, her) who called this morning. _____

9. The lifeguard credited with the rescue was thought to be (he, him). _____

10. If the renter hadn't been (he, him), the apartment might have been left in better shape. _____

11. Professor Susan Foreman declared the scholarship recipient to be (her, she). _____

12. The student club invited David Casper and (she, her) to speak at a campus event. _____

13. Megawati and Jennifer were certain it was not (they, them) who created the shortage. _____

14. The intruder was taken to be (he, him). _____

15. When Christopher opened the door, he expected to see you and (he, him). _____

16. It must have been (they, them) who reported the missing funds. _____

1. they 2. she 3. he 4. me 5. he 6. he 7. she 8. she 9. her 10. them

Want to explore more? Go to: academic.cengage.com/bcomm/guffey or Xtra!

17. We hope to obtain Condoleezza Rice and (he, him) as keynote speakers. _____

18. If the caller is (he, him), please get his telephone number. _____

19. The office staff expected the new manager to be (she, her). _____

20. Are you certain it was (she, her) who created the Web site? _____

C. **Review.** Underline any errors in possessive nouns or personal pronouns in the following sentences. For each sentence write a corrected form in the space provided. Be alert! Some sentences have more than one correction. If a sentence is correct, write *C* in the space.

1. Many attorney's, like Sang-Hee and I, never see the inside of a courtroom. _____

2. On the way to the airport, Jorge and me passed a white stretch limousine that was stalled at the side of the road with it's hood up. _____

3. The Accounting Department processed expense claims for Sally and I, but Sallie's claim was rejected. _____

4. Although I'm sure it was him who sent the e-mail announcement, the CEO doesn't seem to remember it at all. _____

5. Our companys Web site describing our new graphic's capabilities stimulated many inquiries. _____

6. Just between you and I, I think your going to be promoted. _____

7. If chocolate could teach, Galina and me would now be extremely educated. _____

8. I hope that your able to attend the reception because its going to be a lot of fun. _____

9. Theirs just one problem: Neither Craig nor I have credit cards. _____

10. The board has voted to give all employee's a retroactive pay increase. _____

11. Both the network administrator and me are concerned about the increase in personal Web use and it's tendency to slow productivity. _____

12. Although Tonya and me agreed to pay two months rent in advance, the landlord would not rent to her and me. _____

13. No one makes more use of the Web than me. _____

14. All of we accountant's attended a seminar about the Sarbanes-Oxley Act. _____

15. After reviewing our insurance policy and the companys explanation, my wife and I are certain their is a mistake in the reimbursement amount. _____

16. The best manager's believe that recharging one's batteries away from the office really works wonders. _____

17. Us programmers are concerned with the security of customers names and addresses. _____

18. If you were me, would you step into the managers shoes at this time? _____

19. Please send all RSVP's to Tracy or I before December 1. _____

20. Although Neda Mehrabani protested, I'm convinced it was her who sent the gift to Robert and I. _____

Want to explore more? Go to: academic.cengage.com/bcomm/guffey or Xtra!

D. Hotline Review. In the space provided write the correct answer choice.

1. Please send the signed contract to _____ by December 31.
    a. I   b. me   c. myself   _____

2. Because the apartments are so _____, we cannot make exact comparisons.
    a. dis-similar   b. dissimilar   c. dis similar   _____

3. The insurance doesn't cover _____ conditions.
    a. preexisting   b. pre-existing   c. pre existing   _____

4. She hung up after being on hold for _____ long.
    a. to   b. too   _____

5. Her PowerPoint presentation was _____.
    a. un imaginative   b. un-imaginative   c. unimaginative   _____

Want to explore more? Go to: academic.cengage.com/bcomm/guffey or Xtra!

PERSONAL PRONOUNS   I   CHAPTER 6   I   **97**

The following memo contains 32 intentional errors in sentence structure, spelling, and proofreading. When you replace a wordy phrase with one word, it counts as one correction. When you correct a comma splice, run-on, or fragment, the correction counts as two errors. Use proofreading marks to make the corrections here OR make the corrections at the **Guffey Companion Web Site** at **academic.cengage.com/bcomm/guffey.**

MEMORANDUM

DATE: November 15, 200x

TO: Maria S. Damen, Vice President, Marketing   *M S D*

FROM: Ryan Jenkins, Exhibit Manager

SUBJECT: REDUCING A MAJOR EXPENSE AT TRADE SHOWS

As you suggested, Matthew Chavez and myself have been searching for ways to reduce our trade show exhibition costs'. One of our companys major expenses at these shows is the visitors gift that we present.

At last years show we gave away a nine-color, silk-screened T-shirt. Which was designed by a high-priced New York designer. Each shirt cost $15 to produce, however, I've located a Chinese supplier who can produce good-looking T-shirts. For the low cost of only $4 each. Look at the savings we can make:

2,000 silk-screened T-shirts @$15	$30,000
2,000 cheaper T-shirts @$4	8,000
SAVINGS	$22,000

This major saving was immediatley apparent to Matthew and I as we studied the problem. Please examine the enclosed T-shirt sample. If you compare T-shirts, you might expect a cheaper shirt to be dis-similar; but as you can see, this shirt is quiet presentable. What's more, it advertises our name just as well as the more expensive silk-screened T-shirts. If the decision were up to Matthew or I, we would be happy to wear the cheaper shirt.

With increasing travel costs and de-creasing trade show budgets, us in marketing must look carefully at how we spent the companies limited funds for exhibitions. Over the last several years,' we have de-creased the number of shows in which we participate, we have also taken fewer booth staffers then in the passed. This is a significant place to reduce expenses.

For our next major trade show, please authorize the purchase of 2,000 T-shirts. Which can save us $22,000 in exhibition costs. With managements approval before December 1, we can be sure to receive supplys from our Chinese manufacturer for the spring Las Vegas trade show. Matthew and myself look forward to your quick response. If your worried about this suggestion or need more details, please call me at Ext. 480 so that we can talk about it.

Enclosure

Want to explore more? Go to: academic.cengage.com/bcomm/guffey or Xtra!

98 | UNIT 2 | CHAPTER 6 | PERSONAL PRONOUNS

When you are working on your own computer, you will want to *bookmark* or save the URLs of your favorite Web pages.

Goal: To learn to bookmark favorite pages.

1. With your Web browser on the screen, locate the address bar. Key the URL for your book companion site: **academic.cengage.com/ bcomm/guffey.** Locate your book cover. Under **Student,** click **Companion.**

2. Because you will be returning to this page, save the URL by clicking **Favorites** in the upper section of your browser. Click **Add to Favorites** (or whatever your browser says). Click **OK** (or first choose the folder in which to save the URL and then click **OK**).

3. Return to the address bar in your browser and key this URL: **http://www.libraryspot.com.**

4. Examine the main page of *LibrarySpot,* an award-winning library and reference site.

5. Click some of the *LibrarySpot* links that interest you. Return to the main page by clicking **Back.**

6. Gather information about interesting events on a specific date, for example your birthday. Click **What happened on a particular day?** under the **You Asked For It** heading. Make a list of ten of the most interesting events you find. Print one page if possible. Return to the main page. Bookmark this page.

7. Return to the *Guffey Companion Web Site* by clicking **Favorites** and the appropriate link. Click your book cover. Print one page from the Welcome screen.

8. End your session. Turn in your list of interesting events and your printout(s). If your instructor prefers, send an e-mail summarizing what you learned.

Underline the correct pronouns.

1. My colleague and (I, me, myself) will be happy to help you.

2. An e-mail outlining the new procedure was sent to (we, us) employees.

3. I'm convinced that no one will try harder than (she, her).

4. Daryl said it was (they, them) who picked up the order today.

5. Just between you and (I, me), do you know who the new manager will be?

1. I 2. us 3. she 4. they 5. me

Want to explore more? Go to: academic.cengage.com/bcomm/guffey or Xtra!

PERSONAL PRONOUNS | **CHAPTER 6** | **99**

© Jose Luis Pelaez, Inc./Blend Images/Jupiter Images

PRONOUNS AND ANTECEDENTS

OBJECTIVES

When you have studied the materials in this chapter, you will be able to do the following:

LEVEL 1

- Make personal pronouns agree with their antecedents in number and gender.
- Understand the traditional use of common gender and be able to use its alternatives with sensitivity.

LEVEL 2

- Make personal pronouns agree with subjects joined by *or* or *nor*.
- Make personal pronouns agree with indefinite pronouns, collective nouns, organization names, and the antecedents *each*, *every*, and *many a*.

LEVEL 3

- Understand the functions of *who*, *whom*, *whoever*, and *whomever*, and follow a three-step plan in using these words correctly.
- Use the possessive pronoun *whose* correctly.

PRETEST

Underline the correct word.

1. The office manager, along with her staff, submitted (her, their) time sheet.

2. The committee submitted (its, their) recommendation to the board.

3. Either of the branches may send (its, their) manager to the meeting.

1. her 2. its 3. its 4. Whom 5. whoever

100

4. (Who, Whom) did you select for the management trainee position?

5. Send the supplies to (whoever, whomever) placed the order.

Pronouns enable us to communicate efficiently. They provide short forms that save us from the boredom of repetitious nouns. But they can also get us in trouble if the nouns to which they refer—their **antecedents**—are unclear. This chapter shows you how to avoid pronoun–antecedent problems. It also presents solutions to a major problem for sensitive communicators today—how to handle the *his/her* dilemma.

• LEVEL 1 • LEVEL 1 • LEVEL 1 • LEVEL 1 • LEVEL 1 • **LEVEL 1** • LEVEL 1 • L

FUNDAMENTALS OF PRONOUN–ANTECEDENT AGREEMENT

When pronouns substitute for nouns, the pronouns must agree with their antecedents in number (either singular or plural) and gender (either masculine, feminine, or neuter). Here are suggestions for using pronouns effectively.

MAKING PRONOUN REFERENCES CLEAR

Do not use a pronoun if your listener or reader might not be able to identify the noun it represents.

Unclear: Ms. Harrison heard Luke tell Jason that *he* would be late.

Clear: Ms. Harrison heard Luke tell Jason that Luke would be late.

Unclear: In that restaurant *they* do not allow *you* to smoke.

Clear: The restaurant management does not allow its patrons to smoke.

Or: Smoking is not allowed in that restaurant.

Unclear: When Annette Jenkins followed Dawn O'Malley as president, many of *her* policies were reversed.

Clear: When Annette Jenkins followed Dawn O'Malley as president, many of O'Malley's policies were reversed.

MAKING PRONOUNS AGREE WITH THEIR ANTECEDENTS IN NUMBER

Pronouns must agree in number with the nouns they represent. For example, if a pronoun replaces a singular noun, that pronoun must be singular.

Michelangelo felt that *he* was a failure. (Singular antecedent and pronoun)

Great *artists* often doubt *their* success. (Plural antecedent and pronoun)

If a pronoun refers to two nouns joined by *and,* the pronoun must be plural.

The *CEO* and the *employees* discussed *their* differences. (Plural antecedent and pronoun)

Max and *Sarah* need new passwords issued to *them* immediately. (Plural antecedent and pronoun)

Pronoun–antecedent agreement can be complicated when words or phrases come between the pronoun and the word to which it refers. Disregard phrases such as those introduced by *as well as, in addition to,* and *together with.* Find the true antecedent and make the pronoun agree with it.

The *CEO,* together with all department heads, is sending *his* personal thanks. (Singular antecedent and pronoun)

The *department heads,* along with the CEO, are sending *their* personal thanks. (Plural antecedent and pronoun)

A female *member* of the group of protesting employees demanded that *she* be treated equally. (Singular antecedent and pronoun)

MAKING PRONOUNS AGREE WITH THEIR ANTECEDENTS IN GENDER

Pronouns exhibit one of three *genders:* masculine (male), feminine (female), or neuter (neither masculine nor feminine). Pronouns must agree with their antecedents in gender.

Warren Buffet discussed *his* investment strategies. (Masculine gender)

Amy prepared for *her* trip to Russia. (Feminine gender)

The idea had *its* limits. (Neuter gender)

CHOOSING ALTERNATIVES TO COMMON-GENDER ANTECEDENTS

Occasionally, writers and speakers face a problem in choosing pronouns of appropriate gender. English has no all-purpose singular pronoun to represent indefinite nouns (such as *a student* or *an employee*). For this reason writers and speakers have, over the years, used masculine, or common-gender, pronouns to refer to nouns that might be either masculine or feminine. For example, in the sentence *An employee has his rights,* the pronoun *his* referred to its antecedent *employee,* which might name either a feminine or masculine person.

Communicators today, however, avoid masculine pronouns (*he, his*) when referring to indefinite nouns that could be masculine or feminine. Critics call these pronouns "sexist" or "gender biased" because they exclude women. To solve the problem, sensitive communicators rewrite those sentences requiring such pronouns. Although many alternatives exist, here are three options:

Common gender: A passenger must show *his* passport before boarding.

Alternative no. 1: Passengers must show *their* passports before boarding. (Make the subject plural to avoid the need for a singular pronoun. Remember to make the object [*passports*] plural too.)

Alternative no. 2: A passenger must show *a* passport before boarding. (Use an article [*a*] to replace the pronoun. This alternative, however, is less emphatic.)

Alternative no. 3: A passenger must show *his or her* passport before boarding. (Use both masculine and feminine pronouns [*his or her*]. Because this construction is wordy and clumsy, avoid its frequent use.)

Wrong: A passenger must show *their* passport before boarding. (Substituting the plural pronoun *their* is incorrect because *their* does not agree with its singular antecedent, *passenger*.)

Now complete the reinforcement exercises for Level 1.

SPECIAL PRONOUN/ANTECEDENT AGREEMENT CHALLENGES

The following guidelines will help you avoid errors in pronoun-antecedent agreement in special cases. These special instances include sentences in which the antecedents (1) are joined by *or* or *nor*, (2) are indefinite pronouns, or (3) are collective nouns or company names.

ANTECEDENTS JOINED BY *OR* OR *NOR*

When antecedents are joined by *or* or *nor*, the pronoun should agree with the antecedent closer to it.

> Either Sondra or *Janine* left *her* briefcase in the conference room.
>
> Neither the employees nor the *supervisor* expects to see *his* salary increased this year.
>
> Neither the supervisor nor the *employees* expect to see *their* salaries increased this year. (Notice that salaries must also be made plural.)

You may be wondering why antecedents joined by *and* are treated differently from antecedents joined by *or* or *nor*. The conjunction *and* joins one plus one to make two antecedents; hence, a plural pronoun is used. The conjunctions *or* and *nor* require a choice between two antecedents. Always match the pronoun to the closer antecedent.

INDEFINITE PRONOUNS AS ANTECEDENTS

Pronouns such as *anyone, something,* and *anybody* are called *indefinite* because they refer to no specific person or object. Some indefinite pronouns are always singular; others are always plural.

Always Singular		Always Plural
anybody	everything	both
anyone	neither	few
anything	nobody	many
each	no one	several
either	nothing	
everybody	somebody	
everyone	someone	

CAREER TIP

Business and professional people today strive to avoid "sexist" and biased language. For example, use parallel terms (instead of *men and ladies,* say *men and women*). Use neutral titles (*salesperson* instead of *salesman, server* instead of *waitress*). Avoid implied gender (instead of *managers and their wives,* say *managers and their spouses*).

SPOT THE BLOOPER

From NBC's closed captioning of a Miss Teen America pageant: "Each of our contestants have a story."

When indefinite pronouns function as antecedents of pronouns, make certain that the pronoun agrees with its antecedent. Do not let prepositional phrases obscure the true antecedent.

Somebody in the men's league left *his* car lights on.

Each of the corporations had *its* own home office.

Few of our employees have *their* own private parking spaces. (Notice that *spaces* is also plural.)

Several of our branches list *their* job openings on the company's intranet.

STUDY TIP

When *either* or *neither* is followed by an "of" phrase, it is functioning as a singular pronoun (for example, *Either of the books is available*).

The words *either* and *neither* can be confusing. When these words stand alone and function as sentence subjects, they are always considered singular. When they are joined with *or* or *nor* to form conjunctions, however, they may connect plural subjects. These plural subjects, then, may act as antecedents to plural pronouns.

Either of the women *is* able to see *her* personnel record. (*Either* is a singular pronoun and functions as the subject of the sentence. It controls the singular verb *is*. *Either* is also the antecedent of the pronoun *her*.)

Either the woman *or* her friends have left *their* packages. (*Either/or* is used as a conjunction to join the two subjects, *woman* and *friends*. The pronoun *their* agrees with its plural antecedent, *friends*.)

HOT LINK

To reinforce and test your pronoun skills, visit the *University of Houston-Victoria Academic Center:*
http://www.uhv.edu/ac/grammar/pronoun.asp.

COLLECTIVE NOUNS AS ANTECEDENTS

Words such as *jury, faculty, committee, staff, union, team, flock,* and *group* are called *collective* nouns because they refer to a collection of people, animals, or objects. Such words may be either singular or plural depending on the mode of operation of the collection to which they refer. When a collective noun operates as a unit, it is singular. When the elements of a collective noun operate separately, the collective noun is plural.

Our *staff* reaffirmed *its* position on bargaining. (*Staff* operating as one unit)

The *jury* rendered *its* verdict. (*Jury* operating as one unit)

The *jury* were divided in *their* opinions. (*Jury* operating as individuals)

However, if a collective noun is to be used in a plural sense, the sentence can often be made to sound less awkward by the addition of a plural noun (*The jury members were divided in their opinions*).

DID YOU KNOW

English is the first language in history in which the majority of speakers are nonnative. Of the 750 million people who use English regularly, only 375 million are native speakers. It is the universal language of scholarship, science, and trade.

COMPANY AND ORGANIZATION NAMES AS ANTECEDENTS

Company and organization names are generally considered singular. Unless the actions of the organization are attributed to individual representatives of that organization, pronouns referring to organizations should be singular.

Southwest Airlines is adding three new planes to *its* fleet.

The United Nations, in addition to other organizations, is expanding *its* campaign to fight hunger.

Downey, Felker & Torres, Inc., plans to move *its* corporate headquarters.

THE ANTECEDENTS *EACH, EVERY,* AND *MANY A*

When *each, every,* or *many a* precedes a compound subject joined by *and,* the compound subject is considered singular.

> *Each* female player and coach is expected to supply *her* own uniform. [Think *Each single female player and each single coach is expected to supply her own uniform.*]

> *Every* father and son received *his* invitation separately. [Think *Every single father and every single son received his invitation separately.*]

Now complete the reinforcement exercises for Level 2.

· LEVEL 3 · LEVEL 3 · LEVEL 3 · LEVEL 3 · LEVEL 3 · LEVEL **3** · LEVEL 3 ·

ADVANCED PRONOUN USE

The use of *who* and *whom* presents a continuing dilemma for speakers and writers. In conversation the correct choice of *who* or *whom* is especially difficult because of the mental gymnastics necessary to locate subjects and objects. The following guidelines explain when to use *who* and *whom*.

THE CHALLENGE OF *WHO* AND *WHOM*

In conversation, speakers may have difficulty analyzing a sentence quickly enough to use the correct *who* or *whom* form. In writing, however, an author has ample time to scrutinize a sentence and make a correct choice—if the author understands the traditional functions of *who* and *whom*. *Who* is the subjective-case form. Like other subjective-case pronouns, *who* may function as the subject of a verb or as the subject complement of a noun following the linking verb. *Whom* is the objective-case form. It may function as the object of a verb or as the object of a preposition.*

> *Who* do you think will be elected? (*Who* is the subject of *will be elected.*)

> Susan wondered *who* my boss is. (*Who* is the complement of *boss.*)

> *Whom* should we recommend? (*Whom* is the object of *should recommend.*)

> Edmund is the one to *whom* I spoke. (*Whom* is the object of *to.*)

HOW TO CHOOSE BETWEEN *WHO* AND *WHOM*

The choice between *who* and *whom* becomes easier if the sentence in question is approached according to the following procedure:

1. Isolate the *who/whom* clause.
2. Invert the clause, if necessary, to restore normal subject–verb–object order.
3. Substitute the subjective pronoun *he* (*she* or *they*) for *who*. Substitute the objective pronoun *him* (*her* or *them*) for *whom*. If the sentence sounds correct with *him,* replace *him* with *whom*. If the sentence sounds correct with *he,* replace *he* with *who*.

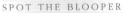

***Whom *may also function as the subject or object of an infinitive. Since little confusion results from these constructions, they will not be discussed.*

Study the following sentences and notice how the choice of *who* or *whom* is made:

Here are the records of those (who/whom) we have selected.

Isolate:	_____ we have selected
Invert:	we have selected _____
Substitute:	we have selected ___him___
Equate:	we have selected ___whom___
Complete:	Here are the records of those *whom* we have selected.

Do you know (who/whom) his doctor is?

Isolate:	_____ his doctor is
Invert:	his doctor is _____ (or _____ is his doctor)
Substitute:	his doctor is ___he___ (or ___he___ is his doctor)
Equate:	his doctor is ___who___ (or ___who___ is his doctor)
Complete:	Do you know *who* his doctor is?

In choosing *who* or *whom*, ignore parenthetical expressions such as *I hope, we think, I believe, they said,* and *you know.*

Edward is the candidate (who/whom) we believe is best.

Isolate:	_____ we believe is best
Ignore:	_____ [we believe] is best
Substitute:	___he___ is best
Equate:	___who___ is best
Complete:	Edward is the candidate *who* we believe is best.

Examples:

Whom do you think we should call? (Invert: You do think we should call him/*whom*.)

The person to *whom* we gave our evaluation was Roshanda. (Invert: The evaluation was given to him/*whom*.)

Do you know *who* the manager is? (Invert: The manager is he/*who*.)

Whom would you like to include in the acknowledgment? (Invert: You would like to include him/*whom* in the acknowledgment.)

THE USE OF *WHOEVER* AND *WHOMEVER*

Whoever, of course, is subjective and *whomever* is objective. The selection of the correct form is sometimes complicated when *whoever* or *whomever* appears in clauses. These clauses may act as objects of prepositions, objects of verbs, or subjects of verbs. Within the clauses, however, you must determine how *whoever* or *whomever* is functioning in order to choose the correct form. Study the following examples and explanations.

Send the supplies to *whoever needs them.* (The clause *whoever needs them* is the object of the preposition *to.* Within the clause itself, *whoever* acts as the subject of *needs* and is therefore in the subjective case.)

A scholarship will be given to *whoever* meets the criteria. (The clause *whoever meets the criteria* is the object of the preposition *for.* Within the clause, *whoever* acts as the subject of *meets* and is therefore in the subjective case.)

We will accept the name of *whomever they nominate*. (The clause *whomever they nominate* is the object of the preposition *of*. Within the clause, *whomever* is the object of *they nominate* and is therefore in the objective case.)

THE USE OF *WHOSE*

The pronoun *whose* functions as a possessive pronoun. Like other possessive pronouns, *whose* has no apostrophe. Do not confuse it with the contraction *who's*, which means "who is" or "who has."

We haven't decided *whose* presentation was more persuasive.

Whose applications were submitted by the deadline?

Please let me know *who's* on call this evening.

Do you know *who's* scheduled to give the keynote address?

Now complete the reinforcement exercises for Level 3.

HOTLINE QUERIES

Answered by Dr. Guffey

Question

Answer

Q: In an article in *U.S. News & World Report* about the U.S. Embassy's proposal to purchase new dishware, I saw this sentence: The location of the crest on the teacups and demitasse cups shall be centered so that when held with the right hand, the crest can be seen by <u>whomever</u> is sitting directly in front of the person holding the cup. Is this correct?

A: Hey, you've found a bona fide blooper! Many writers think that an objective-case pronoun MUST follow the preposition *by*. In this case, however, an entire clause follows the preposition. Within that clause *whoever* functions as the subject. Good detective work! *Whomever* should be *whoever*.

Q: I'm disgusted with and infuriated at a New York University advertisement I just saw in our newspaper. It says, *It's not just <u>who</u> you know . . .* Why would a leading institution of learning use such poor grammar?

A: Because it sounds familiar. But familiarity doesn't make it correct. You're right in recognizing that the proper form is *whom* (isolate the clause *you know him* or *whom*). The complete adage—or more appropriately, cliché—correctly stated is: *It's not what you know but <u>whom</u> you know.*

Q: Here's a sentence we need help with: *We plan to present the contract to whoever makes the lowest bid.* My supervisor recommends *whoever* and I suggest *whomever.* Which of us is right?

A: Your supervisor. The preposition *to* has as its object the entire clause (*whoever makes the lowest bid*). Within that clause *whoever* functions as the subject of the verb *makes*; therefore, the nominative-case form *whoever* should be used.

Q: Please help me decide which *maybe* to use in this sentence: *He said that he (maybe, may be) able to help us.*

A: Use the two-word verb *may be.* Don't confuse it with the adverb *maybe*, which means "perhaps" (*Maybe she will call*).

Q: I don't seem to be able to hear the difference between *than* and *then.* Can you explain it to me?

A: The conjunction *than* is used to make comparisons (*your watch is more nearly accurate than mine*). The adverb *then* means "at that time" (*we must complete this task; then we will take our break*) or "as a consequence" (*if all the angles of the triangle are equal, then it must be equilateral as well*).

Q: What is the order of college degrees, and which ones are capitalized?

A: Two kinds of undergraduate degrees are commonly awarded: the associate's degree, a two-year degree; and the bachelor's degree, a four-year degree. A variety of graduate degrees exist. The most frequently awarded are the master's degree and the doctorate. Notice that these words (*associate's, bachelor's,* and *master's*) are written using the possessive case. In addition, Merriam-Webster dictionaries do not capitalize the names of degrees: *associate of arts degree, bachelor of science, master of arts, doctor of philosophy.* However, when used with an individual's name, the abbreviations for degrees are capitalized: *Craig Bjurstrom, MA; Rhianna Landini, PhD.*

Q: I'm totally confused by job titles for women today. What do I call a woman who is a *fireman,* a *policeman,* a *chairman,* or a *spokesman?* And what about the word *mankind?*

A: As more and more women enter nontraditional careers, some previous designations are being replaced by neutral, inclusive titles. Here are some substitutes:

actor	for *actress*
firefighter	for *fireman*
mail carrier	for *mailman*
police officer	for *policeman*
flight attendant	for *steward* or *stewardess*
reporter or journalist	for *newsman*

Words like *chairman, spokesman,* and *mankind* traditionally have been used to refer to both men and women. Today, though, sensitive writers strive to use more inclusive language. Possible substitutes are *chair, spokesperson,* and *humankind.*

Q: Everyone says "consensus of opinion." Yet, I understand that there is some objection to this expression.

A: Yes, the expression is widely used. However, since *consensus* means "collective opinion," the addition of the word *opinion* results in a redundancy.

Q: Should *undercapitalized* be hyphenated? I can't find it in my dictionary.

A: The prefixes *under* and *over* are not followed by hyphens. These prefixes join the main word: *undercapitalized, underdeveloped, underbudgeted, overbuild, overhang, overjoyed,* and so forth.

LEVEL 1

A. **(Self-check)** Select the correct word(s) to complete the following sentences.

1. When an attorney shows up in court, (he, she, he or she, they) should dress professionally. _____

2. It's important for every applicant to check (his, her, his or her, their) résumé for accuracy. _____

3. The visiting scientist and our resident engineer had (his, her, his or her, their) problems finding the control center. _____

4. No veterinarian's assistant will be assigned to that task until (he is, she is, he or she is, they are) trained. _____

5. One of the members of the girls' gymnastics team set (her, their) personal-best record. _____

6. (They, Researchers) report that the rate of deforestation in Brazil's Amazon rainforest has increased sharply. _____

7. One of the men asked whether (he, they) could use his cell phone during the meeting. _____

8. All flight attendants must have (her, his, his or her, their) uniforms cleaned regularly. _____

9. Robert, after consulting the production staff and others, made (his, their) pricing decision. _____

10. No employee must automatically retire when (he reaches, she reaches, he or she reaches, they reach) the age of 65. _____

Check your answers below.

B. Select the correct word(s) to complete the following sentences.

1. Some people are reluctant to enter (his, their) personal information online. _____

2. An office manager, as well as the other members of management, must do (his, her, his or her, their) best to promote good employee relations. _____

3. A judge often feels that (he, she, he or she, they) should review the charges for the jury. _____

4. Both Dr. Awbrey and Dr. Freeman submitted (her, their) registration forms for the AMA convention. _____

5. Bob Eustes, one of our shipping clerks, submitted (his, their) resignation. _____

6. In many ballparks (you, fans) aren't allowed to smoke in the stands. _____

1. he or she 2. his or her 3. their 4. he or she is 5. her 6. Researchers 7. he 8. their 9. his 10. he or she reaches

Want to explore more? Go to: academic.cengage.com/bcomm/guffey or Xtra!

PRONOUNS AND ANTECEDENTS | **CHAPTER 7** | **109**

7. An employee should know what rights (he has, she has, he or she has, they have) in the workplace.

_____

8. Mr. Petino and Mr. Ramos had already discussed the matter with (his, their) attorneys.

_____

9. If the insured party causes an accident, (he, she, he or she, they) will be charged an additional fee in future premiums.

_____

10. An accountant must double-check (his, her, his or her, their) financial statement figures for accuracy.

_____

C. **Writing Exercise.** Rewrite the following sentences to avoid the use of common-gender pronouns. Show three versions of each sentence.

1. Every resident must display *his* parking permit.

_____

_____

_____

2. Be sure that each new employee has received *his* orientation packet.

_____

_____

_____

3. A doctor must submit *his* insurance paperwork on time.

_____

_____

_____

D. **Writing Exercise.** Rewrite these sentences to make the pronoun references clear.

1. The article reported that Black Dragon Corporation had acquired Gemini Explorations and that it had sold its foreign subsidiaries.

_____

_____

2. They make you wear shoes and shirts in that restaurant.

_____

_____

3. Mr. Williams told Mr. Whitman that he needed to take a vacation.

_____

_____

4. Recruiters like to see job objectives on résumés; however, it may restrict their chances.

_____

_____

5. Mrs. Hartman talked with Courtney about her telecommuting request, but she needed more information.

_____

_____

Want to explore more? Go to: academic.cengage.com/bcomm/guffey or Xtra!

110 | UNIT 2 | CHAPTER 7 | PRONOUNS AND ANTECEDENTS

LEVEL 2

A. **(Self-check)** Select the correct word(s) to complete the following sentences.

1. Anyone at the meeting can share (his, her, his or her, their) opinion on the issue.

   _____

2. Apparently, neither the attachment nor the letters had (its, their) contents proofread very carefully.

   _____

3. Standard & Poor's bases (its, their) bond ratings on many factors.

   _____

4. Someone in the women's choir lost (her, their) voice.

   _____

5. Each man, woman, and child in the club made (his, her, his or her, their) own contribution to the canned food drive.

   _____

6. Either Laurie McDounough or Dorothy Fair will present (her, their) research findings at the meeting.

   _____

7. Nobody in the boisterous crowd could hear (his, her, his or her, their) name when called.

   _____

8. The president asked for budget cuts, and Congress indicated (its, their) willingness to legislate some of them.

   _____

9. Neither of the men would admit (his, their) part in causing the accident.

   _____

10. The Small Business Administration sent (its, their) experts to aid hurricane victims.

    _____

Check your answers below.

B. Select the appropriate pronoun(s) to complete the following sentences.

1. No action can be taken until the committee announces (its, their) decision.

   _____

2. Every employee and manager was told when (his, her, his or her, their) annual performance review would be held.

   _____

3. Neither her dog nor her cat has had (their, its) annual shots.

   _____

4. Not one of the employees would allow (his, her, his or her, their) benefits to be changed.

   _____

5. Someone in this office reported that (his, her, his or her, their) computer had a virus.

   _____

6. The Supreme Court will announce (its, their) decision in June.

   _____

7. Every one of the cars had (its, their) suspension damaged by driving over potholes.

   _____

8. The inspection team will have (its, their) decision on your desk Monday.

   _____

9. Neither the glamour nor the excitement of the job had lost (its, their) appeal.

   _____

10. Any new subscriber may cancel (his, her, his or her, their) subscription within the first ten days.

    _____

11. Union members elected (its, their) officers by electronic ballot.

    _____

12. Many a renter and homeowner (has, have) complained about the tax.

    _____

13. McCormick & Schmick's is proud of (its, their) fresh seafood.

    _____

1. his or her 2. their 3. its 4. her 5. his or her 6. her 7. his or her 8. its 9. his 10. its

Want to explore more? Go to: academic.cengage.com/bcomm/guffey or Xtra!

14. Every renter and homeowner should exercise (his, her, his or her, their) right to vote.

15. If anyone needs assistance, Krista Johns will help (him, her, him or her, them).

LEVEL 3

A. (Self-check) Select the correct word and write it in the space provided.

1. (Who, Whom) do you think we should elect as our new chairperson?

2. I know perfectly well (who, whom) you are.

3. This is the applicant (who, whom) impressed the hiring team.

4. The contract will be awarded to (whoever, whomever) submits the lowest bid.

5. Jackie Harliss-Chang is the investment counselor of (who, whom) I spoke.

6. When I return the call, for (who, whom) should I ask?

7. (Who, Whom) may I say is calling?

8. Will you recommend an attorney (who, whom) can handle this case?

9. The job will be offered to (whoever, whomever) the hiring manager selects.

10. (Whose, Who's) car is blocking the entry?.

Check your answers below.

B. Select the correct word and write it in the space provided.

1. Carmen, (who, whom) left last week, was the most experienced Web designer in our firm.

2. Jake will help (whoever, whomever) is next in line.

3. He is the graphics designer (who, whom) we believe developed their prize-winning Web site.

4. Nadine King, (who, whom) recently passed the bar exam, immediately hung out her shingle.

5. (Who, Whom) have you asked to develop cutting-edge ads for our products?

6. For (who, whom) does the bell toll?

7. I have a pizza for (whoever, whomever) placed the telephone order.

8. The "Father of Accounting" to (who, whom) the professor referred is Luca Pacioli.

9. Leila Nasar is the one (who, whom) we think should be made supervisor.

10. Please tell us the name of (whoever, whomever) you recommend for the position.

11. Adam Smith, (who, whom) is known as the "Father of Capitalism," was born in 1723.

12. Do you know (who, whom) will be taking your place?

13. Please put the call through to (whoever, whomever) is in charge of the project.

14. I wonder (who, whom) the speaker is talking about.

15. In making introductions, who should be introduced to (who, whom)?

1. Whom 2. who (subject complement) 3. who 4. whoever 5. whom 6. whom 7. Who 8. who 9. whomever 10. Whose

Want to explore more? Go to: academic.cengage.com/bcomm/guffey or Xtra!

112 | **UNIT 2** | **CHAPTER 7** | **PRONOUNS AND ANTECEDENTS**

C. In the following sentences determine whether to use *whose* or *who's*. Write the correct word in the space provided.

1. (Whose, Who's) had a chance to study the brief? _____

2. (Whose, Who's) opinion do you respect the most? _____

3. We're not sure (whose, who's) proposal will be adopted. _____

4. It's unclear (whose, who's) planning to take part in tomorrow's walkout. _____

5. (Whose, Who's) on first? _____

D. Skill Maximizer. To make sure you have mastered chapter concepts in all three levels, read the following sentences and underline any faulty pronoun use. Write an improved form(s) in the space provided. Write C if the sentence is correct.

1. The staff adjourned their meeting an hour early. _____

2. Each of the companies calculated their assets and liabilities before the merger. _____

3. *American Demographics* is known for their solid reputation among marketing executives. _____

4. Do you know who Troy is talking about? _____

5. Please direct my inquiry to whoever is in charge of quality control. _____

6. Neither the owner nor his neighbors wanted his address to be revealed. _____

7. Whom would you like to work with? _____

8. Each of the supermarkets featured their advertisements on Thursday. _____

9. Every one of the girls was pleased with their internship program. _____

10. Whose willing to serve as chair of the committee? _____

11. Our entire staff agreed that their response must be unified. _____

12. The instructor whom won the teaching award is Paige Baker. _____

13. An all-expense-paid trip to Florida will be given to whomever wins the sales contest. _____

14. General Motors reported that their sales increased in June. _____

15. It's impossible to determine who's presentation was best. _____

E. Hotline Review. In the space provided write the correct answer choice.

1. Is the newly hired person any better _____ the previous manager?
   a. than   b. then _____

2. If all parties agree, _____ the contract should be approved.
   a. than   b. then _____

3. After completing her associate's degree, Sonia hopes to earn a _____ degree.
   a. Bachelor   b. Bachelor's
   c. bachelor's   d. bachelors _____

4. This _____ our most profitable year yet.
   a. maybe   b. may be _____

5. _____ I'll apply for that position after all.
   a. maybe   b. may be _____

6. Investigators reported that several of the company's buildings were _____.
   a. under-insured   b. underinsured
   c. under insured _____

Want to explore more? Go to: academic.cengage.com/bcomm/guffey or Xtra!

The following e-mail message contains 34 intentional errors in sentence structure, pronouns, spelling, and proof-reading. When you replace a wordy phrase with one word, it counts as one correction. When you correct a comma splice, run-on, or fragment, the correction counts as two errors. Use proofreading marks to make the corrections here OR make the corrections at the **Guffey Companion Web Site** at **academic.cengage.com/bcomm/guffey.**

File | Edit | Mailbox | Message | Transfer | Special | Tools | Window | Help

B | I | U | ⟲ | ≡ ≡ ≡ | A˅ A˄ | ⁙ ⁙ ⁙ ⁙ | A̲ | **Send**

From: Lisa M. Slotsky <lslotsky@dfs.com>
To: Moesha Jenkins <mjenkins@cmc.com>>
Cc:
Subject: Advice for Two People Sharing One Job

I'm happy to hear, Moesha, that you and Sherisa Baldwin plan to ask your manger whether you may share a job. Susan Caminiti and me have had ten years experience in sharing a job here at Deerfield Financial Services, and the arrangement has worked quiet well. As you requested, I'll tell you about our arrangement.

Susan and myself share an office, a desk, a computer, a phone (including an out going voice mail message), and even a monthly parking pass. I'm in the office Monday and Tuesday, Susan is in on Thursday and Friday. We alternate Wednesday's. Communication and organization skills are extremely important to Susan and I. On Sunday afternoon Susan delivers to my home a big manila envelope containing a detailed list of meeting, projects, conferences, and phone calls that took place on my days off. At our mid-week switch, I do the same for her. We strive to insure that our staff has no trouble in it's assignments.

Job sharing, however, can work only when you find the right partner, then it requires a seamless blend of work ethics, personality traits, and egos. During the first year Susan and myself found that we were often both in the office on Wednesdays. I think her and me did more for our boss's then we did for ourselfs. Over the years, however, our arrangement has worked so well that our department now has a staff of 20, and we have earned many bonus.

Of course, an employee who wants to share a job must check with there manager before proceding. We would advice whomever wants to share a job to write a formal proposal that details the division of responsibilitys, schedules, game plans for emergency situations, and so forth. Consider a "two-headed" résumé that explains how your strengths mesh with your partners.

Point out that by sharring a demanding job, two people can work the equivalent of a 60-hour week—without burning out. If you want additional advise, just call Susan or I at 443-6630.

Lisa Slotsky
Investor Relations Department
lslotsky@dfs.com

Want to explore more? Go to: academic.cengage.com/bcomm/guffey or Xtra!

114 | UNIT 2 | CHAPTER 7 | PRONOUNS AND ANTECEDENTS

As you become more familiar with the Web, you may begin to think that the Web is the perfect place for all research. Wrong! Information provided on the Web is not always useful and not always accurate. The following exercise helps you learn to think more critically about what you find on the Web.

Goal: To learn to evaluate Web site credibility.

1. With your Web browser on the screen, go to **http://www.ithaca.edu/library/training/think.html.**
2. Study this page: **ICYou See: Guide to Critical Thinking About What You See on the Web.**
3. Read the six suggestions provided. Click each underlined expression. Use **Back** to move backward.

4. Click **Quiz.** Click **Exhibit One** and **Exhibit Two.** Which of the two exhibit sites looks more reliable?
5. Make a list of five or more questions that you might ask in deciding whether a Web site is reliable. When you finish, submit your list to your instructor or send it in an e-mail.
6. If your instructor advises a longer assignment, click **One more st*p*d assignment.** After examining all seven sites listed for your topic, choose two to evaluate. Follow the instructions by e-mailing your analysis to the author with a cc for your instructor.
7. End your session by clicking the **X** in the upper right corner.

Underline the correct word.

1. Did anyone on the women's softball team leave (her, their) glove on the bus?
2. The entire faculty voted to give (its, their) support to the president.
3. Neither of the companies could identify (its, their) equipment.
4. (Who, Whom) would you like to see as the next department manager?
5. (Whose, Who's) bid is most cost-effective?

1. her 2. its 3. its 4. Whom 5. Whose

Want to explore more? Go to: academic.cengage.com/bcomm/guffey or Xtra!

PRONOUNS AND ANTECEDENTS | CHAPTER 7 | 115

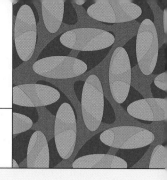

Begin your review by rereading Chapters 4–7. Then test your comprehension of those chapters by filling in the blanks in the exercises that follow. Compare your responses with the key at the end of the book.

LEVEL 1

1. Several (a) childs, (b) children, (c) childrens participated in "Take Your Daughters to Work Day."

2. Each summer I search the farmers' market for the best (a) peachs, (b) peaches.

3. The home of the (a) Ramirezes, (b) Ramirez's, (c) Ramirezes's is located near the bike path.

4. In seven (a) days, (b) day's, (c) days' time, Maxwell will retire.

5. We are giving careful consideration to each (a) company's, (b) companies', (c) companys stock.

6. Many of our (a) students', (b) students, (c) student's have difficulty with possessive constructions.

7. The committee completed (a) it's, (b) its work last week.

8. Let's keep this news between you and (a) me, (b) I.

9. All employees except Ryan and (a) he, (b) him agreed to the reorganization.

10. Ask both of the designers when (a) she, (b) he, (c) he or she, (d) they can give us estimates.

11. When a customer complains, (a) he, (b) she, (c) he or she, (d) they must be treated courteously.

LEVEL 2

12. How did the (a) Sale's, (b) Sales, (c) Sales' Department manage to avoid layoffs?

13. Although he hired two (a) attorneys, (b) attornies, (c) attornies', (d) attorneys' to represent him, he did not prevail.

14. Adriana Herrera consulted her three (a) sister-in-laws, (b) sister-in-law's, (c) sisters-in-law before making a decision.

15. (a) Greg and Patricia's, (b) Greg's and Patricia's new cabin is located on the shores of Lake Tahoe.

16. I certainly hope that today's weather is better than (a) yesterdays, (b) yesterday's.

17. Both George Bush and Bill Clinton served as president during the (a) 1990s, (b) 1990's, (c) 1990s'.

18. Insincerity irritates Dr. Loranjo as much as (a) I, (b) me.

19. Please mail the completed application to (a) I, (b) me, (c) myself.

20. Neither the foreman nor the jury members wanted (a) his name, (b) their names to be released by the media. _____

21. Every clerk and every administrative assistant elected to exercise (a) his, (b) her, (c) his or her, (d) their voting rights. _____

22. Hewlett-Packard was the first company to have (a) it's, (b) its, (c) own "personalized postage." _____

LEVEL 3

23. Following several financial (a) crisis, (b) crises, (c) crisises, the corporation was forced to declare bankruptcy. _____

24. Mathematics (a) is, (b) are Rachel's favorite academic subject. _____

25. We read an announcement that the (a) Harris', (b) Harris's, (c) Harrises, (d) Harrises' son won a scholarship. _____

26. My (a) bosses, (b) boss's, (c) bosses' signature will be forthcoming. _____

27. Tom (a) Hanks' or Hanks's, (b) Hanks, (c) Hankses' new film is doing well at the box office. _____

28. The employee credited with the suggestion was thought to be (a) he, (b) him. _____

29. If I were (a) her, (b) she, I would decline the offer. _____

30. To (a) who, (b) whom did you send your application? _____

31. (a) Who, (b) Whom is available to work overtime this weekend? _____

32. Give the extra supplies to (a) whoever, (b) whomever needs them. _____

33. (a) Who, (b) Whom would you prefer to see in that job? _____

34. (a) Whose, (b) Who's originals were left in the copy machine? _____

35. Do you know (a) whose, (b) who's going to speak at today's seminar? _____

Hotline Review

36. Professor Breuer said it was (a) to, (b) too early to sign up for these classes. _____

37. Shorter, rather (a) then, (b) than longer, training sessions are preferable. _____

38. *Scuba* (from *self-contained underwater breathing apparatus*) is an example of an (a) abbreviation, (b) acronym. _____

39. She drives over the Brooklyn Bridge (a) everyday, (b) every day on her way to work. _____

40. You (a) maybe, (b) may be our most talented Web designer. _____

Name _____

TECHNIQUES FOR EFFECTIVE SENTENCES

The basic unit in writing is the sentence. Sentences come in a variety of sizes, shapes, and structures. As business and professional communicators, we are most interested in functional sentences that say what we want to say correctly and concisely. In this workshop you'll concentrate on two important elements: writing complete sentences and writing concise sentences.

WRITING COMPLETE SENTENCES

To be complete, a sentence must have a subject and a predicate, and it must make sense. As you learned in Chapter 3, incomplete sentences are fragments. Let's consider four common fragment errors you'll want to avoid.

1. The fragment contains a subject and a predicate, but it begins with a subordinate word (such as *because, as, although, since,* or *if*) and fails to introduce a complete clause. You can correct this problem by joining the fragment to a relevant main clause.

   Fragment: Because world markets and economies are becoming increasingly intermixed.

   Revision: Because world markets and economies are becoming increasingly intermixed, Americans will be doing more business with people from other cultures.

   Fragment: Although Americans tend to come to the point directly.

   Revision: Although Americans tend to come to the point directly, people from some other cultures prefer indirectness.

2. The fragment does not contain a subject and a predicate, but a nearby sentence completes its meaning.

   Fragment: In July and August every year in Europe. That's when many Europeans take vacations.

   Revision: In July and August every year in Europe, many Europeans take vacations.

3. The fragment starts with a relative pronoun such as *which, that,* or *who.* Join the fragment to a main clause to form a complete sentence.

   Fragment: Which is a precious item to North Americans and other Westerners.

   Revision: Concise business letters save time, which is a precious item to North Americans and other Westerners.

4. The fragment starts with a noun followed by a *who, that,* or *which* clause. Add a predicate to form a complete sentence.

Fragment: The visiting Asian executive who was struggling to express his idea in English.

Revision: The visiting Asian executive who was struggling to express his idea in English appreciated the patience of his listener.

Skill Check 2.1 Eliminating Sentence Fragments

Each of the following consists of a fragment and a sentence, not necessarily in that order. Use proofreading marks to eliminate the fragment.

Example: Speak in short sentences and use common words. If you want to be understood abroad.

1. Although you should not raise your voice. You should speak slowly and enunciate clearly.

2. A glazed expression or wandering eyes. These alert a speaker that the listener is lost.

3. In speaking with foreign businesspeople, be careful to avoid jargon. Which is special terminology that may confuse listeners.

4. Kevin Chambers, who is an international specialist and consultant. He said that much of the world wants to like us.

5. Graciously accept the blame for not making your meaning clear. If a misunderstanding results.

Skill Check 2.2 Completing Sentences

Expand the following fragments into complete sentences. Add your own ideas. Be ready to explain why each fragment is incomplete and what you did to remedy the problem.

Example: If we keep in mind that Americans abroad are often accused of talking too much.

Revision: If we keep in mind that Americans abroad are often accused of talking too much, we'll become better listeners.

1. The businessperson who engages a translator for important contracts _____

   _____

2. Assuming that a nod, a yes, or a smile indicates agreement _____

   _____

3. If you learn greetings and a few phrases in the language of the country you are visiting _____

   _____

4. Although global business transactions are often conducted in English _____

   _____

5. Which is why Americans sometimes put words in the mouths of foreign friends struggling to express an idea _____

   _____

WRITING CONCISE SENTENCES

Business and professional people value concise, economical writing. Wordy communication wastes the reader's time and sometimes causes confusion. You can make your sentences more concise by avoiding opening fillers, revising wordy phrases, and eliminating redundant words.

Avoiding Opening Fillers

Openers such as *there is, it is,* and *this is to inform you that* fill in sentences but generally add no meaning. These fillers reveal writers spinning their wheels until deciding where the sentence is going. Train yourself to question these constructions. About 75 percent can be eliminated, almost always resulting in more concise sentences.

Wordy:	*There are* three students who volunteered to help.
Revised:	Three students volunteered to help.
Wordy:	*This is to inform you that* our offices will be closed on Monday.
Revised:	Our offices will be closed on Monday.

Revising Wordy Phrases

Some of our most common and comfortable phrases are actually full of "word fat." When examined carefully, these phrases can be pared down considerably.

Wordy Phrases	Concise Substitutes
as per your suggestion	as you suggested
at this point in time	now
due to the fact that	because
for the purpose of	to
give consideration to	consider
in all probability	probably
in spite of the fact that	even though
in the amount of	for
in the event that	if
in the near future	soon
in the neighborhood of	about
in view of the fact that	since
with regard to	about

Notice how you can revise wordy sentences to make them more concise:

Wordy:	*Due to the fact that* fire damaged our distribution center, we must delay some shipments.
Revised:	*Because* fire damaged our distribution center, we must delay some shipments.
Wordy:	We expected growth *in the neighborhood of* 25 percent.
Revised:	We expected *about* 25 percent growth.

Eliminating Redundant Words

Words that are needlessly repetitive are said to be "redundant." Writers must be alert to eliminating redundant words and phrases, such as the following:

advance warning	exactly identical	perfectly clear
alter or change	few in number	personal opinion
assemble together	free and clear	potential opportunity
basic fundamentals	grateful thanks	positively certain
collect together	great majority	proposed plan
consensus of opinion	integral part	reason why
contributing factor	last and final	refer back
dollar amount	midway between	true facts
each and every	new changes	very unique
end result	past history	visible to the eye

Wordy: This paragraph is *exactly identical* to that one.

Revised: This paragraph is *identical* to that one.

Wordy: The *reason why* we are discussing the issue is to reach a *consensus of opinion*.

Revised: The *reason* we are discussing the issue is to reach a *consensus*.

Skill Check 2.3 *Writing Concise Sentences*

In the space provided, rewrite the following sentences to make them more concise.

1. There is a free booklet that shows all the new changes in employee benefits.

   _____

2. In view of the fact that health care benefits are being drastically altered, this is to inform you that an orientation meeting will be scheduled in the near future.

   _____

   _____

3. The reason why we are attending the protest is to make our opinions perfectly clear.

   _____

4. In the event that McDonald's offers new menu items for the purpose of increasing sales, experts think that there is every reason to believe that the effort will be successful.

   _____

   _____

5. There will be a special showing of the orientation training film scheduled at 10 a.m. due to the fact that there were so few in number who were able to attend the first showing.

   _____

   _____

6. This is to give you advance warning that we plan to alter or change the procedures for submitting travel expenses in the very near future.

Skill Check 2.4 Proofreading a Memo

In the memo on page 124, we have deliberately introduced sentence fragments and wordy writing. Use proofreading marks to make all sentences complete and concise. You should make 30 corrections. (When you replace a wordy phrase with one word, it counts as one correction. When you correct a comma splice, run-on, or fragment, the correction counts as two errors.)

Writing Application 2.1.

After you edit the memo on page 124, your instructor may ask you to respond to it. In a memo on a separate sheet, assume that you have received this memo. Show your appreciation to Jason Corzo for his advice. Explain that you are both excited and worried about your new assignment. Use your imagination to tell why. Describe how you expect to prepare for the new assignment. You might say that you plan to start learning the language, to read about the culture, and to talk with colleagues who have worked in Japan. Put this in your own words and elaborate.

Becktelman Worldwide Contractors
Interoffice Memo

TO: Marcia Murphy
FROM: Jason Corzo   *JC*
DATE: August 20, 200x
SUBJECT: CONGRATULATIONS ON YOUR ASSIGNMENT TO JAPAN

Your assignment to Kansai, Japan, as office manager of our International Business Relations Department. That's cause for celebration! This is to inform you that although I'm a little late in responding to your request, I do have some experiences and advice that may interest you.

When I was on assignment in connection with our firm in Japan. My job was to help us break into the construction business. I found it very difficult to locate a Japanese construction firm. That would act as a subcontractor for us. In time, I did find a company and eventually we began to win contracts. In spite of the fact that the process was slow and frustrating.

Despite the slow pace of qualifying for and winning contracts. I am optimistic with regard to expanding our business in Asian countries. In my personal opinion, an important contributing factor in our successful entrance into Pacific Rim markets is how willing we are to play the game according to Asian rules. In the event that we are willing to work from the inside and show our long-term commitment. I am positively certain that we can succeed in gaining a great majority of Asia's construction business in the near future.

On a personal level, Marcia, there are a few things that really helped me in communicating with the Japanese. I learned to smile a lot due to the fact that a smile is perfectly clear to everyone. I also learned to listen without interrupting, and I learned to accept blame each and every time a communication misunderstanding occurred.

Due to the fact that you are in all probability midway between assignments. This message may take a while to catch up with you. Regardless, I congratulate you on this promotion, Marcia. It is the consensus of opinion in our office that you will be very successful in managing our Kansai office in Japan.

SHOWING
THE ACTION

UNIT 1 · UNIT 2 · **UNIT 3** · UNIT 4 · UNIT 5 · UNIT 6

© Goodshoot Images/Jupiter Images

8

VERBS: KINDS,
VOICES, MOODS,
VERBALS

© AL VALEIRO/Pixland/Jupiter Images

9

VERB
TENSES
AND PARTS

© BananaStock/Jupiter Images

10

VERB AND
SUBJECT
AGREEMENT

VERBS: KINDS, VOICES, MOODS, VERBALS

OBJECTIVES

When you have completed the materials in this chapter, you will be able to do the following:

LEVEL 1

- Understand the three main functions of verbs.
- Distinguish between transitive and intransitive verbs.

LEVEL 2

- Recognize the functions and specific uses of active- and passive-voice verbs.
- Understand and apply the subjunctive mood correctly.

LEVEL 3

- Use gerunds, infinitives, and participles correctly.
- Identify and remedy dangling verbal phrases and other misplaced modifiers.

PRETEST

Underline the appropriate answers.

1. In the sentence *Geoffrey scheduled a Web conference,* the verb *scheduled* is (a) transitive, (b) intransitive, (c) linking.

2. In the sentence *The meeting was canceled,* the verb phrase *was canceled* is in the (a) active voice, (b) passive voice, (c) subjunctive mood, (d) intransitive mood.

3. In the sentence *Jane Rada taught the class,* the verb *taught* is in the (a) active voice, (b) passive voice, (c) subjunctive mood, (d) intransitive mood.

4. Emily acts as if she (a) was, (b) were the manager.

5. We appreciate (a) you, (b) your bringing the matter to our attention.

SPOT THE BLOOPER

In *The Denver Post,* a city councilperson was quoted as saying, "I will not be guilted into this idea." (Is this an actual verb?)

1.a 2.b 3.a 4.b 5.b

Verbs are words that energize sentences. They tell what is happening, what happened, and what will happen. The verb is the most complex part of speech. A complete treatment of its forms and uses would require at least a volume. Our discussion of verbs will be limited to practical applications for businesspeople and professionals. In this chapter you'll learn about kinds of verbs, verb voices, and verb moods. You'll also learn about verbals, including gerunds, infinitives, and participles.

KINDS OF VERBS

Verbs express an action, an occurrence, or a state of being.

> Alexandra <u>developed</u> an attractive Web site. (Action)
>
> The winter holidays <u>end</u> the fall term. (Occurrence)
>
> Joe <u>is</u> the new technical writer. (State of being)

In relation to subjects, verbs generally tell what the subject is doing or what is being done to the subject. We'll begin our discussion of verbs by focusing on verbs that express action. These verbs may be divided into two categories: transitive or intransitive. When a verb directs its action toward an object, it is *transitive*. When the action is complete in itself and requires no object, the verb is *intransitive*. Some verbs may be transitive or intransitive, depending on how they function in a sentence.

TRANSITIVE VERBS

A verb expressing an action directed toward a person or thing is said to be **transitive.** A verb used transitively needs, in addition to its subject, a noun or pronoun to complete its meaning. This noun or pronoun functions as the direct object of the transitive verb. Notice in the following sentences that the verbs direct action toward objects.

> <u>Customers</u> <u>bought</u> <u>products</u>.
>
> Yesterday the <u>president</u> <u>called</u> <u>her</u>.
>
> <u>Krispy Kreme</u> <u>sells</u> <u>donuts</u> by the millions.

Objects usually answer the questions *What?* or *Whom?* In the first example, the customers bought *what?* The object is *products.* In the second example, the president called *whom?* The object is *her.*

INTRANSITIVE VERBS

An action verb that does not require an object to complete its action is said to be **intransitive.**

> <u>Tran Phuong</u> <u>worked</u> in our Human Resources Department last summer.
>
> <u>Stan</u> <u>dreams</u> of opening his own business one day.
>
> <u>Francesca</u> <u>listened</u> carefully to the instructions.

Notice that the verbs in these sentences on the previous page do not express actions directed toward persons or things. Prepositional phrases (*in our Human Resources Department, of opening his own business, to the instructions*) and adverbs (*carefully*) do not receive the action expressed by the verbs. Therefore, prepositional phrases and adverbs do not function as objects of verbs.

LINKING VERBS

You will recall that **linking verbs** *link* to the subject words that rename or describe the subject. A noun, pronoun, or adjective that renames or describes the subject is called a **complement** because it *completes* the meaning of the subject.

> Dylan <u>is</u> the new <u>supervisor</u>. (*Supervisor* is a noun complement that completes the meaning of the sentence by renaming *Dylan*.)

> Her salary <u>is</u> <u>excellent</u>. (*Excellent* is an adjective complement that completes the meaning of *salary*.)

> The caller <u>was</u> <u>he</u>. (*He* is a pronoun complement that completes the meaning of *caller*.)

Notice in the preceding sentences that the noun, pronoun, or adjective complements following these linking verbs do not receive action from the verb; instead, the complements *complete* the meaning of the subject.

You are already familiar with those linking verbs that are derived from the *to be* verb form: *am, is, are, was, were, be, being, been*. Other words that often serve as linking verbs are *feels, appears, tastes, seems, sounds, looks*, and *smells*. Notice that many of these words describe sense experiences. Verbs expressing sense experiences may be followed by complements just as the *to be* linking verbs often are.

> She <u>feels</u> <u>bad</u> about her behavior in the meeting. (*Bad* is an adjective complement following the linking verb *feel*. An adjective—not the adverb *badly*—is needed here to describe the senses.)

> Jay <u>appears</u> <u>sad</u>. (*Sad* is an adjective complement following the linking verb *appears*.)

The use of adjectives following such verbs will be discussed more completely in Chapter 11.

The function of a verb in a sentence determines its classification. The verb *write*, for example, is intransitive when it has no object (*Kevin* writes). The same verb is transitive when an object follows (*Kevin writes e-mail*). The verb *felt* is linking when it is used to connect a complement describing the subject (*Maria felt marvelous*). The same verb is transitive when it directs action to an object (*Maria felt the hot sand beneath her feet*). To distinguish between classifications, study carefully the constructions in which the verbs appear.

To review briefly:

- Action verbs—two kinds:

  a. Transitive: need objects to complete their meaning

  b. Intransitive: do not need objects to complete their meaning

- Linking verbs: form a link to words that rename or describe the subject

Now complete the reinforcement exercises for Level 1.

VERB VOICES

You will recall that a verb expressing an action directed toward a person or thing is said to be transitive. Transitive verbs fall into two categories depending on the receiver of the action of the verbs.

ACTIVE VOICE

When the verb expresses an action directed by the subject toward the object of the verb, the verb is said to be in the **active voice.**

> <u>Angie</u> sent the message. (Action directed to the object, *message*.)

Verbs in the active voice are direct and forceful; they clearly identify the doer of the action. For these reasons, writing that frequently uses the active voice is vigorous and effective. Writers of business and professional communications strive to use the active voice; in fact, it is called the **voice of business.**

STUDY TIP

In the passive voice, verbs always require a *helper,* such as *is, are, was, were, being,* or *been.*

PASSIVE VOICE

When the action in a verb is directed toward the subject, the verb is said to be in the **passive voice.** Study the following pairs:

Passive: The <u>figures</u> <u>are</u> <u>totaled</u> daily.

Active: <u>We</u> <u>total</u> the figures daily.

Passive: The <u>lottery</u> <u>was</u> <u>won</u> by Carol Middendorff.

Active: <u>Carol Middendorff</u> <u>won</u> the lottery.

Passive: Three <u>errors</u> <u>were</u> <u>made</u> in the report.

Active: The <u>accountant</u> <u>made</u> three errors in the report.

STUDY TIP

A clue to passive voice is a prepositional phrase beginning with *by.*

Because the passive voice can be used to avoid mentioning the performer of the action, the passive voice is sometimes called the **voice of tact.** Notice how much more tactful the passive version of the last example shown above is. Although directness in business writing is generally preferable, in certain instances the passive voice is used when indirectness is desired.

VERB MOODS

Three verb moods are available to enable a speaker or writer to express an attitude toward a subject: (a) The **indicative mood** is used to express a fact (*We need the contract*); (b) the **imperative mood** is used to express a command (*Send the contract immediately*); (c) the **subjunctive mood** is used to express a doubt, a conjecture, or a suggestion (*If the contract were here, we'd be pleased*). The subjunctive mood may cause speakers and writers difficulty and therefore demands special attention.

CAREER TIP

To be an effective communicator, it's important to use the subjunctive mood correctly. A business or professional person would avoid saying *If I was you,* for example.

SUBJUNCTIVE MOOD

Although the subjunctive mood is seldom used today, it is still employed by careful individuals in the following constructions.

HOT LINK

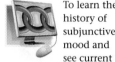

To learn the history of subjunctive mood and see current examples, visit http://www.bartleby.com/64/C001/061.html.

If and *wish* Clauses

When a statement that is doubtful or contrary to fact is introduced by *if, as if,* or *wish,* the subjunctive form *were* is substituted for the indicative form *was.*

> If Lori *were* here, we could proceed. (Lori is *not* here.)
>
> She acts as if she *were* the boss. (She is *not* the boss.)
>
> José wishes he *were* able to snowboard. (José is *not* able to snowboard.)

But if the statement could possibly be true, use the indicative form.

> If Chris *was* in the audience, I missed him. (Chris might have been in the audience.)

That Clauses

When a *that* clause follows a verb expressing a command, recommendation, request, suggestion, or requirement, the subjunctive verb form *be* is used for *to be* verbs. For third-person singular verbs, the *s* or *es* is dropped.

> The director recommended that everyone *be* [not *is*] on time for the meeting.
>
> Our manager ordered that all reports *be* [not *are*] proofread twice.
>
> The Secret Service requires that everyone near the president *receive* [not *receives*] top security clearance.

Motions

When a motion is stated, a subjunctive verb form should be used in the following *that* clause.

> Mario moved that the meeting *be* [not *is*] adjourned.
>
> It has been seconded that the meeting *be* [not *is*] adjourned.

Caution: In a sentence without *that* clauses, do not mix subjunctive and indicative verbs.

> **Right:** If she *were skilled*, she *would receive* job offers. (Both verbs are subjunctive.)
>
> **Right:** If she *is skilled*, she *will receive* job offers. (Both verbs are indicative.)
>
> **Wrong:** If she *were skilled*, she *will receive* job offers. (One subjunctive verb and one indicative verb.)

Now complete the reinforcement exercises for Level 2.

3 · LEVEL 3 · **LEVEL 3** · LEVEL 3 · LEVEL 3 · LEVEL 3 · LEVEL 3 · LEVEL 3 ·

VERBALS

As you learned earlier, English is a highly flexible language in which a given word may have more than one grammatical function. In this level you will study verbals. **Verbals** are words that function as nouns, adjectives, or adverbs. Three kinds of verbals are gerunds (verbal nouns), infinitives, and participles (verbal adjectives).

GERUNDS

A verb form ending in *ing* and used as a noun is called a **gerund.**

> *Marketing* our products on the Web is necessary. (Gerund used as the subject.)
>
> Amarjit enjoys *skiing*. (Gerund used as the direct object.)

In using gerunds, follow this rule: Make any noun or pronoun modifying a gerund possessive, as in *Karen's procrastinating* or *Dale's computing.* Because we sometimes fail to recognize gerunds as nouns, we fail to make their modifiers possessive:

Wrong: The staff objects to *Kevin smoking.*

Right: The staff objects to *Kevin's smoking.*

The staff does not object to Kevin, as the first version states; it objects to his smoking. If we substitute a more easily recognized noun for *smoking,* the possessive form seems more natural: *The staff objects to Kevin's behavior. Behavior* is a noun, just as *smoking* is a gerund; the noun or pronoun modifiers of both must be possessive.

> Mr. Drake resented *his* calling during lunch. (The gerund *calling* requires the possessive pronoun *his*, not the objective-case pronoun *him*.)

> The manager appreciated *your working* late. (Not *you working*)

Not all verbs ending in *ing* are, of course, gerunds. Some are elements in verb phrases and some act as adjectives. Compare these three sentences:

> I saw Benjamin negotiating. (The word *negotiating* functions as an adjective describing Benjamin.)

> I admired Benjamin's negotiating. (As the object of the verb, *negotiating* acts as a gerund.)

> Benjamin is negotiating. (Here *is negotiating* is a verb phrase.)

INFINITIVES

When the present form of a verb is preceded by *to,* the most basic verb form results: the **infinitive.** The sign of the infinitive is the word *to.*

> Try *to call* when you arrive.

> *To write* clearly and concisely requires great skill.

In certain expressions infinitives may be misused. Observe the use of the word *to* in the following infinitive phrases. Do not substitute the conjunction *and* for the *to* of the infinitive.

> Try *to call* when you arrive. (Not *try and call*)

> Be sure *to speak* softly when you use your cell phone in public. (Not *be sure and speak*)

> Check *to see* when the flight is due to arrive. (Not *check and see*)

When any word appears between *to* and the verb (*to* carefully *prepare*), an infinitive is said to be split. At one time split infinitives were considered great grammatical sins. Today most authorities agree that infinitives may be split if necessary for clarity and effect. Avoid, however, split infinitives that result in awkward sentences.

Awkward: Neal Skapura wanted *to,* if he could find time, *take* the online class.

Better: If he could find time, Neal Skapura wanted *to take* the online class.

PARTICIPLES

A **participle** is a verb form that is used with helping verbs to form the present-participle and the past-participle tenses. You'll learn about these tenses in Chapter 9. A participle can also serve as an adjective. As adjectives, participles modify nouns or pronouns, and they do not require helping verbs.

Avoid using participial phrases that sound awkward, such as these:

Awkward:	Pam's having been promoted to office manager was cause for celebration.
Better:	Pam's promotion to office manager was cause for celebration.
Awkward:	Being as you live nearby, should we carpool?
Better:	Since you live nearby, should we carpool?

AVOIDING MISPLACED VERBAL MODIFIERS

Used correctly, verbal modifiers and phrases add clarity and description to your writing. Let's consider the best way to position them within sentences.

INTRODUCTORY VERBAL PHRASES

Introductory verbal phrases must be followed by the words they can logically modify. Such phrases can create confusion or unintended humor when placed incorrectly in a sentence. Consider this sentence: *Sitting in the car, the mountains were breathtaking.* The introductory participial phrase in this sentence is said to *dangle* because it is not followed immediately by a word it can logically modify. The sentence could be improved by revising it to read: *Sitting in the car, we saw the breathtaking mountains.*

After reading an introductory verbal phrase, ask the question *Who?* The answer to that question must immediately follow the introductory phrase. For example, *To find a good job, who?* Answer: *To find a good job, Derek wrote to many companies.* Observe how the following illogical sentences have been improved:

Illogical:	Slipping on the stairs, his back was injured.
Logical:	Slipping on the stairs, *he* injured his back.
Illogical:	Turning on the fan, papers flew about the office.
Logical:	Turning on the fan, *I* caused papers to fly about the office.
Illogical:	After answering the telephone, the doorbell began to ring insistently.
Logical:	After answering the telephone, Jeremy heard the doorbell ring insistently.
Illogical:	Skilled with computers, the personnel director hired Ben Seaberry.
Logical:	Skilled with computers, Ben Seaberry was hired by the personnel director.
But:	To master a language, listen carefully to native speakers. To master a language, (you) listen carefully to native speakers. (In commands, the understood subject is *you.* Therefore, this sentence is correctly followed by the word to which it refers.)

VERBAL PHRASES IN OTHER POSITIONS

In other positions within sentences, verbal phrases must also be placed in logical relation to the words they modify.

Illogical: The missing purchase orders were found by Gordon Young's assistant lying in his top desk drawer.

Logical: Gordon Young's assistant found the missing purchase orders lying in his top desk drawer.

Illogical: Doctors discovered his ankle had been fractured in five places during surgery.

Logical: During surgery, doctors discovered his ankle had been fractured in five places.

Now complete the reinforcement exercises for Level 3.

HOTLINE QUERIES

Answered by Dr. Guffey

Question

Q: I learned that the verb *set* requires an object. If that's true, how can we say that the sun *sets* in the west?

Q: One of my favorite words is *hopefully*, but I understand that it's often used improperly. How should it be used?

Q: I received a magazine advertisement recently that promised me a *free gift* and a *15 percent off discount* if I subscribed. What's wrong with this wording?

Q: When do you use *may* and when do you use *can*?

Answer

A: Good question! The verb *set* generally requires an object, but it does have some standardized uses that do not require an object, such as the one you mention. Here's another: *Some concretes set quickly*. I doubt that anyone would be likely to substitute *sit* in either of these unusual situations. While we're on the subject, the verb *sit* also has some exceptions. Although generally the verb *sit* requires no object, *sit* has a few uses that require objects: *Sit yourself down* and *The waiter sat us at Table 1*.

A: Language purists insist that the word *hopefully* be used to modify a verb (*We looked at the door hopefully, expecting Mr. Guerrero to return momentarily*). The word *hopefully* should not be used as a substitute for *I hope that* or *We hope that*. Instead of saying *Hopefully, interest rates will decline*, one should say *I hope that interest rates will decline*.

A: You've got a double winner here in the category of redundancies. The word *gift* suggests *free*; therefore, to say *free gift* is like *saying I'm studying English English*. It would be better to say *special gift*. In the same way, *15 percent off discount* repeats itself. Omit *off*.

A: Traditionally, the verb *may* is used in asking or granting permission (*yes, you may use that desk*). *Can* is used to suggest ability (*you can succeed in business*). In informal writing, however, authorities today generally agree that *can* may be substituted for *may*.

Q: I just checked the dictionary and found that *cooperate* is now written as one word. It seems to me that years ago it was *co-operate* or *coöperate*. Has the spelling changed?

A: Yes, it has. And so has the spelling of many other words. As new words become more familiar, their spelling tends to become more simplified. For example, *per cent* and *good will* are now shown by most dictionaries as *percent* and *goodwill*. By the same token, many words formerly hyphenated are now written without hyphens: *strike-over* is now *strikeover*, *to-day* is *today*, *editor-in-chief* is *editor in chief*, *vice-president* is *vice president*, and *passer-by* is now *passerby*. Current dictionaries reflect these changes.

Q: On my computer I'm using a program that checks the writer's style. My problem is that it flags every passive-voice verb and tells me to consider using active-voice verbs. Are passive-voice verbs totally forbidden in business and professional writing?

A: Of course not! Computer style checkers capitalize on language areas that can be detected mechanically, and a passive-voice verb is easily identified by a computer. Although active-voice verbs are considered more forceful, passive-voice verbs have a genuine function in business and professional writing. Because they hide the subject and diffuse attention, passive verbs are useful in sensitive messages where indirect language can develop an impersonal, inconspicuous tone. For example, when a lower-level employee must write a persuasive and somewhat negative message to a manager, passive-voice verbs are quite useful.

Q: What's the correct verb in this sentence? *Tim recognized that, if his company (was or were) to prosper, it would require considerable capital.*

A: The verb should be *were* because the clause in which it functions is not true. Statements contrary to fact that are introduced by words such as *if* and *wish* require subjunctive-mood verbs.

Q: Are there two meanings for the word *discreet*?

A: You are probably confusing the two words *discreet* and *discrete*. *Discreet* means "showing good judgment" and "prudent" (*the witness gave a discreet answer, avoiding gossip and hearsay*). The word *discrete* means "separate" or "noncontinuous" (*Alpha, Inc., has installed discrete computers rather than a network computer system*). You might find it helpful to remember that the *e's* are separate in *discrete*.

Q: I saw this in an auction announcement for a Beverly Hills home: *Married to interior decorator Dusty Bartlett, their home saw many of the great Hollywood parties with friends such as Ingrid Bergman and Katharine Hepburn setting by the pool on weekends.* Am I just imagining, or does this sentence say that the home was married to the interior decorator?

A: Amazing, isn't it! But that's what the sentence says. This is a classic misplaced modifier. An introductory verbal phrase must be immediately followed by words that the phrase can logically modify. This sentence doesn't give a clue. Did you see another problem? The verb *setting* should be *sitting*.

LEVEL 1

A. (Self-check) In the spaces provided indicate whether the italicized verbs are transitive (*T*), intransitive (*I*), or linking (*L*).

Example: Kendra *is* our team leader.   L _____

1. Instant messaging *appears* to be growing in popularity in the workplace.   _____

2. The Sanchezes *auctioned* their car on eBay.   _____

3. Before the conference, delegates *met* in the foyer.   _____

4. Jeanette Walgren *is* the professor who won the award.   _____

5. The city *expects* Mayor Newsom to return to the office soon.   _____

6. It *was* he who devised the current work schedule.   _____

7. The production manager *called* over four hours ago.   _____

8. Emily Adams *feels* certain that her work calendar is clear.   _____

9. Well-written business letters *get* results.   _____

10. Personality *opens* doors, but only character keeps them open.   _____

Check your answers below.

B. Each of the following sentences contains a verb that is either transitive or intransitive. If the verb is intransitive, underline it and write *I* in the space provided. If the verb is transitive, underline it, write *T* in the space provided, and also write its direct object.

Examples: After his presentation the manager <u>left</u>.   I _____

Employees <u>brought</u> their lunches.   T (lunches) _____

1. Rich Royka scheduled a meeting to discuss new health care options.   _____

2. The network failed.   _____

3. FedEx maintains a busy Web site for its customers.   _____

4. Our suppliers raised their prices.   _____

5. Storm clouds gathered.   _____

6. Over the years our assets increased.   _____

7. Bill Gates receives many e-mail messages.   _____

1. L, 2. T, 3. I, 4. L, 5. T, 6. L, 7. I, 8. L, 9. T, 10. T

Want to explore more? Go to: academic.cengage.com/bcomm/guffey or Xtra!

VERBS: KINDS, VOICES, MOODS, VERBALS I **CHAPTER 8** I **135**

8. The telephone rang. _____

9. Gregory answered it. _____

10. Jessica expects to pass the CPA exam. _____

C. Linking verbs are followed by complements that identify, rename, or describe the subjects. The most common linking verbs are the forms of *be* (*am, is, are, was,* and so on) and the verbs of the senses (*feels, appears, tastes, smells,* and so on). The following sentences all contain linking verbs. For each sentence underline the linking verb or verb phrase and write its complement in the space provided.

Examples: Leony <u>feels</u> confident in her abilities. confident

Our current team leader <u>is</u> LeRoy Haitz. LeRoy Haitz

1. Florence is known for its beautiful architecture. _____

2. His presentation was professional and convincing. _____

3. That pizza smells fantastic! _____

4. Over the telephone his voice sounds resonant. _____

5. It was she who called you earlier. _____

6. Leonard Goodelman was the wedding photographer. _____

7. He feels comfortable buying items online. _____

8. The manager of that department might be Ignacio. _____

9. That table will be fine. _____

10. It seems unusually cold in here today. _____

D. In the following sentences selected verbs have been italicized. For each sentence indicate whether the italicized verb is transitive (*T*), intransitive (*I*), or linking (*L*). In addition, if the verb is transitive, write its object. If the verb is linking, write its complement.

Examples: The new sales rep *is* Michele Taylor. L (Michele Taylor)

Our Web site *generates* many hits each day. T (hits)

1. The chair of our Curriculum Committee *is* Marie Mueller. _____

2. A virtual keyboard *projects* the image of a full-sized computer keyboard onto any flat surface using laser technology. _____

3. Virtual keyboards *work* best in rooms without bright lighting. _____

4. It *was* she who sent the e-mail. _____

5. Please *check* the links to make sure they're working. _____

6. Her report *appears* accurate, but we must verify some data. _____

7. Todd *feels* marvelous about his recent promotion. _____

8. Producers *move* goods to market to meet seasonal demands. _____

9. It *must have been* they who made the anonymous gift. _____

10. The economy *appears* bright despite interest rate increases. _____

11. Beverly Westbrook *is* the person whom you should call. _____

Want to explore more? Go to: academic.cengage.com/bcomm/guffey or Xtra!

12. Although consumers protested, the airline *ended* its meal service. _____

13. The physician *wrote* a prescription for allergy medicine. _____

14. We *listened* to the presentation with great interest. _____

15. All of us *feel* bad about her transfer. _____

LEVEL 2

A. (Self-check) Transitive verbs in the following sentences have been italicized. For each sentence write *active* or *passive* to indicate the voice of the italicized verb.

Example: Several building code violations *were found* by inspectors. passive _____

1. Mark Messenger *prepared* the certified check. _____

2. The certified check *was prepared* by Mark Messenger _____

3. Communication and computer skills *are required* by many hiring companies. _____

4. Many hiring companies *require* communication and computer skills. _____

5. Janice Salles *owns* a number of apartments and other properties. _____

Select the correct word and write it in the space provided

6. If Wende Ramos (was, were) our manager, morale would be much higher _____

7. Mike Mixon recommended that the meeting (is, be) adjourned at 4:30 p.m. _____

8. If I (was, were) you, I'd apply for the promotion. _____

9. Did your manager suggest that you (be, are) given time off to attend classes? _____

10. If Maggie Sweitzer (was, were) at the opening session, she did not announce herself. _____

Check your answers below.

B. In the spaces provided, write *active* or *passive* to indicate the voice of the italicized verbs in the following sentences.

1. Our company *monitors* the Web activity of all employees. _____

2. The Web activity of all employees *is monitored* by our company. _____

3. You *withdrew* the funds in question on May 29. _____

4. Brad Eckhardt *was told* to submit the expense claim by Friday. _____

Careful writers strive to use the active voice in business and professional communications. This is an important skill for you to develop. To give you practice, rewrite the following sentences changing their passive-voice verbs to active voice. Normally you can change a verb from passive to active voice by making the doer of the action—usually contained in a *by* phrase—the subject of the sentence.

Example: (Passive) Production costs must be reduced by manufacturers.

(Active) Manufacturers must reduce production costs. _____

1. active 2. passive 3. passive 4. active 5. active 6. were 7. be 8. were 9. be 10. was

Want to explore more? Go to: academic.cengage.com/bcomm/guffey or Xtra!

5. Pollution was greatly reduced by General Motors when the company built its new plant. (**Hint:** *Who greatly reduced pollution? Start your new sentence with that name.*)

_____

6. The documents were carefully reviewed by investigators during the audit.

_____

7. Massive short-term financing is used by Nike to pay off its production costs during its slow season.

_____

Some sentences with passive-voice verbs do not identify the doer of the action. Before these sentences can be converted, a subject must be provided.

> **Example:**   (Passive) New subscribers will be offered a bonus. (By whom?—let's say by *BusinessWeek*.)
>
> (Active) *BusinessWeek* will offer new subscribers a bonus.

In each of the following sentences, first answer the question *By whom?* Then rewrite the sentence in the active voice, beginning with your answer as the subject.

8. Our Web site was recently redesigned to increase its attractiveness and effectiveness. (By whom?)

_____

9. Net income before taxes must be calculated carefully when you fill out your tax return. (By whom?)

_____

10. Only a few of the many errors and changes were detected during the first proofreading. (By whom?)

_____

C. Underscore any verbs that are used incorrectly in the following sentences. Write the correct forms in the spaces provided. Write *C* if correct.

1. William wished that he was able to retire at age forty.   _____

2. I move that Alonzo is appointed chair of our Grievance Committee.   _____

3. The CEO recommended that each employee is given full benefits.   _____

4. If a better employee benefit program was available, recruiting would be easier.   _____

5. A stockholder moved that dividends are declared immediately.   _____

6. If he was in my place, he would be more understanding.   _____

7. I wish that our server was working so that I could read my e-mail.   _____

8. Billie Miller Cooper, our management consultant, strongly advised that computer firewalls are installed.   _____

9. Michael said he wished that you were able to accompany him.   _____

10. If Sandy Escalante were in the office that day, I did not see her.   _____

D. **Writing Exercise**. Complete the following sentences.

1. I wish that I (was, were) _____

2. If my boss (was, were) _____

3. If you (was, were) in my position, _____

LEVEL 3

A. (Self-check) In the following sentences gerunds are italicized. Other *ing* words that are not italicized are not functioning as gerunds. Select appropriate modifiers.

1. I appreciate (you, your) *responding* to my e-mail so quickly. _____

2. We saw (Rachel, Rachel's) leaving the office early. _____

3. (His, Him) *traveling* first class was questioned by the auditor. _____

4. Eric's hiring depends on (him, his) *making* a good impression in the interview. _____

5. The (person, person's) picking up the check gets to choose the restaurant. _____

From each of the sets of sentences that follow, select the sentence that is stated in the most logical manner. Write its letter in the space provided.

6. a. Police officers found the suspect hiding in the backyard with the help of a police dog.
   b. With the help of a police dog, police officers found the suspect hiding in the backyard. _____

7. a. Sealed in an airtight crock, the Joneses savored the fine cheese.
   b. Sealed in an airtight crock, the fine cheese was savored by the Joneses. _____

8. a. To complete the accounting equation, one must add liabilities to equity.
   b. To complete the accounting equation, it is necessary to add liabilities to equity. _____

9. a. To graduate early, carry more units.
   b. To graduate early, more units must be carried. _____

10. a. Having completed 20 years of service, Zivi Nunary was presented a gold watch.
    b. Having completed 20 years of service, a gold watch was presented to Zivi Nunary. _____

Check your answers below.

B. Some of the italicized words in the following sentences function as gerunds; others do not. Select appropriate modifiers.

1. We noticed the (president, president's) brisk *walking* as he came down the hall. _____

2. I appreciated (Sandra, Sandra's) *designing* the brochure for us. _____

3. The accuracy of the report resulted largely from (him, his) *proofreading*. _____

4. Their letter complimented you by saying that (you, your) *developing* the new logo made a big difference. _____

5. We appreciate (you, your) not *smoking* on the premises. _____

6. Did the boss recommend (them, their) *attending* the demonstration? _____

7. The (customer, customer's) *paying* his bill complimented the service. _____

8. We are incredulous at (them, their) *winning* the series. _____

9. The (player, player's) *winning* the final game takes the prize. _____

10. (Him, His) *being* on time for the appointment is very important. _____

Want to explore more? Go to: academic.cengage.com/bcomm/guffey or Xtra!

VERBS: KINDS, VOICES, MOODS, VERBALS | CHAPTER 8 | **139**

C. From each of the pairs of sentences shown, select the more acceptable version and write its letter in the space provided.

1. a. She had to, as soon as possible, ask her boss for a day off.
   b. She had to ask her boss for a day off as soon as possible.

_____

2. a. Try to find out when the meeting is scheduled.
   b. Try and find out when the meeting is scheduled.

_____

3. a. We wondered about his ordering so few office supplies.
   b. We wondered about him ordering so few office supplies.

_____

4. a. Our manager started to, as the deadline approached, check the names and addresses.
   b. As the deadline approached, our manager started to check the names and addresses.

_____

5. a. I think their being present at the hearing is crucial.
   b. I think them being present at the hearing is crucial.

_____

D. **Writing Exercise.** Rewrite the following sentences to remedy any gerund or infinitive faults.

1. I plan to, when my visa is issued, work in Japan for a year.

   _____

2. Be sure and call to, if you haven't changed your mind, make your plane reservations.

   _____

3. Please inform your two agents that I appreciate them booking my reservations.

   _____

4. When you travel globally, try and ask good questions about the culture before you leave.

   _____

E. **Writing Exercise.** Each of the following sentences has an illogical introductory verbal phrase. Rewrite each sentence using that introductory phrase so that it is followed by a word it can logically modify. It may be necessary to add a subject. Keep the introductory verbal phrase at the beginning of the sentence.

   Example: Cycling up Mount Diablo, the summit came into view.

   Cycling up Mount Diablo, we saw the summit come into view.

1. Completing her graduate degree, her dream came true.

   _____

2. To be binding, a consideration must support every contract.

   _____

3. As a baboon growing up in the jungle, I realized Kiki had special nutritional needs.

   _____

4. Selected as Employee of the Year, the CEO presented an award to Cecile Chang.

   _____

5. After breaking into the building, the police heard the alarm set off by the burglars.

   _____

Want to explore more? Go to: academic.cengage.com/bcomm/guffey or Xtra!

140 | UNIT 3 | CHAPTER 8 | VERBS: KINDS, VOICES, MOODS, VERBALS

The preceding sentences had misplaced introductory verbal phrases. The next sentences have misplaced verbal phrases in other positions. Rewrite these sentences so that the verbal phrases are close to the words they can logically modify.

6. An autopsy revealed the cause of death to be strangulation by the coroner.

_____

7. A woman said someone stole a necklace from the safe in her closet, which was valued at $3,000.

_____

8. A trellis was designed to divert attention from the large driveway, which is seen walking up to the house.

_____

9. His wallet was found by Dave Evola lying under the front seat of his car.

_____

10. Geologists inspected the site where the boulders broke free from a helicopter.

_____

F. Hotline Review. In the space provided write the correct answer choice.

1. Many Web sites now promise _____ investigative services to locate old friends, competitive information, and deadbeat spouses.
a. discreet   b. discrete   _____

2. The menu was divided into two _____ sections: vegetarian and nonvegetarian.
a. discreet   b. discrete   _____

3. To celebrate the opening of their boutique, owners offered a _____ of designer fragrance.
a. gift   b. free gift   _____

4. Our supervisor wants our _____ in adopting the new policy.
a. co-operating   b. cooperation   _____

5. If I _____ in your shoes, I'd be thrilled.
a. were   b. was   _____

Want to explore more? Go to: academic.cengage.com/bcomm/guffey or Xtra!

VERBS: KINDS, VOICES, MOODS, VERBALS | CHAPTER 8 | **141**

The following interoffice memo contains 27 intentional errors in sentence structure, spelling, and proofreading. Be especially alert to verb problems. Use proofreading marks to make corrections. When you replace a wordy phrase with one word, it counts as one correction. When you correct a comma splice, run-on, or fragment, the correction counts as two errors. Use proofreading marks to make the corrections here OR make the corrections at the **Guffey Companion Web Site** at **academic.cengage.com/bcomm/guffey.**

GRADIENT RESEARCH, INC.
INTEROFFICE MEMORANDUM

TO: Josh Hernandez, Production Manager

FROM: Edward J. Juralski, CEO   *EJJ*

DATE: February 16, 200x

SUBJECT: TELECOMUTING EMPLOYEES' GUIDE

Because telecommuting is becomming increasingly popular, its neccesary for us to be more careful in planing for information security. As well as for our employees health and personal safty. We wish it was possible to talk to each employee individually, but that is impossible. Instead, we have prepared a "Telecommuter Employees Guide." Which includes structured agreements that specify space, equipment, scheduling, communications, and conditions of employment. The complete guide should be given to whomever is about to begin a telecommuting assignment. We appreciate you discussing the following recomendations with any of your staff members whom are considering telecommuting.

Arranging the Home Workspace

- Create a space where you can expect minimal traffic and distraction.
- Make it comfortable but with suficient space for computer, printer, and fax.
- Make your workspace off-limits to family and friend's.
- Provide proper lighting and telephone service.

Ensuring Information Security

- Remember that you're home office is an extension of the company office.
- Be carful to protect information and avoid computer virus's.
- Be sure to backup and store data and other information in a safe place.

We do not recommend at-home meetings for telecommuters. By the same token, we suggest using postal boxes rather then home addresses. We also require smoke detector's in home work areas.

To have any questions answered, my assistant or me can be reached at Ext. 310.

Want to explore more? Go to: academic.cengage.com/bcomm/guffey or Xtra!

142 | UNIT 3 | CHAPTER 8 | VERBS: KINDS, VOICES, MOODS, VERBALS

Many colleges and universities provide grammar hotline services. Generally, you can submit a question by e-mail or by telephone and receive a response from a trained language specialist. Let's assume you want to ask a question and need to know the closest hotline service.

Goal: To learn about online grammar hotlines.

1. With your Web browser on the screen, enter the URL of your favorite search engine. (Do you have it bookmarked? We always try **http://www.google.com** first.)
2. With your search engine on the screen, enter *grammar hotline* as your search term.
3. Click the listing for the **Grammar Hotline Directory** at Tidewater Community College (Writing Center at TCC).
4. Scroll down to see the directory listings.
5. Find a listing for a hotline that is near you or one that seems appropriate. Note the name, telephone number, e-mail address, and/or Web address. If your instructor agrees, send an inquiry. What grammar or mechanics question interests you? Your e-mail inquiry should include a subject line, concise message, and closing information (your name and e-mail address). Print a copy of your outgoing e-mail message and any answer that you receive.
6. End your session and submit your print copies.

Underline the appropriate answers.

1. In the sentence *Peg Luttmann wrote the memo,* the verb *wrote* is (a) transitive, (b) intransitive, (c) subjunctive, (d) passive.

2. In the sentence *Mary Conrad hired four employees,* the verb *hired* is in the (a) active voice, (b) passive voice, (c) subjunctive mood, (d) intransitive mood.

3. In the sentence *Alicia Molitor was given the award,* the verb phrase *was given* is in the (a) active voice, (b) passive voice, (c) subjunctive mood, (d) intransitive mood.

4. If Clara Smith (a) was, (b) were the instructor, the class would be full.

5. Our team celebrated (a) his, (b) him winning the award.

1. a 2. a 3. b 4. b 5. a

Want to explore more? Go to: academic.cengage.com/bcomm/guffey or Xtra!

VERBS: KINDS, VOICES, MOODS, VERBALS | CHAPTER 8 | 143

© AL VALEIRO/Pixland/Jupiter Images

VERB TENSES AND PARTS

OBJECTIVES

When you have completed the materials in this chapter, you will be able to do the following:

LEVEL 1

- Write verbs in the present, past, and future tenses correctly.
- Understand how helping verbs function in verb phrases.

LEVEL 2

- Recognize and use present and past participles.
- Write the correct forms of irregular verbs.

LEVEL 3

- Recognize verb forms in the progressive tenses.
- Recognize verb forms in the perfect tenses.

PRETEST

Underline the correct verb.

1. Virginia (brought, brung) a colleague to the seminar with her.

2. If we had (gone, went) to the training class, we might have learned something.

3. The year-end financial statements are (laying, lying) on your desk.

4. Because prices are (raising, rising), we should look for an apartment immediately.

5. The partially completed building has (set, sat) there untouched for a year.

English verbs change form (**inflection**) to indicate number (singular or plural), person (first, second, or third), voice (active or passive), and tense (time). In contrast to French and German, English verbs are today no longer heavily inflected. That is, our verbs do not change form extensively to indicate number or person. To indicate precise time, however, English employs three rather complex sets of tenses: primary tenses, perfect tenses, and progressive tenses. Level 1 will focus on the primary tenses and helping verbs. Level 2 will consider participles and irregular verbs. Level 3 will treat the progressive and perfect tenses.

· LEVEL 1 · LEVEL 1 · LEVEL 1 · LEVEL 1 · LEVEL 1 · **LEVEL 1** · LEVEL 1 · L

PRIMARY TENSES

Let's begin our discussion of verbs with the primary tenses. These tenses are used to indicate the present, the past, and the future.

PRESENT TENSE

Verbs in the **present tense** express current or habitual action. Present-tense verbs may also be used in constructions showing future action.

> We *celebrate* employees' birthdays once a month. (Current or habitual action)

> He *flies* to Washington tomorrow. (Future action)

PAST TENSE

Verbs in the **past tense** show action that has been completed. Regular verbs form the past tense with the addition of *d* or *ed*.

> The IRS *needed* our tax forms yesterday.

> The report *focused* on changes in our department.

FUTURE TENSE

Verbs in the **future tense** show actions that are expected to occur at a later time. Traditionally, the helper verbs *shall* and *will* have been joined with principal verbs to express future tense. In business and professional writing today, however, the verb *will* is generally used as the helper to express future tense. Careful writers continue to use *shall* in appropriate first-person constructions (*I/We shall attend the meeting*).

> Daniel *will need* extra time to complete his next assignment.

> You *will receive* the contract before June 5.

SUMMARY OF PRIMARY TENSES

The following table summarizes the various forms employed to express the primary tenses:

	Present Tense		Past Tense		Future Tense	
	Sing.	**Plural**	**Sing.**	**Plural**	**Sing.**	**Plural**
First Person:	I need	we need	I needed	we needed	I will need	we will need
Second Person:	you need	you need	you needed	you needed	you will need	you will need
Third Person:	he, she, it, needs	they need	he, she, it needed	they needed	he, she, it will need	they will need

HOT LINK

For ESL (English as a Second Language) students, try searching the Web for *ESL verbs*. You will find many links to sites offering learning tips and helpful exercises.

SPOT THE BLOOPER

In a job applicant's cover letter: "I had strong interpersonal and communication skills."

DID YOU KNOW

In British English some regular verbs are made past tense by adding *t* instead of *ed*. For example, we say *learned*, but in Great Britain they say *learnt*. Other examples include *burned/burnt*, *dreamed/dreamt*, *leaned/leant*, *leaped/leapt*, and *spelled/spelt*.

CHALLENGES USING PRIMARY TENSE

Most adult speakers of our language have few problems using present, past, and future tenses. A few considerations, however, merit mention.

Using the -s Form Verbs

Note that third-person singular verbs require an -s ending (*he needs*).

> She *lives* in a suburb outside of Boston. (Not *live*)

> This printer *breaks* down too often. (Not *break*)

> Randall *checks* his e-mail hourly. (Not *check*)

Expressing "Timeless" Facts

Present-tense verbs are used to express "timeless" facts, even if these verbs occur in sentences with other past-tense verbs.

> What did you say his duties *are?* (Not *were,* if he continues to perform these duties)

> Joan Brault's maiden name is Haitz. (Not *was*)

> What did you say the caller's name *is?* (Not *was*)

Spelling Verbs That Change Form

Use a dictionary to verify spelling of verbs that change form. One must be particularly careful in spelling verbs ending in *y* (*hurry, hurries, hurried*) and verbs for which the final consonant is doubled (*occurred, expelled*).

HELPING (AUXILIARY) VERBS

A verb that combines with a main verb to convey information about tense, mood, or voice functions as a **helping** or **auxiliary verb.** The most common helping verbs are forms of *be (am, is, are, was, were, being, been),* forms of *do (does, did),* and forms of *have (has, had).* As you will recall, the verb *be* and all its forms also function as linking verbs.

> Our manager *is* a funny guy. (The linking verb *is* joins the complement *guy* to the subject.)

> Our manager *is using* his computer. (The helping verb *is* combines with the main verb *using* to form a verb phrase whose object is *computer.*)

Whether functioning as a linking verb or as a helping verb, the verb *be* should be used in standard forms.

> Laura *is applying* for the radiologist position. (Not *be applying*)

> He *is* fortunate to have his certification. (Not *be*)

Now complete the reinforcement exercises for Level 1.

PRESENT AND PAST PARTICIPLES

To be able to use all the tenses of verbs correctly, you must understand the four principal parts of verbs: present, past, present participle, and past participle. You have already studied the present and past forms. Now, let's consider the participles.

PRESENT PARTICIPLE

The **present participle** of a regular verb is formed by adding *ing* to the present tense of the verb. When used in a sentence as part of a verb phrase, the present participle is preceded by a helping verb, such as *am, is, are, was, were, be,* and *been.*

Helping verb   Present participle
↓   ↓
Ryan *is working* at home.

Helping verb   Present participle
↓   ↓
You *are doing* a fine job.

PAST PARTICIPLE

The **past participle** of a regular verb is usually formed by adding a *d* or *t* sound to the present tense of the verb. Like present participles, past participles must combine with one or more helping verbs (such as *has* or *have*):

Helping verb   Past participle
↓   ↓
Mark *has checked* his calculations.

Helping verbs   Past participle
↓   ↓
The figures *have been checked* by his supervisor.

Helping verbs   Past participle
↓   ↓
The accountants *should have calculated* the figures more accurately.

SPOT THE BLOOPER

From a CNN interview: "The warden has came out and gave us his view of the execution."

IRREGULAR VERBS

Up to this point, we have considered only regular verbs. Regular verbs form the past tense by the addition of *d* or *ed* to the present tense form. **Irregular verbs,** however, form the past tense by varying the root vowel and, commonly, adding *en* to the past participle. A list of the more frequently used irregular verbs follows. Learn the forms of these verbs by practicing in patterns such as:

Present tense: Today I __drive__ .

Past tense: Yesterday I __drove__ .

Past participle: In the past I have __driven__ .

FREQUENTLY USED IRREGULAR VERBS

Present	Past	Past Participle
arise	arose	arisen
be (am, is, are)	was, were	been
bear (to carry)	bore	borne
become	became	become

Present	Past	Past Participle
begin	began	begun
bite	bit	bitten
blow	blew	blown
break	broke	broken
bring	brought	brought
build	built	built
buy	bought	bought
choose	chose	chosen
come	came	come
do	did	done
draw	drew	drawn
drink	drank	drunk
drive	drove	driven
eat	ate	eaten
fall	fell	fallen
fight	fought	fought
fly	flew	flown
forget	forgot	forgotten *or* forgot
forgive	forgave	forgiven
freeze	froze	frozen
get	got	gotten *or* got
give	gave	given
go	went	gone
grow	grew	grown
hang (to suspend)	hung	hung
hang (to execute)	hanged	hanged
hide	hid	hidden *or* hid
know	knew	known
lay (to place)	laid	laid
lead	led	led
leave	left	left
lend	lent	lent
lie (to rest)	lay	lain
lie (to tell a falsehood)	lied	lied
lose	lost	lost
pay	paid	paid
prove	proved	proved *or* proven
raise (to lift)	raised	raised

Present	Past	Past Participle
ride	rode	ridden
ring	rang	rung
rise (to move up)	rose	risen
run	ran	run
see	saw	seen
set (to place)	set	set
shake	shook	shaken
shrink	shrank	shrunk
sing	sang	sung
sink	sank	sunk
sit (to rest)	sat	sat
speak	spoke	spoken
spring	sprang	sprung
steal	stole	stolen
strike	struck	struck *or* stricken
swear	swore	sworn
swim	swam	swum
take	took	taken
teach	taught	taught
tear	tore	torn
throw	threw	thrown
wake	woke	woken
wear	wore	worn
write	wrote	written

THREE PAIRS OF FREQUENTLY MISUSED IRREGULAR VERBS

Three pairs of verbs often cause confusion: *lie-lay, sit-set,* and *raise-rise.* The secret to using them correctly lies in (a) recognizing their tense forms and (b) knowing whether they are transitive or intransitive. Recall that transitive verbs require objects; intransitive verbs do not.

LIE–LAY

These two verbs are confusing because the past tense of *lie* is spelled in exactly the same way that the present tense of *lay* is spelled. To be safe, you'll want to memorize these verb forms:

	Present	Past	Past Participle	Present Participle
Intransitive:	lie (to rest)	lay	lain	lying
Transitive:	lay (to place)	laid (not *layed*)	laid	laying

The verb *lie* is intransitive; therefore, it requires no direct object to complete its meaning.

> I *lie* down for a nap every afternoon. (Present tense. Note that *down* is not a direct object.)

> "*Lie* down," Mark told his dog. (Commands are given in the present tense.)

> Yesterday I *lay* down for a nap. (Past tense)

> The originals *have lain* in the copy machine for some time. (Past participle)

> The contract *is lying* on the desk. (Present participle)

The verb *lay* is transitive and must have a direct object to complete its meaning. The objects in the following sentences have been underlined.

> Watch me *lay* three <u>cards</u> down in this round. (Present tense)

> *Lay* the <u>report</u> over there. (Command in the present tense)

> He *laid* the <u>handouts</u> on the conference table. (Past tense)

> He *has laid* bricks all his life. (Past participle)

> The contractor *is laying* new <u>tile</u> in the entryway. (Present participle)

SIT–SET

Less troublesome than *lie–lay,* the combination of *sit–set* is nevertheless perplexing because the sound of the verbs is similar. The intransitive verb *sit* (past tense, *sat;* past participle, *sat*) means "to rest" and requires no direct object.

> Do you *sit* here often? (Present tense. Used intransitively; *here* is not an object.)

> They *sat* in the theater through the closing credits. (Past tense)

> They *had sat* in the waiting room for two hours before they decided to leave (Past participle)

> *Are* you usually *sitting* here in the morning? (Present participle)

The transitive verb *set* (past tense, *set;* past participle, *set*) means "to place" and must have a direct object. The objects in the following sentences have been underlined.

> Letty usually *sets* her coffee <u>mug</u> there. (Present tense)

> We *set* a <u>vase</u> of flowers on the receptionist's desk. (Past tense)

RISE–RAISE

The intransitive verb *rise* (past tense, *rose;* past participle, *risen*) means "to go up" or "to ascend" and requires no direct object.

> The sun *rises* every morning in the east. (Present tense. *Every morning* is an adverbial phrase, not an object.)

> The president *rose* from her chair to greet us. (Past tense)

> The room temperature *has risen* steadily since the meeting began. (Past participle)

> Our elevator *is rising* to the seventh floor. (Present participle)

The transitive verb *raise* (past tense, *raised;* past participle, *raised*) means "to lift up" or "to elevate" and must have a direct object. The objects in the following sentences have been underlined.

> Please *raise* the <u>window</u>. (Present tense)

> AT&T *is raising* prices next month. (Present participle)

Now complete the reinforcement exercises for Level 2.

· LEVEL 3 · LEVEL 3 · LEVEL 3 · LEVEL 3 · LEVEL 3 · LEVEL 3 · LEVEL 3 ·

PROGRESSIVE AND PERFECT TENSES

Thus far in this chapter, you have studied the primary tenses and irregular verbs. The remainder of this chapter focuses on two additional sets of verb tenses: the perfect and the progressive. Most native speakers and writers of English have little difficulty controlling these verb forms because they have frequently heard them used correctly. This largely descriptive section is thus presented for those who are not native speakers and for those who are eager to study the entire range of verb tenses.

PROGRESSIVE TENSES

The **progressive tenses** are used to show continuous or repeated actions. The **present progressive tense** describes ongoing actions that are happening presently. The **past progressive tense** describes ongoing actions that occurred in the past, usually as another action was taking place. The **future progressive tense** describes ongoing actions that will take place in the future. Progressive tenses are formed by adding specific helpers to the present participle (*-ing*) form of a verb, as you can see in the following table.

	Present Progressive Tense		
	First Person	**Second Person**	**Third Person**
Active:	I am hearing we are hearing	you are hearing	he, she, it is hearing they are hearing
Passive:	I am being heard we are being heard	you are being heard	he, she, it is being heard they are being heard

	Past Progressive Tense		
	First Person	**Second Person**	**Third Person**
Active:	I was hearing we were hearing	you were hearing	he, she, it was hearing they were hearing
Passive:	I was being heard we were being heard	you were being heard	he, she, it was being heard they were being heard

Future Progressive Tense		
	First Person	**Second Person**	**Third Person**
Active:	I will be hearing we will be hearing	you will be hearing	he, she, it will be hearing they will be hearing
Passive:	I will be being heard we will be being heard	you will be being heard	he, she, it will be being heard they will be being heard

We *are exporting* grain to numerous countries. (Present progressive tense expresses action in progress.)

We *were sitting* down to dinner when her pager went off. (Past progressive tense indicates action that was begun in the past.)

They *will be receiving* the announcement shortly. (Future progressive tense indicates action in the future.)

PERFECT TENSES

The **perfect tenses** are used to show actions that are already completed or *perfected*. The **present perfect tense** describes actions that began in the past and have continued to the present. The **past perfect tense** describes past actions that took place before other past actions. The **future perfect tense** describes actions that will take place before other future actions. Progressive tenses are formed by adding a form of *to have* to the past participle form of a verb, as you can see in the following table.

Present Perfect Tense		
	First Person	**Second Person**	**Third Person**
Active:	I have heard we have heard	you have heard	he, she, it has heard they have heard
Passive:	I have been heard we have been heard	you have been heard	he she, it has been heard they have been heard

Past Perfect Tense		
	First Person	**Second Person**	**Third Person**
Active:	I had heard we had heard	you had heard	he, she, it had heard they had heard
Passive:	I had been heard we had been heard	you had been heard	he, she, it had been heard they had been heard

Future Perfect Tense		
	First Person	**Second Person**	**Third Person**
Active:	I will have heard we will have heard	you will have heard	he, she, it will have heard they will have heard
Passive:	I will have been heard we will have been heard	you will have been heard	he, she, it will have been heard they will have been heard

She *has worked* for the school district for 15 years. (Present perfect tense expresses action just completed or *perfected*.)

The check *had cleared* the bank before I canceled payment. (Past perfect tense shows an action finished before another action in the past.)

The polls *will have been closed* two hours when the results are telecast. (Future perfect tense indicates action that will be completed before another future action.)

HOT LINK

For a different perspective on verbs and more examples, take a look at *EduFind.com* (http://www.edufind.com). Click **Online English Grammar.** Click **Table of Contents,** and look for **Verbs and Verb Tenses.**

SUMMARY OF TENSES

The following table summarizes verb tenses.

Primary Tenses	Progressive Tenses	Perfect Tenses
Present	Present progressive	Present perfect
Past	Past progressive	Past perfect
Future	Future progressive	Future perfect

Now complete the reinforcement exercises for Level 3.

HOTLINE QUERIES

Answered by Dr. Guffey

Question

Q: As a command, which is correct: *lay down* or *lie down?*

Q: We have a new electronic mail system, and one of its functions is "messaging" people. When folks say, *I'll message you*, it really grates on my nerves. Is this correct?

Answer

A: Commands are given in the present tense. You would never tell someone to *Closed the door* because commands are not given in the past tense. To say *Lay down* (which is the past-tense form of *lie*) is the same as saying *Closed the door.* Therefore, use the present tense: *Lie down.*

A: "Messaging" is certainly a hot term with the explosion of e-mail and instant messaging. As to its correctness, I think we've caught language in the act of evolving. What's happened here is the reinstitution of a noun (*message*) as a verb. Converting nouns into verbs is common in English. It's called *verbing* (he *cornered* the market, we *tabled* the motion, I *penciled* it in on my calendar, the farmer *trucked* the vegetables to market). Actually, *message* was sometimes used as a verb nearly a century ago (in 1896 *the bill was messaged over from the house*). However, its recent use has been almost exclusively as a noun. Today, it is increasingly being used again as a verb. New uses of words usually become legitimate when the words fill a need and are immediately accepted. Some word uses, though, appear to be mere fads, such as *The homeless child could not <u>language</u> her fears.* Forcing the noun *language* to function as a verb is unnecessary since a good word already exists for the purpose: *express.* But other "nouns-made-verbs" have been in use long enough to sound reasonable: I *faxed* the document, he *videotaped* the program, she *keyed* the report.

Q: I'm embarrassed to ask this because I should know the answer—but I don't. Is there an apostrophe in this: *its relevance to our program?*

A: No. Use an apostrophe only for the contraction *it's,* meaning "it is" (*it's a good plan*) or "it has" (*it's been nice working with you*). The possessive pronoun *its,* as used in your example, has no apostrophe (*the car had its oil changed*).

Q: I thought I knew the difference between *principal* and *principle,* but now I'm not so sure. In a report from management I saw this: *The principal findings of the market research are negative.* I thought *principal* always meant your "pal," the school principal.

A: You're partly right and partly wrong. *Principal* may be used as a noun meaning "chief" or "head person." In addition, it may be used as an adjective to mean "chief" or "main." This is the meaning most people forget, and this is the meaning of the word in your sentence. The word *principle* means a "law" or "rule." Perhaps it is easiest to remember *principle = rule.* All other uses require *principal:* the *principal* of the school, the *principal* of the loan, the *principal* reason.

Q: Even when I use a dictionary, I can't tell the difference between *affect* and *effect.* What should the word be in this sentence? *Changes in personnel (affected/effected) our production this month.*

A: No words generate more confusion than do *affect* and *effect.* In your sentence use *affected.* Let's see if we can resolve the *affect/effect* dilemma. *Affect* is a verb meaning "to influence" (*smoking affects health; government policies affect citizens*). *Affect* may also mean "to pretend or imitate" (*he affected a British accent*). *Effect* can be a noun or a verb. As a noun, it means "result" (*the effect of the law is slight*). As a verb (and here's the troublesome part) *effect* means "to produce a result" (*small cars effect gasoline savings; GM effected a new pricing policy*).

Q: I'm editing a screenplay for a studio, and I know something is grammatically wrong with this sentence: *The old man left the room hurriedly after discovering a body laying near the window.*

A: As you probably suspected, the verb *laying* should be *lying. Lay* means "to place" and requires an object (*he is laying the report on your desk now*). *Lie* means "to rest" and requires no object (*the document is lying on your desk*).

Q: My son is studying a foreign language; and he asked me, an English teacher, why we capitalize the personal pronoun *I* in English when we don't capitalize other pronouns.

A: That's a fascinating topic, and a little research on the Web revealed that linguists ponder the same question. In a linguistic journal they discussed some relevant theories. One linguist thought that perhaps the lowercase *i* was too easily confused with the number *1* or with similar looking *i*'s, *u*'s, and *v*'s in medieval handwriting. Another attributed the word's capital letter to our egocentric nature. Another suggested that since the pronoun *I* usually appeared as the first word in a sentence, it was capitalized for that reason. In earlier centuries before the language was standardized, most nouns and pronouns were capitalized haphazardly. One linguist thought that a better question to ask would be why all of the other pronouns lost their capital letters and *I* retained its.

Q: Help! How do I write *fax?* Small letters? Capital letters? Periods? And is it proper to use it as a verb, such as *May we fax the material to you?*

A: The shortened form of *facsimile* is *fax,* written in small letters without periods. Yes, it may be used as a verb, as you did in your sentence.

Q: I'm confused. What is the correct spelling: *all together* or *altogether?* I can never remember whether it's one word or two.

A: It depends on how you're using the word. When spelled as one word, *altogether* means "completely or as a whole" (*Altogether we spent $400 on our vacation*). When spelled as two words, *all together* means "gathered in one location or all acting collectively" (*The committee members were all together in one room*).

REINFORCEMENT EXERCISES

Name _____

LEVEL 1

A. (Self-check) Select the correct verb. Use your dictionary to verify spelling if necessary.

1. Employees learned that their access to certain parts of the company intranet was (denyed, denied). _____

2. What (is, was) the name of the sales rep who stopped by yesterday? _____

3. The machine (jamed, jammed) when conflicting instructions were entered. _____

4. Alexandra knew that the distance between Atlanta and New Orleans (is, was) 470 miles. _____

5. The researcher (tried, tryed) to get her findings published. _____

6. What (is, was) your maiden name? _____

7. Complaints are (refered, referred) to our Customer Service Department. _____

8. Our antique office equipment (need, needs) to be replaced. _____

9. The salespeople who called this morning said that they (be, are, were) with Taylor, Inc. _____

10. She (write, writes) dozens of e-mail messages daily. _____

Check your answers below.

B. In the following sentences, provide three tenses for each verb.

Example: He (arrive) at the office at 7:45 a.m.

Past ___arrived___ Present ___arrives___ Future ___will arrive___

1. Jacqueline (need) Friday off to attend her son's open house.

Past _____ Present _____ Future _____

2. Our supervisor (copy) us on every e-mail message related to the pending merger.

Past _____ Present _____ Future_____

3. Samantha (hurry) to make the elevator.

Past _____ Present _____ Future _____

1. denied 2. is 3. jammed 4. is 5. tried 6. is 7. referred 8. needs 9. are 10. writes

Want to explore more? Go to: academic.cengage.com/bcomm/guffey or Xtra!

VERB TENSES AND PARTS | CHAPTER 9 | **155**

4. Jason (try) to improve his writing skills.

   Past _____   Present _____   Future _____

5. Margaret Britt (cover) the same material in her class.

   Past _____   Present _____   Future _____

6. Monsanto (label) its plastic soft-drink bottle.

   Past _____   Present _____   Future _____

7. Courtney (plan) to major in finance.

   Past _____   Present _____   Future _____

8. The local community college (invest) in child-care facilities for student parents.

   Past _____   Present _____   Future _____

9. Washington Mutual (open) its new branch office downtown today.

   Past _____   Present _____   Future _____

10. Questionnaires (sample) customers' reactions to our new product.

   Past _____   Present _____   Future _____

C. Writing Exercise. Compose sentences using the verbs shown.

   1. (Past tense of *apply*) _____

   2. (Present tense of *fly*) _____

   3. (Future tense of *study*) _____

   4. (Past tense of *cancel*) _____

   5. (Present tense of *learn*) _____

LEVEL 2

A. (Self-check) Write the correct verb. Do not add a helper verb.

   Example: Lori should have (eat) before she left.   eaten _____

   1. Ann Marie Klinko has (teach) business courses for many years.   _____

   2. Have you (see) the changes we made to the Web site?   _____

   3. They have (fly) over Kauai's Na Pali Coast in a helicopter.   _____

   4. Yesterday Chip (wake) before his alarm went off.   _____

   5. Our e-mail and Web-use policy was (write) by Nancy Metzinger.   _____

1. taught 2. seen 3. flown 4. woke 5. written 6. shook 7. gave 8. spoken 9. known 10. gone

Want to explore more? Go to: academic.cengage.com/bcomm/guffey or Xtra!

156 | **UNIT 3** | **CHAPTER 9** | **VERB TENSES AND PARTS**

6. This morning's mild earthquake (shake) the windows in the conference room. _____

7. Over the past year Dr. Karen Howie (give) freely of her services. _____

8. Have you (speak) with the supervisor yet? _____

9. If she had (know) the company had misstated its earnings, she wouldn't have purchased the stock. _____

10. All employees should have (go) to the emergency procedures demonstration. _____

Check your answers on the previous page.

B. Underline any verb errors you find in the following sentences. Write the correct forms in the spaces provided. Do not add helper verbs. Write *C* if the sentence is correct as it stands.

Example: Charles claimed that he <u>seen</u> the accident. saw _____

1. The world has shrank considerably as a result of new communication technologies. _____

2. In order to get more features, Miguel must chose a new wireless carrier. _____

3. Candace buyed a Vespa so that she could get around the city more easily. _____

4. Because stock prices had sank to an all-time low, investors parked their cash. _____

5. Leslie and Mark have went to the lecture in Royce Hall. _____

6. Her friend asked whether Marta had ate lunch yet. _____

7. Her identity was stole by someone who went through her trash. _____

8. We should have thrown out that old printer long ago. _____

9. Why wasn't our electric bill payed last month? _____

10. Is that the dog that has bit two passersby? _____

11. In the late 1800s women fighted for their right to vote. _____

12. The telephone has rang only twice in the past hour. _____

13. I can't believe Claudia brang her dog to work. _____

14. Howling winds have blown all day, making outside work difficult. _____

15. The first pitch of the season was threw out by the president. _____

C. *Lie–Lay.* Write the correct forms of the verb.

Present	Past	Past Participle	Present Participle
lie (to rest):	lay	lain	lying
lay (to place):	laid	laid	laying

Select the correct verb.

1. Norma had to (lay, lie) down until the dizziness passed. _____

2. Stacy (layed, laid) the mail on Mrs. Tong's desk. _____

Want to explore more? Go to: academic.cengage.com/bcomm/guffey or Xtra!

VERB TENSES AND PARTS I CHAPTER 9 I **157**

3. The contracts have been (lying, laying) in her in-box for some time. _____

4. In fact, they had (laid, lain) there for more than a week. _____

5. Shops in Broadway Plaza are (laying, lying) plans for the holiday season. _____

D. **Sit–Set; Rise–Raise.** Write the correct forms of the verbs.

Present	Past	Past Participle	Present Participle
sit (to rest):	sat	sat	sitting
set (to place):	set	set	setting
rise (to go up):	rose	risen	rising
raise (to lift):	raised	raised	raising

Select the correct verb.

1. We'll need to (raise, rise) prices to cover our higher insurance costs. _____

2. How can we finish the project if Aaron (sits, sets) there all day? _____

3. Close the windows if you want to (raise, rise) the temperature in the room. _____

4. My temperature (raises, rises) when I exercise vigorously. _____

5. Have you been (sitting, setting) goals for your future? _____

6. Consumer prices are (rising, raising) faster than consumer income. _____

7. Brenda Woodward (raised, rose) the question of retroactive benefits. _____

8. Julie and Luis Suarez always (sit, set) near the door. _____

9. Our office building (sits, sets) on the corner of Front and Pine. _____

10. Consumer prices have (risen, raised) faster than consumer income. _____

E. **Writing Exercise.** Compose original sentences using the verbs shown.

1. bought _____

2. lent _____

3. lead _____

4. laid _____

5. rose _____

Want to explore more? Go to: academic.cengage.com/bcomm/guffey or Xtra!

158 | UNIT 3 | CHAPTER 9 | VERB TENSES AND PARTS

LEVEL 3

A. (Self-check) Verbs in the following sentences have been italicized. In the space provided, indicate the tense and voice of each of these verbs. Refer to the text to guide you.

Example: Your credit cards *had been recovered* by the time you reported the loss.   past perfect, passive

1. The media *will have gotten* news of the layoffs before employees.   _____

2. The Web site *is being modified* to make it more accessible to the disabled.   _____

3. Mr. Adams's case *will have been heard* in six weeks.   _____

4. I cannot believe what I *am hearing*.   _____

5. Melanie Powell *had been told* to send the payroll reports to the auditor.   _____

6. We *have* just *seen* your product advertised on television.   _____

7. The manager's suggestions for reduced paper use *have been followed* by all employees.   _____

8. We *will be seeing* increased security measures at the airport.   _____

9. Gay Osterello *has worked* for John Muir Hospital for three decades.   _____

10. We *are* now *experiencing* the effects of the last cutback.   _____

Check your answers below.

B. Write the proper verb form.

Example: They (drive) all night before they found a motel. (Past perfect)   had driven

1. By the time the sun came up, William (do) four laps around the track. (Past perfect)   _____

2. When her supervisor called, Viridiana Ponce (get) ready to give her presentation. (Past progressive)   _____

3. By next April, RamCo (open) four branch outlets. (Future perfect)   _____

4. I'm sure they (tell) us about their trip when they return. (Future progressive)   _____

5. Plans (develop) to reduce administrative costs. (Present progressive, passive)   _____

6. Our company (think) about adopting a tuition reimbursement program. (Present progressive)   _____

7. Check to see whether they (receive) the signed contracts. (Present perfect)   _____

8. By 5 p.m. the contract (finish) and faxed to our client. (Past perfect, passive)   _____

1. future perfect, active 2. present progressive, passive 3. future perfect 4. present progressive, active 5. past perfect, passive 6. present perfect, active 7. present perfect, passive 8. future progressive, active 9. present perfect, active 10. present progressive, active

C. Review. These sentences review Chapters 1 through 9. Underline any errors. Then write corrected forms in the spaces provided. Some sentences require more than one correction. If a sentence is correct, write *C* in the space.

1. Teachers salaries have rose steadily over the past few years.

   _____

2. Although Bill Gates' dropped out of college, he has successfully ran a major corporation for years.

   _____

3. Jeff and me could have forgave her if she had softened her tone.

   _____

4. The company hided it's losses by inflating sales.

   _____

5. Every employee must name a beneficiary on their life insurance forms.

   _____

6. During it's first month of operation, the recycling program has broke records for reducing waste.

   _____

7. Everyone except Helen Costigan and I was impressed by the months recycling profits.

   _____

8. Many larger facilitys can recycle at no net cost because there haulers are taking away less trash.

   _____

9. How long have you knowed that you're application was accepted?

   _____

10. Lorraine Ganz contract, which is laying on the desk, must be delivered immediately.

    _____

11. The meeting begun before the CEOs staff arrived.

    _____

12. Not one of the job candidates who we interviewed has wrote a thank-you letter.

    _____

13. Although I told James dog to lay down, it jumped up and knocked me over.

    _____

14. Dylan has wore the same suit to the last four interview's.

    _____

15. You should have saw the e-mails sent to the manager and myself.

    _____

16. The product had sank so low in the eyes of consumers' that it was removed from store shelfs.

    _____

17. Our research shows that the average retail part-time employee has stole over $300 worth of merchandise in a years time.

    _____

18. You and me need to work hard to make sure we don't loose this opportunity.

    _____

19. Cheryl said she seen you and him at Stevens party.

    _____

20. Because to many computers were running, the rooms temperature had raised to 95 degrees.

    _____

Want to explore more? Go to: academic.cengage.com/bcomm/guffey or Xtra!

160 | UNIT 3 | CHAPTER 9 | VERB TENSES AND PARTS

D. Hotline Review. In the space provided write the correct answer choice.

1. The owners plan to sell the company and all of _____ assets.
    a. its   b. it's   _____

2. The _____ difference between a bear and a bull market is simple.
    a. principle   b. principal   _____

3. When stocks are falling, the end _____ is a "bear," or downward, market.
    a. effect   b. affect   _____

4. Rising stocks _____ a market differently; when stocks are increasing,
    it is a "bull" market.
    a. effect   b. affect   _____

5. We have an _____ different situation here.
    a. all together   b. altogether   _____

6. Because he is a person with high _____, he refused the free trip to Hawaii.
    a. principals   b. principles   _____

Want to explore more? Go to: academic.cengage.com/bcomm/guffey or Xtra!

VERB TENSES AND PARTS | CHAPTER 9 | **161**

The following letter has 30 intentional errors in sentence structure, spelling, and proofreading. When you replace a wordy or incorrect phrase with one word, it counts as one correction. When you correct a comma splice, run-on, or fragment, the correction counts as two errors. Count each parenthesis and each dash as a single mark. Use proofreading marks to make the corrections here OR make the corrections at the **Guffey Companion Web Site** at **academic.cengage.com/bcomm/guffey.**

Body Fitness

Training   Massage   Wellness

June 4, 200x

Mr. Allen C. Fineberg
3250 Ponciana Way
Palm Beach Gardens, FL 33410

Dear Mr. Fineburg:

You probably choose Body Fitness because it has became one of the top-rated gyms in the Palm Beach area. Making your workout enjoyable has always been our principle goal. To continue to provide you with the best equipment and programs, my partner and myself need your feedback.

We have build an outstanding program with quality equipment, excellent training programs, and helpful support staff. We feel, however, that we could have a more positive affect and give more individual attention if we could extend our peak usage time. You have probable noticed that attendance at the gym raises from 4 p.m. to 8 p.m. We wish it was possible to accommodate everyone on their favorite equipment during those hours. Although we can't stretch an hour. We would like to make better use of the time between 8 p.m. and 11 p.m. With more members' coming later, we would have less crush from 4 to 8 p.m. Exercise machines that lay idle and strength-training equipment that sets empty could see action.

To encourage you to stay later, security cameras for our parking area are being considered by us. Cameras for some inside facilitys may also be added. We have gave this matter a great deal of thought. Although Body Fitness has never had an incident that endangered a member. We have went to considerable trouble to learn about security cameras because we think that you will feel all together more comfortable with them in action.

Please tell us what you think, fill out the enclosed questionnaire, and drop it the ballot box at the front desk during next weeks visit. We're asking for your feed back. Because we're devoted to serving you better. If you have any other suggestions for reducing the crush at peak times or other ideas that effect our members, please tell us on the enclosed form.

Cordially,

Nicolas Barajas

Nicolas Barajas, Manager

Enclosure

10500 North Military Trail   Palm Beach Gardens, FL 33410   561.799.5302   bodyfitness.pbgardens.com

Want to explore more? Go to: academic.cengage.com/bcomm/guffey or Xtra!

162 | UNIT 3 | CHAPTER 9 | VERB TENSES AND PARTS

Assume you're on the job and a new employee needs a little instruction in the use of e-mail. You decide to use the Web to provide a quick tutorial.

Goal: To learn to use an e-mail tutorial.

1. With your Web browser on the screen, key the following URL for Fraser Valley Regional Library: **http://www.fvrl.bc.ca/learn/tutorial/ e-mail.html.**

2. Read the five sections on this page.
3. How does e-mail save natural resources?
4. How are multiple addresses entered in the **Cc** field?
5. This site provides a quick online tutorial for introducing e-mail, but it suffers from some writing lapses. Can you find two comma splices?
6. Print two pages from this site, underline the answers to our questions, submit your printouts, and end your session.

Underline the correct verb.

1. If you had (saw, seen) how professional she looked, you would have been impressed too.

2. Your telephone has (rung, rang) only twice while you were gone.

3. The contracts have (laid, lain) on your desk for over a week.

4. Have you (payed, paid) the invoice yet?

5. Tony has (worn, wore) the same shirt every day this week.

1. seen 2. rung 3. lain 4. paid 5. worn

Want to explore more? Go to: academic.cengage.com/bcomm/guffey or Xtra!

VERB TENSES AND PARTS | CHAPTER 9 | **163**

VERB AND SUBJECT AGREEMENT

OBJECTIVES

When you have completed the materials in this chapter, you will be able to do the following:

LEVEL 1

- Locate the subjects of verbs despite intervening elements and inverted sentence structure.
- Make verbs agree with subjects joined by *and* and with company names and titles.

LEVEL 2

- Make verbs agree with subjects joined by *or* or *nor*.
- Select the correct verbs to agree with collective nouns and indefinite pronouns.

LEVEL 3

- Make verbs agree with *a number/the number,* quantities and measures, fractions and portions, and *who* clauses.
- Achieve subject–verb agreement with phrases and clauses as subjects and with subject complements.

PRETEST

Underline the correct verb.

1. One of the plant supervisors (plan, plans) to implement a new safety program.
2. The head surgeon, along with her entire operating room team, (was, were) given training on the newest laser technology.
3. Neither the supervisor nor members of his team (is, are) satisfied with the level of service.
4. Behind the reception area (lies, lie) the parking lot and day care center.
5. The number of e-mail messages (is, are) increasing daily.

1. plans 2. was 3. are 4. lie 5. is

Subjects must agree with verbs in number and person. Beginning a sentence with *He don't* damages a speaker's credibility and limits a communicator's effectiveness.

If an error is made in subject–verb agreement, it can generally be attributed to one of three lapses: (a) failure to locate the subject, (b) failure to recognize the number (singular or plural) of the subject after locating it, or (c) failure to recognize the number of the verb. Suggestions for locating the true subject and determining the number of the subject and its verb follow.

· LEVEL 1 · LEVEL 1 · LEVEL 1 · LEVEL 1 · LEVEL 1 · LEVEL 1 · **LEVEL 1** · LEVEL 1 · L

1

LOCATING SUBJECTS

All verbs have subjects. Locating these subjects can be difficult, particularly when (a) a prepositional phrase comes between the verb and its subject, (b) an intervening element separates the subject and verb, (c) sentences begin with *there* or *here,* and (d) sentences are inverted. You practiced locating subjects in Chapter 3, but because this is such an important skill, we provide additional instruction here.

PREPOSITIONAL PHRASES

Subjects of verbs are not found in prepositional phrases. Therefore, you must learn to ignore such phrases in identifying subjects of verbs. Some of the most common prepositions are *of, to, in, from, for, with, at,* and *by.* Notice in these sentences that the italicized prepositional phrases do not contain the subjects of the verbs.

> Each *of our products* is unconditionally guaranteed. (The verb *is* agrees with its singular subject *Each.*)

> It appears that the invoice *for the two shipments* was lost. (The verb *was* agrees with its singular subject *invoice.*)

> The online version *of the magazine's college rankings* is available at its Web site. (The verb *is* agrees with its singular subject *version.*)

Some of the less easily recognized prepositions are *except, but, like,* and *between.* In the following sentences, distinguish the subjects from the italicized prepositional phrases.

> All employees *but Daniel* are qualified to open the store. (The verb *are* agrees with its plural subject *employees.*)

> Everyone *except the managers* is a member of the union. (The verb *is* agrees with its singular subject *everyone.*)

INTERVENING ELEMENTS

Groups of words introduced by *as well as, in addition to, such as, including, together with, plus,* and *other than* do *not* contain sentence subjects.

> Her favorite movie star, *as well as other local celebrities,* is scheduled to attend the fund-raiser.

In this sentence the writer has elected to emphasize the singular subject *star* and to de-emphasize *other local celebrities.* The writer could have given equal weight

to these elements by writing *Her favorite movie star _and_ other local celebrities _are_ scheduled to attend the fund-raiser.* Notice that the number (singular or plural) of the verb changes when both *star* and *celebrities* are given equal emphasis.

Our <u>president</u>, *together with her entire staff of employees*, <u>expects</u> to take this Friday off. (The singular subject *president* agrees with the singular verb *expects*.)

Some <u>entrepreneurs</u> *such as Debbi Fields* <u>have</u> started companies based on a single idea. (The plural subject *entrepreneurs* agrees with the plural verb *have*.)

Our job <u>application</u> *plus three important employment documents* <u>is</u> available on our Web site. (The singular subject *application* agrees with the singular verb *is*.)

SENTENCES BEGINNING WITH *THERE* AND *HERE*

In sentences beginning with *there* or *here,* look for the true subject *after* the verb. The words *here* and *there* are function words that are not classified as subjects.

There <u>are</u> many <u>ways</u> to approach the problem. (The plural subject *ways* follows the verb *are*.)

Here <u>is</u> the fuel oil consumption <u>report</u>. (The singular subject *report* follows the verb *is*.)

Be especially careful when using contractions. Remember that *here's* is the contraction for *here is;* therefore, it should be used only with singular subjects. Likewise, *there's* is the contraction for *there is* and should also be used only with singular subjects.

Incorrect: <u>Here's</u> the <u>documents</u> you requested. (The plural subject *documents* does not agree with the verb *is*.)

Correct: Here <u>are</u> the <u>documents</u> you requested. (The plural subject *documents* agrees with the verb *are*.)

Incorrect: <u>There's</u> three <u>reasons</u> you should hire me for the proofreader position. (The plural subject *reasons* does not agree with the verb *is*.)

Correct: There <u>are</u> three <u>reasons</u> you should hire me for the proofreader position. (The plural subject *reasons* agrees with the verb *are*.)

INVERTED SENTENCE ORDER

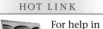
Look for the subject after the verb in inverted sentences and in questions.

On our board of directors <u>are</u> three prominent <u>scientists</u>. (Verb precedes plural subject.)

<u>Have</u> the product <u>specifications</u> <u>been submitted</u>? (Subject separates verb phrase.)

How important <u>are</u> <u>salary</u>, <u>benefits</u>, and <u>job security</u>? (Verb precedes subjects.)

How <u>do</u> <u>law</u> and <u>ethics</u> relate to everyday business? (Verb precedes subjects.)

BASIC RULES FOR SUBJECT–VERB AGREEMENT

Once you have located the sentence subject, decide whether the subject is singular or plural and select a verb that agrees in number.

SUBJECTS JOINED BY *AND*

When one subject is joined to another by the word *and*, the subject is plural and requires a plural verb.

Michael Dell and Meg Whitman are two influential people in the world of technology.

The proposed law and its amendment are before the legislature.

COMPANY NAMES AND TITLES

Even though they may appear to be plural, company names and titles of publications are singular; therefore, they require singular verbs.

Seven Secrets to Successful Investing was an instant bestseller.

JetBlue Airways is advertising the lowest fare to Bermuda.

Richards, Bateman, and Richards, Inc., is offering the bond issue.

Now complete the reinforcement exercises for Level 1.

· LEVEL 2 · LEVEL 2 · LEVEL 2 · LEVEL 2 · LEVEL 2 · LEVEL 2 · LEVEL 2 · L

SPECIAL RULES FOR SUBJECT–VERB AGREEMENT

Making sure your subjects agree with your verbs sometimes requires the application of special rules. This is especially true when dealing with subjects joined by *or* or *nor*, indefinite pronouns as subjects, and collective nouns as subjects.

SUBJECTS JOINED BY *OR* OR *NOR*

When two or more subjects are joined by *or* or *nor*, the verb should agree with the closer subject (the subject that follows *or* or *nor*).

Neither the webmaster nor the clerks know the customer's password.

Neither the clerks nor the webmaster knows the customer's password.

Either Leslie or you are in charge of ordering supplies.

Either you or Leslie is in charge of ordering supplies.

INDEFINITE PRONOUNS AS SUBJECTS

As you may recall from Chapter 7, some indefinite pronouns are always singular, whereas other indefinite pronouns are always plural. In addition, some may be singular or plural depending on the words to which they refer.

Always Singular			Always Plural	Singular or Plural
anyone	every	nobody	both	all
anybody	everyone	nothing	few	more
anything	everybody	someone	many	most
each	everything	somebody	several	some
either	many a	something		any
	neither			none

Either of the two applicants is qualified.

Everybody in the large group of candidates has an equal chance.

Most of the employees are satisfied with the company's benefit package.

Neither of the Web sites is particularly helpful.

Indefinite pronouns such as *all, more,* and *most* provide one of the few instances in which prepositional phrases become important in determining agreement. Although the prepositional phrase does not contain the subject of the sentence, it does contain the noun to which the indefinite pronoun refers.

Most of the applicants are women. (*Most* is plural because it refers to *women*.)

Most of the work is completed. (*Most* is singular because it refers to *work*.)

If the indefinite pronouns *each, every,* or *many a* are used to describe two or more subjects joined by *and,* the subjects are considered separate. As you learned in Chapter 7, this means that each subject is considered to be singular. Therefore, the verb is singular.

Many a semicolon and colon is misused. (Think *Many a semicolon is and many a colon is* . . .)

Every man, woman, and child is affected by the tax relief bill. (Think *Every single man, every single woman, and every single child is* . . .)

The indefinite pronouns *anyone, everyone,* and *someone* are generally spelled as two words when followed by *of* phrases.

Every one of us should commit to learning the new software package.

Any one of those Web sites can be used to book air and hotel reservations.

COLLECTIVE NOUNS AS SUBJECTS

Words such as *faculty, committee,* and *council* may be singular or plural depending on their mode of operation. When a collective noun operates as a single unit, its verb should be singular. When the elements of a collective noun operate separately, the verb should be plural.

Our staff has unanimously approved the board's proposal. (*Staff* is operating as a single unit.)

The council were sharply divided over the budget. (*Council* members were acting separately. Although technically correct, the sentence would be less awkward if it read *The council members were sharply*. . .)

Now complete the reinforcement exercises for Level 2.

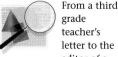

ADDITIONAL RULES FOR SUBJECT–VERB AGREEMENT

In some instances it's difficult to know whether a subject is singular or plural. Here are a few additional rules to guide you in selecting appropriate verbs for such subjects.

THE DISTINCTION BETWEEN *THE NUMBER* AND *A NUMBER*

When the word *number* is the subject of a sentence, its article (*the* or *a*) becomes significant. *The* is specific and therefore implies *singularity; a* is general and therefore implies *plurality.*

> The number of requests for registered domain names is growing annually. (Singular)

> A number of stocks are traded daily. (Plural)

QUANTITIES AND MEASURES

When they refer to *total* amounts, quantities and measures are singular. If they refer to individual units that can be counted, quantities and measures are plural.

> Three years is the period of the loan. (Quantity as a total amount)

> Three years are needed to renovate the property totally. (Quantity as individual units)

FRACTIONS AND PORTIONS

Fractions and portions may be singular or plural depending on the nouns to which they refer.

> Only a third of the students' reading scores are satisfactory. (The fraction *third* is plural because it refers to *scores.*)

> Over half of the contract was ratified. (The fraction *half* is singular because it refers to *contract.*)

> A majority of employees agree with the proposal. (The subject *majority* is plural because it refers to *employees.*)

> A percentage of the budget is allocated to employee benefits. (The subject *percentage* is singular because it refers to *budget.*)

> A percentage of the proceeds go to charity. (The subject *percentage* is plural because it refers to *proceeds.*)

> Part of the proposal is unclear (The subject *part* is plural because it refers to *proposal.*)

WHO CLAUSES

Verbs in *who* clauses must agree in number and person with the nouns to which they refer. In *who* clauses introduced by *one of,* the verb is usually plural because it refers to a plural antecedent. In *who* clauses introduced by *the only one of,* the verb is singular.

> Richard is *one of* those people who always give 100 percent. [Read: Of those people who always give 100 percent, Richard is one.]

SPOT THE BLOOPER

From *The Times-Union* [Albany, New York]: "The interim superintendent of schools said that 'a large number of students arrives without the basic skills we expect them to have.'"

SPOT THE BLOOPER

Article about Meryl Streep in *Parade* magazine: "She's one of the few stars who hasn't nipped and tucked herself into an unrealistic image of youth."

Betty Pearman is *one of* those managers who always get excellent results from their employees. (Read: Of those managers who always get excellent results from their employees, Betty Pearman is one. Note that the pronoun *their* also must agree with its antecedent.)

Maria is *the only one of* our employees who is certified to give CPR. [The adverb *only* limits the number to one.]

Verbs must agree in person with the nouns or pronouns to which they refer.

It is you who are responsible for security.

Could it be I who am to blame?

Was it you who were on the phone?

PHRASES AND CLAUSES AS SUBJECTS

Use a singular verb when the subject of a sentence is a phrase or clause.

Learning about the stock market is fascinating.

That verbs must agree with subjects is accepted.

SUBJECT COMPLEMENTS

In Chapter 8 you learned that linking verbs are followed by complements. Although a complement may differ from the subject in number, the linking verb should always agree with the subject. To avoid awkwardness, reword sentences so that subjects and complements agree in number.

Awkward:	The best part of the Web site is the graphics and video. (Although the singular subject *part* agrees with the singular verb *is*, it sounds awkward because of the plural complement *graphics and video.*)
Better:	The best parts of the Web site are the graphics and video. (The plural subject agrees with the plural complement.)

Awkward:	The reason for his bankruptcy was poor investments in stocks.
Better:	The reasons for his bankruptcy were poor investments in stocks.

Now complete the reinforcement exercises for Level 3.

Answered by Dr. Guffey

Question

Answer

Q: My uncle insists that *none* is singular. My English book says that it can be plural. Who's right?

A: Times are changing. Thirty years ago *none* was almost always used in a singular sense. Today, through usage, *none* may be singular or plural depending on what you wish to emphasize. For example, *None are more willing than we.* But, *None of the students is* (or *are* if you wish to suggest many students) *failing.*

Q: Please help me with this sentence that I'm transcribing for a medical laboratory: *A copy of our analysis, along with our interpretation of its results, (has or have) been sent to you.*

A: The subject of your sentence is *copy;* thus the verb must be *has.* Don't let interrupting elements obscure the real sentence subject.

Q: I'm never sure how to handle words that are used to represent quantities and proportions in sentences. For example, what verb is correct in this sentence: *A large proportion of voters (was or were) against the measure.*

A: Words that represent fractional amounts (such as *proportion, fraction, minimum,* and *majority*) may be singular or plural depending on the words they represent. In your sentence *proportion* represents *voters,* which is plural. Therefore, use the plural verb *were.*

Q: What part of speech is *there* when it begins a sentence, such as *There are two vice presidents*?

A: The word *there* generally is classified as an adverb. But in this position, the word *there* functions as a pronoun. *Merriam-Webster's Collegiate Dictionary,* Eleventh Edition, calls *there* a "function" word when it replaces the grammatical sentence subject.

Q: In a *New York Times* article about singer Michael Jackson and his fight with Sony Music Group, I saw this sentence: *Owning those rights are valuable because once Mr. Jackson owns them outright, he does not have to split royalty payments with Sony as he does now.* It seems to me the phrase *owning those rights* is singular and the verb should be *is.* Am I right?

A: Absolutely! When they act as sentence subjects, phrases and clauses are singular. You deserve a good grammar award!

Q: In a recent *Wall Street Journal* article, I saw this sentence: *At issue is other tax breaks, especially Hope and Lifetime Learning education tax credits.* I don't usually question the *Journal,* but this sentence is weird. What is its problem?

A: Because the sentence order is inverted, the writer had trouble making the subject and verb agree. By moving the subject to the beginning, you can see that it is plural. And a plural subject always demands a plural verb: *Other tax breaks . . . are at issue.*

Q: I have a lot of trouble with verbs in sentences like this: *He is one of the 8 million Americans who (has or have) a drinking problem.*

A: You're not alone. Make your verb agree with its antecedent (*Americans*). One easy way to work with sentences like this is to concentrate on the clause that contains the verb: *Of the 8 million Americans who have a drinking problem, he is one.*

Q: After looking in the dictionary, I'm beginning to wonder about this: *We have alot of work yet to do.* I can't find the word *alot* in the dictionary, but it must be there. Everyone uses it.

A: The two-word phrase *a lot* is frequently used in conversation or in very informal writing (*the copier makes a lot of copies*). *Alot* as one word does not exist. Don't confuse it with *allot* meaning "to distribute" (*the company will allot to each department its share of supplies*).

Q: I confuse *i.e.* and *e.g.* What's the difference?

A: The abbreviation *i.e.* stands for the Latin *id est*, meaning "that is" (*The package exceeds the weight limit, i.e., 5 pounds*). Notice the use of a comma after *i.e.* The abbreviation *e.g.* stands for the Latin *exempli gratia*, meaning "for the sake of example" or "for example" (*The manufacturer may offer a purchase incentive, e.g., a rebate or discount plan*).

LEVEL 1

A. (Self-check) Select the correct word to complete each sentence below. Write it in the space provided.

1. Standing beside me (is, are) my two esteemed colleagues, Ginger Brunell and Edward Trujillo.

_____

2. One desk in our department, along with several on the second and third floors, (is, are) equipped with special ergonomic features.

_____

3. (Has, Have) any of the grant applications been approved?

_____

4. One of the biggest headaches for employers (is, are) dealing with interpersonal relations among employees.

_____

5. No one but the Human Resources director and a few managers ever (talk, talks) about balancing work and family issues.

_____

6. There (is, are) three primary reasons to invest in foreign securities.

_____

7. Addressing the conference (is, are) employees of the Federal Reserve.

_____

8. Southwest Airlines (is, are) known for a fun culture that motivates employees.

_____

9. A set of guidelines to standardize input and output (was, were) developed.

_____

10. *Freakonomics* by Steven D. Levitt and Stephen J. Dubner (appear, appears) to be one of the best-selling economics books of all time.

_____

Check your answers below.

B. Assume that the following phrases serve as sentence subjects. For each item, circle the simple subject(s). Then indicate whether it is singular or plural.

	Singular	Plural
Example: the (controller) and the (treasurer) of the county	_____	✓
1. a list of Web site addresses	_____	_____
2. the office manager together with his staff	_____	_____
3. other services such as Web hosting and HTML coding	_____	_____
4. the production cost and the markup of each item	_____	_____
5. one of the many reasons for developing excellent communication skills	_____	_____
6. current emphasis on product safety and consumer protection	_____	_____
7. Farkas, Evans, & Everett, Inc., an executive placement service	_____	_____
8. the anger and frustration of the passengers	_____	_____

1. are 2. is 3. Have 4. is 5. talks 6. are 7. are 8. is 9. was 10. appears

Want to explore more? Go to: academic.cengage.com/bcomm/guffey or Xtra!

VERB AND SUBJECT AGREEMENT | **CHAPTER 10** | **173**

C. For each of the following sentences, circle the sentence subject. Then, cross out any phrases that separate the verb from its subject. Choose the correct verb and write it in the space provided.

Examples: The (faculty advisor,) ~~along with club members,~~ (is, are) here.   is _____

Our (catalog) ~~of wireless devices~~ (is, are) being sent to you.   is _____

1. The use of cell phones and pagers (is, are) not allowed during meetings.   _____

2. A bachelor's degree from an accredited institution, along with three years of experience, (is, are) necessary for this position.   _____

3. Everyone except temporary workers employed during the last year (has, have) become eligible for retroactive benefits.   _____

4. The wingspan on each of Boeing's latest passenger planes (is, are) longer than the Wright brothers' first flight.   _____

5. All cooperatives except the Lemon Growing Exchange (has, have) been able to show a profit for participating members.   _____

6. Although the economy seems to be booming, only one of the major automobile manufacturers (has, have) been able to show profits.   _____

7. Successful entrepreneurs such as Donald Trump (seem, seems) to possess enormous energy and passion.   _____

8. The range of prices for these models (make, makes) it difficult to provide complete information online.   _____

D. Select the correct verb and write it in the space provided.

1. Here (is, are) a complete list of product features.   _____

2. Outside of Indianapolis (is, are) several new office complexes.   _____

3. Some managers think that grammar and punctuation (doesn't, don't) matter.   _____

4. Lisa (doesn't, don't) mind working extra hours this weekend.   _____

5. Our governor, along with top congressional leaders, (is, are) protesting the budget cuts.   _____

6. Neither Brad nor Janet (is, are) able to attend the meeting.   _____

7. Cisco Systems (has, have) found a way to restructure its finances.   _____

8. Lying on my desk (is, are) my itinerary and plane tickets.   _____

9. Hunter, Knapp, and Huynh, Inc., a legal firm in Oklahoma City, (specializes, specialize) in patent law.   _____

10. Considerable time and money (was, were) spent on the plans.   _____

11. How essential (is, are) experience and education in this field?   _____

12. A task force to solve the budget problems (is, are) to be appointed.   _____

Want to explore more? Go to: academic.cengage.com/bcomm/guffey or Xtra!

174 | UNIT 3 | CHAPTER 10 | VERB AND SUBJECT AGREEMENT

LEVEL 2

A. (Self-check) Write the correct form.

1. Everyone except the president and other management members (is, are) eligible for the early retirement. _____

2. Either Rhonda Behrens or Rona Lee (has, have) already approved the report. _____

3. Every man, woman, and child in the country (is, are) to be counted in the census. _____

4. Each of the Web sites (provides, provide) live support. _____

5. All union members (has, have) to vote on the proposed contract. _____

6. Every one of the new start-up companies (is, are) seeking venture capital. _____

7. Many a server and busser (has, have) complained about rude customers. _____

8. (Everyone, Every one) of the sales reps made quota this month. _____

9. All that work (is, are) yet to be logged in. _____

10. Many surgeons, including Dr. William Inabnet, (listen, listens) to classical or rock music while operating. _____

Check your answers below.

B. Write the correct form.

1. The Department of Labor (report, reports) that 5.3 million jobs have been created in the past three years. _____

2. Neither Judith McDermid nor Bonnie Ideal (is, are) afraid of hard work. _____

3. (Everyone, Every one) of the résumés contained grammatical errors. _____

4. Several of the proposals (contain, contains) complex formulas. _____

5. Either the owner or her partner (is, are) responsible for the taxes. _____

6. The group of players, coaches, and fans (plan, plans) to charter a plane. _____

7. (Is, Are) either of the clients satisfied with our marketing campaign? _____

8. Something about these insurance claims (appear, appears) questionable. _____

9. Every one of the employees who attended the meeting (was, were) opposed to the reductions in benefits. _____

10. An online version of *U.S. News & World Report*'s college rankings (is, are) now available. _____

C. Writing Exercise. Use your imagination in expanding the following sentences.

1. The staff (is, are) _____

_____

2. Our city council (has, have) _____

_____

3. Not one of the plans (was, were) _____

_____

1. is 2. has 3. is 4. provides 5. have 6. is 7. has 8. Every one 9. is 10. listen

Want to explore more? Go to: academic.cengage.com/bcomm/guffey or Xtra!

VERB AND SUBJECT AGREEMENT | CHAPTER 10 | 175

4. Some of the jury members (believe, believes) _____

_____

5. Somebody in the theater filled with patrons (was, were) _____

_____

LEVEL 3

A. **(Self-check)** For each sentence write the correct verb in the space provided.

1. The number of companies performing background checks (is, are) greater than expected. _____

2. Part of the reason for the loss of customers (is, are) poor service. _____

3. Laurie McDonough is one of those accountants who (has, have) earned the respect of their clients. _____

4. Fifteen feet of pipe (is, are) exactly what was specified. _____

5. Didn't you know it is you who (is, are) to be honored at the ceremony? _____

6. A number of problems (is, are) yet to be resolved. _____

7. She is the only one of the service reps who (speak, speaks) three languages. _____

8. Whoever is named for the job (has, have) my approval. _____

9. To take night classes while working (is, are) challenging. _____

10. The hardest part of the job (is, are) the bending and lifting. _____

Check your answers below.

B. Select the correct verb.

1. Five hundred dollars (is, are) required as a damage deposit on the conference facility. _____

2. Our latest advertisements featuring the new digital media server (is, are) an example of the campaign. _____

3. Is it he who (is, are) the new account representative? _____

4. Michael is the only one of the lab assistants who (was, were) able to repair the malfunctioning machine. _____

5. Vacations for employees who are entitled to three or more weeks (is, are) the next item on the agenda. _____

6. Sixty days (is, are) the period of the loan. _____

7. At the rear of the building complex (is, are) the quality control lab and the science department. _____

8. Only a fraction of the conference delegates (was, were) unable to find accommodations at the Mandalay Bay resort. _____

9. Keeping your skills up-to-date (is, are) important in today's economy. _____

10. Over 80 percent of the individuals attending the lecture series (is, are) residents of nearby communities. _____

(. . . . *are job the of parts hardest The* :Better) is .10 is .9 has .8 speaks .7 are .6 are .5 is .4 have .3 is .2 is .1)

Want to explore more? Go to: academic.cengage.com/bcomm/guffey or Xtra!

176 | **UNIT 3** | **CHAPTER 10** | **VERB AND SUBJECT AGREEMENT**

C. Writing Exercise. Some subject-verb constructions are grammatically correct but sound incorrect. Revise the following correct sentences so that they are not only correct but sound so. **Hint:** Make the subject and its complement agree in number.

Example: The best part of my job is meeting people and learning new things ___The best parts of my job are meeting___

___people and learning new things.___

1. The principal task in this office is abstracts and affidavits. _____

_____

2. The primary reason for his wealth is wise stock and other investment choices. _____

_____

3. The main objective this fiscal year is to increase sales and decrease expenses. _____

_____

For further practice in subject-verb agreement, write sentences using the following words as subjects of present-tense verbs. Your sentences should have 12 or more words.

Example: The number of voters is increasing rapidly as we approach the election date. _____

4. A number of voters _____

_____

5. Every one of the new voters _____

_____

6. Some of the new voters _____

_____

D. Skill Maximizer. To offer extra help in areas that cause hesitation for business and professional writers, this proficiency exercise reviews subject-verb agreement. Underline any subject-verb problem and write an improved form in the space provided. Write *C* if the sentence is correct.

1. Persistent inflation and interest rate worries often causes stock prices to drop. _____

2. Was any of the members of the organization present for the final vote? _____

3. After several days of deliberation, the jury has announced its verdict. _____

4. Neither the defendant nor the plaintiffs was satisfied with the judgment. _____

5. Are either of the applicants available to interview on Friday? _____

6. Preparing the dinner for the annual banquet is gourmet chefs from around the world. _____

7. Globalization and the changing ethnic composition of America is causing many organizations to embrace diversity programs. _____

8. The use of UPC scanning devices, computer databases, and thermal-imaging receipts are everywhere in the retail industry. _____

9. One of the problems, in addition to those already mentioned, seem to be resistance to change. _____

10. Both a written proposal and an oral presentation is required for this proposal. _____

Want to explore more? Go to: academic.cengage.com/bcomm/guffey or Xtra!

11. If the level of antioxidants in your diet are low, you may be susceptible to health problems.

_____

12. A host of ethical issues surround business including economic justice, marketing irregularities, executive compensation, and whistle-blowing.

_____

13. Bank of America, along with many other financial institutions, are outsourcing thousands of tech jobs to India.

_____

14. Any one of the stockholders have the right to delegate his or her proxy.

_____

15. Steve is one of those people who always gets along well with fellow workers.

_____

E. Hotline Review. In the space provided write the correct answer choice.

1. Horns blow in different keys and tones; _____ American car horns beep in the tone of F.
a. e.g.,   b. i.e.,

_____

2. Mosquito sprays block the mosquito's sensors so that they don't know you are there; _____ they hide you.
a. e.g.,   b. i.e.,

_____

3. We have _____ of work to do before the end of the day.
a. a lot   b. alot   c. allot

_____

4. Winning both Boeing contracts _____ important because it would generate $57 million in revenues.
a. is   b. are

_____

5. A group of photographers _____ waiting outside the building when we made the announcement.
a. was   b. were

_____

Want to explore more? Go to: academic.cengage.com/bcomm/guffey or Xtra!

178 | UNIT 3 | CHAPTER 10 | VERB AND SUBJECT AGREEMENT

The following e-mail message contains 30 intentional errors in sentence structure, spelling, and proofreading. Be especially alert to verb problems. When you replace a wordy or incorrect phrase with one word, it counts as one correction. When you correct a comma splice, run-on, or fragment, the correction counts as two errors. Count each parenthesis and each dash as a single mark. Use proofreading marks to make the corrections here OR make the corrections at the **Guffey Companion Web Site** at **academic.cengage.com/bcomm/guffey.**

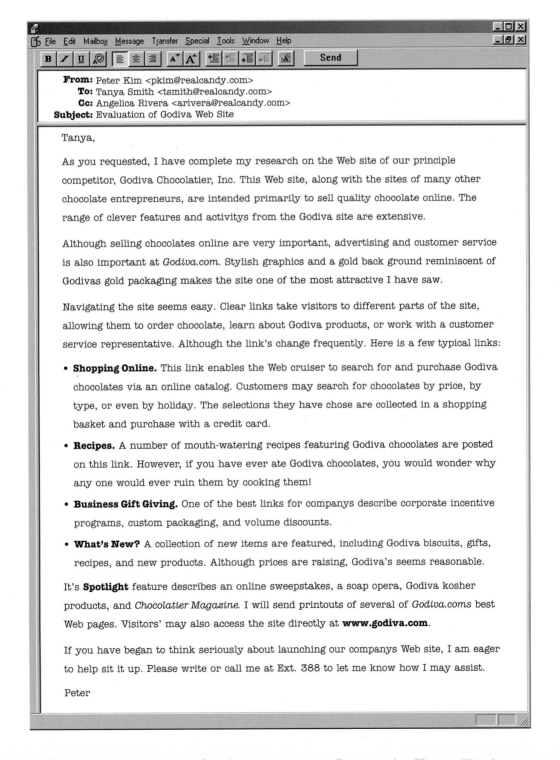

From: Peter Kim <pkim@realcandy.com>
To: Tanya Smith <tsmith@realcandy.com>
Cc: Angelica Rivera <arivera@realcandy.com>
Subject: Evaluation of Godiva Web Site

Tanya,

As you requested, I have complete my research on the Web site of our principle competitor, Godiva Chocolatier, Inc. This Web site, along with the sites of many other chocolate entrepreneurs, are intended primarily to sell quality chocolate online. The range of clever features and activitys from the Godiva site are extensive.

Although selling chocolates online are very important, advertising and customer service is also important at *Godiva.com*. Stylish graphics and a gold back ground reminiscent of Godivas gold packaging makes the site one of the most attractive I have saw.

Navigating the site seems easy. Clear links take visitors to different parts of the site, allowing them to order chocolate, learn about Godiva products, or work with a customer service representative. Although the link's change frequently. Here is a few typical links:

- **Shopping Online.** This link enables the Web cruiser to search for and purchase Godiva chocolates via an online catalog. Customers may search for chocolates by price, by type, or even by holiday. The selections they have chose are collected in a shopping basket and purchase with a credit card.

- **Recipes.** A number of mouth-watering recipes featuring Godiva chocolates are posted on this link. However, if you have ever ate Godiva chocolates, you would wonder why any one would ever ruin them by cooking them!

- **Business Gift Giving.** One of the best links for companys describe corporate incentive programs, custom packaging, and volume discounts.

- **What's New?** A collection of new items are featured, including Godiva biscuits, gifts, recipes, and new products. Although prices are raising, Godiva's seems reasonable.

It's **Spotlight** feature describes an online sweepstakes, a soap opera, Godiva kosher products, and *Chocolatier Magazine.* I will send printouts of several of *Godiva.coms* best Web pages. Visitors' may also access the site directly at **www.godiva.com**.

If you have began to think seriously about launching our companys Web site, I am eager to help sit it up. Please write or call me at Ext. 388 to let me know how I may assist.

Peter

Want to explore more? Go to: academic.cengage.com/bcomm/guffey or Xtra!

VERB AND SUBJECT AGREEMENT | CHAPTER 10 | **179**

"Netiquette" is network etiquette covering the dos and don'ts of online communication. To become familiar with some of the informal "rules of the road" in cyberspace, you will visit the *Business Netiquette International* site.

Goal: To learn about netiquette.

1. With your Web browser on the screen, enter the following URL: **http://www.albion.com/ netiquette/.**
2. Click **The Core Rules of Etiquette;** then click **Introduction.** What is "netiquette"?
3. Click **Next Page** at the bottom of the Introduction to take you to Rule 1. What is Rule 1?

4. Click **Next Page** at the bottom of the Rule 1 page to take you to Rule 2. What is Rule 2?
5. Continue to click **Next Page** until you've read through all ten rules. What should you ask yourself before copying someone on an e-mail message? (**Hint:** Read Rule 4.)
6. How will you be judged online? (**Hint:** Read Rule 5.)
7. After reading all ten rules, click **Netiquette Quiz** to the left. Press the button to begin the quiz.
8. After completing the quiz, print the screen showing your quiz results.
9. End your session and submit your printed page and written answers.

Underline the correct verb.

1. Everyone except the president and other management members (is, are) eligible for early retirement.

2. The cost of supplies, along with service and equipment costs, (is, are) a major problem.

3. There (is, are) many firms we can use to design our new Web site.

4. Appearing next on the program (was, were) Dr. Gwen Hester and Professor Janis Rollins.

5. A number of surprising events (is, are) creating spikes in the stock market.

1. is 2. is 3. are 4. were 5. are

Want to explore more? Go to: academic.cengage.com/bcomm/guffey or Xtra!

180 | **UNIT 3** | **CHAPTER 10** | **VERB AND SUBJECT AGREEMENT**

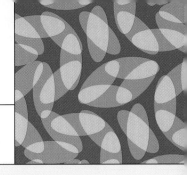

Reread Chapters 8–10. Then test your comprehension of those chapters by completing the exercises that follow. Check your answers at the end of the book.

LEVEL 1

In the blank provided, write the letter of the word or phrase that correctly completes each of the following sentences.

1. In the sentence *An additive makes natural gas smell like rotten eggs,* the verb *smell* is (a) transitive, (b) intransitive, (c) linking. _____

2. In the sentence *We listened carefully to the recording,* the verb *listened* is (a) transitive, (b) intransitive, (c) linking. _____

3. In the sentence *Bob Dameron is the president-elect,* the word *president-elect* is a(n) (a) object, (b) linking verb, (c) complement. _____

4. In the sentence *Maggie framed her diploma,* the word *framed* is (a) transitive, (b) intransitive, (c) linking. _____

5. An ergonomic mouse device (a) has, (b) have been developed for your computer. _____

6. Google, along with other foreign Internet companies, (a) is, (b) are required to abide by China's laws. _____

7. The president and his entire staff (a) send, (b) sends greetings to you. _____

8. Be sure (a) to write, (b) and write the name and address legibly. _____

9. Olsen, Leung, and Miller, Inc., (a) is, (b) are moving to a new location. _____

10. The shipping statement for the equipment and supplies (a) was, (b) were delayed. _____

11. There (a) is, (b) are many kind words we'll be able to say about him at his retirement dinner. _____

12. The tone and wording of a business message (a) are, (b) is very important. _____

13. How effective (a) is, (b) are the company guidelines on Internet use? _____

LEVEL 2

Write the letter of the word or phrase that correctly completes each of the following sentences.

14. She suggested that everyone (a) meet, (b) meets at the café after work. _____

15. He acts as if he (a) was, (b) were the only employee who had to work overtime. _____

16. When converting a verb from the passive to the active voice, the writer must make the doer of the action the (a) subject, (b) object of the active voice verb. _____

17. In the sentence *Our Web site conversion was completed last week,* the verb is in the (a) active, (b) passive voice. _____

18. Many letters and packages have (a) laid, (b) lain, (c) lay on her front step for the past week. _____

19. If you had (a) rode, (b) ridden the subway to work, you would have been on time. _____

20. (a) Is (b) Are either Craigslist or Burger King planning an IPO? _____

21. We think that (a) everyone, (b) every one of the candidates is qualified for the position. _____

22. The jury of six men and seven women (a) has, (b) have been sequestered. _____

23. If I (a) was, (b) were qualified, I would apply for that position. _____

24. The network administrator recommends that employee passwords (a) are, (b) be changed every six months. _____

25. I'm not going to join you because I've already (a) eaten, (b) ate lunch. _____

LEVEL 3

In the blank provided, write the letter that correctly completes each sentence.

26. Nearly everyone in the office objected to (a) Sara, (b) Sara's yelling on her cell phone. _____

27. The number of cable companies offering high-definition television (a) is, (b) are growing rapidly. _____

28. A large percentage of people (a) is, (b) are simplifying their lives. _____

29. It looks as if three fourths of the brochures (a) has, (b) have yet to be assembled. _____

30. She is one of those executives who always (a) tell, (b) tells the truth. _____

For each of the following sentences, indicate whether (a) the sentence is written correctly or (b) the sentence has a verbal phrase placed illogically. Rewrite illogical sentences.

31. To qualify for a full scholarship, applications must be made by January 1. _____

_____

_____

32. Skilled at troubleshooting network problems, the personnel manager hired Eun Park instantly. _____

_____

_____

33. Using two search tools, the Web site was finally located. _____

_____

34. The waiter served a bowl of soup to the woman that was steaming hot. _____

_____

_____

Hotline Review

35. We value one trait in our employees above all others, (a) i.e., (b) e.g., integrity. _____

36. State budget cuts will certainly (a) affect, (b) effect education adversely. _____

37. Researcher Terry Strauss announced her (a) principle, (b) principal findings in a journal article. _____

38. Both plaintiffs and defendants were (a) all together, (b) altogether pleased with the out-of-court settlement. _____

39. Ellen said that she wasted (a) a lot, (b) alot of time on Web searches. _____

40. We trusted that Shannon would be (a) discrete, (b) discreet during the negotiations. _____

TECHNIQUES FOR EFFECTIVE PARAGRAPHS

As you learned in the Writer's Workshop for Unit 2, the basic unit in writing is the sentence. The next unit is the paragraph. Although no rule regulates the length of paragraphs, business writers recognize the value of short paragraphs. Paragraphs with fewer than eight printed lines look inviting and readable, whereas long, solid chunks of print appear formidable. In this workshop you will learn writing techniques for organizing sentences into readable, coherent, and clear paragraphs. The first very important technique involves topic sentences.

ORGANIZING PARAGRAPHS AROUND TOPIC SENTENCES

A well-organized paragraph has two important characteristics. First, it covers just one subject. For example, if you are writing about your booth at the Las Vegas computer expo, you wouldn't throw in a sentence about trouble with the IRS. Keep all the sentences in a paragraph related to one topic. Second, a well-organized paragraph begins with a topic sentence that summarizes what the paragraph is about. A topic sentence helps readers by preparing them for what follows.

Consider the following scenario. Let's say your company promotes an extensive schedule of team sports for employees after hours. One group enjoys weekend bicycling. You've been assigned the task of writing a memo to the members of this group stating that they must wear helmets when cycling. One paragraph of your memo covers statistics about cycling accidents and the incidence of brain injury for unhelmeted riders. Another paragraph discusses the protection offered by helmets:

> *Helmets protect the brain from injury.* They spread the force of a crash from the point of impact to a wider area. When an accident occurs, an unhelmeted head undergoes two collisions. The first occurs when the skull slams into the ground. The second occurs when the brain hits the inside of the skull. A helmet softens the second blow and acts as a shock absorber. Instead of crushing the brain, the impact crushes the foam core of the helmet, often preventing serious brain injury.

Notice how the preceding paragraph focuses on just one topic: how helmets protect the brain from injury. Every sentence relates to that topic. Notice, too, that the first sentence functions as a topic sentence, informing the reader of the subject of the paragraph.

The best way to write a good paragraph is to list all the ideas you may include. Following is a rough draft of ideas for the preceding paragraph. Notice that the fourth item doesn't relate to the topic sentence. By listing the ideas to be included in a paragraph, you can immediately see what belongs—and what doesn't. Once the list is made, you can easily write the topic sentence.

Paragraph Idea List

1. Helmets spread force of impact.

2. Crashes cause two collisions, the first when the skull hits the ground and the second when the brain hits the skull.

3. The foam core of the helmet absorbs the impact.

4. ~~The federal government has issued biking regulations requiring helmets.~~

   Topic Sentence: Helmets protect the brain from injury.

Skill Check 3.1: Organizing a Paragraph

In a memo to the college president, the athletic director is arguing for a new stadium scoreboard. One paragraph will describe the old scoreboard and why it needs to be replaced. Study the following list of ideas for that paragraph.

1. The old scoreboard is a tired warhorse that was originally constructed in the 1960s.

2. It's now hard to find replacement parts for it when something breaks.

3. The old scoreboard is not energy efficient.

4. Coca-Cola has offered to buy a new sports scoreboard in return for exclusive rights to sell soda on campus.

5. The old scoreboard should be replaced for many reasons.

6. It shows only scores for football games.

7. When we have soccer games or track meets, we're without any functioning scoreboard.

   a. Which sentence should be the topic sentence? _____

   b. Which sentence(s) should be developed in a different paragraph? _____

   c. Which sentences should follow the topic sentence? _____

WRITING COHERENT PARAGRAPHS

Effective paragraphs are coherent; that is, they hold together. Coherence is a quality of good writing that doesn't happen accidentally. It is consciously achieved through effective organization and through skillful use of three devices. These writing devices are (a) repetition of key ideas or key words, (b) use of pronouns that refer clearly to their antecedents, and (c) use of transitional expressions.

Repetition of Key Ideas or Key Words. Repeating a key word or key thought from a preceding sentence helps guide a reader from one thought to the next. This redundancy is necessary to build cohesiveness into writing. Notice how the word *deal* is repeated in the second sentence.

> For the past six months, college administrators and Coca-Cola have been working on a *deal* in which the college would receive a new sports scoreboard. The *deal* would involve exclusive rights to sell soda pop on the 12,000-student campus.

Use of Pronouns That Refer Clearly to Their Antecedents. Pronouns such as *this, that, they, these, those,* and *it* help connect thoughts in sentences. But these pronouns are useful only when their antecedents are clear. Often it's better to make the pronoun into an adjective joined with its antecedent to ensure that the reference is absolutely clear. Notice how the pronoun *this* is clearer when it is joined to its antecedent *contract.*

Confusing: The Coca-Cola offer requires an exclusive contract committing the college for ten years without any provision preventing a price increase. *This* could be very costly to students, staff, and faculty.

Improved: The Coca-Cola offer requires an exclusive contract committing the college for ten years without any provision preventing a price increase. *This contract* could be very costly to students, staff, and faculty.

Avoid vague pronouns, such as *it* in the following example.

Confusing: Both Coca-Cola and PepsiCo offered to serve our campus, and we agreed to allow *it* to submit a bid.

Improved: Both Coca-Cola and PepsiCo offered to serve our campus, and we agreed to allow Coca-Cola to submit a bid.

Use of Transitional Expressions. One of the most effective ways to achieve paragraph coherence is through the use of transitional expressions. These expressions act as road signs. They indicate where the message is headed, and they help the reader anticipate what is coming. Some common transitional expressions follow:

although	furthermore	moreover
as a result	hence	nevertheless
consequently	however	of course
for example	in addition	on the other hand
for this reason	in this way	therefore

Other words that act as connectives are *first, second, finally, after, meanwhile, next, after all, instead, specifically, thus, also, likewise, as,* and *as if.*

The following paragraph achieves coherence through use of all three techniques. (1) The key idea of *surprising battle* in the first sentence is echoed in the second sentence with repetition of the word *battle* coupled with *unexpected,* a synonym for *surprising.* (2) The use of a pronoun, *This,* in the second sentence connects the second sentence to the first. (3) The transitional words *however* and *as a result* in the following sentences continue to build coherence.

A *surprising battle* between two global cola giants was recently fought in Venezuela. *This battle* was *unexpected* because Venezuelans had always been loyal Pepsi drinkers. *However,* when the nation's leading bottler sold half of its interest to Coca-Cola, everything changed. *As a result,* Coca-Cola turned the Pepsi-drinking nation of Venezuela into Coke drinkers almost overnight.

Skill Check 3.2: Improving Paragraph Coherence

In the following space or on a separate sheet of paper, use the information from Skill Check 3.1 to write a coherent paragraph about replacing the sports scoreboard. Remember that this paragraph is part of a memo from the athletic director to the college president. Include a topic sentence. Strive to illustrate all three techniques to achieve coherence.

_____

_____

_____

_____

_____

_____

DEVELOPING PARALLEL CONSTRUCTION

Paragraph clarity can be improved by expressing similar ideas with similar grammatical structures. For example, if you are listing three ideas, do not use *ing* words for two of the ideas and a *to* verb with the third idea: *reading, eating, and studying* (not *to study*). Use adjectives with adjectives, verbs with verbs, phrases with phrases, and clauses with clauses. In the following list, use all verbs: *the machine sorted, stamped, and counted* (not *and had a counter*). For phrases, the wording for all parts of the list should be matched; *safety must be improved in the home, in the classroom, and on the job* (not *for office workers*).

Poor: Ms. Tanaga is energetic, resourceful and she can be relied on.

Improved: Ms. Tanaga is energetic, resourceful, and reliable. (Matches adjectives.)

Poor: The new shredder helped us save money, reduce pollution, and paper could be recycled.

Improved: The new shredder helped us save money, reduce pollution, and recycle paper. (Matches verb-noun construction.)

Skill Check 3.3: Improving Parallel Construction

Revise each of the following sentences to improve parallel construction.

1. Your job is to research, design, and the implementation of a diversity program.

   _____

   _____

2. Few managers are able to write letters accurately, concisely, and with efficiency.

   _____

   _____

3. The new software totals all balances, gives weekly reports, and statements are printed.

   _____

   _____

4. Our objectives are to make our stock profitable, to operate efficiently, and developing good employee relations.

   _____

   _____

Writing Application 3.1

On a separate sheet, revise the following paragraph. Add a topic sentence and improve the organization. Correct pronouns with unclear antecedents, wordiness, and misplaced verbal modifiers (which you learned about in Chapter 8). Add transitional expressions if appropriate.

> You may be interested in applying for a new position within the company. The Human Resources Department has a number of jobs available immediately. The positions are at a high level. Current employees may apply immediately for open positions in production, for some in marketing, and jobs in administrative support are also available. To make application, these positions require immediate action. Come to the Human Resources Department. We have a list showing the open positions, what the qualifications are, and job descriptions are shown. Many of the jobs are now open. That's why we are sending this now. To be hired, an interview must be scheduled within the next two weeks.

Writing Application 3.2

On a separate sheet, revise the following poorly written paragraph. Add a topic sentence and improve the organization. Correct misplaced modifiers, pronouns with unclear antecedents, wordiness, and any other writing faults. Add transitional expressions if appropriate.

> As you probably already know, this company (Lasertronics) will be installing new computer software shortly. There will be a demonstration April 18, which is a Tuesday. We felt this was necessary because this new software is so different from our previous software. It will be from 9 to 12 a.m. in the morning. This will show employees how the software programs work. They will learn about the operating system, and this should be helpful to nearly everyone. There will be information about the new word processing program, which should be helpful to administrative assistants and product managers. For all you people who work with payroll, there will be information about the new database program. We can't show everything the software will do at this one demo, but for these three areas there will be some help at the Tuesday demo. Oh yes, Paula Roddy will be presenting the demonstration. She is the representative from Quantum Software.

Writing Application 3.3

Assume you work in the Human Resources Department of Bank of America. You must write an announcement describing a special program of classes for your employees. Use the following information to write a well-organized paragraph announcement. Explain that Bank of America will reimburse any employee the full cost of tuition and books if that employee attends classes. Describe the plan. Skyline Community College, in cooperation with Bank of America, will offer a group of courses for college credit at very convenient locations for our employees. Actually, the classes will be offered at your downtown and East Bay branches. Tell employees that they should call Jean Fujimoto at Ext. 660 if they are interested. You'd better mention the tuition: $180 for a semester course. Explain that we (Bank of America) are willing to pay these fees because we value education highly. However, make it clear that employees must receive a grade of C or higher before they are eligible for reimbursement of course and book fees. It might be a good idea to attach a list of the courses and the times that they will be offered. Include a deadline date for calling Jean.

MODIFYING AND CONNECTING WORDS

UNIT 1 · UNIT 2 · UNIT 3 · UNIT 4 · UNIT 5 · UNIT 6

© BananaStock/Jupiter Images

© Adrian Peacock/Creatas Images/Jupiter Images

© Dynamic Graphics/Creatas Images/Jupiter Images

11
MODIFIERS:
ADJECTIVES
AND ADVERBS

12
PREPOSITIONS

13
CONJUNCTIONS

© BananaStock/Jupiter Images

MODIFIERS: ADJECTIVES AND ADVERBS

OBJECTIVES

When you have completed the materials in this chapter, you will be able to do the following:

LEVEL 1

- Form the comparative and superlative degrees of regular and irregular adjectives and adverbs.
- Use articles, demonstrative adjectives, and possessive adjectives correctly, and avoid double negatives.

LEVEL 2

- Employ adjectives after linking verbs; and use adverbs to modify verbs, adjectives, and other adverbs.
- Punctuate compound and successive independent adjectives correctly.

LEVEL 3

- Compare degrees of absolute adjectives and make comparisons within a group.
- Place adverbs and adjectives close to the words they modify.

PRETEST

Underline the correct word.

1. The (worse, worst) weather in London is in January.

2. (A, An) exceptional job was done on the Web site redesign.

3. If you did (good, well) in the interview, you will be hired.

4. Our (six-year-old, six year old) lease must be renegotiated.

5. The (newly repaired, newly-repaired) copier seems to be working well.

1. worst 2. An 3. well 4. six-year-old 5. newly repaired

190

Both adjectives and adverbs act as modifiers; that is, they describe or limit other words. Many of the forms and functions of adjectives and adverbs are similar. Because of this similarity, these two parts of speech may be confused. That's why we will treat adjectives and adverbs together in this chapter.

· LEVEL 1 · LEVEL 1 · LEVEL 1 · LEVEL 1 · LEVEL 1 · LEVEL 1 · LEVEL 1 · LEVEL 1 · LE

BASIC FUNCTIONS OF ADJECTIVES AND ADVERBS

Adjectives describe or limit nouns and pronouns. As you have already learned, they often answer the questions *What kind? How many?* or *Which one?* Adjectives in the following sentences are italicized.

> *Small, independent* businesses are becoming *numerous*. (Adjectives answer *What kind?*)

> *Two government* grants were awarded to *the eight top* institutions. (Adjectives answer *How many?*)

Adverbs describe or limit verbs, adjectives, or other adverbs. They often answer the questions *When? How? Where?* or *To what extent?*

> *Today* we left work *early*. (Adverbs answer *When? How?*)

> Please take a seat *there*. (Adverb answers *Where?*)

COMPARATIVE AND SUPERLATIVE FORMS

Most adjectives and adverbs have three forms, or degrees: positive, comparative, and superlative. The following examples illustrate how the comparative and superlative degrees of regular adjectives and adverbs are formed.

	Positive	Comparative	Superlative
Adjective:	warm	warmer	warmest
Adverb:	warmly	more warmly	most warmly
Adjective:	careful	more careful	most careful
Adverb:	carefully	more carefully	most carefully

The **positive degree** of an adjective or an adverb is used in merely describing or in limiting another word. The **comparative degree** is used to compare two persons or things. The **superlative degree** is used in the comparison of three or more persons or things.

The comparative degree of short adjectives (nearly all one-syllable and most two-syllable adjectives ending in *y*) is formed by adding *r* or *er* (*warmer*). The superlative degree of short adjectives is formed by the addition of *st* or *est* (*warmest*). Long adjectives, and those difficult to pronounce, form the comparative and superlative degrees, as do adverbs, with the addition of *more* and *most* (*more careful, most beautiful*). The following sentences illustrate degrees of comparison for adjectives and adverbs.

Adjectives:	Sales are unusually *high*.	(Positive degree)
	Sales are *higher* than ever before.	(Comparative degree)
	Sales are the *highest* in years.	(Superlative degree)

Adverbs:	He drives *carefully*.	(Positive degree)
	He drives *more carefully* now.	(Comparative degree)
	He drives *most carefully* at night.	(Superlative degree)

Do not create a double comparative form by using *more* and the suffix *er* together (such as *more neater*) or by using *most* and the suffix *est* together (such as *most fastest*).

IRREGULAR ADJECTIVES AND ADVERBS

A few adjectives and adverbs form the comparative and superlative degrees irregularly.

	Positive	**Comparative**	**Superlative**
Adjectives:	good	better	best
	well	better	best
	bad	worse	worst
	little	less	least
	many, much	more	most
Adverbs:	well	better	best
	many, much	more	most

MODIFIERS THAT DESERVE SPECIAL ATTENTION

A few adjectives and adverbs require special attention because they cause writers and speakers difficulty.

ADJECTIVES AS ARTICLES

The **articles** *a, an,* and *the* must be used carefully. When describing a specific person or thing, use the **definite article** *the,* as in *the film.* When describing persons or things in general, use the **indefinite article** *a* or *an,* as in *a film* (meaning *any* film). The choice of *a* or *an* is determined by the initial sound of the word modified. *A* is used before consonant sounds; *an* is used before vowel sounds.

Before Vowel Sounds		**Before Consonant Sounds**	
an operator		a shop	
an executive		a plan	
an hour }	*h* is not voiced;	a hook }	*h* is voiced
an honor }	vowel is heard	a hole }	
an office }	*o* sounds	a one-man show }	*o* sounds like
an onion }	like a vowel	a one-week trip }	the consonant *w*
an understudy }	*u* sounds	a union }	*u* sounds like
an umbrella }	like a vowel	a unit }	the consonant *y*
an X-ray }	*x* and *m* sound		
an MD }	like vowels		

THE DEMONSTRATIVE ADJECTIVES *THIS/THAT* AND *THESE/THOSE*

Demonstrative adjectives indicate whether a noun is plural or singular and whether it is located nearby or farther away. The demonstrative adjective *this*, and its plural form *these*, indicates something nearby. The demonstrative adjective *that*, and its plural form *those*, indicates something at a distance. Be careful to use the singular forms of these words with singular nouns and the plural forms with plural nouns: *this shoe, that road, these accounts, those records.* Pay special attention to the nouns *kind, type,* and *sort.* Match singular adjectives to the singular forms of these nouns and plural adjectives to the plural forms.

Incorrect:	Job interviewees should be prepared for these type of questions.
Correct:	Job interviewees should be prepared for this type of question.
Correct:	Job interviewees should be prepared for these types of questions.

POSSESSIVE ADJECTIVES

As you learned in Chapters 2 and 6, some possessive pronouns serve as **possessive adjectives** when they describe nouns. Examples of these words include *my, our, your, his, her, its,* and *their.* You can tell that a pronoun is functioning as an adjective when it comes before the noun it's describing.

My job has become demanding lately.

Please visit *our offices* when you're in town.

Please submit *your application* online.

ADVERBS AND DOUBLE NEGATIVES

When a negative adverb (*no, not, nothing, scarcely, hardly, barely*) is used in the same sentence with a negative verb (*didn't, don't, won't*), a substandard construction called a **double negative** results. Among professionals, such constructions are considered to be illogical and illiterate. In the following examples, notice that eliminating one negative corrects the double negative.

Incorrect:	Calling her *won't* do *no* good.
Correct:	Calling her will do no good.
Correct:	Calling her won't do any good.
Incorrect:	We *couldn't hardly* believe the CEO's remarks.
Correct:	We could hardly believe the CEO's remarks.
Correct:	We couldn't believe the CEO's remarks.
Incorrect:	Drivers *can't barely* see in the heavy fog.
Correct:	Drivers can barely see in the heavy fog.
Correct:	Drivers can't see in the heavy fog.
Incorrect:	He *didn't have nothing* to do with it.
Correct:	He had nothing to do with it.
Correct:	He didn't have anything to do with it.

Now complete the reinforcement exercises for Level 1.

ADJECTIVE AND ADVERB CHALLENGES

In the following discussion you will learn to avoid confusing adjectives with adverbs. You will also learn to express compound adjectives and independent adjectives.

CONFUSION OF ADJECTIVES AND ADVERBS

Because they are closely related, adjectives are sometimes confused with adverbs. Here are guidelines that will help you choose the appropriate adjective or adverb.

When to Use Adjectives

Use adjectives to modify nouns and pronouns. Note particularly that adjectives (not adverbs) should follow linking verbs.

> This pasta tastes *delicious.* (Not *deliciously*)
>
> I feel *bad* about the loss. (Not *badly*)
>
> She looks *good* in her business suit. (Not *well*)

When to Use Adverbs

Use adverbs to describe verbs, adjectives, or other adverbs.

> The engine runs *smoothly.* (Not *smooth*)
>
> It runs *more smoothly* than before. (Not *smoother*)
>
> Listen *carefully* to the directions. (Not *careful*)
>
> Time passes *quickly.* (Not *quick*)

A few adverbs have two acceptable forms: *slow, slowly; deep, deeply; direct, directly;* and *close, closely.*

> Drive *slowly.* (Or, less formally, *slow.*)
>
> You may dial us *directly.* (Or, less formally, *direct*)

COMPOUND ADJECTIVES

Writers may form their own adjectives by joining two or more words. When these words act as a single modifier preceding a noun, they are temporarily hyphenated. If these same words appear after a noun, they are generally not hyphenated.

Words Temporarily Hyphenated Before a Noun	Same Words Not Hyphenated After a Noun
never-say-die attitude	attitude of never say die
eight-story building	building of eight stories
state-sponsored program	program that is state sponsored
a case-by-case analysis	analysis that is case by case
follow-up appointment	an appointment to follow up
income-related expenses	expenses that are income related
four-year-old child	child who is four years old
home-based business	business that is home based

Compound adjectives shown in your dictionary with hyphens are considered permanently hyphenated. Regardless of whether the compound appears before or after a noun, it retains the hyphens. Use a current dictionary or reference manual to determine what expressions are always hyphenated. Be sure that you find the dictionary entry that is marked *adjective*. Here are samples:

Permanent Hyphens Before Nouns	Permanent Hyphens After Nouns
first-class seats	seats that are first-class
up-to-date information	the information is up-to-date
old-fashioned attitude	attitude that is old-fashioned
short-term goals	goals that are short-term
well-known expert	expert who is well-known
full-time (part-time) employee	employee who is full-time (part-time)

Don't confuse adverbs ending in *ly* with compound adjectives: *newly decorated office* and *highly regarded architect* would not be hyphenated.

As compound adjectives become more familiar, they are often simplified and the hyphen is dropped. Some familiar compounds that are not hyphenated are *high school student, charge account balance, income tax return, home office equipment, word processing software*, and *data processing center*.

INDEPENDENT (COORDINATE) ADJECTIVES

Independent (coordinate) adjectives occur when two or more successive adjectives independently modify a noun. Writers must separate independent adjectives with commas. Do not use a comma, however, when the first adjective modifies the combined idea of the second adjective and the noun.

Two Adjectives Independently Modifying a Noun	First Adjective Modifying a Second Adjective Plus a Noun
positive, reliable employee	efficient administrative assistant
economical, efficient car	graphite grey sports car
stimulating, provocative book	assistant deputy director

COMMONLY CONFUSED ADJECTIVES AND ADVERBS

The following adjectives and adverbs cause difficulty for some writers and speakers. With a little study, you can master their correct usage.

almost (adv.—nearly): *Almost* (not *Most*) everybody wants to work.

most (adj.— greatest in amount): *Most* people want to work.

farther (adv.—actual distance): How much *farther* is the airport?

further (adv.—additionally): Let's discuss the issue *further*.

sure (adj.—certain): She is *sure* of her decision.

surely (adv.—undoubtedly): He will *surely* be victorious.

later (adv.—after expected time): The contract arrived *later* in the day.

latter (adj.—the second of two things): Of the two options, I prefer the *latter*.

fewer (adj.—refers to numbers): *Fewer* requests for tours were granted this year.

less (adj.—refers to amounts or quantities): *Less* time remains than we anticipated.

SPOT THE BLOOPER

Under a photograph in *Science* magazine: "Museum staffer Ed Rodley checks out 65 million year-old eggs."

STUDY TIP

To determine whether successive adjectives are independent, mentally insert the word *and* between them. If the insertion makes sense, the adjectives are probably independent and require a comma.

SPOT THE BLOOPER

From a radio advertisement for an Internet Service Provider (ISP): "With our Internet service you'll get less annoying pop-up ads."

real (adj.—actual, genuine): The *real* power in the company lies with the board of directors.

really (adv.—actually, truly): Jan is *really* eager to take her vacation.

good (adj.—desirable): A number of *good* plans were submitted.

well { (adv.—satisfactorily): Amy did *well* on her performance evaluation.
{ (adj.—healthy): Jamal feels *well* enough to return to work.

Now complete the reinforcement exercises for Level 2.

LEVEL 3

OTHER USES OF ADJECTIVES AND ADVERBS

In this section you will learn how to use absolute modifiers, how to make comparisons within a group, and how to place adjectives and adverbs appropriately in sentences.

ABSOLUTE MODIFIERS

Adjectives and adverbs that name perfect or complete (absolute) qualities cannot logically be compared. For example, to say that one ball is more *round* than another ball is illogical. Here are some absolute words that should not be used in comparisons.

round	dead	complete
perfect	true	right
unique	correct	straight
perpendicular	endless	unanimous

Authorities suggest, however, that some absolute adjectives may be compared by the use of the words *more nearly* or *most nearly*.

Ron's account of the disagreement was *more nearly accurate* than Sue's version. (Not *more accurate*)

Kris's project is *more nearly complete* than mine. (Not *more complete*)

COMPARISONS WITHIN A GROUP

When the word *than* is used to compare a person, place, or thing with other members of a group to which it belongs, be certain to include the words *other* or *else* in the comparison. This inclusion ensures that the person or thing being compared is separated from the group with which it is compared.

Illogical: Alaska is larger than any state in the United States. (This sentence suggests that Alaska is larger than itself.)

Logical: Alaska is larger than any *other* state in the United States.

Illogical: Our team had better results than any team in the company.

Logical: Our team had better results than any *other* team in the company.

Illogical: Alex works harder than anyone in the office.

Logical: Alex works harder than anyone *else* in the office.

PLACING ADVERBS AND ADJECTIVES

The position of an adverb or adjective can seriously affect the meaning of a sentence. Study these examples.

Only Cathi MacPherson can change the password. (No one else can change it.)

Cathi MacPherson can *only* change the password. (She can't do anything else.)

Cathi MacPherson can change *only* the password. (She can't change anything else.)

To avoid confusion, adverbs and adjectives should be placed close to the words they modify. In this regard, special attention should be given to the words *only, merely, first,* and *last.*

Confusing:	He *merely* said that the report could be improved.
Clear:	He said *merely* that the report could be improved.
Confusing:	Seats in the five *first* rows have been reserved.
Clear:	Seats in the *first* five rows have been reserved.

Now complete the reinforcement exercises for Level 3.

HOTLINE QUERIES

Answered by Dr. Guffey

Question

Answer

Q: Is it necessary to hyphenate a *25 percent* discount?

A: No. Percents are not treated in the same way that numbers appearing in compound adjectives are treated. Thus, you would not hyphenate a *15 percent* loan, but you would hyphenate a *15-year* loan.

Q: Why does the sign above my grocery market's quick-check stand say *Ten or less items*? Shouldn't it read *Ten or fewer items*?

A: Right you are! *Fewer* refers to numbers, as in *fewer items. Less* refers to amounts or quantities, as in *less food*. Perhaps markets prefer *less* because it has fewer letters.

Q: In my writing I want to use *firstly* and *secondly*. Are they acceptable?

A: Both words are acceptable, but most good writers prefer *first* and *second,* because they are more efficient and equally accurate.

Q: How many hyphens should I use in this sentence? *The three, four, and five year plans continue to be funded.*

A: Three hyphens are needed: *three-, four-, and five-year plans*. Hyphenate compound adjectives even when the parts of the compound are separated or suspended

Q: Why can't I remember how to spell *already?* I want to use it in this sentence: *Your account has already been credited with your payment.*

A: You—and many others—have difficulty with *already* because two different words (and meanings) are expressed by essentially the same sounds. The adverb *already* means "previously" or "before this time," as in your sentence. The two-word combination *all ready* means "all prepared," as in *The club members are all ready to board the bus*. If you can logically insert the word *completely* between *all* and *ready,* you know the two-word combination is needed.

Q: I never know how to write *part time*. Is it always hyphenated?

A: The dictionary shows all of its uses to be hyphenated. *She was a part-time employee* (used as an adjective). *He worked part-time* (used as adverb).

Q: Why are these two expressions treated differently: *two-week* vacation and *two weeks'* vacation?

A: Although they express the same idea, they represent two different styles. If you omit the *s*, *two-week* is hyphenated because it is a compound adjective. If you add the *s*, as in *two weeks' vacation,* the expression becomes possessive and requires an apostrophe. Don't use both styles together (not *two-weeks' vacation*).

Q: Here are some expressions that caused us trouble in our business letters. We want to hyphenate all of the following. Right? *Well-produced play, awareness-generation film, decision-making tables, one-paragraph note, swearing-in ceremony, point-by-point analysis, commonly-used book.*

A: All your hyphenated forms are correct except the last one. Don't use a hyphen with an *ly*-ending adverb.

Q: Is this a double negative? *We <u>can't</u> schedule the meeting because we have <u>no</u> room available.*

A: No, this is not regarded as a double negative. In grammar a double negative is created when two negative adverbs modify a verb, such as *can't hardly, won't barely,* or *can't help but.* Avoid such constructions.

11 REINFORCEMENT EXERCISES

Name _____

LEVEL 1

A. (Self-check) Write the correct forms in the spaces provided.

1. This is the (worse, worst) movie I've ever seen. _____

2. The company's profits are (worse, worst) this quarter than last quarter. _____

3. With more (careful, carefuller) planning, this problem could be avoided. _____

4. I can't think of a (better, more better) plan. _____

5. We (can, can't) hardly expect employees to feel good about the layoffs. _____

6. We don't have (nothing, anything) we can offer our guests. _____

7. (This, These) types of computer viruses can be difficult to detect. _____

8. This is the (coldest, most cold) day we've had all year. _____

9. Investing in junk bonds has lost (it's, its, their) appeal. _____

10. The outcome of the race between Connors and Morelli will determine the (faster, fastest) driver. _____

Check your answers below.

B. Write the correct forms in the spaces provided.

1. (This kind, These kinds) of rumors can cause stock prices to plunge. _____

2. Bill Gates is the (more, most) powerful of the software manufacturers. _____

3. Numerous plant workers are considering joining (a, an) union. _____

4. The mortgage company (don't have no, doesn't have any) reason to deny the loan. _____

5. Does (this, these) pair of sunglasses look good on me? _____

6. After paying his taxes, Mark complained that he (has, hasn't) barely a dollar left. _____

7. The biotechnology industry is growing at (a, an) unusually fast pace. _____

8. Susan said she couldn't see (no, any) other way to install the program. _____

9. If you had been (more diligent, diligenter), you would have completed the report on time. _____

10. The company knew that it couldn't give (nothing, anything) to its favorite charity this year. _____

1. worst 2. worse 3. careful 4. better 5. can 6. anything 7. These 8. coldest 9. its 10. faster

Want to explore more? Go to: academic.cengage.com/bcomm/guffey or Xtra!

C. Supply the proper article (*a* or *an*) for the following words.

Example: ___an___ adjustment

1. ____ number
2. ____ honor
3. ____ inventory
4. ____ pattern
5. ____ Hawaiian

6. ____ warehouse
7. ____ agency
8. ____ hour
9. ____ idea
10. ____ utility

11. ____ insult
12. ____ X-ray
13. ____ illegible letter
14. ____ one-year lease
15. ____ eight-year lease

D. In the space provided write the correct comparative or superlative form of the adjective shown in parentheses.

Example: Of the three software packages, which is (good)?   best _____

1. Jordan is the (smart) member of the team.   _____
2. She did (well) on the certification exam than she expected.   _____
3. Please send me the (current) figures you can find.   _____
4. The new accounting software is (easy) to master than the software we were using.   _____
5. I think this meeting room will be (quiet) than the room next door.   _____
6. Of all the employees, Richard is the (little) talkative.   _____
7. Karen Hansen is (businesslike) than the office manager she replaced.   _____
8. Have you ever met a (kind) individual than Lien Phuong Pham?   _____
9. This is the (bad) winter we've had in years.   _____
10. Which is the (interesting) of the two novels?   _____

LEVEL 2

A. **(Self-check)** Write the correct forms in the spaces provided.

1. The airport was (farther, further) away than it appeared on our map.   _____
2. A CEO must be concerned with the (day to day, day-to-day) operations of the organization.   _____
3. We prefer to meet with you (face-to-face, face to face) to finalize the contract.   _____
4. Companies have reported (fewer, less) security breaches this year.   _____
5. Unless sales data can be processed (quicker, more quickly), we will lose business to our competitors.   _____
6. Patricia Franzoia was (real, really) surprised to learn that her boss had resigned.   _____
7. Matthew felt (bad, badly) that he forgot to return your message.   _____
8. Of credit card fraud and auction fraud, the (later, latter) makes up the largest percentage of complaints to the Internet Fraud Compliance Center (IFCC).   _____
9. Some small businesses barely exist from (year-to-year, year to year).   _____
10. Sandra said that she felt (good, well) enough after her surgery to return to work full-time.   _____

Check your answers below.

1. farther 2. day-to-day 3. face to face 4. fewer 5. more quickly 6. really 7. bad 8. latter 9. year to year 10. well

Want to explore more? Go to: academic.cengage.com/bcomm/guffey or Xtra!

B. Write the correct words in the spaces provided.

1. Politicians are finding that blogs work (beautiful, beautifully) for campaigning. _____

2. In an effort to reduce expenses, New Tech will offer employees (fewer, less) benefit options next year. _____

3. Christopher thought that he did (good, well) in his interview. _____

4. Apples and brie cheese taste (good, well) on pizza. _____

5. Global communication has (sure, surely) increased in the last decade. _____

6. Since its tune-up, the engine runs (smoother, more smoothly). _____

7. Lavonda wasn't (real, really) sure she could attend the meeting. _____

8. Please don't take her comments during the meeting (personal, personally). _____

9. Leslie looked (calm, calmly) as she approached the podium. _____

10. Your new suit certainly fits you (good, well). _____

11. The new suit looks very (good, well) on you. _____

12. She wanted to debate the question (further, farther). _____

13. Having prepared for months, we won the bid (easy, easily). _____

14. We had (fewer, less) time to conduct the research than expected. _____

15. Rick feels (sure, surely) that part-time salaries will improve. _____

16. (Most, Almost) everyone agreed that work is the price you pay for money. _____

17. It's wise to keep your résumé (up-to-date, up to date) at all times. _____

18. To reduce legal costs, they pressed for a settlement (quick, quickly). _____

19. Our new ergonomically designed office furniture should keep employees working (comfortable, comfortably). _____

20. Luis feels (good, well) about his presentation to the board. _____

C. Select the correct group of words below. Write its letter in the space provided.

1. a. state of the art technology
   b. state-of-the-art technology _____

2. a. well-documented report
   b. well documented report _____

3. a. child who is ten-years-old
   b. child who is ten years old _____

4. a. ten-year-old child
   b. ten year old child _____

5. a. fully certified nurse
   b. fully-certified nurse _____

6. a. first-class accommodations
   b. first class accommodations _____

7. a. data-processing service
   b. data processing service _____

8. a. strong arm tactics
   b. strong-arm tactics _____

9. a. last-minute preparations
   b. last minute preparations _____

10. a. widely-acclaimed cure
    b. widely acclaimed cure _____

D. Place commas where needed in the following groups of words.

1. yellow sports car

2. honest fair appraisal

3. concise courteous e-mail message

4. snug cheerful apartment

5. imaginative daring designer

6. skilled financial analyst

Want to explore more? Go to: academic.cengage.com/bcomm/guffey or Xtra!

E. Writing Exercise. Compose sentences using the compound adjectives shown. Be sure that the compound adjectives precede nouns.

Example: (up to the minute)

Your up-to-the-minute report arrived today.

1. (three year old)

_____

2. (once in a lifetime)

_____

3. (month by month)

_____

4. (work related)

_____

5. (state of the art)

_____

F. Writing Exercise. Compose sentences using the following words.

1. (farther) _____

_____

2. (latter) _____

_____

3. (fewer) _____

_____

LEVEL 3

A. (Self-check) Underline any errors in the following sentences and write their corrected forms in the spaces provided. If a sentence is correct as it is written, write *C*.

Example: Taylor is the <u>most unique</u> individual I know.   most nearly unique
                                                                                                      _____

1. Of all UPS drivers, Max is the most unique.   _____

2. Professor Anita Musto is the most conscientious teacher I have.   _____

3. She is more conscientious than any teacher I've ever had.   _____

4. We were told to answer the ten last questions.   _____

5. That software company claims to have the most perfect Web browser available.   _____

6. We are concerned only with your welfare and happiness.   _____

7. He merely thought you wanted one page copied.   _____

8. Western mountains are more perpendicular than Eastern mountains.   _____

9. Milan is the most cosmopolitan city in Italy.   _____

10. It is more cosmopolitan than any city in the country.   _____

Check your answers on the next page.

Want to explore more? Go to: academic.cengage.com/bcomm/guffey or Xtra!

B. Underline errors and write corrected forms in the spaces provided. If correct, write *C.*

1. Her three last books have been best-sellers. _____

2. He discovered a straighter route from Tampa to Miami _____

3. Colonel Bauer asserted that the U.S. Army was safer for women than any organization in America. _____

4. Is this the most correct answer among all the applicants' tests? _____

5. I only have one idea for solving the security problem. _____

6. Portland is the largest city in Maine. _____

7. Portland is larger than any city in Maine. _____

8. That version of software is only sold on Symantec's Web site. _____

9. Kinko's offers the most complete office service in town. _____

10. The two first applicants presented excellent résumés. _____

C. Skill Maximizer. The following sentences review Levels 1, 2, and 3. For each sentence underline errors and write a corrected form in the space provided. If a sentence is correct, write *C* in the space.

1. The employees were dismayed to learn about the layoffs in a e-mail message. _____

2. Which of the three advertising campaigns do you like better? _____

3. Sandy said that she couldn't barely hear you on your cell phone. _____

4. Because of excessive costs, designer Donna Karan made less trips to the Far East and Africa in search of "creative inspiration." _____

5. Mr. Wu interviewed a Canadian official and an European diplomat concerning the proposed two-year trade program. _____

6. Their daughter, who is three-years-old, is already reading. _____

7. One applicant felt that he had done good on the skills test. _____

8. I like this job better than any job I've ever had. _____

9. The city council thought that most everyone would vote in favor of protecting the open space. _____

10. Sally Stouder's only task was to make a point by point comparison of the programs. _____

D. Hotline Review. In the space provided write the correct answer choice.

1. If you sign the contract today, we'll give you a _____ discount.
   a. 15 percent   b. 15-percent _____

2. She is looking for a _____ job for the summer.
   a. part time   b. part-time _____

3. Do you prefer a _____ loan?
   a. 24, 36, or 48 month   b. 24-, 36-, or 48-month _____

4. Jeff was _____ to purchase a new car when his loan fell through.
   a. all ready   b. already _____

5. He had _____ selected the model and all of its accessories.
   a. all ready   b. already _____

1. most nearly unique 2. C 3. any other teacher 4. last ten questions 5. most nearly perfect 6. with only 7. you merely wanted or you wanted merely 8. more nearly perpendicular 9. C 10. any other city

Want to explore more? Go to: academic.cengage.com/bcomm/guffey or Xtra!

The following letter contains intentional errors representing language principles covered thus far, spelling, and proofreading. You should mark 30 changes. If one word replaces three, it's considered one change. When you replace a wordy or incorrect phrase with one word, it counts as one correction. When you correct a comma splice, run-on, or fragment, the correction counts as two errors. Count each parenthesis and each dash as a single mark. Use proofreading marks to make the corrections here OR make the corrections at the **Guffey Companion Web Site** at **academic.cengage.com/bcomm/guffey.**

Elite Tropical Cruise Lines

8567 West Broadway Phone: 305-555-5555
Suite 2398 Fax: 305-222-2222
Miami Beach, FL 3313 Website: http://www.elitetropical.com

November 2, 200x

Ms. Jessica Stoudenmire
Holiday Travel Agency
520 West Third Street
New York, NY 10013

Dear Ms. Stoudemire:

At Elite Tropical Cruise Lines, my colleagues and myself genuinely appreciate the loyalty of Holiday Travel Agency and its continuing use of the "Voyager Ship" line for your holiday tour packages for travelers' of all ages. As our customers know, the "Voyager Ship" is more luxurious than any cruise ship in the world, offering the enjoyablest activities on the seas.

A wide range of guests have experienced unforgettable cruises to unique and exotic ports of call. These type of positive experiences have inspired our guests to return year after year. It is our long standing policy to try and offer fun, sun, and exciting tours to these guests, including high school and college students. Recently, however, some of our younger guests has been loud and disruptive. Last year we raised the drinking age from 18 to 21, but this plan didn't work very good. Because of unruly young people, some passengers couldn't barely enjoy their travel aboard our cruise ships.

As a result, we are now instituting a new policy. Effective immediately, any passenger under the age of 21 will be excepted only when accompanied by a adult over 25. If this new policy will effect your student tour packages, we hope you will agree that the reasons behind us instituting this new policy required serious action. Elite Tropicals goal is to provide a real relaxing environment for all its passengers. Promoting family packages are one way in which we help high-school and college students join their family's for vacation fun away from the stresses of every day life.

Expecting carefree fun filled vacations, your customers will not be dissappointed by Elite Tropical. We attract more guests then any cruise line in the world, and 98 percent of our guests reports that they are very satisfied. If you would be willing to work with me to plan new packages for your New York customers. My staff and I will call you during the week of January 5.

Sincerely,

Stephanie Carroll

Stephanie Carroll
Vice President, Customer Service

Want to explore more? Go to: academic.cengage.com/bcomm/guffey or Xtra!

204 | UNIT 4 | CHAPTER 11 | **MODIFIERS: ADJECTIVES AND ADVERBS**

Goal: To locate quotations online.

You will be giving a presentation during an awards ceremony and would like to include inspirational quotations in your introduction and conclusion. You decide to search for relevant, business-related quotations on the Web.

1. With your Web browser on the screen, go to **http://www.quoteland.com.**
2. Click **Quotations by Topic.**
3. Scroll through the list of topics, and click on topics that sound appropriate for a business presentation. Select five quotations that you could include in your presentation, and copy them into a Word document. Be sure to copy both the quotation and the name of the person who is responsible for the quote.
4. To look at another source for quotations, key this URL: **http://www.woopidoo.com.** Click **Research tools;** then click **U.S. and World Newspapers.** Click a topic under **Famous Business Quotes.**
5. Find five more quotations that you like, and copy them into your Word document.
6. End your session and submit your list of quotations.

Underline the correct word.

1. Gelato has (fewer, less) calories than ice cream.

2. It would be (a, an) honor to meet the author.

3. Jason was certain that he had done (good, well) on his CPA exam.

4. Erin completed a (page by page, page-by-page) check of the book.

5. Employees liked their (completely-redecorated, completely redecorated) office.

1. fewer 2. an 3. well 4. page-by-page 5. completely redecorated

Want to explore more? Go to: academic.cengage.com/bcomm/guffey or Xtra!

MODIFIERS: ADJECTIVES AND ADVERBS | **CHAPTER 11** | **205**

© Adrian Peacock/Creatas Images/Jupiter Images

12

PREPOSITIONS

OBJECTIVES

When you have completed the materials in this chapter, you will be able to do the following:

LEVEL 1

- Use objective-case pronouns as objects of prepositions.
- Avoid using prepositions in place of verbs and adverbs.

LEVEL 2

- Use troublesome prepositions correctly.
- Omit unnecessary prepositions, retain necessary ones, and construct formal sentences that avoid terminal prepositions.

LEVEL 3

- Recognize idioms and idiomatic constructions.
- Use idioms involving prepositions correctly.

PRETEST

Underline the correct word.

1. Lydia is frustrated because she receives (to, too) much spam.

2. She felt (as if, like) these spam messages were affecting her productivity.

3. Do you plan (on taking, to take) a two-week vacation?

4. Management and workers alike agreed (to, with) the contract.

5. Please plan to sit (beside, besides) the CEO at the banquet.

Prepositions are connecting words. They show the relationship of a noun or pronoun to another word in a sentence. This chapter reviews the use of objective-case pronouns following prepositions. It also focuses on common problems that communicators have with troublesome prepositions. Finally, it presents many words in our language that require specific prepositions (idiomatic expressions) to sound "right."

COMMON USES OF PREPOSITIONS

In the following list, notice that prepositions may consist of one word or several.

about	below	from	on
according to	beside	in	on account of
after	between	in addition to	over
along with	but	in spite of	to
among	by	into	under
around	during	like	until
at	except	of	upon
before	for	off	with

OBJECTIVE CASE FOLLOWING PREPOSITIONS

As you will recall from Chapter 6, pronouns that are objects of prepositions must be in the objective case.

> We received quotes *from him* and *her* for our June newsletter.
>
> The disagreement is with the distributor, not *with* you and *me*.
>
> Give the account balances *to them*.

Less frequently used prepositions are *like, between, except,* and *but* (meaning "except"). These prepositions may lead to confusion in determining pronoun case. Consider the following examples.

> Just *between you and me*, would you invest in this risky stock? (Not *between you and I*)
>
> Volunteers *like Mr. Sheldon and him* are rare. (Not *like Mr. Sheldon and he*)
>
> Applications from everyone *but them* have arrived. (Not *but they*)

FUNDAMENTAL PROBLEMS WITH PREPOSITIONS

In even the most casual speech or writing, the following misuses of prepositions should be avoided.

Of for *have*
The verb phrases *should have* and *could have* should never be written as *should of* or *could of*. The word *of* is a preposition and cannot be used in verb phrases.

> Juan *should have* called first. (Not *should of*)
>
> I *would have* covered for you if I had been available. (Not *would of*)

Off for *from*
The preposition *from* should never be replaced by *off* or *off of*.

> Marsha borrowed a highlighter *from me*. (Not *off of*)
>
> Shannon said she got the information *from you*. (Not *off* or *off of*)

SPOT THE BLOOPER

From a job applicant's cover letter: "I would be prepared to meet with you at your earliest convenience to discuss what I can do to your company."

SPOT THE BLOOPER

Photo caption in *The Tribune* [Greeley, Colorado]: "West's David Shaw hits the winning shot for he and Tom White."

SPOT THE BLOOPER

From the *Chicago Tribune:* "Sammy Sosa's late arrival at the Cubs' training camp turned into a hug-in between he and manager Don Baylor."

To for *too*

The preposition *to* means "in a direction toward." Do not use the word *to* in place of the adverb *too*, which means "additionally," "also," or "excessively." The word *to* may also be part of an infinitive construction.

> Dividends are not distributed *to* stockholders unless declared by directors. (*To* meaning "in a direction toward")

> Profits were *too* small to declare dividends. (*Too* meaning "excessively")

> Contributions of services will be accepted *too*. (*Too* meaning "also")

> She is learning *to* program in HTML and Java. (*To* as part of the infinitive *to program*)

Now complete the reinforcement exercises for Level 1.

LEVEL 2

TROUBLESOME PREPOSITIONS

Use special caution in regard to the following prepositions.

Among, between

Among means "in or through the midst of" or "surrounded by." It is usually used to speak of three or more persons or things; *between* means "shared by" and is usually used for two persons or things.

> The disagreement was *between* him and his partner.

> Profits were distributed *among* the four partners.

Beside, besides

Beside means "next to"; *besides* means "in addition to."

> The woman sitting *beside* me on the plane was Carly Fiorina, former CEO of Hewlett-Packard.

> *Besides* a résumé, you should bring a list of your references to the interview.

Except

The preposition *except*, meaning "excluding" or "but," is sometimes confused with the verb *accept*, which means "to receive."

> Everyone *except* Melanie and her was able to come.

> Did you *accept* the job offer from CitiGroup?

In, into, in to

In indicates a position or location. *Into* can mean several things, including (1) entering something, (2) changing form, or (3) making contact. Some constructions may employ *in* as an adverb preceding an infinitive:

> The meeting was held *in* the conference room. (Preposition *in* indicates location.)

> I ran *into* Stan on the way to the meeting. (Preposition *into* indicates making contact with someone.)

> They went *in* to see the manager. (Adverb *in* precedes infinitive *to see*.)

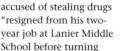

Like

The preposition *like* should be used to introduce a noun or pronoun. Do not use *like* to introduce a clause (a group of words with a subject and a predicate). To introduce clauses, use *as, as if,* or *as though.*

> She looks very much *like* Jennifer Lopez. (*Like* used as a preposition to introduce the object, *Jennifer Lopez.*)
>
> She looks *as if* she is tired. (*As if* used to introduce the clause *she is tired.*)
>
> *As* I said in my e-mail message, the production deadline has changed. (Do not use *like* to introduce the clause *I said in my e-mail message.*)

NECESSARY PREPOSITIONS

Don't omit those prepositions necessary to clarify a relationship. Be particularly careful when two prepositions modify a single object.

> We have every desire *for* and hope *of* an early settlement. (Do not omit *for.*)
>
> What type *of* firewall would you like to install? (Do not omit *of.*)
>
> Don Foster is unsure *of* how to approach the problem. (Do not omit *of.*)
>
> Benefits for exempt employees seem to be higher than *for* nonexempt employees. (Do not omit *for.*)
>
> When did you graduate *from* high school? (Do not omit *from.*)*

UNNECESSARY PREPOSITIONS

Omit unnecessary prepositions.

> Leave the package *inside* the door. (Better than *inside of*)
>
> Both Web sites are useful. (Better than *both of the Web sites*)
>
> Where is the meeting? (Better than *meeting at*)
>
> She could not help laughing. (Better than *help from laughing*)
>
> Keep the paper near the printer. (Better than *near to*)
>
> He met with the new manager at lunch. (Better than *met up with*)

ENDING A SENTENCE WITH A PREPOSITION

In the past, language authorities warned against ending a sentence (or a clause) with a preposition. In formal writing today most careful authors continue to avoid terminal prepositions. In conversation, however, terminal prepositions are acceptable.

Informal:	What organization is he a member *of?*
Formal:	*Of* what organization is he a member?
Informal:	What is this tool used *for?*
Formal:	*For* what is this tool used?
Informal:	We missed the television news program he appeared on.
Formal:	We missed the television news program on which he appeared.
Informal:	When you called, whom did you speak to?
Formal:	When you called, *to* whom did you speak?

Now complete the reinforcement exercises for Level 2.

See the Hotline Query on page 211 regarding the expression "graduating from college."

SPOT THE BLOOPER

Headline in the *Lodi* [California] *News Sentinel:* "College bond looks like it may be close to passage."

SPOT THE BLOOPER

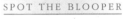

From an Ann Landers column: ". . . [They] might get their eyes opened up."

SPOT THE BLOOPER

From a job applicant's résumé: "Education: Bachelor of engineering. Passed out in top 2 percent."

IDIOMATIC USE OF PREPOSITIONS

Every language has **idioms,** which are word combinations that are peculiar to that language. These combinations have developed through usage and often cannot be explained rationally. A native speaker usually is unaware of idiom usage until a violation jars his or her ear, such as "He is capable *from* (rather than *of*) violence."

The following list shows words that require specific prepositions to denote precise meanings. This group is just a sampling of the large number of English idioms. Consult a dictionary or reference manual when you are unsure of the correct preposition to use with a particular word.

HOT LINK

An excellent place to learn more about prepositions is Capital Community College's site at http://grammar.ccc.commnet.edu/grammar/prepositions.htm.

acquainted with	Are you *acquainted with* the new CEO?
addicted to	Jeremy is *addicted to* surfing the Web.
adept in	Are you *adept in* negotiation tactics?
adhere to	All employees must *adhere to* certain Web-use policies.
agree on (mutual ideas)	Our team members *agree on* nearly everything.
agree to (a proposal)	Did they *agree to* reduced benefits?
agree with (a person)	I *agree with* you on this issue.
all of (when followed by a pronoun)	All *of us* contributed. (For efficiency omit *of* when *all* is followed by a noun, as *All members contributed*.)
angry at (a thing)	Many employees are *angry at* the change in benefits.
angry with (a person)	Are you *angry with* me for being late?
both of (when followed by a pronoun)	Both *of them* were hired. (For efficiency omit *of* when *both* is followed by a noun, as *Both men were hired*.)
buy from	You may *buy from* any one of our approved vendors.
capable of	She is *capable of* remarkable accomplishments.
comply with	We must *comply with* governmental regulations.
conform to	Your products do not *conform to* our specifications.
contrast with	The angles *contrast with* the curves in that logotype.
correspond to (match)	A company's success *corresponds to* its leadership.
correspond with (write)	We *correspond with* our clients regularly.
differ from (things)	Debit cards *differ from* credit cards.
differ with (person)	I *differ with* you in small points only.
different from (not *than*)	This product is *different from* the one I ordered.
disagree with	Do you *disagree with* him?
expert in	Dr. Rand is an *expert in* electronics.
guard against	We must *guard against* complacency.
identical with or to	Our strategy is *identical with* (or *to*) our competitor's.
independent of	Living alone, the young man was *independent of* his parents.

infer from	I *infer from* your remark that you are dissatisfied.
interest in	Matt has a great *interest in* the bond market.
negligent of	Pat was *negligent of* the important duties of his position.
oblivious of or to	He is often *oblivious of* (or *to*) what goes on around him.
plan to (not on)	We *plan to* expand our target market.
prefer to	Do you *prefer to* work a four-day week?
reason with	We tried to *reason with* the unhappy customer.
reconcile with (match)	Checkbook figures must be *reconciled with* bank figures.
reconcile to (accept)	He has never become *reconciled to* retirement.
responsible for	William is *responsible for* locking the building.
retroactive to	The salary increase is *retroactive to* last July 1.
sensitive to	He is unusually *sensitive to* his employees' needs.
similar to	Your proposal topic is *similar to* mine.
standing in (not *on*) line	How long have you been *standing in* line?
talk to (tell something)	The speaker *talked to* the large group.
talk with (exchange remarks)	Let's *talk with* Theresa about our mutual goals.

Now complete the reinforcement exercises for Level 3.

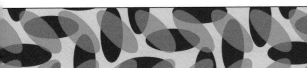

HOTLINE QUERIES

Answered by Dr. Guffey

Question

Q: What's wrong with saying *Lisa graduated college last year?*

Q: I have a sentence that begins *Beside(s) providing financial aid . . . .* Is there any real difference between *beside* and *besides?*

Q: I'm writing a sentence that reads *Please proceed to the podium . . . .* Is this correct, or should I use *precede* instead of *proceed?*

Answer

A: The preposition *from* must be inserted for syntactical fluency. Two constructions are permissible: *Lisa graduated from college* or *Lisa was graduated from college.* The first version is more popular; the second is preferred by traditional grammarians.

A: Yes, indeed! *Beside* is a preposition meaning "by the side of" (*come sit beside me*). *Besides* is an adverb meaning "in addition to" (*besides paper we must order cartridges*). In your sentence use *besides.*

A: You're correct to use *proceed*, which means "to go forward or continue," in this sentence. The word *precede* means "to go before" (*A discussion will precede the final vote*).

Q: I was always taught that you should never end a sentence with a preposition. But sometimes following this rule sounds so stuffy and unnatural, such as saying *From where are you?* instead of *Where are you from?* Is it ever acceptable to end a sentence with a preposition?

A: In the past, language authorities warned against ending a sentence (or a clause) with a preposition. In formal writing today most careful authors continue to avoid terminal prepositions. In conversation and informal writing, however, terminal prepositions are acceptable.

Q: Can you tell me what sounds strange in this sentence and why? *The building looks like it was redesigned.*

A: The word *like* should not be used as a conjunction, as has been done in our sentence. Substitute *as if* (*the building looks as if it was redesigned*).

Q: Should *sometime* be one or two words in the following sentence? *Can you come over (some time) soon?*

A: In this sentence you should use the one-word form. *Sometime* means "an indefinite time" (*the convention is sometime in December*). The two-word combination means "a period of time" (*we have some time to spare*).

Q: I saw this printed recently: *Some of the personal functions being reviewed are job descriptions, job specifications, and job evaluations.* Is *personal* used correctly here?

A: Indeed not! The word *personal* means "private" or "individual" (*your personal letters are being forwarded to you*). The word *personnel* refers to employees (*all company personnel are cordially invited*). The sentence you quote requires *personnel*.

Q: Is there any difference between *proved* and *proven?*

A: As a past participle, the verb form *proved* is preferred (*he has proved his point*). However, the word *proven* is preferred as an adjective form (*that company has a proven record*). *Proven* is also commonly used in the expression *not proven*.

Q: How should I write *industry wide?* It's not in my dictionary.

A: A word with the suffix *wide* is usually written solid: *industrywide, nationwide, countrywide, statewide, worldwide.*

LEVEL 1

A. (Self-check) Select the correct word and write it in the space provided.

1. Everyone in the office except (he, him) uses instant messaging regularly. _____

2. Bill Gates (could of, could have) kept his fortune, but he chose to give much of it to a charitable foundation. _____

3. Many believe that Federal Reserve announcements are (to, too) cryptic to understand. _____

4. Everyone received the e-mail announcement but (I, me). _____

5. We were able to get her e-mail address (off of, from) Zachary. _____

6. Will invitations be sent to Jonathan and (her, she)? _____

7. Government, too, has (to, too) consider the effects of inflation. _____

8. Can you borrow a stapler (off of, from) Enrique? _____

9. With more experience Alex (would of, would have) landed the job. _____

10. Let's keep this news between you and (I, me). _____

Check your answers below.

B. Underline any errors you find in the following sentences. Write the correct forms in the spaces provided. Write *C* if the sentence is correct as written.

Example: Performers like Hayley and <u>she</u> are crowd pleasers. her

1. Everyone on the train except <u>she</u> was talking on a cell phone. _____

2. Vincent Donofino <u>could of</u> been the one who called. _____

3. I'm going to try to get the price quote <u>off of</u> Richard. _____

4. You should make an appointment with Dr. Rosen or <u>she</u>. _____

5. Our union said that management's offer was "too little and <u>to</u> late." _____

6. Diana Abernathy told Andrew and me that we should have read the directions more carefully. _____

7. It's <u>to</u> soon to tell whether voice recognition will become standard. _____

8. CEO Christine Gerbig spoke with the marketing manager and I about sales. _____

Want to explore more? Go to: academic.cengage.com/bcomm/guffey or Xtra!

PREPOSITIONS I **CHAPTER 12** I **213**

9. Just between you and I, the difference between a job and a career is the difference between 40 and 60 hours a week. _____

10. You should of attended the sales training session last week. _____

11. Our manager, together with Tanya and he, helped to close the sale. _____

12. Last year we tried to order supplies off of them too. _____

13. You can always rely on coworkers like Michelle and she when you need extra help to meet a deadline. _____

14. Everyone except him and I received the announcement too late to respond. _____

15. To address the letter properly, you must use information off of their stationery. _____

LEVEL 2

A. (Self-check) Select the correct word(s).

1. The net profits will be divided (between, among) the three partners. _____

2. Web 2.0 technology is making its way (in, into) corporate offices. _____

3. We engrave identification serial numbers (inside, inside of) all new equipment. _____

4. The office suite (besides, beside) ours has been vacant for months. _____

5. It looks (like, as if) our firm will get the government contract. _____

6. Have you decided whether you will (except, accept) the position? _____

7. Despite his salary and new title, Tony feels (like, as) a technician. _____

8. Differences (between, among) the two brothers affected their management styles. _____

9. When the door was opened, the contracts blew (off, off of) the desk. _____

10. In her job search, Marcia used many resources (beside, besides) the Web. _____

Check your answers below.

B. In the following sentences, cross out unnecessary prepositions and insert necessary ones.

Examples: What type network security is needed?
               ^of

               Where are you going to?

1. Where should I send the check to?

2. A new café is opening opposite to the park.

3. Special printing jobs must be done outside of the office.

4. Charles had great respect and interest in the stock market.

5. Who can tell me where the meeting is scheduled at?

6. What style clothes is recommended for the formal dinner?

7. Leah couldn't help from laughing when Noah spilled his latte as he walked into the conference room.

Want to explore more? Go to: academic.cengage.com/bcomm/guffey or Xtra!

8. Where shall we move the extra desks and chairs to?

9. Lee Montgomery graduated college with a degree in graphic design.

10. What type smart card does Sun Microsystems manufacture?

11. Please write up her performance appraisal quickly.

12. Our appreciation and interest in the program remain strong.

C. Select the correct word(s).

1. Relief funds were divided (among, between) all hurricane victims. _____

2. (As, Like) we mentioned yesterday, Friday will be a half day. _____

3. The new research specialist will move into the office (beside, besides) mine. _____

4. He ran (in, into) an old college buddy at the airport. _____

5. Your laptop computer looks just (like, as) mine. _____

6. The advertising campaign looks (like, as if) it will be quite successful. _____

7. Has anyone been (in to, into) see me this morning? _____

8. You're going to have to (accept, except) the changes. _____

9. Employees are required to turn expense reports (in to, into) their supervisors within one week. _____

10. If he (accepts, excepts) the position, he will have to move to Boise, Idaho. _____

11. (Beside, Besides) Randy Marks and Nan Goodman, whom have you invited? _____

12. It looks (like, as if) Dr. Helen Grattan will be the next CEO. _____

D. **Writing Exercise.** The following sentences have prepositions that end clauses. Rewrite the sentences so that the prepositions precede their objects.

Example: Here is the information you asked about.

Here is the information about which you asked. _____

1. Whom did you send payment to?

_____

2. Please locate the file you put the contract in.

_____

3. What did I come into this room for?

_____

4. We have a number of loyal members we can rely upon.

_____

5. What company did you purchase these supplies from?

_____

Want to explore more? Go to: academic.cengage.com/bcomm/guffey or Xtra!

PREPOSITIONS | CHAPTER 12 | 215

LEVEL 3

A. (Self-check) Underline any errors in the use of prepositions in the following sentences, and write the correct form in the space provided. Write *C* if the sentence is correct as written.

1. Al Fernandez is exceptionally <u>adept with</u> troubleshooting. _____

2. Public companies must <u>comply to</u> Sarbanes-Oxley requirements. _____

3. In a televised address, the president will <u>talk with</u> the nation at 6 p.m. _____

4. How long do you <u>plan on staying</u> at the conference? _____

5. His management philosophy is quite <u>different than</u> mine. _____

6. Are you <u>angry at</u> me for disagreeing with you during the meeting? _____

7. How can one reconcile this new business venture with their recent bankruptcy? _____

8. Jordan is an <u>expert at</u> bioengineering. _____

9. Your work ethic is <u>similar with</u> mine. _____

10. Because she was <u>negligent to</u> her duties, she received a poor performance review. _____

Check your answers below.

B. Underline any errors in the use of prepositions in the following sentences, and write a correction in the space provided. Write *C* if the sentence is correct as written.

1. How does common stock <u>differ with</u> preferred stock? _____

2. It was a pleasure <u>talking to</u> you yesterday during the interview. _____

3. The company <u>plans on developing</u> a new interactive Web site. _____

4. Customers were upset after standing <u>on line</u> for an hour. _____

5. Have you become <u>acquainted to</u> the new intern yet? _____

6. That film is much <u>different than</u> what I expected. _____

7. All procedures must <u>adhere with</u> the company manual. _____

8. The light background on the Web page <u>contrasts to</u> the font color. _____

9. Do you hire an interpreter when your company <u>corresponds to</u> Chinese customers? _____

10. A firewall will help guard against unauthorized access to our intranet. _____

C. Writing Exercise. Write complete sentences using the expressions shown in parentheses.

1. (oblivious to) _____

2. (reconcile with) _____

3. (retroactive to) _____

4. (independent of) _____

5. (differs from) _____

1. adept in 2. comply with 3. talk to 4. plan to stay 5. different from 6. angry with 7. C 8. expert in 9. similar to 10. negligent of

Want to explore more? Go to: academic.cengage.com/bcomm/guffey or Xtra!

216 | UNIT 4 | CHAPTER 12 | PREPOSITIONS

D. Hotline Review. In the space provided write the correct answer choice.

1. Josh said that he hopes to _____ college within two years.
   a. graduate   b. graduate from   _____

2. Diandra will take her vacation _____ in August.
   a. some time   b. sometime   _____

3. All _____ matters are now handled by our Human Resources Department.
   a. personal   b. personnel   _____

4. If you have _____ to spare on Saturday, please drop by to help us.
   a. some time   b. sometime   _____

5. Employees are not allowed to send _____ e-mail messages during work hours.
   a. personal   b. personnel   _____

6. New _____ standards should make it easier to distribute our products internationally.
   a. industry wide   b. industrywide   c. industry-wide   _____

Want to explore more? Go to: academic.cengage.com/bcomm/guffey or Xtra!

The following memo contains intentional errors representing spelling, proofreading, and language principles covered thus far. You should mark 30 changes. When you replace a wordy or incorrect phrase with one word, it counts as one correction. When you correct a comma splice, run-on, or fragment, the correction counts as two errors. Count each parenthesis and each dash as a single mark. Use proofreading marks to make the corrections here OR make the corrections at the **Guffey Companion Web Site** at **academic.cengage.com/bcomm/guffey.**

HIGH TECH SOLUTIONS
INTEROFFICE MEMO

DATE: July 1, 200x
TO: All Employees
FROM: Craig Abrams, Human Resources   *CA*
SUBJECT: New E-Mail and Web Policy

Over the past few month's, supervisors have provided datum about e-mail and Web use to top management and I. Beside using e-mail and the Web for work related purposes, some employees are useing these tools for personal bussiness. This, of course, is having serious implications for our company and its productivity. Improper use can also led to larger problems such as lawsuits. We have, therefore, hired two attornies who is expert at writing e-mail and Web policies to help write a policy for our firm. We plan on implementing the policy on September 1.

During the month of August, workshops will be given by my staff and I to help employees learn how to comply to the new policy. You can also schedule an appointment with your immediate supervisor to talk to them about the new policy. In addition, you can turn any comments or suggestions into me before September 1. Finally, you can obtain a rough draft of the policy off of my receptionist after July 31. She can also let you know where training sessions will be held at.

I think we can all understand that to much personnel e-mail and Web use can negatively effect our company. Thats why this policy is needed, and we are confident that you will all except it's provisions. The policy we develop will be similar with policies used by other company's in our industry. As we develop the policy, we will remain sensitive of the needs of all employees to make sure that the policy is something to which everyone can agree. If you have an interest and a desire to assist us with this important task, please contact my assistant or I at Ext. 452 before August 15.

Want to explore more? Go to: academic.cengage.com/bcomm/guffey or Xtra!

218 | UNIT 4 | CHAPTER 12 | PREPOSITIONS

Goal: To learn about weblogs (blogs).

Your company is thinking about using blogs for research purposes, and you want to learn more about this communication tool.

1. With your Web browser on the screen, go to **http://en.wikipedia.org/wiki/Blog.**
2. Read the Wikipedia article to learn what blogs are, their history, types of blogs, and how blogs are used. Take notes on any interesting fact you learn about blogs.
3. Now go to *Google Blog Search* at **http://blogsearch.google.com/** to find a blog related to your major, profession, or hobby. Type a relevant search term in the search box and click **Search Blogs.**
4. Once you find a blog that interests you, read some of the most recent entries. List three interesting facts or opinions that you learned from these entries. How do blogs differ from other communication tools you have used?
5. Print one page from the blog.
6. End your session by clicking the **X** in the upper right corner of your browser. Turn in all printed pages and your answers to the questions.

POSTTEST

Underline the correct word.

1. Her presentation is still three minutes (to, <u>too</u>) long
2. It looks (like, <u>as if</u>) we'll be able to avoid layoffs.
3. Is it necessary for all documents to comply (to, <u>with</u>) the new guidelines?
4. Dividends will be distributed (between, <u>among</u>) stockholders.
5. (Beside, <u>Besides</u>) Jeffrey, who is able to work Saturday?

1. too 2. as if 3. with 4. among 5. Besides

Want to explore more? Go to: academic.cengage.com/bcomm/guffey or Xtra!

PREPOSITIONS | **CHAPTER 12** | **219**

© Dynamic Graphics/Creatas Images/Jupiter Images

13

CONJUNCTIONS

OBJECTIVES

When you have completed the materials in this chapter, you will be able to do the following:

LEVEL 1

- Distinguish between simple and compound sentences.
- Punctuate compound sentences using coordinating conjunctions such as *and, or, nor,* and *but*.
- Punctuate compound sentences using conjunctive adverbs such as *therefore, however,* and *consequently*.

LEVEL 2

- Distinguish among phrases, dependent clauses, and independent clauses.
- Punctuate introductory and terminal dependent clauses.
- Punctuate parenthetical, essential, and nonessential dependent clauses.

LEVEL 3

- Recognize correlative conjunctions such as *either . . . or, not only . . . but also,* and *neither . . . nor*.
- Recognize simple, compound, complex, and compound-complex sentences.
- Convert simple sentences into a variety of more complex patterns.

PRETEST

Insert commas and semicolons to punctuate the following sentences correctly.

1. All employees must be able to communicate effectively therefore we evaluate communication skills during employment interviews.

2. Sherilyn said that Travis Garcia who works in our Marketing Department will be leaving next month.

1. effectively; therefore. 2. Garcia, Department. 3. New York City, 4. attachment, 5. b

3. Eleanor Uyeda prefers to remain in New York City but Bonnie Albert is considering the Albany area.

4. When you receive an e-mail attachment be sure to check it for a virus.

Underline the letter of the sentence that is more effective.

5. a. Not only is this wireless service more reliable but it also is cheaper than the other.
   b. This wireless service is not only more reliable but also cheaper than the other.

Conjunctions are connecting words. They may be separated into two major groups: those that join grammatically equal words or word groups and those that join grammatically unequal words or word groups. Recognizing conjunctions and understanding their patterns of usage will, among other things, enable you to use commas and semicolons more appropriately.

COORDINATING CONJUNCTIONS

Coordinating conjunctions connect words, phrases, and clauses of equal grammatical value or rank. The most common coordinating conjunctions are *and, or, but,* and *nor.* Notice in these sentences that coordinating conjunctions join grammatically equal elements.

> The qualities I admire most are *honesty, integrity,* and *reliability.* (Here the word *and* joins equal words.)

> Open your mind *to new challenges* and *to new ideas.* (Here *and* joins equal phrases.)

> *Samantha opens the mail,* but *Antonio delivers it to employees.* (Here *but* joins equal clauses.)

Three other coordinating conjunctions should also be mentioned: *yet, for,* and *so.* The words *yet* and *for* may function as coordinating conjunctions, although they are infrequently used as such.

> We use e-mail extensively, *yet* we still prefer personal contact with our customers.

> The weary traveler was gaunt and ill, *for* his journey had been long and arduous.

The word *so* is sometimes informally used as a coordinating conjunction. In more formal contexts the conjunctive adverbs *therefore* and *consequently* should be substituted for the conjunction *so.* You'll study conjunctive adverbs later in this chapter.

| **Informal:** | The plane leaves at 2:15, *so* you still have time to pack. |
| **Improved:** | The plane leaves at 2:15; *therefore,* you still have time to pack. |

To avoid using *so* as a conjunction, try starting your sentence with *because* or *although.*

| **Informal:** | Cell phone calls in public can be intrusive, so they are banned in some places. |
| **Improved:** | Because cell phone calls in public can be intrusive, they are banned in some places. |

PHRASES AND CLAUSES

A group of related words without a subject and a verb is called a **phrase.** You are already familiar with verb phrases and prepositional phrases. It is not important

HOT LINK

For a colorful look at "A Brief Explanation of Conjunctions," visit this site: **http://www.gsu.edu/ ~wwwesl/egw/bryson.htm.** If the site is not available, search for *conjunctions* with your favorite search tool.

SPOT THE BLOOPER

From a column in *The Miami Herald:* "But the famous are not like you and I."

SPOT THE BLOOPER

From the *Patriot-Ledger* [Quincy, Massachusetts]: "Clemens is able to come off the disabled list Sunday, but tests by Dr. Arthur Pappas led to the conclusion that Clemens' groin is still too weak to pitch in a game."

that you be able to identify the other kinds of phrases (infinitive, gerund, participial), but it is very important that you be able to distinguish phrases from clauses.

The alarm was coming from another part of the building.

      phrase   phrase   phrase

A group of related words including a subject and a verb is a **clause.**

We interviewed three applicants, and we decided to hire Richard Royka.

     clause   clause

Karen is interested in a job in accounting, but she wants to travel also.

     clause   clause

SIMPLE AND COMPOUND SENTENCES

A **simple sentence** has one **independent clause,** that is, a clause that can stand alone. A **compound sentence** has two or more independent clauses.

> Many people are concerned about identity theft. (Simple sentence)

> Our Travel Department planned the sales trip, but some salespeople also made private excursions. (Compound sentence)

PUNCTUATING COMPOUND SENTENCES USING COORDINATING CONJUNCTIONS

When coordinating conjunctions (*and, or, but,* and *nor*) join clauses in compound sentences, a comma generally precedes the conjunction. However, if the sentence is short (up to 12 or 13 total words), the comma may be omitted.

> We can handle our employee payroll internally, *or* we can outsource it to a reputable firm.

> Ship the package by UPS *or* ship it by FedEx. (Clauses are too short to require a comma.)

Place a comma before the coordinating conjunction when an independent clause follows the conjunction.

> The bank will notify you of each transfer, *or* it will send you a monthly statement. (Comma used because *or* joins two independent clauses.)

> Analyze all your possible property risks, *and* protect yourself with adequate liability insurance. (Comma needed to join two independent clauses; the subject of each clause is understood to be *you.*)

Do not use commas when coordinating conjunctions join compound verbs, objects, or phrases.

> The bank will notify you of each transfer or will send you a monthly statement. (No comma needed because *or* joins the compound verbs of a single independent clause.)

> Our CEO said that employees should not have to choose between working overtime *and* spending time with their families. (No comma needed because *and* joins the compound objects of a prepositional phrase.)

> Stockholders are expected to attend the meeting *or* to send their proxies. (No comma needed because *or* joins two infinitive phrases.)

CONJUNCTIVE ADVERBS

Conjunctive adverbs may also be used to connect equal sentence elements. Because conjunctive adverbs are used to effect a transition from one thought to another, and because they may consist of more than one word, they have also been called **transitional expressions.** The most common conjunctive adverbs follow:

accordingly	in fact	on the other hand
consequently	in the meantime	that is
furthermore	moreover	then
hence	nevertheless	therefore
however	on the contrary	thus

In the following compound sentences, observe that conjunctive adverbs join clauses of equal grammatical value. Note that semicolons (*not* commas) are used before conjunctive adverbs that join independent clauses. Commas should immediately follow conjunctive adverbs of two or more syllables. Note also that the word following a semicolon is not capitalized—unless, of course, it is a proper noun.

> Sarah did her best; *nevertheless,* she did not pass her CPA exam the first time.

> Equipment expenditures are great this quarter; *on the other hand,* new equipment will reduce labor costs.

> The growing use of handheld phones in cars endangers safety; thus several communities are giving away free bumper stickers that say "Drive Now, Talk Later."

Generally, no comma is used after one-syllable conjunctive adverbs such as *hence, thus,* and *then* (unless a strong pause is desired).

STUDY TIP

Some authorities call the conjunctive adverb a "conjunctive joiner." Such a term may help you remember its function.

DISTINGUISHING CONJUNCTIVE ADVERBS FROM PARENTHETICAL ADVERBS

Many words that function as conjunctive adverbs may also serve as parenthetical adverbs. **Parenthetical adverbs,** such as *however, therefore,* and *consequently,* are used to effect transitions from one thought to another. Use semicolons *only* with conjunctive adverbs that join independent clauses. Use commas to set off parenthetical adverbs that interrupt the flow of a sentence.

STUDY TIP

Use a semicolon only when you are joining two complete sentences.

> The Federal Reserve System, *therefore,* is a vital force in maintaining a sound banking system and a stable economy. (Adverb used parenthetically.)

> The Federal Reserve System is a vital force in maintaining a sound banking system; *therefore,* it is instrumental in creating a stable economy. (Conjunctive adverb joins two clauses.)

> We believe, *however,* that cellular phone sales will continue to grow. (Adverb phrase used parenthetically.)

> We agree that cell phones are convenient; *however,* they must be used responsibly. (Conjunctive adverb phrase used to join two clauses.)

Now complete the reinforcement exercises for Level 1.

SUBORDINATING CONJUNCTIONS

To join unequal sentence elements, such as independent and dependent clauses, use **subordinating conjunctions.** A list of the most common subordinating conjunctions follows.

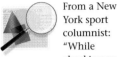
after	because	provided	until
although	before	since	when
as	even though	so that	where
as if	if	that	whether
as though	in order that	unless	while

You should become familiar with this list of conjunctions. But don't feel that you need to recall them from memory. Generally, you can recognize a subordinating conjunction by the way it limits, or subordinates, the clause it introduces. In the clause *because he wants to go to graduate school,* the subordinating conjunction *because* limits the meaning of the clause it introduces. The clause is incomplete and could not stand alone as a sentence.

INDEPENDENT AND DEPENDENT CLAUSES

Main clauses that can stand alone are said to be **independent.** They have subjects and verbs and make sense by themselves. Clauses that cannot stand alone are said to be **dependent.** They have subjects and verbs, but they depend on other clauses for the completion of their meaning. Dependent clauses are often introduced by subordinating conjunctions. Dependent clauses may precede or follow independent clauses.

Dependent clause	Independent clause

When we want a quick reply, we send an e-mail message.

Independent clause	Dependent clause

We send an e-mail message when we want a quick reply.

PUNCTUATION OF SENTENCES WITH DEPENDENT CLAUSES

Business and professional writers are especially concerned with clarity and accuracy. A misplaced or omitted punctuation mark can confuse a reader by altering the meaning of a sentence. The following guidelines for using commas help ensure clarity and consistency in writing. Some professional writers, however, take liberties with accepted conventions of punctuation, particularly in regard to comma usage. These experienced writers may omit a comma when they feel that such an omission will not affect the reader's understanding of a sentence. Beginning writers, though, are well advised to first develop skill in punctuating sentences by following traditional guidelines.

INTRODUCTORY DEPENDENT CLAUSES

Use a comma after a dependent (subordinate) clause that precedes an independent clause.

> *Even though* Philo Farnsworth invented the television in 1927, he was never able to personally introduce it to consumers.

> *Because* President Franklin D. Roosevelt passed a series of securities laws in the 1930s, he helped create the Securities and Exchange Commission (SEC) to enforce them.

Use a comma after an introductory dependent clause even though the subject and verb may not be stated.

> *As* [it is] expected, the opening will be delayed.

> *If* [it is] possible, send a replacement immediately.

> *When* [they are] printed, your brochures will be distributed.

TERMINAL DEPENDENT CLAUSES

Generally, a dependent clause introduced by a subordinating conjunction does not require a comma when the dependent clause is **terminal,** meaning that it falls at the end of a sentence.

> We must complete our research *before* we write the report.

> We cannot continue *until* he returns.

If, however, the dependent clause at the end of a sentence interrupts the flow of the sentence, provides nonessential information, or sounds as if it were an afterthought, a comma should be used.

> I am sure I paid the bill, *although* I cannot find my receipt. (Dependent clause adds unnecessary information.)

> We will ship the goods within the week, *if* that is satisfactory with you. (Dependent clause adds unnecessary information.)

PARENTHETICAL CLAUSES

A **parenthetical clause** adds additional information to a sentence. Within sentences, dependent parenthetical clauses that interrupt the flow and are unnecessary for the grammatical completeness of the sentence are set off by commas.

> The motion, *unless* you want further discussion, will be tabled until our next meeting.

> At our next meeting, *provided* we have a quorum, the motion will be reconsidered.

RELATIVE CLAUSES

The **relative pronouns** *who, whom, whose, which,* and *that* actually function as conjunctions when they introduce dependent clauses. *Who* is used to refer to persons. It may introduce essential (restrictive) or nonessential (nonrestrictive) clauses. *That* refers to animals or things and should be used to introduce essential clauses. *Which* refers to animals or things and introduces nonessential clauses. The tricky part is deciding whether a clause is essential or nonessential. In some cases, only the writer knows whether a clause is intended to be essential or nonessential.

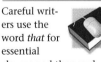

An **essential clause** is needed to identify the noun to which it refers; therefore, no commas should separate this clause from its antecedent.

> Any employee *who wants an August vacation* must apply soon. (The relative pronoun *who* refers to a person, and it introduces an essential clause. The dependent clause is essential because it is needed to identify which employees must apply soon. No commas are needed.)

> A company *that* (not *who* or *which*) values its employees is likely to succeed. (The relative pronoun *that* introduces an essential clause. The dependent clause is essential because it is needed to identify which company is likely to succeed. No commas are needed.)

A **nonessential clause** contains information that the reader does not need to know; the main clause is understandable without this extra information. If the clause is nonessential, it should be set off from the rest of the sentence by commas. Notice that *two* commas are used to set off internal nonessential dependent clauses.

> Software giant Microsoft, *which* is headquartered in Redmond, has many other offices in the state of Washington. (The relative pronoun *which* introduces a nonessential clause and is set off by commas. The antecedent of the dependent clause, *Microsoft*, is clearly identified)

> Jamie Langelier, *who* has excellent recommendations, is applying for a position in our department. (The relative pronoun *who* introduces a nonessential clause and is set off by commas. The antecedent of the dependent clause, *Jamie Langelier,* is clearly identified.)

PUNCTUATION REVIEW

The following three common sentence patterns are very important for you to study and understand. Notice particularly how they are punctuated.

Independent clause (,) + { and / or / nor / but } + Independent clause.   (Comma used when a coordinating conjunction joins independent clauses.)

Independent clause (;) + { therefore, / consequently, / however, / nevertheless, } + Independent clause.   (Semicolon used when a conjunctive adverb joins independent clauses.)

{ Since / If / As / When } Dependent clause (,) + Independent clause.   (Comma used after a dependent clause introduced by a subordinate conjunction.)

Now complete the reinforcement exercises for Level 2.

CORRELATIVE CONJUNCTIONS

Correlative conjunctions, like coordinating conjunctions and conjunctive adverbs, join grammatically equal sentence elements. Correlative conjunctions are always paired: *both . . . and, not only . . . but (also), either . . . or,* and *neither . . . nor.* When greater emphasis is desired, these paired conjunctions are used instead of coordinating conjunctions.

> Your best chances for advancement are in the marketing department *or* in the sales department.

> Your best chances for advancement are *either* in the marketing department *or* in the sales department. (More emphatic)

In using correlative conjunctions, place them so that the words, phrases, or clauses being joined are parallel in construction.

Not Parallel:	*Either* Molly was flying to Chicago *or* to Peoria.
Parallel:	Molly was flying *either* to Chicago *or* to Peoria.
Not Parallel:	She was *not only* talented, *but* she was *also* intelligent.
Parallel:	She was *not only* talented *but also* intelligent.
Not Parallel:	I *neither* have the time *nor* the energy for this.
Parallel:	I have *neither* the time *nor* the energy for this.

SENTENCE VARIETY

To make messages more interesting, good writers strive for variety in sentence structure. Notice the monotony and choppiness of a paragraph made up entirely of simple sentences:

> Leila Peters founded a dessert business in 2001. She specialized in molded containers made of French chocolate. Her 350 designs were unique. She copyrighted them. Another chocolatier copied her spiral chocolate seashell. Leila sued. She won.

Compare the following version of this paragraph, which uses dependent clauses and other structures to achieve greater sentence variety:

> Leila Peters, who founded a dessert business in 2001, specialized in molded containers made of French chocolate. Because her 350 designs were unique, she copyrighted them. When another chocolatier copied her spiral chocolate seashell, Leila sued and won.

Recognizing the kinds of sentence structures available to writers and speakers is an important step in achieving effective expression. Let's review the three kinds of sentence structures that you have been studying and include a fourth category as well.

SPOT THE BLOOPER

From an article in *The Press* [Atlantic City] about Tom Cruise's appearance on the *Today* show: "Next time, instead of jumping on a couch, Cruise should consider laying on one."

Kind of Sentence	Minimum Requirement	Example
Simple	One independent clause	Leila Peters founded a dessert business in 2001.
Compound	Two independent clauses	Leila founded a dessert business in 2001, and she specialized in molded containers of French chocolate.
Complex	One independent clause and one dependent clause	Leila Peters, who founded a dessert business in 1995, specialized in molded containers of French chocolate.
Compound-complex	Two independent clauses and one dependent clause	Leila's chocolate designs were copyrighted; therefore, when another chocolatier copied one, she sued and won.

Developing the ability to use a variety of sentence structures to facilitate effective communication takes practice and writing experience.

Now complete the reinforcement exercises for Level 3.

HOTLINE QUERIES

Answered by Dr. Guffey

Question

Answer

Q: A friend of mine gets upset when I say something like, *I was so surprised by her remark.* She thinks I'm misusing *so.* Am I?

A: Your friend is right, if we're talking about formal expression. The intensifier *so* requires a clause to complete its meaning. For example, *I was so surprised by her remark that I immediately protested.* It's like waiting for the other shoe to drop when one hears *so* as a modifier without a qualifying clause. *He was so funny.* So funny that what? *He was so funny that he became a stand-up comedian.*

Q: My English-teacher aunt says that I should say, *My cell phone is not so clear as yours* instead of *My cell phone is not as clear as yours.* Is she right?

A: As a matter of style in negative comparisons, some people prefer to use *not so . . . as.* However, it is just as acceptable to say *not as . . . as.* (For example, *Price is not as (or so) important as location.*

Q: I don't think I'll ever be able to know the difference between *that* and *which.* They sound alike to me. Any advice for keeping them straight?

A: The problem usually is the substitution of *which* for *that.* Whenever you're tempted to use *which,* remember that it requires a comma. Think *which + comma.* If the sentence doesn't sound right with a comma, then you know you need *that.* One eminent language specialist, William Strunk, advised careful writers to go *which*-hunting and remove all defining *whiches.* Examples: *The contract that we sent in June was just returned* (defines which one). *The Wilson contract, which we sent in June, was just returned* (adds a fact about the only contract in question).

Q: Can the word *that* be omitted from sentences? For example, *She said [that] she would come.*

A: The relative pronoun *that* is frequently omitted in conversation and casual writing. For absolute clarity, however, skilled writers include it.

Q: Does *Ms.* have a period after it? Should I use this title for all women in business today?

A: *Ms.* is probably a blend of *Miss* and *Mrs.* It is written with a period following it. Some women in business prefer to use *Ms.,* presumably because it is a title equal to *Mr.* Neither title reveals one's marital status. Many other women, however, prefer to use *Miss* or *Mrs.* as a title. It's always wise, if possible, to determine the preference of the individual.

Q: Another employee and I are collaborating on a report. I wanted to write this: *Money was lost due to poor attendance.* She says the sentence should read: *Money was lost because of poor attendance.* My version is more concise. Which of us is right?

A: Most language authorities agree with your coauthor. *Due to* is acceptable when it introduces an adjective phrase, as in *Success was due to proper timing.* In this sense, *due to* is synonymous with *attributable to.* However, *because of* should introduce adverbial phrases and should modify verbs: *Money was lost because of poor attendance. Because of* modifies the verb phrase *was lost.*

Q: I'm not sure which word to use in this sentence: *They have used all (they're, their, there) resources in combating the disease.*

A: Use *their,* which is the possessive form of *they.* The adverb *there* means "at that place" or "at that point" (*we have been there before*). *There* is also used as an expletive or filler preceding a linking verb (*there are numerous explanations*). *They're* is a contraction of *they* and *are* (*they're coming this afternoon*).

Q: Can you help me with the words *averse* and *adverse?* I've never been able to straighten them out in my mind.

A: *Averse* is an adjective meaning "disinclined" and generally is used with the preposition *to* (*The little boy was averse to bathing*). *Adverse* is also an adjective, but it means "hostile" or "unfavorable" (*Adverse economic conditions halted the company's growth*). In distinguishing between these two similar words, it might help you to know that the word *averse* is usually used to describe animate (living) objects.

Q: Should *reevaluate* be hyphenated?

A: No. It is not necessary to use a hyphen after the prefix *re* unless the resulting word may be confused with another word (*to re-mark the sales ticket, to re-cover the chair*).

LEVEL 1

A. (Self-check) Select *a, b,* or *c* to identify the following sentences.

a. A comma correctly punctuates a compound sentence.

b. The sentence is not compound; thus the comma should be omitted.

c. Although the sentence is compound, the clauses are too short to require a comma.

Example: In 1913 the U.S. government created the Federal Reserve, and Henry Ford introduced the assembly line.

a

1. Glide Memorial Church will auction off a lunch with Warren Buffett, and bidding will start at $25,000.

2. A New York restaurant received so many complaints about cell phone users that it set up a cell phone lounge, and banished their use elsewhere.

3. E-mail your resume, or fax it.

4. Listen well, and look carefully.

5. Albert Einstein was four years old before he could speak, and seven years old before he could read.

In the following sentences, insert commas and semicolons. In the space provided, indicate the number of punctuation marks you added. Be prepared to explain your choices.

Example: Too many staff members missed the seminar$_\wedge$therefore$_\wedge$future attendance will be mandatory.

2

6. Mother Teresa was best known for her work in Calcutta however she also founded facilities for the poor in the United States.

7. Karla read that the best time to ask for a raise is at 9 a.m. or 1 p.m. midweek thus she made an appointment to see her boss.

8. She was disappointed however when he was unavailable until Friday.

9. Ozana Costellano appears to be best qualified on the other hand Shanell Alexander has excellent recommendations.

10. We were late for the meeting thus we did not hear the introductions.

Check your answers below.

1. a 2. b 3. c 4. c 5. b 6. (2) Calcutta; however, 7. (1) midweek; 8. (2) disappointed, however, 9. (2) qualified; on the other hand, 10. (1) meeting;

Want to explore more? Go to: academic.cengage.com/bcomm/guffey or Xtra!

CONJUNCTIONS | CHAPTER 13 | **231**

B. A simple sentence has one independent clause. A compound sentence has two or more independent clauses. Indicate with a check mark whether the following sentences, all of which are punctuated correctly, are simple or compound. **Hint:** A sentence is not compound unless the words preceding and following a conjunction form independent clauses. If these groups of words could not stand alone as sentences, the sentence is not compound.

	Simple	Compound
1. Sharon Forrester conducted research on blogs and shared her findings with other department members.	_____	_____
2. Sharon Forrester conducted research on blogs, and she shared her findings with other department members.	_____	_____
3. Management trainees are sent to all our branch offices in this country and to some of the branch offices in South America and Europe.	_____	_____
4. Fill in all answer blanks on the application, and send the completed form to the human resources director.	_____	_____
5. The best companies embrace their mistakes and learn from them.	_____	_____

C. Insert commas and semicolons where appropriate in the following sentences. Then, in the space provided, indicate the number of punctuation marks you have added for each sentence. If no punctuation mark is needed, write *0*. Be prepared to explain your choices.

Example: Kevin came to work on Monday, but he was absent on Tuesday.   1 _____

Example: Some loans must be secured; therefore, the borrower must supply collateral.   2 _____

1. Some employees think their e-mail should be confidential but courts generally uphold an employer's right to monitor messages. _____

2. Women are outpacing men on college campuses and now earn the majority of diplomas in fields once dominated by men. _____

3. Periods of stock market growth are called *bull markets* and periods of stock market decline are known as *bear markets*. _____

4. Please copy this contract and fax it immediately. _____

5. The best time to ask for a raise is at 9 a.m. in the middle of the work week or at 1 p.m. after your boss has had lunch. _____

6. Many people fear becoming victims of identity theft however identity theft rarely results in actual financial loss for consumers. _____

7. Microwave relay stations have reduced telephone costs moreover cable and satellite circuits reduce costs even more. _____

8. Our company is faced nevertheless with unusually expensive communication costs. _____

9. Click fraud has become a huge problem thus many companies are no longer advertising on Web sites such as Google. _____

10. The Equal Pay for Equal Work Act was passed in 1963 consequently women's wages became more equitable. _____

Want to explore more? Go to: academic.cengage.com/bcomm/guffey or Xtra!

D. Write sentences using the conjunctions shown below. Be sure to punctuate each sentence correctly.

1. (*consequently* as a conjunctive adverb) _____

_____

2. (*consequently* as a parenthetical adverb) _____

_____

3. (*but* as a coordinating conjunction) _____

_____

4. (*nevertheless* as a conjunctive adverb) _____

_____

5. (*nevertheless* as a parenthetical adverb) _____

_____

LEVEL 2

A. **(Self-check)** Indicate whether the following word groups are phrases (*P*), independent clauses (*I*), or dependent clauses (*D*). (Remember that phrases do not have both subjects and verbs.)

Example: in the spring of this year   P _____

1. when you account for cultural differences   _____
2. Microsoft and Google approved of the new Internet regulations   _____
3. recently they acquired an option to purchase the property   _____
4. before anyone had an opportunity to examine it carefully   _____
5. during the middle of the four-year fiscal period from 2005 through 2009   _____

Where appropriate, insert commas in the following sentences. In the space provided after each sentence, indicate the number of commas you have added to that sentence. Do not add any commas that you cannot justify.

Example: Before we make the investment, we want to do some research.   1 _____

6. Proctor and Gamble which made a fortune with Ivory soap discovered the
formula by accident.   _____
7. As predicted interest rates will climb during any period of inflation.   _____
8. A magazine that features the 100 best places to work is now on the newsstands. _____
9. Tiffany English who was the top salesperson in the country received a
Porsche convertible as a bonus.   _____
10. Any salesperson who sells more than the weekly quota will receive a bonus. _____

Check your answers below.

1. D 2. I 3. I 4. D 5. P 6. (2) Gamble, soap, 7. (1) predicted, 8. (0) 9. (2) English, country, 10. (0)

Want to explore more? Go to: academic.cengage.com/bcomm/guffey or Xtra!

B. Indicate whether the following word groups are phrases (*P*), independent clauses (*I*), or dependent clauses (*D*). For the clauses, underline the subjects once and the verbs twice.

> **Example:** until we are able to assess the damage   D _____

1. as you prepare for a behavioral employment interview   _____

2. on the first page of the Web site   _____

3. many businesses sell services rather than products   _____

4. after she complimented Gregorio Morales's work   _____

5. during the final briefing last week   _____

C. After each sentence write the correct word in the space provided. Remember that the relative pronoun *which* should be used only to introduce nonessential clauses and, as such, requires commas.

1. The city council needs to come up with a plan (which, that) will satisfy all residents.   _____

2. Are you the one (who, that, which) handles employee grievances?   _____

3. The IRS, (who, that, which) audits only 2 percent of all income tax returns, is choked with paperwork.   _____

4. Amazon.com is known as an organization (who, that, which) emphasizes innovation and customer service.   _____

5. Employers are looking for workers (who, that, which) have good vocabularies, grammar, and manners.   _____

D. Sort this group of words into three lists and write them below: *and, however, if, but, moreover, although, nor, because, consequently, or, thus, since.*

Coordinating Conjunctions	Conjunctive Adverbs	Subordinating Conjunctions
_____	_____	_____
_____	_____	_____
_____	_____	_____
_____	_____	_____

E. Where appropriate, insert commas in the following sentences. In the space provided after each sentence, indicate the number of commas that you added. Be prepared to discuss the reasons for the commas you use.

1. Philip Knight who was the cofounder and former CEO of Nike was tattooed with the company's "swoosh" logo.   _____

2. If you have any further budget questions please e-mail them to Kris Bertrand.   _____

3. We were notified that the computer server would be down for six hours although we were not told why.   _____

4. When completed the newly created Web site will enable customers to track shipments.   _____

5. The warranty that you refer to in your recent letter covers only merchandise brought to our shop for repair.   _____

Want to explore more? Go to: academic.cengage.com/bcomm/guffey or Xtra!

6. John Halamka who serves as Harvard Medical School's chief information officer was among the first to have a radio-frequency chip put into his arm to help doctors locate his medical records in an emergency. _____

7. A secretary who joined our staff only two months ago received this month's merit award. _____

8. Zone Improvement Program codes which are better known as zip codes are designed to expedite the sorting and delivery of mail. _____

9. The Senate will surely when it convenes in its regular session discuss defense spending. _____

10. Marketers who develop advertising targeted at heavy users are attempting to build brand loyalty. _____

F. **Writing Exercise.** Use your imagination to write the following complete sentences. Remember that clauses must contain subjects and verbs.

1. A sentence using *and* to connect two independent clauses. _____

_____

2. A sentence using *but* to connect two independent clauses. _____

_____

3. A sentence using *because* to introduce a dependent clause. _____

_____

4. A sentence using *although* to introduce a dependent clause. _____

_____

5. A sentence using *after* to introduce a dependent clause. _____

_____

LEVEL 3

A. **(Self-check)** Select the more effective version of each of the following pairs of sentences. Write its letter in the space provided.

1. a. Either she will go to veterinary school or to medical school.
   b. She will go either to veterinary school or to medical school. _____

2. a. Lisa Gores is not available to conduct the meeting, and neither is James O'Malley
   b. Neither Lisa Gores nor James O'Malley is available to conduct the meeting. _____

3. a. Our objectives are both to improve customer relations and to increase sales.
   b. Our objectives are both to improve customer relations and increasing sales. _____

4. a. Cheryl needed more time for her studies, so she asked for a part-time assignment.
   b. Because Cheryl needed more time for her studies, she asked for a part-time assignment. _____

5. a. The new network is not only faster but also more efficient.
   b. Not only is the new network faster, but it is also more efficient. _____

Want to explore more? Go to: academic.cengage.com/bcomm/guffey or Xtra!

CONJUNCTIONS | CHAPTER 13 | **235**

Indicate the structure of the following sentences by writing the appropriate letter in the spaces provided.

a = simple sentence   c = complex sentence
b = compound sentence d = compound-complex sentence

Example: Because some business owners want to avoid Sarbanes-Oxley requirements, they
are securing funding using creative methods.   c _____

6. Netscape's initial public offering (IPO) in 1995 was the catalyst to the Internet
   stock explosion of the late 1990s.   _____

7. Because the needs of today's luxury travelers are changing, Ritz-Carlton is
   retraining its employees.   _____

8. Virtual worlds are all the rage, and IBM CEO Samuel Palmisano was the first
   corporate CEO to appear in a virtual-world setting.   _____

9. We have no working backup system, and other departments face a similar
   problem.   _____

10. Allen was offered a sales position in Grand Rapids; therefore, he eagerly
    made plans to travel to Michigan, where he looked forward to beginning
    his sales career.   _____

11. We may have to lay off employees unless we can cut costs by 30 percent.   _____

12. U.S. airlines reduced services and cut jobs, but it continued to lose money. _____

13. Although the letter was concise, its message was clear; moreover, it
    promoted goodwill.   _____

14. Laura Cooper, Lynn Seaman, My Bui, and Jane Bennett will be honored.   _____

15. Because pictures are worth a thousand words, your report should include
    photos or graphics.   _____

Check your answers below.

B.   Which of these sentence pairs is more effective?

1. a. Either bankruptcy can be declared by the debtor or it can be requested
      by the creditors.
   b. Bankruptcy can be either declared by the debtor or requested by the
      creditors.   _____

2. a. Our travel counselor will both plan your trip and make your reservations.
   b. Our travel counselor will both plan your trip and reservations will be made. _____

3. a. Either send the proposal to Tracy Orr or to me.
   b. Send the proposal either to Tracy Orr or to me.   _____

4. a. Not only do banks use computers to sort checks, but they also use
      computers for disbursing cash automatically.
   b. Banks use computers not only to sort checks but also to disburse cash
      automatically.   _____

5. a. Neither the employees nor the managers were happy with the proposed
      cutbacks in benefits.
   b. Neither the employees were happy with the proposed cutbacks in benefits,
      and nor were the managers.   _____

1. b 2. b 3. a 4. b 5. a 6. a 7. c 8. b 9. b 10. d 11. c 12. b 13. d 14. a 15. c

Want to explore more? Go to: academic.cengage.com/bcomm/guffey or Xtra!

236 | UNIT 4 | CHAPTER 13 | CONJUNCTIONS

C. Rewrite the following sentences to make them more effective.

1. Either stocks can be purchased online or they can be purchased from a broker.

_____

_____

2. Neither the staff was happy with the proposed cutbacks in class offerings, and nor were the students.

_____

_____

3. Not only does the Small Business Administration (SBA) provide training, but it also guarantees loans.

_____

4. Users of cell phones are often guilty of boorish behavior, so many restaurants and other public places have imposed bans.

_____

_____

_____

5. Old computer hardware creates hazardous dump sites, so computer manufacturers are starting recycling programs.

_____

_____

_____

D. Rewrite the following groups of simple sentences into *one* sentence for each group. Add coordinating conjunctions, conjunctive adverbs, and subordinating conjunctions as needed to create more effective complex, compound, and compound-complex sentences.

Example: Lucent Technologies needed an executive assistant. It advertised online. It finally hired a recent graduate. The graduate had excellent skills.

After advertising for an executive assistant online, Lucent Technologies finally hired a recent graduate who had excellent skills.

1. Rusty was recently hired as a transportation engineer. She will work for Werner Enterprises. Werner Enterprises is located in Omaha, Nebraska.

_____

_____

2. Marlon Lodge is a British linguist and musician. He taught English to German employees of HSBC. He discovered that his students caught on more quickly when he set new vocabulary to music.

_____

_____

_____

Want to explore more? Go to: academic.cengage.com/bcomm/guffey or Xtra!

CONJUNCTIONS | CHAPTER 13 | **237**

3. Cows will respond to beeps. Some Japanese ranchers learned of this phenomenon and equipped their cattle with pagers. Now they herd cattle with beepers. These ranchers need fewer workers as a result.

_____

_____

4. Skilled writers save time for themselves. They also save it for their readers. They organize their ideas into logical patterns. They do this before sitting down at their computers.

_____

_____

5. Nancy Burnett is a single parent. She has merchandising experience. Nancy started a mall-based chain of stores. These stores sell fashionable, durable clothing for children.

_____

_____

E. **Hotline Review.** In the space provided write the correct answer choice.

1. Please wait right over _____ until the interviewer is ready.
   a. their   b. they're   c. there   _____

2. _____ airline tickets will be issued electronically.
   a. Their   b. They're   c. There   _____

3. Because of _____ weather conditions, several airlines had to delay flights.
   a. adverse   b. averse   _____

4. Management is _____ to any decrease in employee health benefits.
   a. adverse   b. averse   _____

5. Which is preferable for business and professional writing?
   a. Everyone thought the new Web design was so beautiful.
   b. Everyone thought the new Web design was beautiful.   _____

6. I'm calling to _____ my appointment.
   a. re-confirm   b. reconfirm   _____

Want to explore more? Go to: academic.cengage.com/bcomm/guffey or Xtra!

238 I UNIT 4 I CHAPTER 13 I CONJUNCTIONS

The following e-mail message contains intentional errors representing spelling, proofreading, punctuation, and language principles covered thus far. You should mark 30 changes. When you replace a wordy or incorrect phrase with one word, it counts as one correction. When you correct a comma splice, run-on, or fragment, the correction counts as two errors. Count each parenthesis and each dash as a single mark. Use proofreading marks to make the corrections here OR make the corrections at the **Guffey Companion Web Site** at **academic.cengage.com/bcomm/guffey.**

File Edit Mailbox Message Transfer Special Tools Window Help

B *I* U | | A˅ A˄ | | | | | | | | | | **Send**

From: Sebastian Fox, Manager, Legal Support Services <sfox@jayco.com>
Date: May 24, 200x
To: Claudia Eckelmann, Vice President, Employee Relations <ceckelmann@jayco.com>
Cc:
Subject: CONDUCTING EMPLOYEE EVALUATIONS

Claudia,

I recently learn that one of our employee's has filed a law suit against the company because of comments a supervisor made during a performance evaluation. This is a unfortunate event that could of been prevented. Here are a list of tips that you should share with all manager's.

1. Before you can accurately evaluate an employees performance you need to establish a system to measure that performance. You; therefore, need to develop performance standards and goals for each employee. Remember to remain sensitive of the employees needs. Plan on sharing these standards and goals in writeing with the employee.

2. Monitor the preformance of each employee throughout the year. Keep a log for each worker and note memorable incidents or projects involving that worker. Although many managers are understandably adverse to placing negative comments in files, such comments must be included as part of the evaluation process. Any employee, who does something exceptional, should be given immediate feed back. If you give this feedback orally make a written note of the conversation for the employees personnell file.

3. At least once a year, formally evaluate the worker by writing a performance appraisal and by meeting with the worker. At the meeting let your employee know what you think they did good, and which areas the employee maybe able to improve. Be sure and discuss the standards and goals you set earlier. Listen carefully to your employee's comments and take good notes.

Giving evaluations can be difficult, however, careful planning and preparation is necessary to make the process go smooth. Be specific, give deadlines, be honest, and be realistic. Following these steps is an excellent way to help the company avoid legal problems. Please e-mail me with any questions.

Sebastian

Want to explore more? Go to: academic.cengage.com/bcomm/guffey or Xtra!

CONJUNCTIONS | CHAPTER 13 | **239**

Goal: To learn about spyware.

You've heard that spyware is dangerous and can be used to gather sensitive information from your computer. You decide to find out more.

1. With your Web browser on the screen, go to the **Security at Home** page of the Microsoft site at **http://www.microsoft.com/athome/ security/**.

2. Click Spyware in the menu to the left to read articles about spyware. Read **What is Spyware?**

Click the arrow at the bottom of the page to learn the signs of spyware infection, how to get rid of spyware, and how to prevent spyware. Print at least two pages of this article.

3. What is spyware? How can you tell whether you have it on your computer? What are five things you can do to protect your computer against spyware?

4. End your session by clicking the **X** in the upper right corner of your browser. Turn in all printed pages and your answers.

Add commas or semicolons to the following sentences.

1. Technology is changing rapidly therefore most employees need regular retraining.

2. If your organization requires real-time communication try instant messaging.

3. We are posting the job announcement online and we are also asking for employee referrals.

4. The software demonstration by Victor Castro who represents Custom Systems will be Friday.

Underline the letter of the sentence that is more effective.

5. (a) Neither can we ship the printer nor the computer until April 1.
   (b) We can ship neither the printer nor the computer until April 1.

1. rapidly; therefore, 2. communication, 3. online, 4. Castro, Systems, 5. b

Want to explore more? Go to: academic.cengage.com/bcomm/guffey or Xtra!

240 | UNIT 4 | CHAPTER 13 | CONJUNCTIONS

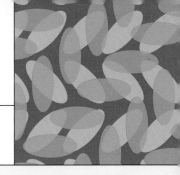

UNIT	**UNIT REVIEW**
4	*Chapters 11–13*

Name _____

Begin your review by rereading Chapters 11–13. Then test your comprehension with the following exercises. Compare your responses with those provided at the end of the book.

LEVEL 1

Write the letter of the correct answer choice.

1. I've never read a (a) worst, (b) worse executive summary. _____

2. In comparing the three shipping companies, we decided that DHL is (a) fastest, (b) faster. _____

3. If you need (a) a, (b) an example of her work, take a look at her e-portfolio. _____

4. The board members (a) would have, (b) would of been impressed with your presentation. _____

5. The service contract is (a) to, (b) too expensive. _____

6. We are fortunate to have exceptional employees like William and (a) him, (b) he. _____

7. We're seeking a bright young person (a) which, (b) whom we can train. _____

8. The group of words *if you will write us* is a(n) (a) phrase, (b) independent clause, (c) dependent clause. _____

Insert appropriate commas and semicolons in the following sentences. In the space provided, indicate the number of punctuation marks you added. Write *0* if you add none.

9. Gina first took a job in Knoxville and later decided to move to Charlotte. _____

10. Hai Nguyen might be assigned to work in our legal office or he might be assigned to our administrative headquarters. _____

11. Amy's payroll service was a huge success consequently she is opening a second office. _____

12. Kristin wrote a chronological résumé but Cameron preferred a functional strategy for his résumé. _____

LEVEL 2

Write the letter of the correct answer choice.

13. Let's discuss these ideas (a) further, (b) farther over lunch. _____

14. We'll hear complaints on a (a) case by case, (b) case-by-case basis. _____

15. If you have (a) less, (b) fewer than ten items, you may use the quick-check lane. _____

16. President Jaunett Neighbors agreed that the contract was written (a) satisfactorily, (b) satisfactory. _____

17. Power in our government is balanced (a) among, (b) between its three branches. _____

18. You must turn your paperwork (a) into, (b) in to me by Monday. _____

19. Does anyone (a) beside, (b) besides you know the password? _____

Insert appropriate commas and semicolons in the following sentences. In the space provided, indicate the number of marks you added.

20. Alice Waters who owns Chez Panisse in Berkeley is a champion of locally grown organic food. _____

21. Before sending her résumé Holly made sure it was flawless. _____

22. The employee who asked for a transfer will be moving to Atlanta. _____

23. Send all checks to Gina Caracas who is in charge of contributions. _____

24. As reported our division shows declining sales and dwindling profits. _____

LEVEL 3

Write the correct answer choice.

25. Jacksonville is larger than (a) any other city, (b) any city in Florida. _____

26. Examine carefully the (a) 50 first, (b) first 50 pages of the booklet. _____

27. Air France (a) plans to fly, (b) plans on flying to China. _____

28. The approved contract is not very different (a) than, (b) from the first version. _____

29. We asked that our salary increase be retroactive (a) to, (b) from the first of the year. _____

Insert appropriate commas and semicolons in the following sentences. In the space provided, indicate the number of marks you added.

30. If you want to create a good impression be sure to write a thank-you letter after a job interview. _____

31. When Pat Cramer joined our West Virginia office sales immediately increased. _____

32. I was unable to locate the figures you requested when you called our office last week. _____

33. Sales in your district have risen markedly moreover service requests are decreasing. _____

34. Although he had no use for bodyguards Elvis Presley is said to have had a very special use for two highly trained CPAs. _____

35. The meek will inherit the earth however the strong will retain the mineral rights. _____

Hotline Review

36. She has (a) all ready, (b) already handled the customer inquiry. _____

37. (a) Adverse, (b) Averse working conditions caused many employees to resign. _____

38. When you visit New York, be sure to spend (a) sometime, (b) some time at the Metropolitan Museum of Art. _____

39. All (a) personnel, (b) personal matters are now handled in our Human Resources Department. _____

40. Microsoft Office (a) maybe, (b) may be facing some tough competition from Google. _____

Name _____

E-MAIL MESSAGES AND MEMOS

E-mail messages and memos are increasingly important forms of internal communication for most companies today. Organizations are downsizing, flattening chains of command, forming work teams, and empowering rank-and-file employees. Given more power in making decisions, employees find that they need more information. They must collect, exchange, and evaluate information about the products and services they offer. Management also needs input from employees to respond rapidly to local and global market actions. This growing demand for information results in an increasing use of memos and especially e-mail. That's why anyone entering a business or profession today should know how to write good e-mail messages and memos.

CHARACTERISTICS OF E-MAIL MESSAGES AND MEMOS

E-mail messages and memos have a number of characteristics in common:

- They begin with *To, From, Date,* and *Subject.*
- They generally cover just one topic.
- They are informal.
- They are concise.

E-mail messages and memos use efficient standard formats, such as you see in Figure 4.1. So that they can be acted on separately, e-mail messages and memos should discuss only one topic. Let's say you send your supervisor an e-mail message requesting a copier repair. You also add a comment about an article you want to appear in the company newsletter. The supervisor may act on one item and overlook the other. He might also want to forward your request for a copier repair directly to the operations manager, but he has to edit or rekey the message because of the second topic. Thus, e-mail messages and memos are most helpful when they cover just one subject.

Because they replace conversation, these messages tend to be informal. They may include first-person pronouns, such as *I* and *me,* as well as occasional contractions, such as *can't* or *haven't.* The tone, however, should not become familiar or unbusinesslike. Moreover, memos and e-mail messages should not be wordy. Concise messages save time and often are more easily understood than longer documents.

Writing Plan

For most informational and procedural messages, follow a direct writing plan that reveals the most important information first. Here are specific tips for writing the subject line, first sentence, body, and closing of e-mail messages and memos.

Figure 4.1
Comparing E-mail Messages and Memos

```
File  Edit  Mailbox  Message  Transfer  Special  Tools  Window  Help

  B  I  U                                              Send

      To:   Sondra Rios <sondra.rios@mail.onyx.com>
    From:   Michael E. Wynn <mewynn@mail.onyx.com>
 Subject:   Adding New Dependents to Your Health Coverage  •——————
      Cc:
     Bcc:
 Attached:

    Dear Sondra:  •——————————

    Yes, you may add new dependents to your health plan coverage. Since you are a regular, active
    employee, you are eligible to add unmarried dependent children (natural, adopted, step, and
    foster) under age 19 or under age 26, if they are full-time students. You may also be eligible to
    enroll your domestic partner as your dependent, as part of a pilot program.

    For any new dependent, you must submit a completed "Verification of Dependent Eligibility
    Form." You must also submit a photocopy of a document that verifies the dependent's eligibility.
    An acceptable verification document for a spouse is a photocopy of your marriage certificate.
    For children, submit a photocopy of a birth certificate, adoption certificate, or guardianship
    certificate. Please call the Health Insurance Unit at Ext. 2559 for more information or to ask for
    an application.

    Michael E. Wynn  •——————————
    Health Benefits Coordinator
```

Includes descriptive subject line

Starts with optional salutation to show friendliness and to identify the message opening

Uses single spacing within paragraphs and double spacing between

Closes with name and title to ensure identification

Starts dateline 2 inches from top on full sheet or 1 inch from top on half sheet

Includes descriptive subject line

Omits salutation

Uses single spacing within paragraphs and double spacing between

Omits closing and writer's identification

Onyx Enterprise
Interoffice Memo

DATE: May 3, 200x

TO: Sondra Rios, Sales and Marketing Department

FROM: Michael E. Wynn, Health Benefits Coordinator *MEW*

SUBJECT: ADDING NEW DEPENDENTS TO YOUR HEALTH COVERAGE

Yes, you may add new dependents to your health plan coverage. Since you are a regular, active employee, you are eligible to add unmarried dependent children (natural, adopted, step, and foster) under age 19 or under age 26, if they are full-time students. You may also be eligible to enroll your domestic partner as your dependent, as part of a pilot program.

For any new dependent, you must submit a completed "Verification of Dependent Eligibility Form." You must also submit a photocopy of a document that verifies the dependent's eligibility. An acceptable verification document for a spouse is a photocopy of your marriage certificate. For children, submit a photocopy of a birth certificate, adoption certificate, or guardianship certificate. Please call the Health Insurance Unit at Ext. 2559 for more information or to ask for an application.

Subject Line. In the subject line, summarize the message. Although brief, a subject line must make sense and should capture the reader's interest. Instead of *Meeting,* for example, try *Meeting to Discuss Hiring Two New Employees.* A subject line is like a newspaper headline. It should snag attention, create a clear picture, and present an accurate summary. It should not be a complete sentence and should rarely occupy more than one line.

First Sentence. Although an explanation occasionally may precede the main idea, the first sentence usually tells the primary idea of the message. For example, an appropriate first sentence in a memo announcing a new vacation procedure follows:

> Here are new guidelines for employees taking two- or three-week vacations between June and September.

The opening of the message may issue a polite command (*Please answer the following questions about . . .*), make a request (*Please begin research on a summer internship program*), or ask a question (*Can your department complete the printing of a . . .*). Try not to begin with a lengthy explanation. Get to the point as quickly as possible.

Skill Check 4.1 Openings for E-Mail Messages and Memos

Which subject line is better for an e-mail or memo? Circle its letter.

1. a. SUBJECT: Inventory
   b. SUBJECT: Annual Pharmacy Inventory Scheduled for June 2

2. a. SUBJECT: This Memo Announces Revised Procedures for Applying for Dental Benefits
   b. SUBJECT: Revised Procedures for Dental Benefits Applications

Which opening sentence is better for an e-mail or memo?

3. a. Employees interested in learning about new communication technologies are invited to a workshop on January 31.
   b. For some time now we have been thinking about the possibility of holding a workshop about new communication technologies for some of our employees.

4. a. We have noticed recently a gradual but steady decline in the number of customers purchasing items from our Web site.
   b. Please conduct a study and make recommendations regarding the gradual but steady decline of online customer purchases.

5. Write a subject line for a memo that describes the possibility of a new sports scoreboard sponsored by Coca-Cola, a topic to be discussed at the next management council meeting.

   _____

   _____

6. Write a subject line for an e-mail or memo announcing a demonstration of new software for all employees to be given Thursday, November 16.

   _____

   _____

Body of Message. Provide details of the message in the body. If you are asking for information, arrange your questions in a logical order. If you are providing information, group similar information together. Think about using side headings in bold print, such as you see in these paragraphs. They help readers understand, locate, and reference information quickly.

You can also improve the readability of any message by listing items with numbers or bullets. Compare the two sets of instructions that follow:

Hard to Read

The instructions for operating our copy machine include inserting your meter in the slot, loading paper in the upper tray, and then copies are fed through the feed chute.

Improved

Here are instructions for using the copy machine:
- Insert your meter in the slot.
- Load paper in the upper tray.
- Feed copies through the feed chute.

Notice that all the items in the preceding bulleted list are parallel in construction. That means that each item uses the same form. All begin with verbs. This kind of balanced writing helps readers anticipate and understand information more readily.

Skill Check 4.2 Listing Information

In the space provided, revise the following paragraph so that it includes an introductory sentence and a list of four items.

> We are trying to improve budget planning, and we'd also like to control costs. To accomplish these goals, we must change our procedures for submitting requests in the future for outside printing jobs. The new procedures include first determining your exact printing specifications for a particular job. Then we want you to obtain two estimates for the job. These estimates should be submitted in writing to Kelly. Finally, you may place the outside print order—but only after receiving approval.

_____

_____

_____

_____

_____

_____

Closing an E-Mail Message or Memo. E-mail messages and memos frequently end with (a) a request for action, (b) a summary of the message, or (c) a closing thought. If action on the part of the reader is sought, be sure to spell out that action clearly. A vague request such as _Drop by to see this customer sometime_ is ineffective because the reader may not understand exactly what is to be done. A better request might be worded as follows: _Please make an appointment to see Rebecca Johnson before June 2 when she will be leaving_. Notice that an _end date_ is given. This technique, particularly when coupled with a valid reason, is effective in prompting people to act.

Another way to close an internal message is by summarizing its major points. A closing summary is helpful if the message is complicated. When no action request is made and a closing summary is unnecessary, the writer may prefer to end the memo with a simple closing thought, such as _I'll appreciate your assistance, What do you think of this proposal?_ or _Call me if I may answer questions_. Avoid tired, mechanical phrases such as _Don't hesitate to call on me,_ or _Thank you for your cooperation_. If you wish to express these thoughts, find a fresh way to say them.

Figure 13.1 shows how the four parts of a writing plan combine to create a readable, efficient interoffice memo. For more information on memo and e-mail formats, see Appendix C.

SPECIAL TIPS FOR SENDING E-MAIL MESSAGES

Instead of using paper to send memos, increasing numbers of businesspeople are turning to e-mail to send messages. To make the best use of e-mail, you may wish to implement the following suggestions:

- **Compose off line.** Instead of dashing off hasty messages online, take the time to compose off line. Consider using your word processing program and then cutting and pasting your message to the e-mail compose box. This avoids "self-destructing" online (losing all your writing through some glitch or pressing the wrong key).

- **Get the address right.** E-mail addresses are sometimes complex, often illogical, and always unforgiving. Omit one character or misread the letter *l* for the number *1*, and your message bounces. Solution: Use your electronic address book for people you write to frequently. And double-check every address that you key in manually. Also be sure that you don't reply to a group of receivers when you intend to answer only one.

- **Keep lines, paragraphs, and messages short.** Try to keep your lines under 65 characters in length and your paragraphs no longer than eight lines. Above all, keep your message short. If it requires more than three screens, consider sending it in hard-copy form.

- **Care about correctness.** Senders and receivers of e-mail tend to be casual about spelling, grammar, and usage. However, people are still judged by their writing; and you never know how far your message will travel. Read and edit any message before hitting the **Send** button!

- **Don't send anything you wouldn't want published.** Because e-mail seems like a telephone call or a person-to-person conversation, writers sometimes send sensitive, confidential, inflammatory, or potentially embarrassing messages. Beware! E-mail creates a permanent record that often does not go away even when deleted. And every message is a corporate communication that can be used against you or your employer. Don't write anything that you wouldn't want your boss, your family, or a judge to read.

SPECIAL TIPS FOR REPLYING TO E-MAIL MESSAGES

Before replying to an e-mail message, think about some of the suggestions provided here. You can save yourself time and heartache by developing good reply procedures.

- **Scan all messages in your inbox before replying to each individually.** Because subsequent messages often affect the way you respond, read them all first (especially all those from the same individual).

- **Don't automatically return the sender's message.** When replying, cut and paste the relevant parts. Avoid irritating your recipients by returning the entire "thread" (sequence of messages) on a topic.

- **Revise the subject line if the topic changes.** When replying or continuing an e-mail exchange, revise the subject line as the topic changes.

- **Never respond when you're angry.** Always allow some time to cool off before shooting off a response to an upsetting message. You often come up with different and better alternatives after thinking about what was said. If possible, iron out differences in person.

Finally, remember that office computers are meant for work-related communication. Unless your company specifically allows it, never use your employer's computers for personal messages, personal shopping, or entertainment. Assume that all e-mail is monitored. Employers legally have the right to eavesdrop on employee e-mail messages, and many do.

Writing Application 4.1

At your computer, revise the following poorly written message. It suffers from wordiness, indirectness, and confusing instructions. Include a numbered list in your revision, and be sure to improve the subject line. Prepare this as an e-mail message or as an internal memo.

TO: All Staff Members
FROM: Roy Minami, Manager
DATE: July 11, 200x
SUBJECT: COPIER RULES

Some of you missed the demonstration of the operation of our new Turbo X copier last week. I thought you might appreciate receiving this list of suggestions from the salesperson when she gave the demonstration. This list might also be helpful to other employees who saw the demo but didn't take notes and perhaps can't remember all these pointers. It's sometimes hard to remember how to operate a machine when you do it infrequently. Here's what she told us to do. There are two paper loading trays. Load 8 1/2-x-11-inch or 8 1/2-x-14-inch paper in the two loading trays. The paper should curve upward in the tray. You should take your copy and feed it into the machine face up. However, if you have small sheets or book pages or cut-and-pasted copy, lift the copier door and place your copy face down on the glass.

Before you begin, select the number of copies to be made by pressing the touch selector panel. Don't push too hard. If copies become jammed, open the front door and see where the paper got stuck in the feed path. Remove jammed paper. Oh yes, your meter must be inserted before the machine will operate. We urge you, of course, to make only as many copies as you really need. Keep this list to use again.

Don't hesitate to call on me if you need a private demonstration.

Writing Application 4.2

As the manager of Reprographic Services, write an e-mail message to Kevin Suzuki, manager, Technical Services. You are very worried that one of the computers of your operators may be infected with a virus. The computer belongs to Jackie Jimenez. Jackie says that each time she opens a previously stored document in her Word program, the contents of the document are immediately deleted. Fortunately, because Jackie has backup files, she hasn't lost anything yet. But obviously she can't go on using this computer. You plan to assign Jackie some temporary tasks for the rest of the day; however, she must have her computer up and running by tomorrow. You want a technician to inspect her machine before 5 p.m. today. You know that Kevin likes to learn as much about a computer problem as possible before he sends a technician, so include sufficient details to help him identify the problem.

Writing Application 4.3

As the manager of the Customer Services Division, Milwaukee Breweries, write an e-mail message to Melissa Miller, supervisor, Customer Services. Ask Melissa to draft a form letter that can be sent to groups requesting plant tours. In your memo, explain that the brewery has always encouraged tour groups to see your home plant brewery. However, you cannot sponsor tours at this time because of extensive remodeling. You are also installing a new computer-controlled bottling system. Tours are expected to resume in September. You need a form letter that can be sent to all groups but that can be personalized for individual responses. You want the letter draft by Monday, April 6. The letter should build good customer relations, a primary goal of your tour policy. The letter might enclose a free product coupon and a brochure picturing your operations. Tell Melissa to add any information that she feels would improve the letter.

PUNCTUATING
SENTENCES

© Ingram Publishing/Jupiter Images

14

COMMAS

© David Buffington/Blend Images/Jupiter Images

15

SEMICOLONS
AND COLONS

© Image Source/Jupiter Images

16

OTHER
PUNCTUATION

© Ingram Publishing/Jupiter Images

14

COMMAS

OBJECTIVES

When you have completed the materials in this chapter, you will be able to do the following:

LEVEL 1

- Use commas correctly in series, direct address, and parenthetical expressions.
- Use commas correctly in punctuating dates, time zones, addresses, geographical items, and appositives.

LEVEL 2

- Use commas correctly in punctuating independent adjectives, verbal phrases, and prepositional phrases.
- Use commas correctly in punctuating independent, introductory, terminal, and nonessential clauses.

LEVEL 3

- Use commas correctly in punctuating degrees, abbreviations, and numerals.
- Use commas correctly to indicate omitted words and contrasting statements, for clarity, and with short quotations.

PRETEST

Insert appropriate commas in the following sentences.

1. Your interview Ms. Diaz will take place on Tuesday June 9 at 10 a.m.

2. Zappos ships its shoes from Shepherdsville Kentucky to U.S. addresses only.

3. The attorney had reason to believe by the way that the judge was not impartial and might even be biased against this case.

1. interview, Ms. Diaz,   Tuesday, June 9,   2. Shepherdsville, Kentucky,   3. believe, by the way,   4. 1956,   5. tired,   evening,   morning,

250

4. America's interstate highway system began in 1956 and it has given birth to many new industries.

5. Although tired employees preferred the evening not the morning in-service training programs.

When you talk with a friend, you are probably unaware of the "invisible" commas, periods, and other punctuation marks that you are using. In conversation your pauses and voice inflections punctuate your thoughts and clarify your meaning. In writing, however, you must use a conventional set of symbols, punctuation marks, to help your reader understand your meaning.

Over the years we have gradually developed a standardized pattern of usage for all punctuation marks. This usage has been codified (set down) in rules that are observed by writers who wish to make their writing as precise as possible. As noted earlier, some professional writers may deviate from conventional punctuation practices. In addition, some organizations, particularly newspapers and publishing houses, maintain their own style manuals to establish a consistent "in-house" style.

The punctuation guidelines presented in this book represent a consensus of punctuation styles that are acceptable in business and professional writing. Following these guidelines will enable you to write with clarity, consistency, and accuracy.

· LEVEL 1 · LEVEL 1 · LEVEL 1 · LEVEL 1 · LEVEL 1 · LEVEL 1 · LEVEL 1 · LEVEL 1 · LE

BASIC GUIDELINES FOR USING COMMAS

The most used and misused punctuation mark, the **comma,** indicates a pause in the flow of a sentence. *Not all sentence pauses, however, require commas.* It is important for you to learn the standard rules for the use of commas so that you will not be tempted to clutter your sentences with needless, distracting commas. Here are the guidelines for basic comma usage.

SERIES

Commas are used to separate three or more equally ranked (coordinate) elements (words, phrases, or short clauses) in a series. A comma before the conjunction ensures separation of the last two items. Some writers omit the comma before the conjunction in a series. Business writers, however, are encouraged to use this comma to ensure clarity and ease of reading. No commas are used when conjunctions join all the items in a series.

> Only in October, November, and December are discounts offered. (Series of words. Notice that a comma precedes *and*, but no comma follows the last item, *December*.)

> Wireless technology enables you to respond to customers' requests, change sales forecasts, and manage suppliers even when you are away from the office. (Series of phrases)

> Denise Morita is the owner, Chuck Risby is the marketing manager, and Cheryl Summers is the executive assistant. (Series of clauses)

> We need wireless access to e-mail and Web sites and the home office. (No commas needed when conjunctions are repeated.)

DIRECT ADDRESS

Words and phrases of direct address are set off with commas.

> I do believe, *Ms. Adams*, that you have outdone yourself.

> I respectfully request, *sir*, that I be transferred.

PARENTHETICAL EXPRESSIONS

Parenthetical words, phrases, and clauses may be used to create transitions between thoughts. These expressions interrupt the flow of a sentence and are unessential to its grammatical completeness. These commonly used expressions, some of which are listed below, are considered nonessential because they do not answer specifically questions such as *When? Where? Why?* or *How?* Set off these expressions with commas when they are used parenthetically.

after all	however	needless to say
as a matter of fact	in addition	nevertheless
as a result	in conclusion	no doubt
as a rule	incidentally	of course
at the same time	in fact	on the other hand
by the way	in general	otherwise
consequently	in my opinion	that is
finally	in other words	therefore
for example	in the first place	under the circumstances
furthermore	in the meantime	unfortunately

In addition, we'd like to order the extended warranty. (At beginning of sentence)

This report is not, *however*, one that must be classified. (Inside sentence)

You have checked your résumé for accuracy, *no doubt*. (At end of sentence)

The words in question are set off by commas only when they are used parenthetically and actually interrupt the flow of a sentence.

However the vote goes, we will abide by the result. (No comma needed after *however*.)

We have *no doubt* that you'll be able to fulfill the duties of this position. (No commas needed to set off *no doubt*.)

Don't confuse short introductory essential prepositional phrases for parenthetical expressions. Notice that the following phrases are essential and therefore require no commas.

In the summer more rental units become available. (No comma is needed because the short prepositional phrase answers the question *When?*)

For that reason our competitors are lowering their prices. (No comma is needed because the short prepositional phrase answers the question *Why?*)

With your help our production team can meet its goal. (No comma is needed because the short prepositional phrase answers the question *How?*)

DATES AND TIME ZONES

When dates contain more than one element, the second and succeeding elements are normally set off by commas. Commas also set off time zones used with clock times. Study the following illustrations.

STUDY TIP

Phrases are essential (no commas) when they answer the questions *When? Where? Why?* or *How?*

SPOT THE BLOOPER

Sign outside a restaurant in Grenada, Mississippi: "LETS EAT SENIOR CITIZENS."

Dates

On January 8 we opened for business. (No comma needed for one element.)

On January 8, 2007, we opened for business. (Two commas set off second element.)

On Monday, January 8, 2007, we opened for business. (Commas set off second and third elements.)

In June 2008 the reorganization was effected. (Commas are not used with the month and year only.)

STUDY TIP

In separating dates and years, many writers remember the initial comma but forget the final one (*On January 10, 2009, the new fiscal year begins*).

Time Zones

Our flight leaves Newark at 8:05 a.m., EST, and arrives in Salt Lake City at 1:35 p.m., MST.

He placed his online bid at 6:38 p.m., PST, which was two minutes before the auction closed.

ADDRESSES AND GEOGRAPHICAL ITEMS

When dates, addresses, and geographical items contain more than one element, the second and following elements should be set off by commas, as shown in these examples.

Addresses

Please send the application to Ms. Barbara Briggs, 1913 Piazza Court, Baton Rouge, Louisiana 70817, by Friday. (Commas are used between all elements except the state and zip code, which are considered a single unit in this special instance.)

STUDY TIP

When separating cities and states, remember to include the comma after the state if the sentence continues (*my friend from Wheeling, West Virginia, called*).

Geographical Items

He moved from Bangor, Maine, to Lexington, Kentucky. (Two commas set off the state unless it appears at the end of the sentence.)

APPOSITIVES

You will recall that **appositives** rename or explain preceding nouns or pronouns. An appositive that provides information not essential to the identification of its antecedent should be set off by commas.

Nancy Deason, *the Sun Microsystems sales representative*, is here. (The appositive adds nonessential information; commas set it off.)

The sales representative *Nancy Deason* is here to see you. (The appositive is needed to identify which sales representative has arrived; therefore, no commas are used.)

Closely related one-word appositives do not require commas.

My supervisor *Doug* sometimes uses my computer.

Now complete the reinforcement exercises for Level 1.

SPOT THE BLOOPER

From *The Union-Leader* [Manchester, New Hampshire]: "Prince Louis Ferdinand of Prussia, a grandson of Germany's last emperor who worked in a Detroit auto plant in the 1930s and later opposed Nazi dictator Adolf Hitler, has died at age 86." [Could a comma help clarify who worked in the auto plant?]

SPECIAL GUIDELINES FOR USING COMMAS

At this level we will review comma usage guidelines that you studied in previous chapters, and we will add one new guideline.

INDEPENDENT ADJECTIVES

Separate two or more adjectives that equally modify a noun (see Chapter 11).

> Online customers can conduct *secure, real-time* banking transactions.

> We're looking for an *industrious, ambitious* person to hire.

INTRODUCTORY VERBAL PHRASES

Verbal phrases (see Chapter 8) that precede main clauses should be followed by commas. Prepositional phrases containing verb forms are also followed by commas.

> *To qualify for the position*, you must have two years' experience. (Infinitive verbal phrase)

> *Working overtime*, we completed the project before the deadline. (Participial verbal phrase)

> *By enrolling early*, you will receive our special discount. (Prepositional phrase with a verb form)

PREPOSITIONAL PHRASES

One or more introductory prepositional phrases totaling four or more words should be followed by a comma.

> *On the first Tuesday of each month,* museum admission is free.

> *During the winter months*, production usually declines.

Introductory prepositional phrases of fewer than four words require *no* commas.

> *In 2010* we plan to expand to India.

> *In some instances* a single parent must work alternate hours.

Prepositional phrases in other positions do not require commas when they are essential and do not interrupt the flow of the sentence.

> We have installed *in our Chicago office* a centralized telecommunications system. (No commas are needed around the prepositional phrase because it answers the question *Where?* and does not interrupt the flow of the sentence.)

> You may *at your convenience* stop by to pick up your check. (No commas are needed because the prepositional phrase answers the question *When?* and does not interrupt the flow of the sentence.)

INDEPENDENT CLAUSES

When a coordinating conjunction (see Chapter 13) joins independent clauses, use a comma before the coordinating conjunction, unless the clauses are very short (up to 12 or 13 total words).

> In Japan the wireless Internet has become wildly successful, and companies are pushing for even more sophisticated services.

James uses his cell phone and Jan prefers her Blackberry. (No comma is needed since both clauses are short.)

INTRODUCTORY CLAUSES

Dependent clauses that precede independent clauses are followed by commas.

> *When you have finished*, please turn out the lights and lock the door.
>
> *If you have any questions*, please call me at Ext. 306.
>
> *Because we rely on e-mail*, we have cut back on voice mail.

TERMINAL DEPENDENT CLAUSES

Whether to use a comma to separate a dependent clause at the end of a sentence depends on whether the added information is essential. Generally, terminal clauses add information that answers questions such as *When? Why?* and *How?* Such information is essential; thus no comma is necessary. Only when a terminal clause adds unnecessary information or an afterthought should a comma be used.

> Please turn out the lights and lock the door *when you have finished*. (No comma is needed because the terminal clause provides essential information and answers the question *When?*)
>
> Please call me at Ext. 306 *if you have any questions*. (No comma is needed because the terminal clause provides essential information and answers the question *Why?*)
>
> I plan to leave at 3:30, *although I could stay if you need me*. (A comma is needed because the terminal clause provides additional unnecessary information.)

NONESSENTIAL CLAUSES

Use commas to set off clauses that are used parenthetically or that supply information unneeded for the grammatical completeness of a sentence.

> An increase in employee benefits, *as you can well understand*, must be postponed until profits improve. (Commas are needed because the italicized clause adds unnecessary information.)
>
> We received a letter from Senator Joseph Biden, *who will be speaking to our organization next week*. (Commas are necessary because the italicized clause adds unnecessary information.)
>
> The culprit behind the spam, which advertised everything from cable descramblers to herbal remedies, was finally apprehended. (Commas are necessary because the italicized clause adds unneeded information. The relative pronoun *which* is a clue that the clause is unnecessary.)

Do *not* use commas to set off clauses that contain essential information. You might want to review this topic in Chapter 13.

> An executive *who is preparing proposals* certainly needs an up-to-date reference manual. (No commas are necessary because the italicized clause is essential; it tells what executive needs an up-to-date reference manual.)

Now complete the reinforcement exercises for Level 2.

ADDITIONAL GUIDELINES FOR USING COMMAS

The last guidelines for commas include suggestions for punctuating degrees, abbreviations, numerals, omitted words, contrasting statements, and short quotations.

DEGREES AND ABBREVIATIONS

Except for *Jr.* and *Sr.*, degrees, personal titles, and professional designations following individuals' names are set off by commas.

> John T. O'Dell Jr. is frequently confused with John T. O'Dell Sr.
>
> Norman Rosen, MD, uses telemedicine connections to keep in touch with his patients.
>
> Judith Lounsbury, PhD, believes in using holistic methods in her practice.
>
> We have retained Robin Cittenden, Esq., to represent us.

The abbreviations *Inc.* and *Ltd.* are set off by commas only if the company's legal name includes the commas.

> Printrak International, Inc., helps law enforcement agencies ensure safety and security by integrating cross-platform applications. (Company's legal name includes comma.)
>
> Global Industries Ltd. provides offshore construction in the Gulf of Mexico and West Africa. (Legal name does not include comma before *Ltd.*)

NUMERALS

Unrelated figures appearing side by side should be separated by commas.

> By 2010, 228 million subscribers will be using wireless devices worldwide.
>
> On page 10, two illustrations show the wiring diagram.

Numbers of more than three digits require commas.

> 1,760   47,950   6,500,000

However, calendar years and zip codes are written without commas within the numerals.

Calendar Years:	1776	1945	2008
Zip Codes:	02116	45327	90265

Telephone numbers, house numbers, decimals, page numbers, serial numbers, and contract numbers are also written without commas within the numerals.

Telephone Number:	(415) 937-5594
House Number:	5411 Redfield Circle
Decimal Number:	.98651, .0050
Page Number:	Page 1036
Serial Number:	36-5710-1693285763
Contract Number:	No. 359063420

OMITTED WORDS

A comma is used to show the omission of words that are understood.

> Last summer we hired 12 interns; this summer, only 3 interns. (Comma shows omission of *we hired* after *summer.*)

CONTRASTING STATEMENTS

Commas are used to set off contrasting or opposing expressions. These expressions are often introduced by such words as *not, never, but,* and *yet.*

SPOT THE BLOOPER

From *The Boston Globe:* "Then her hair caught fire while sitting in a front seat during a fireworks display."

We chose Tommaso's, not Steps of Rome, to cater our World Cup celebration party. (Two commas set off a contrasting statement that appears in the middle of a sentence.)

Our earnings this year have been lower, yet quite adequate.

The more he protests, the less we believe him. (One comma sets off a contrasting statement that appears at the end of a sentence.)

CLARITY

Commas are used to separate words repeated for emphasis and words that may be misread if not separated.

Susan Keegan said that it was a very, very complex contract.

Whoever goes, goes at his or her own expense.

No matter what, you know you have our support.

In business, time is money.

SHORT QUOTATIONS

A comma is used to separate a short quotation from the rest of a sentence. If the quotation is divided into two parts, two commas are used.

STUDY TIP

Here's a good rule to follow in relation to the comma: *When in doubt, leave it out!*

Alice Beasley said, "The first product to use a bar code was Wrigley's gum."

"The first product to use a bar code," said Alice Beasley, "was Wrigley's gum."

Now complete the reinforcement exercises for Level 3.

HOTLINE QUERIES

Answered by Dr. Guffey

Question

Q: I remember when company names with "Inc." and "Ltd." always had commas around these abbreviations. Has this changed?

Q: When the company name *Sun Microsystems, Inc.,* appears in the middle of a sentence, is there a comma following *Inc.?*

Answer

A: Today's practice involves using commas only if the official company name includes the commas. For example, the following company names are written without commas: Phizer Inc., Canon Inc., Caterpillar Inc. However, other companies include the commas: Motorola, Inc.; Novell, Inc.; Cisco Systems, Inc.; Castle Rock Entertainment, Inc. One way to check on the official name is to search for the company's Web site and look at it there.

A: Current authorities recommend the following practice in punctuating *Inc.*: If the legal company name includes a comma preceding *Inc.*, then a comma should follow *Inc.* if it is used in the middle of a sentence (*we learned that Sun Microsystems, Inc., has an education software program*).

Q: My boss always leaves out the comma before the word *and* when it precedes the final word in a series of words. Should the comma be used?

A: Although some writers omit that comma, careful writers favor its use so that the last two items in the series cannot be misread as one item. For example, *The departments participating are Engineering, Accounting, Marketing, and Advertising.* Without that final comma, the last two items might be confused as one item.

Q: Should I use a comma after the year in this sentence? *In 2007 we began operations.*

A: No. Commas are not required after short introductory prepositional phrases (fewer than four words) unless confusion might result without them. If two numbers, for example, appear consecutively, a comma would be necessary to prevent confusion: *In 2007, 156 companies used our services.*

Q: Are these three words interchangeable: *assure, ensure,* and *insure?*

A: Good question! Although all three words mean "to make secure or certain," they are not interchangeable. *Assure* refers to persons and may suggest setting someone's mind at rest (*let me assure you that we are making every effort to locate it*). *Ensure* and *insure* both mean "to make secure from loss," but only *insure* is now used in the sense of protecting or indemnifying against loss (*the building and its contents are insured*). Use *ensure* to mean "to make certain" (*the company has ensured the safety of all workers*).

Q: It seems to me that the word *explanation* should be spelled as *explain* is spelled. Isn't this unusual?

A: Many words derived from root words change their grammatical form and spelling. Consider these: *disaster, disastrous; maintain, maintenance; repeat, repetition; despair, desperate, desperation; pronounce, pronunciation.*

Q: Is *appraise* used correctly in this sentence? *We will appraise stockholders of the potential loss.*

A: No, it's not. Your sentence requires *apprise*, which means "to inform or notify." The word *appraise* means "to estimate" (*he will appraise your home before you set its selling price*).

Q: Which word is correct in this sentence? The officer (*cited, sited, sighted*) me for speeding?

A: Your sentence requires *cited*, which means "to summon" or "to quote." *Site* means "a location," as in *a building site* or *a Web site. Sight* means "a view" or "to take aim," as in *the building was in sight.*

Q: When the word *too* appears at the end of a sentence, should it be preceded by a comma?

A: When the adverb *too* (meaning "also") appears at the end of a clause, it requires no comma (*His friend is coming too*). However, when *too* appears in the middle of the sentence, particularly between the subject and the verb, it requires two commas to set it off (*His friend, too, is coming*). When *too* means "to an excessive extent," it requires no commas (*The speech was too long*).

LEVEL 1

A. (Self-check) Insert necessary commas. In the space provided indicate briefly the reason for the comma (for example, *series, parenthetical, direct address, date, address, essential appositive,* and so forth). Write *C* if the sentence is correct.

Example: He stated, on the contrary, that he would decline the offer.   parenthetical

1. Tuesday September 11 2001 is a day that cannot be forgotten.   _____

2. Hong Kong is on the other hand one of the most densely populated areas in the world.   _____

3. Bronte Tennyson Athens Florence London Paris and Tarzan are all towns in the state of Texas.   _____

4. Herb Kelleher grew up in Haddon Heights New Jersey before he moved to Dallas Texas to start Southwest Airlines in 1971.   _____

5. Clarence Darrow the famous trial lawyer defended John Scopes in the evolution trial.   _____

6. The famous journalist H. L. Mencken covered the Scopes Trial.   _____

7. The fax arrived at 11:37 a.m. CST.   _____

8. Your reservation Mr. Takeda has been confirmed.   _____

9. We have no doubt that such practices are widespread.   _____

10. Organize your thoughts and jot down some notes and then keyboard the message from your notes.   _____

Check your answers below.

B. Insert necessary commas. In the space provided indicate briefly the reason for the comma (for example, *series, parenthetical, direct address, date, time zone, address, essential appositive,* and so forth). Write *C* if the sentence is correct.

1. Please tell us Mr. Trump what it's like to produce and star in *The Apprentice*.   _____

2. *The Apprentice* has had contestants work for such companies as Gillette Norwegian Cruise Line Arby's and General Motors.   _____

3. As a matter of fact the contestants even did a project for the Boys and Girls Club of America.   _____

4. Applications for *The Apprentice* should be sent to the Casting Department 149 South Barrington Avenue Los Angeles CA 90049 by the deadline.   _____

1. Tuesday, September 11, 2001, (date) 2. Hong Kong is, hand, (parenthetical) 3. Bronte, Tennyson, Athens, Florence, London, Paris, (series) 4. Haddon Heights, New Jersey, Dallas, Texas, (address) 5. Darrow, lawyer, (nonessential appositive) 6. C 7. 11:37 a.m., (time zone) 8. reservation, Mr. Takeda, (direct address) 9. C 10. C

Want to explore more? Go to: academic.cengage.com/bcomm/guffey or Xtra!

COMMAS | CHAPTER 14 | **259**

5. Sam Walton the founder of Wal-Mart started out by opening a small store in Arkansas.

6. Wal-Mart opened its first store in Shanghai on July 28 2005 in the Pudong area.

7. This store in China opened of course 13 years after Sam Walton's death.

8. Nevertheless his family has continued to run the business with great success.

9. Popular places for destination weddings include Hawaii Mexico and the Caribbean because of their warm weather.

10. My sister Susan and her husband Gary traveled to Barbados in the Caribbean for the wedding of friends.

11. Phone companies cable companies and Internet companies all want to get into the on-demand video business.

12. Strict rules are needed however to make sure that companies don't start charging for access to public information.

13. In February 1935 Parker Brothers started selling the board game *Monopoly*.

14. Charles B. Darrow who was a heater salesman in Pennsylvania was the first to patent the board game *Monopoly*.

15. The National Monopoly Championship will be aired on ESPN at 8 p.m. EST.

C. Insert necessary commas. In the space provided for each sentence, write the number of commas that you inserted. If the sentence is correct, write *C*. Be prepared to explain each comma.

1. I hope Mark that you will accept the position in Hannibal Missouri as soon as possible.

2. The author Mark Twain was born in the town of Florida Missouri on Sunday November 30 1835 and was raised in Hannibal.

3. Mark Twain was a printer's apprentice he was a licensed riverboat pilot and he was a newspaper reporter.

4. Damon Washington the chief security officer responded to a disturbance that awoke nearly everyone in the building at 1:30 a.m. PST.

5. With your assistance we should be able to finish the report by Friday April 4.

6. Send your application to Cathy Verrett 160 East Tolman Drive Philadelphia Pennsylvania 19106 before August 4.

7. For that reason our next sales letter of course must target key decision makers.

8. In the meantime our sales letter must include more than facts testimonials and guarantees.

9. Incidentally we have shipped your wood sample to our designers in Portland Oregon and Tampa Florida for their inspection.

10. Members may choose from many martial arts Pilates aqua fitness and salsa classes offered at Bally Total Fitness.

11. I have no doubt in my mind about his competency and integrity.

12. Our analysis Mr. and Mrs. Carter shows that you owe additional taxes for 2004 2005 and 2006.

13. Most people by the way don't like the idea of passengers using cell phones while flying on planes.

Want to explore more? Go to: academic.cengage.com/bcomm/guffey or Xtra!

14. The Small Business Administration which celebrated its fiftieth anniversary in 2003 helps entrepreneurs start manage and finance small companies. _____

15. The famous investor Warren Buffett agreed to give $37 billion to charity. _____

LEVEL 2

A. (Self-check) Insert necessary commas. In the space provided indicate briefly the reason for the comma (for example, *independent adjectives, introductory verbal phrase, independent clauses,* and so forth). Write *C* if the sentence is correct.

Example: Jeremy made several constructive͵imaginative suggestions. independent adjectives _____

1. To succeed in life you must be willing to learn from your mistakes. _____

2. At the end of each fiscal year we prepare several financial statements. _____

3. By November we are able to predict with considerable accuracy the year's profits. _____

4. It takes 43 facial muscles to frown but it takes only 17 muscles to smile. _____

5. If your computer seems to be working more slowly lately you may be the victim of spyware. _____

6. You may be the victim of spyware if your computer has seemed slower lately. _____

7. The work in this office is strictly confidential as I am sure you are well aware. _____

8. The person who designed your Web site is talented. _____

9. Dr. Morris Edelson plans to attend the conference in London and later he expects to vacation in Europe. _____

10. We expect honest thorough answers during the interview process. _____

Check your answers below.

B. Insert necessary commas. In the space provided indicate briefly the reason for the comma (for example, *independent adjectives, introductory verbal phrase, introductory clause,* and so forth). Write *C* if the sentence is correct.

1. Digital camera users are looking for reliable long-lasting batteries. _____

2. Agreeing to serve as our leader Frances Sheppard worked with students and faculty to devise an online learning program. _____

3. If I were you I would invest in real estate. _____

4. In 2006 the Oxford English Dictionary database reached 1 billion words and it now contains words like "inner-child" and "wiki." _____

5. When you look up the meaning of "wiki" in an online dictionary you learn that it is a type of Web site that allows users to quickly add and edit information. _____

1. life, (intro. verbal phrase) 2. year, (long intro. prep. phrase) 3. C 4. frown, (independent clauses) 5. lately, (introductory clause) 6. C 7. confidential, (unnecessary terminal clause) 8. C 9. London, (independent clauses) 10. honest, (independent adjectives)

Want to explore more? Go to: academic.cengage.com/bcomm/guffey or Xtra!

COMMAS | CHAPTER 14 | **261**

6. Dan Bricklin who created the first spreadsheet has now developed a multiuser wiki spreadsheet program. _____

7. The man who created the first spreadsheet has now developed a multi-user wiki spreadsheet program. _____

8. Because today's college graduates owe an average of $30,000 each in student loans some refer to these graduates as "Generation Broke." _____

9. Many of these college graduates are moving back home because they can't afford to live on their own. _____

10. Only college graduates will be considered and only those with technical skills will be hired. _____

11. Any increase in salaries as you might have expected is presently impossible because of declining profits. _____

12. For a period of at least six months we cannot increase salaries. _____

13. In 2006 the letter "W" was officially added to the Swedish dictionary. _____

14. Clearing the papers from his desk he finally located the contract. _____

15. The sportswriter charged that professional football players are overpaid overprivileged athletes. _____

C. Insert necessary commas. For each sentence write in the space provided the number of commas that you inserted. If the sentence is correct, write *C*. Be prepared to explain each comma.

1. If scientists are correct the Earth's surface is composed of a number of shifting plates that move a few inches each year. _____

2. Our current liability insurance in view of the new law that went into effect April 1 needs to be increased. _____

3. The happy carefree students celebrated the completion of their examinations although many had to leave immediately for their jobs. _____

4. Agreeing to serve as our chair Patrick Leong made valuable contributions to our committee. _____

5. She wants a peppy sporty Mini Cooper for her fortieth birthday. _____

6. By the spring of next year we hope to have completed our telecommunications network. _____

7. Antonio Perez who is chief executive of Eastman Kodak said that Kodak needs more change if it hopes to survive the advent of digital imaging. _____

8. Some companies have excellent voice mail systems but others use impersonal systems that frustrate and irritate callers. _____

9. In June 2006 an estimated 55 billion e-mail spam messages were sent each day. _____

10. Although it represents a small share of our total sales the loss of the Phoenix territory would negatively affect our profits. _____

11. We do not at this time see any reason for continuing this inefficient profitless practice. _____

12. When you send an e-mail message remember that it may be forwarded to someone else. _____

Want to explore more? Go to: academic.cengage.com/bcomm/guffey or Xtra!

13. As Professor Brunton predicted the resourceful well-trained graduate was hired immediately. _____

14. We hope that the new year will be prosperous for you and that we may have many more opportunities to serve you. _____

15. You were probably concerned about your increased insurance rates but you didn't know where to find adequate economical coverage. _____

LEVEL 3

A. (Self-check) Insert necessary commas. In the space provided indicate briefly the reason for the comma (for example *omitted words, contrasting statement, clarity, short quotation,* and so forth). Write *C* if the sentence is correct.

1. What it is is a matter of principle. _____

2. The first loan was made on February 3; the second June 1. _____

3. "Those who cannot remember the past" said George Santayana "are condemned to repeat it." _____

4. In the fall we'll open a branch in Peoria; in the spring in Wichita. _____

5. Andy Kivel PhD specializes in information management. _____

6. In December 2001 286 Enron employees received bonuses totaling $72 million. _____

7. We were pleased that 1489 new customers signed up for service this year. _____

8. We were expecting Ms. Weber not Mr. Allen to conduct the audit. _____

9. "A résumé is a balance sheet without any liabilities" said personnel specialist Robert Half. _____

10. The octogenarians had known each other for a long long time. _____

Check your answers below.

B. Insert necessary commas. In the space provided indicate briefly the reason for the comma (for example, *omitted words, contrasting statement, clarity, short quotation,* and so forth). Write *C* if the sentence is correct.

1. "Nothing you can't spell" said humorist Will Rogers "will ever work." _____

2. By February 2006 $88 billion in aid was allocated for emergency relief for Hurricane Katrina victims. _____

3. On January 1 your Policy No. 8643219 will expire. _____

4. Lynn Craig LVN and Annette Juarez RN work at St. Elizabeth's. _____

5. On paper diets often sound deceptively simple. _____

6. The better we treat our customers the more loyal they will be to our company. _____

1. is, (clarity) 2. second, (omitted words) 3. past," Santayana, (short quotation) 4. spring, (omitted words) [**Note:** Do not use a comma after a short introductory prepositional phrase.] 5. Kivel, PhD, (abbreviation) 6. 2001, (adjacent numerals) 7. 1,489 (numerals) 8. Weber, Allen, (contrasting statement) 9. liabilities," (short quotation) 10. long, (clarity)

Want to explore more? Go to: academic.cengage.com/bcomm/guffey or Xtra!

COMMAS | CHAPTER 14 | **263**

7. Major responsibility for the loan lies with the signer; secondary responsibility with the cosigner. _____

8. We are looking for stable not risky stocks in which to invest. _____

9. Motion-picture producer Samuel Goldwyn said "A verbal contract isn't worth the paper it's written on." _____

10. In short employees must be more considerate of others. _____

11. Donna Meyer PhD and Victor Massaglia MD spoke at the opening session. _____

12. In 2005 18 050 631 total vehicles were recalled in the United States. _____

13. It was Ford Motor Co. not General Motors Corp. that had the most recalls. _____

14. Ford Motor Co. recalled 6 million vehicles; General Motors Corp. 5 million. _____

15. What it was was an international power struggle. _____

C. **Writing Exercise.** Select five comma rules that you think are most important. Name the rule; then write an original sentence illustrating that rule.

Comma Rule	**Sentence Illustration**
1. _____	_____
2. _____	_____
3. _____	_____
4. _____	_____
5. _____	_____

D. **Skill Maximizer.** To make sure you have mastered the use of commas, try your skill on these challenging sentences that cover all levels. Insert needed commas and write the number that you added in the space provided. Write *C* if the sentence is correct. Be prepared to discuss the rule for each comma you add.

1. On October 24 1901 Annie Taylor at the age of 64 became the first person to go over Niagara Falls in a barrel. _____

2. John D. Rockefeller Sr. who founded Standard Oil was known as a driven determined and philanthropic man. _____

3. Rockefeller by the way was born in Richland New York in July 1839. _____

4. Denise Minor who was our first team leader moved to Worcester Massachusetts. _____

5. The person who became our next team leader was from Cambridge Massachusetts. _____

6. At a recent meeting of our team we decided that members should at their convenience complete an online training module. _____

7. Although *National Geographic* prints only about 30 photographs for each article the photographer takes about 14,000 images. _____

8. If you work in an office with open cubicles it is rude to listen to Web radio any kind of streaming audio or your iPod without headphones. _____

9. Renouncing her wealthy social background Florence Nightingale became a nurse and is considered the founder of modern nursing. _____

Want to explore more? Go to: academic.cengage.com/bcomm/guffey or Xtra!

10. For three years you have worked here during the summer and you have always been an asset to the firm. _____

11. Although bored students managed to stay awake during the lecture. _____

12. Whatever it is it is not very amusing. _____

13. Our yearly budget was over $2 000 000 for equipment supplies and utilities. _____

14. Cooperation not competition is what is needed at this time. _____

15. "There is no such thing" said Tom Peters "as a minor lapse in integrity." _____

E. Hotline Review. In the space provided write the correct answer choice.

1. The Rileys could not _____ their home because they live in the potential path of hurricanes.
a. ensure   b. insure   c. assure
_____

2. Mrs. Riley tried to _____ the agent that their house was stable and secure.
a. ensure   b. insure   c. assure
_____

3. A realtor should _____ your property before you list it for sale.
a. apprise   b. appraise
_____

4. Our insurance agent _____ all clients of the limitations of home ownership policies.
a. apprises   b. appraises
_____

5. Luckily, the officer did not _____ him for speeding.
a. sight   b. cite   c. site
_____

6. Have you checked out their new Web _____?
a. sight   b. cite   c. site
_____

Want to explore more? Go to: academic.cengage.com/bcomm/guffey or Xtra!

This letter contains 35 intentional errors representing spelling, proofreading, punctuation, and language princi-ples covered thus far. When you replace a wordy or incorrect phrase with one word, it counts as one correc-tion. When you correct a comma splice, run-on, or fragment, the correction counts as two errors. Use proof-reading marks to make the corrections here *OR* make the corrections at the **Guffey Companion Web Site** at **academic.cengage.com/bcomm/guffey.**

Briggs Mills, Inc.

440 Vine Street   www.briggsmills.com
Cincinnati, OH 45202   513-579-3100

May 12, 200x

Ms. Julie Perzel
Director Human Resources
Clayton Manufacturing
10001 East Industrial Park Road
Cleveland, OH 44101

Dear Ms. Pretzel:

Mr. Martin A. Anderson whom is applying for the position of manger of manufacturing support at your organization requested that I write this confidential letter of reccommendation. Mr. Anderson has worked under my supervision as a manufacturing support supervisor for three year's at Briggs Mills Inc.

As a supervisor of manufacturing support Mr. Anderson helped to hire, evaluate and supervise a team of four machine technicians. Him and his team was responsible for the preventive maintance, troubleshooting and repair of machines on three production lines. Because of his strong interpersonal skills Mr. Anderson expected and obtained high performance from his machine technicians. Each technician whom was evaluated ranked in the upper two levels of performance for the past three year's. In addition Mr. Andersons own performance was evaluated at our highest level for the last two year's.

Mr. Andersons team developed a highly-effective maintenance and calibration program, that reduced line shutdowns by 10 percent. Furthermore, in addition to his supervisory work Mr. Anderson initiated improvements in machine documentation.

These changes enabled support personal to repair machines without relying on production engineers. Although documentation changes were cumbersome for our engineers Mr. Anderson brang about needed change without alienating engineers or technicians. His enthusiastic upbeat personality has had a positive affect on the entire organization.

Im sorry that Mr. Andersen may leave Briggs Mills but I am confident that his technical, interpersonal and leadership skills will serve you well in your organization. I recommend him highly, and would be happy to have him return to us in the future.

Sincerly,

Mark A. Summers

Mark A. Summers
Vice President, Operations

Want to explore more? Go to: academic.cengage.com/bcomm/guffey or Xtra!

266 I UNIT 5 I CHAPTER 14 I COMMAS

LEARNING WEB WAYS

Goal: To gather job-search and career information.

Soon you will be looking for a job. You decide to learn as much as possible about wages and trends in your career area.

1. With your Web browser on the screen, go to **http://www.salary.com.**
2. Click **All titles** in the "Salary Wizard" section. Then choose your job category from the drop-down menu. Enter your zip code and press **Search.**
3. Study the list of job titles. Select one by clicking **Base pay** below it. For this job title what is the

median salary in your geographic area? What are the high and low salary figures listed?
4. At the top of the graph, click **Benefits.** What benefits does someone in this position generally receive? What is the dollar value of these benefits? (Hint: Subtract the base salary from the total amount.)
5. Click **Net Paycheck Estimate** at the top of the graph. What would your net paycheck for this position be? How often would you be paid each year?
6. End your session and submit your answers.

POSTTEST

Insert appropriate commas in the following sentences.

1. Please let us know Ms. Knox what we can do to ensure a pleasant smooth transition.
2. The manager thinks on the other hand that all service calls must receive prior authorization and that current service contracts must be honored.
3. Connie Jo Clark PhD and Patricia Flood CPA have been asked to speak at our Scottsdale Arizona conference.
4. When trained all employees in this company should be able to offer logical effective advice to customers.
5. To meet the deadline make sure your application fee is received by January 25 2009 at 5 p.m. PST.

1. know, Ms. Knox,   2. thinks,   hand,   3. Clark PhD,   Flood, CPA,   Scottsdale, Arizona,   4. trained,   logical,   5. deadline,   January 25,   2009,   5 p.m.,

Want to explore more? Go to: academic.cengage.com/bcomm/guffey or Xtra!

COMMAS | **CHAPTER 14** | **267**

SEMICOLONS AND COLONS

OBJECTIVES

When you have completed the materials in this chapter, you will be able to do the following:

LEVEL 1

- Use semicolons correctly in punctuating compound sentences.
- Use semicolons when necessary to separate items in a series.

LEVEL 2

- Learn the proper and improper use of colons to introduce listed items.
- Correctly use colons to introduce quotations and explanatory sentences.

LEVEL 3

- Distinguish between the use of commas and semicolons preceding expressions such as *namely*, *that is*, and *for instance* as well as when separating certain independent clauses joined by *and*, *or*, *nor*, or *but*.
- Use colons appropriately and be able to capitalize words following colons when necessary.

PRETEST

Insert commas and semicolons to punctuate the following sentences correctly.

1. "Green" technologies are gaining a strong following consequently many industries are beginning to produce green products and recycling programs.

2. The following experts were invited to speak Jan Lee Valley College Roietta Fulgham American River College and Kathy Green Phoenix College.

1. following; consequently, 2. speak: Lee, College; Fulgham, College; Green, College. 3. history, 4. sure, however, 5. choose, following;
namely,

3. The Ford Edsel was one of the most famous failures in history Coca-Cola's New Coke was another well-known disappointment.

4. We're not sure however that instant messaging is right for everyone.

5. Although the committee had many cities from which to choose it decided to focus on the following namely San Francisco, Denver, or New Orleans.

This chapter introduces semicolons and colons, which can be two powerful punctuation marks in business writing. Skilled writers use semicolons and colons to signal readers about the ideas that will follow. You can improve your writing and look more professional if you know how to use them correctly. In this chapter you'll learn basic uses and advanced applications of semicolons and colons.

BASIC USES OF THE SEMICOLON

Semicolons tell readers that two closely related ideas should be thought of together. The semicolon is a stronger punctuation mark than a comma, which signifies a pause; but the semicolon is not as strong as a period, which signifies a complete stop. Understanding the use of semicolons will help you avoid fundamental writing errors, such as the comma splice and the run-on sentence. The most basic use of the semicolon occurs in compound sentences. Many business and professional communicators use a comma when they should be using a semicolon. Study the following examples to make sure you don't make this error.

INDEPENDENT CLAUSES SEPARATED BY CONJUNCTIVE ADVERBS

Semicolons are used primarily when two independent clauses are separated by a conjunctive adverb or a transitional expression. You studied this basic semicolon use in Chapter 13. Here are some review examples.

> Courtney wanted to improve her presentation skills; *consequently,* she joined Toastmasters. (Semicolon separates two independent clauses joined by the conjunctive adverb *consequently.*)

> Companies make no profits until they recover costs; *therefore,* most companies use a cost approach in pricing. (Semicolon separates two independent clauses joined by the conjunctive adverb *therefore.*)

> Manuel Gonzales worked for the university for over 20 years; *thus* he had witnessed many changes. (Semicolon separates two independent clauses joined by the conjunctive adverb *thus.*)

INDEPENDENT CLAUSES WITHOUT A COORDINATING CONJUNCTION OR A CONJUNCTIVE ADVERB

Two or more closely related independent clauses not separated by a conjunctive adverb or a coordinating conjunction (*and, or, nor, but*) require a semicolon.

> Sales meetings during prosperous times were lavish productions that focused on entertainment; meetings today focus on training and motivation.

> Not all job openings are found in classified ads or in job databases; the "hidden" job market accounts for as many as two thirds of all available positions.

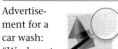

Occasionally, skillful writers use a comma to separate short, closely related independent clauses. As a business or professional writer, however, you'll never be wrong if you use a semicolon to separate two independent clauses.

Acceptable: Layda provided the business experience, Shaun provided the capital.

Better: Layda provided the business experience; Shaun provided the capital.

SERIES CONTAINING INTERNAL COMMAS OR COMPLETE THOUGHTS

Semicolons are used to separate items in a series when one or more of the items contain internal commas.

> Only the company branches in Wilmington, Delaware; Tucson, Arizona; and Cincinnati, Ohio, are showing substantial profits.

> Attending the conference were Merv Maruyama, executive vice president, Cabrillo Industries; Carla Chambers, president, Santa Rosa Software; and Paul Christiansen, program director, Club Mediterranean.

Semicolons are used to separate three or more serial independent clauses.

> The first step consists of surveying all available information related to the company objective so that an understanding of all problems can be reached; the second step involves interviewing consumers, wholesalers, and retailers; and the third step consists of developing a research design in which the actual methods and procedures to be used are indicated.

A series of short independent clauses, however, may be separated by commas.

> Amazon.com was founded in 1994, it unveiled its Web site in 1995, and it went public in 1997.

Now complete the reinforcement exercises for Level 1.

BASIC USES OF THE COLON

Although it has a variety of functions, the **colon** is most often used to introduce lists, quotations, and explanatory sentences.

FORMALLY LISTED ITEMS

Use a colon after an independent clause that introduces one item, two items, or a formal list. A list may be shown vertically or horizontally and is usually introduced by such words as *the following, as follows, these,* or *thus.* A colon is also used when words like these are implied but not stated.

> Any good leader must possess *one* important trait: integrity. (Independent clause introduces single item.)

> Text messages are now used to deliver *the following* types of information: medical, financial, educational, and political. (Formal list with introductory expression stated)

> Our company uses several delivery services for our important packages: UPS, FedEx, and DHL. (Formal list with introductory expression only implied)

These are some of the financial services the Federal Reserve provides to member banks:
1. Collecting checks, payments, and other credit instruments
2. Electronically transferring funds
3. Distributing and receiving cash and coins (Formal list shown vertically)

Do not use a colon unless the list is introduced by an independent clause. Lists often function as sentence complements or objects. When this is the case and the statement introducing the list is incomplete, no colon should be used. It might be easiest to remember that lists introduced by verbs or prepositions require no colons (because the introductory statement is incomplete).

> Three requirements for this position are a master's degree, computer knowledge, and five years' experience in systems analysis. (No colon is used because the introductory statement is not complete; the list is introduced by a *to be* verb and functions as a complement to the sentence.)

> Awards of merit were presented to Professor Loncorich, Ms. Harned, and Dr. Konishi. (No colon is used because the introductory statement is not an independent clause; the list functions as an object of the preposition *to*.)

Do not use a colon when an intervening sentence falls between the introductory statement and the list.

> According to a recent survey, these are the top convention cities in North America. The survey was conducted by *Tradeshow Week*.

> Las Vegas   New York
>
> Toronto   Chicago

QUOTATIONS

Use a colon to introduce long one-sentence quotations and quotations of two or more sentences.

> Franklin D. Roosevelt said: "It is common sense to take a method and try it. If it fails, admit it freely and try another. But above all, try something."

Incomplete quotations not interrupting the flow of a sentence require no colon, no comma, and no initial capital letter.

> The River Walk area of San Antonio is sometimes described as "the Venice of the Southwest."

EXPLANATORY SENTENCES

Use a colon to separate two independent clauses if the second clause explains, illustrates, or supplements the first.

> The company's new directors faced a perplexing dilemma: they had to choose between declaring bankruptcy and investing more funds to recoup previous losses.

> One of the traits of highly successful people is this: they never give up on themselves.

Now complete the reinforcement exercises for Level 2.

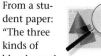

SPECIAL USES OF SEMICOLONS

You've just studied basic uses for semicolons. Occasionally, though, semicolons are used in circumstances demanding special attention.

INTRODUCTORY EXPRESSIONS SUCH AS *NAMELY, FOR INSTANCE,* AND *THAT IS*

When introductory expressions (such as *namely, for instance, that is,* and *for example*) immediately follow independent clauses, they may be preceded by either commas or semicolons. Generally, if the words following the introductory expression appear at the end of the sentence and form a series or an independent clause, use a semicolon before the introductory expression. If not, use a comma.

STUDY TIP

Notice that a comma follows *namely, for instance, that is,* and *for example* when these words are used as introductory expressions.

Numerous fringe benefits are available to employees; *namely,* stock options, life insurance, health insurance, dental care, and vision care. (A semicolon is used because *namely* introduces a series at the end of the sentence.)

Several books give additional information you might find useful when opening your own business; *for example,* Steve Mariotti's *The Young Entrepreneur's Guide to Starting and Running a Business* is an excellent resource. (A semicolon is used because *for example* introduces an independent clause.)

We are proposing many new additions to the health care package, *for example,* holistic medicine and chiropractic benefits. (A comma is used because *for example* introduces neither a series nor an independent clause.)

These same introductory expressions may introduce parenthetical words within sentences. Commas usually punctuate individual items introduced parenthetically within sentences. If the introductory expression introduces several items punctuated by internal commas, then use dashes or parentheses. Dashes and parentheses will be treated in detail in Chapter 16.

SPOT THE BLOOPER

From a column in *The Chicago Tribune:* "[A] letter from her mother, written in Polish, for example, has the date (for we dummies in the audience) written in English."

The biggest health problem facing employees, *namely,* work-related stress, costs a large employer about $3.5 million annually. (Commas are used because the introductory expression *namely* introduces a single item.)

The pursuit of basic job issues—*for instance,* wages, job security, and working conditions—has been the main concern of American workers. (Dashes are used because the introductory expression *for instance* introduces several items punctuated with internal commas.)

INDEPENDENT CLAUSES WITH COORDINATING CONJUNCTIONS

Normally, a comma precedes a coordinating conjunction (*and, or, nor, but*) when it joins two independent clauses. If, however, either of the independent clauses contains additional commas and if the reader might be confused, a semicolon may be used instead of the normally expected comma.

We have examined your suggestions carefully, and it appears that they have considerable merit. (Comma precedes coordinating conjunction because no additional punctuation appears within either clause.)

The first three cities recommended by our relocation committee were Atlanta, Dallas, and Cincinnati; but Miami, San Diego, and Seattle were also mentioned. (Semicolon precedes coordinating conjunction to show where the second independent clause begins and to prevent confusion.)

SPECIAL USES OF COLONS

Colons also have other uses that are common in business writing.

BUSINESS LETTER SALUTATIONS

Colons are placed after the salutation of a business letter when mixed punctuation is used.

Dear Mr. Paniccia: Dear Customer Service: Dear Felicia:

TIME

In expressions of time, use a colon to separate hours from minutes.

10:15 a.m.   9:45 p.m.

PUBLICATION TITLES

Place a colon between titles and subtitles of books, articles, and other publications.

Engineering Your Start-Up: A Guide for the High-Tech Entrepreneur (Book title)

"Oil Prices: How High Can They Go?" (Article title)

WORKS CITED AND BIBLIOGRAPHIES

A colon is used between the place of publication and the name of publisher when preparing bibliographies and lists of works cited.

Guffey, Mary Ellen. *Essentials of Business Communication.* Cincinnati: South-Western Cengage Learning, 2007.

CAPITALIZATION FOLLOWING COLONS

Do not capitalize the initial letter of words or of phrases listed following a colon unless the words so listed are proper nouns or appear as a vertical array.

The six Cs of effective business communication are the following: clarity, courtesy, conciseness, completeness, correctness, and confidence.

These cities will receive heavy promotional advertising: Omaha, Lincoln, Sioux City, and Council Bluffs.

To be legally enforceable, a contract must include at least three elements:
1. Mutual assent of competent parties
2. A consideration
3. A lawful purpose

Do not capitalize the first letter of an independent clause following a colon if that clause explains or supplements the first one (unless, of course, the first word is a proper noun).

You will be interested in opening a Roth IRA for one special reason: all earnings are tax free if you meet certain requirements.

Capitalize the first letter of an independent clause following a colon if that clause states a formal rule or principle.

In business the Golden Rule is often stated in the following way: He with the gold rules.

For a quotation following a colon, capitalize the initial letter of each complete sentence.

In their book *Clicks and Mortar,* David S. Pottruck and Terry Pierce say: "To distinguish one business from others, the people in the company have to be personally dedicated to the culture of the company. Their dedication needs to be such that they will automatically take the actions that make the company's culture live."

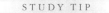

A FINAL WORD

Semicolons are excellent punctuation marks when used carefully and knowingly. After reading this chapter, though, some students are guilty of semicolon overkill. They begin to string together two—and sometimes even three—independent clauses with semicolons. Remember to use semicolons in compound sentences *only* when two ideas are better presented together. Now complete the reinforcement exercises for Level 3.

HOTLINE QUERIES

Answered by Dr. Guffey

Question

Q: My partner and I are preparing an announcement describing our new Web business. We don't agree on how to punctuate this sentence: *We offer a wide array of network services; such as design, support, troubleshooting, and consulting, etc.*

Q: When I list items vertically, should I use a comma or semicolon after each item? Should a period be used after the final item? For example,

Please inspect the following rooms and equipment:
1. *The control room*
2. *The power transformer and its standby*
3. *The auxiliary switchover equipment*

Q: Which word should I use in this sentence? *Our department will (disburse or disperse) the funds shortly.*

Answer

A: First, drop the semicolon before *such as*. No comma or semicolon is necessary before a list introduced by *such as*. Second, do not use *etc.* at the end of a series. If you have other services to offer, name them. Tacking on *etc.* suggests that you have more items but for some reason you are not listing them.

A: Do not use commas or semicolons after items listed vertically, and do not use a period after the last item in such a list. However, if the listed items are complete sentences or if they are long phrases that complete the meaning of the introductory comment, periods may be used after each item.

A: Use *disburse*. *Disperse* means "to scatter" (*Police dispersed the unruly crowd*) or "to distribute" (*Information will be dispersed to all divisions*). *Disburse* means "to pay out." Perhaps this memory device will help you keep them straight: associate the *b* in *disburse* with *bank* (*Banks disburse money*).

Q: I've been told that I should spell *judgment* without the *e*. Why, then, do I sometimes see this word spelled *judgement?* Are both spellings acceptable?

A: Most dictionaries will give both the preferred and any alternate spellings of a word. The preferred spelling will always be listed first. Although *judgement* is included in many dictionaries as an alternate spelling, it should not be used in business or any other type of writing because most people would identify it as being misspelled. If you use this spelling in Word, it will be flagged as being misspelled. In addition, if you look this word up in any law dictionary using this spelling, you won't find it because *judgment* is the only accepted spelling in the legal field.

Q: I can never keep the words *capital* and *capitol* straight. Which one would I use in the sentence *He invested $150,000 of his own (capital, capitol) in his new business?*

A: This sentence requires the noun *capital,* which means "the wealth of an individual or firm." The noun *capital* refers to a city serving as the seat of government (*Montpelier is the capital of Vermont*). As an adjective, *capital* describes (a) an uppercase letter (*capital letter*), (b) something punishable by death (*capital punishment*), or (c) something excellent (*a capital idea*). The noun *capitol* is used to describe a building used by the U.S. Congress (always capitalized) or a building where a state legislature meets (capitalized only to describe the full building name). *They visited the United States Capitol on their recent trip to Washington, DC. They had visited their state capitol building many times before their trip.*

Q: I'm setting up advertising copy, and this sentence doesn't look right to me: *This line of fishing reels are now priced . . .*

A: Your suspicion is correct. The subject of the verb in this sentence is *line;* it requires the singular verb *is.*

Q: A memo from our vice president said, *The new benefits package is equally as good as the previous package.* Is *equally as* correct English?

A: Writers should use *equally* or *as* but not both together. *The new benefit package is as good as the previous package.* OR *The new benefit package equals the previous package.* OR *The new benefit package and the previous package are equally good.*

Q: The other day I said, *Do you think he meant to infer that employees might be laid off?* A coworker corrected me. What's wrong with what I said?

A: You should have used *imply* in your sentence. The word *imply* means "to suggest without stating." The word *infer* means to read a conclusion (*From the survey results, we inferred that customers want live online customer support*).

Q: I work in an office where we frequently send letters addressed to people on a first-name basis. Should I use a comma or a colon after a salutation like *Dear Antonio?*

A: The content of the letter, not the salutation (greeting), determines the punctuation after the salutation. If the letter is a business letter, always use a colon. If the letter is totally personal, a comma may be used, although a colon would also be appropriate.

LEVEL 1

A. **(Self-check)** For each of the following sentences, underline any errors in punctuation. Then in the space provided write the correct punctuation mark plus the word preceding it. Write *C* if the sentence is correct.

Example: The price of our stock has been steadily increasing, therefore, I will make quite a profit when I sell.

increasing;

1. Jeff Bezos worked for years to build Amazon.com, it was years before the company made a profit.

_____

2. Many people buy and sell items on eBay, it is the most widely used online auction site.

_____

3. Investors' expectations were high consequently, competitive bidding for the new IPO was brisk.

_____

4. Our equipment costs have tripled in the last five years, salary expenses have increased even more.

_____

5. E-business has always been a risky undertaking, online companies seem to disappear as quickly as they appear.

_____

6. According to Red Herring, four of the top European entertainment companies are Double Fusion, Jerusalem, Israel; Echovox, Geneva, Switzerland; IceMobile, Amsterdam, The Netherlands; and Mobix Interactive, London, United Kingdom.

_____

7. The United Kingdom has the most companies on the list, and France and Israel tie for second place.

_____

8. Communications is the largest sector on the list Internet services make up the second-largest sector.

_____

9. One of the hottest areas is mobile communications, a number of companies offer chipsets and software to manage the downloading of video and other rich media to handsets and mobile phones.

_____

10. Consumers are also looking for alternative sources of power, thus some companies are offering such products as paper-thin batteries for compact devices.

_____

Check your answers below.

1. Amazon.com; 2. eBay; 3. high; 4. years; 5. undertaking; 6. C 7. list; 8. list; 9. communications; 10. power;

Want to explore more? Go to: academic.cengage.com/bcomm/guffey or Xtra!

SEMICOLONS AND COLONS | CHAPTER 15 | **277**

B. Add any necessary commas or semicolons to the following sentences. (Do not add periods.) In the spaces provided write the number of punctuation marks you inserted. Write *C* if a sentence is correct as written.

Example: Check 21 went into effect in October 2004 however many consumers still don't understand this law.

2 _____

1. Check 21 allows checks to be processed electronically consequently checks clear much more quickly.

_____

2. German shoppers generally bring their own plastic or cloth bags for groceries therefore they were unaccustomed to Wal-Mart's bagging techniques.

_____

3. Greenland is the largest island in the world it is about ten times the size of Great Britain.

_____

4. Buildings swayed lights flickered and dishes rattled.

_____

5. Some of the cities expected to bid on the 2016 Summer Olympics are Cape Town South Africa New Dehli India Lisbon Portugal Havana Cuba and San Francisco California.

_____

6. London England will host the 2012 Summer Olympics London was chosen over Paris New York Moscow and Madrid.

_____

7. The shortest recorded reign of any monarch was that of Louis XIX of France it lasted only 15 minutes.

_____

8. Toyota wants to expand beyond automobiles hence the company has moved into consulting, prefab houses, advertising, health care support, and sweet potatoes.

_____

9. Jeremy worked Jennifer supervised and Jean entertained.

_____

10. Web advertising attempts to reach large international audiences television advertising is aimed at national or local audiences.

_____

11. Google hired 800 new employees last year this is triple the total from two years ago.

_____

12. Computer hackers can easily decode short passwords thus passwords should be at least six to eight characters long and be a mix of letters and numerals.

_____

13. We have hired "white hat" hackers their job is to test how well our computer systems withstand assaults by real hackers.

_____

14. Smart companies assume their computer networks will be broken into consequently they develop computer-use policies to limit the damage.

_____

15. Among the oddly named towns in the United States are Boring, Maryland; Truth or Consequences, New Mexico; Rough and Ready, California; and Slap Out, Alabama.

_____

16. Recent speakers at the Commonwealth Club include Katie Couric anchor *CBS Evening News* George Lakoff Professor of Linguistics University of California and Alberto Gonzalez attorney general U.S. Department of Justice.

_____

Want to explore more? Go to: academic.cengage.com/bcomm/guffey or Xtra!

278 | UNIT 5 | CHAPTER 15 | SEMICOLONS AND COLONS

17. Consumers expect anytime anywhere access to businesses therefore wireless cell phone use is growing.

18. Women now earn the majority of bachelor's degrees in business, biological sciences, social sciences and history in addition women outpace men in degrees in education and psychology.

19. If you open your account immediately your first 500 checks will be supplied free moreover you will receive a bonus gift if you are among our first 50 customers.

20. Some of the most famous product failures in history, along with the companies responsible, have included the Hula Burger McDonald's the Betamax Sony and Breakfast Mates Kellogg's.

LEVEL 2

A. (Self-check) For each of the following sentences, underline any errors in punctuation. Then in the space provided write the correct punctuation plus the preceding word. If a colon should be omitted, write *Omit colon.* Write *C* if the sentence is correct.

Example: Business model patents were awarded to: Netflix, TiVo, and Priceline.   Omit colon

1. Three factors on which auto insurers frequently base rates are: a driver's safety record, miles driven, and years of driving experience.

2. The American Association of Retired Persons (AARP) selected the following cities as the best places to "reinvent your life": Fort Collins, Colorado; Bellingham, Washington; and Raleigh, North Carolina.

3. Smart phones are available from the following three companies: Please check on prices.

Motorola   Nokia   Samsung.

4. Dr. Marlyn Wiswall said; "Never underestimate the value of stories and humor in delivering and organizing your speech. People forget facts and graphs; they remember and retell memorable stories and anecdotes that illustrate your points."

5. The head of the computer security firm admitted one big problem: finding good people without criminal records.

6. Five of the worst computer passwords are: your first name, your last name, the Enter key, *Password,* and the name of a sports team.

7. We have requests for information from three local companies: Sterling Laboratories, Putnam Brothers, and Big Dog, Inc.

8. The computer virus was called: "Backdoor Winker."

Want to explore more? Go to: academic.cengage.com/bcomm/guffey or Xtra!

SEMICOLONS AND COLONS I CHAPTER 15 I **279**

9. The most commonly observed holidays are the following: Thanksgiving, Labor Day, Christmas, July Fourth, and New Year's Day. _____

10. Shane proposed a solution to our day-care problem: open a home office and share child-care duties. _____

Check your answers below.

B. For the following sentences, add any necessary but missing punctuation marks. For each sentence indicate in the space provided the number of additions you have made. Mark *C* if the sentence is correct as it stands.

Example: According to the Federal Trade Commission (FTC) the following scams are most likely to arrive in your e-mail box business opportunities chain letters work-at-home schemes and investment opportunities.   5 _____

1. Three similar types of tropical storms with different names are cyclones typhoons and hurricanes. _____

2. American Apparel, maker of trendy clothing, unveiled its latest, hippest retail outlet a computer-generated boutique operating as a simulation game. _____

3. Polygraph examinations generally consist of four elements a preexamination interview, a demonstration, questioning of the examinee, and a postexamination interview. _____

4. Sam Walton, founder of Wal-Mart, once said "Outstanding leaders go out of their way to boost the self-esteem of their personnel. If people believe in themselves, it's amazing what they can accomplish." _____

5. Experts suggest the following tips for choosing a business name
   1. Avoid generic names.
   2. Keep it brief.
   3. Don't be too narrow or too literal. _____

6. Each balance sheet is a statement of assets liabilities and owner's equity. _____

7. Google offers many services in addition to its Web-search tool including the following Google Maps Google Finance Google News Gmail Google Talk and Froogle. _____

8. Energy in this country is supplied from a number of sources oil natural gas coal nuclear fission and hydropower. _____

9. For graduation you must complete courses in mathematics, accounting, English, management, and computer applications. _____

10. The law of supply and demand can function only under the following condition: producers must know what consumers want. _____

11. Professor Marilyn Simonson asked that research reports contain the following sections introduction body summary and bibliography. _____

12. Additional costs in selling the house are title examination, title insurance, transfer tax, preparation of documents, and closing fee. _____

Want to explore more? Go to: academic.cengage.com/bcomm/guffey or Xtra!

13. Warren Bennis said "The factory of the future will have only two employees, a man and a dog. The man will be there to feed the dog. The dog will be there to keep the man from touching the equipment." _____

14. Of all the discoveries and inventions in human history, the four greatest are said to be these speech, fire, agriculture, and the wheel. _____

15. Ritz employees follow these four rules build strong relationships with guests, create memorable experiences for guests, seek opportunities to innovate, and continuously learn and grow. _____

C. **Writing Exercise.** Write original sentences to illustrate the following. Talk about your experience in using e-mail. For example: *I generally use the Internet for e-mail; however, I plan to get better at using it for research.*

1. (Semicolon with conjunctive adverb) _____

_____

2. (Semicolon without conjunctive adverb) _____

_____

3. (Colon with listed items) _____

_____

LEVEL 3

A. **(Self-check)** Insert necessary punctuation. In the space provided, write the number of punctuation marks that you inserted. Write *C* if the sentence is correct.

1. Four employees have been recognized for achievement awards; namely, Michelle Taylor, Corrine Chan, Todd Wilde, and Lorenda Carty. _____

2. Many new words have been added to the dictionary; for example, *ringtone, biodiesel, spyware,* and *agritourism.* _____

3. Many airlines, including American and Delta, no longer provide free meals in coach; and Northwest Airlines, which is trying to offset rising fuel prices, has stopped offering free magazines, pillows, and movies on its domestic flights. _____

4. The meeting started promptly at 1:15 p.m. and ended at 3:45 p.m. _____

5. "Smart kitchens" are now offered in many new homes for example some smart kitchens come with ovens that can cook food on demand via a cell phone. _____

6. All employees are urged to observe the following rule: When in doubt, consult the company style manual. _____

7. The writer of a research report should include a variety of references; for example, books, periodicals, government publications, and newspapers. _____

Want to explore more? Go to: academic.cengage.com/bcomm/guffey or Xtra!

8. A must-read book for investors is *Against the Gods The Remarkable Story of Risk.*

9. For the opening session of the convention, the keynote speaker will be systems analyst Barb Kaldenberger; and for the afternoon general membership meeting, the speaker will be NASA representative Catherine Peck.

10. You may pay your deposit using any of the following methods: credit card, check, or wire transfer.

Check your answers below.

B. For the following sentences, add necessary punctuation. For each sentence indicate the number of additions you made. Mark *C* if correct.

Example: If she completes the proposal Sharon Allen will fly to Washington on Tuesday, if not she will leave on Thursday.   3 _____

1. I am looking for many factors in a job for example pleasant working environment good benefits and opportunity for growth. _____

2. Because of her computer expertise Kay Stephan was chosen as our network administrator and because of her people skills Karley Cooper was chosen as trainer. _____

3. The book group will discuss Eric Schlosser's *Fast Food Nation The Dark Side of the All-American Meal* at next week's meeting. _____

4. Companies that plan to expand in China should be aware of several important factors for example regulatory environment cultural differences and technologies in use. _____

5. Large and small companies have an important reason for expanding in China that is by 2025 China is predicted to become the world's largest economy. _____

6. Three times have been designated for the interviews Thursday at 6 30 p.m. Friday at 3 30 p.m. and Monday at 10 a.m. _____

7. An author, composer, or photographer may protect his or her product with a government-approved monopoly namely a copyright. _____

8. Ben Bernanke, the chair of the Federal Reserve, promised to use plain English in his communications however many complain that he is using "Fedspeak" instead. _____

9. Stories circulated about Henry Ford founder Ford Motor Company Lee Iacocca former CEO Chrysler Motor Company and Shoichiro Toyoda former chief Toyota Motor Company. _____

10. AT&T plans to provide the following to low-income families computer equipment Internet access and training. _____

Want to explore more? Go to: academic.cengage.com/bcomm/guffey or Xtra!

282 | UNIT 5 | CHAPTER 15 | SEMICOLONS AND COLONS

C. **Hotline Review.** In the space provided write the correct answer choice.

1. We admired the architecture on the _____ building in Providence, Rhode Island.
   a. capital   b. capitol   _____

2. Carson City is the _____ of Nevada.
   a. capital   b. capitol   _____

3. Reimbursements will be _____ to employees on Friday.
   a. disbursed   b. dispersed   _____

4. Some cities use fogging machines to _____ mosquito-control pesticides.
   a. disburse   b. disperse   _____

5. We _____ from our research study that customers prefer the new taste.
   a. inferred   b. implied   _____

6. Did her comment _____ that she's looking for another job?
   a. infer   b. imply   _____

Want to explore more? Go to: academic.cengage.com/bcomm/guffey or Xtra!

SEMICOLONS AND COLONS | CHAPTER 15 | **283**

The following memo contains intentional errors representing spelling, proofreading, punctuation, and language principles covered thus far. You should mark 40 changes. When you replace a wordy or incorrect phrase with one word, it counts as one correction. When you correct a comma splice, run-on, or fragment, the correction counts as two errors. Use proofreading marks to make the corrections here OR make the corrections at the **Guffey Companion Web Site** at **academic.cengage.com/bcomm/guffey.**

Software Unlimited

Interoffice Memo

DATE: February 3, 200x
TO: Doug Rincon
FROM: Jennifer Tejada   *JT*
SUBJECT: RECOMMENDED FREE E-MAIL PROGRAMS

As you requested I am submitting this list of three of the best free e-mail cites that I could find on the Web. All of the cites seems to provide basic e-mail service with various features, however a few features are available only for a fee.

1. Gmail <www.gmail.com>

Gmail is quickly becoming one of the most popular free e-mail programs on the Web. This program which has no pop-ups or banner ads offers many attractive features. In addition the number of features are growing everyday. The most-popular features are the following, 2,500 megabytes of storage, spam protection, automatic forwarding and virus scanning.

Messages can even be sent and read in over 40 languages, some of which are: Arabic, Tagalog, Latvian and Portuguese. Gmail also offers an unique feature, that is, Gmail integrates instant messaging in to the e-mail experience. In order to sign up for a Gmail account you must be invited by someone whom all ready has one.

2. Yahoo Mail <www.mail.yahoo.com>

Yahoo Mail is another free e-mail service thats easy to use. In addition to e-mail a Yahoo Mail account includes the following free features, spam protection, virus protection, 1 gigabyte of storage and access from anywhere a user has a Web connection. For just $19.99 a year you can get a Yahoo Mail Plus account. This premium account offers: virus cleaning, SpamGuardPlus and 2 gigabytes of e-mail storage.

3. Hotmail <www.hotmail.com>

Hotmail which is owned by Microsoft is a third free e-mail program. This program offers: powerful spam filters, virus scanning and virus cleaning. When a user first enrolls they receive 25 megabytes of storage, however, after 30 days this amount increases to 250 megabytes.

Gmail is the program I recommend, Yahoo Mail and Hotmail are not as robust. Be sure and check out these sites, and then let me know whether you have any question.

Want to explore more? Go to: academic.cengage.com/bcomm/guffey or Xtra!

284 | UNIT 5 | CHAPTER 15 | SEMICOLONS AND COLONS

Goal: To find valuable career information on the Web.

You're now ready to hunt for a job, and you decide to learn what you can to make your job search a success.

1. With your Web browser on the screen, go to the *Quintessential Careers* site: **http://www. quintcareers.com.**

2. At the *Quintessential Careers* site, click **Open Our Career Toolkit.**

3. On the "Career Resources Toolkit for Job-Seekers" site, click **Career, College, and Job-Related Articles.** Click **Job Hunting Do's and Don'ts Articles.**

4. Scroll down to read the article titles, and click the article of your choice.

5. Read and print the article.

6. Use the **Back** button to repeat the process for another article. Choose a second article to read and print.

7. To explore more of this career site, press the **Back** button to return to the main page, or reenter **http://wwwquintcareers.com.**

8. End your session and submit two printed pages with the articles you read.

Add appropriate semicolons, colons, and commas.

1. Gas prices are rising dramatically therefore more people are walking and riding their bikes to work.

2. The following instructors have been chosen to represent their schools at the professional meeting Joyce Birch Normandale Community College Sandra Farrar Louisiana Technical College and Paul Murphey Southwest Wisconsin Technical College.

3. All morning sessions begin at 9 a.m. all afternoon sessions begin at 1 p.m.

4. The Allen & Company conference which is one of the most high-profile get-togethers in the country is attended by 300 billionaires for example, Bill Gates, Warren Buffett, Rupert Murdoch, and Steve Jobs.

5. Have you read Robert K. Greenleaf's book *Servant Leadership A Journey Into the Nature of Legitimate Power and Greatness?*

1. dramatically; therefore. 2. meeting: Birch, College; Farrar, College; Murphey. 3. 9 a.m.; 4. conference, country, billionaires. 5. *Leadership*

Want to explore more? Go to: academic.cengage.com/bcomm/guffey or Xtra!

SEMICOLONS AND COLONS | CHAPTER 15 | 285

16

OTHER PUNCTUATION

OBJECTIVES

When you have completed the materials in this chapter, you will be able to do the following:

LEVEL 1

- Use periods to correctly punctuate statements, commands, indirect questions, polite requests, abbreviations, initials, and numerals.
- Use question marks and exclamation points correctly.

LEVEL 2

- Recognize acceptable applications for dashes and parentheses.
- Correctly punctuate and capitalize material set off by parentheses and dashes.

LEVEL 3

- Use double and single quotation marks properly, and correctly place other punctuation marks in relation to quotation marks.
- Use underscores, italics, and brackets appropriately.

PRETEST

Use proofreading marks to insert appropriate punctuation in the following sentences.

1. Please invite Radene Schroeder PhD and M L Vasquez

2. Dr Stanier Ms Ling and Mr Ramirez have been appointed to the SEC

3. The chapter titled How Companies Cope was the best one in the book *The World Is Flat* by Thomas L Friedman

1. Schroeder, PhD, M. L. Vasquez. 2. Dr. Stanier, Ms. Ling, Mr. SEC. 3. "How Companies Cope" L. Friedman. 4. degrees. 5. Dr. say, "If more, yourself?"

4. I wonder whether all candidates for the CEO position completed MBA degrees

5. Did Dr Phil say If you want more you have to require more from yourself

This chapter teaches you how to use periods, question marks, and exclamation points correctly. It also includes suggestions for punctuating with dashes, parentheses, single quotation marks, double quotation marks, brackets, and underscores (italics).

USES FOR THE PERIOD

The period can be used to punctuate sentences, abbreviations, initials, and numerals. Guidelines for each use are covered in this section.

TO PUNCTUATE STATEMENTS, COMMANDS, AND INDIRECT QUESTIONS

Use a period at the end of a statement, a command, or an indirect question.

> In 1809 Mary Kies became the first woman to be issued a U.S. patent. (Statement)
>
> Deliver the food for the office party before 5 p.m. (Command)
>
> Liz asked whether we had sent the price list. (Indirect question)

TO PUNCTUATE POLITE REQUESTS

Use a period, not a question mark, to punctuate a polite request. A **polite request** is a command or suggestion phrased as a request. Such a request asks the reader to perform a specific action instead of responding with a *yes* or *no*.

> Could you please check the latest prices on MP3 players. (Polite request)
>
> May I suggest that you submit your application online. (Polite request)
>
> Will you be sure to lock the door when you leave. (Polite request)

If you are asking a favor or if you think the reader may feel that your request is presumptuous, use a question mark rather than a period.

> May I ask you to fill in for me at the next board meeting? (Request that asks a favor)

If you are uncomfortable using a period at the end of a polite request, rephrase the sentence:

> Will you please send me a list of available properties. (Polite request)
>
> Please send me a list of available properties. (Polite request rephrased)

TO PUNCTUATE ABBREVIATIONS

Because of their inconsistencies, abbreviations present problems to writers. The following suggestions will help you organize certain groups of abbreviations and provide many models. In studying these models, note the spacing, capitalization, and use of periods. For a more thorough list of acceptable abbreviations, consult an up-to-date reference manual or dictionary.

a. Use periods after most abbreviations beginning with lowercase letters. Notice that the internal periods are not followed by spaces.

a.m. (ante meridiem)	i.e. (that is)	et al. (and others)
p.m. (post meridiem)	e.g. (for example)	ft. (foot or feet)

Exceptions: mph (miles per hour), wpm (words per minute), mm (millimeter), and kg (kilogram).

b. Use periods for most abbreviations containing capital and lowercase letters.

Dr. (Doctor)	Esq. (Esquire)	Mr. (Mister)
Ms. (blend of Miss and Mrs.)	No. (number)	Sat. (Saturday)

Exceptions: PhD (doctor of philosophy) and EdD (doctor of education)

c. Use all capital letters without periods or internal spaces for the abbreviations of many business organizations, educational institutions, governmental agencies, radio and television stations, professional organizations, job titles, professional designations, academic degrees, and business and technology terms.

AT&T (American Telephone & Telegraph)	IBM (International Business Machines)
UGA (University of Georgia)	RIT (Rochester Institute of Technology)
IRS (Internal Revenue Service)	EPA (Environmental Protection Agency)
NPR (National Public Radio)	PBS (Public Broadcasting Service)
BBB (Better Business Bureau)	STC (Society of Technical Communication)
CEO (chief executive officer)	CFO (chief financial officer)
RN (registered nurse)	CPA (certified public accountant)
BA (bachelor of arts)	MBA (master of business administration)
DSL (digital subscriber line)	HDTV (high-definition television)
VAT (value-added tax)	EST (eastern standard time)
FAQ (frequently asked question)	GDP (gross domestic product)
FYI (for your information)	URL (universal resource locator)

Exceptions: Periods and spaces are included when initials are used for a person's first and middle names (*Mr. J. A. Jones*). In addition, some abbreviations have two forms (*c.o.d., COD* [collect on delivery], *f.o.b., FOB* [free on board]).

d. Use all capital letters without periods or internal spaces for the abbreviations of geographical areas, two-letter state abbreviations, and Canadian province abbreviations. For a complete list of two-letter state and Canadian province abbreviations, consult Figure C.4 in Appendix C.

USA (United States of America)	UK (United Kingdom)
AR (Arkansas)	HI (Hawaii)
NS (Nova Scotia)	BC (British Columbia)

Exception: In business writing use periods when using the abbreviation for *United States* as an adjective (*U.S. Postal Service, U.S. currency*).

TO PUNCTUATE NUMERALS

For a monetary sum, use a period (decimal point) to separate dollars from cents.

> The two items in question, $13.92 and $98.67, were both charged in the month of October.

Use a period (decimal point) to mark a decimal fraction.

> Only 35.3 percent of eligible voters voted in Tuesday's election.

USES FOR THE QUESTION MARK

The question mark punctuates direct questions and questions added to statements.

TO PUNCTUATE DIRECT QUESTIONS

Use a question mark at the end of a direct question.

> What can we do to improve communication among departments?

> Has the music industry been successful in stopping illegal file sharers?

TO PUNCTUATE QUESTIONS ADDED TO STATEMENTS

Place a question mark after a question that is added to the end of a statement. Use a comma to separate the statement from the question.

> Starbucks offers wireless Internet networks in many locations, doesn't it?

> This order should be sent by e-mail, don't you think?

USES FOR THE EXCLAMATION POINT

Because the exclamation point expresses strong emotion, business and professional writers use it sparingly.

TO EXPRESS STRONG EMOTION

After a word, phrase, or clause expressing strong emotion, use an exclamation point.

> Impossible! I will never be able to meet such a tight deadline.

> Unbelievable! Have you seen these sales figures?

> What a work of art!

Do not use an exclamation point after mild interjections, such as *oh* and *well*.

> Oh, now I see what you mean.

> Now complete the reinforcement exercises for Level 1.

· LEVEL 2 · LEVEL 2 · LEVEL 2 · LEVEL 2 · LEVEL 2 · **LEVEL 2** · LEVEL 2 · L

USES FOR THE DASH

The dash is a legitimate and effective mark of punctuation when used according to accepted conventions. It is often used to show emphasis. As an emphatic punctuation mark, however, the dash loses effectiveness when it is overused. With a word processor, you can create a dash by typing two hyphens with no space before, between, or after the hyphens. In printed or desktop publishing-generated material, a dash appears as a solid line (an *em* dash). Most current word processors will automatically convert two hyphens to an *em* dash. Study the following suggestions for and illustrations of appropriate uses of the dash.

TO SET OFF PARENTHETICAL ELEMENTS AND APPOSITIVES

Within a sentence, parenthetical elements and appositives are usually set off by commas. If, however, the parenthetical element or appositive itself contains internal commas, use dashes (or parentheses) to set it off.

> Sources of raw materials—farming, mining, fishing, and forestry—are all dependent on energy.

> Four legal assistants—Priscilla Alvarez, Vicki Evans, Yoshiki Ono, and Edward Botsko—received cash bonuses for outstanding service.

TO INDICATE AN INTERRUPTION

An interruption or abrupt change of thought may be separated from the rest of a sentence by a dash. However, sentences with abrupt changes of thought or with appended afterthoughts can usually be improved through rewriting.

> We will refund your money—you have my guarantee—if you are not completely satisfied. (Interruption of thought)

> You can submit your report on Friday—no, we must have it by Thursday at the latest. (Abrupt change of thought)

TO SET OFF A SUMMARIZING STATEMENT

Use a dash (not a colon) to separate an introductory list from a summarizing statement.

> Flexibility, communication skills, intelligence—these are the qualities I appreciate most in a manager.

> Cell phones, pagers, personal organizers—these are some of the most frequently used mobile communication devices.

TO ATTRIBUTE A QUOTATION

Place a dash between a quotation and its source.

> "Live as if you were to die tomorrow. Learn as if you were to live forever."
> —Mahatma Gandhi

> "The future belongs to those who believe in the beauty of their dreams."
> —Eleanor Roosevelt

USES FOR PARENTHESES

Parentheses are generally used in pairs. This section covers guidelines for using parentheses correctly.

TO SET OFF NONESSENTIAL SENTENCE ELEMENTS

Generally, nonessential sentence elements may be punctuated as follows: (a) with commas, to make the lightest possible break in the normal flow of a sentence; (b) with dashes, to emphasize the enclosed material; and (c) with parentheses, to de-emphasize the enclosed material.

> Figure 17, which appears on page 9, clearly illustrates the process. (Normal punctuation)

SPOT THE BLOOPER

A gardening article about the dwarf amaryllis, published in *Florida Today*: "They are an ideal compliment to the larger blooming amaryllis or can be stunning as a mass planting of their own." (See this chapter's Hotline Queries.)

Figure 17—which appears on page 9—clearly illustrates the process. (Dashes emphasize enclosed material.)

Figure 17 (which appears on page 9) clearly illustrates the process. (Parentheses de-emphasize enclosed material.)

Explanations, references, and directions are often enclosed in parentheses.

The bank's current business hours (9 a.m. to 5 p.m.) will be extended in the near future (to 6 p.m.).

I recommend that we direct more funds (see the budget on page 14) to research and development.

A small studio apartment in Florence, Italy, rents for about 1.100 euros ($1,385) per month.

TO MARK NUMERALS AND ENCLOSE ENUMERATED ITEMS

In legal documents and contracts, numerals may appear in both word and figure form. Parentheses enclose the figures. However, business writers are not encouraged to use this wordy technique for most messages.

Your contract states that the final installment payment is due in ninety (90) days.

When using numbers or letters to enumerate lists within sentences, enclose the numbers or letters in parentheses. Use letters for items that have no particular order. Use numbers for items that suggest a sequence.

The Federal Trade Commission (FTC) has initiated several programs to protect individual privacy, including (a) the National Do Not Call Registry, (b) the Fair Credit Reporting Act, and (c) an identity theft Web site.

To post your résumé online, (1) prepare and save your résumé using your word processor, (2) log in to your Monster.com account, (3) click the **Résumé** link, (4) click the **Attach an Existing Résumé** link, (5) type in a résumé headline and career objective, (6) attach your résumé, and (7) click the **Save** button.

PUNCTUATING AROUND PARENTHESES

If the material enclosed by parentheses is embedded within another sentence, a question mark or exclamation point may be used where normally expected. Do not, however, use a period after a statement embedded within another sentence.

I visited the new business travel Web site (have you seen it?) last night.

Photoshop's "hints palette" feature (see Chapter 5) provides helpful illustrations and tips.

If the material enclosed by parentheses is not embedded in another sentence, use whatever punctuation is required.

Report writers must document all references. (See Appendix A for a guide to current documentation formats.)

In sentences involving expressions within parentheses, a comma, semicolon, or colon that would normally occupy the position occupied by the second parenthesis is then placed after that parenthesis.

When we complete the redesign (in late June), we can begin testing the Web site. (Comma follows parenthesis.)

Your tax return was received before the deadline (April 15); however, you did not include your payment. (Semicolon follows parenthesis.)

Now complete the reinforcement exercises for Level 2.

USES FOR QUOTATION MARKS

Guidelines for using quotation marks to enclose direct quotations, quotations within quotations, short expressions, definitions, and literary titles are covered in this section. You will also learn how to place other punctuation in relation to quotation marks.

TO ENCLOSE DIRECT QUOTATIONS

Double quotation marks are used to enclose direct quotations. Unless the exact words of a writer or speaker are being repeated, however, quotation marks are not used.

> "Never trust a computer you can't throw out a window," said Apple Computer Corporation cofounder Steve Wozniak. (Direct quotation enclosed)

> Abraham Lincoln said that we cannot escape tomorrow's responsibility by evading it today. (Indirect quotation requires no quotation marks.)

Capitalize only the first word of a direct quotation.

> "The human race has only one really effective weapon," said Mark Twain, "and that is laughter." (Do not capitalize *and*.)

Single quotation marks (apostrophes on most keyboards) are used to enclose quoted passages cited within quoted passages.

> Delores Tomlin remarked, "In business writing I totally agree with Aristotle, who said, 'A good style must, first of all, be clear.'" (Single quotation marks within double quotation marks)

TO ENCLOSE SHORT EXPRESSIONS

Slang, words used in a special sense, and words following *stamped* or *marked* are often enclosed within quotation marks.

> Cheryl feared that her presentation would "bomb." (Slang)

> Computer criminals are often called "hackers." (Words used in a special sense)

> Some companies are employing Web logs, better known as "blogs," to improve the flow of information among employees. (Words used in a special sense)

> The package was stamped "Handle with Care." (Words following *stamped*)

TO ENCLOSE DEFINITIONS

Quotation marks are used to enclose specific definitions of words or expressions. The word or expression being defined is underscored or set in italics.

> The term *arbitration* refers to "a form of alternative dispute resolution in which a neutral third party hears arguments and evidence and renders a decision."

> Businesspeople use the term *working capital* to indicate an "excess of current assets over current debts."

TO ENCLOSE TITLES

Quotation marks are used to enclose the titles of subdivisions of literary and artistic works, such as magazine and newspaper articles, chapters of books, episodes of television shows, poems, lectures, and songs. However, italics (or underscores) are used to enclose the titles of complete works, such as the names of books, magazines, Web sites, pamphlets, movies, television series, music albums, and newspapers (see next section).

> I loved *The Wall Street Journal* article titled "Why Does 'Everybody' Now Put 'Everything' in Quotation Marks?"

> One source of information for your proposal might be the article "The ADA's Next Step: Cyberspace," which appeared in *BusinessWeek* recently.

> In the episode of *The Office* titled "Diversity Day," the boss, played by Steve Carell, managed to offend everyone.

PUNCTUATING AROUND QUOTATION MARKS

Periods and commas are always placed inside closing quotation marks, whether single or double. Semicolons and colons are, on the other hand, always placed outside closing quotation marks.

> Bernadette Ordian said, "I'm sure the package was stamped 'First Class.'"

> The article is titled "Corporate Espionage," but I don't have a copy.

> Our contract stipulated that "both parties must accept arbitration as binding"; therefore, the decision reached by the arbitrators is final.

> Three dates have been scheduled for the seminar called "Successful E-Business": April 1, May 3, and June 5.

Question marks and exclamation points may go inside or outside closing quotation marks, as determined by the form of the quotation.

> Kalonji Watts said, "How may I apply for that position?" (Quotation is a question.)

> "The next time your cell phone rings," fumed the CEO, "we will ask you to leave!" (Quotation is an exclamation.)

> Do you know who it was who said, "You've got to love what you do to really make things happen"? (Incorporating sentence asks question; quotation does not.)

> I can't believe that the check was stamped "Insufficient Funds"! (Incorporating sentence is an exclamation; quotation is not.)

> When did the manager say, "Who wants to leave early on Friday?" (Both incorporating sentence and quotation are questions. Use only one question mark inside the quotation marks.)

USES FOR ITALICS

Italics (or underscore if italics are not accessible) are normally used for titles of books, magazines, pamphlets, newspapers, and other complete published or artistic works that contain subdivisions. In addition, words under discussion in the sentence and used as nouns are italicized.

> *If You Think You're Not Buying It, You Probably Are*, a book by author Joe Cappo, was favorably reviewed in *The Wall Street Journal*.

> Two of the most frequently misspelled words are *definitely* and *separate*. (Words used as nouns)

STUDY TIP

In the United States, periods and commas are always inside of quotation marks. Semicolons and colons are always outside. Question marks and exclamation points depend on the material quoted.

SPOT THE BLOOPER

Crime report in the *Record-Herald* [Washington Court House, Ohio]: A young man was arrested for "possession of underage alcohol."

STUDY TIP

With today's sophisticated software programs and printers, you can, like professional printers, use italics instead of underscoring for titles and special words.

USES FOR BRACKETS

Within quotations, brackets are used by writers to enclose their own inserted remarks. Such remarks may be corrective, illustrative, or explanatory. Brackets are also used within quotations to enclose the word *sic,* which means "thus" or "so." This Latin form is used to emphasize the fact that an error obvious to all actually appears thus in the quoted material.

> "A British imperial gallon," reported Eli Greenstein, "is equal to 1.2 U.S. gallons [4.54 liters]."

> "The company's reorganization program," wrote President Theodore Bailey, "will have its greatest affect [*sic*] on our immediate sales."

Now complete the reinforcement exercises for Level 3.

HOTLINE QUERIES

Answered by Dr. Guffey

Question

Answer

Q: My team and I are writing a proposal in which we say that *some of the current dot coms are undervalued.* We can't agree on how to write *dot coms.*

A: This playful reference to Internet companies is a little slangy, but it has become part of our common language. The standard way to write this expression is with a hyphen (*dot-com*).

Q: Should a period go inside or outside quotation marks? At the end of a sentence, I have typed the title "*Positive Vs. Negative Values.*" The author of the document wants the period outside because she says the title does not have a period in it.

A: In the United States typists and printers have adopted a uniform style: when a period or comma falls at the same place quotation marks would normally fall, the period or comma is always placed inside the quotation marks—regardless of the content of the quotation. In Britain a different style is observed.

Q: I have a phone extension at work, and I often want to tell people to call me at this extension. Can I abbreviate the word *extension?* If so, what is the proper abbreviation?

A: The abbreviation for *extension* is *Ext.* Notice that the abbreviation is capitalized and ends with a period. When you use this abbreviation in conjunction with a phone number, place a comma before and after (*To reserve your spot, please call me at 685-1230, Ext. 2306, before November 30.*)

Q: We're having an argument in our office about abbreviations. Can *department* be abbreviated *dep't?* How about *manufacturing* as *mf'g?*

A: In informal writing or when space is limited, words may be contracted or abbreviated. If a conventional abbreviation for a word exists, use it instead of a contracted form. Abbreviations are simpler to write and easier to read. For example, use *dept.* instead of *dep't;* use *natl.* instead of *nat'l;* use *cont.* instead of *cont'd.* Other accepted abbreviations are *ins.* for *insurance; mfg.* for *manufacturing; mgr.* for *manager;* and *mdse.* for *merchandise.* Notice that all abbreviations end with periods.

Q: Where should the word *sic* be placed when it is used?

A: *Sic* means "thus" or "so stated," and it is properly placed immediately following the word or phrase to which it refers. For example, *The kidnappers placed a newspaper advertisement that read "Call Monna* [sic] *Lisa."* *Sic* is used within a quotation to indicate that a quoted word or phrase, though inaccurately spelled or used, appeared thus in the original. *Sic* is italicized and placed within brackets.

Q: I've looked in the dictionary but I'm still unsure about whether to hyphenate *copilot*.

A: The hyphen is no longer used in most words beginning with the prefix *co* (*coauthor, cocounsel, codesign, cofeature, cohead, copilot, costar, cowrite*). Only a few words retain the hyphen (*co-anchor, co-edition, co-official*). Check your dictionary for usage. In reading your dictionary, notice that centered periods are used to indicate syllables (*co•work•er*); hyphens are used to show hyphenated syllables (*co-own*).

Q: I sometimes see three periods in a row in documents I'm reading and in book and film reviews. Does this use of periods have a name? When is this type of punctuation used?

A: A series of three periods, with spaces before, between, and after each period, is called an *ellipsis* (. . .). Ellipses are usually used to show that information has been left out of quoted material. (*Roger Ebert's review of* Chicago *includes these words:* "By filming it in its own spirit, by making it frankly a stagy song-and-dance revue . . . the movie is big, brassy fun.") The ellipsis shows that this is not Roger Ebert's complete quote and that words have been omitted between *revue* and *the*.

Q: I recently received an invitation to my high school reunion that used the apostrophe like this: *the class of '96.* Is this a correct use of the apostrophe?

A: Yes. In addition to forming noun possession and contractions, the apostrophe has several other uses. It can be used to take the place of omitted letters or figures (*He stops by Dunkin' Donuts every morning on his way to work*). This is especially common when expressing a year (*Music, films, and fashions of the '70s are suddenly popular again*). In technical documents the apostrophe can be used as the symbol for *feet*. A quotation mark is used as the symbol for *inches* (*She is only 5' 1", but she can overpower a room*).

Q: Should I use *complimentary* or *complementary* to describe free tickets?

A: Use *complimentary*, which can mean "containing a compliment, favorable, or free" (*the dinner came with complimentary wine; he made a complimentary remark*). *Complementary* means "completing or making perfect" (*The online edition of* The Wall Street Journal *is the perfect complement to your print subscription. The complementary colors enhanced the room*). An easy way to remember *compliment* is by thinking "*I* like to receive a *compliment*."

LEVEL 1

A. (Self-check) In the spaces provided after each sentence, indicate whether a period, question mark, or exclamation point is needed. Use the symbol. If no additional punctuation is required, write *C*.

Example: Would you please send me your latest catalog⊙   ._____

1. May I suggest that you contact the manager directly   _____

2. What a fantastic presentation   _____

3. The meeting is at 2 p.m., isn't it   _____

4. Has anyone checked the FedEx Web site to see whether our package
   was delivered   _____

5. Download a trial version of our file transfer protocol (FTP) software today   _____

6. Wow! My new boss is amazing   _____

7. Warren asked whether our company will start using the smart cards
   manufactured by Fargo Electronics, Inc   _____

8. Did Tracy mail the test results when she left at 5 p.m.   _____

9. I wonder whether he's checked with the three credit reporting bureaus to
   find out whether his credit card has been used fraudulently   _____

10. Dr. Helen C. Haitz and Emile Brault, PhD, will appear on TV at 2 p.m., EST.   _____

Check your answers below.

B. Write the letter of the correctly punctuated sentence.

1. a. Wyatt asked whether Google's original name was Googol.
   b. Wyatt asked whether Google's original name was Googol?
   c. Wyatt asked, whether Google's original name was Googol.   _____

2. a. Did our CEO interview Ms. E. W. Rasheen for the C.P.A. position?
   b. Did our C.E.O. interview Ms. E. W. Rasheen for the C.P.A. position?
   c. Did our CEO interview Ms. E. W. Rasheen for the CPA position?   _____

3. a. Many more MBA programs are available in the USA than in the UK.
   b. Many more M.B.A. programs are available in the U.S.A. than in the U.K.
   c. Many more M.B.A. programs are available in the USA than in the UK.   _____

4. a. Advertisements will air on the following radio stations: KFOG, KGO,
   and KCSM.
   b. Advertisements will air on the following radio stations: K.F.O.G., K.G.O.,
   and K.C.S.M..
   c. Advertisements will air on the following radio stations; KFOG, KGO,
   and KCSM.   _____

1. directly. 2. presentation! 3. it? 4. delivered? 5. today. 6. amazing! 7. Inc. 8. 5 p.m.? 9. fraudulently. 10. C

Want to explore more? Go to: academic.cengage.com/bcomm/guffey or Xtra!

OTHER PUNCTUATION | CHAPTER 16 | **297**

5. a. The No 1 official at the EPA has a B.A. from MSU Mankato.
    b. The No. 1 official at the EPA has a BA from MSU Mankato.
    c. The No. 1 official at the EPA has a B.A. from MSU Mankato.   _____

6. a. The recipient's address is 5 Sierra Drive, Rochester, N.Y. 14616.
    b. The recipient's address is 5 Sierra Drive, Rochester, NY 14616.
    c. The recipient's address is 5 Sierra Drive, Rochester, Ny. 14616.   _____

C. In the following sentences, all punctuation has been omitted. Insert commas, periods, question marks, colons, and exclamation points. Some words have extra spaces between them so that punctuation may be inserted; however, a space does not mean that punctuation is necessary. Use a caret (∧) to indicate each insertion. In the space at the right, indicate the number of punctuation marks you inserted. Consult a reference manual or a dictionary for abbreviation style if necessary.

Example: Virginia asked whether William M◦Curran Sr◦was hired as C F O at
             ∧   ∧
             Apple Computer, Inc◦   3 _____
             ∧

1. Will you please contact Sandra B Stone Ph D about her P D A order   _____

2. The H T M L workshop will be held from 9 a m until 4 p m   _____

3. Dr Delores K Garland will travel from the U S A to the R O C in 2010   _____

4. You did change your P I N as the bank requested didn't you   _____

5. Thu Thi Tran M B A was recognized for her work with the S E C   _____

6. What a dilemma the latest F C C regulations have created   _____

7. Stop That's an emergency exit   _____

8. Deliver the signed contracts to Ms C M Gigliotti before 6 p m E S T   _____

9. If I B M offers a full-service contract we would be interested   _____

10. What a great story on the A B C news   _____

11. Dan wondered whether he had earned enough units for his A A degree   _____

12. After completing her B S degree at U N L V Kim transferred and began
    working on an M S degree   _____

13. Ms J S Neighbors has been appointed consultant for educational
    services to the A F L - C I O   _____

14. Does he often use the abbreviations e g and i e in his e-mail messages   _____

15. Since the funds were earned in the U K I must consult my C P A about
    paying taxes in the U S A   _____

16. Some users wonder whether the F A Q s on the U S P S Web site are current _____

17. Has the erroneous charge of $45 95 been removed from my account   _____

18. The guest list includes the following individuals Dr Lyn Clark Ms Frances
    Hendricks and Professor Jean Sturgill   _____

19. Lt Gen Maxwell asked whether the U S Census Bureau office will be
    open until 6 p m   _____

20. You did check the U R L for that Web site didn't you   _____

Want to explore more? Go to: academic.cengage.com/bcomm/guffey or Xtra!

298 | UNIT 5 | CHAPTER 16 | OTHER PUNCTUATION

LEVEL 2

A. **(Self-check)** Write the letter of the correctly punctuated sentence in the space provided.

1. a. Luke Wilkinson scored a perfect 800 (can you believe it) on the GMAT.
    b. Luke Wilkinson scored a perfect 800 (can you believe it?) on the GMAT.
    c. Luke Wilkinson scored a perfect 800 (can you believe it) on the G.M.A.T.? _____

2. a. Mission statement, management bios, product fact sheet, list of clients: these
       are documents that can boost a company's professionalism.
    b. Mission statement, management bios, product fact sheet, list of clients—
       these are documents that can boost a company's professionalism.
    c. Mission statement, management bios, product fact sheet, list of clients;
       these are documents that can boost a company's professionalism. _____

3. a. "Sometimes it is better to lose and do the right thing than to win and
       do the wrong thing."—Tony Blair
    b. "Sometimes it is better to lose and do the right thing than to win and
       do the wrong thing," Tony Blair
    c. "Sometimes it is better to lose and do the right thing than to win and
       do the wrong thing": Tony Blair _____

4. (Emphasize parenthetical element.)
    a. Currently our basic operating costs: rent, utilities, and wages, are
       10 percent higher than last year.
    b. Currently our basic operating costs (rent, utilities, and wages) are
       10 percent higher than last year.
    c. Currently our basic operating costs—rent, utilities, and wages—are
       10 percent higher than last year. _____

5. a. Removing the back panel (see the warning on page 1) should be done
       only by authorized repair staff.
    b. Removing the back panel, see the warning on page 1, should be done
       only by authorized repair staff.
    c. Removing the back panel: see the warning on page 1, should be done
       only by authorized repair staff. _____

6. a. Recently you applied for a position (executive assistant); however, you
       did not indicate for which branch your application is intended.
    b. Recently you applied for a position; (executive assistant) however, you
       did not indicate for which branch your application is intended.
    c. Recently you applied for a position (executive assistant;) however, you
       did not indicate for which branch your application is intended. _____

7. (Emphasize.)
    a. Sales, sales, and more sales: that's what we need to succeed.
    b. Sales, sales, and more sales—that's what we need to succeed.
    c. Sales, sales, and more sales; that's what we need to succeed. _____

8. (De-emphasize.)
    a. Four features—maps, instant messaging, Web searching, and e-mail—are
       what Americans want most on their cell phones.
    b. Four features, maps, instant messaging, Web searching, and e-mail,
       are what Americans want most on their cell phones.
    c. Four features (maps, instant messaging, Web searching, and e-mail)
       are what Americans want most on their cell phones. _____

Check your answers below.

1.b 2.b 3.a 4.c 5.a 6.a 7.b 8.c

Want to explore more? Go to: academic.cengage.com/bcomm/guffey or Xtra!

OTHER PUNCTUATION | CHAPTER 16 | 299

B. Insert dashes or parentheses in the following sentences. In the space provided after each sentence, write the number of punctuation marks you inserted. Count each parenthesis and each dash as a single mark.

Example: (Emphasize.) Consumers use retail Web sites for basic product
information‒price, availability, quality‒and for customer service.   2 _____

1. "To succeed in life in today's world, you must have the will and tenacity to finish the job." Ching-Ning Chu.   _____

2. (De-emphasize.) The Tony Award-winning production of *The History Boys* have you seen the reviews will be opening here shortly.   _____

3. Podcasting, mashups, and wikis these are all features you'll find on Web 2.0.   _____

4. (De-emphasize.) Five start-up companies Digg, Last.fm, Newsvine, Tagworld, and YouTube are expected to play major roles in developing the social media content for Web 2.0.   _____

5. (Emphasize.) Three of the biggest problems with e-mail privacy, overuse, and etiquette will be discussed.   _____

6. Funds for the project will be released on the following dates see Section 12.3 of the original grant : January 1, March 14, and June 30.   _____

7. (De-emphasize.) As soon as you are able to make an appointment try to do so before December 30 , we will process your passport application.   _____

8. Voice recorder, photo album, laser pointer, language translator these are just some of the many ways an iPod can be used.   _____

9. (De-emphasize.) Readers of *Condé Nast Traveler* selected four U.S. cities San Francisco, New York, Chicago, and New Orleans as having the best restaurants.   _____

10. The BlackBerry warranty contract is limited to sixty 60 days.   _____

C. Using three different forms of punctuation, correctly punctuate the following sentence. In the space provided explain how the three methods you have employed differ.

1. Numerous appeals all of which came from concerned parents prompted us to rethink the school closure.   _____

2. Numerous appeals all of which came from concerned parents prompted us to rethink the school closure.   _____

3. Numerous appeals all of which came from concerned parents prompted us to rethink the school closure.   _____

Explanation: _____

_____

LEVEL 3

A. **(Self-check)** Indicate whether the following statements are true (*T*) or false (*F*).

1. Double quotation marks are used to enclose the exact words of a writer or speaker.   _____

2. Names of books, magazines, Web sites, pamphlets, and newspapers should be enclosed in quotations.   _____

3. Periods and commas are always placed inside closing quotation marks.   _____

Want to explore more? Go to: academic.cengage.com/bcomm/guffey or Xtra!

4. Brackets are used by writers to enclose their own remarks inserted into a quotation. _____

5. A quotation within a quotation is shown with single quotation marks. _____

6. Semicolons and colons are always placed outside closing quotation marks. _____

7. Titles of articles, book chapters, poems, and songs should be italicized or underlined. _____

8. If both a quotation and its introductory sentence are questions, use a question mark before the closing quotation marks. _____

9. The word *sic* is used to show that a quotation is free of errors. _____

10. A single quotation mark is typed by using the apostrophe key. _____

Check your answers below.

B. Many, but not all, of the following sentences contain direct quotations. Insert all necessary punctuation. Underlines may be used for words that might be italicized in print.

Example: The term _preferred stock_ means "stock having priority over common stock in the distribution of dividends."

1. In the arena of human life, said Aristotle, the honors and rewards fall to those who show their good qualities in action _____

2. The word *mashup* is a technology term that is defined as a Web site that uses content from more than one source to create a completely new service _____

3. Kym Anderson's chapter titled Subsidies and Trade Barriers appears in the book *How to Spend $50 Billion to Make the World a Better Place* _____

4. Did Donald Trump really say Anyone who thinks my story is anywhere near over is sadly mistaken _____

5. In his speech the software billionaire said Our goal is to link the world irregardless [sic] of national boundaries and restrictions _____

6. Oprah Winfrey said that the best jobs are those we'd do even if we didn't get paid _____

7. Garth said he was stoked about his upcoming vacation to Mexico _____

8. The postal worker said Shall I stamp your package Fragile _____

9. Did you see the article titled The Patented Path to Profits in *Forbes* _____

10. The French expression *répondez s'il vous plaît* means respond if you please _____

11. Would you please send a current catalog to Globex, Inc _____

12. (Direct quotation.) The man who does not read good books said Mark Twain has no advantage over the man who cannot read them _____

13. (Emphasize.) Three of the largest manufacturers Dell, IBM, and Hewlett-Packard submitted bids _____

14. In *BusinessWeek* I saw an article titled U S Fashion's Passage to India _____

15. (De-emphasize.) Albert Einstein once said that only two things the universe and human stupidity are infinite _____

1. T 2. F 3. T 4. T 5. T 6. T 7. F 8. T 9. F 10. T

C. Writing Practice. On a separate sheet, write a paragraph describing your ideal job. Try to include as many of the punctuation marks you have studied as possible. Include commas, semicolons, periods, question marks, exclamation points, dashes, parentheses, quotation marks, italics, and possibly even brackets. Include a quotation from your boss. Make up the name of a book or article that you could publish about this job.

D. Hotline Review. In the space provided, write the correct answer choice.

1. When the economy slowed, many _____ went out of business.
    a. dot.coms   b. dot-coms   c. dot coms   _____

2. Which sentence is punctuated correctly?
    a. Have you read the article titled "Does Motorola Have Nokia's Number"?
    b. Have you read the article titled "Does Motorola Have Nokia's Number?"
    c. Have you read the article titled "Does Motorola Have Nokia's Number?"?   _____

3. One of the best ways to motivate employees is to _____ their work.
    a. compliment   b. complement   _____

4. Companies often make acquisitions in order to acquire _____ products.
    a. complimentary   b. complementary   _____

5. He gets along well with his _____.
    a. co-workers   b. co workers   c. coworkers   _____

Want to explore more? Go to: academic.cengage.com/bcomm/guffey or Xtra!

302 I UNIT 5 I CHAPTER 16 I OTHER PUNCTUATION

The following letter contains intentional errors representing spelling, proofreading, punctuation, and language principles covered thus far. You should mark 40 changes. When you replace a wordy or incorrect phrase with one word, it counts as one correction. When you correct a comma splice, run-on, or fragment, the correction counts as two errors. Count each parenthesis and each dash as a single mark. Use proofreading marks to make the corrections here OR make the corrections at the **Guffey Companion Web Site** at **academic.cengage.com/bcomm/guffey.**

2419 Branch Lane
Austin, TX 78214
August 23, 200x

Mr. Doug Young, Manager
Tejas Grill
3210 South Congress Avenue
Austin, TX 78704

Dear Mr. Young,

Even when us servers has given good service some customers don't leave a tip. This is a serious problem for we servers at Tejas Grill. Many of us has gotten together and decided to bring the problem—and a possible solution, to your attention in this letter. Please read our ideas carefully, then plan on meeting with us to discuss them.

Some restaurants (such as the Coach House in New York—now automatically adds a 15 percent tip to the bill. Other restaurants are printing gratuity guideline's on checks. In fact American Express now provides a calculation feature on it's terminals so that restaurants can chose the tip levels they want printed. The following tip levels are included; 10, 15, or 20 percent. You can read about these procedures in an article titled Forcing the Tip, which appeared recently in "The New York Times." Ive enclosed a copy.

A mandatory tip printed on checks would work good at Tejas don't you think. We give good service and receive many complements, however, some customers forget to tip. By printing a suggested tip on the check we remind customers so that they won't forget. A printed mandatory tip also does the math for customers which is an advantage for those who are not to good with figures!

Printing mandatory tips on checks not only help customers but also prove to the staff that you support them in there goal to recieve decent wages for the hard work they do. A few customers might complain but these customers can always cross out the printed tip if they wish. If you have any doubts about the plan we could try it for a six month period and monitor customer's reactions.

We urge you to begin printing a mandatory 15 percent tip on each customers bill. Our American Express terminals are already equipped to do this. Will you please let us know your feelings about this proposal as soon as possible. Its a serious concern to we servers.

Sincerely,

Brenda Vasquez

Brenda Vasquez
Server

Enclosure

Want to explore more? Go to: academic.cengage.com/bcomm/guffey or Xtra!

OTHER PUNCTUATION | CHAPTER 16 | **303**

Goal: To locate some of the best business-related sites on the Web.

You want to conduct business research on the Web, but you want to make sure that the sites you visit are credible. You just found out that the American Library Association (ALA) has put together a list of reputable business sites, and you want to learn more.

1. With your Web browser on the screen, go to the American Library Association's *Best of the Best Business Web sites* site (**http://www.ala.org/ala/rusa/rusaourassoc/ rusasections/brass/brass.htm**). Click the **Best of the Best Business Web Sites** icon.

2. In the **Subject Index** section, click your major or business area of interest.

3. Read the description for each related Web site. Click the link for the site that sounds most interesting or relevant. (Note: The site will open in a separate browser window.)

4. Find two or three facts or pieces of information on the site that will help you in your studies or career. Write down what you learn and explain how it will help you in your studies or in your career.

5. Print two pages from this Web site. End your session. Submit your printouts and answers to the questions posed here.

Use proofreading marks to insert necessary punctuation.

1. Will you please send me a copy of the article titled Winning Negotiation Strategies

2. When did we receive this package marked Confidential

3. The only guests who have not sent RSVPs are Miss Mendoza Mrs Gold and Mr Sims

4. Taking pictures, surfing Web sites, watching TV shows these are just some of the things people do with their cell phones.

5. Did Dr Simanek say "I'd like to put you on an exercise program"

1. "Winning Negotiation Strategies." 2. "Confidential"? 3. Mendoza, Mrs. Gold, and Mr. Sims. 4. shows— 5. Dr. say, "I'd program."?

Want to explore more? Go to: academic.cengage.com/bcomm/guffey or Xtra!

304 | UNIT 5 | CHAPTER 16 | OTHER PUNCTUATION

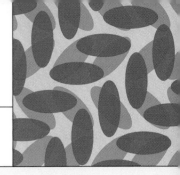

First, review Chapters 14–16. Then, test your comprehension of those chapters by completing the exercises that follow and comparing your responses with those shown at the end of the book.

LEVEL 1

Insert necessary punctuation in the following sentences. Write *C* if the sentence is correct.

1. Because employers want to hire the right people many conduct Web searches to discover more about candidates.   _____

2. However the matter is resolved, the goodwill of the customer is paramount.   _____

3. Using a technology called "telesensing " cell phones can be used to take someone's pulse check on sick relatives and warn police about criminals hiding behind walls.   _____

4. Tod Sizer a researcher at Bell Labs is developing ways to read cell phone signals bounced off the body.   _____

5. A jogger who has a phone with a telesensing chip will be able to monitor heart and respiration rates.   _____

6. Nearby mobile phones however can cause interference with telesensing.   _____

Select a, b, or c to indicate the correctly punctuated sentence.

7. a. Unethical behavior that results in personal gain is reprimanded unethical behavior that results in corporate gain is also reprimanded.
  b. Unethical behavior that results in personal gain is reprimanded, unethical behavior that results in corporate gain is also reprimanded.
  c. Unethical behavior that results in personal gain is reprimanded; unethical behavior that results in corporate gain is also reprimanded.   _____

8. a. Reports have arrived from our offices in Bonn, Switzerland, Munich, Germany, and Vienna, Austria.
  b. Reports have arrived from our offices in Bonn, Switzerland; Munich, Germany; and Vienna, Austria.
  c. Reports have arrived from our offices in: Bonn, Switzerland; Munich, Germany; and Vienna, Austria.   _____

9. a. Small businesses can benefit from having a logo; therefore, we recommend working with a logo development company.
  b. Small businesses can benefit from having a logo, therefore, we recommend working with a logo development company.
  c. Small businesses can benefit from having a logo; therefore we recommend working with a logo development company.   _____

10. a. Would you please check the BBB Web site.
  b. Would you please check the B.B.B. Web site.
  c. Would you please check the BBB Web site?   _____

11. a. We are astonished needless to say about the misstatement of profits.
  b. We are astonished, needless to say, about the misstatement of profits.
  c. We are astonished, needless to say; about the misstatement of profits.   _____

12. a. She said she held AA and BS degrees didn't she?
    b. She said she held A.A. and B.S. degrees, didn't she?
    c. She said she held AA and BS degrees, didn't she?

LEVEL 2

Select a, b, or c to indicate the correctly punctuated sentence.

13. a. Wow! A total of 89.9 percent of the voters approved!
    b. Wow, a total of 89 point 9 percent of the voters approved!
    c. Wow. A total of 89.9 percent of the voters approved!

14. a. *Forbes* selected the top U.S. cities for business and careers; Albuquerque, Raleigh, and Houston.
    b. *Forbes* selected the top U.S. cities for business and careers, Albuquerque, Raleigh, and Houston.
    c. *Forbes* selected the top U.S. cities for business and careers: Albuquerque, Raleigh, and Houston.

15. a. In addition, the list included Boise, Knoxville, and Phoenix.
    b. In addition, the list included, Boise, Knoxville, and Phoenix.
    c. In addition, the list included: Boise, Knoxville, and Phoenix.

16. a. Jack Welch said, "I've learned that mistakes can often be as good a teacher as success."
    b. Jack Welch said: "I've learned that mistakes can often be as good a teacher as success."
    c. Jack Welch said; "I've learned that mistakes can often be as good a teacher as success."

17. a. Three of the best U.S. cities for singles: Austin, Houston, and Dallas-Fort Worth, are located in Texas.
    b. Three of the best U.S. cities for singles—Austin, Houston, and Dallas-Fort Worth—are located in Texas.
    c. Three of the best U.S. cities for singles, Austin, Houston, and Dallas-Fort Worth, are located in Texas.

18. a. Citigroup, General Electric, Bank of America, AIG, and HSBC—these are the five largest companies in the world.
    b. Citigroup, General Electric, Bank of America, AIG, and HSBC: these are the five largest companies in the world.
    c. Citigroup, General Electric, Bank of America, AIG, and HSBC, these are the five largest companies in the world.

19. (Emphasize.)
    a. Three airlines, Cathay Pacific, Singapore Airlines, and Thai Airways, offer the best first-class service.
    b. Three airlines: Cathay Pacific, Singapore Airlines, and Thai Airways, offer the best first-class service.
    c. Three airlines—Cathay Pacific, Singapore Airlines, and Thai Airways—offer the best first-class service.

20. a. The largest U.S. charities are United Way, Salvation Army, and Feed the Children.
    b. The largest U.S. charities are: United Way, Salvation Army, and Feed the Children.
    c. The largest U.S. charities are—United Way, Salvation Army, and Feed the Children.

21. (De-emphasize.)
    a. A pilot project—refer to page 6 of the report—may help us justify the new system.
    b. A pilot project, refer to page 6 of the report, may help us justify the new system.
    c. A pilot project (refer to page 6 of the report) may help us justify the new system.

22. a. When I last saw him (in late June?), he agreed to my salary raise.
    b. When I last saw him (in late June) he agreed to my salary raise.
    c. When I last saw him (in late June); he agreed to my salary raise.

LEVEL 3

Select a, b, or c to indicate the correctly punctuated sentence.

23. a. Incidentally "telematics" enables a car to wirelessly exchange data with external sources such as cell phones, MP3 players, and navigation systems.
b. Incidentally—"telematics" enables a car to wirelessly exchange data with external sources such as cell phones, MP3 players, and navigation systems.
c. Incidentally, "telematics" enables a car to wirelessly exchange data with external sources such as cell phones, MP3 players, and navigation systems. _____

24. a. Our goal is to encourage, not hamper, good communication.
b. Our goal is to encourage—not hamper, good communication.
c. Our goal is to encourage, not hamper good communication. _____

25. a. Only one department submitted its report on time, namely the Legal Department.
b. Only one department submitted its report on time, namely, the Legal Department.
c. Only one department submitted its report on time: namely, the Legal Department. _____

26. a. Four women are considered the most powerful in the world, namely, Condoleezza Rice, Wu Yi, Yulia Tymoshenko, and Gloria Arroyo.
b. Four women are considered the most powerful in the world; namely, Condoleezza Rice, Wu Yi, Yulia Tymoshenko, and Gloria Arroyo.
c. Four women are considered the most powerful in the world; namely Condoleezza Rice, Wu Yi, Yulia Tymoshenko, and Gloria Arroyo. _____

27. a. The computer was producing "garbage," that is, the screen showed gibberish.
b. The computer was producing "garbage"; that is, the screen showed gibberish.
c. The computer was producing "garbage;" that is, the screen showed gibberish. _____

28. a. Boston is often called Beantown" and "The Hub of the Universe".
b. Boston is often called 'Beantown' and 'The Hub of the Universe.'
c. Boston is often called "Beantown" and "The Hub of the Universe." _____

29. a. The Economist, a British magazine, featured an article called "Of Gambling, Grannies, and Good Sense."
b. *The Economist,* a British magazine, featured an article called "Of Gambling, Grannies, and Good Sense."
c. "The Economist," a British magazine, featured an article called *Of Gambling, Grannies, and Good Sense.* _____

30. a. "It has been my observation, said Henry Ford, that most people get ahead during the time that others waste."
b. "It has been my observation," said Henry Ford, "That most people get ahead during the time that others waste."
c. "It has been my observation," said Henry Ford, "that most people get ahead during the time that others waste." _____

31. a. Who was it who said, "If I'm going to do something, I do it spectacularly or I don't do it at all."?
b. Who was it who said, "If I'm going to do something, I do it spectacularly or I don't do it at all?"
c. Who was it who said, "If I'm going to do something, I do it spectacularly or I don't do it at all"? _____

32. a. Did the office manager really say, "Stamp this package 'Confidential'?"
b. Did the office manager really say, "Stamp this package 'Confidential'"?
c. Did the office manager really say, "Stamp this package "Confidential"? _____

33. a. Rudy Giuliani said, "When you confront a problem, you begin to solve it."

b. Rudy Giuliani said; "When you confront a problem, you begin to solve it."

c. Rudy Giuliani said, "When you confront a problem you begin to solve it".

_____

Hotline Review

Write the letter of the word or phrase that correctly completes each sentence.

34. Every measure has been taken to (a) insure, (b) ensure your safety.

_____

35. Because few stockholders were (a) appraised, (b) apprised of the CEO's total salary package, no complaints were heard.

_____

36. Have you ever been (a) cited, (b) sited, (c) sighted for a speeding violation?

_____

37. You can request a refund by visiting our Web (a) cite, (b) site, (c) sight.

_____

38. We offer (a) complimentary, (b) complementary shipping for all purchases.

_____

39. Paul invested $20,000 as (a) capitol, (b) capital to start a new business.

_____

40. All rebates will be (a) dispersed, (b) disbursed next month.

_____

INFORMATIONAL BUSINESS LETTERS

Business letters are important forms of external communication. That is, they deliver information to individuals outside an organization. Although e-mail has become incredibly successful for both internal and external communication, many important messages still require written letters. Business letters are necessary when a permanent record is required, when formality is significant, and when a message is sensitive and requires an organized, well-considered presentation. Business letters may request information, respond to requests, make claims, seek adjustments, order goods and services, sell goods and services, recommend individuals, develop goodwill, or achieve many other goals. All business and professional people have to write business letters of various kinds, but a majority of those letters will be informational.

CHARACTERISTICS OF BUSINESS LETTERS

Writers of good business letters—whether the messages are informational, persuasive, or bad news—are guided by the four Cs: conciseness, clarity, correctness, and courtesy. In earlier Writing Workshops, you learned techniques for making your writing concise and clear. You've also studied many guidelines for correct grammar and usage throughout this textbook. At this point we'll review some of these techniques briefly as they relate to business letters.

Conciseness. Concise letters save the reader's time by presenting information directly. You can make your letters concise by avoiding these writing faults: (a) wordy phrases (such as *in addition to the above* and *in view of the fact that*), (b) excessive use of expletives (such as *There are four reasons that explain . . .* or *It is a good plan*), (c) long lead-ins (such as *This message is to inform you that* or *I am writing this letter to*), (d) needless adverbs (such as *very, definitely, quite, extremely,* and *really*), and (e) old-fashioned expressions (such as *attached please find* and *pursuant to your request*).

Clarity. Business letters are clear when they are logically organized and when they present enough information for the reader to understand what the writer intended. Informational letters are usually organized directly with the main idea first. Clarity can be enhanced by including all the necessary information. Some authorities estimate that one third of all business letters are written to clarify previous correspondence. To ensure that your letters are clear, put yourself in the reader's position and analyze what you have written. What questions may the reader ask? Does your information proceed logically from one point to another? Are your sentences and paragraphs coherent?

Correctness. Two aspects of correctness are accuracy of facts and accuracy of form. In regard to facts, good writers prepare to write by gathering relevant information. They collect supporting documents (previous letters, memos, and reports), they make inquiries, they jot down facts, and they outline the message. Correct letters require thorough preparation. In the same manner, correct letters require careful proofreading and attention to form.

Typographical errors, spelling irregularities, and grammatical faults distract the reader and damage the credibility of the writer. Correct business letters also follow one of the conventional formats, such as block or modified block, shown in Appendix C.

Courtesy. You develop courtesy in business letters by putting yourself in the place of the reader. Imagine how you would like to be treated and show the same consideration and respect for the individual receiving your message. The ideas you express and the words used to convey those ideas create an impression on the reader. Be alert to words that may create a negative feeling, such as *you claim, unfortunately, you neglected, you forgot, your complaint,* and so forth. Create a positive feeling by presenting your message from the point of view of the reader. Try to use the word *you* more than the words *I* and *we.* Create a warm tone in business letters by using conversational language. How can you make your writing sound like conversation? Think of your reader as if he or she were sitting across from you having a friendly chat. Avoid formal, pretentious, and stuffy language, such as *the undersigned is pleased to grant your request.* In your business messages you can develop goodwill toward your company and toward yourself by putting yourself in the place of the reader, by developing a friendly tone, and by using conversational language.

Skill Check 5.1 Reviewing the Four Cs

1. Which of the following is most concise?
    a. Due to the fact that we had a warehouse fire, your shipment is delayed.
    b. This is to inform you that your shipment will be delayed.
    c. Because of a warehouse fire, your shipment is delayed.
    d. There was a warehouse fire, which explains why your shipment is delayed. _____

2. Which of the following is clear and logical?
    a. If the strike is not settled quickly, it may last a while.
    b. Flying over the rain forests of Indonesia, the trees form a solid and menacing green carpet.
    c. This is not to suggest that Salt Lake, Denver, and Houston are not the most affordable areas for housing.
    d. Prince Charles complained that the citizens of Britain speak and write their language poorly. _____

3. Which of the following is grammatically correct?
    a. We hope that you and he will be in town for our next seminar.
    b. A host of ethical issues involve business, including e-mail privacy, whistleblowing, and mission statements.
    c. We must develop a policy on returning merchandise. So that they know about it before they are made.
    d. Jeffrey has 20 years experience in the software industry. _____

4. Which of the following is most courteous?
    a. During your interview, I informed you that if we were not successful in finding a suitable candidate, I would contact you.
    b. We appreciate receiving your letter describing your treatment by our store security personnel.
    c. In your letter of June 1, you claim that you were harassed by our store security personnel.
    d. Unfortunately, we are unable to complete your entire order because you neglected to provide a shirt size. _____

5. Which of the following sounds most conversational?
   a. Attached herewith is the form you requested.
   b. Pursuant to your request, we are forwarding the form you requested.
   c. Under separate cover we are sending the form you requested.
   d. You'll receive the form you requested in a separate mailing.

Writing Plan

Most business letters have three parts: opening, body, and closing. This three-part writing plan will help you organize the majority of your business messages quickly and effectively.

Opening. The opening of a business letter may include a subject line that refers to previous correspondence or summarizes the content of the message. A subject line should make sense but should not be a complete sentence; it is not followed by a period.

The first sentence of a business letter that requests or delivers information should begin directly with the main idea. If you are asking for information, use one of two approaches. Ask the most important question first, such as *Do you have a two-bedroom cottage on Devil's Lake available for the week of July 8–15?* A second approach involves beginning with a summary statement, such as *Please answer the following questions regarding . . . .* If the letter delivers information, begin with the most important information first, such as *Yes, we have a two-bedroom cottage on Devil's Lake available for . . . .* or *Here is the information you requested regarding . . . .* Most informational business letters should *not* begin with an explanation of why the letter is being written.

Body. The body of the letter provides explanations and additional information to clarify the first sentence. Use a separate paragraph for each new idea, being careful to strive for concise writing. If the message lends itself to enumeration, express the items in a bulleted or numbered list. Be certain, of course, to construct the list so that each item is parallel.

Think about the individual reading your message. Will that person understand what you are saying? Have you included enough information? What may seem clear to you may not be so evident to your reader. In responding to requests, don't hesitate to include more information than was requested—if you feel it would be helpful. Maintain a friendly, conversational, and positive tone.

Closing. Business letters that demand action should conclude with a specific request, including end dating if appropriate. That is, tell the reader when you would like the request complied with, and, if possible, provide a reason (for example, *Please send me this information by June 1 so that I can arrange my vacation*).

Letters that provide information may end with a summary statement or a pleasant, forward-looking thought (for example, *I hope this information helps you plan your summer vacation*). Business organizations may also use the closing to promote products or services. Avoid ending your letters with mechanical phrases such as *If I can be of further service, don't hesitate to call on me,* or *Thanks for any information you can provide.* Find a fresh way to express your desire to be of service or to show appreciation.

Figure 5.1
Information Request

GraphicPros

264 South Halsted Street
Chicago Heights, IL 60412
FAX (708) 345-2210   VOICE (708) 345-8329   WEB: http://www.graphicpros.com

March 5, 200x

Ms. Kesha Scott
Micro Supplies and Software
P.O. Box 800
Fort Atkinson, WI 53538-2900

Dear Ms. Scott:

SUBJECT: AVAILABILITY AND PRICE OF EQUIPMENT SECURITY DEVICES   *Summarizes main idea*

Please provide information and recommendations regarding security equipment to prevent the theft of office computers, keyboards, monitors, faxes, and printers.   *Introduces purpose immediately*

Our office now has 18 computer workstations and 6 printers that we must secure to desks or counters. Answers to the following questions will help us select the best devices for our purpose.   *Explains need for information*

1. What device would you recommend that can secure a workstation consisting of a computer, monitor, and keyboard?

2. What expertise and equipment are required to install and remove the security device?   *Groups open-ended questions into list for quick comprehension and best feedback*

3. How much is each device? Do you offer quantity discounts, and, if so, how much?

Because our insurance rates will be increased if the security devices are not installed before May 12, we would appreciate your response by March 20.   *Courteously provides end date and reason*

Sincerely,

Brent R. Barnwell

Brent R. Barnwell
Office Manager

Figure 5.1 illustrates the application of the writing plan to an information request. Notice that the subject line summarizes the main topic of the letter, while the first paragraph provides more information about the reason for writing. The body of the letter explains the main idea and includes a list of questions so that the reader can see quickly what information is being requested. The closing includes an end date with a reason.

Skill Check 5.2 Reviewing the Writing Plan

In the space provided, write a, b, or c to identify the letter part where each of the following might logically be found.

     a. Opening   b. Body   c. Closing

1. Explanation and details   _____

2. Subject line that summarizes main idea   _____

3. End dating with reason   _____

4. Enumerated or bulleted list   _____

5. Main idea   _____

6. Summary statement or forward-looking thought   _____

Writing Application 5.1

At a computer revise the following poorly written letter. Use block style (every line starts at the left margin) and mixed punctuation. This is a personal business letter; follow the format shown in Figure C.2 in Appendix C. Remember that the following letter is poorly written. Improve it!

1435 Sunrise Circle
Upland, CA 91786
Current date

Ms. Barbara L. Hernandez
Manager, Rainbow Resort
1102 West Brannan Island Road
Isleton, CA 95641-1102

Dear Ms. Hernandez:

I saw an advertisement recently in *Sunset* magazine where Rainbow Resort rents houseboats. My family and I (there are three kids and my wife and me) would like to take a vacation on a houseboat from July 17 through July 24 in the California Delta area. We've never done this before but it sounds interesting.

Please send me any information you may have. I'll have to make my vacation plans soon.

I have no idea how much this might cost. If we rent a houseboat, we want to know do you provide bedding, dishes, pots and pans, and the like? I'm wondering about navigating a houseboat. Will we have to take a course or training on how to operate it? It may be too difficult for us to operate. How far can we travel in the Delta area in one of your houseboats? What if we decide to stay on more than one week? I actually have two weeks of vacation, but we may want to travel in our RV part of the time. Does insurance come with the rental fee? Our kids want to know if it has TV.

Yours,

Leslie E. Childers

Writing Application 5.2

Assume you are Barbara Hernandez. Write a response to Mr. Childers' letter. Use modified block style and mixed punctuation. Tell Mr. Childers that the rental fee, which is $175 per day or $1,000 per week, does include insurance. You have a houseboat available for July 17–24, but definite reservations must be made for that time and for the week following, if Mr. Childers decides to stay two weeks. Your houseboats can travel about 100 miles on the inland waterways of the Delta. Rainbow Resort provides bedding, dishes, and kitchenware. Yes, each houseboat has a TV set. You also provide an AM/FM radio and a CD player. Your houseboats accommodate four to ten people, and you require a deposit of $500 for a one-week reservation. Reservations must be received by June 1 to ensure a July vacation. Your houseboats are easy to operate. No special training is required, but you do give each operator about 30 minutes of instruction. Send Mr. Childers a brochure describing Rainbow Resort and the memorable holiday he and his family can enjoy. The scenery and attractions are good.

Writing Application 5.3

Write a personal business letter in response to the following problem. For your home office you ordered a VoIP phone system called the VTech IP8100-2. This system comes with two cordless handsets, each with its own charging dock. It had many other attractive features, and you were eager to try it. When the system arrived, however, you followed all installation instructions and discovered that an irritating static sound interfered with every telephone call you made or received. You don't know what is causing the static, but the product description promised the following: "You'll experience excellent signal clarity with Frequency Hopping Digital Spread Spectrum (FHDSS) transmission, and a frequency of 5.8GHz. 95-channel auto-search ensures a clear signal." Because you must rely on clear calls for your business, you returned the VoIP phone system January 15 by UPS Next Business Day shipping service to ElectroWare, Inc., the Web-based supplier from whom you purchased the system. You still have a copy of the invoice, which states that merchandise may be returned for any reason within 30 days after purchase. You also have the UPS receipt proving that you returned it. However, your Visa statement (No. 5390-3390-2219-0002) has not shown a credit for the return. Your last two statements show no credit for $188.90. You're wondering what happened. Did ElectroWare receive the returned VoIP phone system? Why hasn't your account been credited? If ElectroWare did not receive the shipment, you want UPS to trace it. Write to ElectroWare, Inc., 22121 Crystal Creek Boulevard, Bothell, Washington 98201-2212. You have complied with their instructions regarding returning merchandise, and you want them to credit your account. You do not want another VoIP phone system from ElectroWare. Be sure to open your letter with a direct request for the action you want taken.

WRITING
WITH STYLE

UNIT 1 · UNIT 2 · UNIT 3 · UNIT 4 · UNIT 5 · UNIT 6 ·

17

CAPITALIZATION

18

NUMBERS

© Goodshoot/Jupiter Images

CAPITALIZATION

OBJECTIVES

When you have completed the materials in this chapter, you will be able to do the following:

LEVEL 1

- Recognize proper nouns and proper adjectives for purposes of capitalization.
- Determine when to capitalize sentence beginnings, geographic locations, organization names, academic courses and degrees, and seasons.

LEVEL 2

- Understand when to capitalize personal titles, numbered and lettered items, and points of the compass.
- Correctly capitalize departments, divisions, committees, government terms, product names, and literary titles.

LEVEL 3

- Capitalize beginning words, celestial bodies, ethnic references, and words following *marked* and *stamped*.
- Apply special rules in capitalizing personal titles and terms.

PRETEST

Use proofreading marks to show any letters that should be capitalized in the following sentences.

1. The securities and exchange commission will meet at trump tower in new york city on april 29 to discuss requirements for using plain english in proxy statements.

2. Last spring father traveled to the midwest to visit his mother in des moines, iowa.

3. After receiving a master's degree from the university of rhode island, cerise became director of the merchant services department in the corporate offices of bank of america.

4. Our company president and vice president met with several supervisors on the west coast to discuss how to compete against google's new online offerings.

5. The internal revenue service requires corporations to complete form 1040 before the april 15 deadline.

Rules governing capitalization reflect conventional practices; that is, they have been established by custom and usage. By following these conventions, a writer tells a reader, among other things, what words are important. In earlier times writers capitalized most nouns and many adjectives at will; few conventions of capitalization or punctuation were consistently observed. Today most capitalization follows definite rules that are fully accepted and practiced at all times. Dictionaries are helpful in determining capitalization practices, but they do not show all capitalized words. To develop skill in controlling capitals, study the rules and examples shown in this chapter.

LEVEL 1 • LEVEL 1 • LEVEL 1 • LEVEL 1 • LEVEL 1 • **LEVEL 1** • LEVEL 1 • LE

BASIC RULES OF CAPITALIZATION

In this level you will learn the basic rules of capitalization, including capitalizing proper nouns, proper adjectives, beginnings of sentences, geographic locations, organization names, academic courses and degrees, and seasons.

PROPER NOUNS

Capitalize proper nouns, including the *specific* names of persons, places, schools, streets, parks, buildings, religions, holidays, events, months, nicknames, agreements, Web sites, software programs, historical periods, and so forth. Do *not* capitalize common nouns that make *general* reference.

Proper Nouns	Common Nouns
Alexander Graham Bell	the man who invented the telephone
Mexico, Canada	neighboring countries of the United States
College of the Redwoods, Purdue University	a community college and a university
Abbey Road, Baker Street	famous streets in London
Fenway Park, Wrigley Field	legendary baseball parks
Episcopalian, Buddhist	representatives of two religions
Redwood Room, Clift Hotel	a room in the hotel
Veterans Day, New Year's Day	two holidays
Boston Marathon, World Series, World Cup	well-known sporting events
Golden Gate Bridge, Brooklyn Bridge	bridges over bodies of water
Supreme Court, Senate	components of government
October, November, December	last three months of the year

Proper Nouns	Common Nouns
the Windy City, the Big Easy	nicknames of cities
European Union	an agreement among several countries
Wikipedia	a Web site
PowerPoint, QuickBooks, FrontPage	software programs
U.S. Postal Service	a trip to the post office
Great Depression, Digital Age	periods of time

STUDY TIP

Most proper nouns retain their capital letters when they become adjectives—for example, French toast, Russian roulette, Persian cat, Spanish moss, Italian marble, and Swedish massage.

PROPER ADJECTIVES

Capitalize most adjectives that are derived from proper nouns.

Renaissance art	British rock
Freudian slip	Spanish language
Keynesian economics	Heimlich maneuver
Jamaican dollar	Internet access

Do not capitalize those adjectives originally derived from proper nouns that have become common adjectives (without capitals) through usage. Consult your dictionary when in doubt.

plaster of paris	venetian blinds
french fries	china dishes
manila folder	diesel engine
monarch butterfly	charley horse

BEGINNING OF SENTENCE

Capitalize the first letter of a word beginning a sentence.

Many companies that recruit on college campuses use the Web to conduct background checks on job candidates.

GEOGRAPHIC LOCATIONS

Capitalize the names of *specific* places such as continents, countries, states, cities, counties, mountains, valleys, lakes, rivers, seas, oceans, and geographic regions. Capitalize *county* and *state* when they follow proper nouns.

South America, Asia	Snake River, Mississippi River
Chile, Taiwan	Sea of Cortez, Arctic Ocean
Maine, New Hampshire, Vermont	Pacific Northwest, Texas Panhandle
Kansas City, Minneapolis	European Community (EC)
Broward County, Cook County	New York State
Mount Everest, Yosemite Valley	Upper West Side, Chinatown
Lake Louise, Lake Tahoe	Southeast, Northwest

Do not capitalize words such as *city of, state of,* or *county of* when they come before the geographic locations they are describing.

the city of Chicago	state of Washington
county of Crawford	town of Cape Vincent

ORGANIZATION NAMES

Capitalize the principal words in the names of all business, civic, educational, governmental, labor, military, philanthropic, political, professional, religious, sports, and social organizations.

United States Air Force	American Cancer Society
Green Party	National Basketball Association
Habitat for Humanity	Intel Corporation
Securities and Exchange Commission	National Park Service
Screen Actors Guild	The Boeing Company*

Generally, do *not* capitalize *committee, company, association, board,* and other shortened name forms when they are used to replace full organization names. If these shortened names, however, are preceded by the word *the* and are used in formal or legal documents (contracts, bylaws, minutes, etc.), they may be capitalized.

> Does the company offer tuition reimbursement benefits? (Informal document)

> The Treasurer of the *Association* is herein authorized to disburse funds. (Formal document)

ACADEMIC COURSES AND DEGREES

Capitalize the names of numbered courses and specific course titles. Do not capitalize the names of academic subject areas unless they contain a proper noun.

> Marina plans to take Accounting 181, Psychology 101, and Management 120 next semester.

> Anna excelled in business management, Japanese, and computer programming.

> All accounting majors must take business English and business law.

Capitalize abbreviations of academic degrees whether they stand alone or follow individuals' names. Do not capitalize general references to degrees.

> Cathy Overby earned AA, BS, and MS degrees before her thirtieth birthday. (Associate of Arts, Bachelor of Science, and Master of Science degrees)

> Matthew hopes to earn bachelor's and master's degrees in business administration. (General reference to degrees and major)

> Elizabeth S. Wright, PhD, teaches psychology in the spring semester.

> Glenda R. Hanson is a certified PLS. (Professional Legal Secretary)

SEASONS

Do not capitalize seasons unless they are **personified** (spoken of as if alive) or combined with a year.

> Our annual sales meeting is held each spring.

> "Come, Winter, with thine angry howl . . ."—Burns

> Lynn Spiesel will begin working on her master's degree during the Fall 2009 semester.

Now complete the reinforcement exercises for Level 1.

---

*Capitalize the *only when it is part of an organization's official name (as it would appear on the organization's stationery).*

SPECIAL RULES OF CAPITALIZATION

In this level you will learn several rules for capitalizing titles of people. You will also learn how to properly capitalize numbered and lettered items, compass points departments and committees, government terms, brand names, and published and artistic titles.

TITLES OF PEOPLE

Many rules exist for capitalizing personal and professional titles of people.

Titles Preceding Names

Capitalize courtesy titles (such as *Mr., Mrs., Ms., Miss,* and *Dr.*) when they precede names. Also capitalize titles representing a person's profession, company position, military rank, religious station, political office, family relationship, or nobility when the title precedes the name and replaces a courtesy title.

> The staff greeted *Mr. and Mrs.* Gary Smith. (Courtesy titles)
>
> Speakers included *Professor* Jackie Harless-Chang and *Dr.* Ann Lee. (Professional titles)
>
> Sales figures were submitted by *Budget Director* Magee and *Vice President* Anderson. (Company titles)
>
> Will *Major General* Donald M. Franklin assume command? (Military title)
>
> Appearing together were *Rabbi* David Cohen, *Archbishop* Sean McKee, and *Reverend* Cecil Williams. (Religious titles)
>
> We expect *President* Bush to meet with *Prime Minister* Tony Blair. (Political titles)
>
> Only *Aunt* Brenda and *Uncle* Skip had been to Alaska. (Family relationship)
>
> Onlookers waited for *Prince* Charles and *Queen* Elizabeth to arrive. (Nobility)

Titles Followed by Appositives

Do not capitalize a person's title—professional, business, military, religious, political, family, or one related to nobility—when the title is followed by an appositive. You will recall that **appositives** rename or explain previously mentioned nouns or pronouns.

> Only one *professor*, Malcolm Randall, favored a tuition hike.
>
> University employees asked their *president*, Diane Scott-Summers, to help raise funds.
>
> Reva Hillman discovered that her *uncle*, Paul M. Hillman, had named her as his heir.

Titles or Offices Following Names

Do not capitalize titles or offices following names.

> Klaus Entenmann, *president* of DaimlerChrysler, met with Janet Marzett, *vice president* of Human Resources and Administrative Services.
>
> After repeated requests, Rose Valenzuela, *supervisor*, Document Services, announced extended hours.
>
> George W. Bush, *president* of the United States, conferred with Mike Enzi, *senator* from Wyoming.
>
> John G. Roberts, *chief justice* of the U.S. Supreme Court, promised a ruling in June.

Titles or Offices Replacing Names

Generally, do not capitalize a title or office that replaces a person's name.

> Neither the *president* nor the *general counsel* of the company could be reached for comment.

> An ambitious five-year plan was developed by the *director of marketing* and the *sales manager*.

> The *president* conferred with the *joint chiefs of staff* and the *secretary of defense*.

> At the reception the *mayor* of Oklahoma spoke with the *governor* of Arkansas.

Titles in Business Correspondence

Capitalize titles in addresses and closing lines of business correspondence.

> Ms. Carol A. Straka
> Executive Vice President, Planning
> Energy Systems Technology, Inc.
> 8907 Canoga Avenue
> Canoga Park, CA 91371

> Very sincerely yours,

> Benelle H. Robinson
> Marketing Manager

Family Titles

Do not capitalize family titles used with possessive pronouns or possessive nouns.

> We're meeting my *mother* and Victoria's *sister* for lunch at L'Osteria del Forno.

> Did you hear that his *father* met Leonard's *cousin* at the sales conference?

But do capitalize titles of close relatives when they are used without pronouns.

> Please call *Father* and *Uncle* Joe immediately.

> What do you think about my decision, *Mom*?

NUMBERED AND LETTERED ITEMS

Capitalize nouns followed by numbers or letters except in *page, paragraph, line, size,* and *verse* references.

> United Flight 8828 to Rome will depart from Gate A28.

> Volume II, Appendix A, contains a copy of Medicare Form 72T. Instructions are on page 6, line 12.

> Take Exit 12 off State Highway 5 and follow the signs to Building I-63-B.

POINTS OF THE COMPASS

Capitalize *north, south, east, west,* and their derivatives when they represent *specific* regions.

> the Middle East, the Far East

> the Midwest, the Southeast

> the East Coast, the West Coast

> Easterners, Southerners

> Northern Hemisphere

> Northern California, South Georgia

Do not capitalize the points of the compass when they are used in directions or in general references.

> turn east on Roswell Road

> located in the west of town

> drive south on Highway 1

> eastern Maine, western Illinois

DEPARTMENTS, DIVISIONS, AND COMMITTEES

Capitalize the principal words in the official name of a division, department, or committee. When a department or division is referred to by its function because the official name is unknown, do not capitalize this reference. Outside your organization capitalize only *specific* department, division, or committee names.

> Contact our Client Support Department for more information. (Specific department)

> Miguel Zuliani works with the International Division of Apple. (Specific division)

> You have been appointed to our Process Improvement Committee. (Specific committee)

> I'm sending my resume to human resources. (Unofficial or unknown department name)

> A steering committee has not yet been named. (Unofficial or unknown name)

GOVERNMENTAL TERMS

Do not capitalize the words *federal, government, national,* or *state* unless they are part of a specific title.

> Neither the state government nor the federal government would fund the proposal.

> The Department of Labor administers a variety of federal labor laws that apply to employees in all the states.

PRODUCT NAMES

Capitalize product names only when they represent trademarked items. Except in advertising, common names following manufacturers' names are not capitalized.

Coca-Cola	Wite-Out correction fluid	Ping-Pong
Kleenex tissues	Ray-Ban sunglasses	Starbucks coffee
Gap jeans	Maytag washer	Styrofoam cup
Xerox copier	Apple computer	Chrysler Jeep
Q-Tip swab	Velcro adhesive	Excel spreadsheet
Ace bandage	Boogie Board	Scotch tape

PUBLISHED AND ARTISTIC TITLES

Capitalize the principal words in the titles of books, magazines, newspapers, articles, movies, plays, songs, poems, Web sites, and reports. Do *not* capitalize articles (*a, an, the*), conjunctions (*and, but, or, nor*), and prepositions with three or fewer letters (*in, to, by, for,* etc.) unless they begin or end the title. The word *to* in infinitives (*to run, to say, to write*) and the word *as* are also not capitalized unless it they appear as the first word of a title or subtitle.

By the way, remember that the titles of published works that contain subdivisions (such as books, magazines, pamphlets, newspapers, TV series, plays, albums, Web sites, and musicals) are italicized or underscored. Titles of literary or artistic works without subdivisions (such as chapters, newspaper articles, magazine articles, songs, poems, and episodes in a TV series) are placed in quotation marks.

> Ann Lee's *Financial Strategies You Can Bank On* (Book with preposition at end of title)

> "How to Get the Most From a Placement Service" appearing in *Newsweek* (Article in magazine)

Late Night With David Letterman (TV series)

Robert Frost's "Stopping by Woods on a Snowy Evening" (Poem)

Life Is Beautiful (Movie.)

Bob Dylan's "When the Ship Comes In" on *The Times They Are A-Changin'* (Song and album)

"Ask the Career Doctor," a link at *Quintessential Careers* (Link and Web site)

Now complete the reinforcement exercises for Level 2.

· LEVEL 3 · LEVEL 3 · LEVEL 3 · LEVEL 3 · LEVEL 3 · LEVEL 3 · LEVEL 3 · l

ADDITIONAL RULES OF CAPITALIZATION

In this level you will learn some additional rules of capitalization, including properly capitalizing beginning words, celestial bodies, ethnic references, and words following *marked* and *stamped*. Finally you will learn how to capitalize special uses of personal titles and terms.

BEGINNING WORDS

In addition to capitalizing the first word of a complete sentence, capitalize the first words in quoted sentences, independent phrases, enumerated items, formal rules or principles following colons, and some components of business correspondence.

Daniel Boorstin of the Library of Congress said, "Trying to plan for the future without a sense of the past is like trying to plant cut flowers." (Quoted sentence)

No, not at the present time. (Independent phrase)

Follow these steps to apply for a student visa:
1. Complete the visa application for the appropriate country.
2. Gather required information and arrange for an application fee.
3. Submit your application in person prior to traveling to the country. (Enumerated items)

Our office manager repeated his favorite rule: Treat the customer as you would like to be treated. (Rule following colon)

SUBJECT: Monthly Sales Meeting on June 9 (Capitalize the first letter of all primary words in e-mail and memo *subject lines;* an alternative is to type the subject line in all capital letters.)

Dear Mr. Steinbeck: (Capitalize the first word and all nouns in a *salutation.*)

Sincerely yours, (Capitalize only the first word of a *complimentary* close)

CELESTIAL BODIES

Capitalize the names of **celestial bodies** including planets, planet satellites, stars, constellations, and asteroids. Do not capitalize the terms *earth, sun,* or *moon* unless they are used as the names of specific bodies in the solar system.

Why on earth did you vote against the resolution?

The planets closest to the sun are Mercury, Mars, and Earth.

ETHNIC REFERENCES

Terms that relate to a particular culture, language, or race are capitalized.

> In Hawaii, Asian and Western cultures merge.
>
> Both English and Hebrew are spoken by Jews in Israel.
>
> African Americans and Latinos turned out to support their candidates.

Note: Hyphenate terms such as *African-American* and *French-Canadian* when they are used as adjectives (*African-American collection* or *French-Canadian citizens*). Do not hyphenate these terms when they are nouns.

WORDS FOLLOWING *MARKED* AND *STAMPED*

Capitalize words that follow the words *marked* and *stamped*.

> Although it was stamped "Fragile," the postal carrier threw it into the back of the truck.
>
> The check came back marked "Insufficient Funds."

SPECIAL USES OF PERSONAL TITLES AND TERMS

Generally, titles are capitalized according to the specifications set forth earlier. However, when a title of an official appears in that organization's minutes, bylaws, or other official documents, it is capitalized.

> The Controller will have authority over departmental budgets. (Title appearing in bylaws.)
>
> By vote of the stockholders, the President is empowered to declare a stock dividend. (Title appearing in annual report)

When the terms *ex, elect, late,* and *former* are used with capitalized titles, they are not capitalized.

> We went to hear ex-President Carter speak at the symposium.
>
> Mayor-elect Cortazzo addressed the city council.

Titles other than *sir, madam, ladies,* and *gentlemen* are capitalized when used in direct address.

> Yes, *Professor*, your research project will be funded. (Direct address)
>
> You'll soon learn, *ladies and gentlemen*, how this new procedure can reduce your workload.

Now complete the reinforcement exercises for Level 3.

Answered by Dr. Guffey

Question

Answer

Q: I'm having trouble not capitalizing *president* when it refers to the president of the United States. It used to be capitalized. Why isn't it now?

A: For some time the trend has been away from "upstyle" capitalization. Fewer words are capitalized. My two principal authorities (*Merriam-Webster Collegiate Dictionary* and *The Chicago Manual of Style*) both recommend lowercase for *president of the United States*. In addition, many publications, including *The New York Times*, capitalize the word *president* only when it's used as a title with a last name (*President Bush*). However, other authorities maintain that the term should always be capitalized because of high regard for the office.

Q: I don't know how to describe the copies made from our copy machine. Should I call them *Xerox* copies or something else?

A: They are *Xerox* copies only if made on a Xerox copier. Copies made on other machines may be called *xerographic* copies, *machine* copies, *photocopies,* or *copies.*

Q: In the doctor's office where I work, I see the word *medicine* capitalized, as in *the field of Medicine.* Is this correct?

A: No. General references should not be capitalized. If it were part of a title, as in the Northwestern College of *Medicine*, it would be capitalized.

Q: I'm writing a paper for my biology class on *in vitro fertilization.* Since this is a medical term, shouldn't I capitalize it?

A: Don't capitalize medical procedures or diseases unless they are named after individuals (*Tourette's syndrome*). *In vitro* means "outside the living body." Specialists in the field use the abbreviation *IVF* after the first introduction of the term.

Q: I work for a state agency, and I'm not sure what to capitalize or hyphenate in this sentence: *State agencies must make forms available to non-English-speaking applicants.*

A: Words with the prefix *non* are usually not hyphenated (*nonexistent, nontoxic*). But when *non* is joined to a word that must be capitalized, it is followed by a hyphen. Because the word *speaking* combines with *English* to form a single-unit adjective, it should be hyphenated. Thus, the expression should be typed *non-English-speaking applicants.*

Q: When we use a person's title, such as *business manager*, in place of a person's name, shouldn't the title always be capitalized?

A: No. Business titles are capitalized only when they precede an individual's name, as in *Business Manager Smith*. Do not capitalize titles when they replace an individual's name: *Our business manager will direct the transaction.*

Q: How do you spell *marshal*, as used in *the Grand Marshal of the Rose Parade?*

A: The preferred spelling is with a single *l*: *marshal*. In addition to describing an individual who directs a ceremony, the noun *marshal* refers to a high military officer or a city law officer who carries out court orders (*the marshal served papers on the defendant*). As a verb, *marshal* means "to bring together" or "to order in an effective way" (*the attorney marshaled convincing arguments*). The similar-sounding word *martial* is an adjective and means "warlike" or "military" (*martial law was declared after the riot*). You'll probably need a dictionary to keep those words straight!

Q: My boss has just placed me in charge of editing a new company newsletter, which will be published bimonthly. I hate to admit it, but I was afraid to ask my boss what *bimonthly* means. Does this mean that the newsletter will come out twice a month? That's a lot of work!

A: You can relax! *Bimonthly* means that your company newsletter will be published every other month. If your boss had said the newsletter would be published *semi-monthly*, you would have been editing two newsletters every month.

Q: How can I keep the words *advice* and *advise* straight? I can never decide which one to use.

A: It's best to remember that *advice* is a noun meaning "a suggestion or recommendation" (*She went to her attorney for tax advice*). The word *advise* is a verb meaning "to counsel or recommend" (*Her attorney advised her to open an IRA*).

LEVEL 1

A. (Self-check) In the following sentences, use standard proofreading marks to correct errors you find in capitalization. Use three short lines (≡) under a lowercase letter to indicate that it is to be changed to a capital letter. Draw a diagonal (/) through a capital letter you wish to change to a lowercase letter. Indicate at the right the total number of changes you have made in each sentence.

Example: The B̸andit Henry McCarthy was also known as Billy the k̲id.   2 _____

1. All Employees will attend a Training Session on our new e-mail Program to be held on Monday, October 5.   _____

2. Born in new jersey, herb kelleher, former CEO of southwest airlines, grew up in the State of texas.   _____

3. Starbucks ensures high standards by training its Baristas in Coffee preparation techniques and Customer Service.   _____

4. In the Fall Darija Walker plans to study italian, accounting, Marketing, and Project Management.   _____

5. Sondra uses comcast for her internet access at home.   _____

6. Pelee island is located on the canadian side of lake erie.   _____

7. Regulations of the Occupational Safety and health administration resulted in costly expenses for our Company.   _____

8. Salt lake city, in the State of Utah, was founded by Brigham Young and a small Party of Mormons in 1847.   _____

9. The boston marathon is an annual Sporting Event hosted by the City of Boston, Massachusetts, on patriot's day, the third Monday of April.   _____

10. Elise hopes to complete AA, BA, and MA Degrees at different Colleges.   _____

Check your answers below.

B. Use proofreading marks to correct any capitalization errors in these sentences. Indicate the total number of changes at the right. If no changes are needed, write *0*.

1. The Jackson Family visited Florida during the Winter and soon learned why it's known as the "sunshine state."   _____

2. Representatives from the methodist, presbyterian, baptist, and catholic faiths will hold a Conference in the City of Boise, Idaho.   _____

Want to explore more? Go to: academic.cengage.com/bcomm/guffey or Xtra!

CAPITALIZATION | CHAPTER 17 | **327**

3. Kendra Hawkins was sent to our Kansas city branch office for the Months of April and May, but she hopes to return by Summer.

    _____

4. Our Company encourages Employees to earn Associate's and Bachelor's Degrees at nearby Colleges and Universities.

    _____

5. Nontraditional students face the herculean challenge of juggling full-time jobs while working on their Degrees.

    _____

6. All company representatives gathered in kansas city in the chouteau room of the hyatt regency crown center for the annual Spring sales meeting.

    _____

7. Work schedules will have to be adjusted in november for veterans day.

    _____

8. Last Fall Tricia Rojas took out a policy with the prudential life insurance company. (The word *the* is part of the company name.)

    _____

9. The green bay packers won the first super bowl in 1967.

    _____

10. Professor Solis employed the socratic method of questioning students to elicit answers about Business Management.

    _____

11. After driving through New York state, we stayed in New York city and visited the Empire State building.

    _____

12. Members of the sierra club work hard to make sure that the endangered species act protects the Gray Wolf, which makes its home in the northern rockies.

    _____

13. Dennis O'Rourke completed the requirements for a master's degree at the Massachusetts institute of technology.

    _____

14. His report on diesel engines contained many greek symbols in the engineering equations.

    _____

15. The Hip-Hop Music mogul's customized lincoln navigator sported big wheels, satellite radio, three dvd players, six tv screens, a sony playstation 3, and vibrating front seats.

    _____

LEVEL 2

A. **(Self-check)** Use proofreading marks to correct errors you find in capitalization. Indicate at the right the total number of changes you make. If no changes are needed, write *0*.

    Example: Project manager Karen O'Brien was promoted to Vice President.   3 _____

1. Mary Minnick, Executive Vice President of the Coca-Cola company, also serves as President of the Company's Marketing, Strategy, and Innovation Department.

    _____

2. Additional information on the features of our new Security Software is available on Page 41 in appendix B.

    _____

3. Personnel director Rosenburg will head our new intellectual property committee.

    _____

4. Both my Mother and my Sister received Nokia Cell Phones as christmas gifts.

    _____

5. The Fishing Industry in the Pacific northwest is reeling from the impact of recent Federal regulations.

    _____

6. Our business manager and our executive vice president recently attended an e-business seminar in southern California.

    _____

Want to explore more? Go to: academic.cengage.com/bcomm/guffey or Xtra!

328 I UNIT 6 I CHAPTER 17 I CAPITALIZATION

7. My Uncle recommended that I read the article titled "The 100 best companies to work for." _____

8. Please send the order to Ms. Milagros Ojermark, manager, customer services, Atlas Fitness Equipment inc., 213 Summit Drive, Spokane, Washington 99201. _____

9. The president met with the secretary of state to discuss peace talks in the Middle East. _____

10. Illy, a company founded in the Northern part of Italy during World war I, produces coffee made from pure arabica beans. _____

Check your answers below.

B. Use proofreading marks to correct errors in the following sentences. Indicate the number of changes you make for each sentence.

1. Health minister Anbumani Ramadoss announced that India will become the first Country to ban images of smoking in all tv shows and new films. _____

2. My uncle Eduardo recently purchased a t-mobile sidekick to use for his phone and e-mail. _____

3. Because brazil, australia, and argentina are located in the southern hemisphere, their Summers and Winters are the opposite of ours. _____

4. When the president, the secretary of state, and the secretary of labor traveled to the State of Minnesota, stringent security measures were effected. _____

5. To locate the exact amount of federal funding, look on Line 7, Page 6 of supplement no. 4. _____

6. Akio Morita, the Founder of Sony corporation, hurried to gate 16 to catch flight 263 to north Carolina. _____

7. My Father suggested that I read the book *The Seven Habits Of Highly Successful People.* _____

8. Send all inquiries in writing to Gene Montesano, ceo, Lucky Brand Jeans corporation, 5233 Alcoa avenue, vernon, california 90058. _____

9. We have trouble with excel spreadsheets from our overseas offices because they are set up on european A4 paper, not american-size letterhead. _____

10. Google was originally named googol; however, an Angel Investor made a check out to "Google, inc.," and this typo became the Company's name. _____

11. Memorial Day is a Federal Holiday; therefore, Banks will be closed. _____

12. Franklin became an assistant to the administrator of the Governor Bacon Health center, which is operated by the department of health and social services of the State of Delaware. _____

13. Many Cybercriminals are now using the telephone as part of fraudulent schemes, commonly known as "Phishing," to obtain personal information from victims. _____

14. For lunch Ahmal ordered a big mac, french fries, and a coca-cola. _____

15. A midwesterner who enjoys sunshine, Mr. Franco travels south each Winter to vacation in Southern Georgia. _____

1. (6) executive vice president Company's 2. (4) security software page Appendix 3. (4) Director Intellectual Property Committee 4. (5) mother sister cell phones Christmas 5. (4) fishing industry Northwest federal 6. (1) Southern 7. (5) uncle Best Companies to Work For 8. (4) Manager Customer Services Inc. 9. (0) 10. (3) northern War Arabica

Want to explore more? Go to: academic.cengage.com/bcomm/guffey or Xtra!

CAPITALIZATION | CHAPTER 17 | 329

LEVEL 3

A. (Self-check) Use standard proofreading marks to indicate necessary changes. Write the total number of changes at the right.

Example: Mercury, venus, earth, and mars are dense and solid.   3 _____

1. Because the letter was marked "confidential," Sandy delivered it personally to her Boss. _____

2. The guiding principle of capitalization is this: capitalize *specific* names and references, but do not capitalize *general* references. _____

3. In South America most Brazilians speak portuguese, most Surinamese speak dutch, and most Guyanese speak english. _____

4. The Late President Franklin D. Roosevelt, who served in Office during the great depression, is remembered for his policies aiding the recovery of the american economy. _____

5. The following users are most likely to be sued by the record industry association of america for illegal music downloading and file sharing:

    1. those who download a minimum of a few hundred songs

    2. those who share downloaded music with others

    3. those internet users who live in the united states

6. How on Earth do you think you'll get away with this? _____

7. Money traders watched carefully the relation of the american dollar to the chinese yuan, the european euro, and the japanese yen. _____

8. The library of congress featured a collection of african-american writers. _____

9. You, Sir, are in danger of being held in contempt of court. _____

10. Our Organization's bylaws state the following: "The Secretary of the Association will submit an agenda two weeks before each meeting." _____

Check your answers below.

B. Use proofreading marks to indicate necessary changes. Write the total number of changes at the right.

1. As the Sun beat down on the crowd, Ex-president Clinton continued his Graduation Address to the students of the university of Mississippi. _____

2. Would you like a ride home? yes, thank you very much. _____

3. Warren Buffett, one of the World's greatest investors, says that everyday investors should follow this rule: never lose the money. _____

4. Terry noticed that the english spoken by asians in hong kong sounded more british than american. _____

5. Our accounting department should mark this Invoice "paid." _____

6. The Minutes of our last meeting contained the following statement: "the vice president acted on behalf of the president, who was attending a conference in the far East." _____

Want to explore more? Go to: academic.cengage.com/bcomm/guffey or Xtra!

7. Our Office Manager always uses "Best Regards" as his complimentary close. _____

8. Tell me, doctor, how dangerous this procedure really is. _____

9. Three brands owned by the Coca-Cola company are the following:

    1. canada dry

    2. minute maid

    3. nescafé _____

10. SUBJECT: June 24 staff meeting _____

C. **Review.** Select a or b to indicate correct capitalization.

1.	a. our finance manager	b. our Finance Manager	_____
2.	a. the Washington monument	b. the Washington Monument	_____
3.	a. awarded a Bachelor's degree	b. awarded a bachelor's degree	_____
4.	a. courses in Farsi and anatomy	b. courses in farsi and anatomy	_____
5.	a. the Pacific Room at the Marriott	b. the pacific room at the Marriott	_____
6.	a. French fries and a pepsi-cola	b. french fries and a Pepsi-Cola	_____
7.	a. a file marked "urgent"	b. a file marked "Urgent"	_____
8.	a. a fall sale	b. a Fall sale	_____
9.	a. the president's speech	b. the President's speech	_____
10.	a. a Television show on PBS	b. a television show on PBS	_____

D. **Writing Exercise.** On a separate sheet, write one or two paragraphs summarizing an article from a local newspaper. Choose an article with as many capital letters as possible. Apply the rules of capitalization you learned in this chapter.

E. **Hotline Review.** In the space provided write the correct answer choice.

1. Please make a _____ of the contract to send to Washington.
   a. xerox   b. photocopy _____

2. We have made provisions for any _____ candidate.
   a. non-english-speaking   b. non-English-speaking _____

3. The fire _____ suspected that arson was involved in the fire.
   a. marshal   b. martial _____

4. Our e-mail newsletter is sent to customers _____, on the 15th and the last day of the month.
   a. bimonthly   b. semimonthly _____

5. Brooke's counselor gave her good _____ about what courses to take.
   a. advice   b. advise _____

6. Our network administrator will _____ you about how often to change your password.
   a. advice   b. advise _____

Want to explore more? Go to: academic.cengage.com/bcomm/guffey or Xtra!

CAPITALIZATION | CHAPTER 17 | 331

The following letter report contains intentional errors representing spelling, proofreading, punctuation, capitalization, and language principles covered thus far. You should mark 50 changes. Use three short lines (≡) under a lowercase letter to indicate that it is to be changed to a capital letter. Draw a diagonal (/) through a capital letter you wish to change to a lowercase letter. When you replace a wordy or incorrect phrase with one word, it counts as one correction. When you correct a comma splice, run-on, or fragment, the correction counts as two errors. Count each parenthesis and each dash as a single mark. Use proofreading marks to make the corrections here OR make the corrections at the **Guffey Companion Web Site** at **academic.cengage.com/bcomm/guffey.**

National Association for Retail Marketing

540 Campus Place
Oshkosh, WI 54901   (920) 233-0948   www.narm.org

January 5, 200x

Ms. Jamie Owens, President
Retail Group, Inc.
240 Pacific Avenue
Seattle, WA 98403

Dear Ms. Owens,

Please consider giving a presentation at the annual meeting of the National Association For Retail Marketing in the City of Oshkosh, Wisconsin on April 6. Your presentation would proceed a lavishly-catered banquet.

In the passed you have said "retail has to feel relevant or its dead." Thats why were turning to you for guidance.

Many of we retailers have little experience in attracting Generation y shoppers and we realize that their going to represent 41 percent of the u.s. population in the next Decade. Its depressing for us to realize that only 15 percent of this group shops in Department Stores. Attracting this segment of shoppers are critical to future profitability and that's why we are turning to you for help.

You have been the driving force behind a number of retail makeovers, including blockbuster video, nike, sears and starbucks. Our members were especially impressed by your startling redesign of Mega Mart, making it one of the highest grossing sellers of consumer electronic's in north America. With your finger on the changing pulse of american retail you were the first choice of our Committee to be keynote speaker at our annual meeting.

Will you be available to give our keynote address on April 6. Although our honorarium is only $3,000 we can offer you the opportunity to share your expertise with 1500 of the top retailers in the Country. Many of them are struggling, and would enthusiastically welcome your presentation. In addition you may find that many would become future client's.

Enclosed is a brochure and pamphlets describing previous conferences. If you will call me at (405) 499-3928 I can provide details and answer questions. So that we may continue our conference planning procedures please let me know by November 10 whether you will become our Featured Speaker. This is you're chance to have a huge affect on future retailer's.

Sincerely Yours,

Douglas Eamon

Douglas Eamon
Events Coordinator

Enclosure

Want to explore more? Go to: academic.cengage.com/bcomm/guffey or Xtra!

332 I UNIT 6 I CHAPTER 17 I CAPITALIZATION

Goal: To keep up with business news online.

Even if you read your local paper daily, breaking news happens all the time. As a business student, you should know how to keep up with the latest happenings. You know that many Web sites offer up-to-the-minute business news.

1. With your Web browser on the screen, go to Reuters, a highly respected global information company, at **http://www.reuters.com.**

Click **Business** in the menu to the left of your screen.

2. Click on the link for a business news story that interests you.
3. Click **Print This Article** to print a copy of the article from this Web site; then read the article.
4. In a paragraph of three or four sentences, summarize the story. What did you learn about business from the story?
5. End your session. Submit your printouts and answers to the questions posed here.

Use proofreading marks to correct errors you find in capitalization.

1. Our Company President and Marketing Manager are fluent in spanish and german.
2. Blanca studied english literature, Accounting, and psychology at central wyoming college.
3. The Engineers will meet in the san marino room of the red lion inn next thursday.
4. Applicants must have a Master's Degree to be considered for the Controller position.
5. My Father attended a Training Session on Dragon NaturallySpeaking, a Voice-Recognition Software program, in the midwest.

1. company president   marketing manager   Spanish   German   2. English   accounting   Central Wyoming College   3. engineers   San Marino Room   Red Lion Inn   Thursday   4. master's degree   controller   5. father   training session   voice-recognition software   Midwest

Want to explore more? Go to: academic.cengage.com/bcomm/guffey or Xtra!

CAPITALIZATION | CHAPTER 17 | **333**

© John Lund/Sam Diephuis/Blend Images/Jupiter Images

NUMBERS

OBJECTIVES

When you have completed the materials in this chapter, you will be able to do the following:

LEVEL 1

- Correctly choose between figure and word forms to express general numbers and numbers beginning sentences.
- Express money, dates, clock time, addresses, and telephone and fax numbers appropriately.

LEVEL 2

- Use the correct form in writing related numbers, consecutive numbers, periods of time, ages, anniversaries, and round numbers.
- Use the correct form in expressing numbers used with words, abbreviations, and symbols.

LEVEL 3

- Express correctly weights, measurements, and fractions.
- Use the correct form in expressing percentages, decimals, and ordinals.

PRETEST

Underline any incorrect expression of numbers, and write an improved form in the blank provided. For example, *$10* or *ten dollars*?

1. Please plan to attend the 1st informational meeting on September 18th at ten a.m. _____

2. When Megan reached 21 years of age, she assumed ownership of over fifty acres of property in 2 states. _____

1. first 18 10 a.m. 2. twenty-one 50 acres two 3. $17 fifty 39-cent 4. 34 November 23 5. 9 by 12 inches $2 million

334

3. Please take seventeen dollars to pick up 50 thirty-nine-cent stamps at the post office.

      _____

4. Of the thirty-four students who took the notary public class on November 23rd, only two didn't pass the test.

      _____

5. The art treasure measures only nine inches by twelve inches, but it is said to be worth nearly two million dollars.

      _____

Just as capitalization is governed by convention, so is the expression of numbers. Usage and custom determine whether numbers are to be expressed in the form of a figure (for example, *5*) or in the form of a word (for example, *five*). Numbers expressed as figures are shorter and more easily comprehended, yet numbers used as words are necessary in certain instances. The following guidelines are observed in expressing numbers that appear in written *sentences*. Numbers that appear in business documents such as invoices, statements, and purchase orders are always expressed as figures.

BASIC GUIDELINES FOR EXPRESSING NUMBERS

In this level you will learn the general rules for expressing numbers. You'll also learn how to correctly express items that appear frequently in business correspondence, including monetary amounts, dates, clock time, addresses, and telephone and fax numbers.

GENERAL RULES

The numbers *one* through *ten* are generally written as words. Numbers above *ten* are written as figures.

> The committee consisted of *nine* regular members and *one* chair.

> Of the *32* IPOs backed by private-equity firms, only *13* resulted in a positive return to investors.

Numbers that begin sentences are written as words. If a number involves more than two words, however, the sentence should be rewritten so that the number no longer falls at the beginning. When expressing numbers as words, hyphenate all compound numbers between 21 and 99.

> *Thirty-four* people applied for the Web application developer position.

> A total of *320* distributors agreed to market the product. (Not *Three hundred twenty* distributors agreed to market the product.)

MONEY

Sums of money $1 or greater are expressed as figures. If a sum is a whole dollar amount, most writers omit the decimal and zeros (even if the amount appears with fractional dollar amounts). Always include commas in monetary figures $1,000 or greater.

> Although she budgeted only *$200*, Andrea spent *$314.95* for her digital camera.

> This statement shows purchases of *$7.13*, *$10*, *$43.50*, *$90*, and *$262.78*.

> A ticket for a first-class parlor suite on the Titanic cost $4,350 (about $69,600 today).

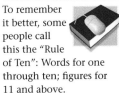

Sums less than $1 are written as figures that are followed by the word *cents*. If they are part of sums greater than $1, use a dollar sign and a decimal instead of the word *cents*.

Jack needed *50 cents* to buy the morning newspaper.

Our monthly petty cash statement showed purchases of $7.13, *$.99*, $2.80, $1, and *$.40*.

DATES

In dates, numbers that appear after the name of the month are written in **cardinal figures** (*1, 2, 3,* etc.). Those that stand alone or appear before the name of a month are written in **ordinal figures** (*1ˢᵗ, 2ⁿᵈ, 3ʳᵈ,* etc.).

The New York Stock Exchange was formed on *May 17, 1792*.

On the *2ⁿᵈ* of January and again on the *12ᵗʰ*, we called for service.

Most American communicators express dates in the following form: month, day, year. An alternative form, used primarily in military and international correspondence, begins with the day of the month. Some business organizations prefer the international date style for its clarity since it separates the numerical date of the month from the year.

On *July 17, 1861,* the first paper money, known as *greenbacks*, was issued by the United States government. (General date format)

Our lease expires on *31 July 2010*. (Military and international format)

CLOCK TIME

Figures are used when clock time is expressed with *a.m.* or *p.m.* Omit the colon and zeros with whole hours. When exact clock time is expressed with *o'clock,* either figures or words may be used. Note that phrases such as *in the afternoon* or *in the morning* may follow clock time expressed with *o'clock* but not with time expressed with *a.m.* and *p.m.*

The first shift starts at *8 a.m.;* the second, at *3:30 p.m.*

Department mail is usually distributed at *ten* (or *10*) *o'clock* in the morning.

ADDRESSES

Except for the number *One*, house numbers are expressed as figures. Apartment numbers, suite numbers, box numbers, and route numbers are also written in figure form.

5 Sierra Drive	27321 Van Nuys Boulevard
One Peachtree Plaza, Suite 900	1762 Cone Street, Apt. 2B
P.O. Box 8935	Rural Route 19

Street names that involve the number *ten* or a lower number are written as ordinal words (*First, Second, Third*). In street names involving numbers greater than *ten,* the numeral portion is written in ordinal figure form (*11ᵗʰ, 22ⁿᵈ, 33ʳᵈ*).

201 Third Street	1190 54th Street
2320 West 22nd Street	3261 South 103rd Avenue

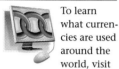

HOT LINK

To learn what currencies are used around the world, visit *Oanda* at **http://www.oanda.com/**.

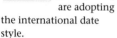

CAREER TIP

As American companies become more global, many are adopting the international date style.

SPOT THE BLOOPER

From *The Suburban & Wayne Times* [Wayne, Pennsylvania]: "Cases of Lyme disease, which is transmitted by deer carrying ticks, are on the rise."

TELEPHONE AND FAX NUMBERS

Telephone and fax numbers are expressed with figures. When used, the area code is placed in parentheses preceding the telephone number. As an alternate form, you may separate the area code from the telephone number with a hyphen. A third format that has gained acceptance is to separate the parts of the number with periods. When you include an extension, separate it from the phone number with a comma.

> Please call us at *555-1101* for further information.
>
> You may reach me at *(801) 643-3267, Ext. 244*, after 9:30 a.m.
>
> Call our toll-free number at *800-340-3281* for the latest stock quotes.
>
> Please fax your order to 415.937.5594.

Now complete the reinforcement exercises for Level 1.

· LEVEL 2 · LEVEL 2 · LEVEL 2 · LEVEL 2 · LEVEL 2 · LEVEL 2 · LEVEL 2 · L

SPECIAL GUIDELINES FOR EXPRESSING NUMBERS

Special guidelines exist for expressing related and consecutive numbers. In this level you will also learn how to use numbers to express periods of time, ages and anniversaries, numbers used in conventional phrases, numbers used with abbreviations and symbols, and round numbers.

RELATED NUMBERS

Related numbers are those used similarly in the same document. They should be expressed as the largest number is expressed. Thus, if the largest number is greater than *ten,* all the numbers should be expressed as figures.

> Only *7* customers out of *238* failed to complete the comment card.
>
> Of the *98* e-mail documents Casey received today, *19* were marked "Urgent" and 7 were marked "Confidential."
>
> Nearly *20* employees will be expected to share the *15* computers, *8* printers, and *3* fax machines. (Note that items appearing in a series are always considered to be related.)

Unrelated numbers within the same reference are written as words or figures according to the general guidelines presented earlier in this chapter.

> *Twenty-three* contract changes will be discussed by *89* employees working in *eight* departments.
>
> During the *four* peak traffic hours, *three* bridges carry at least *20,000* cars.

CONSECUTIVE NUMBERS

Consecutive numbers occur when two numbers appear one after the other, both modifying a following noun (such as *ten 39-cent stamps*). Express the first number in words and the second in figures. If, however, the first number cannot be

STUDY TIP

With consecutive numbers, remember that the second number is ALWAYS a figure. The first number is usually a word, unless it requires three or more words (*120 5-year-old* children.)

expressed in *one or two words,* place it in figures also (*120 39-cent* stamps). Do not use commas to separate the figures.

> Historians divided the era into *four 25-year* periods. (Use word form for the first number and figure form for the second.)

> Erich purchased *two 512MB* memory cards for his digital camera. (Use word form for the first number and figure form for the second.)

> Did you request *twenty 100-watt* bulbs? (Use word form for the first number and figure form for the second.)

> We'll need at least *150 100-watt* bulbs. (Use figure form for the first number since it requires more than two words.)

PERIODS OF TIME

Periods of time (seconds, minutes, hours, days, weeks, months, and years) are treated as any other general number. That is, numbers ten and below are written in word form. Numbers above *ten* are written in figure form.

> Heather has designed the Web site so that each page loads in *one* to *three* seconds.

> After a *183*-day strike, workers returned to their jobs.

> Congress has regulated minimum wages for over *69 years.*

> Employees earn a *two-week* vacation after being with the company for *one* year.

STUDY TIP

Figures are easier to understand and remember than words are. That's why business terms, even for numbers under ten, are generally written as figures.

Figures are used to achieve special emphasis in expressing business concepts such as discount rates, interest rates, contracts, warranty periods, credit terms, loan periods, and payment terms.

> Your loan must be repaid within *60 days* in accordance with its terms.

> Higher interest rates are offered on *6-* to *9-month* certificates of deposit.

SPOT THE BLOOPER

Classified advertisement in the help-wanted section of a newspaper: "Three-year-old teacher needed for preschool. Experience preferred."

AGES AND ANNIVERSARIES

Ages and anniversaries that can be expressed in one or two words are generally written in word form. Those that require more than two words are written in figures. Figures are also used when an age (a) appears immediately after a name; (b) is expressed in exact years, months, and sometimes days; or (c) is used in a legal or technical sense.

> When he was *fifty-five,* Ernest Hemingway was awarded the Nobel Prize in Literature. (Use word form for age expressed in two or fewer words.)

> In 2007 LucasArts Entertainment celebrated the *twenty-fifth* anniversary of the company's founding. (Use word form for an anniversary expressed in two or fewer words.)

> Bill Gates, *52,* plans to work full-time for Microsoft through July 2008, after which he will devote more time to the Bill & Melinda Gates Foundation. (Use figure form for age appearing immediately after a name.)

> The child was adopted when he was *3 years 8 months and 24 days* old. (Use figure form for age expressed in terms of exact years and months. Notice that commas are not used to separate age expressions.)

> Although the legal voting age is *18,* young people must be *21* to purchase alcohol. (Use figure form for age used in a legal sense.)

ROUND NUMBERS

Round numbers are approximations. They may be expressed in word or figure form, although figure form is shorter and easier to comprehend.

> Approximately *300* (or *three hundred*) new homeowners have installed solar panels.

> At last count we had received about *20* (or *twenty*) reservations.

For ease of reading, round numbers in the millions or billions should be expressed with a combination of figures and words.*

> The federal deficit is about *$8.5 trillion.*

> The world population is approximately *6.5 billion,* and the U.S. Census Bureau expects this figure to grow to around *9.2 billion* by 2050.

> Nearly *1.5 million* imported cars were sold this year.

NUMBERS USED WITH WORDS, ABBREVIATIONS, AND SYMBOLS

Numbers used with words are expressed as figures.

page 28	Policy 04-168315	Area Code 213
Room 232	Volume 5	Section 8
Option 3	Form 1040	Public Law 96-221

Numbers used with abbreviations are expressed as figures.

Apt. 23	Serial No. 265188440	Nos. 199 and 202
Ext. 3206	Account No. 08166-05741	Social Security No. 535-52-2016

Notice that the word *number* is capitalized and abbreviated when it precedes a number. However, if the word *number* begins a sentence, do not abbreviate it. Notice, too, that no commas are used in serial, account, and policy numbers.

Symbols (such as #, %, ¢) are usually avoided in contextual business writing (sentences). In other business documents where space is limited, however, symbols are frequently used. Numbers appearing with symbols are expressed as figures.

> 45%   39¢   #2 can   2/10, n/60

Now complete the reinforcement exercises for Level 2.

---

* *Note that only when* one million *is used as an approximation, use word form; otherwise, use* 1 million.

ADDITIONAL GUIDELINES FOR EXPRESSING NUMBERS

The following guidelines will help you use appropriate forms for weights and measurements, fractions, percentages, decimals, and ordinals.

WEIGHTS AND MEASUREMENTS

Weights and measurements, including temperatures, are expressed as figures. When one weight or measure consists of several words treated as a single unit (*3 feet 4 inches*), do not use a comma to separate the units.

> My new Sony Cyber-shot digital camera measures only *3.5 by 2.2 by 1.0 inches* and weighs just *8 ounces.*
>
> Our specifications show the weight of the printer to be *7 pounds 9 ounces.*
>
> The truck required *21 gallons* of gasoline and *2 quarts* of oil to travel *250 miles.*
>
> The highest temperature ever recorded was *134 degrees* in 1922 in El Azizia, Libya.

In sentences the nouns following weights and measurements should be spelled out (for example, *21 gallons* instead of *21 gal.*). In business forms or in statistical presentations, however, such nouns may be abbreviated.

> 8′ × 10′   #10   7 oz.   3,500 sq. ft.   2 lb.   12 qt.

FRACTIONS

Simple fractions are fractions in which both the numerator and denominator are whole numbers. They are expressed as words. If a fraction functions as a noun, no hyphen is used. If it functions as an adjective, a hyphen separates its parts.

> Linguists predict that as many as *one half* of the world's 6,800 languages could disappear over the next century. (Fraction used as a noun)
>
> A *two-thirds* majority is needed to carry the measure. (Fraction used as an adjective)

Long or awkward fractions appearing in sentences may be written either as figures or as a combination of figures and words.

> The computer will execute a command in *1 millionth* of a second. (Combination of words and figures is easier to comprehend.)
>
> Flight records revealed that the emergency system was activated *13/200* of a second after the pilot was notified. (Figure form is easier to comprehend.)

Mixed fractions, which are whole numbers combined with fractions, are always expressed by figures.

> Office desks are expected to be *35¼ inches* long, not *35½ inches.*

Use the extended character set of your word processing program to insert fractions that are written in figures. Fractions written in figures that are not found in extended character sets of word processing programs are formed by using the diagonal to separate the two parts. When fractions that are constructed with

diagonals appear with key fractions, be consistent by using the diagonal construction for all the fractions involved.

> The shelves were supposed to be *36 5/8* inches wide, not *26 3/8* inches. (Notice that fractions that must be constructed with diagonals are separated from their related whole numbers.)

PERCENTAGES AND DECIMALS

Percentages are expressed with figures followed by the word *percent*. The percent sign (%) is used only on business forms or in statistical presentations.

> Interest rates have been as low as *4½ percent* and as high as *19 percent*.

> Top executives at U.S. multinationals say business ethics and corporate governance have increased by *63 percent*.

Decimals are expressed with figures. If a decimal does not contain a whole number (an integer) and does not begin with a zero, a zero should be placed before the decimal.

> Lance Armstrong had the highest average speed in the Tour de France when he maintained an average speed of *25.882* miles per hour in 2005. (Contains a whole number)

> Close examination revealed the settings to be *.005* inch off. (Begins with a zero)

> Less than *0.1* percent of the operating costs will be borne by taxpayers. (Zero placed before decimal that neither contains a whole number nor begins with a zero)

ORDINALS

Ordinal numbers are used to show the position in an ordered sequence. Although ordinal numbers are generally expressed in word form (*first, second, third,* etc.), three exceptions should be noted: (a) Figure form is used for dates appearing before a month or appearing alone; (b) figure form is used for street names involving numbers greater than *ten;* and (c) figure form is used when the ordinal would require more than two words.

Most Ordinals

> City Lights Books recently celebrated its *fiftieth anniversary*.

> Before the *eighteenth century*, spelling was not standardized.

> Of more than 350 cities analyzed worldwide, Zurich, Switzerland, ranks *first* in quality of living.

> Alcee Hastings represents the *Twenty-third Congressional District*.

Dates

> Your payment must be received by the *30*[th] to qualify for the cash discount.

> Paychecks are issued on the *1*[st] and the *15th* of each month.

Streets

> Traffic lights installed on *Second Street* have improved pedestrian safety.

> Our headquarters will move to 3589 *23*[rd] *Street* on the 6th of September.

Larger ordinals

Levi Strauss ranked *484th* on *Forbes* list of the 500 largest American corporations.

First Federal Bank ranks *103rd* in terms of capital investments.

Some word processing programs automatically make superscripts from ordinals. If you dislike this program feature, you may turn it off.

Now complete the reinforcement exercises for Level 3.

HOTLINE QUERIES

Answered by Dr. Guffey

Question

Q: I recently saw the following format used by a business to publish its telephone number on its stationery and business cards: 212.582.0903. Is it now an option to use periods in telephone numbers?

Q: My manager is preparing an advertisement for a charity event. She has written this: *Donors who give $100 dollars or more receive plaques.* I know this is not right, but I can't exactly put my finger on the problem.

Q: I'm never sure when to hyphenate numbers, such as *thirty-one*. Is there some rule to follow?

Q: A fellow team member wants to show dollar amounts in two forms, such as the following: *The consultant charges two hundred dollars ($200) an hour.* I think this is overkill. Do we have to show figures in two forms?

Answer

A: Yes, this is now an acceptable option for writing telephone and fax numbers that perhaps reflect European influences. To some, the style is upscale and chic; to others, it's just confusing. Telephone and fax numbers written in the traditional formats are most readily recognized. That's why it's probably safer to stick with hyphens or parentheses: 212-582-0903 or (212) 582-0903.

A: The problem is in *$100 dollars*. That is like saying *dollars dollars*. Drop the word *dollars* and use only the dollar sign: *Donors who give $100 or more . . . .*

A: When written in word form, the numbers *twenty-one* through *ninety-nine* are hyphenated. Numbers are also hyphenated when they form compound adjectives and precede nouns (*ten-year-old* child, *16-story* building, *four-year* term, *30-day* lease).

A: In formal legal documents, amounts of money may be expressed in words followed by figures in parentheses. However, business writers do not follow this practice because it is unnecessary, wordy, and pretentious. In fact, some readers are insulted because the practice suggests they are not bright enough to comprehend just one set of figures.

Q: Should I put quotation marks around figures to emphasize them? For example, *Your account has a balance of "$2,136.18."*

A: Certainly not! Quotation marks are properly used to indicate an exact quotation, or they may be used to enclose the definition of a word. They should not be used as a mechanical device for added emphasis.

Q: What should I write: *You are our No. 1 account*, or *You are our number one account?* Should anything be hyphenated?

A: Either is correct, but we prefer *No. 1* because it is more easily recognizable. No hyphen is required.

Q: How should I spell the word *lose* in this sentence: *The employee tripped over a (lose or loose) cord?*

A: In your sentence use the adjective *loose*, which means "not fastened," "not tight," or "having freedom of movement." Perhaps you can remember it by thinking of the common expression *loose change*, which suggests unattached, free coins jingling in your pocket. If you *lose* (*mislay*) some of those coins, you have less money and fewer *o's*.

Q: I'm having trouble telling the difference between these two words: *aid* and *aide*. Can they be used interchangeably?

A: Absolutely not! The word *aid* is a verb meaning "to help or assist" (*Ben & Jerry's aids many environmental organizations*). *Aid* is also a noun meaning "assistance" (*The United States plans to send foreign aid to several African countries*). The word *aide* is also a noun but refers to "a person who acts as an assistant" (*The student aide assisted her professor with grading*).

Q: The following three sentences appeared in an assignment my daughter received from her fifth grade teacher: *It's going to be interesting! For each state list it's geographical region. On your map identify each state and note its' capital.* I always have trouble myself with *its* and *it's*, but it seems as if something is wrong here.

A: You're right! Even teachers have trouble with *its* and *it's*. In the first sentence, *it's*, a contraction for *it is*, has been used correctly (*It is going to be interesting!*). In the last two sentences, the teacher should have used the possessive form of *it*, which is *its*, to show possession. In fact, the word *its'* does not exist. Now your only decision is whether you should point out these errors to your daughter's teacher!

LEVEL 1

A. **(Self-check)** Choose (a) or (b) to complete the following sentences.

1. All (a) eleven, (b) 11 employers surveyed said that they use Google to run background checks on potential employees. _____

2. (a) 23, (b) Twenty three (c) Twenty-three call centers in India announced that they will be switching from customer service to mortgage processing. _____

3. *The Wall Street Journal* began running front-page ads on the (a) 17th, (b) seventeenth of September. _____

4. Companies pay search engine companies (a) 18 cents, (b) $.18 each time their ads are clicked. _____

5. Cecilia spends (a) $30.00, (b) $30 each month for her Internet-access service. _____

6. The new Emporis buildings are located at (a) Three, (b) 3 Peachtree Pointe in Atlanta. _____

7. Financial institutions are clustered on (a) Seventh, (b) 7th Avenue. _____

8. Send the letter to (a) 320 27th Street, (b) 320 27 Street. _____

9. Organizers expect (a) 38000, (b) 38,000 to attend the Macworld Conference & Expo. _____

10. We plan to meet again at (a) 9:00 a.m., (b) 9 a.m. Tuesday. _____

Check your answers below.

B. Assume that the following phrases appear within sentences (unless otherwise noted) in business correspondence. Write the preferred forms in the spaces provided. If a phrase is correct as shown, write *C*.

Example: 1135 54 Street   1135 54th Street _____

1. fourteen new blog entries _____

2. on Fourth Street _____

3. charged $.50 for a coffee refill _____

4. received 4 e-mail messages _____

5. on April ninth _____

6. located on 5th Avenue _____

7. charges of $3.68, 79 cents, and $40.00 _____

8. on the sixteenth of October _____

1. b 2. c 3. a 4. a 5. b 6. b 7. a 8. a 9. b 10. b

Want to explore more? Go to: academic.cengage.com/bcomm/guffey or Xtra!

NUMBERS | CHAPTER 18 | 345

9. meeting at 11:00 a.m. _____

10. arrived at ten o'clock _____

11. a total of seventy-nine orders _____

12. on August 31st _____

13. moved to 12655 32nd Street _____

14. costs $49 dollars _____

15. (Beginning of sentence) 27 interviewees _____

16. exactly thirty-two dollars _____

17. the address is 7 Hampton Square _____

18. the address is 1 Hampton Square _____

19. has sixty-six rooms _____

20. at 8 o'clock _____

21. (International style) on April 15, 2009 _____

22. located at 2742 8th Street _____

23. at five thirty p.m. _____

24. the first of June _____

25. for one hundred dollars _____

26. cost exactly 90¢ _____

27. at 18307 Eleventh Street _____

28. call 800/598-3459 _____

29. all 50 states _____

30. bought 2 laptops _____

C. Rewrite these sentences correcting any errors you note.

1. On April 15th Alicia submitted the following petty cash disbursements: $2.80, 95 cents, $5.00, and 25 cents.

   _____

2. Tonja James moved from seventeen sixteen Sunset Drive to 1 Bellingham Court.

   _____

3. 24 different wireless packages are available from our 3 local dealers.

   _____

4. On the 18 of March, I sent you 3 e-mail messages about restricting Internet use.

   _____

5. Although McDonald's advertised a sandwich that cost only ninety-nine cents, most customers found that lunch cost between three dollars and three dollars and ninety-nine cents.

   _____

6. Regular work breaks are scheduled at 10:00 a.m. in the morning and again at 3:30 p.m. in the afternoon.

   _____

Want to explore more? Go to: academic.cengage.com/bcomm/guffey or Xtra!

7. We want to continue operations through the thirtieth, but we may be forced to close by the twenty-second.

_____

8. 1319 people visited our Web site when it launched on July 1st.

_____

LEVEL 2

A. **(Self-check)** Select (a) or (b) to complete each of the following sentences.

1. Consultants distributed (a) 4 55-page, (b) four 55-page proposals.   _____

2. Laura Lozano has worked in Phoenix for (a) twenty-seven, (b) 27 years.   _____

3. The annual stockholders' meeting will be held in (a) Room Two, (b) Room 2.   _____

4. Of the 235 e-mail messages sent, only (a) 7, (b) seven bounced back.   _____

5. Although she is only (a) 25, (b) twenty-five, Heather owns her own
restaurant in Las Vegas.   _____

6. Google paid (a) $4.95 million, (b) $4,950,000 to settle a click-fraud case.   _____

7. Have you completed your IRS Form (a) Ten Forty, (b) 1040?   _____

8. In 2006 San Francisco observed the (a) 100th, (b) one hundredth anniversary of
the great earthquake.   _____

9. Your short-term loan covers a period of (a) 60, (b) sixty days.   _____

10. The serial number on my monitor is (a) 85056170, (b) 85,056,170.   _____

Check your answers below.

B. For the following sentences, underscore any numbers or words that are expressed inappropriately and write the correct forms in the spaces provided. If a sentence is correct as written, write _C._

Example: The documentation group has prepared 4 twenty-page reports.   four 20-page   _____

1. Our board of directors is composed of 15 members, of whom three are
doctors, four are nurses, and eight are other health care professionals.   _____

2. We plan to print two hundred twenty-five-page booklets.   _____

3. After a period of sixteen years, ownership reverts to the state.   _____

4. One New York spammer sent more than 825,000,000 unsolicited e-mail
messages.   _____

5. The following policy Nos. are listed for Lisa Orta: No. 1355801 and No. 1355802.   _____

6. Model 8,400 costs $10,000 and can be leased for $275 a month.   _____

7. Over 53,000,000 Chinese visit online forums regularly.   _____

8. Of the 65 typed pages, nine pages require minor revisions and six pages
demand heavy revision.   _____

1. b 2. b 3. b 4. a 5. b 6. a 7. b 8. b 9. a 10. a

Want to explore more? Go to: academic.cengage.com/bcomm/guffey or Xtra!

NUMBERS | CHAPTER 18 | **347**

9. John Edwards, forty-one, and Emily Downing, thirty-three, were interviewed for the two executive positions.

_____

10. On page forty-four of Volume two, the total deficit is listed at nearly $34,000,000,000.

_____

11. Warranties on all flat-panel monitors are limited to ninety days.

_____

12. The total book club membership of eight hundred thousand received the four bonus books.

_____

13. Only seven of the 57 staff members were unable to attend the two-day training session.

_____

14. About thirty people will be laid off from the Boise office.

_____

15. When the child was two years six months old, his parents established a trust fund for $1.6 million.

_____

16. Bill Gates' mansion on Lake Washington features a wall of twenty-four video screens, parking for twenty cars, and a reception hall for one hundred people.

_____

17. Taking 7 years to construct, the 40,000-square-foot home reportedly cost more than fifty million dollars.

_____

18. Volkswagen has sold more than 21,500,000 Beetles since 1934, making it the most successful car ever built.

_____

C. Assume that the following phrases appear in business or professional correspondence. Write the preferred forms in the spaces provided. If a phrase is correct as shown, write _C._

1. nine offices with eleven computers and fifteen desks

_____

2. three seventy-five pound weights

_____

3. loan period of sixty days

_____

4. Joan Brault, seventy, and

Frank Brault, sixty-eight

_____

5. Account No. 362,486,012

_____

6. three point two billion dollars

_____

7. Gate Twenty-three

_____

8. a period of seventeen years

_____

9. fifty-nine customer comments

_____

10. about two hundred guests

_____

11. four point four million people

_____

12. Section three point two

_____

13. 9 three-bedroom apartments

_____

14. warranty period of two years

_____

15. insurance for 15 computers, 12 printers, and 3 scanners

_____

Want to explore more? Go to: academic.cengage.com/bcomm/guffey or Xtra!

348 I **UNIT 6** I **CHAPTER 18** I **NUMBERS**

LEVEL 3

A. **(Self-check)** Choose (a) or (b) to complete the following sentences.

1. The size of carry-on baggage should not exceed (a) 22" × 14" × 9", (b) 22 by 14 by 9 inches. _____

2. Most airlines do not allow carry-on baggage that weighs more than (a) 40, (b) forty pounds. _____

3. Spam makes up more than (a) one fifth, (b) one-fifth, (c) 1/5 of all e-mail messages sent. _____

4. Coca-Cola controls more than (a) 30 percent, (b) thirty percent of the total soft-drink market in Japan. _____

5. Darrell Issa represents the (a) 49th, (b) Forty-ninth Congressional District. _____

6. Surprising pollsters, Senator Williams received a (a) two-thirds, (b) two thirds majority. _____

7. This copier can make copies up to (a) 11 by 17 inches, (b) eleven by seventeen inches. _____

8. Maintenance costs are only (a) 0.5, (b) .5 percent above last year's. _____

9. Some hybrid vehicles can get over (a) fifty, (b) 50 miles per gallon. _____

10. Did you know that many office buildings have no (a) 13th, (b) thirteenth floor? _____

Check your answers below.

B. Rewrite the following sentences with special attention to appropriate number usage.

1. "Kingda Ka," which claims to be the world's fastest and tallest roller coaster, travels one hundred twenty eight miles per hour and is four hundred fifty six feet high.

_____

_____

2. On May 20th nearly 1/3 of the visitors to Six Flags Great Adventure in New Jersey lined up for a high-speed joyride on four eighteen-passenger rail cars.

_____

_____

3. Swiss engineers used precise instruments to ensure that Kingda Ka's three thousand one hundred eighteen feet of steel track were within 0.05 inches of specifications.

_____

_____

4. To ride Kingda Ka, you must be at least fifty-four inches but less than 6' 5" tall.

_____

Want to explore more? Go to: academic.cengage.com/bcomm/guffey or Xtra!

NUMBERS | CHAPTER 18 | 349

5. Only the Kingda Ka ride can reach speeds of one hundred twenty-eight mph in three point three seconds, achieving a negative gravity force with 6.5 seconds of weightlessness at the top before taking a forty-one-story plunge.

_____

_____

6. Located in the 4th Congressional District, Six Flags Great Adventure is seventy-four miles from New York City and attracts over three million visitors each summer.

_____

_____

7. The square mileage of Washington, DC, is 68 point 2; and its population is about 550 thousand.

_____

8. Washington, DC's, population decreased 3.8% between 2000 and 2005.

_____

9. Females make up approximately fifty-two point seven percent of the population in Washington, DC.

_____

10. A little more than 1/2 of eligible Americans voted in the last presidential election.

_____

C. **Writing Exercise.** In your local newspaper, find ten sentences with numbers. Write those sentences on a separate sheet. After each one, explain what rule the number style represents. Strive to find examples illustrating different rules.

D. **Hotline Review.** In the space provided write the correct answer choice.

1. Your contribution of _____ to the Animal Rescue Foundation is greatly appreciated.
   a. $100   b. 100 dollars   c. $100 dollars   _____

2. _____ interns were hired for the summer.
   a. Twenty-one   b. 21   c. Twenty one   _____

3. The United States sent foreign _____ to tsunami victims in Indonesia.
   a. aide   b. aid   _____

4. Lyle is training to become an _____ in a psychiatric facility.
   a. aide   b. aid   _____

5. Investors were afraid that they would _____ money on junk bonds.
   a. loose   b. lose   _____

6. Sharon hunted for _____ change for the parking meter.
   a. loose   b. lose   _____

Want to explore more? Go to: academic.cengage.com/bcomm/guffey or Xtra!

350 I UNIT 6 I CHAPTER 18 I NUMBERS

The following e-mail message contains intentional errors representing language principles covered throughout all textbook chapters. Use proofreading marks to make 50 changes. Use three short lines (≡) under a lowercase letter to indicate that it is to be changed to a capital letter. Draw a diagonal (/) through a capital letter you wish to change to a lowercase letter. When you replace a wordy or incorrect phrase with one word, it counts as one correction. When you correct a comma splice, run-on, or fragment, the correction counts as two errors. Count each parenthesis and each dash as a single mark. Use proofreading marks to make the corrections here OR make the corrections at the **Guffey Companion Web Site** at **academic.cengage.com/bcomm/guffey.**

October 1, 200x

CERTIFIED MAIL, RETURN RECEIPT REQUESTED

Mr. Charles Smith
Customer Relations
Sony USA

1 Sony Drive
Park Ridge, NY 07656

Dear Mr. Smith,

Pictures from a once in a lifetime trip are irreplaceable. Thats why I put my trust in Sonys Cyber-shot DSC-W100 Digital Camera, which I bought for a cruise I took to the french caribbean last Summer to celebrate my 40th birthday. Experience, dependability and customer service, these are the quality's that I associate with the name "Sony."

I took 100's of pictures on my twenty day trip. Although I checked some of the early shots using the lcd screen I didn't check any pictures for the last 1/2 of the trip in order to conserve my battery. When I come home however I learned that most of the pictures I took latter in the trip did not turn out because the camera had malfunctioned. 98 of the pictures I took the last week of my trip were faded to a near white color. Enclosed is the camera, the memory card I used, the printed photos and my receipt for the camera.

As you must realize the value of these photographs are far greater then the cost of the printing, or the purchase price of the camera. The real loss is the complete record of a beautiful trip. Without pictures, I will not remember how I felt and looked standing in front of diamond rock in the Southern part of Martinique or shopping in the town of marigot in St. Martin. I will not remember dancing with children around a fire in a Guadalupe Village. 11 days of my dream vacation was essentially unrecorded. This represents more than 50% of my vacation.

Replacing the film or camera are not enough. Without pictures I feel like I never took the trip. I have suffered a tremendous emotional loss and I am requesting that sony pay me $7500 so that I may repeat my trip, and replace the pictures lost because of this faulty camera.

I know that Sony enjoys a excellent reputation with consumers, therefore, I trust that you will do the right thing in helping me replace my lost memories. Please contact me by October 30th so that I may begin making plans for a Spring cruise.

Sincerely,

Daniella Davidson

Daniella Davidson

Enclosures: Sony Cyber-shot camera, memory card, printed photos, receipt

Want to explore more? Go to: academic.cengage.com/bcomm/guffey or Xtra!

NUMBERS | CHAPTER 18 | **351**

Goal: To learn how to avoid being a victim of Internet fraud.

You've heard a lot about Internet fraud and want to learn how to avoid becoming a victim yourself.

1. With your Web browser on the screen, go to the U.S. Department of Justice *Internet Fraud* site at **http://www.internetfraud.usdoj.gov/.** Click **What Is Internet Fraud?**

2. Read the description of Internet fraud. Next scroll down to learn about major types of

Internet fraud. Finally, read what the U.S. Department of Justice is doing to combat Internet fraud and how you can deal with Internet fraud.

3. Copy the information you found most helpful into a Word document and print it.

4. On a separate sheet list five strategies that could help you avoid becoming a victim of Internet fraud.

5. End your session. Submit your printouts and answers.

Underline numbers that are expressed inappropriately. Write corrected forms in the spaces provided.

1. If you save only five hundred dollars annually, you'll have fifty-four thousand dollars after twenty-five years if it earns an average of 10%.

   _____

2. Approximately 7,500,000 millionaires in the United States control about 11 trillion dollars in assets.

   _____

3. By the June 30th application deadline, we received ninety-eight applications for a job that pays $10.00 an hour.

   _____

4. Please call our office, located at 3549 6th Avenue, at 585/663-0785, to schedule an appointment.

   _____

5. Flight thirty-seven will depart from Gate five at 5:00 p.m.

   _____

1. $500 $54,000 25 10 percent 2. 7.5 millionaires, $11 trillion 3. June 30, 98, $10 4. 3549 Sixth Avenue, (585) 663-0785 5. Flight 37, Gate 5, 5 p.m.

Want to explore more? Go to: academic.cengage.com/bcomm/guffey or Xtra!

352 I UNIT 6 I CHAPTER 18 I NUMBERS

UNIT 6 REVIEW
Chapters 17–18

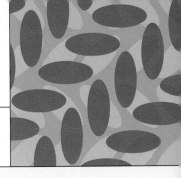

Name _____

First, review Chapters 17–18. Then test your comprehension of those chapters by completing the exercises that follow. Compare your responses with those shown at the end of the book.

LEVEL 1

Select *a* or *b* to describe the group of words that is more acceptably expressed.

1.	a. courses in Marketing, German, and Anatomy	b. courses in marketing, German, and anatomy	_____
2.	a. living in Sweetwater county	b. living in Sweetwater County	_____
3.	a. the State of Kansas	b. the state of Kansas	_____
4.	a. a fall promotional event	b. a Fall promotional event	_____
5.	a. plaster of Paris	b. plaster of paris	_____
6.	a. the 17th of May	b. the seventeenth of May	_____
7.	a. forty-five dollars	b. $45	_____
8.	a. on 16th Avenue	b. on Sixteenth Avenue	_____
9.	a. on July 4th	b. on July 4	_____

Use proofreading marks to correct any errors in capitalization or number usage in the following sentences. In the space at the right, indicate how many changes you made.

10. 35 Graduate Students are enrolled in 5 sections of Accounting. _____

11. One share of google stock initially sold for 100 dollars on its 1st day of trading on August 19th, 2004. _____

12. You must navigate through 9 Web pages to send an e-mail message to the President. _____

LEVEL 2

Select *a* or *b* to describe the group of words that is more acceptably expressed.

13.	a. your Mom and Dad	b. your mom and dad	_____
14.	a. travel south on Highway 1	b. travel South on Highway 1	_____
15.	a. our manager, Jean Hunnicutt	b. our Manager, Jean Hunnicutt	_____
16.	a. our Legal Department	b. our legal department	_____
17.	a. a message from Lisa Cantrell, Sales Director	b. a message from Lisa Cantrell, sales director	_____
18.	a. a message from Sales Director Cantrell	b. a message from sales director Cantrell	_____

19. a. for the past four years   b. for the past 4 years   _____

20. a. 4 twenty-story buildings   b. four 20-story buildings   _____

21. a. nine paralegals assigned to   b. 9 paralegals assigned to   14 cases   14 cases   _____

Use proofreading marks to correct any errors in capitalization or number usage in the following sentences. In the space at the right, indicate how many changes you made.

22. His lunch consisting of a big mac, french fries, and a coca-cola cost three dollars and seventy-five cents.   _____

23. Carolyn Pleck, President, traveled South on highway 85 to attend the party celebrating her company's 10th anniversary.   _____

24. My Father recommended that I read the book *Success Built To Last,* which has sold approximately 2,000,000 copies.   _____

LEVEL 3

Select the correct group of words below and write its letter in the space provided.

25. a. a world of possibilities   b. a World of possibilities   _____

26. a. Mayor-Elect   b. Mayor-elect   _____

27. a. an e-mail marked "confidential"   b. an e-mail marked "Confidential"   _____

28. a. have a seat, Sir   b. have a seat, sir   _____

29. a. less than 0.3 percent   b. less than .3 percent   _____

30. a. 89 degrees   b. eighty-nine degrees   _____

31. a. a 90% test score   b. a 90 percent test score   _____

32. a. a one third interest   b. a one-third interest   _____

33. a. a Mormon temple   b. a mormon temple   _____

34. a. italian and greek cultures   b. Italian and Greek cultures   _____

35. a. 3rd place   b. third place   _____

Hotline Review

Write the letter of the word or phrase that correctly completes each sentence.

36. Do you have any _____ you can give me about graduate programs?
a. advise   b. advice   _____

37. Our newsletter comes out _____, on the 1st and the 15th of each month.
a. bimonthly   b. semimonthly   _____

38. The Red Cross immediately sent _____ following the hurricane.
a. aid   b. aide   _____

39. The guard will _____ top-seeded runners to the start line.
a. marshal   b. martial   _____

40. Ramona doesn't want to _____ her opportunity to travel abroad.
a. loose   b. lose   _____

Name _____

SHORT REPORTS

Reports are a fact of life in the business world today. They are important because they convey needed information, and they help decision makers solve problems. Organizing information into a meaningful report is an important skill you will want to acquire if your field is business.

CHARACTERISTICS OF REPORTS

As an introduction to report writing, this workshop focuses on the most important characteristics of reports. You'll learn valuable tips about the format, data, headings, and writing plan for short business reports and internal proposals.

Format. How should a business report look? Three formats are commonly used. *Letter format* is appropriate for short reports prepared by one organization for another. A letter report, as illustrated in Figure 6.1, is like a letter except that it is more carefully organized. It includes side headings and lists where appropriate. *Memo format* is common for reports written within an organization. These internal reports look like memos—with the addition of side headings. *Report format* is used for longer, more formal reports. Printed on plain paper (instead of letterhead or memo forms), these reports begin with a title followed by carefully displayed headings and subheadings.

Data. Where do you find the data for a business report? Many business reports begin with personal observation and experience. If you were writing a report on implementing flex-time for employees, you might begin by observing current work schedules and by asking what schedules employees preferred. Other sources of data for business reports include company records, surveys, questionnaires, and interviews. If you want to see how others have solved a problem or collect background data on a topic, you can consult magazines, journals, and books. Much information is available electronically through online library indexes or from searching databases and the Web.

Headings. Good headings in a report highlight major ideas and categories. They guide the reader through a report. In longer reports they divide the text into inviting chunks, and they provide resting places for the eyes. Short reports often use *functional* heads (such as *Problem, Summary,* and *Recommendations*). Longer reports may employ *talking heads* (such as *Short-Term Parking Solutions*) because they provide more information to the reader. Whether your heads are functional or talking, be sure they are clear and parallel. For example, use *Visible Costs* and *Invisible Costs* rather than *Visible Costs* and *Costs That Don't Show*. Don't enclose headings in quotation marks, and avoid using headings as antecedents for pronouns. For example, if your heading is *Laser Printers,* don't begin the next sentence with *These produce high-quality output . . . .*

Figure 6.1
Short Report—Letter Format

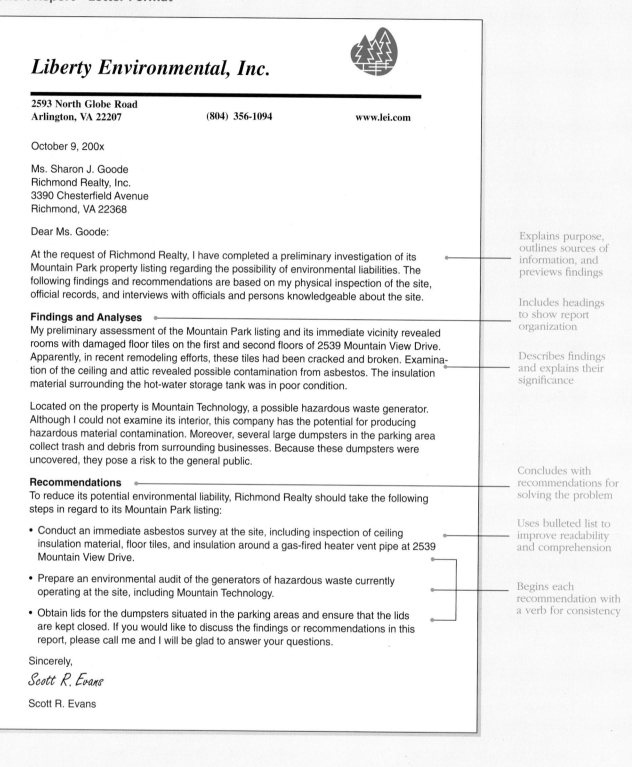

Liberty Environmental, Inc.

2593 North Globe Road
Arlington, VA 22207   **(804) 356-1094**   **www.lei.com**

October 9, 200x

Ms. Sharon J. Goode
Richmond Realty, Inc.
3390 Chesterfield Avenue
Richmond, VA 22368

Dear Ms. Goode:

At the request of Richmond Realty, I have completed a preliminary investigation of its Mountain Park property listing regarding the possibility of environmental liabilities. The following findings and recommendations are based on my physical inspection of the site, official records, and interviews with officials and persons knowledgeable about the site.

Findings and Analyses

My preliminary assessment of the Mountain Park listing and its immediate vicinity revealed rooms with damaged floor tiles on the first and second floors of 2539 Mountain View Drive. Apparently, in recent remodeling efforts, these tiles had been cracked and broken. Examination of the ceiling and attic revealed possible contamination from asbestos. The insulation material surrounding the hot-water storage tank was in poor condition.

Located on the property is Mountain Technology, a possible hazardous waste generator. Although I could not examine its interior, this company has the potential for producing hazardous material contamination. Moreover, several large dumpsters in the parking area collect trash and debris from surrounding businesses. Because these dumpsters were uncovered, they pose a risk to the general public.

Recommendations

To reduce its potential environmental liability, Richmond Realty should take the following steps in regard to its Mountain Park listing:

• Conduct an immediate asbestos survey at the site, including inspection of ceiling insulation material, floor tiles, and insulation around a gas-fired heater vent pipe at 2539 Mountain View Drive.

• Prepare an environmental audit of the generators of hazardous waste currently operating at the site, including Mountain Technology.

• Obtain lids for the dumpsters situated in the parking areas and ensure that the lids are kept closed. If you would like to discuss the findings or recommendations in this report, please call me and I will be glad to answer your questions.

Sincerely,

Scott R. Evans

Scott R. Evans

Explains purpose, outlines sources of information, and previews findings

Includes headings to show report organization

Describes findings and explains their significance

Concludes with recommendations for solving the problem

Uses bulleted list to improve readability and comprehension

Begins each recommendation with a verb for consistency

Skill Check 6.1 *Reviewing the Characteristics of Short Reports*

Select a letter to indicate the best format for the report described.

   a. Memo format   b. Letter format   c. Report format

   1. A short report to a company from an outside consultant   _____

   2. A short report from a product manager to her boss   _____

   3. A long report describing a company's diversity program   _____

   4. If you were writing a report to persuade management to purchase more computers,
      the best way to begin collecting data would be to
      a. observe current use
      b. consult books and journals
      c. search the Internet   _____

   5. Which combination of report headings is best?
      a. Delivery costs, Suppliers
      b. Reduction of delivery costs, Recommendations
      c. "Delivery costs," "Supply Costs"
      d. Reducing delivery costs, Finding new suppliers   _____

WRITING PLAN FOR A SHORT REPORT

Short reports often have three parts: introduction, findings, and recommendations. If the report is purely informational, a summary may be made instead of recommendations.

Introduction. This part of a report may also be called *Background*. In this section, you'll want to explain why you are writing. You may also (a) describe what methods and sources you used to gather information and why they are credible, (b) provide any special background information that may be necessary, and (c) offer a preview of your findings.

Findings. This section may also be called *Observations, Facts, Results,* or *Discussion.* Important points to consider in this section are organization and display. You may wish to organize the findings (a) chronologically (for example, to describe the history of a problem), (b) alphabetically (if you were, for example, evaluating candidates for a position), (c) topically (for example, discussing sales by regions), or (d) from most to least important (such as listing criteria for evaluating equipment). To display the findings effectively, you could (a) use side headings, (b) number each finding, (c) underline or boldface the key words, or (d) merely indent the paragraphs.

Summary or Recommendations. Some reports just offer information. Such reports may conclude with an impartial summary. Other reports are more analytical, and they generally conclude with recommendations. These recommendations tell readers how to solve the problem and may even suggest ways to implement the necessary actions. To display recommendations, number each one and place it on a separate line.

   Notice that the letter report in Figure 6.1 includes an introduction, findings and analyses, and recommendations.

WRITING PLAN FOR AN INTERNAL PROPOSAL

Both managers and employees must occasionally write reports that justify or recommend something such as buying equipment, changing a procedure, hiring an employee, consolidating departments, or investing funds. Here is a writing plan for an internal proposal that recommends a course of action.

Introduction. In this section, identify the problem briefly. Use specific examples, supporting statistics, and authoritative quotes to lend credibility to the seriousness of the problem. If you think your audience will be receptive, announce your recommendation, solution, or action immediately and concisely. If you think your audience will need to be persuaded or educated, do not announce your solution until after you have explained its advantages.

Body. In writing the body of an internal proposal, you may want to include all or some of the following elements. Explain more fully the benefits of the recommendations or steps to be taken to solve the problem. Include a discussion of pros, cons, and costs. If appropriate, describe the factual and ethical negative consequences of the current situation. For example, if your internal proposal recommends purchasing new equipment, explain how much time, effort, money, and morale are being lost by continuing to use outdated equipment that needs constant repairs. Quantification through accurate facts and examples builds credibility and persuasive appeal. Explain the benefits of your proposal. A bulleted list improves readability and emphasis. Anticipate objections to your proposal and discuss ways to counter those objections. The body should also provide a plan and schedule for implementing your proposal. If many people will be included in implementing the proposal, prepare a staffing section. Describe who will be doing what. You may also describe alternative solutions and show how they will not work as well as your proposal.

Conclusion. In the conclusion summarize your recommendation. Describe the specific action to be taken. Ask for authorization to proceed. To motivate the reader, you might include a date for the action to take place and a reason for the deadline.

An internal proposal is generally formatted as a memo such as the one shown in Figure 6.2. In this memo report the writer expects the reader to be receptive to the recommendation of pilot testing smart tires. Thus, the proposal begins directly with the recommendations announced immediately. The body discusses how the recommendation would work, and it itemizes benefits. It anticipates objections and counters them. The closing summarizes what action is to be taken and presents a deadline.

Writing Application 6.1

Organize the following information into a short letter report. As Cynthia M. Chavez, president, Chavez and Associates, you have been hired as a consultant to advise the St. Petersburg, Florida, City Council. The City Council has asked you and your associates to investigate a problem with Pinellas Park Beachway.

In 1979 St. Petersburg constructed a 12-foot pathway, now called the Pinellas Park Beachway. It was meant originally for bicycle riders, but today it has become very popular for joggers, walkers, bikers, in-line skaters, skateboarders, sightseers, and people walking their dogs. In fact, it's become so popular that it is dangerous. Last year the St. Petersburg Police Department reported an amazing 65 collisions in the area. And this doesn't count the close calls and minor accidents that no one reported. The City Council wants your organization to identify the problem and come up with some workable recommendations for improving safety.

As you look into the matter, you immediately decide that the council is right. A problem definitely exists! In addition to the many pedestrians and riders, you see that families with rented pedal-powered surreys clog the beachway. Sometimes they even operate these vehicles on the wrong side. Your investigation further reveals that bicyclists with rental bikes do not always have bells to alert walkers. And poor lighting makes nighttime use extremely dangerous. You've noticed that conditions seem to be worst on Sundays. This congestion results from nearby art and crafts fairs and sales, attracting even more people to the crowded area.

continued on page 360

Figure 6.2
Internal Proposal—Memo Format

DATE: September 20, 200x
TO: Kevin West, Vice President
FROM: James Worthington, Operations Manager *JW*
SUBJECT: PILOT TESTING SMART TIRES

Next to fuel, truck tires are our biggest operating cost. Last year we spent $211,000 replacing and retreading tires for 495 trucks. This year the costs will be greater because prices have jumped at least 12 percent and because we've increased our fleet to 550 trucks. Truck tires are an additional burden since they require labor-intensive paperwork to track their warranties, wear, and retread histories. To reduce our long-term costs and to improve our tire tracking system, I recommend that we do the following:

- Purchase 24 Goodyear smart tires.
- Begin a one-year pilot test on six trucks.

How Smart Tires Work

Smart tires have an embedded computer chip that monitors wear, performance, and durability. The chip also creates an electronic fingerprint for positive identification of a tire. By passing a handheld sensor next to the tire, we can learn where and when a tire was made (for warranty and other identification), how much tread it had originally, and its serial number.

How Smart Tires Could Benefit Us

Although smart tires are initially more expensive than other tires, they could help us improve our operations and save us money in four ways:

1. **Retreads.** Goodyear believes that the wear data is so accurate that we should be able to retread every tire three times, instead of our current two times. If that's true, in one year we could save at least $27,000 in new tire costs.
2. **Safety.** Accurate and accessible wear data should reduce the danger of blowouts and flat tires. Last year, drivers reported six blowouts.
3. **Record keeping and maintenance.** Smart tires could reduce our maintenance costs considerably. Currently, we use an electric branding iron to mark serial numbers on new tires. Our biggest headache is manually reading those serial numbers, decoding them, and maintaining records to meet safety regulations. Reading such data electronically could save us thousands of dollars in labor.
4. **Theft protection.** The chip can be used to monitor each tire as it leaves or enters the warehouse or yard, thus discouraging theft.

Summary and Action

Specifically, I recommend that you do the following:

- Authorize the special purchase of 24 Goodyear smart tires at $450 each, plus one electronic sensor at $1,200.
- Approve a one-year pilot test in our Atlanta territory that equips six trucks with smart tires and tracks their performance.

Please let me have your authorization by September 30 so that I can begin the pilot test before the winter driving season is upon us.

Introduces problem briefly but with concrete facts

Presents recommendations immediately

Justifies recommendation by explaining proposal and benefits

Offers counter-argument to possible objection

Explains recommendation in more detail

Specifies action to be taken

Concludes with deadline and reason

continued from page 358

Your investigation confirms that the beachway is dangerous. But what to do about it? In a brainstorming session, your associates make a number of suggestions for reducing the dangers to users. By the way, the council is particularly interested in lessening the threat of liability to the city. One of your associates thinks that the beachway should be made at least 15 or more feet wide. Another suggests that the beachway be lighted at night. Someone thinks that a new path should be built, on the beach side of the existing beachway; this path would be for pedestrians only. Educating users about safety rules and etiquette would certainly be wise for everyone. One suggestion involves better striping or applying colors to designate different uses for the beachway. And why not require that all rental bicycles be equipped with bells? One of the best recommendations involved hiring uniformed "beach hosts" who would monitor the beachway, give advice, offer directions, and generally patrol the area.

In a short report, outline the problem and list your recommendations. Naturally, you would be happy to discuss your findings and recommendations with the St. Petersburg City Council.

Writing Application 6.2

Assume that your office needs a piece of equipment such as a photocopier, fax, scanner, digital camera, computer, printer, or the like. Do the research necessary to write a convincing internal proposal to your boss. Because you feel that your boss will be receptive to your request, you can use the direct approach.

Developing Spelling Skills

WHY IS ENGLISH SPELLING SO DIFFICULT?

No one would dispute the complaint that many English words are difficult to spell. Why is spelling in our language so perplexing? For one thing, our language has borrowed many of its words from other languages. English has a Germanic base on which a superstructure of words borrowed from French, Latin, Greek, and other languages of the world has been erected. For this reason, its words are not always formed by regular patterns of letter combinations. In addition, spelling is made difficult because the pronunciation of English words is constantly changing. Today's spelling was standardized nearly 300 years ago, but many words are pronounced differently today than they were then. Therefore, pronunciation often provides little help in spelling. Consider, for example, the words *sew* and *dough*.

WHAT CAN BE DONE TO IMPROVE ONE'S SPELLING?

Spelling is a skill that can be developed, just as arithmetic, keyboarding, and other skills can be developed. Because the ability to spell is a prerequisite for success in business and in most other activities, effort expended to acquire this skill is effort well spent.

Three traditional approaches to improving spelling have met with varying degrees of success.

1. RULES OR GUIDELINES

The spelling of English words is consistent enough to justify the formulation of a few spelling rules, perhaps more appropriately called **guidelines** since the generalizations in question are not invariably applicable. Such guidelines are, in other words, helpful but not infallible.

2. MNEMONICS

Another approach to improving one's ability to spell involves the use of mnemonics or memory devices. For example, the word *principle* might be associated with the word *rule,* to form in the mind of the speller a link between the meaning and the spelling of *principle.* To spell *capitol,* one might think of the *dome* of the capitol building and focus on the *o*'s in both words. The use of mnemonics can be an effective device for the improvement of spelling only if the speller makes a real effort to develop the necessary memory hooks.

3. ROTE LEARNING

A third approach to the improvement of spelling centers on memorization. The word is studied by the speller until it can be readily reproduced in the mind's eye.

THE 1-2-3 SPELLING PLAN

Proficiency in spelling is not attained without concentrated effort. Here's a plan to follow in mastering the 400 commonly misspelled words included in this appendix. For each word, try this 1-2-3 approach.

1. Is a spelling guideline applicable? If so, select the appropriate guideline and study the word in relation to that guideline.
2. If no guideline applies, can a memory device be created to aid in the recall of the word?
3. If neither a guideline nor a memory device will work, the word must be memorized. Look at the word carefully. Pronounce it. Write it or repeat it until you can visualize all its letters in your mind's eye.

Before you try the 1-2-3 plan, become familiar with the six spelling guidelines that follow. These spelling guidelines are not intended to represent all the possible spelling rules appearing in the various available spelling books. These six guidelines are, however, among the most effective and helpful of the recognized spelling rules.

GUIDELINE 1: WORDS CONTAINING *IE* OR *EI*

Although there are exceptions to it, the following familiar rhyme can be helpful.

(a) Write *i* before *e*
(b) Except after *c*,
(c) Or when sounded like *a*
     As in *neighbor* and *weigh*.

Study these words illustrating the three parts of the rhyme.

(a) *i* Before *e*		(b) Except After *c*	(c) or When Sounded Like *a*
achieve	grief	ceiling	beige
belief	ingredient	conceive	eight
believe	mischief	deceive	freight
brief	niece	perceive	heir
cashier	piece	receipt	neighbor
chief	shield	receive	reign
convenient	sufficient		their
field	view		vein
friend	yield		weight

Exceptions: These exceptional *ei* and *ie* words must be learned by rote or with the use of a mnemonic device.

caffeine	height	seize
either	leisure	sheik
financier	neither	sleight
foreigner	protein	weird

GUIDELINE 2: WORDS ENDING IN *E*

For most words ending in an *e*, the final *e* is dropped when the word is joined to a suffix beginning with a vowel (such as *ing, able,* or *al*). The final *e* is retained when a suffix beginning with a consonant (such as *ment, less, ly,* or *ful*) is joined to such a word.

Final *e* Dropped	Final *e* Retained
believe, believing	arrange, arrangement
care, caring	require, requirement
hope, hoping	hope, hopeless
receive, receiving	care, careless
desire, desirable	like, likely
cure, curable	approximate, approximately
move, movable	definite, definitely
value, valuable	sincere, sincerely
disperse, dispersal	use, useful
arrive, arrival	hope, hopeful

Exceptions: The few exceptions to this spelling guideline are among the most frequently misspelled words. As such, they deserve special attention. Notice that they all involve a dropped final *e*.

acknowledgment	ninth
argument	truly
judgment	wholly

GUIDELINE 3: WORDS ENDING IN *CE* OR *GE*

When *able* or *ous* is added to words ending in *ce* or *ge*, the final *e* is retained if the *c* or *g* is pronounced softly (as in *change* or *peace*).

advantage, advantageous	change, changeable
courage, courageous	service, serviceable
outrage, outrageous	manage, manageable

GUIDELINE 4: WORDS ENDING IN *Y*

Words ending in a *y* that is preceded by a consonant normally change the *y* to *i* before all suffixes except those beginning with an *i*.

Change *y* to *i* Because *y* Is Preceded by a Consonant	Do Not Change *y* to *i* Because *y* Is Preceded by a Vowel
accompany, accompaniment	employ, employer
study, studied, studious	annoy, annoying, annoyance
duty, dutiful	stay, staying, stayed
industry, industrious	attorney, attorneys
carry, carriage	valley, valleys
apply, appliance	

Change *y* to *i* Because *y* Is Preceded by a Consonant	Do Not Change *y* to *i* When Adding *ing*
try, tried	accompany, accompanying
empty, emptiness	apply, applying
forty, fortieth	study, studying
secretary, secretaries	satisfy, satisfying
company, companies	try, trying
hurry, hurries	

Exceptions: day, daily; dry, dried; mislay, mislaid; pay, paid; shy, shyly; gay, gaily.

GUIDELINE 5: DOUBLING A FINAL CONSONANT

If one-syllable words or two-syllable words accented on the second syllable end in a single consonant preceded by a single vowel, the final consonant is doubled before the addition of a suffix beginning with a vowel.

Although complex, this spelling guideline is extremely useful and therefore well worth mastering. Many spelling errors can be avoided by applying this guideline.

One-Syllable Words	Two-Syllable Words
can, canned	acquit, acquitting, acquittal
drop, dropped	admit, admitted, admitting
fit, fitted	begin, beginner, beginning
get, getting	commit, committed, committing
man, manned	control, controller, controlling
plan, planned	defer, deferred (but deference*)
run, running	excel, excelled, excelling
shut, shutting	occur, occurrence, occurring
slip, slipped	prefer, preferring (but preference*)
swim, swimming	recur, recurred, recurrence
ton, tonnage	refer, referring (but reference*)

Because the accent shifts to the first syllable, the final consonant is not doubled.

Here is a summary of conditions necessary for application of this guideline.

1. The word must end in a single consonant.
2. The final consonant must be preceded by a single vowel.
3. The word must be accented on the second syllable (if it has two syllables).

Words derived from *cancel, offer, differ, equal, suffer,* and *benefit* are not governed by this guideline because they are accented on the first syllable.

GUIDELINE 6: PREFIXES AND SUFFIXES

For words in which the letter that ends the prefix is the same as the letter that begins the main word (such as in *dissimilar*), both letters must be included. For words in which a suffix begins with the same letter that ends the main word (such as in *coolly*), both letters must also be included.

Prefix	Main Word	Main Word	Suffix
dis	satisfied	accidental	ly
ir	responsible	incidental	ly
il	literate	clean	ness
mis	spell	cool	ly
mis	state	even	ness
un	necessary	mean	ness

On the other hand, do not supply additional letters when adding prefixes to main words.

Prefix	Main Word
dis	appoint (*not* dissappoint)
dis	appearance
mis	take

Perhaps the most important guideline one can follow in spelling correctly is to use the dictionary whenever in doubt.

400 Most Frequently Misspelled Words* (Divided into 20 Lists of 20 Words Each)

List 1

1. absence
2. acceptance
3. accessible
4. accidentally
5. accommodate
6. accompaniment
7. accurately
8. accustom
9. achievement
10. acknowledgment, acknowledgement
11. acquaintance
12. acquire
13. across
14. actually
15. adequately
16. admitted
17. adolescence
18. advantageous
19. advertising
20. advice, advise

List 2

21. afraid
22. against
23. aggressive
24. all right
25. almost
26. alphabetical
27. already
28. although
29. amateur
30. among
31. amount
32. analysis
33. analyze
34. angel, angle
35. annoyance
36. annual
37. answer
38. apologized
39. apparent
40. appliance

Compiled from lists of words most frequently misspelled by students and businesspeople.

List 3

41. applying
42. approaches
43. appropriate
44. approximately
45. arguing
46. argument
47. arrangement
48. article
49. athlete
50. attack
51. attendance, attendants
52. attitude
53. attorneys
54. auxiliary
55. basically
56. beautiful
57. before
58. beginning
59. believing
60. benefited

List 4

61. biggest
62. breath, breathe
63. brief
64. business
65. calendar
66. capital, capitol
67. career
68. careless
69. carrying
70. cashier
71. ceiling
72. certain
73. challenge
74. changeable
75. chief
76. choose, chose
77. cloths, clothes
78. column
79. coming
80. committee

List 5

81. companies
82. competition
83. completely
84. conceive
85. conscience
86. conscientious
87. conscious
88. considerably
89. consistent
90. continuous
91. controlling
92. controversial
93. convenience
94. council, counsel
95. cylinder
96. daily
97. deceive
98. decision
99. define
100. dependent

List 6

101. description
102. desirable
103. destroy
104. development
105. difference
106. dining
107. disappearance
108. disappoint
109. disastrous
110. discipline
111. discussion
112. disease
113. dissatisfied
114. distinction
115. divide
116. doesn't
117. dominant
118. dropped
119. due
120. during

List 7

121. efficient	128. especially	135. explanation
122. eligible	129. exaggerate	136. extremely
123. embarrass	130. excellence	137. familiar
124. encourage	131. except	138. families
125. enough	132. exercise	139. fascinate
126. environment	133. existence	140. favorite
127. equipped	134. experience	

List 8

141. February	148. forty, fourth	155. generally
142. fictitious	149. forward, foreword	156. government
143. field	150. freight	157. governor
144. finally	151. friend	158. grammar
145. financially	152. fulfill	159. grateful
146. foreigner	153. fundamentally	160. guard
147. fortieth	154. further	

List 9

161. happiness	168. humorous	175. importance
162. hear, here	169. hungry	176. incidentally
163. height	170. ignorance	177. independent
164. heroes	171. imaginary	178. indispensable
165. hopeless	172. imagine	179. industrious
166. hoping	173. immediately	180. inevitable
167. huge	174. immense	

List 10

181. influential	188. interrupt	195. kindergarten
182. ingredient	189. involve	196. knowledge
183. initiative	190. irrelevant	197. laboratory
184. intelligence	191. irresponsible	198. laborer
185. interest	192. island	199. laid
186. interference	193. jealous	200. led, lead
187. interpretation	194. judgment	

List 11

201. leisurely
202. library
203. license
204. likely
205. literature
206. lives
207. loneliness
208. loose, lose
209. losing
210. luxury
211. magazine
212. magnificence
213. maintenance
214. manageable
215. maneuver
216. manner
217. manufacturer
218. marriage
219. mathematics
220. meant

List 12

221. mechanics
222. medicine
223. medieval
224. mere
225. miniature
226. minutes
227. mischief
228. misspell
229. mistake
230. muscle
231. mysterious
232. naturally
233. necessary
234. neighbor
235. neither
236. nervous
237. nickel
238. niece
239. ninety
240. ninth

List 13

241. noticeable
242. numerous
243. obstacle
244. occasionally
245. occurrence
246. off
247. offered
248. official
249. omitted
250. operate
251. opinion
252. opportunity
253. opposite
254. organization
255. origin
256. original
257. paid
258. pamphlet
259. parallel
260. particular

List 14

261. passed, past
262. pastime
263. peaceable
264. peculiar
265. perceive
266. performance
267. permanent
268. permitted
269. persistent
270. personal, personnel
271. persuading
272. phase, faze
273. philosophy
274. physical
275. piece
276. planned
277. pleasant
278. poison
279. political
280. possession

List 15

281. possible
282. practical
283. precede
284. preferred
285. prejudice
286. preparation
287. prevalent
288. principal, principle
289. privilege
290. probably
291. proceed
292. professor
293. prominent
294. proving
295. psychology
296. pursuing
297. quantity
298. quiet, quite
299. really
300. receipt

List 16

301. receiving
302. recognize
303. recommend
304. reference
305. referring
306. regard
307. relative
308. relieving
309. religious
310. reminiscent
311. repetition
312. representative
313. requirement
314. resistance
315. responsible
316. restaurant
317. rhythm
318. ridiculous
319. sacrifice
320. safety

List 17

321. satisfying
322. scenery
323. schedule
324. science
325. secretaries
326. seize
327. sense, since
328. sentence
329. separate
330. sergeant
331. serviceable
332. several
333. shining
334. shoulder
335. significance
336. similar
337. simply
338. sincerely
339. site, cite
340. source

List 18

341. speak, speech
342. specimen
343. stationary, stationery
344. stopped
345. stories
346. straight, strait
347. strenuous
348. stretch
349. strict
350. studying
351. substantial
352. subtle
353. succeed
354. success
355. sufficient
356. summary
357. suppose
358. surprise
359. suspense
360. swimming

List 19

361. syllable
362. symbol
363. symmetrical
364. synonymous
365. technique
366. temperament
367. temperature
368. tendency
369. than, then
370. their, there
371. themselves
372. theories
373. therefore
374. thorough
375. though
376. through
377. together
378. tomorrow
379. tragedies
380. transferred

List 20

381. tremendous
382. tried
383. truly
384. undoubtedly
385. unnecessary
386. until
387. unusual
388. useful
389. using
390. vacuum
391. valuable
392. varies
393. vegetable
394. view
395. weather, whether
396. weird
397. were, where
398. wholly, holy
399. writing
400. yield

Developing Vocabulary Skills

If you understand the meanings of many words, you can be said to have a "good vocabulary." Words are the basis of thought. We think with words, we understand with words, and we communicate with words.

A large working vocabulary is a significant asset. It allows us to use precise words that say exactly what we intend. In addition, we understand more effectively what we hear and read. A large vocabulary also enables us to score well on employment and intelligence tests. Lewis M. Terman, who developed the Stanford-Binet IQ tests, believes that vocabulary is the best single indicator of intelligence.

In the business world, where precise communication is extremely important, surveys show a definite correlation between vocabulary size and job performance. Skilled workers, in the majority of cases, have larger vocabularies than unskilled workers. Supervisors know the meanings of more words than the workers they direct, and executives have larger vocabularies than employees working for them.

Having a good vocabulary at our command doesn't necessarily ensure our success in life, but it certainly gives us an advantage. Improving your vocabulary will help you expand your options in an increasingly complex world.

Vocabulary can be acquired in three ways: accidentally, incidentally, and intentionally. Setting out intentionally to expand your word power is, of course, the most efficient vocabulary-building method. One of the best means of increasing your vocabulary involves using 3-by-5 cards. When you encounter an unfamiliar word, write it on a card and put the definition of the word on the reverse side. Just five to ten minutes of practice each day with such cards can significantly increase your vocabulary.

Your campaign to increase your vocabulary can begin with the 18 lists of selected business terms and words of general interest included in this appendix. You may already know partial definitions for some of these words. Take this opportunity to develop more precise definitions for them. Follow these steps in using the word lists:

1. Record the word on a 3-by-5 card.
2. Look up the word in your dictionary. Compare the dictionary definitions of the word with the definition alternatives shown after the word in your copy of *Business English*. Select the correct definition, and write its letter in the space provided in your textbook. (The definitions provided in your textbook are quite concise but should help you remember the word's most common meaning.)
3. On the reverse side of your card, write the phonetic spelling of the word and the word's part of speech. Then write its definition using as much of the dictionary definition as you find helpful. Try also to add a phrase or sentence illustrating the word.
4. Study your 3-by-5 cards often.
5. Try to find ways to use your vocabulary words in your speech and writing.

1. adjacent = (a) previous, (b) similar, (c) overdue, (d) nearby _____

2. ambivalence = having (a) uncertainty, (b) ambition, (c) compassion, (d) intelligence _____

3. belligerent = (a) overweight, (b) quarrelsome, (c) likable, (d) believable _____

4. contingent = (a) conditional, (b) allowable, (c) hopeless, (d) impractical _____

5. decadent = in a state of (a) repair, (b) happiness, (c) decline, (d) extreme patriotism _____

6. entitlement = (a) label, (b) tax refund, (c) screen credit, (d) legal right _____

7. equivalent = (a) subsequent, (b) identical, (c) self-controlled, (d) plentiful _____

8. paramount = (a) foremost, (b) high mountain, (c) film company, (d) insignificant _____

9. plausible = (a) quiet, (b) acceptable, (c) notorious, (d) negative _____

10. unilateral = (a) powerful, (b) harmonious, (c) one-sided, (d) indelible _____

1. affluent = (a) rich, (b) slippery, (c) persistent, (d) rebellious _____

2. autocrat = one who (a) owns many cars, (b) is self-centered, (c) has power, (d) collects signatures _____

3. benevolent = for the purpose of (a) religion, (b) doing good, (c) healing, (d) violence _____

4. entrepreneur = (a) business owner, (b) traveler, (c) salesperson, (d) gambler _____

5. impertinent = (a) stationary, (b) bound to happen, (c) obsolete, (d) rude and irreverent _____

6. imprudent = (a) unwise, (b) crude, (c) vulnerable, (d) lifeless _____

7. mediator = one who seeks (a) overseas trade, (b) profits, (c) safe investment, (d) peaceful settlement _____

8. preponderance = (a) thoughtful, (b) exclusive right, (c) superiority, (d) forethought _____

9. recipient = (a) receiver, (b) respondent, (c) voter, (d) giver _____

10. reprehensible = (a) obedient, (b) independent, (c) blameworthy, (d) following _____

1. affable = (a) cheap, (b) pleasant, (c) strange, (d) competent _____

2. consensus = (a) population count, (b) attendance, (c) tabulation, (d) agreement _____

3. criterion = (a) standard, (b) command, (c) pardon, (d) law _____

4. diligent = (a) gentle, (b) industrious, (c) prominent, (d) intelligent _____

5. hydraulic = operated by means of (a) air, (b) gasoline; (c) liquid, (d) mechanical parts _____

6. hypothesis = (a) triangle, (b) promulgate, (c) highest point, (d) theory _____

7. phenomenon = (a) imagination, (b) rare event, (c) appointment, (d) clever saying _____

8. reticent = (a) silent, (b) strong-willed, (c) inflexible, (d) disagreeable _____

9. sanctuary = a place of (a) healing, (b) refuge, (c) rest, (d) learning _____

10. stimulus = something that causes (a) response, (b) light, (c) pain, (d) movement _____

List 4

1. beneficiary = one who (a) receives a license, (b) creates goodwill, (c) receives proceeds, (d) makes friends _____

2. constrain = (a) restrict, (b) filter, (c) use, (d) inform _____

3. corroborate = (a) contradict, (b) recall, (c) erode, (d) confirm _____

4. dun (n) = a demand for (a) legal action, (b) payment, (c) credit information, (d) dividends _____

5. equitable = (a) fair, (b) profitable, (c) similar, (d) clear _____

6. fluctuate = (a) rinse out, (b) magnetic field, (c) pricing schedule, (d) swing back and forth _____

7. indolent = (a) self-indulgent, (b) lazy, (c) pampered, (d) uncertain _____

8. nullify = (a) disappear, (b) imitate, (c) invalidate, (d) enhance _____

9. obsolete = (a) ugly, (b) outmoded, (c) audible, (d) scant _____

10. stabilize = to make (a) pleasant, (b) congenial, (c) traditional, (d) firm _____

List 5

1. arbitrate = (a) decide, (b) construct, (c) conquer, (d) ratify _____

2. coalition = (a) deliberation, (b) allegiance, (c) adherence, (d) alliance _____

3. collate = (a) assemble, (b) denounce, (c) supersede, (d) uninformed _____

4. conglomerate = combination of (a) executives, (b) companies, (c) investments, (d) countries _____

5. franchise = (a) fictitious reason, (b) right, (c) obligation, (d) official announcement _____

6. logistics = (a) speculations, (b) analytic philosophy, (c) reasonable outcome, (d) details of operation _____

7. proxy = authority to (a) act for another, (b) write checks, (c) submit nominations, (d) explain _____

8. subsidiary = (a) below expectations, (b) country dominated by another, (c) company controlled by another, (d) depressed financial condition _____

9. termination = (a) end, (b) inception, (c) identification, (d) evasive action _____

10. virtually = (a) absolutely, (b) precisely, (c) almost entirely, (d) strictly _____

List 6

1. affiliate = (a) trust, (b) attract, (c) effect, (d) join _____

2. alter = (a) table for religious ceremony, (b) solitary, (c) attribute, (d) modify _____

3. boisterous = (a) vociferous, (b) masculine, (c) cheerful, (d) brusque _____

4. configuration = (a) stratagem, (b) foreign currency, (c) form, (d) comprehension _____

5. conveyance = (a) vehicle, (b) transformation, (c) baggage, (d) consortium _____

6. infringe = (a) ravel, (b) decorative border, (c) encroach, (d) frivolous _____

7. jurisdiction = (a) science of law, (b) enunciation, (c) justice, (d) authority _____

8. nonpartisan = (a) unbiased, (b) antisocial, (c) ineffective, (d) untenable _____

9. parity = (a) price index, (b) justice under law, (c) plenitude, (d) equality of purchasing power _____

10. usury = (a) method of operation, (b) implementation, (c) illegal interest, (d) customary _____

List 7

1. anonymous = (a) multiplex, (b) powerless, (c) vexing, (d) nameless _____

2. cartel = (a) combination to fix prices, (b) ammunition belt, (c) partnership to promote competition, (d) placard _____

3. conjecture = (a) coagulation, (b) gesticulation, (c) guesswork, (d) connection _____

4. disparity = (a) unlikeness, (b) separation, (c) lacking emotion, (d) repudiation _____

5. environment = (a) urban area, (b) zenith, (c) surroundings, (d) latitude _____

6. impetus = (a) oversight, (b) stimulus, (c) hindrance, (d) imminent _____

7. portfolio = a list of (a) books, (b) security analysts, (c) corporations, (d) investments _____

8. quiescent = (a) presumptuous, (b) latent, (c) immoderate, (d) volatile _____

9. surrogate = (a) substitute, (b) accused, (c) authenticate, (d) suspend _____

10. tariff = (a) marsupial, (b) announcement, (c) ship, (d) duty _____

List 8

1. accrue = (a) conform, (b) accumulate, (c) diminish, (d) multiply _____

2. amortize = (a) pay off, (b) reduce, (c) romance, (d) kill _____

3. commensurate = (a) infinitesimal, (b) erroneous, (c) reliable, (d) proportional _____

4. consortium = (a) configuration, (b) partnership or association, (c) royal offspring, (d) rental property _____

5. discernible = (a) perceptive, (b) pretentious, (c) recognizable, (d) dissident _____

6. frugal = (a) thrifty, (b) wasteful, (c) judicious, (d) profligate _____

7. pecuniary = (a) rudimentary, (b) eccentric, (c) financial, (d) distinctive _____

8. retract = (a) disavow, (b) reorganize, (c) reciprocate, (d) hide _____

9. scrutinize = (a) cheerfully admit, (b) baffle, (c) persist, (d) examine carefully _____

10. tenacious = (a) falling apart, (b) holding on, (c) immobile, (d) chagrined _____

List 9

1. amiable	= (a) contumacious, (b) impetuous, (c) feasible, (d) congenial	_____
2. credible	= (a) plausible, (b) deceitful, (c) religious, (d) tolerant	_____
3. defendant	= one who (a) sues, (b) answers suit, (c) judges, (d) protects	_____
4. dissipate	= (a) accumulate, (b) partition, (c) liquify, (d) scatter or waste	_____
5. incentive	= (a) impediment, (b) support, (c) motive, (d) remuneration	_____
6. innocuous	= (a) harmless, (b) injection, (c) facetious, (d) frightening	_____
7. oust	= (a) install, (b) instigate, (c) shout, (d) expel	_____
8. pittance	= (a) tiny amount, (b) tithe, (c) abyss, (d) pestilence	_____
9. plaintiff	= one who (a) defends, (b) is sad, (c) sues, (d) responds	_____
10. superfluous	= (a) extraordinary, (b) very slippery, (c) shallow, (d) oversupplied	_____

List 10

1. adroit	= (a) ideal, (b) resilient, (c) witty, (d) skillful	_____
2. derogatory	= (a) minimal, (b) degrading, (c) originating from, (d) devious	_____
3. escrow	= (a) international treaty, (b) public registration, (c) licensed by state, (d) type of deposit	_____
4. facsimile	= (a) principle, (b) prototype, (c) exact copy, (d) counterfeit	_____
5. inordinate	= (a) unwholesome, (b) excessive, (c) unimportant, (d) treacherous	_____
6. logical	= (a) reasoned, (b) irrelevant, (c) lofty, (d) intricate	_____
7. malfeasance	= (a) prevaricate, (b) injurious, (c) superstitious, (d) misconduct	_____
8. noxious	= (a) pernicious, (b) unusual, (c) pleasant, (d) inconsequential	_____
9. résumé	= (a) budget report, (b) minutes of meeting, (c) photo album, (d) summary of qualifications	_____
10. spasmodic	= (a) paralyzing, (b) intermittent or fitful, (c) internal, (d) painful	_____

List 11

1. animosity	= (a) happiness, (b) deep sadness, (c) hatred, (d) study of animals	_____
2. caveat	= (a) headwear, (b) warning, (c) neckwear, (d) prerogative	_____
3. conscientious	= (a) meticulous, (b) productive, (c) cognizant, (d) sophisticated	_____
4. cosmopolitan	= (a) provincial, (b) multicolored, (c) heavenly, (d) worldly	_____
5. decipher	= (a) preclude, (b) decode, (c) demise, (d) reproach	_____
6. euphemism	= (a) religious discourse, (b) facial expression, (c) figurative speech, (d) inoffensive term	_____
7. fraudulent	= (a) loquacious, (b) candid, (c) deceitful, (d) despotic	_____
8. peripheral	= (a) supplementary, (b) imaginary, (c) visionary, (d) supernatural	_____
9. pungent	= (a) knowledgeable, (b) wise religious man, (c) acrid, (d) vulnerable	_____
10. requisite	= (a) essential, (b) demand, (c) skillful, (d) discreet	_____

List 12

1. ad valorem = (a) esteemed, (b) genuine, (c) recompense, (d) proportional

2. carte blanche = (a) white carriage, (b) credit terms, (c) full permission, (d) geographical expression

3. de facto = (a) prejudicial, (b) actual, (c) valid, (d) unlawful

4. esprit de corps = (a) group enthusiasm, (b) strong coffee, (c) central authority, (d) government overturn

5. modus operandi = (a) method of procedure, (b) practical compromise, (c) business transaction, (d) flexible arbitration

6. per capita = per unit of (a) income, (b) population, (c) birth, (d) household

7. per diem = (a) daily, (b) weekly, (c) yearly, (d) taxable

8. prima facie = (a) self-taught, (b) apparent, (c) principal, (d) artificial effect

9. status quo = (a) haughty demeanor, (b) steadfast opinion, (c) position of importance, (d) existing condition

10. tort = (a) rich cake, (b) extended dream, (c) wrongful act, (d) lawful remedy

List 13

1. acquit = (a) discharge, (b) pursue, (c) interfere, (d) impede

2. annuity = (a) yearly report, (b) insurance premium, (c) tuition refund, (d) annual payment

3. complacent = (a) appealing, (b) self-satisfied, (c) sympathetic, (d) scrupulous

4. contraband = (a) discrepancy, (b) opposing opinion, (c) smuggled goods, (d) ammunition

5. insolvent = (a) uncleanable, (b) unexplainable, (c) bankrupt, (d) unjustifiable

6. malicious = marked by (a) good humor, (b) ill will, (c) great pleasure, (d) injurious tumor

7. negligent = (a) careless, (b) fraudulent, (c) unlawful, (d) weak

8. nominal = (a) enumerated, (b) beneficial, (c) extravagant, (d) insignificant

9. rescind = (a) consign, (b) oppose, (c) repeal, (d) censure

10. stringent = (a) rigid, (b) expedient, (c) compliant, (d) resilient

List 14

1. affirm = (a) business organization, (b) validate, (c) elevate, (d) encircle

2. exonerate = (a) commend, (b) declare blameless, (c) banish, (d) emigrate

3. expedite = (a) elucidate, (b) get rid of, (c) amplify, (d) rush

4. hamper (v) = (a) impede, (b) delineate, (c) release, (d) assuage

5. implement (v) = (a) suppress, (b) ameliorate, (c) carry out, (d) attribute

6. induce = (a) teach, (b) construe, (c) persuade, (d) copy

7. obliterate = (a) obstruct, (b) prevent, (c) minimize, (d) erase

8. quandary = a state of (a) doubt, (b) certainty, (c) depression, (d) apprehension

9. surmount = (a) hike, (b) overcome, (c) interpret, (d) specify   _____

10. veracity = (a) truthfulness, (b) swiftness, (c) efficiency, (d) persistence   _____

List 15

1. aggregate = constituting (a) hostile crowd, (b) word combination,
   (c) total group, (d) sticky mass   _____

2. ambiguous = (a) peripatetic, (b) uncertain, (c) enterprising, (d) deceptive   _____

3. amend = (a) alter, (b) pray, (c) praise, (d) utter   _____

4. apportion = (a) sanction, (b) ratify, (c) estimate, (d) divide   _____

5. collaborate = (a) scrutinize, (b) cooperate, (c) surrender, (d) accumulate   _____

6. ingenuity = (a) innocence, (b) torpor, (c) cleverness, (d) self-composure   _____

7. irretrievable = not capable of being (a) sold, (b) identified, (c) explained,
   (d) recovered   _____

8. lenient = (a) liberal, (b) crooked, (c) benevolent, (d) explicit   _____

9. retrench = (a) dig repeatedly, (b) curtail, (c) reiterate, (d) enlighten   _____

10. trivial = (a) composed of three parts, (b) momentous, (c) paltry,
    (d) economical   _____

List 16

1. audit = (a) examine, (b) speak, (c) exchange, (d) expunge   _____

2. arrears = (a) old-fashioned, (b) gratuity, (c) overdue debt, (d) option   _____

3. curtail = (a) obstruct, (b) restore, (c) rejuvenate, (d) shorten   _____

4. encumber = (a) grow, (b) substantiate, (c) burden, (d) illustrate   _____

5. exemplify = (a) segregate, (b) divulge, (c) illustrate, (d) condone   _____

6. extension = (a) unusual request, (b) prolonged journey,
   (c) haphazard results, (d) extra time   _____

7. fortuitous = (a) accidental, (b) courageous, (c) radical, (d) assiduous   _____

8. innovation = (a) reorganization, (b) occupancy, (c) introduction, (d) solution   _____

9. syndicate = (a) union of writers, (b) council of lawmakers,
   (c) group of symptoms, (d) association of people   _____

10. venture = (a) speculative business transaction, (b) unsecured loan,
    (c) stock split, (d) gambling debt   _____

List 17

1. acquiesce = (a) gain possession of, (b) confront, (c) implore, (d) comply   _____

2. enumerate = (a) articulate, (b) list, (c) enunciate, (d) see clearly   _____

3. erratic = (a) pleasurable, (b) wandering, (c) exotic, (d) serene   _____

4. expedient = serving to promote (a) fellowship, (b) one's self-interests,
   (c) good of others, (d) speedy delivery   _____

5. feasible = (a) auspicious, (b) profuse, (c) reasonable, (d) extraneous   _____

6. literal = (a) exact, (b) devout, (c) apropos, (d) noticeable   _____

7. lucrative = (a) providential, (b) swift, (c) pleasant, (d) profitable   _____

8. negotiable = (a) essential, (b) adequate, (c) open to discussion, (d) economical _____

9. nonchalant = (a) dull, (b) cool, (c) unintelligent, (d) sagacious _____

10. reconcile = (a) resolve differences, (b) calculate, (c) modify, (d) remunerate _____

List 18

1. apprehensive = (a) knowledgeable, (b) fearful, (c) reticent, (d) autonomous _____

2. circumspect = (a) cautious, (b) uncertain, (c) cooperative, (d) frugal _____

3. collateral = (a) revenue, (b) secret agreement, (c) book value, (d) security for a loan _____

4. insinuation = (a) disagreeable proposal, (b) indirect suggestion, (c) elucidating glimpse, (d) flagrant insult _____

5. liaison = (a) legal obligation, (b) treaty, (c) connection between groups, (d) quarantine _____

6. procrastinate = (a) predict, (b) reproduce, (c) postpone, (d) advance _____

7. ratification = the act of (a) confirming, (b) reviewing, (c) evaluating, (d) inscribing _____

8. renovate = (a) renegotiate, (b) restore, (c) supply, (d) deliver _____

9. saturate = to fill (a) slowly, (b) dangerously, (c) as expected, (d) to excess _____

10. vendor = (a) seller, (b) manufacturer, (c) tradesman, (d) coin collector _____

Reference Guide to Document Formats

Business and professional documents carry two kinds of messages. Verbal messages are conveyed by the words chosen to express the writer's ideas. Nonverbal messages are conveyed largely by the appearance of a document. If you compare an assortment of letters and memos from various organizations, you will notice immediately that some look more attractive and more professional than others. The nonverbal message of the professional-looking documents suggests that they were sent by people who are careful, informed, intelligent, and successful. Understandably, you're more likely to take seriously documents that use attractive stationery and professional formatting techniques.

Over the years certain practices and conventions have arisen regarding the appearance and formatting of documents. Although these conventions offer some choices (such as letter and punctuation styles), most business documents follow standardized formats. To ensure that your documents carry favorable nonverbal messages about you and your organization, you'll want to give special attention to the appearance and formatting of your letters, envelopes, memos, e-mail messages, and fax cover sheets.

APPEARANCE

To ensure that a message is read and valued, you need to give it a professional appearance. Two important elements in achieving a professional appearance are stationery and placement of the message on the page.

Stationery Most organizations use high-quality stationery for printed business documents. This stationery is printed on select paper that meets two qualifications: weight and cotton-fiber content.

Paper is measured by weight and may range from 9 pounds (thin onionskin paper) to 32 pounds (thick card and cover stock). Most office stationery is in the 16- to 24-pound range. Lighter 16-pound paper is generally sufficient for internal documents including memos. Heavier 20- to 24-pound paper is used for printed letterhead stationery.

Paper is also judged by its cotton-fiber content. Cotton fiber makes paper stronger, softer in texture, and less likely to yellow. Good-quality stationery contains 25 percent or more cotton fiber.

Spacing After Punctuation For some time typists left two spaces after end punctuation (periods, question marks, and so forth). This practice was necessary, it was thought, because typewriters did not have proportional spacing and sentences were easier to read if two spaces separated them. Professional typesetters, however, never followed this practice because they used proportional spacing, and readability was not a problem. Fortunately, today's word processors now make available the same fonts used by typesetters.

The question of how many spaces to leave after concluding punctuation is one of the most frequently asked questions at the Modern Language Association Web site (**http://www.mla.org**). MLA experts point out that most publications in this country today have the same spacing after a punctuation mark as between words on the same line. Influenced by the look of typeset publications, many writers now leave only one space after end punctuation. As a practical matter, however, it is not wrong to use two spaces.

Letter Placement The easiest way to place letters on the page is to use the defaults of your word processing program. These are usually set for side margins of 1 to 1¼ inches. Many companies today find these margins acceptable.

If you want to adjust your margins to better balance shorter letters, use the following chart:

Words in Body of Letter	Side Margins	Blank Lines After Date
Under 200	1 ½ inches	4 to 10
Over 200	1 inch	2 to 3

Experts say that a "ragged" right margin is easier to read than a justified (even) margin. You might want to turn off the justification feature of your word processing program if it automatically justifies the right margin.

LETTER PARTS

Professional-looking business letters are arranged in a conventional sequence with standard parts. Following is a discussion of how to use these letter parts properly. Figure C.1 illustrates the parts in a block-style letter.

Letterhead Most business organizations use 8½- × 11-inch paper printed with a letterhead displaying their official name, street address, Web address, e-mail address, and telephone and fax numbers. The letterhead may also include a logo and an advertising message such as *Frontier Bank: A new brand of banking.*

Dateline On letterhead paper you should place the date two blank lines below the last line of the letterhead or 2 inches from the top edge of the paper (line 13). On plain paper place the date immediately below your return address. Since the date goes on line 13, start the return address an appropriate number of lines above it. The most common dateline format is as follows: *June 9, 2009.* Don't use *th* (or *rd*) when the date is written this way. For European or military correspondence, use the following dateline format: *9 June 2009.* Notice that no commas are used.

Addressee and Delivery Notations Delivery notations such as *FAX TRANSMISSION, FEDERAL EXPRESS, MESSENGER DELIVERY, CONFIDENTIAL,* or *CERTIFIED MAIL* are typed in all capital letters two blank lines above the inside address.

Inside Address Type the inside address—that is, the address of the organization or person receiving the letter—single-spaced, starting at the left margin. The number of lines between the dateline and the inside address depends on the size of the letter body, the type size (point or pitch size), and the length of the typing lines. Generally, two to ten blank lines are appropriate.

Be careful to duplicate the exact wording and spelling of the recipient's name and address on your documents. Usually, you can copy this information from the letterhead of the correspondence you are answering. If, for example, you are responding to *Jackson & Perkins Company,* don't address your letter to *Jackson and Perkins Corp.*

Always be sure to include a courtesy title such as *Mr., Ms., Mrs., Dr.,* or *Professor* before a person's name in the inside address—for both the letter and the envelope.

Figure C.1
Block and Modified Block Letter Styles

Block style
Mixed punctuation

Letterhead ——————————•

Island Graphics
893 Dillingham Boulevard
Honolulu, HI 96817-8817

(808)493-2310
http://www.islandgraphics.com

↓ Dateline is 2 inches from the top or 1 blank line below letterhead

Dateline ——————————• September 13, 200x

↓ 2 to 10 blank lines

Inside address ——————————• Mr. T. M. Wilson, President
Visual Concept Enterprises
1901 Kaumualii Highway
Lihue, HI 96766

↓ 1 blank line

Salutation ——————————• Dear Mr. Wilson:

↓ 1 blank line

Subject line ——————————• SUBJECT: BLOCK LETTER STYLE

↓ 1 blank line

This letter illustrates block letter style, about which you asked. All typed lines begin at the left margin. The date is usually placed 2 inches from the top edge of the paper or one blank line below the last line of the letterhead, whichever position is lower.

Body ——————————• This letter also shows mixed punctuation. A colon follows the salutation, and a comma follows the complimentary close. Open punctuation requires no colon after the salutation and no comma following the close; however, open punctuation is seldom seen today.

If a subject line is included, it appears two lines below the salutation. The word *SUBJECT* is optional. Most readers will recognize a statement in this position as the subject without an identifying label. The complimentary close appears one blank line below the end of the last paragraph. Enclosed are examples for your inspection.

↓ 1 blank line

Complimentary close ——————————• Sincerely,

↓ 3 blank lines

Mark H. Wong

Signature block ——————————• Mark H. Wong
Graphics Designer

↓ 1 blank line

MHW:pil
Enclosures

Modified block style,
Mixed punctuation

In the modified block style letter shown at the left, the date is centered or aligned with the complimentary close and signature block, which start at the center. Mixed punctuation includes a colon after the salutation and a comma after the complimentary close, as shown above and at the left.

Although many women in business today favor *Ms.*, you'll want to use whatever title the addressee prefers.

Remember that the inside address is not included for readers (who already know who and where they are). It's there to help writers accurately file a copy of the message.

In general, avoid abbreviations (such as *Ave.* or *Co.*) unless they appear in the printed letterhead of the document being answered.

Attention Line An attention line allows you to send your message officially to an organization but to direct it to a specific individual, officer, or department. However, if you know an individual's complete name, it's always better to use it as the first line of the inside address and avoid an attention line. Here are two common formats for attention lines:

MultiMedia Enterprises
931 Calkins Road
Rochester, NY 14301

ATTENTION MARKETING DIRECTOR

MultiMedia Enterprises
Attention: Marketing Director
931 Calkins Road
Rochester, NY 14301

Attention lines may be typed in all caps or with upper- and lowercase letters. The colon following *Attention* is optional. Notice that an attention line may be placed two lines below the address block or printed as the second line of the inside address. You'll want to use the latter format if you're composing on a word processor because the address block may be copied to the envelope and the attention line will not interfere with the last-line placement of the zip code. (Mail can be sorted more easily if the zip code appears in the last line of a typed address.)

Whenever possible, use a person's name as the first line of an address instead of putting that name in an attention line. Some writers use an attention line because they fear that letters addressed to individuals at companies may be considered private. They worry that if the addressee is no longer with the company, the letter may be forwarded or not opened. Actually, unless a letter is marked "Personal" or "Confidential," it will very likely be opened as business mail.

Salutation For most letter styles, place the letter greeting, or salutation, one blank line below the last line of the inside address or the attention line (if used). If the letter is addressed to an individual, use that person's courtesy title and last name (*Dear Mr. Lanham*). Even if you are on a first-name basis (*Dear Leslie*), be sure to add a colon (not a comma or a semicolon) after the salutation. Do not use an individual's full name in the salutation (not *Dear Mr. Leslie Lanham*) unless you are unsure of gender (*Dear Leslie Lanham*).

For letters with attention lines or those addressed to organizations, the selection of an appropriate salutation has become more difficult. Formerly, *Gentlemen* was used generically for all organizations. With the prevalence of women in business management today, however, *Gentlemen* is problematic. Because no universally acceptable salutation has emerged as yet, you could use *Ladies and Gentlemen* or *Gentlemen and Ladies*. One way to avoid the salutation dilemma is to address a document to a specific person.

Subject and Reference Lines Although experts suggest placing the subject line one blank line below the salutation, many organizations actually place it above the salutation. Use whatever style your organization prefers. Reference lines often show policy or file numbers; they generally appear one blank line above the salutation. Use initial capital letters for the main words or all capital letters.

Body Most business letters and memorandums are single-spaced, with double-spacing between paragraphs. Very short messages may be double-spaced with indented paragraphs.

Complimentary Close Typed one blank line below the last line of the letter, the complimentary close may be formal (*Very truly yours*) or informal (*Sincerely* or *Cordially*).

Signature Block In most letter styles the writer's typed name and optional identification appear three blank lines below the complimentary close. The combination of name, title, and organization information should be arranged to achieve a balanced look. The name and title may appear on the same line or on separate lines, depending on the length of each. Use commas to separate categories within the same line, but not to conclude a line.

Sincerely,

Jeremy M. Wood

Jeremy M. Wood, Manager
Technical Sales and Services

Cordially yours,

Casandra Baker-Murillo

Casandra Baker-Murillo
Executive Vice President

Courtesy titles (*Ms., Mrs.,* or *Mr.*) should be used before names that are not readily distinguishable as male or female. They should also be used before names containing only initials and international names. The title is usually placed in parentheses, but it may appear without them.

Yours truly,

Ms. K. C. Tripton

(Ms.) K. C. Tripton
Project Manager

Sincerely,

Mr. Leslie Hill

(Mr.) Leslie Hill
Public Policy Department

Some organizations include their names in the signature block. In such cases the organization name appears in all caps one blank line below the complimentary close, as shown here.

Cordially,

LITTON COMPUTER SERVICES

Ms. Shelina A. Simpson

Ms. Shelina A. Simpson
Executive Assistant

Reference Initials Reference initials identify who keyed and formatted the letter. If used, the initials of the preparer and writer are typed one blank line below the writer's name and title. Generally, the writer's initials are capitalized and the preparer's are lowercased, but this format varies. Today the writer's initials are usually omitted.

Enclosure Notation When an enclosure or attachment accompanies a document, a notation to that effect appears one blank line below the reference initials. This notation reminds the typist to insert the enclosure in the envelope, and it reminds the recipient to look for the enclosure or attachment. The notation may be spelled out (*Enclosure, Attachment*), or it may be abbreviated (*Enc., Att.*). It may indicate the number of enclosures or attachments, and it may also identify a specific enclosure (*Enclosure: Form 1099*).

Copy Notation If you make copies of correspondence for other individuals, you may use *cc* to indicate courtesy copy, or merely *c* for any kind of copy. A colon following the initial(s) is optional.

Second-Page Heading When a letter extends beyond one page, use plain paper of the same quality and color as the first page. Identify the second and succeeding pages with a heading consisting of the name of the addressee, the page number, and the date. Use either of the following two formats:

Ms. Rachel Ruiz	2	May 3, 200x

Ms. Rachel Ruiz
Page 2
May 3, 200x

Both headings appear 1 inch from the top of the paper followed by two blank lines to separate them from the continuing text. Avoid using a second page if you have only one line or the complimentary close and signature block to fill that page.

LETTER STYLES

Business letters are generally prepared in one of two formats. The most popular is the block style.

Block Style In the block style, shown in Figure C.1, all lines begin at the left margin. This style is a favorite because it is easy to format.

Modified Block Style The modified block style differs from block style in that the date and closing lines appear in the center, as shown at the bottom of Figure C.1. The date may be (a) centered, (b) begun at the center of the page (to align with the closing lines), or (c) backspaced from the right margin. The signature block—including the complimentary close, writer's name and title, or organization identification—begins at the center. The first line of each paragraph may begin at the left margin or may be indented five or ten spaces. All other lines begin at the left margin.

Personal Business Style When business and professional writers prepare letters on plain paper, they often use the personal business style. It includes the writer's street and city address on two lines above the date, as shown in Figure C.2. Notice that the writer's name does not appear here; it is typed and signed at the end of the letter. The personal business letter may be formatted in (a) full block style with all lines starting at the left margin, (b) modified block with blocked paragraphs, or (c) modified block style with indented paragraphs. In the modified block style, notice that the date and closing lines both start at the center of the page.

PUNCTUATION STYLES

Two punctuation styles are commonly used for letters. *Mixed* punctuation, shown in Figure C.1, requires a colon after the salutation and a comma after the complimentary close. *Open* punctuation contains no punctuation after the salutation or complimentary close.

With mixed punctuation, be sure to use a colon—not a comma or semicolon—after the salutation. Even when the salutation is a first name, the colon is appropriate.

ENVELOPES

An envelope should be of the same quality and color of stationery as the letter it carries. Because the envelope introduces your message and makes the first impression, you need to be especially careful in addressing it. Moreover, how you fold the letter is important.

Return Address The return address is usually printed in the upper left corner of an envelope, as shown in Figure C.3. In large companies some form of identification (the writer's initials, name, or location) may be typed above the company

Figure C.2
Personal Business Style

2 inches

2230 Turtle Creek Drive
Monroeville, PA 15146
May 29, 200x

Mr. Richard M. Jannis
Vice President, Operations
Sports World, Inc.
4807 Allegheny Boulevard
Pittsburgh, PA 16103

Dear Mr. Jannis:

Today's Pittsburgh *Examiner* reports that your organization plans to expand its operations to include national distribution of sporting goods, and it occurs to me that you will be needing highly motivated, self-starting sales representatives and marketing managers. I have these significant qualifications to offer:

- Four years of formal training in business administration, including specialized courses in sales management, retailing, marketing promotion, and consumer behavior.

- Practical experience in demonstrating and selling consumer products, as well as successful experience in telemarketing.

- A strong interest in most areas of sports and good communication skills (which helped me become a sportscaster at Penn State radio station WGNF).

I would like to talk with you about how I can put these qualifications, and others summarized in the enclosed résumé, to work for Sports World as it develops its national sales force. I'll call during the week of June 6 to discuss your company's expansion plans and the opportunity for an interview.

Sincerely,

Donald W. Vinton

Donald W. Vinton

Enclosure

Callouts:

Includes street address, city, state, zip code, and date—but not name

Useful for personal messages such as this letter of application

Bulleted items to improve readability may be blocked or indented

Paragraphs may be blocked or indented

Includes typewritten name and signature

---

name and return address. This identification helps return the letter to the sender in case of nondelivery.

On an envelope without a printed return address, single-space the return address in the upper left corner. Beginning on line 3 on the fourth space (½ inch) from the left edge, type the writer's name, title, company, and mailing address.

Mailing Address On legal-sized No. 10 envelopes (4½ × 9½ inches), begin the address on line 13 about 4½ inches from the left edge, as shown in Figure C.3. For small envelopes (3⅝ × 6½ inches), begin typing on line 12 about 2½ inches from the left edge. The easiest way to correctly position the mailing address on the envelope is to use your word processor's envelope feature.

In addressing your envelopes for delivery in the United States or in Canada, use the two-letter state and province abbreviations shown in Figure C.4. Notice that

Figure C.3
Envelope Formats

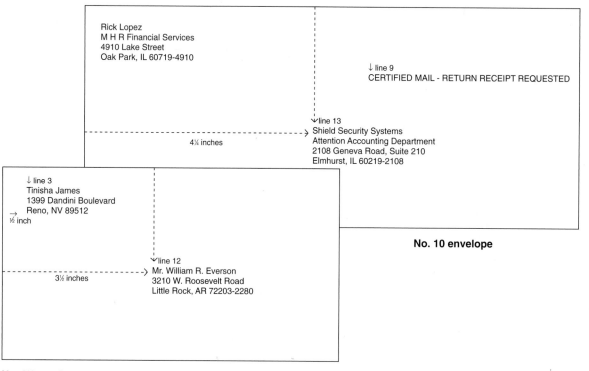

Rick Lopez
M H R Financial Services
4910 Lake Street
Oak Park, IL 60719-4910

↓ line 9
CERTIFIED MAIL - RETURN RECEIPT REQUESTED

⌄line 13
Shield Security Systems
Attention Accounting Department
2108 Geneva Road, Suite 210
Elmhurst, IL 60219-2108

4¼ inches

No. 10 envelope

↓ line 3
Tinisha James
1399 Dandini Boulevard
Reno, NV 89512
→
½ inch

⌄line 12
Mr. William R. Everson
3210 W. Roosevelt Road
Little Rock, AR 72203-2280

3½ inches

No. 6¾ envelope

these abbreviations are in capital letters without periods. Also use the U.S. Postal Service's zip + 4 zip codes whenever possible.

Folding The way a letter is folded and inserted into an envelope sends additional nonverbal messages about a writer's professionalism and carefulness. Most businesspeople follow the procedures shown here, which produce the least number of creases to distract readers.

For large No. 10 envelopes, begin with the letter face up. Fold slightly less than one third of the sheet toward the top, as shown in the following diagram. Then fold down the top third to within ½ inch of the bottom fold. Insert the letter into the envelope with the last fold toward the bottom of the envelope.

For small No. 6¾ envelopes, begin by folding the bottom up to within ½ inch of the top edge. Then fold the right third over to the left. Fold the left third to within ½ inch of the last fold. Insert the last fold into the envelope first.

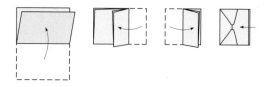

Figure C.4
Abbreviations of States, Territories, and Provinces

State or Territory	Two-Letter Abbreviation	State or Territory	Two-Letter Abbreviation
Alabama	AL	North Dakota	ND
Alaska	AK	Ohio	OH
Arizona	AZ	Oklahoma	OK
Arkansas	AR	Oregon	OR
California	CA	Pennsylvania	PA
Canal Zone	CZ	Puerto Rico	PR
Colorado	CO	Rhode Island	RI
Connecticut	CT	South Carolina	SC
Delaware	DE	South Dakota	SD
District of Columbia	DC	Tennessee	TN
Florida	FL	Texas	TX
Georgia	GA	Utah	UT
Guam	GU	Vermont	VT
Hawaii	HI	Virgin Islands	VI
Idaho	ID	Virginia	VA
Illinois	IL	Washington	WA
Indiana	IN	West Virginia	WV
Iowa	IA	Wisconsin	WI
Kansas	KS	Wyoming	WY
Kentucky	KY		
Louisiana	LA	**Canadian Province**	**Two-Letter Abbreviation**
Maine	ME		
Maryland	MD	Alberta	AB
Massachusetts	MA	British Columbia	BC
Michigan	MI	Labrador	LB
Minnesota	MN	Manitoba	MB
Mississippi	MS	New Brunswick	NB
Missouri	MO	Newfoundland	NF
Montana	MT	Northwest Territories	NT
Nebraska	NE	Nova Scotia	NS
Nevada	NV	Ontario	ON
New Hampshire	NH	Prince Edward Island	PE
New Jersey	NJ	Quebec	PQ
New Mexico	NM	Saskatchewan	SK
New York	NY	Yukon Territory	YT
North Carolina	NC		

MEMORANDUMS

Memorandums deliver messages within organizations, although e-mail is quickly replacing the use of printed memos. Some offices use memo forms imprinted with the organization name and, optionally, the department or division names. Although the design and arrangement of memo forms vary, they usually include the basic elements of *TO, FROM, DATE,* and *SUBJECT.* Large organizations may include other identifying headings, such as *FILE NUMBER, FLOOR, EXTENSION, LOCATION,* and *DISTRIBUTION.*

Because of the difficulty of aligning computer printers with preprinted forms, many business writers use a standardized memo template (sometimes called a "wizard"). This template automatically provides attractive headings with appropriate spacing and formatting. Other writers store their own preferred memo formats. Either method eliminates alignment problems.

If no printed or stored computer forms are available, memos may be typed on company letterhead or on plain paper, as shown in Figure C.5. On a full sheet of

Figure C.5
Memo on Plain Paper

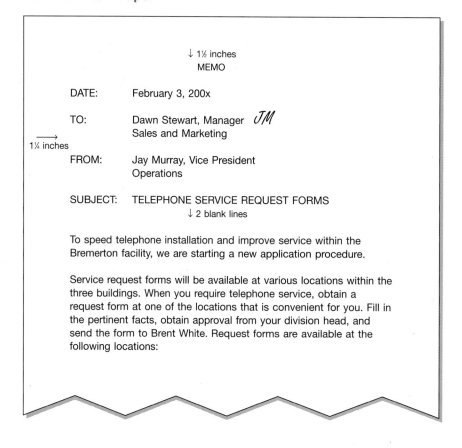

paper, leave a 1½-inch top margin; on a half sheet, leave a 1-inch top margin. Double-space and type in all caps the guide words *TO:, FROM:, DATE:, SUBJECT:*. Align all the fill-in information two spaces after the longest guide word (*SUBJECT:*). Leave two blank lines after the last line of the heading and begin typing the body of the memo. Like business letters, memos are single-spaced.

Memos are generally formatted with side margins of 1¼ inches, or they may conform to the printed memo form.

E-MAIL MESSAGES

E-mail has become the most popular form of communication in today's workplace. The following suggestions may guide you in setting up the parts of an e-mail message. Always check, however, with your organization so that you can follow its practices.

To Line Include the receiver's e-mail address after *To*. If the receiver's address is recorded in your address book, you just have to click on it. Be sure to enter all addresses very carefully since one mistyped letter prevents delivery.

From Line Most mail programs automatically include your name and e-mail address after *From*.

Cc and Bcc Insert the e-mail address of anyone who is to receive a copy of the message. *Cc* stands for carbon copy or courtesy copy. Don't be tempted, though, to send needless copies just because it's so easy. *Bcc* stands for blind carbon copy.

Some writers use *bcc* to send a copy of the message without the addressee's knowledge. Writers are also using the *bcc* line for mailing lists. When a message is being sent to a number of people and their e-mail addresses should not be revealed, the *bcc* line works well to conceal the names and addresses of all receivers.

Subject Identify the subject of the e-mail message with a brief but descriptive summary of the topic. Be sure to include enough information to be clear and compelling. Capitalize the first letters of principal words, or capitalize the entire line if space permits. Subject lines in all lowercase letters look unimportant and unprofessional. Most important, never leave a subject line blank.

Salutation Include a brief greeting, if you like. Some writers use a salutation such as *Dear Sondra* followed by a comma or a colon. Others are more informal with *Hi, Sondra!,* or *Good morning* or *Greetings*. Some writers simulate a salutation by including the name of the receiver in an abbreviated first line, as shown in Figure C.6. Other writers treat an e-mail message like a memo and skip the salutation entirely.

Message Cover just one topic in your message, and try to keep your total message under two screens in length. Single-space and be sure to use both upper- and lowercase letters. Double-space between paragraphs.

Closing Conclude an external message, if you like, with *Sincerely, Best wishes,* or *Warm regards,* followed by your name. If the recipient is unlikely to know you, it's a good idea to include your title, organization, and contact information. Some e-mail users include a signature file with identifying information that is automatically inserted at the end of each message they send. Writers of e-mail messages sent within organizations may omit a closing but should still type at least their first names at the end of e-mail messages to personalize them.

Figure C.6
Typical E-Mail Message

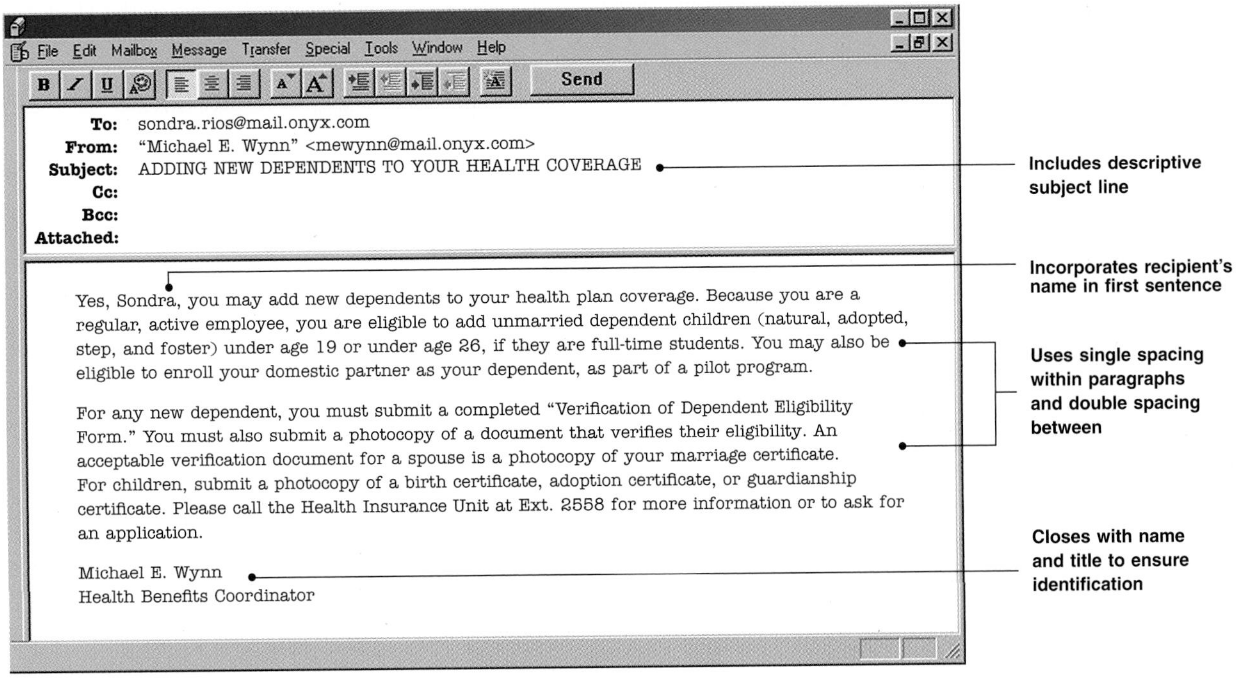

Includes descriptive subject line

Incorporates recipient's name in first sentence

Uses single spacing within paragraphs and double spacing between

Closes with name and title to ensure identification

Attachment Use the attachment window or button to select the path and file name of any file you wish to send with your e-mail message. When attaching a file to an e-mail message, call attention to the attachment in the body of the message.

FAX COVER SHEET

Documents transmitted by fax are usually introduced by a cover sheet, such as that shown in Figure C.7. As with memos, the format varies considerably. Important items to include are (a) the name and fax number of the receiver, (b) the name and fax number of the sender, (c) the number of pages being sent, and (d) the name and telephone number of the person to notify in case of unsatisfactory transmission.

When the document being transmitted requires little explanation, you may prefer to attach an adhesive note (such as a Post-it™ fax transmittal form) instead of a full cover sheet. These notes carry essentially the same information as shown in our printed fax cover sheet. They are perfectly acceptable in most business organizations and can save considerable paper and transmission costs.

Figure C.7
Fax Cover Sheet

FAX TRANSMISSION

DATE: _____

TO: _____   FAX NUMBER: _____
_____
_____

FROM: _____   FAX NUMBER: _____
_____
_____

NUMBER OF PAGES TRANSMITTED INCLUDING THIS COVER SHEET:____

MESSAGE:

If any part of this fax transmission is missing or not clearly received, please call:

NAME: _____

PHONE:_____

CHAPTER

1

Self-Help Exercises
Reference Skills

Name _____

Nearly every student who takes this English course says, "I wish I had more exercises to try my skills on." Because of the many requests, we provide this set of self-help exercises for extra reinforcement. Immediate feedback is an important ingredient in successful learning. Therefore, a key to these exercises begins on p. 457. Don't check the key, of course, until you complete each exercise.

Use a current dictionary to complete the following exercise.

1. In grammar the word *neuter* means
   a. asexual
   b. neutral
   c. neither feminine nor masculine
   d. both feminine and masculine _____

2. An *autocrat* is one who enjoys
   a. owning many cars
   b. ruling by himself or herself
   c. democratic relationships
   d. racing automobiles _____

3. The words *in so much as* should be written
   a. in so much as
   b. in somuchas
   c. insomuch as
   d. in somuch as _____

4. The word *logistics* is
   a. plural but may be used with a singular verb
   b. plural and always requires a plural verb
   c. singular
   d. neither singular nor plural _____

5. The abbreviation *MST* stands for
   a. master in statistical technology
   b. Mountain Standard Time
   c. manual or standard transmission
   d. master _____

6. *Amanuensis* originally meant
   a. deterioration of sight
   b. coarse herbs including pigweeds
   c. a slave with secretarial duties
   d. a female warrior _____

7. The word *(non)productive* should be written
   a. non-productive
   b. nonproductive
   c. non productive
   d. non-Productive _____

8. When the word *notwithstanding* is used to mean "nevertheless," it functions as what part of speech?
   a. conjunction
   b. adverb
   c. preposition
   d. adjective _____

9. The plural of the word *proxy* is
   a. proxies'
   b. proxys
   c. proxy's
   d. proxies _____

10. The word *filibuster* comes from a _____ word meaning "freebooter."
    a. French
    b. Spanish
    c. Italian
    d. Russian _____

11. *Foggy Bottom* is the site of
    a. a cathedral in London
    b. the U.S. Department of State
    c. a famous Irish castle
    d. a San Francisco nightclub _____

Parts of Speech

Name _____

WORKSHEET 1

A. This exercise is designed to help you develop a better understanding of the parts of speech. Using Chapter 2, write a brief definition or description of the eight parts of speech listed here. Then list three words as examples of each part of speech.

		Brief Definition	**Three Examples**		
1.	noun	names person, place, thing, concept	Anthony	paper	truth
2.	pronoun	_____	_____	_____	_____
3.	verb	_____	_____	_____	_____
4.	adjective	_____	_____	_____	_____
5.	adverb	_____	_____	_____	_____
6.	preposition	_____	_____	_____	_____
7.	conjunction	_____	_____	_____	_____
8.	interjection	_____	_____	_____	_____

B. Fill in the parts of speech for all the words in these sentences. Use a dictionary if necessary.

We sent an e-mail message to Jennifer, but she was very busy.

1. We _____   **5.** message _____   **9.** she _____

2. sent _____   **6.** to _____   **10.** was _____

3. an _____   **7.** Jennifer _____   **11.** very _____

4. e-mail _____   **8.** but _____   **12.** busy _____

Gosh, the computer and printer processed this lengthy report in 20 seconds.

13. Gosh _____   **17.** printer _____   **21.** report _____

14. the _____   **18.** processed _____   **22.** in _____

15. computer _____   **19.** this _____   **23.** 20 _____

16. and _____   **20.** lengthy _____   **24.** seconds _____

We arrived promptly, but the committee meeting started late.

25. We _____   **28.** but _____   **31.** meeting _____

26. arrived _____   **29.** the _____   **32.** started _____

27. promptly _____   **30.** committee _____   **33.** late _____

WORKSHEET 2

Fill in the parts of speech for all the words in these sentences. Use a dictionary if necessary.

I sold property in Fresno, but one transaction may not clear escrow.

1. I _____	**5.** Fresno _____	**9.** may _____
2. sold _____	**6.** but _____	**10.** not _____
3. property _____	**7.** one _____	**11.** clear _____
4. in _____	**8.** transaction _____	**12.** escrow _____

Oh, did Lee really think he could change that method of operation?

13. Oh _____	**17.** think _____	**21.** that _____
14. did _____	**18.** he _____	**22.** method _____
15. Lee _____	**19.** could _____	**23.** of _____
16. really _____	**20.** change _____	**24.** operation _____

The old accounting system was neither accurate nor efficient, but one company had used it faithfully for the past 40 years.

25. The _____	**32.** nor _____	**39.** it _____
26. old _____	**33.** efficient _____	**40.** faithfully _____
27. accounting _____	**34.** but _____	**41.** for _____
28. system _____	**35.** one _____	**42.** the _____
29. was _____	**36.** company _____	**43.** past _____
30. neither _____	**37.** had _____	**44.** 40 _____
31. accurate _____	**38.** used _____	**45.** years _____

Kerry quietly slipped into an empty seat during the long class film.

46. Kerry _____	**50.** an _____	**54.** the _____
47. quietly _____	**51.** empty _____	**55.** long _____
48. slipped _____	**52.** seat _____	**56.** class _____
49. into _____	**53.** during _____	**57.** film _____

E-mail has completely changed the way we communicate with our customers.

58. E-mail _____	**62.** the _____	**66.** with _____
59. has _____	**63.** way _____	**67.** our _____
60. completely _____	**64.** we _____	**68.** customers _____
61. changed _____	**65.** communicate _____	

WORKSHEET 1

LOCATING SUBJECTS AND VERBS

Action verbs tell what the subject is doing or what is being done to the subject. For each of the following sentences, locate the action verb and underline it twice. Then locate the subject of the verb and underline it once. To locate the subject, use the verb preceded by *Who?* or *What?* In the example the verb is *answered.* To help you find the subject, ask, *Who answered?*

Example: A <u>group</u> of applicants <u>answered</u> the advertisement.

1. The applicant with the best qualifications received the first interview.

2. In the afternoon session the speaker made a dynamic presentation.

3. During the sales campaign our telephones rang constantly.

4. In the winter we will hire four new workers for this department.

5. Our management team built a strong program of sales and service.

6. The most successful salespeople received trips to Hawaii.

7. In the meantime, our human resources manager will send you an application form.

8. Last week we released our new line of upscale, stylish cell phones.

9. One of the vice presidents was given a promotion recently.

10. Today's computers require managers to think with new clarity and precision.

11. The printout with all the customers' names and addresses was accurate.

12. One of our top salespeople sold $2 million worth of life insurance.

13. A list of restaurants with low-priced meals is available in the lobby.

14. Everything except labor and parts is covered by your warranty.

15. A committee consisting of 11 employees plus the manager was appointed to investigate.

Linking verbs (such as *am, is, are, was, were, be, being,* and *been*) often join to the sentence words that describe or rename the subject. In the following sentences, underline the linking verbs twice and the subjects once.

Examples: <u>E. J. Todd</u> <u>was</u> president of the organization last year.
   In the morning the <u>air</u> <u>is</u> cool.

16. Mr. Thomas is the office manager for Ryerson Metals Corporation.

17. The new copiers are very dependable.

18. Ms. Seymour is the person for the job.

19. Mr. Torres has been office manager for nine years.

20. Our new offices are much brighter than our previous ones.

WORKSHEET 2

SENTENCE PATTERNS

Finish the following sentences in the patterns indicated.

SUBJECT–VERB

Example: Cell phones ___ring___ .

1. Stockholders _____.
2. Stock prices _____.
3. Employees _____.

4. The security alarm _____.
5. In 1945 World War II _____.
6. Last year's sales _____.

SUBJECT–ACTION VERB–OBJECT

Example: The sales director made a ___call___ .

7. Our salesperson sold a _____.
8. The network was infected with a _____.
9. Ricky mailed the _____.

10. I telephoned _____.
11. Someone locked _____.
12. The clerk filed all the _____.

SUBJECT–LINKING VERB–COMPLEMENT

Examples: She is very ___friendly___ .
Eric could have been the ___manager___ .

13. Sales have been _____.
14. Susan is the new _____.
15. Last year the owner was _____.

16. I am _____.
17. The writer could have been _____.
18. The caller was _____.

Compose original sentences in the following patterns.

19. (Subject–verb) _____.
20. (Subject–verb) _____.
21. (Subject–action verb–object) _____.
22. (Subject–action verb–object) _____.
23. (Subject–linking verb–complement) _____.

WORKSHEET 3

SENTENCE TYPES

From the following list, select the letter that accurately describes each of the following groups of words. Add end punctuation marks.

a = fragment   d = question
b = statement   e = exclamation
c = command

1. The management of a multinational corporation with branch offices in several cities _____

2. Send me a brochure describing your latest workout equipment _____

3. Will you be working next weekend or during the week _____

4. The work schedule is usually posted late in the week _____

5. Wow, his presentation was amazing _____

6. If you have an opportunity to be promoted to a managerial position _____

7. For a generous return on your funds, invest in second trust deeds _____

8. In all levels of business, written and spoken English is extremely important in achieving success _____

9. Because it is difficult to improve your language skills on your own _____

SENTENCE FAULTS

From the following list, select the letter that accurately describes each of the following groups of words.

a = correctly punctuated sentence   c = comma splice
b = fragment   d = run-on sentence

10. I'll have the answer soon, first I must make a telephone call. _____

11. If you consider all the pros and cons before you make a decision. _____

12. We have no idea what to order only Ms. Sanchez can do that. _____

13. Your entire department is entitled to overtime compensation. _____

14. You check the current address list, and I'll check the old one. _____

15. You check the current address list, I'll check the old one. _____

16. You check the current address list I'll check the old one. _____

17. Although we have complete confidence in our products and prices. _____

18. When you return from the conference, please submit a brief report describing the information you learned. _____

19. We must focus our charitable contributions on areas that directly relate to our business, therefore, we are unable to send a check this year. _____

20. If you agree that this memo accurately reflects our conversation. _____

Self-Help Exercises
Nouns

Name _____

LEVEL 1

Write the preferred plural forms of the nouns shown below. Use a dictionary if necessary.

1. giraffe _____
2. foot _____
3. switch _____
4. Bush _____
5. box _____
6. language _____
7. fax _____
8. sandwich _____
9. income tax _____
10. child _____
11. success _____
12. value _____
13. dress _____
14. branch _____
15. recommendation _____
16. woman _____
17. mismatch _____
18. taxi _____
19. loaf (of bread) _____
20. annex _____
21. belief _____
22. Ross _____
23. storm _____
24. ranch _____
25. Jones _____
26. Chavez _____
27. letter _____
28. business _____
29. computer _____
30. wish _____

LEVEL 2

Write the preferred plural forms of the nouns shown below. Use a dictionary if necessary.

1. wharf _____
2. chief of police _____
3. 2000 _____
4. Wolf _____
5. embargo _____
6. LVN _____
7. size 10 _____
8. amt. _____
9. faculty _____
10. by-product _____
11. entry _____
12. looker-on _____
13. company _____
14. knife _____
15. court-martial _____
16. A _____
17. Sherman _____
18. memo _____
19. valley _____
20. zero _____
21. life _____
22. yr. _____
23. Murphy _____
24. runner-up _____
25. oz. _____
26. journey _____
27. MBA _____
28. wolf _____
29. Kelly _____
30. minority _____

LEVEL 3

Write the preferred plural forms of the nouns shown below. Use a dictionary if necessary.

1. datum _____

2. thesis _____

3. bacterium _____

4. Chinese _____

5. parenthesis _____

6. headquarters _____

7. alumna _____

8. millennium _____

9. genus _____

10. news _____

11. p. (page) _____

12. f. (and following pages) _____

13. larva _____

14. basis _____

15. memorandum _____

Select the correct word in parentheses and complete the sentences in your own words.

16. The goods produced in that factory (is, are) _____

_____

17. Politics in Washington (is, are) _____

_____

18. Several (formula, formulas) _____

_____

19. Four separate (analysis, analyses) _____

_____

20. In the business curriculum economics (is, are) _____

_____

LEVEL 1

WORKSHEET 1

Before you begin this exercise, review the five-step plan for placing apostrophes:

1. Look for possessive construction. (Usually two nouns appear together.)

2. Reverse the nouns. (Use a prepositional phrase, such as *interest of three years.*)

3. Examine ownership word. (Does it end in an *s* sound?)

4. If the ownership word does *not* end in an *s* sound, add an apostrophe and *s.*

5. If the ownership word does end in an *s* sound, usually add only an apostrophe.

Using apostrophes, change the following prepositional phrases into possessive constructions.

Example: interest of three years   three years' interest _____

1. passwords of all employees   _____

2. office of this company   _____

3. uniforms of the women   _____

4. rent of two months   _____

5. signature of the supervisor   _____

6. opinions of all members   _____

7. the landing of the pilot   _____

8. agreement of both partners   _____

9. notebook of Jeffrey   _____

10. strengths of the department   _____

11. time of two years   _____

12. customs of those people   _____

13. merger of last week   _____

14. credit from the bank   _____

15. savings of citizens   _____

16. mountains of Canada   _____

17. requirements of the employer   _____

18. résumés of all candidates   _____

19. policies of the government   _____

20. fees of both attorneys   _____

WORKSHEET 2

Write the correct possessive form of the word in parentheses in the space provided.

1. Applicants will have at least a (year) wait for an apartment. _____

2. Several (drivers) inquiries prompted the posting of a better sign. _____

3. We found the (carpenter) tools after he left the building. _____

4. The electronics store installed a hidden video camera to observe a suspected (thief) activities. _____

5. The (day) news is summarized every hour on WABC. _____

6. Our new (employees) cafeteria is busy from 11 a.m. to 1 p.m. _____

7. Only the (CEO) car may be parked in the special zone. _____

8. Most (readers) letters supported the magazine's editorial position. _____

9. Where is the (caller) message? _____

10. All (authors) rights are protected by copyright law. _____

Correct any errors in the following sentences by underlining the errors and writing the correct forms in the spaces provided. If a sentence is correct as written, write *C*.

11. Like its clothing, the Gaps headquarters are simple, clean, and comfortable. _____

12. The names of these customers are not alphabetized. _____

13. Some of the countrys biggest manufacturers are being investigated. _____

14. This account has been credited with four months interest. _____

15. Your organizations voice mail system is excellent. _____

16. The vice presidents resignation left a vital position unfilled. _____

17. Are you researching your familys genealogy? _____

18. I am prepared to protest the bill of my attorney, William Glass. _____

19. In three years time the software paid for itself. _____

20. Not a single farmers crop was undamaged by the storm. _____

21. A citizens committee was formed to address parking problems. _____

22. One years interest on the account amounted to $120. _____

23. Each customers complimentary game tickets were mailed today. _____

24. Childrens clothing is on the first floor. _____

25. The announcement of new benefits for employees was made in the supervisors memo, which she sent out yesterday. _____

LEVEL 2

Correct any errors in the following sentences by underlining the errors and writing the correct form in the spaces provided. If the sentence is correct as written, write *C*.

1. The document required the notary publics signature and his seal. _____

2. At least one companies' records are computerized. _____

3. During lunch Juan stopped at the stationers for supplies. _____

4. My uncle's lawyer's suggestions in this matter were excellent. _____

5. The editor's in chief office is on the fifth floor. _____

6. We borrowed my aunt's and uncle's motor home. _____

7. All RNs' uniforms must now be identical. _____

8. This month's expenses are somewhat less than last months. _____

9. Debbie's and Julie's iPods have similar song lists. _____

10. The president's assistant's telephone number has been changed. _____

11. Have you called the new sales' representative? _____

12. My two brothers-in-law's beards are neat and well trimmed. _____

13. The union meeting will be held at Larrys. _____

14. I'm going over to Ricks to pick him up. _____

15. We spent our vacation enjoying New Englands' historical towns. _____

16. CBS's report on the vote was better than any other station's. _____

17. Clark's and Clark's reference manual is outstanding. _____

18. The Los Angeles' symphony planned an evening of Beethoven. _____

19. The two architects licenses were issued together. _____

20. Our sales this year are greater than last years. _____

21. All FBI agents must pass rigorous security investigations. _____

22. Diana's and Jason's marriage license was lost. _____

23. The First Lady answered all the reporters questions carefully. _____

24. Workers said they expected a days pay for an honest days work. _____

25. Robin and John's new car came with a five-year warranty. _____

LEVEL 3

Write the correct form of the words shown in parentheses.

Example: The (Stivers) cat is missing.   Stiverses' _____

1.   I see that (someone else) books got wet also.   _____

2.   Lee (Ross) office is on the south side of the campus.   _____

3.   Both (class) test results were misplaced.   _____

4.   Beth (Saunders) home is farther away than anyone else's.   _____

5.   The bank is reconsidering the (Rodriguez) loan application.   _____

6.   I have no idea where (Les) car is parked.   _____

7.   Only my (boss) desk is cluttered.   _____

8.   The other (boss) desks are rather neat.   _____

9.   Did you hear that the (Horowitz) are moving?   _____

10.   Several (actress) costumes were so valuable that insurance policies were
taken out to insure them.   _____

11.   I think that was Mr. (Harris) parking spot you just took.   _____

12.   Ms. (Burns) history class met outside on that balmy day.   _____

13.   Who is (James) partner for the team project?   _____

14.   That (waitress) station consists of four tables.   _____

15.   None of the (Garvey) belongings were missing.   _____

16.   Have you visited the (Morris) vacation home?   _____

17.   Only Ms. (Betz) car remained in the parking lot.   _____

18.   It looks as if the (Walker) home is getting a new roof.   _____

19.   Mr. (Simons) driver's license was renewed automatically.   _____

20.   Mr. (Jones) property is on Kelton Avenue.   _____

21.   Professor (White) lecture was well organized and informative.   _____

22.   Have you seen the (Williams) four-room tent that they took camping
last weekend?   _____

23.   We heard that the (Kimball) may be moving.   _____

24.   Visitors at Graceland swore they saw (Elvis) ghost.   _____

25.   Fans of the (Los Angeles) Dodgers cheered their team.   _____

Self-Help Exercises

Personal Pronouns

Name _____

LEVEL 1

WORKSHEET 1

List seven pronouns that could be used as subjects of verbs.

1. _____   3. _____   5. _____   7. _____

2. _____   4. _____   6. _____

List seven pronouns that could be used as objects of verbs or objects of prepositions.

8. _____   10. _____   12. _____   14. _____

9. _____   11. _____   13. _____

PRONOUNS AS SUBJECTS

Select the correct pronoun to complete each sentence below. All the omitted pronouns function as subjects of verbs.

15. Ms. Georges and (I, me) submitted purchase requisitions.   _____

16. In the afternoon training session, the manager and (she, her) will
    make presentations.   _____

17. Will you and (he, him) be going to the sales meeting?   _____

18. Mr. North and (they, them) expect to see you Saturday.   _____

19. It is difficult to explain why Matt and (her, she) decided to move.   _____

20. Of all the applicants only (we, us) agreed to be tested now.   _____

21. Ramon and (she, her) deserve raises because of their hard work.   _____

22. After Ms. Cortez and (he, him) had returned, customers were handled
    more rapidly.   _____

23. Only you and (her, she) will participate in the demonstration.   _____

24. After the spring sales campaign ends, the marketing manager and (he, him)
    will be promoted.   _____

25. Because we are most familiar with the project, you and (I, me) must complete
    the report.   _____

WORKSHEET 2

Select the correct pronoun to complete each of the following sentences. All the omitted pronouns function as objects of verbs or prepositions. Prepositions have been underlined to help you identify them.

1. Just <u>between</u> you and (I, me), our branch won the sales trophy.   _____

2. Michelle said that she had seen you and (he, him) at the airport.   _____

3. We hope to show (they, them) the billing procedure this afternoon.   _____

4. Everybody <u>but</u> (I, me) is ready to leave.   _____

5. Have you talked <u>with</u> Brad and (her, she) about this change?   _____

6. We need more workers <u>like</u> Maria and (him, he) to finish the job.   _____

7. All supervisors <u>except</u> Mrs. Young and (her, she) approved the plan.   _____

8. This insurance program provides you and (they, them) with equal benefits.   _____

9. Terms of the settlement were satisfactory <u>to</u> (we, us).   _____

10. Every operator <u>but</u> Maddie and (I, me) had an opportunity for overtime.   _____

POSSESSIVE-CASE PRONOUNS

Remember that possessive-case pronouns (*yours, his, hers, its, whose,* and *theirs*) do not contain apostrophes. Do not confuse these pronouns with the following contractions: *it's* (it is), *there's* (there is), *who's* (who is), and *you're* (you are). In the following sentences select the correct word.

11. Do you think (its, it's) necessary for us to sign in?   _____

12. Is (theirs, their's) the white house at the end of the street?   _____

13. The contract and all (its, it's) provisions must be examined.   _____

14. (There's, Theirs) a set of guidelines for us to follow.   _____

15. Jack's car and (hers, her's) are the only ones left in the lot.   _____

16. The check is good only if (its, it's) signed.   _____

17. I was told that Sue's and (yours, your's) were the best departments.   _____

18. (Who's, Whose) umbrella is that lying in the corner?   _____

19. Most car registrations were sent April 1, but (our's, ours) was delayed.   _____

20. (You're, Your) taking Courtney's place, aren't you?   _____

LEVEL 2

Select the correct pronoun to complete these sentences.

1. Do you expect Mr. Jefferson and (they, them) to meet you?   _____

2. No one could regret the error more than (I, me, myself).   _____

3. These photocopies were prepared by Charles and (she, her).   _____

4. (We, Us) policyholders are entitled to group discounts.   _____

5. Procrastination disturbs Steven as much as (I, me, myself).   _____

6. For the summer only, Universal Parcel is hiring James and (I, me, myself).   _____

7. Have you corresponded with the authors, Dr. Lee and (she, her)?   _____

8. On that project no one works as hard as (he, him, himself).   _____

9. Everyone but Mr. Foster and (he, him) can help customers if necessary.   _____

10. Do you know whether Gary and (I, me, myself) signed it?   _____

11. Only Erik (himself, hisself) knows what is best for him.   _____

12. We asked two women, Denise and (she, her), to come along.   _____

13. The proceeds are to be divided among Mr. Shelby, Ms. Huerra, and (she, her).   _____

14. Ms. Greerson thinks that Mr. Cardillo is a better salesperson than (she, her).   _____

15. All property claims must be submitted to my lawyer or (I, me, myself)
    before April 15.   _____

16. The new contract was acceptable to both management and (us, we).   _____

17. When reconciling bank statements, no one is more accurate than (she, her).   _____

18. The best time for you and (he, him) to enroll is in January.   _____

19. The president and (I, me, myself) will inspect the facility.   _____

20. Everyone except Kevin and (I, me, myself) was able to join the program.   _____

21. Send an application to Human Resources or (I, me, myself) immediately.   _____

22. (She and I, Her and me, Her and I) are among the best-qualified candidates.   _____

23. Have you invited Jon and (she, her, herself) to our picnic?   _____

24. Most of the e-mail messages sent to (us, we) employees are considered spam.   _____

25. Only Rasheed and (I, me, myself) were given cell phones by the company.   _____

LEVEL 3

WORKSHEET 1

Remember that pronouns that rename the subject and that follow linking verbs must be in the subjective case: (*It was* _he_ *who placed the order*). When the infinitive *to be* has no subject (and that subject must immediately precede the infinitive *to be*), the pronoun that follows must be in the subjective case (*My sister is often taken to be* _I_).

In the following sentences, select the correct word.

1. It must have been (her, she) who called this morning. _____
2. I certainly would not like to be (he, him). _____
3. Do you think that it was (they, them) who complained? _____
4. Tram answered the telephone by saying, "This is (her, she)." _____
5. Ms. Richards thought the salesperson to be (he, him). _____
6. If you were (she, her), would you take the job? _____
7. Cecile is sometimes taken to be (her, she). _____
8. Jim said that yesterday's driver could have been (he, him). _____
9. Ms. Soriano asked Frank and (I, me) to help her. _____
10. Was it (they, them) who made the contribution? _____
11. The most accurate proofreader seems to be (he, him). _____
12. Producer Edwards would not allow me to be (he, him) in the production. _____
13. Mr. Fox wants to assign you and (her, she) the project. _____
14. Are you sure it was (I, me) who was called to the phone? _____
15. The visitor was thought to be (she, her). _____
16. If it had not been (she, her) who made the announcement, I would not have believed it. _____
17. How could anyone have thought that Courtney was (I, me)? _____
18. I do not wish to discourage either you or (he, him). _____
19. If anyone is disappointed, it will be (I, me). _____
20. What makes Joan wish to be (she, her)? _____
21. Do you think it was (he, him) who made the large contribution? _____
22. Mr. Rivera selected you and (he, him) because of his confidence in your abilities. _____
23. If it had been (she, her), we would have recognized her immediately. _____
24. Everyone thought the new manager would be (she, her). _____
25. Because the president is to be (he, him), Mr. Thomas will act as CEO. _____

WORKSHEET 2

Select the correct word to complete the following sentences.

1. Only the president and (he, him) can grant leaves of absence. _____

2. The manager mistook Danielle to be (I, me). _____

3. The body of the manuscript is followed by (its, it's) endnotes. _____

4. Our staff agreed that you and (she, her) should represent us. _____

5. How can you believe (us, we) to be guilty? _____

6. I'm not sure (their's, there's) enough time left. _____

7. Everyone thought the new manager would be (he, him). _____

8. My friend and (I, me) looked for jobs together. _____

9. This matter will be kept strictly between you and (I, me). _____

10. Good employees like you and (she, her) are always on time. _____

11. Judge Waxman is fully supported by (we, us) consumers. _____

12. We agree that (your, you're) the best person for the job. _____

13. Send the announcement to Ms. Nguyen and (she, her) today. _____

14. All employees except Kim and (he, him) will be evaluated. _____

15. Many locker combinations are listed, but (your's, yours) is missing. _____

16. Apparently the message was intended for you and (I, me, myself). _____

17. Was it (he, him, himself) who sent the mystery e-mail message? _____

18. The bank is closed, but (it's, its) ATM is open. _____

19. Please submit the report to (him or me, he or I) before May 1. _____

20. (There's, Theirs) only one path for us to follow. _____

21. For you and (he, him), I would suggest careers in marketing. _____

22. These personnel changes affect you and (I, me, myself) directly. _____

23. My friend and (I, me, myself) are thinking of a trip to Hawaii. _____

24. Only two branches plan to expand (they're, their) display rooms. _____

25. The operator thought it was (she, her) calling for assistance. _____

26. Because you are a member of the audit review team, you have a better overall picture of the operations than (I, me, myself). _____

27. Though you may not agree with our decision, I hope you'll support Todd and (I, me) in our effort to get the job done. _____

28. Some of the recent decisions made by (us, we) supervisors will be reviewed by the management council when it meets in January. _____

29. I wonder if it was (she, her) who was reprimanded for excessive e-mail use. _____

30. Do you think (theirs, their's, there's) any real reason to change our computer passwords every month? _____

LEVEL 1

Pronouns must agree with the words for which they substitute. Don't let words and phrases that come between a pronoun and its antecedent confuse you.

> **Examples:** Every one of the women had *her* forms ready. (Not *their*)
>
> Our supervisor Bob, along with four assistants, offered *his* support. (Not *their*)

Select the correct word(s) to complete these sentences.

1. Ms. Kennedy, in addition to many other members of the staff, sent (her, their) best wishes. _____

2. Every employee must have (his, her, his or her, their) physical examination completed by December 31. _____

3. After a job well done, everyone appreciates (his, her, his or her, their) share of credit. _____

4. Several office workers, along with the manager, announced (his or her, their) intention to vote for the settlement. _____

5. Individuals like Mr. Herndon can always be depended on to do (her, his, his or her, their) best in all assignments. _____

6. If a policyholder has a legitimate claim, (he, she, he or she, they) should contact us immediately. _____

7. Every one of the employees brought (her or his lunch, their lunches) to the outdoor event. _____

8. When a customer walks into our store, treat (him, her, him or her, them) as you would an honored guest in your home. _____

9. Carolyn Davis, along with several other company representatives, volunteered to demonstrate (her, his, his or her, their) equipment. _____

10. A few of the members of the touring group, in addition to their guide, wanted (his or her picture, their pictures) taken. _____

11. Any female member of the project could arrange (her, their) own accommodations if desired. _____

12. Every player on the men's ball team complained about (his, their) uniform. _____

Rewrite this sentence to avoid the use of a common-gender pronoun. Show three versions.

> Every employee must obtain his parking permit in the supervisor's office.

13. _____

14. _____

15. _____

LEVEL 2

Underline any pronoun–antecedent errors in the following sentences. Then write a corrected form in the space provided. If a sentence is correct, write *C.*

1. Last Friday either Ms. Monahan or Ms. Chavez left their computer on.

2. The Federal Drug Administration has not yet granted it's approval for the drug.

3. Every clerk, every manager, and every executive will be expected to do their part in making the carpooling program a success.

4. Somebody left their cell phone in the tray at the airport security check.

5. Neither one of the men wanted to have their remarks quoted.

6. Every one of the delegates to the women's conference was wearing their name tag.

7. The vice president and the marketing director had already made their reservations.

8. Each of the pieces of equipment came with their own software.

9. The firm of Higgins, Thomas & Keene, Inc., is moving their offices to Warner Plaza.

10. Every manager expects the employees who report to them to be willing to earn their salaries.

11. Neither of the women had her driver's license in the car.

12. We hoped that someone in the office could find their copy of the program.

13. Either the first telephone caller or the second one did not leave their number.

14. If everybody will please take their seats, we can get started.

15. The faculty agreed to publicize their position on budget cuts.

16. We saw that HomeCo reduced their prices on lawn mowers.

17. Few of the color printers had the sale price marked on it.

18. Every one of the male employees agreed to be more careful in protecting their computer password.

19. Each bridesmaid will pay for their own gown.

20. All managers and employees know that she or he must boost productivity.

LEVEL 3

WORKSHEET 1

In selecting *who* or *whom* to complete the following sentences, apply these five steps:

1. Isolate the *who* clause: (*who, whom*) the contract names
2. Invert to normal subject–verb order: the contract names (*who, whom*)
3. Substitute pronouns: the contract names *him*
4. Equate: the contract names *whom*
5. Complete: We do not know *whom* the contract names.

Example: We do not know (who, whom) the contract names.   whom _____

1. (Who, Whom) will you invite to your party?   _____
2. Rick Nash is the employee (who, whom) the CEO asked to present to the board.   _____
3. Do you know (who, whom) will be taking your place?   _____
4. To (who, whom) did she refer in her letter?   _____
5. Did Mr. Glade say (who, whom) he wanted to see?   _____
6. Dr. Truong is a man (who, whom) everyone respects.   _____
7. (Who, Whom) was president of your organization last year?   _____
8. (Who, Whom) do you want to work with?   _____
9. (Who, Whom) has the best chance to be elected?   _____
10. I know of no one else (who, whom) plays so well.   _____

In choosing *who* or *whom* to complete these sentences, ignore parenthetical phrases such as *I think, we know, you feel,* and *I believe.*

11. Julie is a person (who, whom) I know will be successful on the job.   _____
12. The human resources director hired an individual (who, whom) he thought would be the best performer.   _____
13. Is Ms. Hastings the dealer (who, whom) you think I should call?   _____
14. Major Kirby, (who, whom) I think will be elected, is running in the next election.   _____
15. (Who, Whom) do you believe will be given the job?   _____

WORKSHEET 2

In the following sentences, selecting *who, whom, whoever,* or *whomever* first requires isolating the clause within which the pronoun appears. Then, *within the clause,* determine whether a nominative- or objective-case pronoun is required.

Example: Give the package to (whoever, whomever) opens the door.
(*He* or *she* opens the door = *whoever* opens the door.)   whoever _____

1. A bonus will be given to (whoever, whomever) sells over $100,000.   _____

2. Discuss the problem with (whoever, whomever) is in charge of the program.   _____

3. We will interview (whoever, whomever) you recommend.   _____

4. You may give the tickets to (whoever, whomever) you wish.   _____

5. Johnson said to give the parking pass to (whoever, whomever) asked for it.   _____

6. The committee members have promised to cooperate with (whoever, whomever) is selected to chair the committee.   _____

7. Please call (whoever, whomever) you believe can repair the machine.   _____

8. (Whoever, Whomever) is nominated for the position must be approved by the full membership.   _____

9. Reservations have been made for (whoever, whomever) requested them in advance.   _____

10. (Whoever, Whomever) is chosen to lead the delegation will command attention at the caucus.   _____

In choosing *who* or *whom* to complete these sentences, be especially alert to pronouns following the linking verbs. Remember that the nominative *who* is required as a subject complement.

Example: Was it (who, whom) I thought it was? (It was *he* = *who*.)   who _____

11. (Who, Whom) is the customer who wanted a replacement?   _____

12. The visitor who asked for me was (who, whom)?   _____

13. Was the new CEO (who, whom) we thought it would be?   _____

14. The winner will be (whoever, whomever) is tops in sales.   _____

15. For (who, whom) was this new printer ordered?   _____

WORKSHEET 3

In the following sentences, select the correct word.

1. (Who, Whom) did you call for assistance? _____

2. Mr. Lincoln, (who, whom) we thought would never be hired, did well in his first assignment. _____

3. By (who, whom) are you currently employed? _____

4. You should hire (whoever, whomever) you feel has the best qualifications. _____

5. Did the caller say (who, whom) he wanted to see? _____

6. The man (who, whom) I saw yesterday walked by today. _____

7. (Whoever, Whomever) is first on the list will be called next. _____

8. The sales rep sent notices to customers (who, whom) she felt should be notified. _____

9. Is the manager (who, whom) we thought it would be? _____

10. The manager praised the clerk (who, whom) worked late. _____

11. She is the one (who, whom) Kevin helped yesterday. _____

12. Many of us thought Mr. Alison was a nice person with (who, whom) to work. _____

13. (Who, Whom) is Stacy often mistaken to be? _____

14. (Who, Whom) did you say to call for reservations? _____

15. Please make an appointment with (whoever, whomever) you consider to be the best internist. _____

16. Here is a list of satisfied customers (who, whom) you may wish to contact. _____

17. (Whoever, Whomever) is suggested by Mr. Arthur must be interviewed. _____

18. The candidate (who, whom) the party supports will win. _____

19. Marcia is one on (who, whom) I have come to depend. _____

20. For (who, whom) are these contracts? _____

21. Do you know (whose, who's) jacket this is? _____

22. Do you know (whose, who's) working overtime tonight? _____

23. We're not sure (whose, who's) signed up for Friday's seminar. _____

24. It doesn't matter (whose, who's) comments those are. _____

25. You'll never guess (whose, who's) running for president! _____

Self-Help Exercises
Verbs: Kinds, Voices, Moods, Verbals

Name _____

LEVEL 1

Fill in the answers to the following questions with information found in your text.

1. What kind of action verbs direct action toward a person or thing? _____

2. What kind of action verbs do not require an object to complete their action? _____

3. What kind of verbs link to the subject words that rename or describe the subject? _____

4. What do we call the nouns, pronouns, and adjectives that complete the meaning of a sentence by renaming or describing the subject? _____

In each of the following sentences, indicate whether the underlined verb is transitive (*T*), intransitive (*I*), or linking (*L*). In addition, if the verb is transitive, write its object. If the verb is linking, write its complement. The first two sentences are followed by explanations to assist you.

5. Jeff <u>ran</u> along the dirt path back to his home. (The verb *ran* is intransitive. It has no object to complete its meaning. The phrase *along the dirt path* tells where Jeff ran; it does not receive the action of the verb.) _____

6. It <u>might have been</u> Jessica who called yesterday. (The verb phrase ends with the linking verb *been*. The complement is *Jessica,* which renames the subject *it.*) _____

7. Juan <u>input</u> the addresses of our most recent customers. _____

8. Customers <u>crowded</u> into the store at the beginning of the sale. _____

9. Sherry <u>was</u> a consultant on the software conversion project. _____

10. Levi Strauss first <u>sold</u> pants to miners in San Francisco in the 1800s. _____

11. The bank <u>faxed</u> you the loan application. _____

12. Chocolate fudge ice cream <u>tastes</u> better than chocolate mint. _____

13. Do you think it <u>was</u> he who suggested the improvement? _____

14. We <u>walked</u> around the shopping mall on our lunch hour. _____

15. Our company recruiter <u>asks</u> the same questions of every candidate. _____

16. Many corporations <u>give</u> gifts to important foreign clients. _____

17. This dictionary <u>is</u> the best on the market for office workers. _____

18. All employees <u>listened</u> intently as the CEO discussed annual profits. _____

19. Ellen <u>feels</u> justified in asking for a raise. _____

20. Customers <u>have</u> high expectations from most advertised products. _____

LEVEL 2

WORKSHEET 1

Transitive verbs that direct action toward an object are in the active voice. Transitive verbs that direct action toward a subject are in the passive voice. Writing that incorporates active-voice verbs is more vigorous and more efficient than writing that contains many passive-voice verbs. To convert a passive-voice verb to the active voice, look for the doer of the action. (Generally the agent of the action is contained in a *by* phrase.) In the active voice the agent becomes the subject.

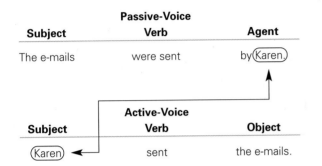

For each of the following sentences, underline the agent (doer of the action). Write that word in the space provided. Then rewrite the sentence changing the passive-voice verbs to active voice. Your rewritten version should begin with the word (and its modifiers) that you identified as the agent.

Agent

1. The text message was not received by Mark until Monday morning.

   _____

   _____

   _____

2. Our order was shipped last week by Dell.

   _____

   _____

   _____

3. Withdrawals must be authorized by Sherri Bradford beginning next week.

   _____

   _____

   _____

4. Wyatt was asked by Mr. Stern to be responsible for turning out the lights at the end of the day.

   _____

   _____

   _____

5. Employees who travel a great deal were forced by management to surrender their frequent-flier mileage awards.

   _____

   _____

   _____

WORKSHEET 2

Some sentences with passive-voice verbs do not identify the doer of the action. Before these sentences can be converted, a subject must be provided. Use your imagination to supply subjects.

Passive: Interest will be paid on all deposits. (*By whom?* By First Federal.)
Active: First Federal will pay interest on all deposits.

By whom?

1. Our departmental report must be completed before 5 p.m. _____

   _____

   _____

2. Checks were written on an account with insufficient funds. _____

   _____

   _____

3. Decisions are made in the courts that affect the daily lives of all Americans. _____

   _____

   _____

4. Employees working with computers were warned to change their passwords frequently. _____

   _____

   _____

5. Our accounting records were scrutinized during the audit. _____

   _____

   _____

WORKSHEET 3

Write the correct answers in the spaces provided.

1. If I (was, were) you, I would complete my degree first. _____

2. If Mr. Greer (was, were) in the office yesterday, he did not sign the checks. _____

3. One of the stockholders moved that a committee (be, is) constituted to study the problem immediately. _____

4. If the manager were here, he (will, would) sign the work order and we could proceed. _____

5. Government officials recommend that all homes (are, be) stocked with an emergency supply of food and water. _____

6. Dr. Washington suggested that the patient (rest, rests) for the next two days. _____

7. Angela wished that she (was, were) able to fly to Phoenix to visit her sister. _____

8. Under the circumstances, even if the voter registration drive (was, were) successful, we might lose the election. _____

9. After consulting management, our manager suggested that all employees (are, be) given three-week vacations. _____

10. It has been moved and seconded that the meeting (is, be) adjourned. _____

LEVEL 3

WORKSHEET 1

A verb form ending in *ing* and used as a noun is a gerund.

> *Passing* the examination is important. (Gerund used as subject.)

A noun or pronoun modifying a gerund should be possessive.

> *Your* passing the examination is important.

Don't confuse verbals acting as nouns with those acting as adjectives.

> The man *passing* the test received his license. (*Passing* functions as an adjective describing *man*.)

> The man's *passing* the test is important. (Verbal noun *passing* functions as the subject of the verb *is*.)

In the following sentences, underline any gerunds and write their modifiers in the space provided. If a sentence contains no gerund, write *None*.

Example: It is your <u>smoking</u> that disturbs the others.   your _____

1.   This job offer is contingent on your passing our physical examination.   _____

2.   Our office certainly did not approve of his investing in high-risk securities.   _____

3.   It was Mr. Cortina's gambling that caused him to lose his job.   _____

Some of the remaining sentences contain gerunds. If any error appears in the modifier, underline the error and write the correct form in the space provided. If the sentence is correct, write *C.*

Example: Jamie Salazar was instrumental in <u>us</u> acquiring the Collins' account.   our _____

4.   The individual receiving the award could not be present to accept it.   _____

5.   Do you think you criticizing the manager had anything to do with your transfer?   _____

6.   We deeply appreciate you calling us to give us this news at this time.   _____

7.   An employee taking a message must write clearly.   _____

8.   Ms. Fackler said that me working overtime was unnecessary this weekend.   _____

WORKSHEET 2

From the sets of sentences that follow, select the sentence that is the more logically stated. Write its letter in the space provided.

1. a. Try and come to lunch with us on Friday.
   b. Try to come to lunch with us on Friday. _____

2. a. To get to the meeting quickly, a shortcut was taken by Mike.
   b. To get to the meeting quickly, Mike took a shortcut. _____

3. a. In investing money in the stock market, one must expect risks.
   b. In investing money in the stock market, risks must be expected. _____

4. a. After filling out an application, the human resources manager gave me an interview.
   b. After filling out an application, I was given an interview by the human resources manager. _____

5. a. Driving erratically down the street, the driver was stopped by the officer.
   b. Driving erratically down the street, the officer stopped the driver. _____

Check your answers to the preceding five questions. Using the better versions of the sentence sets as models, rewrite the following sentences to make them logical. Add words as necessary, but retain the verbal expressions as sentence openers.

6. Completing the examination in only 20 minutes, a perfect score was earned by Maria.

   _____

   _____

   _____

7. To locate the members' names and addresses, the current directory was used.

   _____

   _____

   _____

8. Driving through the desert, the highway seemed endless.

   _____

   _____

   _____

9. Addressing an audience for the first time, my knees shook and my voice wavered.

   _____

   _____

   _____

LEVEL 1

Select the correct verb.

1. Did you tell me that the caller's name (is, was) Scott? _____

2. A bad accident (occured, occurred) late last evening. _____

3. Mr. Anderson says that the car you are driving (is, was) red. _____

4. Are you sure that her maiden name (is, was) Spitnale? _____

5. We were taught that an ounce of prevention (is, was) worth a pound of cure. _____

In the space provided, write the verb form indicated in parentheses.

> **Example:** Joan (carry) a heavy workload every day. (present tense) carries

6. The software company (plan) to expand its markets abroad. (present tense) _____

7. A Kentucky Fried Chicken franchise (sell) American-style fast food in Japan. (future tense) _____

8. The giant Mitsubishi conglomerate (supply) the Colonel with chicken in Japan. (past tense) _____

9. The marketing director (study) possible sales sites in foreign countries. (present tense) _____

10. We (analyze) such factors as real estate, construction costs, and local attitudes toward fast food. (future tense) _____

11. Management (apply) a complex formula to forecast the profitability of the new business. (past tense) _____

12. We (consider) the vast differences between the two cultures. (past tense) _____

13. A local franchise (vary) the side dishes to accommodate cultural preferences. (present tense) _____

14. Kentucky Fried Chicken (insist) on retaining its original recipe in foreign stores. (present tense) _____

15. It (appeal) to the average customer in Japan. (future tense) _____

16. Doing business in Japan (require) an appreciation of rituals and formalities. (present tense) _____

17. In East Asia the presentation of business cards (demand) special attention to ceremony. (future tense) _____

18. Western businesspeople (try) to observe local customs. (past tense) _____

WORKSHEET 1

Select the correct verb.

1. If her cell phone had (rang, rung), she would have heard it. _____

2. Ice (froze, freezed) in the pipes last night. _____

3. Before leaving on her vacation, Ms. Stanton (hid, hide) her silver and other valuables. _____

4. Have you (chose, chosen) a location for the new equipment? _____

5. Three new homes were recently (builded, built) on Fairfax Avenue. _____

6. He had already (drank, drunk) two bottles of water when he asked for more. _____

7. We must have (forget, forgotten) the keys. _____

8. Are you sure you have (gave, given) him the correct combination? _____

9. Andre and the others had (went, gone) on the hike earlier. _____

10. The smaller dog was (bit, bitten) by a larger neighborhood dog. _____

Underline any errors in the following sentences. Write the correct form in the space provided. Write *C* if the sentence is correct as written. Do not add helping verbs.

Example: After we <u>run</u> out of food, we had to return to camp headquarters. ran _____

11. We had ate a small snack before we ordered dinner. _____

12. The TV commercial was sang by an actress whose lips did not match the sound track. _____

13. Mr. Jefferson was stricken just as he left the witness stand. _____

14. Hundreds of mushrooms sprung up after the rain. _____

15. Many people were shook by the minor earthquake yesterday. _____

16. Tracy had wore her stylish new boots only twice. _____

17. Fortunately, he had wrote most of his report before his computer crashed. _____

18. Their car was stole from its parking place overnight. _____

19. Because of a threatening storm, she should have took a cab. _____

20. If we had went to the movie premier, we would have seen the stars. _____

WORKSHEET 2

LIE–LAY

Use the following chart to help you select the correct form of *lie* or *lay* in these sentences.

Present	Past	Past Participle	Present Participle
lie (rest)	lay (rested)	lain (have, has, or had rested)	lying (resting)
lay (place)	laid (placed)	laid (have, has, or had placed)	laying (placing)

Example: This afternoon I must (rest) down before dinner.   lie _____

1. I am sure that I (placed) the book on the desk yesterday. _____

2. Andrea angrily told her dog to (rest) down. _____

3. This month's bills have been (resting) in the drawer for weeks. _____

4. Kim (placed) her books on the desk near the entrance. _____

5. The worker was (placing) concrete blocks for the foundation. _____

6. This evening I must (rest) down before we leave. _____

7. Yesterday I (rested) in my room, worrying about today's exam. _____

8. (Place) the papers in a stack over there. _____

9. That old candy has (rested) on the shelf for several weeks. _____

10. Let the fabric (rest) there for several hours until it dries. _____

Now try these sentences to test your skill in using the forms of *lie* and *lay*.

11. Will you be able to (lie, lay) down before dinner? _____

12. How long have these papers been (laying, lying) here? _____

13. Please tell your very friendly dog to (lay, lie) down. _____

14. Will the mason (lay, lie) bricks over the concrete patio? _____

15. The contract has (laid, lain) on his desk for over two weeks. _____

16. Yesterday I (laid, lay) down in the afternoon. _____

17. Mothers complain about clothes that are left (laying, lying) around. _____

18. Returned books (lie, lay) in a pile at the library until the staff can return them to the stacks. _____

19. I'm sure I (laid, layed, lied) my keys on this counter. _____

20. When you were (lying, laying) the groceries down, did you see my keys? _____

LEVEL 3

Use Chapter 9 to look up the verb tenses required in the following sentences.

Example: By June 1 you (employ) here one full year. (future perfect, passive)

will have been employed

1. McDonald's (open) many restaurants in foreign countries. (present perfect) _____

2. McDonald's (plan) to launch a franchise program. (present progressive) _____

3. We (call) for service at least three times before a technician arrived. (past perfect) _____

4. She (work) on that project for the past six months. (present perfect) _____

5. We (see) the very first screening of the documentary. (past progressive) _____

6. The mayor (sign) the proclamation at this afternoon's public ceremony. (future progressive) _____

7. The water main (broke) by the bulldozer working on street repairs. (past perfect, passive) _____

8. I (see) two good movies recently. (present perfect) _____

9. We (consider) the installation of a new e-mail system. (present progressive) _____

10. The president's message (hear) across the country by Americans in four time zones. (past progressive, passive) _____

The next sentences review Level 2.

11. The alarm had (rang, rung) three times before we responded. _____

12. Yesterday we (drank, drunk) many glasses of water because of the heat. _____

13. You must (chose, choose) a new Internet service provider. _____

14. The car has been (drove, driven) many miles. _____

15. Steve claims he (saw, seen) the report yesterday. _____

16. If Rasheed had (went, gone) earlier, he would have told us. _____

17. Daphne said she (seen, saw) an accident on her way to work. _____

18. The tour guide checked to see whether everyone had (ate, eaten) before we left the lunch stop. _____

19. Rodney had (wrote, written) four e-mail messages before he realized they were not being received. _____

20. The price of our stocks (raised, rose) again yesterday. _____

21. Witnesses had (swear, swore, sworn) to tell the truth during the trial. _____

22. Stock prices (sank, sunk) so low that investors were sitting on their cash. _____

23. Because it was washed in hot water, the cashmere sweater (shrank, shrunk). _____

24. If we had (began, begun) the report earlier, we could have met the deadline. _____

25. Employees had been (forbade, forbidden) to use company computers for games or shopping. _____

Self-Help Exercises
Verb and Subject Agreement

Name

chapter 10

LEVEL 1

WORKSHEET 1

For each of the following sentences, cross out any phrase that comes between a verb and its subject. Then select the correct verb and write it in the space provided.

Example: One ~~of the most interesting books on all the lists~~ (is, are)
Becoming a Millionaire at 21.   is _____

1. Many Web sites on the government's prohibited list (provide, provides) games or amusement that employees may not access.   _____

2. The supervisor, together with two technicians, (is, are) working on the faulty circuit.   _____

3. This company's supply of raw materials (come, comes) from South America.   _____

4. A good many workers in addition to Jennifer (think, thinks) the work shifts should be rearranged.   _____

5. Everyone except you and John (is, are) to repeat the test.   _____

6. The table as well as two chairs (was, were) damaged.   _____

7. A list with all the customers' names and addresses (is, are) being sent. _____

8. Other equipment such as our terminals and printers (need, needs) to be reevaluated.   _____

9. One of the online shopping sites (has, have) a section devoted to clearance items.   _____

10. Several copies of the report (is, are) being prepared for distribution. _____

11. The furniture, as well as all the equipment including computers, (is, are) for sale.   _____

12. Effects of the disease (is, are) not known immediately.   _____

13. Three salespeople, in addition to their district sales manager, (has, have) voiced the same suggestion.   _____

14. Profits from his home business (is, are) surprising.   _____

15. Every one of the potential businesses that you mention (sounds, sound) good. _____

16. A shipment of 8,000 drill sets (was, were) sent to four warehouses.   _____

17. Everyone except the evening employees (is, are) coming.   _____

18. We learned that two subsidiaries of the corporation (is, are) successful. _____

19. Officials in several levels of government (has, have) to be consulted.   _____

20. A letter together with several enclosures (was, were) mailed yesterday. _____

WORKSHEET 2

For each of the following sentences, underline the subject. Then select the correct verb and write it in the space provided.

Example: Here (is, are) a <u>copy</u> of the findings for your files.   is _____

Suggestion: If you know that a subject is singular, temporarily substitute *he, she,* or *it* to help you select the proper verb. If you know that a subject is plural, temporarily substitute *they* for the subject.

1. The flow of industrial goods (travel, travels) through different distribution channels from the flow of consumer goods.   _____

2. Here (is, are) the newspaper and magazines you ordered.   _____

3. Coleman, Harris & Juarez, Inc., one of the leading management consultant firms, (is, are) able to accept our business.   _____

4. The books on the open shelves of our company's library (is, are) available to all employees.   _____

5. There (appear, appears) to be significant points omitted from the report.   _____

6. The various stages in the life cycle of a product (is, are) instrumental in determining profits for that product.   _____

7. No one except the Cunninghams (was, were) able to volunteer.   _____

8. A member of the organization of painters and plasterers (is, are) unhappy about the recent settlement.   _____

9. The size and design of its container (is, are) influential in the appeal of a product.   _____

10. Just one governmental unit from the local, state, or national levels (is, are) all we need to initiate the project.   _____

11. American Airlines (has, have) improved service while cutting costs.   _____

12. Only two seasons of the year (provide, provides) weather that is suitable for gliding.   _____

13. (Has, Have) the moving van of the Wongs arrived yet?   _____

14. At present the condition of the company's finances (is, are) extremely strong as a result of the recent bond sale.   _____

15. Incoming luggage from three flights (is, are) now being sorted.   _____

16. The salary of Maria Chavez, along with the earnings of several other employees, (has, have) been increased.   _____

17. One of the best designs (appear, appears) to have been submitted by your student.   _____

18. Trying to improve relations between doctors and patients, the American Medical Association, along with several dozen medical societies, (is, are) helping doctors embrace online consultations.   _____

19. Certainly the ease and convenience of shopping at any hour of the day or night—and getting fast delivery without ever leaving home—(is, are) very appealing.   _____

20. Aggressiveness and delinquency in boys (is, are) linked to high levels of lead in their bones, according to a recent study.   _____

LEVEL 2

For each of the following sentences, underline the subject. Then select the correct word and write it in the space provided.

1. Most of the salary compensation to which he referred (is, are) beyond basic pay schedules. _____

2. The Committee on Youth Activities (has, have) enlisted the aid of several well-known athletes. _____

3. Each of the young men and women (deserve, deserves) an opportunity to participate in local athletics. _____

4. Either your company or one of your two competitors (is, are) going to win the government contract. _____

5. The work for our Special Products Division (is, are) yet to be assigned. _____

6. Either of the two small businesses (is, are) able to secure a loan. _____

7. City council members (was, were) sharply divided along partisan lines. _____

8. Neither the packing list nor the two invoices (mention, mentions) the missing ottoman. _____

9. Every one of your suggestions (merit, merits) consideration. _____

10. Our survey shows that (everyone, every one) of the owner-managed businesses was turning a profit. _____

11. Either Steven or you (is, are) expected to return the call. _____

12. Each of the machines (has, have) capabilities that are suitable for our needs. _____

13. Mrs. Roberts said that most of the credit for our increased sales (belong, belongs) to you. _____

14. First on the program (is, are) the group of Indo-European folk dancers. _____

15. Some of the enthusiasm (is, are) due to the coming holiday. _____

16. After 10 p.m. the staff (has, have) to use the front entrance only. _____

17. (Was, Were) any of the supervisors absent after the holiday? _____

18. The union (has, have) made an agreement with management. _____

19. We were informed that neither management nor the employees (has, have) special privileges. _____

20. Most of the work that was delivered to us four days ago (is, are) completed. _____

LEVEL 3

In the following sentences, select the correct word.

1. Reed says that 75 feet of plastic pipe (has, have) been ordered. _____

2. The number of women in the labor force (is, are) steadily increasing. _____

3. Phillip said that he is one of those individuals who (enjoy, enjoys) a real challenge. _____

4. Over two thirds of the stock issue (was, were) sold immediately after it was released. _____

5. Gerald is the only one of the four applicants who (was, were) prepared to complete the application form during the interview. _____

6. That most offices are closed on weekends (is, are) a factor that totally escaped Mr. Brotherton. _____

7. The majority of the employees (favor, favors) the reorganization plan. _____

8. Telephones (is, are) one item that we must install immediately. _____

9. At least four fifths of the women in the audience (is, are) willing to participate in the show. _____

10. How could it be I who (am, is) responsible, when I had no knowledge of the agreement until yesterday? _____

11. Let it be recorded that on the second vote, the number of members in favor of the proposal (is, are) less than on the first vote. _____

12. Only half of the box of highlighters (is, are) left in the supply cabinet. _____

13. Are you one of those people who (like, likes) to sleep late? _____

14. I'm sure that it is you who (is, are) next on the list. _____

15. It looks as if 20 inches of extra cord (is, are) what we need. _____

16. Our office manager reports that a number of printers (need, needs) repair. _____

17. At least one third of the desserts purchased for the party (was, were) uneaten. _____

18. Hiking in Europe and sailing to Scandinavia (is, are) what I plan for my future vacations. _____

19. Sherry Lansing is one of our e-mail users who (complain, complains) about the system. _____

20. Whoever submitted an application earliest (has, have) the right to be interviewed first. _____

Name _____

LEVEL 1

Write the correct comparative or superlative form of the adjective shown in parentheses.

Example: Carmen is (neat) than her sister.   neater _____

1. We hope that the new procedures prove to be (effective) than previous procedures.   _____

2. Of all the suggestions made, Mr. Bradley's suggestion is the (bad).   _____

3. Mrs. Schrillo's daughter is certainly (friendly) than she is.   _____

4. Of the three individuals who volunteered, Ted is the one about whom I am (less) certain.   _____

5. I don't believe I've ever seen a (beautiful) sunset than this one.   _____

6. We make many printers, but the Model SX6 is the (fast).   _____

7. No restaurant makes (good) hamburgers than Clown Alley.   _____

8. Located next to the airport, Westchester is probably the (noisy) area in the city.   _____

9. Living in the suburbs provides (quiet) surroundings than in the city.   _____

10. Of all the applications we have received, this one seems the (sincere).   _____

11. For this job we need the (skilled) employee in the department.   _____

12. I'm afraid Andrea has the (less) chance of being selected in the lottery. _____

13. No one works (slow) than Bob.   _____

14. DataSource is (likely) to be awarded the contract than CompuPro.   _____

15. This is probably the (unusual) request I've ever received.   _____

16. Juan has had (few) citations than any other driver.   _____

17. The office is certainly looking (good) today than yesterday.   _____

18. Everyone watching the video thought that Thomas looked (credible) than any other actor.   _____

19. It was the (bad) accident I've ever seen.   _____

20. Sharon's report had the (less) errors of all those submitted.   _____

LEVEL 2

If the underlined word or words in the sentences below are correctly expressed, write *C*. If they are incorrect, write a corrected form in the space provided.

Example: Because <u>less</u> people made contributions, we failed to reach our goal.   fewer _____

1. He played his Internet music so <u>loud</u> that we couldn't work.   _____

2. We have decided to increase our <u>point-of-purchase</u> advertising.   _____

3. How much <u>further</u> will we proceed in our study of business ethics?   _____

4. <u>Less</u> employment opportunities exist in that field; therefore, I'm transferring to a different major.   _____

5. The machine is running <u>quieter</u> since we installed a hood.   _____

6. Todd and I felt <u>badly</u> about Kurt's accident.   _____

7. The general manager should not become involved in this <u>conflict of interest</u> issue.   _____

8. Ms. Edelstein was dressed <u>neatly</u> for the interview.   _____

9. At present we're searching for a source of <u>inexpensive, accessible</u> raw materials.   _____

10. My organization has selected the <u>later</u> of the two proposals you submitted.   _____

11. Sam said he was sure he did <u>good</u> on his examination.   _____

12. Most candidates completed the examinations <u>satisfactory</u>.   _____

13. We are conducting the campaign from <u>house-to-house</u>.   _____

14. Ms. Wharton appeared to be looking quite <u>well</u> despite her recent illness.   _____

15. You can <u>sure</u> depend on my help whenever you need it.   _____

16. The children were playing <u>quiet</u> when the guests arrived.   _____

17. We employees are <u>real</u> concerned about the new parking fee.   _____

18. You are a preferred <u>charge-account</u> customer at our store.   _____

19. We expect a signed contract in the <u>not too distant</u> future.   _____

20. Unfortunately, we've had <u>less</u> applications this year than ever before.   _____

LEVEL 3

In the following sentences, select the correct word(s).

1. Only the (a) two last, (b) last two speakers made relevant comments.

2. No one could be more (a) perfect, (b) nearly perfect for the job.

3. Craig is more stubborn than (a) anyone else, (b) anyone I know.

4. He is the most (a) nearly stubborn, (b) stubborn of all my friends.

5. (a) Mrs. Smith reports that she has only one volunteer.

    (b) Mrs. Smith only reports that she has one volunteer.

6. Applications will be given to the (a) first five, (b) five first job candidates.

7. Los Angeles is larger than (a) any other city, (b) any city in California.

8. I recommend this reference manual because it is (a) more nearly complete, (b) more complete than other reference manuals.

For each of the following sentences, underline any errors in the use of adjectives and adverbs. Then write the correct form. Mark *C* if the sentence is correct as written.

9. He can be counted on to paint the room as neat as a professional would do the job.

10. The uniform you are required to wear certainly fits you good.

11. Because we have less work to do this week, we should finish soon.

12. The recently-enacted law has received great support.

13. Apparently we have picked the worse time of the year to list an office for rent.

14. Although it is a honorary position, the chairmanship is important.

15. We hadn't hardly reached shelter when it began to rain.

16. The Andersons made a round the world tour last year.

17. Because of their many kindnesses to us, I feel badly that we cannot reciprocate in some way.

18. If less people were involved, the new procedures could have been implemented earlier.

19. He only said that he would work hard to complete the contract.

20. Festival promoters rented a 840 acre farm in Ulster County.

LEVEL 1

Underline any errors in the following sentences. Then write the correct form. If the sentence is correct as written, write *C*.

1. You should of seen the looks on their faces! _____

2. No one except Mr. Levine and he had access to the company records. _____

3. I read the book and plan to attend the lecture too. _____

4. Just between you and I, this engine has never run more smoothly. _____

5. Some of the software programs we borrowed off of Jeffrey. _____

6. If you will address your inquiry too our Customer Relations Department, you will surely receive a response. _____

7. The director of human resources, along with the office manager and she, is planning to improve our hiring procedures. _____

8. We could of done something about the error if we had known earlier. _____

9. Because we are receiving to many spam messages, we are adding filters. _____

10. All salespeople except Ms. Berk and he were reassigned. _____

11. Did you obtain your copy of the team proposal off him? _____

12. Please get your passes from either Mrs. Bowman or he. _____

13. See whether you can get some change for the machine off of her. _____

14. Both the project coordinator and he should have verified the totals before submitting the bid. _____

15. The commission for the sale has to be divided between Ms. Carpenter and he. _____

16. Because to few spaces are available, additional parking must be found on nearby streets. _____

17. If you and he could of come yesterday, we might have been able to help you. _____

18. So that we may better evaluate your application, please supply references too. _____

19. You could of had complimentary tickets if you had called her. _____

20. The marketing manager assigned too many customers to Ann and I. _____

LEVEL 2

For each of the following sentences, underline any errors in the use of prepositions. Then write a correct form. Mark *C* if the sentence is correct as written.

1. We think that beside salary the major issue is working conditions. _____

2. Your support and participation in this new Web program are greatly appreciated. _____

3. The warranty period was over with two months ago. _____

4. Please come into see me when you are ready for employment. _____

5. Just inside of the office entrance is the receptionist. _____

6. The senior Mr. Wiggins left $3 million to be divided between three heirs. _____

7. Will you be able to deliver the goods like you said you would? _____

8. For most of us, very few opportunities like this ever arise. _____

9. Exactly what type software did you have in mind? _____

10. Some of the trucks were moved in to the garage at dusk. _____

11. When can we accept delivery of the electrical components ordered from Hellman, Inc.? _____

12. Because of your concern and involvement in our community action campaign, we have received thousands of dollars in contributions. _____

13. I know the time and date of our next committee meeting, but I do not know where it is at. _____

14. If you were willing to accept further responsibility, I would assign you the committee chairmanship. _____

15. Joanna could not help from laughing when she saw her e-mail. _____

16. Please hurry up so that we may submit our proposal quickly. _____

17. What style furniture is most functional for the waiting room? _____

18. After going into meet the supervisor, Carla was hired. _____

19. All parking lots opposite to the corporate headquarters will be cleaned. _____

20. Immediately after Kathy graduated high school, she started college. _____

LEVEL 3

In the following sentences, select the correct word.

1. Halle found that her voice was rising as she became more and more angry (a) at, (b) with the caller. _____

2. We know of no one who is more expert (a) in, (b) with cell phone technology than Dr. France. _____

3. Our specifications must comply (a) with, (b) to those in the request for proposal (RFP). _____

4. After corresponding (a) to, (b) with their home office, I was able to clear up the error in my account. _____

5. The houses in that subdivision are identical (a) to, (b) with each other. _____

6. If you (a) plan to attend, (b) plan on attending the summer session, you'd better register immediately. _____

7. A few of the provisions are retroactive (a) for, (b) to January 1. _____

8. Jeff talked (a) to, (b) with his boss about the company's future plans. _____

9. Standing (a) on, (b) in line is not my favorite activity. _____

10. She made every effort to reason (a) to, (b) with the unhappy customer. _____

11. Apparently the letters on the screen do not sufficiently contrast (a) with, (b) to the background. _____

12. The courses, faculty, and students in this school are certainly different (a) from, (b) than those at other schools. _____

13. Do you dare to disagree (a) to, (b) with him? _____

14. Being the leader of a business team is similar (a) with, (b) to coaching a sports team. _____

15. I am angry (a) at, (b) with the recommendation that we share offices. _____

16. The president insisted that he was completely independent (a) of, (b) from his campaign contributors. _____

17. He went on working oblivious (a) from, (b) to the surrounding chaos. _____

18. The figures on the balance sheet could not be reconciled (a) to, (b) with the actual account totals. _____

19. A number of individuals agreed (a) to, (b) with the plan. _____

20. If you are desirous (a) about, (b) of taking a June vacation, you had better speak to the office manager soon. _____

LEVEL 1

WORKSHEET 1

Name four coordinating conjunctions:

1. _____   2. _____   3. _____   4. _____

When coordinating conjunctions connect independent clauses (groups of words that could stand alone as sentences), the conjunctions are preceded by commas. The two independent clauses form a compound sentence.

Compound Sentence: We hope to increase sales in the South, *but* we need additional sales personnel.

Use a comma only if the sentence is compound. When the words preceding or following the coordinating conjunction do not form an independent clause, no comma is used.

Simple Sentence: The bank will include the check with your monthly statement *or* will send the check to you immediately.

In the following sentences, selected coordinating conjunctions have been underlined. Mark *a* or *b* for each sentence.

    a = No punctuation needed   b = Insert a comma before the
                                                underlined conjunction

5. Marc Green is a specialist in information systems <u>and</u> he will be responsible for advising and assisting all our divisions.   _____

6. Marc Green is a specialist in information systems <u>and</u> will be responsible for advising and assisting all our divisions.   _____

7. This is an orientation session designed for all new employees <u>but</u> topics of interest for all employees will also be discussed.   _____

8. I have studied the plan you are developing <u>and</u> feel that it has real merit.   _____

9. We seek the reaction of the council <u>and</u> of others who have studied the plan.   _____

10. Our executive vice president will make the presentation in New York <u>or</u> he will unveil the plan in London.   _____

WORKSHEET 2

1. Name five conjunctive adverbs:

   1. _____   3. _____   5. _____

   2. _____   4. _____

2. When a conjunctive adverb joins independent clauses, what punctuation mark precedes the conjunctive adverb?   _____

3. Many words that serve as conjunctive adverbs can also function as parenthetical adverbs. When used parenthetically, adverbs are set off by what punctuation marks?   _____

In the following sentences, words acting as conjunctive or parenthetical adverbs are underlined. Add necessary commas and semicolons to punctuate the sentences.

4. The company is planning <u>nevertheless</u> to proceed with its expansion.   _____

5. Tour prices are contingent on double occupancy <u>that is</u> two people must share accommodations.   _____

6. This organization <u>on the other hand</u> is quite small in the industry.   _____

7. Our group will travel first to New York for the first product presentation <u>then</u> we will proceed to Paris for additional presentations.   _____

8. Today's job market is very competitive <u>however</u> recent graduates can find jobs if they are well trained and persistent.   _____

9. Most recruiters prefer chronological résumés <u>consequently</u> we advise our graduates to follow the traditional résumé format.   _____

10. Human resource professionals spend little time reading a cover letter <u>therefore</u> it is wise to keep your letter short.   _____

LEVEL 2

WORKSHEET 1

Use *T* or *F* to indicate whether the following statements are true or false.

1. A phrase is a group of related words *without* a subject and a verb. _____

2. A clause is a group of related words containing a subject and a verb. _____

3. An independent clause has a subject and a verb and makes sense by itself. _____

4. A dependent clause contains a subject and a verb but depends for its meaning on another clause. _____

5. Conjunctions such as *because, if,* and *when* are used preceding independent clauses. _____

Indicate whether the following groups of words are phrases (*P*), independent clauses (*I*), or dependent clauses (*D*). If you indicate that a group of words is an independent clause, capitalize the first word (use ≡) and place a period at the end of the group of words.

Example: he stood in a very long line.   I _____

6. in the past year _____

7. although she came to every meeting _____

8. she came to every meeting _____

9. during the period from spring to fall _____

10. if sales continue to climb as they have for the past four months _____

11. the director asked for additional personnel _____

12. as soon as we can increase our production _____

13. we can increase our production _____

14. because your organization has financial strength _____

15. in the future _____

16. when he returns to the office _____

17. fill out and mail the enclosed card _____

18. by next fall _____

19. we are reworking our original plans _____

20. because your old résumé listed your work history and then went on to describe previous jobs in grim and boring detail disregarding their current relevance _____

WORKSHEET 2

Add necessary commas to the following sentences. If a sentence requires no punctuation, write *C* next to it.

1. If you follow my suggestions you will help to improve the efficiency of our department.

2. You will help to improve the efficiency of our department if you follow my suggestions.

3. When completed the renovation should make the seventh floor much more attractive.

4. Let's discuss the problem when Ms. Gardner returns.

5. Drivers who park their cars in the restricted area are in danger of being ticketed.

6. Our latest company safety booklet which was submitted over six weeks ago is finally ready for distribution.

7. As you may know we have paid dividends regularly for over 70 years.

8. These payments provided there is no interruption in profits should continue for many years to come.

9. If necessary you may charge this purchase to your credit card.

10. Any employee who wishes to participate may contact our Human Resources Department.

11. James Gilroy who volunteered to head the program will be organizing our campaign.

12. I assure you that you will hear from Ms. Higgins as soon as she returns.

13. Before you send in the order may I see the catalog?

14. May I see the catalog before you send in the order?

15. We will submit the proposal within four working days if that schedule meets with your approval.

WORKSHEET 3

Use the information provided within parentheses to construct dependent clauses for the following sentences. Add subordinating conjunctions such as *who, which, although,* and *since.*

Example: Dr. Cushman recently moved his practice to Miami Beach. (Dr. Cushman specializes in pediatrics.)

Dr. Cushman, who specializes in pediatrics, recently moved his practice to Miami Beach. _____

1.   The original agreement was drawn between Mr. Hightower and Columbia Communications. (The agreement was never properly signed.) _____

_____

_____

2.   Thank you for informing us that your credit card is missing. (This credit card has an expiration date of April 30.) _____

_____

_____

Combine the following clauses into single sentences.

3.   (Your account is four months past due.) We will be forced to take legal action. We must hear from you within seven days. _____

_____

_____

4.   Sally Horton won an award as this month's outstanding employee. (She works in the Quality Control Department.) Ms. Horton is an assistant to the manager in that department. _____

_____

_____

5.   We are sending you four poster advertisements. They will appear in advertisements in magazines in April. (April marks the beginning of a national campaign featuring our sports clothes.) _____

_____

_____

LEVEL 3

The correlative conjunctions *both . . . and, either . . . or, neither . . . nor,* and *not only . . . but (also)* should be used in parallel constructions. That is, the words these conjunctions join should be similarly patterned. Compare the words that *follow* the conjunctions. For example, if a verb follows *either,* a verb should follow *or.* If the active voice is used with *neither,* then the active voice should be used with *nor.* Study the following examples.

Not Parallel: *Either* Vicki is typing the Collins' report *or* proofreading it. (The subject follows *either* and a verb follows *or.*)

Parallel: Vicki is *either* typing the Collins' report *or* proofreading it. (Both conjunctions are followed by verbs.)

Not Parallel: *Neither* have I pumped the gas *nor* was the oil checked. (An active voice construction follows *neither* while a passive voice construction follows *nor.*)

Parallel: I have *neither* pumped the gas *nor* checked the oil.

In the following items, write the letters of the sentences that are constructed in parallel form.

1.   a.   We have neither the energy to pursue this litigation nor do we have the finances.
   b.   To pursue this litigation, we have neither the energy nor the finances.   _____

2.   a.   You may either write a research report or a book report can be made.
   b.   You may either write a research report or make a book report.   _____

3.   a.   He is not only clever but also witty.
   b.   Not only is he clever but he is also witty.   _____

4.   a.   The Web site contains both information and it has an application form.
   b.   The Web site contains both information and an application form.   _____

Revise the following sentences so that the correlative conjunctions are used in parallel construction.

5.   Either you can fax him your response or you can send him an e-mail message.   _____

   _____

   _____

6.   Our goals are both to educate motorists and also lives may be saved.   _____

   _____

   _____

7.   Neither does Tony have a job offer nor does he even have an interview lined up.   _____

   _____

   _____

8.   We knew either that we had to raise more money or begin selling stock.   _____

   _____

   _____

9.   Not only are businesses looking for employees who can work in teams but also can learn effectively in teams.   _____

   _____

   _____

LEVEL 1

Add necessary commas to the following sentences. For each sentence indicate the number of commas that you added. If a sentence is correct, write *C*.

1. Your organization's use of cross-functional teams Mr. Wilson explains why your company is able to develop so many innovative products. _____

2. By the way do all of your teams work well together and collaborate effectively? _____

3. To be most successful however all teams require training coaching and other support. _____

4. Our team leader is from Ames Iowa but is now working in Des Moines. _____

5. Developing effective collaborative teams on the other hand is not always possible. _____

6. The CEO's son Mark will be joining our team for the summer. _____

7. Send the shipment to MicroTech Systems 750 Grant Road Tucson Arizona 85703 as soon as possible. _____

8. It appears sir that an error has been made in your billing. _____

9. You have until Friday April 30 to make complete payment on your past-due account. _____

10. Mr. Franklin T. Molloy who is an advertising executive has been elected chairman of the council. _____

11. Anyone who is interested in applying for the job should see Ms. Sheridan. _____

12. The bidding closes at 10 p.m. EST. _____

13. You will in addition receive a free brochure outlining our wireless devices. _____

14. Our latest wireless technology provides support for high-traffic areas such as airports shopping centers and college campuses. _____

15. All things considered the company will be obligated to pay only those expenses directly related to the installation. _____

16. Only Mr. Hudson who is a specialist in information systems is qualified to write that report. _____

17. You can avoid patent trademark and copyright problems by working with an attorney. _____

18. We are convinced incidentally that our attorney's fees are most reasonable. _____

19. Mr. Van Alstyne developed the policy Ms. Thorson worked on the budget and Mr. Seibert handled compensation issues. _____

20. Sasha will travel to Italy Greece and Croatia next summer. _____

LEVEL 2

Add necessary commas to the following sentences. For each sentence indicate the number of commas that you added. If a sentence is correct, write *C*.

1. We must find a practical permanent solution to our Internet access problems. _____

2. For a period of six months it will be necessary to reduce all expenditures. _____

3. Melissa Meyer speaking on behalf of all classified employees gave a welcoming address. _____

4. We held a marketing meeting last week and we included representatives from all divisions. _____

5. I am looking forward to getting together with you when you are again in Rochester. _____

6. We do appreciate as I have told you often your continuing efforts to increase our sales. _____

7. Consumer patterns for the past five years are being studied carefully by our marketing experts. _____

8. For some time we have been studying the growth in the number of working women and minorities. _____

9. After you have examined my calculations please send the report to Bill Thompson. _____

10. Please send the report to Bill Thompson after you have examined my calculations. _____

11. Would you please after examining my calculations send the report to Bill Thompson. _____

12. Our human resources director is looking for intelligent articulate young people who desire an opportunity to grow with a start-up company. _____

13. Call me as soon as you return or send me an e-mail message within the next week. _____

14. Beginning on the 15th of June Dell is slashing prices on laptop computers. _____

15. In 2009 we will unveil our most innovative hybrid vehicle. _____

16. As soon as I can check the inventory we will place an order. _____

17. On October 25 the president and I visited Sandra Goodell who is president of Sandra Goodell Public Relations. _____

18. You may at your convenience submit a report describing when where and how we should proceed. _____

19. To begin the purchase process we will need your request by Thursday June 1 at the latest. _____

20. Any student who has not signed up for a team by this time must see the instructor. _____

LEVEL 3

Add necessary commas to the following sentences. For each sentence indicate the number of commas that you added. If a sentence is correct, write *C.*

1. Michael Ferrari PhD has written another book on consumer buying.   _____

2. In 2008 our company expanded its marketing to include the United Kingdom.   _____

3. By 2009 12 of our competitors were also selling in Great Britain.   _____

4. In 2007 our staff numbered 87; in 2008 103.   _____

5. It was in Taiwan not in mainland China where the lightest racing bike in the world was made.   _____

6. Long before our president conducted his own research into marketing trends among youthful consumers. (Tricky!)   _____

7. "We prefer not to include your name" said the auditor "when we publish the list of inactive accounts."   _____

8. You may sign your name at the bottom of this sheet and return it to us as acknowledgment of this letter.   _____

9. The provisions of your Policy No. 85000611 should be reviewed every five years.   _____

10. Irving Feinstein MD will be the speaker at our next meeting.   _____

11. Dr. Feinstein received both a BA and an MBA from Northwestern University.   _____

12. Ever since we have been very careful to count the number of boxes in each shipment.   _____

13. In his lecture Dr. Hawkins said "One species of catfish reproduces by hatching eggs in its mouth and growing them to about three inches before releasing them."   _____

14. Did you say it was Mr. Samuels not Ms. Lambert who made the sale?   _____

15. Ten computers were sold in January; nine in February.   _____

16. Our figures show that 17365000 separate rental units were occupied in September.   _____

17. "The function of a supervisor" remarked Sid Stern "is to analyze results not to try to control how the job is done."   _____

18. By the way it was the president not the vice president who ordered the cutback.   _____

19. "A diamond" said the therapist "is a chunk of coal that made good under pressure."   _____

20. Whoever signs signs at her own risk.   _____

LEVEL 1

Punctuate the following groups of words as single sentences. Add commas and semicolons. Do not add words or periods to create new sentences.

Example: Come in to see our new branch office, meet our friendly tellers and manager.

1. Our principal function is to help management make profits however we can offer advice on staffing problems as well.

2. Delegates came from as far as Brownsville Texas Seattle Washington and Bangor Maine.

3. Jerry looked up names Andrea addressed envelopes and Janelle stuffed the envelopes.

4. Thank you for your order it will be filled immediately.

5. Employees often complain about lack of parking space on the other hand little interest was shown in a proposed carpooling program.

6. Computers are remarkable however they are only as accurate as the people who program them.

7. This sale is not open to the general public we are opening the store to preferred customers only.

8. Some of the employees being promoted are Jill Roberts secretary Legal Department Lea Lim clerk Human Resources and Mark Cameron dispatcher Transportation Department.

9. We will be happy to cooperate with you and your lawyers in settling the estate however several matters must be reviewed.

10. In the morning I am free at 10 a.m. in the afternoon I have already scheduled an appointment.

11. The book was recently selected for a national award thus its sales are soaring.

12. Look over our online catalog make your selections and click to submit your order.

13. We hope that we will not have to sell the property but that may be our only option.

14. The film that you requested is now being shown to law students in Michigan it will be shown during June in California and it will be used during July and August in the states of Florida and North Carolina.

15. We do not sell airline seats we sell customer service.

16. Our convention committee is considering the Hyatt Regency Hotel Columbus Ohio Plaza of the Americas Hotel Dallas Texas and the Brown Palace Hotel Denver Colorado.

17. As requested the committee will meet Thursday May 4 however it is unable to meet Friday May 5.

18. Market research involves the systematic gathering recording and analyzing of data.

LEVEL 2

Add colons, semicolons, or commas to the following sentences. Do not add words or periods. Write *C* after the sentence if it is correct.

1. Three phases of our business operation must be scrutinized purchasing, production, and shipping.

2. The candidates being considered for supervisor are Ned Bingham, Sean Davis, and Anna Donato.

3. George Steinbrenner, New York Yankees owner, said "I want this team to win. I'm obsessed with winning, with discipline, with achieving. That's what this country's all about."

4. Following are four dates reserved for counseling. Sign up soon.
   September 28   January 4
   September 30   January 6

5. At its next meeting the board of directors must make a critical decision should the chief executive officer be retained or replaced?

6. This year's seminar has been organized to give delegates an opportunity to exchange ideas, plans, techniques, and goals.

7. The three Cs of credit are the following character, capacity, and capital.

8. Our Boston tour package included visits to these interesting historical sites the House of Seven Gables, Bunker Hill, the Boston Tea Party Ship and Museum, and Paul Revere's home.

9. I recommend that you take at least three courses to develop your language arts skills Essentials of College English 105, Business Communication 201, and Managerial Communication 305.

10. The speaker said that "membership is voluntary" but that contributions would be greatly appreciated.

11. Several of the tax specialists on the panel were concerned with the same thought government spending continues to rise while taxes are being reduced.

12. To determine an individual's FICO credit rating, companies use the following factors payment history, outstanding debt, credit history, inquiries and new accounts, and types of credit in use.

13. Scholarships will be awarded to Jill Hofer Jeremy Stone and Carolena Garay.

14. Our favorite Colorado resort is noted for fly fishing, mountain biking, tennis and hiking.

15. Our favorite Colorado resort is noted for the following fly fishing, mountain biking, and hiking.

LEVEL 3

Add colons, semicolons, dashes, or commas as needed. If a word following a colon should not be capitalized, use a proofreading mark (/) to indicate lowercase. Show words to be capitalized with (≡). Mark *C* if a sentence is correct as it stands.

1. There are three primary ways to make a credit check namely by e-mail, by U.S. mail, or by telephone.

2. Please order the following supplies Cartridges, paper, and labels.

3. Although we are expanding our services we continue to do business according to our original philosophy that is we want to provide you with flexible and professional investment services on a highly personal basis.

4. Employees who conduct Web research are taught this rule Evaluate the validity of all data found on the Web.

5. Dr. Ruglio's plane departed at 2 15 and should arrive at 6 45.

6. We invited Jeff, Kevin, Tony, and Tom but Tony was unable to come.

7. Three of our top executives namely Mr. Thomas, Mr. Estrada, and Mrs. Stranahan are being transferred to the Milwaukee office.

8. On our list of recommended reading is *Investment an Introduction to Analysis.*

9. The library, as you are already aware, needs space for additional books, particularly in the nonfiction field and even greater space will be required within the next five years.

10. Our airline is improving service in several vital areas for example baggage handling, food service, and weather forecasts.

11. Julie Schumacher was hired by a brokerage house and given the title of "registered representative" that is she is able to buy and sell securities.

12. Professor Wilson listed five types of advertising Product, institutional, national, local, and corrective.

13. We considered only one location for our fall convention namely San Francisco.

14. Many important questions are yet to be asked concerning our program for instance how can we meet our competitor's low prices in the Southwest?

15. If possible, call him as soon as you return to the office however I doubt that he is still at his desk.

LEVEL 1

Add any necessary punctuation to the following sentences. If a sentence is correct, write *C.*

1. Will you please send this c o d shipment as soon as possible

2. You did say the meeting is at 10 a m didn't you

3. Mr Kephart is a C P A working for Berman, Inc

4. Do you know whether Donald L Cullens Jr applied for the job

5. Help The door is jammed

6. Will you please Ms. Juarez visit our Web site and register for your gift

7. What a day this has been

8. Although most candidates had A A degrees two applicants had B A degrees

9. Our C E O and C F O normally make all budget decisions

10. Cynthia asked whether invitations had been sent to Miss Tan Mr Roe and Ms Rich

11. All calls made before 9 a m E S T are billed at a reduced rate

12. Alan Bennett M D and Gina Caracas Ph D were our keynote speakers

13. How many FAQs (frequently asked questions) do you think we should post at our Web site

14. We're expanding marketing efforts in China France and the U K

15. Surprisingly, the C P U of this computer is made entirely of parts from the U S A

16. Please send the package to Laurie Adamski 5 Sierra Drive Rochester N Y 14616.

17. Would you please check Policy Nos 44657001 and 44657002 to see whether each includes $50000 comprehensive coverage

18. Did you say the order was received at 5 p m P S T

19. Wow How much was the lottery prize

20. After Mike completed his M A he was hired to develop scripts for movie D V Ds.

LEVEL 2

Write *T* (true) or *F* (false) after the following statements.

1. In typewritten or simple word processing—generated material, a dash is formed by typing two successive underscores. _____

2. Parentheses are often used to enclose explanations, references, and directions. _____

3. Dashes must be avoided in business writing since they have no legitimate uses. _____

4. Question marks and exclamation points may be used to punctuate parenthetical statements (enclosed within parentheses) within other sentences. _____

5. If a comma falls at the same point where words enclosed by parentheses appear, the comma should follow the final parenthesis. _____

Write the letter of the correctly punctuated sentence in the space provided.

6. a. I am busy on all those dates—oh, perhaps October 18 is free.
   b. I am busy on all those dates: oh, perhaps October 18 is free.
   c. I am busy on all those dates, oh, perhaps October 18 is free. _____

7. (De-emphasize)
   a. Directions for assembly, see page 15, are quite simple.
   b. Directions for assembly—see page 15—are quite simple.
   c. Directions for assembly (see page 15) are quite simple. _____

8. a. Eat, sleep, and read: that's what I plan to do on my vacation.
   b. Eat, sleep, and read—that's what I plan to do on my vacation.
   c. Eat, sleep, and read, that's what I plan to do on my vacation. _____

9. a. To file a complaint with the Better Business Bureau (BBB), call during normal business hours.
   b. To file a complaint with the Better Business Bureau, (BBB) call during normal business hours.
   c. To file a complaint with the Better Business Bureau (BBB) call during normal business hours. _____

10. (Normal emphasis)
   a. Sharon Hunt (who is an excellent manager) may be promoted.
   b. Sharon Hunt, who is an excellent manager, may be promoted.
   c. Sharon Hunt—who is an excellent manager—may be promoted. _____

11. a. "What is needed for learning is a humble mind." (Confucius)
   b. "What is needed for learning is a humble mind.": Confucius
   c. "What is needed for learning is a humble mind."—Confucius _____

12. a. You missed the due date (July 1;) however, your payment is welcome.
   b. You missed the due date; (July 1) however, your payment is welcome.
   c. You missed the due date (July 1); however, your payment is welcome. _____

13. a. Only one person knows my password—Denise Powell, and I have confidence in her.
   b. Only one person knows my password (Denise Powell), and I have confidence in her.
   c. Only one person knows my password; Denise Powell, and I have confidence in her. _____

14. (Emphasize)
   a. Our current mortgage rates: see page 10 of the enclosed booklet—are the lowest in years.
   b. Our current mortgage rates (see page 10 of the enclosed booklet) are the lowest in years.
   c. Our current mortgage rates—see page 10 of the enclosed booklet—are the lowest in years. _____

LEVEL 3

Write *T* (true) or *F* (false) for each of the following statements.

1. When the exact words of a speaker are repeated, double quotation marks are used to enclose the words. _____

2. To indicate a quotation within another quotation, single quotation marks (apostrophes on most keyboards) are used. _____

3. When a word is defined, its definition should be underscored. _____

4. The titles of books, magazines, newspapers, and other complete works published separately may be underscored or italicized. _____

5. The titles of chapters of books and magazine articles may be underscored or enclosed in quotation marks. _____

6. In the United States periods and commas are always placed inside closing quotation marks. _____

7. Brackets are used when a writer inserts his or her own remarks inside a quotation. _____

8. The Latin word *sic* may be used to call attention to an error in quoted material. _____

9. Semicolons and colons are always placed outside closing quotation marks. _____

10. Question marks and exclamation points may be placed inside or outside closing quotation marks, depending on the wording of the sentence and quotation. _____

Write the letter of the correctly punctuated statement.

11. a. "Jobs," said Mr. Steele, "will be scarce this summer."
    b. "Jobs, said Mr. Steele, will be scarce this summer."
    c. "Jobs", said Mr. Steele, "will be scarce this summer." _____

12. a. The manager said, "This file was clearly marked Confidential."
    b. The manager said, "This file was clearly marked 'Confidential'."
    c. The manager said, "This file was clearly marked 'Confidential.'" _____

13. a. A *chattel* is defined as a "piece of movable property."
    b. A "chattel" is defined as a *piece of movable property.*
    c. A "chattel" is defined as a "piece of movable property." _____

14. a. Do you know who it was who said, "Forewarned is forearmed."
    b. Do you know who it was who said, "Forewarned is forearmed"?
    c. Do you know who it was who said, "Forewarned is forearmed."? _____

15. a. "We warn all e-mail users to avoid messages that are 'flaming,'" said the CEO.
    b. "We warn all e-mail users to avoid messages that are "flaming," said the CEO.
    c. "We warn all e-mail users to avoid messages that are 'flaming'", said the CEO. _____

COMPLETE PUNCTUATION REVIEW

Insert all necessary punctuation in the following sentences. Correct any incorrect punctuation. Do not break any sentences into two sentences.

1. Did you see the article titled Soaring Salaries of C E O s that appeared in The New York Times

2. This years budget costs are much higher than last years, therefore I will approve overtime only on a case by case basis.

3. The S.E.C. has three new members Dr. Carla Chang Professor Mark Rousso and Robert Price Esq

4. Needless to say all contract bids must be received before 5 pm E S T

5. We formerly depended on fixed-rate not variable rate mortgages.

6. The following representatives have been invited Christine Lenski DataCom Industries, Mark Grant LaserPro, Inc., and Ivan Weiner Image Builders.

7. Last year we moved corporate headquarters to Orlando Florida but maintained production facilities in Atlanta.

8. (Quotation) Did Dr. Tran say We will have no class Friday.

9. Graduation ceremonies for B.A. candidates are at 11 am, graduation ceremonies for M.B.A. candidates are at 2 pm.

10. As we previously discussed the reorganization will take effect on Monday August 8.

11. We feel however that the cars electrical system should be fully warranted for five years.

12. Will you please send copies of our annual report to Anna Golan and D A Rusterholz?

13. Although he had prepared carefully Mitchell feared that his presentation would bomb.

14. In the event of inclement weather we will close the base and notify the following radio stations KJOW KLOB and KOB-TV.

15. (Emphasize) Three excellent employees Gregorio Morales, Dawna Capps, and DaVonne Williams will be honored at a ceremony Friday June 5.

16. (Quotation) "Your attitude not your aptitude will determine your altitude, said Zig Ziglar.

17. By May 15 our goal is to sell 15 cars, by June 15 20 additional cars.

18. The full impact of the E P A ruling is being studied you will receive information as it becomes available.

19. If the fax arrives before 9 pm we can still meet our June 1 deadline.

20. Send the contract to Ms Courtney Worthy Administrative Assistant Globex Industries 7600 Normandale Boulevard Milwaukee WI 53202 as soon as possible.

21. (De-emphasize) Please return the amended budget proposal see page 2 for a summary of the report to the presidents office by Friday March 4.

22. Prospective entrepreneurs were told to read a Success magazine article titled A Venture Expert's Advice.

23. Larry Zuckerman our former manager now has a similar position with I B M.

24. If you really want to lose weight you need give up only three things, namely breakfast, lunch, and dinner.

25. As expected this years expenses have been heavy, consequently we may have to freeze hiring for the next six months.

CHAPTER 17

Name _____

LEVEL 1

Write the letter of the group of words that is correctly capitalized.

1. (a) a case of german measles   (b) a case of German measles   _____

2. (a) in the field of marketing   (b) in the field of Marketing   _____

3. (a) the Hancock Building   (b) the Hancock building   _____

4. (a) for all Catholics, Protestants, and Muslims   (b) for all catholics, protestants, and muslims   _____

5. (a) an order for china and crystal   (b) an order for China and crystal   _____

6. (a) both Master's and Doctor's degrees   (b) both master's and doctor's degrees   _____

7. (a) the state of Oklahoma   (b) the State of Oklahoma   _____

8. (a) a class in conversational French   (b) a class in Conversational French   _____

9. (a) a memo from our Sacramento Office   (b) a memo from our Sacramento office   _____

10. (a) a salad with French dressing   (b) a salad with french dressing   _____

11. (a) our web site   (b) our Web site   _____

12. (a) traffic in the big apple   (b) traffic in the Big Apple   _____

13. (a) the King Edward room   (b) the King Edward Room   _____

14. (a) a holiday on Memorial Day   (b) a holiday on Memorial day   _____

15. (a) the waters of Delaware bay   (b) the waters of Delaware Bay   _____

Use proofreading marks to capitalize (≡) or to show lowercase (/) letters in the following sentences.

16. Bob's Chevron Station is located on Speedway Avenue in the next County.

17. Many employees of the Meredith Corporation plan to participate in the Company's profit-sharing plan.

18. Investigators from the securities and exchange commission insisted on seeing all E-Mail messages.

19. During the Winter I will enroll in management, english composition, and accounting.

20. The American Association Of Nurses will open its annual meeting in the Pacific ballroom of the Regency hotel in San Francisco.

21. Our persian cat and russian wolfhound cohabit quite peacefully.

22. Last Summer my family and I visited the grand canyon in arizona.

23. The two companies signed a Contract last april.

24. Interior designers recommended italian marble for the entry and spanish tiles for the patio.

25. A limousine will take guests from kansas city international airport directly to the alameda plaza hotel.

LEVEL 2

Write the letter of the group of words that is correctly capitalized.

1. (a) my uncle and my aunt   (b) my Uncle and my Aunt   _____

2. (a) Very sincerely yours,   (b) Very sincerely Yours,   _____

3. (a) Send it to Vice President Lee   (b) Send it to vice president Lee _____

4. (a) Volume II, Page 37   (b) Volume II, page 37   _____

5. (a) located in western Indiana   (b) located in Western Indiana   _____

6. (a) stored in building 44   (b) stored in Building 44   _____

7. (a) within our Human Resources   (b) within our human resources
         Department   department   _____

8. (a) the Federal Communications   (b) the federal communications
         Commission   commission   _____

9. (a) in appendix III   (b) in Appendix III   _____

10. (a) heading South on Highway 5   (b) heading south on Highway 5   _____

11. (a) the book *Ethics and Business*   (b) the book *Ethics And Business* _____

12. (a) both federal and state laws   (b) both Federal and State laws   _____

13. (a) Q-tips and kleenexes   (b) Q-Tips and Kleenexes   _____

14. (a) orders from Sales Director Ali   (b) orders from sales director Ali _____

15. (a) a trip to the east coast   (b) a trip to the East Coast   _____

Use proofreading marks to capitalize (≡) or to show lowercase letters (/) in the following sentences.

16. We received a directive from Ruth Jones, Supervisor, Administrative Services Division.

17. The President of our Company gave an address entitled "Leadership: What Effective Managers do and how They do it."

18. Gina Schmidt, customer service representative, attended a convention in the east.

19. To reach my home, proceed north on highway 10 until you reach exit 7.

20. Mayor Bruno visited the governor in an attempt to increase the city's share of State funding.

21. The best article is "Does your training measure up?" by Leslie Brokaw.

22. John placed his ray-ban sunglasses on the formica counter.

23. Sue's Mother and Father were scheduled to leave on flight 37 from gate 6 at phoenix sky harbor international airport.

24. In April our data entry and data verification departments will be merged into the technical services division.

25. Taxicab, Bus, and Limousine service is available from the airport to the ritz-carlton hotel.

LEVEL 3

Write the letter of the group of words that is correctly capitalized.

1. (a) photographs sent from Venus to Earth   (b) photographs sent from Venus to earth   _____

2. (a) a room marked "private"   (b) a room marked "Private"   _____

3. (a) the Egyptian Room and the Sahara Room   (b) the Egyptian room and the Sahara room   _____

4. (a) the finest production on earth   (b) the finest production on Earth   _____

5. (a) from Senator-Elect Ross   (b) from Senator-elect Ross   _____

6. (a) When, sir, are you free?   (b) When, Sir, are you free?   _____

7. (a) some asian cultures   (b) some Asian cultures   _____

8. (a) an envelope stamped "confidential   (b) an envelope stamped "Confidential"   _____

9. (a) our sales director, Joe Hines   (b) our Sales Director, Joe Hines   _____

10. (a) to ex-President Clinton   (b) to Ex-President Clinton   _____

Use proofreading marks to capitalize (≡) or to show lowercase (/) letters in the following sentences.

11. The returned check was stamped "Insufficient funds."

12. A paddleboat traveled south down the Mississippi river.

13. No one recognized ex-senator Thurston when he toured Napa valley.

14. We wonder, professor, if the gravity of Mars might be similar to that of earth.

15. The Organization's bylaws state: "On the third Monday of every month the Club's Treasurer will prepare the financial report."

16. The President of our Company has traveled to Pacific Rim Countries to expand foreign markets.

17. The secretary of state met with the president to discuss this country's National policy toward african nations.

18. British english is the Dialect taught in most countries where english is not a native language.

19. In malaysia we soon learned that muslims do not eat pork and that buddhists and hindus do not eat beef.

20. Although he was known as a "banker's banker," Mr. Lee specialized in Mortgage Financing.

LEVEL 1

In the space provided write the letter of the correctly expressed group of words.

1. (a) for 24 employees   (b) for twenty-four employees   _____

2. (a) only 9 days left   (b) only nine days left   _____

3. (a) twenty-five dollars   (b) $25   _____

4. (a) on the thirtieth of May   (b) on the 30th of May   _____

5. (a) it cost 20 cents   (b) it cost twenty cents   _____

6. (a) (military style) 5 April 2009   (b) April 5, 2009   _____

7. (a) $2.05, 85¢, and $5.00   (b) $2.05, $.85, and $5   _____

8. (a) we started at 9 a.m.   (b) we started at nine a.m.   _____

9. (a) 2 Highland Avenue   (b) Two Highland Avenue   _____

10. (a) 226 Sixth Street   (b) 226 6th Street   _____

Underline any errors in the expression of numbers in the following sentences. Write the correct forms.

11. 194 businesses were sent the ethics survey on December 1st.   _____

12. 2 companies have moved their corporate offices to twenty-fifth avenue.   _____

13. Three of the least expensive items were priced at $5.00, $3.29, and 99 cents.   _____

14. If your payment of $100.00 is received before the 2 of the month, you will
    receive a discount.   _____

15. On February 1st the guidelines for all fifteen departments went into effect.   _____

16. Our office, formerly located at Two Ford Place, is now located at
    One Kent Avenue.   _____

17. Please call me at 815 611-9292, Ext. Three, before 4 p.m.   _____

18. On May 15th 2 performances will be given: one at two p.m. and another
    at eight p.m.   _____

19. 3 of our employees start at 8:00 a.m., and 5 start at 8:30 a.m.   _____

20. If reservations are made before the fifteenth of the month, the fare will be
    204 dollars.   _____

21. Grossmont College offers a fifteen-hour training course that costs one hundred
    twenty-five dollars.   _____

22. Classes meet Monday through Thursday from 11:45 a.m. until one p.m.   _____

23. The Werners moved from 1,762 Milburn Avenue to 140 East 14 Street.   _____

24. Lisa had only $.25 left after she purchased supplies for forty-four dollars.   _____

25. On the third of January and again on the 18th, our copy machine needed
    service.   _____

LEVEL 2

Write the letter of the correctly expressed group of words.

1. (a) for 82 students in 3 classes   (b) for 82 students in three classes   _____

2. (a) an interest period of ninety days   (b) an interest period of 90 days   _____

3. (a) over the past thirty years   (b) over the past 30 years   _____

4. (a) two 35-day contracts   (b) 2 35-day contracts   _____

5. (a) he is 45 years old   (b) he is forty-five years old   _____

6. (a) line three   (b) line 3   _____

7. (a) nearly 2.6 billion units   (b) nearly 2,600,000,000 units   _____

8. (a) fifteen 50-page pamphlets   (b) 15 fifty-page pamphlets   _____

9. (a) Lois Lamb, 65, and John Lamb, 66   (b) Lois Lamb, sixty-five, and John Lamb, sixty-six   _____

10. (a) exactly two years and seven months ago   (b) exactly 2 years and 7 months ago   _____

Underline any errors in the expression of numbers in the following sentences. Write the corrected form.

11. We have received fifty reservations over the past 14 days.   _____

12. Tour guests will be transported in three thirty-five-passenger air-conditioned motor coaches throughout the fifteen-day excursion.   _____

13. 53 of the corporations had operating budgets that exceeded one million dollars.   _____

14. Only 10 telephones are available for the forty-eight employees in 5 offices.   _____

15. Chapter eight in Volume two provides at least three references to pumps.   _____

16. About 100 chairs are stored in Room Four, and another eight chairs are in Room 14.   _____

17. We ordered two thirty-inch desks and three chairs.   _____

18. Of the twenty requests we received, five were acted on immediately and three had to be tabled.   _____

19. The 2 loans must be repaid within 90 days.   _____

20. When she was only 24 years old, Mrs. Markham supervised more than 120 employees.   _____

21. Only two of the 125 mailed surveys were undeliverable.   _____

22. Frank Morris, sixty-four, plans to retire in one year.   _____

23. Linda Hannan and her fifteen-person company signed a three million dollar contract.   _____

24. She purchased new equipment to beam fifty-two World Cup games from nine locations to forty million avid soccer fans in Pacific Rim countries.   _____

25. The thirty-year mortgage carries an interest rate of eight percent.   _____

LEVEL 3

Assume that all of the following phrases appear in complete sentences. Write the letter of the phrase that is appropriately expressed.

1. (a) the tank holds just 9 gallons   (b) the tank holds just nine gallons   _____
2. (a) only a three percent gain   (b) only a 3 percent gain   _____
3. (a) 4/5 of the voters   (b) four fifths of the voters   _____
4. (a) a 50% markup   (b) a 50 percent markup   _____
5. (a) a one-half share   (b) a one half share   _____
6. (a) a decline of .5 percent   (b) a decline of 0.5 percent   _____
7. (a) he placed 3rd in the state   (b) he placed third in the state   _____
8. (a) in the nineteenth century   (b) in the 19th century   _____
9. (a) a 5-pound box of candy   (b) a five-pound box of candy   _____
10. (a) at least 95% of the   (b) at least 95 percent of the
        stockholders   stockholders   _____

Underline any errors in the expression of numbers. Write the corrected form.

11. A No. Ten envelope actually measures four and a half by nine and a half inches.   _____

12. The two candidates in the 33d Congressional District waged hard-hitting campaigns.   _____

13. Tests show that the driver responded in less than seven two hundredths of a second.   _____

14. Great strides in communication technology have been made in the 21st century.   _____

15. The desk top measured thirty and three-fourths inches by sixty and a half inches.   _____

16. Payment must be received by the thirtieth to qualify for a three percent discount.   _____

17. Our office was moved about fifty blocks from 7th Street to 58th Street.   _____

18. Temperatures in Phoenix were over one hundred degrees for 8 consecutive days.   _____

19. The notebook computer weighs just seven point nine four pounds and is fifteen and a half inches wide.   _____

20. Appropriation measures must be passed by a 2/3 majority.   _____

21. She ordered a nine by twelve rug to cover two-thirds of the floor.   _____

22. After completing Form Ten Forty, the accountant submitted his bill for 800 dollars.   _____

23. By the year 2,010, the number of employees over the age of 55 will increase by 52%.   _____

24. Nine different airlines carry over one hundred thousand passengers daily.   _____

25. The company car was filled with fifteen gallons of gasoline and one quart of oil.   _____

Chapter 1 Self-Help Answers

1. c **2.** b **3.** c **4.** a **5.** b **6.** c **7.** b **8.** b **9.** d **10.** b **11.** b

Chapter 2 Self-Help Answers

Worksheet 1

A. 2. substitutes for a noun *he she it* **3.** shows action or joins words that describe the subject *jumps works is* **4.** describes nouns or pronouns *tall soft five* **5.** modifies verbs, adjectives, or other adverbs *hurriedly very nicely* **6.** joins nouns and pronouns to the sentence *to for at* **7.** connects words or groups of words *and but or* **8.** shows strong feelings *Wow! Gosh! No!*

B. 1. pronoun **2.** verb **3.** adj **4.** adj **5.** noun **6.** prep **7.** noun **8.** conj **9.** pronoun **10.** verb **11.** adverb **12.** adj **13.** interj **14.** adj **15.** noun **16.** conj **17.** noun **18.** verb **19.** adj **20.** adj **21.** noun **22.** prep **23.** adj **24.** noun **25.** pronoun **26.** verb **27.** adverb **28.** conj **29.** adj **30.** adj **31.** noun **32.** verb **33.** adv

Worksheet 2

1. pronoun **2.** verb **3.** noun **4.** prep **5.** noun **6.** conj **7.** adj **8.** noun **9.** verb **10.** adv **11.** verb **12.** noun **13.** interj. **14.** verb **15.** noun **16.** adverb **17.** verb **18.** pronoun **19.** verb **20.** verb **21.** adj **22.** noun **23.** prep **24.** noun **25.** adj **26.** adj **27.** adj **28.** noun **29.** verb **30.** conj **31.** adj **32.** conj **33.** adj **34.** conj **35.** adj **36.** noun **37.** verb **38.** verb **39.** pronoun **40.** adverb **41.** prep **42.** adj **43.** adj **44.** adj **45.** noun **46.** noun **47.** adverb **48.** verb **49.** prep **50.** adj **51.** adj **52.** noun **53.** prep **54.** adj **55.** adj **56.** adj. **57.** noun **58.** noun **59.** verb **60.** adverb **61.** verb **62.** adj **63.** noun **64.** pronoun **65.** verb **66.** prep **67.** adj **68.** noun

Chapter 3 Self-Help Answers

Worksheet 1

1. (S) applicant (V) received **2.** (S) speaker (V) made **3.** (S) telephones (V) rang **4.** (S) we (V) will hire **5.** (S) team (V) built **6.** (S) salespeople (V) received **7.** (S) manager (V) will send. **8.** (S) we (V) released **9.** (S) one (V) was given **10.** (S) computers (V) require **11.** (S) printout (V) was **12.** (S) One (V) sold **13.** (S) list (V) is **14.** (S) Everything (V) is covered **15.** (S) committee (V) was appointed **16.** (S) Mr. Thomas (V) is **17.** (S) copiers (v) are **18.** (S) Ms. Seymour (V) is **19.** (S) Mr. Torres (V) has been **20.** (S) offices (V) are

Worksheet 2

Answers will vary. **1.** voted **2.** fell **3.** arrived **4.** rang **5.** ended **6.** dropped **7.** policy **8.** virus **9.** package **10.** him **11.** the door **12.** documents **13.** good **14.** manager **15.** Mr. Jones **16.** Mary **17.** Mr. Smith **18.** John **19–23.** *Answers will vary.*

Worksheet 3

1. a **2.** c **3.** d **4.** b **5.** e **6.** a **7.** c **8.** b **9.** a **10.** c **11.** b **12.** d **13.** a **14.** a **15.** c **16.** d **17.** b **18.** a **19.** c **20.** b

Chapter 4 Self-Help Answers

LEVEL 1

1. giraffes **2.** feet **3.** switches **4.** the Bushes **5.** boxes **6.** languages **7.** faxes **8.** sandwiches **9.** income taxes **10.** children **11.** successes **12.** values **13.** dresses **14.** branches **15.** recommendations **16.** women **17.** mismatches **18.** taxis **19.** loaves **20.** annexes **21.** beliefs **22.** the Rosses **23.** storms **24.** ranches **25.** the Joneses **26.** the Chavezes **27.** letters **28.** businesses **29.** computers **30.** wishes

LEVEL 2

1. wharves **2.** chiefs of police **3.** 2000s **4.** the Wolfs **5.** embargoes **6.** LVNs **7.** size 10s **8.** amts. **9.** faculties **10.** by-products **11.** entries **12.** lookers-on **13.** companies **14.** knives **15.** courts-martial **16.** A's **17.** the Shermans **18.** memos **19.** valleys **20.** zeros **21.** lives **22.** yrs. **23.** the Murphys **24.** runners-up **25.** oz. **26.** journeys **27.** MBAs **28.** wolves **29.** the Kellys **30.** minorities

LEVEL 3

1. data **2.** theses **3.** bacteria **4.** Chinese **5.** parentheses **6.** headquarters **7.** alumnae **8.** millennia **9.** genera **10.** news **11.** pp. **12.** ff. **13.** larvae **14.** bases **15.** memoranda or memorandums **16.** are **17.** is or are **18.** formulas **19.** analyses **20.** is

Chapter 5 Self-Help Answers

LEVEL 1

Worksheet 1

1. all employees' passwords **2.** this company's office **3.** the women's uniforms **4.** two months' rent **5.** the supervisor's signature **6.** all members' opinions **7.** the pilot's landing **8.** both partners' agreement **9.** Jeffrey's notebook **10.** the department's strengths **11.** two years' time **12.** those people's customs **13.** last week's merger **14.** the bank's credit **15.** citizens' savings **16.** Canada's mountains **17.** the employer's requirements **18.** all candidates' résumés **19.** the government's policies **20.** both attorneys' fees

Worksheet 2

1. year's **2.** drivers' **3.** carpenter's **4.** thief's **5.** day's **6.** employees' **7.** CEO's **8.** readers' **9.** caller's **10.** authors' **11.** Gap's **12.** C **13.** country's **14.** months' **15.** organization's **16.** president's **17.** family's **18.** C **19.** years' **20.** farmer's **21.** citizens' **22.** year's **23.** customer's **24.** Children's **25.** supervisor's

LEVEL 2

1. public's **2.** company's **3.** stationer's **4.** The suggestions of my uncle's lawyer **5.** editor in chief's **6.** aunt and uncle's **7.** C **8.** last month's **9.** C **10.** telephone number of the president's assistant **11.** sales **12.** C or beards of my two brothers-in-law **13.** Larry's **14.** Rick's **15.** England's **16.** C **17.** Clark and Clark's **18.** Angeles **19.** architects' **20.** last year's **21.** C **22.** Diana and Jason's **23.** reporters' **24.** day's day's **25.** C

LEVEL 3

1. someone else's **2.** Ross' or Ross's **3.** classes' **4.** Saunders' or Saunders's **5.** Rodriguezes' **6.** Les' or Les's **7.** boss's **8.** bosses' **9.** Horowitzes **10.** actresses' **11.** Harris' or Harris's **12.** Burns' or Burns's **13.** James' or James's **14.** waitress's **15.** Garveys' **16.** Morrises' **17.** Betz' or Betz's **18.** Walkers' **19.** Simons' or Simons's **20.** Jones' or Jones's **21.** White's **22.** Williamses' **23.** Kimballs **24.** Elvis' or Elvis's **25.** Los Angeles

Chapter 6 Self-Help Answers

LEVEL 1

Worksheet 1

1–14. *Order of answers may vary.* **1–7.** I, you, he, she, it, we, they **8–14.** me, you, him, her, it, us, them **15.** I **16.** she **17.** he **18.** they **19.** she **20.** we **21.** she **22.** he **23.** she **24.** he **25.** I

Worksheet 2

1. me **2.** him **3.** them **4.** me **5.** her **6.** him **7.** her **8.** them **9.** us **10.** me **11.** it's **12.** theirs **13.** its **14.** There's **15.** hers **16.** it's **17.** yours **18.** Whose **19.** ours **20.** You're

LEVEL 2

1. them **2.** I **3.** her **4.** We **5.** me **6.** me **7.** her **8.** he **9.** him **10.** I **11.** himself **12.** her **13.** her **14.** she **15.** me **16.** us **17.** she **18.** him **19.** I **20.** me **21.** me **22.** She and I **23.** her **24.** us **25.** I

LEVEL 3

Worksheet 1

1. she **2.** he **3.** they **4.** she **5.** him **6.** she **7.** she **8.** he **9.** me **10.** they **11.** he **12.** him **13.** her **14.** I **15.** she **16.** she **17.** I **18.** him **19.** I **20.** she **21.** he **22.** him **23.** she **24.** she **25.** he

Worksheet 2

1. he **2.** me **3.** its **4.** she **5.** us **6.** there's **7.** he **8.** I **9.** me **10.** her **11.** us **12.** you're **13.** her **14.** him **15.** yours **16.** me **17.** he **18.** its **19.** him or me **20.** There's **21.** him **22.** me **23.** I **24.** their **25.** she **26.** I **27.** me **28.** us **29.** she **30.** there's

Chapter 7 Self-Help Answers

LEVEL 1

1. her **2.** his or her **3.** his or her **4.** their **5.** their **6.** he or she **7.** his or her lunch **8.** him or her **9.** her **10.** their pictures **11.** her **12.** his **13.** Every employee must obtain his or her . . . **14.** Every employee must obtain a parking permit . . . **15.** All employees must obtain their parking permits. . . .

LEVEL 2

1. use *her* instead of *their* **2.** *its* instead of *it's* **3.** *his* or *her* instead of *their* **4.** *his* or *her* for *his* **5.** *his* for *their* **6.** *her* for *their* **7.** C **8.** *its* for *their* **9.** *its* for *their* **10.** *him* or *her* for *them* **11.** C **12.** *his* or *her* for *their* **13.** *his* or *her* for *their* **14.** *his* or *her seat* for *their seats.* **15.** *its* for *their* **16.** *its* for *their* **17.** *them* for *it* **18.** *his* for *their* **19.** *her* for *their* **20.** *they* for *she* or *he*

LEVEL 3

Worksheet 1

1. Whom **2.** whom **3.** who **4.** whom **5.** whom **6.** whom **7.** Who **8.** Whom **9.** Who **10.** who **11.** who **12.** who **13.** whom **14.** who **15.** Who

Worksheet 2

1. whoever **2.** whoever **3.** whomever **4.** whomever **5.** whoever **6.** whoever **7.** whoever **8.** Whoever **9.** whoever **10.** Whoever **11.** Who **12.** who **13.** who **14.** whoever **15.** whom

Worksheet 3

1. Whom **2.** who **3.** whom **4.** whoever **5.** whom **6.** whom **7.** Whoever **8.** who **9.** who **10.** who **11.** whom **12.** whom **13.** Who **14.** Whom **15.** whomever **16.** whom **17.** Whoever **18.** whom **19.** whom **20.** whom **21.** whose **22.** who's **23.** who's **24.** whose **25.** who's

Chapter 8 Self-Help Answers

LEVEL 1

1. transitive **2.** intransitive **3.** linking **4.** complements **5.** I **6.** L—Jessica **7.** T—addresses **8.** I **9.** L—consultant **10.** T—pants **11.** T—application **12.** L—better **13.** L—he **14.** I **15.** T—questions **16.** T—gifts **17.** L—best **18.** I **19.** L—justified **20.** T—expectations

LEVEL 2

Worksheet 1

1. Mark did not receive the text message until Monday morning. **2.** Dell shipped our order last week. **3.** Sherri Bradford must authorize withdrawals beginning next week. **4.** Mr. Stern asked Wyatt to be responsible for turning out the lights at the end of the day. **5.** Management forced employees who travel a great deal to surrender their frequent-flier awards.

Worksheet 2

Answers may vary. **1.** We must complete our departmental report before 5 p.m. **2.** Mr. Smith wrote checks on an account with insufficient funds. **3.** Judges make decisions in the courts that affect the daily lives of all Americans. **4.** Management warned employees working with computers to change their passwords frequently. **5.** Our CPA scrutinized our accounting records during the audit.

Worksheet 3

1. were **2.** was **3.** be **4.** would **5.** be **6.** rest **7.** were **8.** were **9.** be **10.** be

LEVEL 3

Worksheet 1

1. your passing **2.** his investing **3.** Mr. Cortina's gambling **4.** C **5.** your criticizing **6.** your calling **7.** C **8.** my working

Worksheet 2

1. b **2.** b **3.** a **4.** b **5.** a
6. Completing the examination in only 20 minutes, Maria earned a perfect score.
7. To locate the members' names and addresses, we used a current directory.
8. Driving through the desert, we thought the highway seemed endless.
9. My knees shook and my voice wavered when I addressed the audience for the first time.

Chapter 9 Self-Help Answers

LEVEL 1

1. is **2.** occurred **3.** is **4.** is **5.** is **6.** plans **7.** will sell **8.** supplied **9.** studies **10.** will analyze **11.** applied **12.** considered **13.** varies **14.** insists **15.** will appeal **16.** requires **17.** will demand **18.** tried

LEVEL 2

Worksheet 1

1. rung **2.** froze **3.** hid **4.** chosen **5.** built **6.** drunk **7.** forgotten or forgot **8.** given **9.** gone **10.** bitten **11.** eaten **12.** sung **13.** C or struck **14.** sprang **15.** shaken **16.** worn **17.** written **18.** stolen **19.** taken **20.** gone

Worksheet 2

1. laid **2.** lie **3.** lying **4.** laid **5.** laying **6.** lie **7.** lay **8.** Lay **9.** lain **10.** lie **11.** lie **12.** lying **13.** lie **14.** lay **15.** lain **16.** lay **17.** lying **18.** lie **19.** laid **20.** laying

LEVEL 3

1. has opened **2.** is planning **3.** had called **4.** has worked **5.** were seeing **6.** will be signing **7.** had been broken **8.** have seen **9.** are considering **10.** was being heard **11.** rung **12.** drank **13.** choose **14.** driven **15.** saw **16.** gone **17.** saw **18.** eaten **19.** written **20.** rose **21.** sworn **22.** sank **23.** shrank **24.** begun **25.** forbidden

Chapter 10 Self-Help Answers

LEVEL 1

Worksheet 1

1. provide (subject: sites) **2.** is (subject: supervisor) **3.** comes (subject: supply) **4.** think (subject: workers) **5.** is (subject: everyone) **6.** was (subject: table) **7.** is (subject: list) **8.** needs (subject: equipment) **9.** has (subject: One) **10.** are (subject: copies) **11.** is (subject: furniture) **12.** are (subject: Effects) **13.** have (subject: salespeople) **14.** are (subject: Profits) **15.** sounds (subject: one) **16.** was (subject: shipment) **17.** is (subject: Everyone) **18.** are (subject: subsidiaries) **19.** have (subject: Officials) **20.** was (subject: letter)

Worksheet 2

1. travels (subject: flow) **2.** are (subject: newspapers and magazines) **3.** is (subject: Coleman, Harris & Juarez, Inc.) **4.** are (subject: books) **5.** appear (subject: points) **6.** are (subject: stages) **7.** was (subject: No one) **8.** is (subject: member) **9.** are (subject: size and design) **10.** is (subject: unit) **11.** has (subject: American Airlines) **12.** provide (subject: seasons) **13.** Has (subject: van) **14.** is (subject: condition) **15.** is (subject: luggage) **16.** has (subject: salary) **17.** appears (subject: One) **18.** is (subject: American Medical Association) **19.** are (subject: ease and convenience) **20.** are (subject: Aggressiveness and delinquency)

LEVEL 2

1. is (subject: Most) **2.** has (subject: The Committee on Youth Activities) **3.** deserves (subject: Each) **4.** is (subject: one [of your two competitors]) **5.** is (subject: work) **6.** is (subject: Either) **7.** were (subject: members) **8.** mention (subject: invoices) **9.** merits (subject: one) **10.** every one **11.** are (subject: you) **12.** has (subject: Each) **13.** belongs (subject: most) **14.** is (subject: group) **15.** is (subject: Some) **16.** has (subject: staff) **17.** Were (subject: any) **18.** has (subject: union) **19.** have (subject: employees) **20.** is (subject: Most)

LEVEL 3

1. has **2.** is **3.** enjoy **4.** was **5.** was **6.** is **7.** favor **8.** are **9.** are **10.** am **11.** is **12.** is **13.** like **14.** are **15.** is **16.** need **17.** were **18.** are **19.** complain **20.** has

Chapter 11 Self-Help Answers

LEVEL 1

1. more effective **2.** worst **3.** friendlier or more friendly **4.** least certain **5.** more beautiful **6.** fastest **7.** better **8.** noisiest **9.** quieter **10.** most sincere **11.** most skilled **12.** least **13.** slower or more slowly **14.** more likely **15.** most unusual **16.** fewer **17.** better **18.** more credible **19.** worst **20.** fewest

LEVEL 2

1. loudly **2.** C **3.** C **4.** Fewer **5.** more quietly **6.** bad **7.** conflict-of-interest **8.** C **9.** C **10.** latter **11.** well **12.** satisfactorily **13.** house to house **14.** C **15.** surely **16.** quietly **17.** really **18.** charge account **19.** not-too-distant **20.** fewer

LEVEL 3

1. b **2.** b **3.** a **4.** b **5.** a **6.** a **7.** a **8.** a **9.** neatly **10.** well (for *good*) **11.** C **12.** recently enacted **13.** worst (for *worse*) **14.** an (for *a*) **15.** had hardly **16.** round-the-world **17.** bad (for *badly*) **18.** fewer people **19.** said only **20.** an 840-acre

Chapter 12 Self-Help Answers

LEVEL 1

1. should have (for *should of*) **2.** him (for *he*) **3.** C **4.** me (for *I*) **5.** from (for *off of*) **6.** to (for *too*) **7.** her (for *she*) **8.** could have (for *could of*) **9.** too (for *to*) **10.** him (for *he*) **11.** from (for *off*) **12.** him (for *he*) **13.** from (for *off of*) **14.** C **15.** him (for *he*) **16.** too (for *to*) **17.** could have (for *could of*) **18.** C **19.** could have (for *could of*) **20.** me (for *I*)

LEVEL 2

1. besides (for *beside*) **2.** support of **3.** omit *with* **4.** in to (for *into*) **5.** inside the office **6.** among (for *between*) **7.** as (for *like*) **8.** C **9.** type of software **10.** into (for *in to*) **11.** C **12.** concern for **13.** omit *at* **14.** C **15.** omit *from* **16.** omit *up* **17.** style *of* **18.** going *in to* meet **19.** omit *to* **20.** graduated *from*

LEVEL 3

1. b **2.** a **3.** a **4.** b **5.** b **6.** a **7.** b **8.** b **9.** b **10.** b **11.** a **12.** a **13.** b **14.** b **15.** a **16.** a **17.** b **18.** b **19.** a **20.** b

Chapter 13 Self-Help Answers

LEVEL 1

Worksheet 1

The order of Answers 1–4 may vary. **1.** and **2.** or **3.** nor **4.** but (students may also list *yet, for,* and *so*) **5.** b **6.** a **7.** b **8.** a **9.** a **10.** b

Worksheet 2

Answers may vary. **1.** therefore, however, consequently, moreover, then, in the meantime **2.** semicolon **3.** commas **4.** planning, nevertheless, **5.** occupancy; that is, **6.** organization, on the other hand, **7.** presentation; then **8.** competitive; however, **9.** résumés; consequently, **10.** letter; therefore,

LEVEL 2

Worksheet 1

1. T **2.** T **3.** T **4.** T **5.** F **6.** P **7.** D **8.** I **9.** P **10.** D **11.** I **12.** D **13.** I **14.** D **15.** P **16.** D **17.** I **18.** P **19.** I **20.** D

Worksheet 2

1. suggestions, **2.** C **3.** completed, **4.** C **5.** C **6.** booklet, which was submitted over six weeks ago, **7.** know, **8.** payments, provided there is no interruption in profits, **9.** necessary, **10.** C **11.** Gilroy, who volunteered to head the program, **12.** C **13.** order, **14.** C **15.** days,

Worksheet 3

Answers will vary

1. Although never signed, the original agreement was drawn between Mr. Hightower and Columbia Communications.
2. Thank you for informing us that your credit card, which has an expiration date of April 30, is missing.
3. Because your account is four months past due, we will be forced to take legal action unless we hear from you within seven days.
4. Sally Horton, who works as assistant to the manager in the Quality Control Department, won an award as this month's outstanding employee.
5. We are sending you four poster advertisements that will appear in magazines in April, which marks the beginning of a national campaign featuring our sports clothes.

LEVEL 3

1. b **2.** b **3.** a **4.** b
5. You can either fax your response or send an e-mail message.
6. Our goals are both to educate motorists and to save their lives.
7. Tony has neither a job interview nor even an interview lined up.
8. We knew that we had to either raise more money or begin selling stock.
9. Businesses are looking for employees who not only can work in teams but also can learn effectively in teams.

Chapter 14 Self-Help Answers

LEVEL 1

1. (2) teams, Mr. Wilson, **2.** (1) By the way, **3.** (4) successful, however, training, coaching, **4.** (2) Ames, Iowa, **5.** (2) teams, on the other hand, **6.** C **7.** (4) MicroTech Systems, 750 Grant Road, Tucson, Arizona 85703, **8.** (2) appears, sir, **9.** (2) Friday, April 30, **10.** (2) Molloy, who is an advertising executive, **11.** C **12.** 10 p.m., **13.** (2) will, in addition, **14.** (2) airports, shopping centers, **15.** (1) considered, **16.** (2) Hudson, who is a specialist in information systems, **17.** (2) patent, trademark, **18.** (2) convinced, incidentally, **19.** (2) policy, budget, **20.** Italy, Greece,

LEVEL 2

1. (1) practical, **2.** (1) months, **3.** (2) Meyer, employees, **4.** (1) week, **5.** C **6.** (2) appreciate, often, **7.** C **8.** C **9.** (1) calculations, **10.** C **11.** (2) please, calculations, **12.** (1) intelligent, **13.** (1) return, **14.** (1) June, **15.** C **16.** (1) inventory, **17.** (1) Goodell, who **18.** (2) when, where, **19.** (3) process, Thursday, June 1, **20.** C

LEVEL 3

1. (2) Ferrari, PhD, **2.** C **3.** (1) 2009, **4.** (1) 2008, **5.** (2) Taiwan, China, **6.** (1) before, **7.** (2) name," said the auditor, **8.** C **9.** C **10.** (2) Feinstein, MD, **11.** C **12.** (1) since, **13.** (1) said, **14.** (2) Samuels, not Ms. Lambert, **15.** (1) nine, **16.** (2) 17,365,000 **17.** (3) supervisor," remarked Sid Stern, results, **18.** (3) way, president, vice president, **19.** (2) diamond," said the therapist, **20.** (1) signs, signs

Chapter 15 Self-Help Answers

LEVEL 1

1. profits; however, **2.** Brownsville, Texas; Seattle, Washington; and Bangor, **3.** names, envelopes, **4.** order; **5.** space; on the other hand, **6.** remarkable; however, **7.** public; **8.** Roberts, secretary, Legal Department; Lea Lim, clerk, Human Resources; and Mark Cameron, dispatcher, **9.** estate; however, **10.** 10 a.m.; **11.** award; **12.** catalog, selections, **13.** property, **14.** Michigan; California; **15.** seats; (preferred) **16.** Hyatt Regency Hotel, Columbus, Ohio; Plaza of the Americas Hotel, Dallas, Texas; and the Brown Palace Hotel, Denver, Colorado **17.** requested, Thursday, May 4; however, Friday, **18.** gathering, recording,

LEVEL 2

1. scrutinized: **2.** C **3.** said: **4.** C **5.** decision: **6.** C **7.** following: **8.** sites: **9.** skills: **10.** C **11.** thought: **12.** factors: **13.** Hofer, Stone, **14.** tennis, **15.** following:

LEVEL 3

1. check; namely, **2.** supplies: cartridges **3.** services, philosophy; that is, **4.** rule: **5.** 2:15 6:45 **6.** Tom; **7.** executives—namely, Mr. Thomas, Mr. Estrada, and Mrs. Stranahan—**8.** *Investment: An* **9.** field; **10.** areas; for example, **11.** representative"; that is, **12.** advertising: product **13.** convention, namely, **14.** program; for instance, **15.** office; however,

Chapter 16 Self-Help Answers

LEVEL 1

1. c.o.d. possible. **2.** 10 a.m., didn't you? **3.** Mr. CPA Inc. **4.** Donald L. Cullens Jr. job? **5.** Help! jammed! **6.** please, Ms. Juarez, gift. [**Note:** If you don't feel comfortable using a period after a polite request, rephrase the sentence so that it is clearly a command: *Please visit our Web site and register for your gift.*] **7.** been! **8.** AA degrees, BA degrees. **9.** CEO and CFO decisions. **10.** Tan, Mr. Roe, and Ms. Rich. **11.** 9 a.m., EST, rate. **12.** Bennett, MD, Caracas, PhD, speakers. **13.** site? **14.** China, France, and the UK. **15.** CPU USA. **16.** Adamski, Drive, Rochester, NY 14616. **17.** Nos. $50,000 coverage. **18.** 5 p.m., PST? **19.** Wow! prize? **20.** MA, DVDs.

LEVEL 2

1. F (use two hyphens) **2.** T **3.** F **4.** T **5.** T **6.** a **7.** c **8.** b **9.** a **10.** b **11.** c **12.** c **13.** b **14.** c

LEVEL 3

1. T **2.** T **3.** F (enclose definition in quotation marks) **4.** T. **5.** F (enclose in quotation marks) **6.** T **7.** T **8.** T **9.** T **10.** T **11.** a **12.** c **13.** a **14.** b **15.** a

Complete Punctuation Review

1. "Soaring Salaries of CEOs" The New York Times? [In print, use underscore or italics.] **2.** This year's last year's; therefore, case-by-case **3.** SEC members: Dr. Carla Chang, Professor Mark Rousso, and Robert Price, Esq. **4.** say, 5 p.m., EST. **5.** fixed-rate, not variable-rate, **6.** invited: Christine Lenski, DataCom Industries; Mark Grant, LaserPro, Inc.; and Ivan Weiner, **7.** Orlando, Florida, **8.** say, "We Friday"? **9.** BA 11 a.m.; MBA 2 p.m. **10.** discussed, Monday, August 8. **11.** feel, however, car's **12.** D. A. Rusterholz. **13.** carefully, "bomb." **14.** weather, stations: KJOW, KLOB, and KOB-TV. **15.** employees—Gregorio Williams—Friday, June 5. **16.** attitude, aptitude, altitude," **17.** cars; by June 15, **18.** EPA studied; **19.** 9 p.m., **20.** Ms. Courtney Worthy, Administrative Assistant, Globex Industries, 7600 Normandale Boulevard, Milwaukee, WI 53202, **21.** (see page 2 for a summary of the report) to the president's Friday, **22.** Success "A Venture Expert's Advice." **23.** Zuckerman, our former manager, IBM. **24.** weight, things; namely, **25.** expected, this year's heavy; consequently,

Chapter 17 Self-Help Answers

LEVEL 1

1. b **2.** a **3.** a **4.** a **5.** a **6.** b **7.** a **8.** a **9.** b **10.** a **11.** b **12.** b **13.** b **14.** a **15.** b **16.** station county **17.** company's **18.** Securities Exchange Commission e-mail **19.** winter English **20.** of Ballroom Hotel **21.** Persian Russian **22.** summer Grand Canyon Arizona **23.** contract April **24.** Italian Spanish **25.** Kansas City International Airport Alameda Plaza Hotel

LEVEL 2

1. a **2.** a **3.** a **4.** b **5.** a **6.** b **7.** a **8.** a **9.** b **10.** b **11.** a **12.** a **13.** b **14.** a **15.** b **16.** supervisor **17.** president company Do How Do It **18.** East **19.** Highway Exit **20.** Governor state **21.** "Does Your Training Measure Up?" **22.** Ray-Ban Formica **23.** mother and father Flight 37 Gate 6 Phoenix Sky Harbor International Airport **24.** Data Entry and Data Verification Departments Technical Services Division **25.** bus limousine Ritz-Carlton Hotel

LEVEL 3

1. a **2.** b **3.** a **4.** a **5.** b **6.** a **7.** b **8.** b **9.** a **10.** a **11.** Funds **12.** River **13.** Senator Valley **14.** Professor Earth **15.** organization's **16.** president company countries **17.** national African **18.** English dialect English **19.** Malaysia Muslims Buddhists Hindus **20.** mortgage financing

Chapter 18 Self-Help Answers

LEVEL 1

1. a **2.** b **3.** b **4.** b **5.** a **6.** a **7.** b **8.** a **9.** a **10.** a **11.** A total of 194 December 1 **12.** Two 25th Avenue **13.** $5 $.99 **14.** $100 2nd **15.** February 1 15 departments. **16.** 2 Ford Place **17.** (815) 611-9292, Ext. 3 *or* 805-611-9292, Ext. 3 **18.** May 15 two 2 p.m. 8 p.m. **19.** Three 8 a.m. five **20.** 15th $204 **21.** 15-hour $125 **22.** 1 p.m. **23.** 1762 14th **24.** 25 cents $44 **25.** 3rd

LEVEL 2

1. b **2.** b **3.** b **4.** a **5.** b **6.** b **7.** a **8.** a **9.** a **10.** b **11.** 50 **12.** three 35-passenger 15-day **13.** Fifty-three $1 million **14.** ten 48 five **15.** Chapter 8 Volume 2 **16.** Room 4 8 chairs **17.** 30-inch **18.** 20 requests 5 3 **19.** two loans **20.** twenty-four years **21.** Only 2 **22.** 64 **23.** 15-person $3 million **24.** 52 40 million **25.** 30-year 8 percent

LEVEL 3

1. a **2.** b **3.** b **4.** b **5.** a **6.** b **7.** b **8.** a **9.** a **10.** b **11.** No. 10 4 1/2 by 9 1/2 inches **12.** Thirty-third **13.** 7/200 **14.** twenty-first **15.** 30

3/4 inches by 60 1/2 inches **16.** 30th 3 percent **17.** 50 blocks Seventh **18.** 100 degrees eight **19.** 7.94 pounds 15 1/2 inches **20.** two-thirds **21.** 9 by 12 two thirds **22.** Form 1040 $800 **23.** 2010 fifty-five 52 percent **24.** 100,000 **25.** 15 gallons 1 quart

Answers to Unit Reviews

Unit 1 Review (Chapters 1–3)

1. F **2.** T **3.** T **4.** F **5.** T **6.** F **7.** T **8.** F **9.** T **10.** T **11.** b **12.** c **13.** d **14.** b **15.** a **16.** c **17.** a **18.** d **19.** c **20.** a **21.** b **22.** c **23.** a **24.** b **25.** c **26.** b **27.** a **28.** d **29.** a **30.** b **31.** a **32.** c **33.** d **34.** a **35.** c **36.** c **37.** a **38.** b **39.** b **40.** c

Unit 2 Review (Chapters 4–7)

1. b **2.** b **3.** a **4.** c **5.** a **6.** b **7.** b **8.** a **9.** b **10.** d **11.** c **12.** b **13.** a **14.** c **15.** a **16.** b **17.** a **18.** b **19.** b **20.** b **21.** c **22.** b **23.** b **24.** a **25.** d **26.** b **27.** a **28.** a **29.** b **30.** b **31.** a **32.** a **33.** b **34.** a **35.** b **36.** b **37.** b **38.** b **39.** b **40.** b

Unit 3 Review (Chapters 8–10)

1. c **2.** b **3.** c **4.** a **5.** a **6.** a **7.** a **8.** a **9.** a **10.** a **11.** b **12.** a **13.** b **14.** a **15.** b **16.** a **17.** b **18.** b **19.** b **20.** a **21.** b **22.** a **23.** b **24.** b **25.** a **26.** b **27.** a **28.** b **29.** b **30.** a **31.** b **32.** b **33.** b **34.** b **35.** a **36.** a **37.** b **38.** b **39.** a **40.** b

Unit 4 (Chapters 11–13)

1. b **2.** a **3.** b **4.** a **5.** b **6.** a **7.** b **8.** c **9.** (0) **10.** (1) office, **11.** (2) succes; consequently, **12.** (1) résumé, **13.** a **14.** b **15.** b **16.** a **17.** a **18.** b **19.** b **20.** (2) Waters, Berkeley, **21.** (1) résumé **22.** (0) **23.** (1) Caracas, **24.** (1) reported, **25.** a **26.** b **27.** a **28.** b **29.** a **30.** (1) impression, **31.** (1) office, **32.** (0) **33.** (2) markedly; moreover, **34.** (1) bodyguards, **35.** (2) earth; however, **36.** b **37.** a **38.** b **39.** a **40.** b

Unit 5 (Chapters 14–16)

1. (1) people, **2.** C **3.** (3) "telesensing," pulse, relatives **4.** (2) Sizer, Labs **5.** C **6.** (2) phones, however **7.** c **8.** b **9.** a **10.** a **11.** b **12.** c **13.** a **14.** c **15.** a **16.** a **17.** b **18.** a **19.** c **20.** a **21.** c **22.** a **23.** c **24.** a **25.** b **26.** b **27.** b **28.** c **29.** b **30.** c **31.** c **32.** b **33.** a **34.** b **35.** b **36.** a **37.** b **38.** a **39.** b **40.** b

Unit 6 (Chapters 17–18)

1. b **2.** b **3.** b **4.** a **5.** b **6.** a **7.** b **8.** a **9.** b **10.** (5) Thirty-five graduate students five accounting **11.** (4) Google $100 first August 19 **12.** (2) nine president **13.** b **14.** a **15.** a **16.** a **17.** b **18.** a **19.** a **20.** b **21.** a **22.** (5) Big Mac Coca-Cola $3.75 **23.** (4) president south Highway tenth **24.** (3) father *to* 2 million **25.** a **26.** b **27.** b **28.** b **29.** a **30.** a **31.** b **32.** b **33.** a **34.** b **35.** b **36.** b **37.** b **38.** a **39.** a **40.** b

Index

Prefixes, 89, 108, 295, 325, 364–365
Prepositional phrases, 29, 128, 165, 252, 254, 258
Prepositions, 19, 84, 165, 206, 322
  common uses of, 207–208
  ending a sentence with, 209, 212
  idiomatic use of, 210–211
  necessary and unnecessary, 209
  troublesome, 208–209
Present participles, 147
Present perfect tense, 152
Present progressive tense, 151
Present tense, 145
president, capitalization of, 325
Primary tense, 145–146
principal, principle, 154
Principle verb, 29
Product names, capitalization of, 322
Progressive tense, 151–152
Pronouns, 17, 18, 83. *See also*
  Antecedents; Personal pronouns
  advanced use of, 105–107
  antecedent agreement and, 101–105
  indefinite, as subjects, 167–168
  reflexive, 86, 88
  relative, 225–226
  types of, 88
  vague, 185
Pronunciation, in dictionaries, 6
Proofreading, 8, 45
Proper adjectives, capitalization of, 318
Proper nouns, 49, 52, 69, 317–318
Proposal, 357–359
proved, proven, 212
Publication titles, colons in, 273
Punctuation. *See also individual punctuation marks*
  around parentheses, 291
  of commands, 34
  of compound sentences, 222
  dependent clauses and, 224–226
  of exclamations, 34
  of introductory verbal phases, 254
  of letter salutations, 275
  mixed, in business letters, 381
  of nonessential clauses, 255
  open, in business letter, 384
  of questions, 34
  reference manual as guide for, 10
  of sentences with dependent clauses, 224–225
  spacing after, 379–380
  of statements, 33
Purdue University Online Writing Lab
  hot links, 27, 49, 166, 254, 292

Q

Quantifiable data, 49
Quantities and measures, subject-verb agreement and, 169
Question mark, 289, 293
Questions, 34, 287, 289
Quotation marks, 292–295
Quotations, 205, 257, 271, 290, 292

R

Radio stations, call letters of, 89
Random House Compact Unabridged Dictionary (CD-ROM), 8
Random House Webster's College Dictionary, 4
re-, 229
real, really, 196
Reciprocal pronouns, 88
Recommendations, in a report, 357
Redundant words, 122
Reference initials, 383
Reference lines, in business letters, 382
Reference manuals, 9–10
References, importance of using, 4
Reference skills, 4–10
Reflexive pronouns, 86, 88
Related numbers, 337
Relative clauses, 225–226
Relative pronouns, 88, 225–226
Reports, 355–357

Restrictive and nonrestrictive clauses, 225–226
Return address, on envelopes, 384–385
rise, raise, 150–151
Rote learning, for spelling, 361
Round numbers, 339
"Rule of Ten," 335
Run-on sentence, 33

S

Salutations, 22, 244, 273, 275, 381, 382, 389
Search engines, 10, 143
Search tools, 42
Seasons, capitalization of, 319
Second-page heading, 383–384
-*self, -selves*, 86
Semicolons, 226, 293
  basic uses, 269–270
  caution about, 274
  special uses, 272
Sentence fragment, 32, 119–120
Sentences. *See also specific forms of punctuation;* Subject, of sentence; Topic sentences
  capitalization in, 318
  comma splice, 33
  complete, 29, 119–120
  compound, coordinating conjunctions, punctuation, and, 222
  concise, 121–123
  effective, techniques for, 119–124
  elements in, 29–30
  ending with a preposition, 209, 212
  faults, 32–33
  numbers beginning, 335
  opening fillers, avoiding, 121
  patterns, 30–32, 172
  punctuating, 33–34, 224–225, 271, 287
  simple, 222
  variety in, 227–228
Serial numbers, commas and, 256
Series, commas and semicolons in, 251, 270
Sexist language, 102, 103
-*s* form verbs (third-person singular), 146
sic, 295
Signature block, in a letter, 381, 383
Simple fractions, 340
Simple predicate, 29
Simple subject, 29
Singular nouns, 50
sit, set, 133, 134, 150
so, 221, 228
someone, 168
sometime, some time, 212
Special noun plurals, 54–55
Spell checker, 8
Spelling, 128, 146, 275, 361–370
Spyware, 240
Sr., 256
Stamped, words following, 324
State abbreviations, 89, 288, 387
Statements, punctuating, 33, 287, 289
Statements of comparison, 85
stationary, stationery, 56
Stationery, 379
Streets. *See* Addresses
Style checkers, 134
Subject, of sentence. *See also* Subject-verb agreement
  complements and, 128
  complete, 29
  compound, personal pronouns and, 85
  locating, 29–30, 165–166
  simple, 29
  subjects joined by *and*, 167
  subjects joined by *or* or *nor*, 167
Subject–action verb–object sentence pattern, 31
Subject complement, subjective-case pronouns and, 86–87
Subject complements, 170
Subjective-case pronouns, 83, 86–88
Subject line, 245, 381, 382, 388, 389

Subject–linking verb–complement sentence pattern, 31
Subject-verb agreement, 164, 275
  collective nouns as subjects, 168
  company names and titles and, 167
  distinction between *the number* and *a number*, 169
  errors in, 165
  fractions and portions, 169, 171
  indefinite pronouns as subjects, 167–168
  intervening elements and, 165–166
  inverted sentence order and, 166, 172
  it, they substitutions, 167
  locating subjects, 165–166
  one of those who, 169
  phrases and clauses as subjects, 170
  prepositional phrases and, 165
  Purdue University Online Writing Lab hot link, 166
  quantities and measures, 169
  sentences beginning with *there* and *here*, 166, 171
  subject complements and, 170
  who clauses, 169–170
Subject–verb sentence pattern, 30
Subjunctive mood, of verbs, 129–130, 134
Subordinating conjunctions, 224. *See* Conjunctions
such as, 274
Suffixes, spelling guidelines for, 364–365
Summarizing statements, 290
Summary, for reports, 357
Superlative forms, of adjectives and adverbs, 7, 191–192
sure, surely, 195
Surnames, plural of, 52
Syllabication, 5–6
Symbols, numbers used with, 339
Synonyms, 4, 7, 8

T

Talking heads, in reports, 355
Telephone numbers, 256, 337, 342
Television stations, call letters of, 89
Tense, 144–154
Terminal dependent clauses, 225, 255
Textbook vs. reference manual, 10
than, 196
than, then, 108
thank you, thank-you, 35
that, as relative pronoun, 229
that, which, 225–226, 228
that clauses, subjective verb forms and, 130
that is, 272
TheFreeDictionary.com (online), 9
"*the*" preceding a name, 69
there, here, at beginning of sentence, 30, 166, 171
there, they're, their, 229
Thesaurus, 4, 7, 8
Third-person singular verbs, 146
this/that, these/those, 193
Tidewater Community College Writing Center, 143
Time, 273, 336, 338
"Timeless" facts, present-tense verbs and, 146
Time period, possessive construction of, 70
Time zones, commas in, 252–253
Titles, 35, 103, 167
  capitalization in, 320–325
  courtesy, in business letters, 380, 383
  job, abbreviation of, 288
  quotation marks and, 293
to, too, 89, 208
to be. See Infinitives
To line, 387, 388, 389, 390
too, commas and, 258
Topic sentences, 183–184
toward, towards, 22
Trademarks, 322
Transitional expressions, 185, 223, 252
Transitive verbs, 127

U

Unabridged dictionary, 5
under, 108
Units of measurement, plural of, 53
University of Houston-Victoria Academic Center hot link (testing pronoun skills), 104
University of Ottawa hot link (verb overview), 127
University of Wisconsin, *The Writing Center* hot link (semicolons), 274
Unrelated numbers, 337
URLs (uniform resource locators), style of, 15
Usage labels, in dictionary entries, 7
Utah Valley State College *Online Writing Lab* hot link (sentence practice), 33

V

Verbal messages, 379
Verbals
  gerunds, 130–131
  infinitives, 131
  introductory verbal phrases, 132
  misplaced modifiers and, 132–133
  participles, 132
  phrases in other positions, 133
Verbing, 153
Verb phrase, 29
Verbs, 18, 126. *See also* Subject-verb agreement; Tense
  action, 31, 127–128
  antecedents and, 172
  functions of, 18, 128
  helping/auxiliary, 29, 146
  intransitive, 127–128
  irregular, 7, 147–151
  linking, 18, 29, 31, 34, 128
  misplaced modifiers and, 134
  moods, 129–130
  placement of, 30
  principle, 29
  pronouns as object of, 84
  -*s* form (third-person singular), 146
  that change form, spelling of, 146
  transitive, 127
  University of Ottawa hot link, 127
  voice of, 129
Vocabulary skills, developing, 371–378
Voice, of verbs, 129
Voice of business (verbs), 129
Voice of tact (verbs), 129

W

Web browser, 15
Web site, 21
Webster's New World College Dictionary, 5
Weights, number style in, 340
who, which, that, 225–226
who, whom, 105–106, 107
who clauses, 169–170
whoever, whomever, 106–107, 108
whose, 107
-*wide*, 212
Wikipedia hot link (capitalization), 323
-*wise*, 35
Word processing programs, dictionary/ thesaurus feature, 8
Wordy sentences, 121
Workplace communication, importance of, 3–4
Works cited, colons in, 273
World Wide Web, 8–10
Writing skills, value of, 29

X

xerox, 325

Y

Yahoo! search engine, 42
yet, 221

Z

Zip codes, commas and, 256